FINANCIAL INSTITUTIONS AND SERVICES SERIES

TAX HAVEN BANKS

FINANCIAL INSTITUTIONS AND SERVICES SERIES

Stock Exchanges, IPO's and Mutual funds
E. Klein (Editor)
2004. ISBN: 1-59454-173-6

Global Banking Issues
E. Klein (Editor)
2005. ISBN: 1-59454-172-8

Financial Institutions and Development
E. Klein (Editor)
2005. ISBN: 1-59454-177-9

Capital Formation, Governance and Banking
E. Klein (Editor)
2005. ISBN: 1-59454-191-4

Information Sellers and Resellers
Shane C. Leger (Editor)
2009. ISBN: 978-1-60692-228-6

Hedge Funds: Regulation and Nonregulation
Yeram E. Torrey (Editor)
2009. ISBN: 978-1-60692-041-1

Securitization of Subprime Mortgages
Milton R. Spotgeste (Editor)
2009. ISBN: 978-1-60692-200-2

Reforming Risk in Financial Markets
Melvin R. Turley (Editor)
2009. ISBN: 978-1-60692-445-7

Liquidity, Interest Rates and Banking
Jeffrey Morrey and Alexander Guyton (Editors)
2009. ISBN: 978-1-60692-775-5

U. S. Coins: The Price of a Penny
Walter M. Carvalho (Editor)
2009. ISBN: 978-1-60692-939-1

Econometric Modeling of Value-at-Risk
Timotheos Angelidis and Stavros Degiannakis
2009. ISBN: 978-1-60741-040-9

Global Banking Regulation and Supervision: What are the Issues and What Are the Practices?
James R. Barth, Jie Gan and Daniel E. Nolle
2009. ISBN: 978-1-60741-315-8

Stock Returns: Cyclicity, Prediction and Economic Consequences
George I. Ellison (Editor)
2009. ISBN: 978-1-60741-458-2

Tax Haven Banks
Wade D. Brookins (Editor)
2009. ISBN: 978-1-60692-283-5

FINANCIAL INSTITUTIONS AND SERVICES SERIES

TAX HAVEN BANKS

WADE D. BROOKINS
EDITOR

Nova Science Publishers, Inc.
New York

For permission to use material from this book please contact us:
Telephone 631-231-7269; Fax 631-231-8175
Web Site: http://www.novapublishers.com

LIBRARY OF CONGRESS CATALOGING-IN-PUBLICATION DATA

Tax haven banks / editor, Wade D. Brookins.
p. cm.
Includes index.
ISBN 978-1-60692-283-5 (hardcover)
1. Tax evasion--United States. 2. Tax havens. 3. Banks and banking, Foreign--Taxation--United States. I. Brookins, Wade D.
KF6334.T395 2009
343.7305'23--dc22

2009028851

Published by Nova Science Publishers, Inc. ✝ New York

CONTENTS

PREFACE

This book provides information on an issue of critical importance to tax administration in this country; the practice of sheltering U.S. earned income in foreign jurisdictions as a means of avoiding U.S. taxation. Each year, the United States loses an estimated $100 billion in tax revenues due to offshore tax abuses. Offshore tax havens today hold trillions of dollars in assets provided by citizens of other countries, including the United States. A related issue is the extent to which financial institutions in tax havens may be facilitating international tax evasion. About 50 tax havens operate in the world today with their twin hallmarks being secrecy and tax avoidance. Billions and billions of dollars worth of U.S. assets find their way into these secrecy tax havens, aided by banks, trust companies, accountants, lawyers, and from offshore tax abuses. This book discusses such sources of tax havens, as well as the steps that the IRS has taken to alleviate this problem.

In: Tax Haven Banks
Editor: Wade D. Brookins
ISBN: 978-1-60692-283-5

Chapter 1

TAX HAVEN BANKS AND U.S. TAX COMPLIANCE STAFF REPORT PERMANENT SUBCOMMITTEE ON INVESTIGATIONS UNITED STATES SENATE (STAFF REPORT, PERMANENT SUBCOMMITTEE ON INVESTIGATIONS, UNITED STATES SENATE)

U.S. SENATE PERMANENT SUBCOMMITTEE ON INVESTIGATIONS

STAFF REPORT ON TAX HAVEN BANKS AND U.S. TAX COMPLIANCE

July 17, 2008

Each year, the United States loses an estimated $100 billion in tax revenues due to offshore tax abuses.[1] Offshore tax havens today hold trillions of dollars in assets provided by citizens of other countries, including the United States.[2] The extent to which those assets represent funds hidden from tax authorities by taxpayers from the United States and other countries outside of the tax havens is of critical importance.[3] A related issue is the extent to which financial institutions in tax havens may be facilitating international tax evasion.

In February 2008, a global tax scandal erupted after a former employee of a Liechtenstein trust company provided tax authorities around the world with data on about 1,400 persons with accounts at LGT Bank in Liechtenstein. On February 14, 2008, German tax authorities, having obtained the names of 600-700 German taxpayers with Liechtenstein accounts, executed multiple search warrants and arrested a prominent businessman for allegedly using Liechtenstein bank accounts to evade €1 million ($1.45 million) in tax.[4] About a week later, the U.S. Internal Revenue Service (IRS) announced it had "initiat[ed] enforcement action involving more than 100 U.S. taxpayers to ensure proper income reporting and tax payment in connection accounts in Liechtenstein."[5] The United Kingdom, Italy, France, Spain, and Australia made similar announcements on the same day.[6] Altogether since February, nearly a dozen countries have announced plans to investigate taxpayers with Liechtenstein accounts,[7] demonstrating not only the worldwide scope of the tax scandal, but also a newfound international determination to contest tax evasion facilitated by a tax haven bank.

In May 2008, a second international tax scandal broke when the United States arrested a private banker formerly employed by UBS AG, one of the largest banks in the world, on charges of having conspired with a U.S. citizen and a business associate to defraud the IRS of $7.2 million in taxes owed on $200 million of assets hidden in offshore accounts in Switzerland and Liechtenstein. The United States had earlier detained as a material witness in that prosecution a senior UBS private banking official from Switzerland traveling on business in Florida, allegedly seizing his computer and other evidence. In June 2008, the former UBS private banker, Bradley Birkenfeld, pleaded guilty to conspiracy to defraud the IRS.[8] His alleged co-conspirator, Mario Staggl, part owner of a trust company, remains at large in Liechtenstein. The current UBS senior private banking official, Martin Liechti, remains under travel restrictions. This enforcement action appears to represent the first time that the United States has criminally prosecuted a Swiss banker for helping a U.S. taxpayer evade payment of U.S. taxes.[9]

On June 30, 2008, the United States took another step. It filed a petition in the U.S. District Court for the Southern District of Florida requesting leave to file an IRS administrative summons with UBS asking the bank to disclose the names of all of its U.S. clients who have opened accounts in Switzerland, but for which the bank has not filed forms with the IRS disclosing the Swiss accounts.[10] The court approved service of the summons on UBS on July 1, 2008.[11] The summons has apparently been served, but according to Swiss authorities the Swiss and American governments are negotiating over its execution.[12] This John Doe summons represents the first time that the United States has attempted to pierce Swiss bank secrecy by compelling a Swiss bank to name its U.S. clients.

The U.S. Senate Permanent Subcommittee on Investigations has long had an investigative interest in U.S. taxpayers who use offshore tax havens to hide assets and evade taxes.[13] As part of this effort, the Subcommittee has undertaken an investigation into the extent to which tax haven banks may be assisting U.S. taxpayers to evade taxes, in particular by urging U.S. clients to open accounts abroad, assisting them in structuring those accounts to avoid disclosure to U.S. authorities, and providing financial services in ways that do not alert U.S. authorities to the existence of the foreign accounts. Of particular concern in this investigation has been the extent to which tax haven banks may be manipulating their reporting obligations under the Qualified Intermediary ("QI") Program, which was established by the U. S. government in 2001, to encourage foreign financial institutions to report and withhold tax on U.S. source income paid to foreign bank accounts. QI participant institutions sign an agreement to report and withhold U.S. taxes on an aggregate basis in return for being freed of the legal obligation to disclose the names of their non-U.S. clients. Evidence is emerging, however, that tax haven banks are taking manipulative and deceptive steps to avoid their QI obligation to disclose their U.S. clients.

To illustrate the issues, this Report presents two case histories showing how banks in Liechtenstein and Switzerland have employed banking practices that can facilitate, and have resulted in, tax evasion by their U.S. clients.

I. EXECUTIVE SUMMARY

A. Subcommittee Investigation

The Subcommittee began this bipartisan investigation into tax haven banks in February 2008. Since then, the Subcommittee has issued more than 35 subpoenas and conducted numerous interviews and depositions with bankers, trust officers, taxpayers, tax and estate planning professionals, and others. The Subcommittee has consulted with experts in the areas of tax, trusts, estate planning, securities, anti-money laundering, and international law, and spoken with domestic and foreign government officials and international organizations involved with tax administration and enforcement. During the investigation, the Subcommittee reviewed hundreds of thousands of pages of documents, including bank account records, internal bank memoranda, trust agreements, incorporation papers, correspondence, and electronic communications, as well as materials in the public domain, such as legal pleadings, court rulings, SEC filings, and information on the Internet. In addition, the Subcommittee has consulted with the governments of Liechtenstein and Switzerland, and expresses appreciation for their cooperation with the Subcommittee.

B. Overview of Case Histories

This Chapter presents case histories, involving LGT Bank in Liechtenstein and UBS AG of Switzerland, that lend insight into how these banks work with U.S. clients and execute their U.S. tax compliance obligations.

(1) LGT bank case history

The LGT Group ("LGT"), which includes LGT Bank in Liechtenstein, LGT Treuhand, a trust company, and other subsidiaries and affiliates, is a leading Liechtenstein financial institution that is owned by and financially benefits the Liechtenstein royal family. From at least 1998 to 2007, LGT employed practices that could facilitate, and in some instances have resulted in, tax evasion by U.S. clients. These LGT practices have included maintaining U.S. client accounts which are not disclosed to U.S. tax authorities; advising U.S. clients to open accounts in the name of Liechtenstein foundations to hide their beneficial ownership of the account assets; advising clients on the use of complex offshore structures to hide ownership of assets outside of Liechtenstein; and establishing "transfer corporations" to disguise asset transfers to and from LGT accounts. It was also not unusual for LGT to assign its U.S. clients code words that they or LGT could invoke to confirm their respective identities. LGT also advised clients on how to structure their investments to avoid disclosure to the IRS under the QI Program. Of the accounts examined by the Subcommittee, none had been disclosed by LGT to the IRS. These and other LGT practices contributed to a culture of secrecy and deception that enabled LGT clients to use the bank's services to evade U.S. taxes, dodge creditors, and ignore court orders.

LGT's trust office in Liechtenstein managed an estimated $7 billion in assets and more than 3,000 offshore entities for clients during the years 2001 to 2002; it is unclear what percentage was attributable to U.S. clients. Seven LGT accounts help illustrate LGT practices of concern to the Subcommittee.

Marsh Accounts: Hiding $49 Million Over Twenty Years. James Albright Marsh, a U.S. citizen from Florida in the construction business, formed four Liechtenstein foundations, two in 1985, one in 1998, and one in 2004, and transferred substantial sums to them. LGT assisted him in establishing the two 1985 foundations, using documents that gave Mr. Marsh and his sons substantial control over the foundations and strong secrecy protections. By 2007, the assets in his four foundations had a combined value of more than $49 million. Although LGT became a participant in the QI Program in 2001, which requires foreign banks to report information on accounts with U.S. securities, LGT did not report the Marsh accounts. Instead it advised Mr. Marsh to divest his LGT foundations of U.S. securities, and treated the accounts as owned by non-U.S. persons, the Liechtenstein foundations that LGT had formed. After Mr. Marsh's death in 2006, the IRS apparently discovered the Liechtenstein foundations through the documents released by the former LGT employee. Mr. Marsh's family is now in negotiation with the IRS over back taxes, interest and penalties owed on the $49 million in undeclared assets.

Wu Accounts: Hiding Ownership of Assets. William S. Wu is a U.S. citizen who was born in China and has lived for many years with his family in New York. His sister is a U.S. citizen living in Hong Kong. LGT helped Mr. Wu establish a Liechtenstein foundation in 1996, and a second one in 2006, while helping his sister establish a Liechtenstein foundation that operated for four years, from 1997-2001, before transferring its assets to another foundation in Hong Kong. LGT documents indicate that these foundations were used to conceal certain Wu ownership interests. For example, in 1997, three months after forming his foundation, Mr. Wu pretended to sell his home in New York to what appeared to be an unrelated party from Hong Kong. In fact, the buyer, Tai Lung Worldwide Ltd., was a British Virgin Islands company with a Hong Kong address, and it was wholly owned by a Bahamian corporation called Sandalwood International Ltd., which was, in turn, wholly owned by Mr. Wu's Liechtenstein foundation. His sister's foundation was used in a similar manner. In her case, the documents indicate that her Liechtenstein foundation was the sole owner of a bearer share corporation formed in Samoa, called Manta Company Ltd., which owned a Hong Kong corporation called Bowfin Co. Ltd. which, in turn, held real estate, a vehicle, a mobile telephone, and two bank accounts. LGT documentation indicates that the bank was fully aware of these arrangements and expressed no concerns. LGT documents also show that Mr. Wu transferred substantial sums to his foundation and, over the years, withdrew substantial amounts, ranging from $100,000 to $1.5 million at a time. In one instance, LGT arranged for Mr. Wu to withdraw $100,000 using a HSBC bank check drawn on an LGT correspondent account, which made the funds difficult to trace. By 2006, Mr. Wu's first foundation had been dissolved, while his second foundation had assets in excess of $4.6 million.

Lowy Account: Using a U.S. Corporation to Hide Beneficiaries. Frank Lowy, an Australian citizen, was a pre-existing client of LGT when, in 1996, he formed a new Liechtenstein foundation at LGT to benefit himself and his three sons, David, Peter and Stephen. LGT documents show that Mr. Lowy informed LGT that he wished to hide his ownership of the foundation assets from Australian tax authorities, and rather than express concern, LGT took a number of measures to accomplish that objective. LGT allowed the foundation instruments to be signed, for example, not by the Lowys, but by a Lowy family lawyer, J.H. Gelbard. LGT did not transfer assets from other Lowy-affiliated entities directly to the new foundation, but instead routed them through an offshore corporation, Sewell Services Ltd., to prevent any direct link to other Lowy entities. The foundation instruments did not name the Lowys as beneficiaries. Instead, the foundation instruments included a complex mechanism providing that the beneficiaries would be named by the last corporation in which Beverly Park Corporation, formed in Delaware, held the stock. Despite this provision which authorized a future company to name the beneficiaries, internal LGT documents were explicit that Mr. Lowy and his three sons were the true beneficiaries of the foundation. Documents obtained by the Subcommittee indicate that the Lowys exercised control over the Beverly Park Corp. because it was ultimately owned by the Frank Lowy Family Trust, and Peter Lowy, a U.S. citizen living in California, was appointed the company's president and director. In 2001, when the Lowys decided to dissolve the foundation and move its assets to Switzerland, Beverly Park Corp. formed a new British Virgin Islands corporation named Lonas Inc., whose sole director and officer was the Lowy family lawyer, J.H. Gelbard. After receiving instructions from Lonas to send the foundation assets to accounts in Geneva that did not bear the Lowys' names, LGT telephoned David Lowy twice to confirm the arrangements, recording one of those conversations. These telephone calls indicate that LGT continued to view the Lowys as the true beneficiaries of the foundation. In December 2001, LGT transferred assets valued at about $68 million to a Geneva bank and dissolved the foundation.

Greenfield Accounts: Pitching A Transfer to Liechtenstein. Harvey and Steven Greenfield, father and son, are New York businessmen who are longtime participants in the U.S. toy industry. In 1992, LGT helped Harvey Greenfield establish a Liechtenstein foundation, for which he is the sole primary beneficiary and his son holds power of attorney. This foundation used two British Virgin Islands corporations as conduits to transfer funds, which at the end of 2001, had a combined value of about $2.2 million. In March 2001, at its Liechtenstein offices, LGT held a five-hour meeting with the Greenfields attended by three LGT private bankers and Prince Philipp, Chairman of the Board of the LGT Group and brother to the reigning sovereign. The meeting was primarily a sales pitch to convince the Greenfields to transfer to their LGT foundation assets valued at "around U.S. $30 million" from a Bank of Bermuda office in Hong Kong. An LGT memorandum describing the meeting states:

> "The Bank of Bermuda has indicated to the client that it would like to end the business relationship with him as a U.S. citizen. Due to these circumstances, the client is now on the search for a safe haven for his offshore assets. ... There follows a long discussion about the banking location Liechtenstein, the banking privacy law as well as the security and stability, that Liechtenstein, as a banking location and sovereign nation, can guarantee its clients. The Bank ... indicate[s] strong interest in receiving the U.S. $30 million. ... The clients are very careful and eager to dissolve the Trust with the Bank of Bermuda leaving behind as few traces as possible."

The LGT memorandum expresses no concern about Bank of Bermuda's decision to end its relationship with the Greenfields or their desire to move their funds with "as few traces as possible." The memorandum shows that LGT uses its "banking privacy law" as a selling point, employs the royal family to secure new business, and is more than willing to provide advice and assistance to help U.S. clients move substantial funds in secrecy.

Gonzalez Accounts: Inflating Prices and Frustrating Creditors. Jorge and Conchita Gonzalez, and their son Ricardo, operated a car dealership in the United States for many years. Beginning in 1986, LGT helped them form two Liechtenstein foundations and two Liechtenstein corporations primarily to assist their car dealership, which was located in Puerto Rico and specialized in selling Volvos. Two of these Liechtenstein entities provided financing for the dealership. One of the Liechtenstein corporations, Auto und Motoren AG ("AUM"), represented itself to Volvo as a "guarantor" of the dealership's debts, apparently without revealing that AUM and the dealership were both beneficially owned by the Gonzalezes. As a result, Volvo sent AUM copies of the invoices it sent the dealership for the cars being purchased for sale in Puerto Rico. As disclosed in a civil lawsuit asserting that Volvo, the dealership, and the Gonzalezes had fraudulently overcharged for certain cars, AUM had not merely taken receipt of the Volvo invoices, but had sent additional invoices to the dealership for selected cars, specifying a higher cost for them than Volvo had charged. Because of this "double invoicing scheme," a jury found Volvo liable and assessed damages of $130 million.[14] The court applied the same damages to the dealership and Gonzalezes. The dealership declared bankruptcy, and the Gonzalezes formed a new Liechtenstein foundation to better hide their assets. LGT documents show that the bank was aware of the litigation and, "[f]or the purpose of protection from creditors, who are litigating the family in Puerto Rico," helped the Gonzalezes transfer assets from the prior foundation and companies to the new entity. The Gonzalezes eventually settled the lawsuit for much less. At the end of 2001, the new foundation's accounts held assets with a combined value of about $4.4 million.

Chong Accounts: Moving Funds Through Hidden Accounts. Richard M. Chong is a U.S. citizen, California resident, and venture capitalist. After his father died and left a Liechtenstein foundation to Mr. Chong's mother, LGT helped her reorganize it into four funds benefiting herself and her three children. The funds, called "Fund Mother," "Fund Son R," "Fund Daughter T," and "Fund Son C," held assets that, in 2002, had a combined value of about $9.4 million. LGT records show that, beginning in 1999, Mr. Chong moved large sums into and out of the foundation accounts in transactions that appear related to his business ventures. In 2004, LGT set up for the foundation's exclusive use what LGT has sometimes referred to as a "transfer corporation" to help disguise asset flows into and out of a foundation's accounts. This transfer corporation acts as a pass-through entity that breaks the direct link between the foundation and other persons with whom it is exchanging funds, making it harder to trace those funds. Here, LGT's Hong Kong office acquired Apex Assets Ltd., using a Hong Kong corporate service provider, arranged a mailing address in Samoa, and opened a new account for Apex at the bank. Financial documents show that, afterward, virtually all funds deposited into or withdrawn from the foundation accounts were routed through Apex, a practice that continued into 2007. In 2008, LGT notified Chong of the disclosure of some of its accounts by a former employee, apologized, and provided him with the names of several U.S. lawyers.

Miskin Accounts: Hiding Assets from Courts and a Spouse. Michael Miskin, a U.K. citizen, has claimed residency in Bermuda, but lived in California for a decade, from 1991 to 2002. In 2003, after his wife of nearly 40 years filed for divorce, he effectively disappeared from view, ignored court orders to transfer California real estate and £3 million in alimony to his ex- wife, and hid assets from the court in offshore jurisdictions around the world, including possibly at LGT. LGT documents show that, in the early 1 990s, LGT helped Mr. Miskin open an account in Liechtenstein and deposit millions of Swiss francs, apparently transferred from another Liechtenstein bank that had been disclosed to his wife's legal counsel. In 1998, having obtained information indicating that Mr. Miskin was hiding assets from his wife and tax authorities, LGT nevertheless helped him form a Liechtenstein foundation and transfer into its account his existing LGT funds, then valued at nearly 10 million Swiss francs or $6.6 million. Also in 1998, Mr. Miskin purchased a $700,000 condominium in California, hiding his ownership by making the purchase in the name of a Guernsey corporation owned by a Guernsey trust. Despite evidence that he lived in the condominium for years, Mr. Miskin denied being a U.S. resident; an internal LGT memorandum noted approvingly: "The financial beneficiary has his PLACE OF RESIDENCE IN BERMUDA and not in the U.S. Hence, he pays no taxes in the U.S.!!!!! !" At the end of 2001, $6 million in assets remained at LGT. In 2003, a U.K. court ordered Mr.

Miskin to pay £3 million in alimony and transfer the California realty to his ex-wife. He failed to acknowledge or comply with the court order. When Ms. Miskin filed papers to enforce the U.K. court order in a California court, Mr. Miskin unsuccessfully contested the case. In the end, the U.S. court awarded Ms. Miskin the real estate, but she was unable to obtain the alimony. The existence of the Liechtenstein foundation and funds were not disclosed to the courts or his ex- wife.

These LGT accounts together portray a bank whose personnel too often viewed LGT's role as, not just a guardian of client assets or trusted financial advisor, but also a willing partner to clients wishing to hide their assets from tax authorities, creditors, and courts. In that context, bank secrecy laws have served as a cloak not only for client misconduct, but also for bank personnel colluding with clients to evade taxes, dodge creditors, and defy court orders.

(2) UBS AG case history

UBS AG of Switzerland is one of the largest financial institutions in the world, and has one of the world's largest private banks catering to wealthy individuals. From at least 2000 to 2007, UBS made a concerted effort to open accounts in Switzerland for wealthy U.S. clients, employing practices that could facilitate, and have resulted in, tax evasion by U.S. clients. These UBS practices included maintaining for an estimated 19,000 U.S. clients "undeclared" accounts in Switzerland with billions of dollars in assets that have not been disclosed to U.S. tax authorities; assisting U.S. clients in structuring their accounts to avoid QI reporting requirements; and allowing its Swiss bankers to market securities and banking services on U.S. soil without an appropriate license in apparent violation of U.S. law and UBS policy. In 2007, after its activities within the United States came to the attention of U.S. authorities, UBS banned its Swiss bankers from traveling to the United States and took action to revamp its practices.

The information obtained by the Subcommittee about UBS practices in the United States was obtained, in part, from former UBS employee, Bradley Birkenfeld, a U.S. citizen who worked as a private banker in Switzerland from 1996, until his arrest in the United States in 2008. Mr. Birkenfeld worked for UBS in its private banking operations in Geneva from 2001 to 2005, until he resigned from the bank. In 2007, while in the United States, Mr. Birkenfeld voluntarily provided documentation and testimony to the Subcommittee related to his employment as a private banker. In a sworn deposition before Subcommittee staff, Mr. Birkenfeld provided detailed information about a wide range of issues related to UBS business dealings with U.S. clients. In 2008, Mr. Birkenfeld was arrested, indicted, and pled guilty to conspiring with a U.S. taxpayer, Igor Olenicoff, to hide $200 million in assets in Switzerland and Liechtenstein, and to evade $7.2 million in U.S. taxes.

Maintaining Undeclared Accounts with Billions in Assets. From at least 2000 to 2007, UBS maintained Swiss accounts for thousands of U.S. clients with billions of dollars in assets that have not been disclosed to U.S. tax authorities. Although UBS AG signed a QI agreement with the United States in 2001, UBS has never filed 1099 Forms reporting these accounts to the IRS, contending that these U.S. client accounts fall outside its QI reporting obligations. UBS refers to these accounts internally as "undeclared accounts."

In response to Subcommittee inquiries, UBS has estimated that it today has about 20,000 accounts in Switzerland for U.S. clients, of which roughly 1,000 are declared accounts and 19,000 are undeclared accounts that have not been disclosed to the IRS. UBS also estimates that those accounts contain assets with a combined value of about 18.2 billion in Swiss francs or about $17.9 billion. UBS was unable to specify the breakdown in assets between the undeclared and declared accounts, except to note that the amount of assets in the undeclared accounts would be much greater.

These figures suggest that the number of U.S. client accounts in Switzerland and the amount of assets contained in those accounts have increased significantly since 2002, when a UBS document reported that the Swiss private banking operation then had more than 11,000 accounts for clients in the United States and Canada, with combined assets in excess of 20 billion Swiss francs or about $13.3 billion.

The UBS figures for 2008 are also consistent with internal UBS documents from 2004 and 2005, which suggest that a substantial portion of the UBS Swiss accounts opened for U.S. clients at that time were undeclared, and that these undeclared accounts held more assets, brought in more new money, and were more profitable for the bank than the declared accounts. This information is contained in a set of monthly reports for select months in 2004 and 2005, which tracked key information for the Swiss accounts opened for U.S. clients, breaking down the data for both declared and undeclared accounts. Each report appears to show substantially greater assets in the undeclared accounts than in the declared accounts. In October 2005, for example, the data indicates a total of about 18.5 billion Swiss francs of assets in the undeclared accounts and 2.6 billion Swiss francs in the declared accounts. The October 2005 report also suggests that the undeclared accounts had acquired 1 billion Swiss francs in net new money for UBS, while the declared accounts had collectively lost 333 million Swiss francs over the same time period. The monthly reports also indicate that UBS earned significantly more in revenues from the undeclared accounts. For example, the October 2005 data shows that UBS obtained year-to-date revenues of about 180 million Swiss francs from the undeclared accounts versus 22.1 million Swiss francs from the declared accounts. These statistics suggest that the undeclared U.S. client accounts were more popular and more lucrative for the bank.

In the recent U.S. criminal prosecution of Mr. Birkenfeld, the U.S. government filed a Statement of Facts, signed by Mr. Birkenfeld, stating that UBS in Switzerland had "$20 billion of assets under management in the United States undeclared business, which earned the bank approximately $200 million per year in revenues."

Ensuring Bank Secrecy. UBS has not only opened undeclared Swiss accounts for U.S. clients, UBS has assured its U.S. clients with undeclared accounts that U.S. authorities would not learn about them, because the bank is not required to disclose them; UBS procedures, practices and services protect against disclosure; and the account information is further shielded by Swiss bank secrecy laws. In November 2002, for example, senior officials in the UBS private banking operations in Switzerland sent the following letter to U.S. clients about their Swiss accounts which states in part:

> "[W]e should like to underscore that a Swiss bank which runs afoul of Swiss privacy laws will face sanctions by its Swiss regulator ... [I]t must be clear that information relative to your Swiss banking relationship is as safe as ever and that the possibility of putting pressure on our U.S. units does not change anything. ...
>
> UBS (as all other major Swiss banks) has asked for and obtained the status of a Qualified Intermediary under U.S. tax laws. The QI regime fully respects client confidentiality as customer information are only disclosed to U.S. tax authorities based on the provision of a W-9 form. Should a customer choose not to execute such a form, the client is barred from investments in US securities but under no circumstances will his/her identity be revealed. Consequently, UBS's entire compliance with its QI obligations does not create the risk that his/her identity be shared with U.S. authorities."

This letter plainly asserts that UBS will not disclose to the IRS a Swiss account opened by a U.S. client, so long as that account contains no U.S. securities, even if UBS knows the accountholder is a U.S. taxpayer obligated under U.S. law to report the account and all income to the IRS.

UBS not only maintained secret, undeclared accounts for U.S. clients, it also took steps to assist its U.S. clients to structure their Swiss accounts to avoid QI reporting requirements. UBS informed the Subcommittee that, after it joined the QI Program in 2001, and informed its U.S. clients about its QI disclosure obligations, many U.S. clients elected to sell their U.S. securities so that their identities would not be disclosed to the IRS under the QI agreement UBS told the Subcommittee that, in 2001, these U.S. clients sold over $2 billion in U.S. securities from their Swiss accounts to avoid QI reporting. UBS allowed these U.S. clients to continue to maintain accounts in Switzerland, and helped them reinvest in other types of assets that did not trigger reporting obligations to the IRS, despite evidence that the U.S. clients were using the accounts to hide assets from the IRS. In addition, UBS told the Subcommittee that, in 2001, at least 250 of its U.S. clients with Swiss accounts opened new accounts in the names of offshore corporations, trusts, foundations, or other entities, and transferred assets including, in a number of instances, U.S. securities from their personal accounts to those new accounts. UBS treated the new accounts as held by non-U.S. persons whose identities did not have to be disclosed to the IRS, even though UBS knew that the true beneficial owners were U.S. persons. UBS was unable to estimate for the Subcommittee by the time this Chapter was prepared the total volume of assets that were transferred to these new accounts in 2001, although it said it was working to gather that data.

The Subcommittee also asked UBS whether, after 2001, its Swiss employees had assisted any U.S. clients to avoid QI reporting requirements, either by opening accounts with no U.S. securities or opening accounts in the names of foreign entities that, as non-U.S. persons, were not required to be disclosed to the IRS. UBS told the Subcommittee that it did not have reliable data on the extent to which its Swiss employees may have continued to engage in this conduct from 2002 to the present.

These facts indicate that, soon after it joined the QI Program, UBS helped its U.S. clients structure their Swiss accounts to avoid reporting billions of dollars in assets to the IRS. Among other actions, UBS helped U.S. clients establish offshore structures to assume nominal ownership of assets and allowed U.S. clients to continue to hold undisclosed accounts that were not reported to the IRS. Such actions, while not per se violations of the QI Program, were aimed at circumventing its intended purpose of increasing disclosure of U.S. client accounts, and led to the formation of offshore structures and undeclared accounts that could facilitate, and have resulted in, tax evasion by U.S. clients.

The Statement of Facts in the Birkenfeld criminal case characterizes these actions as follows: "By concealing the U.S. clients' ownership and control in the assets held offshore, defendant Birkenfeld, the Swiss Bank, its managers and bankers evaded the requirements of the Q.I. program, defrauded the IRS and evaded United States income taxes."[15]

Targeting U.S. Clients. Although UBS has extensive banking and securities operations in the United States that could accommodate its U.S. clients, from at least 2000 to 2007, UBS directed its Swiss bankers to target U.S. clients to open more bank accounts in Switzerland. Until recently, UBS encouraged its Swiss bankers to travel to the United States to recruit new U.S. clients, organized events to help them meet wealthy U.S. individuals, and set annual performance goals for obtaining new U.S. business. UBS Swiss bankers also marketed securities and banking products and services while in the United States, and accepted orders for securities transactions from clients in the United States, without an appropriate license and in apparent violation of U.S. law and UBS policy.

U.S. securities law prohibits persons from advertising securities products or services or executing securities transactions within the United States, unless registered with the Securities and Exchange Commission (SEC). In addition, securities products offered to U.S. persons must comply with U.S. securities laws, which generally means they must be registered with the SEC, a condition that may not be met by non-U.S. securities, mutual funds, and other investment products. State securities laws may have similar prohibitions. Moreover, U.S. tax laws may require foreign financial institutions to report sales of non-U.S. securities on 1099 Forms if the sales are effected in the United States, such as through a broker physically in the United States or telephone calls or emails originating in the United States. In addition, although UBS AG is itself licensed to operate as a bank and broker-dealer in the United States, its banking and securities licenses do not extend to its non-U.S. offices or affiliates providing services to U.S. residents.

To avoid violating U.S. law, exceeding their licenses, or triggering 1099 reporting requirements, since at least 2002, UBS has maintained written policies restricting the marketing and client-related activities that may be undertaken in the United States by UBS bankers from outside of the country. For example, 2002 UBS guidelines instruct its Swiss bankers to ensure that there is "no use of US mails, e-mail, courier delivery or facsimile regarding the client's securities portfolio;" "no use of telephone calls into the US regarding the client's securities portfolio;" "no account statements, confirmations, performance reports or any other communications" while in the United States; "no further instructions ... from ... clients while they are in the US;" "no marketing of advisory or brokerage services regarding securities;" "no discussion of or delivery of documents concerning the client's securities portfolio while on visits in the US:" "no discussion of performance, securities purchased or sold or changes in the investment mandate for the client" while in the United States; and "no delivery of documents regarding performance, securities purchased or sold or changes in the investment mandate for the client." The 2004 and 2007 versions of this UBS policy are even more restrictive.

Despite these explicit and extensive restrictions on allowable U.S. activities, from at least 2000 to 2007, UBS routinely authorized and paid for its Swiss bankers to travel to the United States to develop new business and service existing clients. In his deposition, Mr. Birkenfeld told the Subcommittee that, during his four years at UBS, the private bankers from Switzerland who targeted U.S. clients typically traveled to the United States four to six times per year, using their trips to recruit new clients and provide financial services to existing clients. He estimated: "As I remember, there [were] around 25 people in Geneva, 50 people in Zurich, and five to ten in Lugano. This is a formidable force."

Mr. Birkenfeld testified that UBS also provided its Swiss bankers with tickets and funds to go to events attended by wealthy U.S. individuals, so that they could solicit new business for the bank in Switzerland. He said that UBS sponsored U.S. events likely to attract wealthy clients, such as the Art Basel Air Fair in Miami; performances in major U.S. cities by the UBS Vervier Orchestra featuring talented young musicians; and U.S. yachting events attended by the elite Swiss yachting team, Alinghi, which was also sponsored by UBS. A UBS document laying out marketing strategies to attract U.S. clients confirms that the bank "organized VIP events" and engaged in the "Sponsorship of Major Events" such as "Golf, Tennis Tournaments, Art, Special Events." This document even identified the 25 most affluent housing areas in the United States to provide "targeted locations where to organize events."

To gauge the extent of UBS efforts to target U.S. clients while on U.S. soil, the Subcommittee conducted an analysis of more than 500 travel records compiled by the Department of Homeland Security, at the Subcommittee's request, of persons travelling from Switzerland to the United States from 2001 to 2008, to identify UBS Swiss bankers who serviced U.S. clients. The Subcommittee determined that, from 2001 to 2008, roughly twenty UBS Swiss client advisors made an aggregate total of over 300 visits to the United States. Only two of these visits took place from 2001 to 2002; the rest occurred from 2003 to 2008. On several occasions, the visits appear to have involved multiple client advisors travelling together to UBS-sponsored events in the United States. Some of these client advisors designated their visits as travel for a non-business purpose on the I-94 Customs declaration forms that all visitors must complete prior to entry into the United States. Closer analysis, however, reveals that the dates and ports of entry for such trips coincided with the UBS-sponsored events, suggesting the visits were, in fact, business-related. The data also disclosed UBS bankers who made regular U.S. visits. One UBS employee, for example, travelled to the United States three times per year, at roughly four-month intervals, from 2003 to 2007. Another senior UBS Swiss private bank official – Michel Guignard – visited the United

States nearly every other month for a significant portion of the period examined by the Subcommittee. Martin Liechti, an even more senior Swiss private banking official who heads Wealth Management Americas, visited the United States up to eight times in a year.

NNM Performance Goals. UBS not only encouraged its Swiss bankers to travel to the United States to recruit new U.S. clients, it also assigned its Swiss bankers specific performance goals for bringing new money into the bank from the United States. Mr. Birkenfeld told the Subcommittee that, during his tenure at the bank, his superiors at UBS assigned him a specific monetary goal, referred to as a "net new money" or "NNM" target, that he was expected to bring into the bank by the end of the year from U.S. clients. He said that a NNM target was assigned to each Swiss Client Advisor who dealt with U.S. clients, depending upon their seniority and past performance. He told the Subcommittee that it was his "job as a private banker ... to bring in net new money ... probably $50 million a year or $40 million."

A 2007 email from Mr. Liechti indicates that the bank's focus on net new money continued after Mr. Birkenfeld left UBS in 2005. His email wishes his colleagues a "Happy New Year" and then urges them to increase their NNM efforts. He states:

> "The markets are growing fast, and our competition is catching up. ... The answer to guarantee our future is GROWTH. We have grown from CHF 4 million per Client Advisor in 2004 to 17 million in 2006. We need to keep up with our ambitions and go to 60 million per Client Advisor! ...
>
> In the Chinese Horoscope, 2007 is the year of the pig. In many cultures, the pig is a symbol for 'luck'. While it's always good to have [a] bit of luck, it is not luck that leads to success. Success is the result of vision and purpose, hard work and passion. ... Together as a team I am convinced we will succeed!"[16]

The Liechti email indicates that in two years, from 2004 to 2006, UBS Swiss bankers had quadrupled the amount of net new money being drawn into UBS from the "Americas," and that the bank's management sought to quadruple that figure again in a single year, 2007. This email helps to convey the pressure that UBS placed on its Swiss private bankers to bring in new money from the United States into Switzerland.

Mr. Birkenfeld told the Subcommittee that the overall effort of the UBS Swiss private banking operation to secure U.S. clients was the most extensive he had observed in his 12 years working in Swiss private banking. He said the Swiss bankers he worked with typically had an "existing book of business," with numerous U.S. clients, and "a very regimented cycle of going out and acquiring new clients, taking care of your existing clients, make sure the revenue was there." He described one private banker who would see as many as 30 or 40 existing clients on a single trip. He said, "This was a massive machine. I had never seen such a large bank making such a dedicated effort to market to the U.S. market."

A UBS business plan for the years 2003 through 2005, provides context for the Swiss focus on obtaining U.S. clients. This document observes that "3 1% of World's UHNWIs [Ultra High Net Worth Individuals] are in North America (USA + Canada)." It also observes that the United States has 222 billionaires with a combined net worth of $706 billion. This type of information helps explain why UBS dedicated significant resources to obtaining U.S. clients for its private banking operations in Switzerland. It also explains why the Swiss effort to attract billions to their tax haven may have contributed to the huge tax loss to the U.S. treasury.

Servicing U.S. Clients with Swiss Accounts. UBS not only allowed U.S. clients to open undeclared accounts in Switzerland, it also took steps to ensure that its Swiss bankers serviced their U.S. clients in ways that minimized disclosure of information to U.S. authorities. Mr. Birkenfeld told the Subcommittee that UBS private bankers were supposed to keep a low profile during their business trips to avoid attracting attention from U.S. authorities. He noted, for example, that UBS business cards did not include a reference to a private banker's involvement in "wealth management." He also said that some UBS Swiss private bankers who visited the United States on business told U.S. customs officials that they were instead in the country for non-business reasons. UBS also provided its private bankers with explicit training on how to detect -- and avoid – surveillance by U.S. customs agents and law enforcement officers, and how to react if confronted.

Protecting client-specific account information was also a concern. Mr. Birkenfeld explained, for example, that client account statements were normally kept in Switzerland rather than mailed to the United States. He said that Swiss bankers traveling to the United States to meet with specific clients took elaborate measures to disguise or encrypt the account information they brought with them, to prevent it from falling into the wrong hands. He said, for example, some bankers took "cryptic notes" of the account information, created handwritten spreadsheets with no identifying information other than a code name, or used computers equipped to receive only highly encrypted information that, allegedly, "[e]ven if the [U.S.] Customs opened it, for instance, they wouldn't see anything."

Mr. Birkenfeld also told the Subcommittee that, despite U.S. laws and UBS policies restricting securities activities that could be undertaken in the United States by non-U.S. personnel, some UBS Swiss bankers communicated with their U.S. clients by telephone, fax, mail and email, to market securities products and services, and to carry out securities transactions. The facts suggest, until recently, UBS was not enforcing its own policies. This lack of enforcement, in turn, raises concerns that UBS Swiss bankers with U.S. clients may have been routinely violating UBS policy and U.S. law.

Olenicoff Accounts. These concerns are further illustrated by the recent criminal prosecution involving UBS accounts opened in Switzerland by Mr. Birkenfeld for Igor Olenicoff. Mr. Olenicoff is a billionaire real estate developer, U.S. citizen, and resident of Florida and California. From 2001 until 2005, Mr. Birkenfeld and Mario Staggl, a trust officer from Liechtenstein helped Mr. Olenicoff open multiple bank accounts in the names of offshore companies he controlled at UBS in Switzerland and Neue Bank in Liechtenstein. For a time, Mr. Olenicoff was Mr. Birkenfeld's largest private banking client. To service these accounts, Mr. Birkenfeld met with Mr. Olenicoff in the United States and elsewhere, communicated with him by telephone, fax, and email in the United States, and advised him on how to avoid disclosure of his accounts and assets to the IRS. In 2007, Mr. Olenicoff pled guilty to one criminal count of filing a false income tax return by failing to disclose the foreign bank accounts he controlled. He was sentenced to two years probation and 120 hours of community service, and paid six years of back taxes, interest, and penalties totaling $52 million. In 2008, Mr. Birkenfeld pled guilty to conspiring with Mr. Olenicoff to defraud the IRS and avoid payment of taxes owed on $200 million in assets hidden in accounts in

Switzerland and Liechtenstein. Their alleged coconspirator, Mr. Staggl, remains at large in Liechtenstein.

2007 Overhaul. In November 2007, after its U.S. activities had come to the attention of U.S. authorities, UBS imposed a travel ban prohibiting its Swiss bankers from going to the United States. In addition, UBS re-issued a policy statement with more extensive restrictions on allowable activities within the United States by its non-U.S. personnel. UBS is currently under investigation by the SEC, IRS, and Department of Justice.

C. Report Findings and Recommendations

Based upon its investigation, the Subcommittee staff makes the following findings of fact and recommendations.

Report findings

Based upon its investigation, the Subcommittee staff makes the following findings of fact.

1. **Bank Secrecy.** Bank secrecy laws and practices are serving as a cloak, not only for client misconduct, but also for misconduct by banks colluding with clients to evade taxes, dodge creditors, and defy court orders.
2. **Bank Practices That Facilitate Tax Evasion.** From at least 2000 to 2007, LGT and UBS employed banking practices that could facilitate, and have resulted in, tax evasion by their U.S. clients, including assisting clients to open accounts in the names of offshore entities; advising clients on complex offshore structures to hide ownership of assets; using client code names; and disguising asset transfers into and from accounts.
3. **Billions in Undeclared U.S. Client Accounts.** Since 2001, LGT and UBS have collectively maintained thousands of U.S. client accounts with billions of dollars in assets that have not been disclosed to the IRS. UBS alone has an estimated 19,000 accounts in Switzerland for U.S. clients with assets valued at $18 billion. The IRS has identified at least 100 accounts with U.S. clients at LGT.
4. **QI Structuring.** LGT and UBS have assisted their U.S. clients in structuring their foreign accounts to avoid QI reporting to the IRS, including by allowing U.S. clients who sold their U.S. securities to continue to hold undisclosed accounts and by opening accounts in the name of non-U.S. entities beneficially owned by U.S. clients. While these banking practices did not technically violate the banks' QI agreements, the result is that the banks helped keep accounts secret from the IRS and thereby facilitated tax evasion by their U.S. clients.

Report recommendations

Based upon its investigation and factual findings, the Subcommittee staff makes the following recommendations.

1. **Strengthen QI Reporting of Foreign Accounts Held by U.S. Persons.** In addition to prosecuting misconduct under existing law, the Administration should strengthen the Qualified Intermediary Agreement by requiring QI participants to file 1099 forms for: (1) all U.S. persons who are clients (whether or not the client has U.S. securities or receives U.S. source income); and (2) accounts beneficially owned by U.S. persons, even if the accounts are held in the name of a foreign corporation, trust, foundation, or other entity. The IRS should also close the "QI-KYC Gap" by expressly requiring QI participants to apply to their QI reporting obligations all information obtained through their know-your-customer procedures to identify the beneficial owners of accounts.
2. **Strengthen 1099 Reporting.** Congress should strengthen the statutory 1099 reporting requirements by requiring any domestic or foreign financial institution that obtains information that the beneficial owner of a foreign-owned financial account is a U.S. taxpayer to file a 1099 form reporting that account to the IRS.
3. **Penalize Tax Haven Banks that Impede U.S. Tax Enforcement.** Treasury should penalize tax haven banks that impede U.S. tax enforcement or fail to disclose accounts held directly or indirectly by U.S. clients by terminating their QI status, and Congress should amend Section 311 of the Patriot Act to allow Treasury to bar such banks from doing business with U.S. financial institutions.
4. **Attribute Presumption of Control to U.S. Taxpayers Using Tax Havens.** Congress should amend U.S. tax laws to create a presumption in enforcement proceedings that legal entities, such as corporations, trusts, and foundations, are under the control of the U.S. persons who formed them, sent them assets, or received assets from them, where those entities are located or operating in an offshore secrecy jurisdiction.
5. **Allow More Time to Combat Offshore Tax Abuses.** Congress should extend from three years to six years the amount of time IRS has after a return is filed to investigate and propose assessments of additional tax if the case involves an offshore tax haven with secrecy laws and practices.
6. **Enact Stop Tax Haven Abuse Act.** Congress should enact the Stop Tax Haven Abuse Act to strengthen the United States ability to combat offshore tax abuse.

II. BACKGROUND

A. The Problem of Offshore Tax Abuse

Each year, the United States loses an estimated $100 billion in tax revenues due to offshore tax abuses.[17] These funds represent a substantial portion of the annual U.S. tax gap, which is the difference between what U.S. taxpayers owe and what they pay, most recently estimated by the IRS at $345 billion.[18]

In 2006, the Subcommittee released a report and held a hearing on six case studies showing how a mature offshore industry, using an armada of tax attorneys, accountants, bankers, brokers, corporate service providers, trust administrators, and others, aggressively promotes the use of tax havens to U.S. citizens as a means to avoid U.S. taxes.[19] In one case history, from 1992 to 2005, two brothers from Texas created a network consisting of 58 offshore trusts and corporations, transferred $190 million in assets to that network, and directed the investment of those offshore assets, without paying taxes on either the initial transfers or the offshore income of more than $600 million subsequently generated.[20] Three other case histories showed how U.S. businessmen used offshore trusts and shell companies to hide substantial funds and other assets from U.S. tax authorities.[21] The remaining two case histories focused on how a U.S. offshore promoter helped U.S. citizens open offshore accounts and establish offshore structures, while a U.S. securities firm used offshore entities and a phony offshore securities portfolio in an abusive tax shelter that offset billions of dollars in taxable income within the United States.[22]

The 2006 Subcommittee hearing focused primarily on the roles played by U.S. professionals, such as tax attorneys, accountants, investment advisors, and bankers, in assisting U.S. taxpayers in moving assets offshore and using those offshore assets to further their personal or business aims. The roles played by tax haven professionals and financial institutions received less extensive review. The Liechtenstein tax scandal and the arrest of a former UBS private banker, however, demonstrate anew the key role played by tax haven financial institutions in facilitating, knowingly or unknowingly, U.S. tax dodges.

B. Initiatives to Combat Offshore Tax Abuse

Concerns about offshore tax abuses and the role of tax havens in facilitating tax evasion are longstanding. This Subcommittee held a hearing in 1983 on U.S. taxpayers using offshore secrecy jurisdictions to hide assets and evade U.S. taxes.[23] Over the years, the United States and the international community have undertaken an array of initiatives to combat offshore tax abuses. In recent years, this effort has intensified. A brief summary of major initiatives over the last ten years to combat offshore tax abuses follows.

Tax Information Exchange Agreements. One major effort undertaken by the United States to combat offshore tax abuse is its ongoing work to obtain tax treaties or tax information exchange agreements (TIEAs) with foreign countries.[24] A major objective of these treaties and agreements is to establish arrangements for the United States to obtain information from its counterpart to advance its tax enforcement efforts.[25]

The United States has entered into more than 60 tax treaties with other countries.[26] A United States Model Income Tax Convention establishes the basic format and provisions that the United States seeks to include in its tax treaties.[27] Article 26 of the Model Convention focuses on tax information exchange. The model Article 26 states that the treaty partners "shall exchange such information as may be relevant for carrying out the provisions of this Convention or of the domestic laws of the Contracting States concerning taxes of every kind ... including information relating to the assessment or collection of, the enforcement or prosecution in respect of, or the determination of appeals in relation to, such taxes." Article 26 requires the treaty partners to protect the confidentiality of the information received from the other country and to disclose the information only to persons, administrative bodies, and courts involved in tax administration. Article 26 also allows a treaty partner to refuse to share information in certain limited circumstances, such as if obtaining the information would be at variance with the country's laws.

In addition, the United States has entered into more than 20 TIEAs, many with known tax havens. TIEAs first came into use about 20 years ago, after Congress enacted a 1983 law authorizing the U.S. Treasury Department to negotiate bilateral or multilateral tax information exchange agreements with certain countries in the Caribbean and Central America.[28] TIEAs received another boost in 2000, when the OECD began obtaining written commitments from a number of offshore jurisdictions promising to enter into tax information exchange agreements with other countries in order to avoid being identified as an uncooperative tax haven.[29]

TIEAs, by their nature, are more limited than tax treaties, since they deal with only one issue, tax information exchange. Typically, TIEAs require the tax authorities of the two countries to agree to exchange information upon request in both criminal and civil tax matters. The parties also typically promise to provide the requested information whether or not the person at issue is a resident or citizen of either country, and whether or not the matter would constitute a violation of the tax laws of the country being asked to supply the information. In addition, the parties typically promise to provide each other with the requested information regardless of laws or practices relating to bank secrecy.

For many years, few offshore tax havens would agree to enter into a tax treaty or TIEA with the United States requiring the exchange of tax information. During the Bush Administration, however, the Treasury Department made a concerted effort to obtain TIEAs with known tax havens, in an effort to strengthen their cooperation with U.S. tax enforcement efforts. Since 2000, the Bush Administration has signed more than a dozen TIEAs. Many of these TIEAs have only recently gone into effect, and opinion is divided on whether tax havens are fully complying with the agreements.[30]

A few countries that have resisted signing either a tax treaty or TIEA with the United States have instead entered into tax information exchange arrangements as part of a Mutual Legal Assistance Treaty ("MLAT").[31] MLATs typically establish the parameters for the signatory countries to cooperate in criminal investigations and prosecutions. By using this mechanism to respond to tax information requests, the signatory country agrees to provide tax information only in criminal tax matters. Since most U.S. tax matters are handled in civil rather than criminal proceedings, this approach severely restricts tax information exchanges between the two countries.[32]

Liechtenstein has never entered into either a tax treaty or TIEA with the United States.[33] In 2002, Liechtenstein did enter into a Mutual Legal Assistance Treaty with the United States, and agreed to participate in tax information exchanges in the context of criminal proceedings.[34] Under the MLAT, Liechtenstein agreed to provide assistance in U.S. criminal matters where the conduct at issue "constitutes tax fraud, defined as tax evasion committed by means of the intentional use of false, falsified or incorrect business records or other documents, provided the tax due ... is substantial."[35] Diplomatic notes exchanged in connection with the MLAT list five types of intentional conduct that presumptively qualify as "tax fraud" entitled to assistance under the treaty, including the preparation or filing of false documents, the destruction of records, or the concealment of assets.[36]

Switzerland has a longer history of cooperation with the United States on tax matters, although, like Liechtenstein, that cooperation has been limited to criminal tax matters. Switzerland first entered into a tax treaty with the United States in 1951.[37] Under that treaty, Switzerland agreed to exchange information only in criminal cases involving "tax fraud," a criminal offense narrowly defined in Swiss law.[38] In 1996, Switzerland and the United States updated the tax treaty and, among other changes, modernized the tax information exchange provisions.[39] A revised Article 26 now states that the treaty partners "shall exchange such information ... as is necessary for carrying out the provisions of the present Convention or for the prevention of tax fraud or the like."[40] A Protocol agreed to in connection with the revised tax treaty provides a new definition of "tax fraud" than what was applied in the earlier tax treaty or in Swiss law. The Protocol states that "the term 'tax fraud' means fraudulent conduct that causes or is intended to cause an illegal and substantial reduction in the amount of the tax paid."[41] The Protocol also states: "Fraudulent conduct is assumed in situations when a taxpayer uses, or has the intention to use a forged or falsified document ... or, in general , a false piece of documentary evidence, and in situations where the taxpayer uses, or has the intention to use a scheme of lies ('Lugengebaude') to deceive the tax authority." The U.S. State Department, when submitting the new treaty for ratification by the U.S. Senate, stated that the new provisions had "significantly expand[ed] the scope of the exchange of information between the United States and Switzerland."[42] Other observers, while conceding the improvements achieved in the 1996 tax treaty, remain critical of Swiss assistance in U.S. tax matters.

Qualified Intermediary Program. In addition to its systematic effort to obtain tax treaties or tax information exchange agreements with foreign governments, the United States launched a new initiative in 2000, which took effect in 2001, called the Qualified Intermediary ("QI") Program.[43] The QI Program is intended to encourage foreign financial institutions to report U.S. source income to the IRS and withhold taxes on that income as required by U.S. tax law. Thousands of foreign financial institutions have become voluntary QI participants.[44]

The QI Program is focused primarily on U.S. source income.[45] U.S. source income refers to income that originates in the United States, such as dividends paid on U.S. stock; capital gains paid on sales of U.S. stock or real estate; royalties paid on U.S. assets; rent paid on U.S. property; interest paid on U.S. deposits; and other types of "fixed, determinable, annual, or periodic income."[46] Most of this income, when paid to a U.S person, is taxable; most of it is not taxable when paid to a non-U.S. person, in an apparent effort to attract foreign investment to the United States. But a few categories of U.S. source income, such as U.S. stock dividends, are taxable even when paid to a non-U.S. person.

The QI Program seeks to enlist foreign financial institutions in the U.S. effort to collect and remit U.S. taxes owed primarily on U.S. source income, by offering participating institutions reduced paperwork and disclosure obligations. The QI Program applies only to foreign financial institutions that buy and sell U.S. securities on behalf of their clients through securities accounts opened at U.S. financial institutions. Treasury regulations, which took effect in 2001, require U.S. financial institutions to withhold 30 percent of the income earned on U.S. investments maintained in a foreign financial account, unless the foreign financial institution provides the U.S. withholding agent with the names of the beneficial owners of the accounts.[47] In effect, these regulations require foreign financial institutions doing business with U.S. financial institutions to disclose their clients by name or risk 30 percent of their client's income being withheld by the U.S. financial institution. Even with this 30 percent penalty, many foreign financial institutions were reluctant to provide their client names, not only because it opened the door to competition from the U.S. financial institution over the clients, but also because it undermined bank secrecy. The QI Program was designed, in part, to resolve this dilemma for foreign financial institutions.

To participate in the QI program, a foreign financial institution must voluntarily sign a 65-page standardized agreement with the IRS.[48] By signing the agreement, the foreign financial institution agrees to act as the U.S. withholding agent and comply with the withholding obligations set out in U.S. tax law for certain clients. In addition, it must have "know-yourcustomer" ("KYC") procedures in place that ensure the foreign financial institution verifies and documents the beneficial owner of any account at its institution.

To carry out its withholding obligations, the foreign financial institution agrees to obtain a W-9 or W8BEN Form from all of its clients who buy or sell U.S. securities through any account for which the foreign financial institution is a designated QI participant. These forms, which each client must fill out and provide to the foreign financial institution, identify the client as either a U.S. or non-U.S. person.[49] For every client who completes a W-9 Form – indicating the client is a U.S. person -- the foreign financial institution agrees to file an annual, individualized 1099 Form with the IRS, reporting the client's name, taxpayer identification number, and all "reportable payments" made to the client's accounts.[50] In contrast, for every non-U.S. person filing a W8BEN Form, the foreign financial institution is not required to file an individualized 1042S Form reporting account information to the IRS. Instead, QI participants calculate the "reportable amounts" of U.S. source income paid to all of their non-U.S. accounts in the QI Program, file a single 1042 Form for each category of U.S. source income paid to those accounts – also called "pooled reporting" – and remit any withheld taxes to the IRS on an aggregated basis.

The 1042 forms filed by QI participants for non-U.S. accountholders do not contain any client names or client-specific information; instead each form contains a single aggregate figure for a single category of U.S. source income paid by the foreign financial institution during the year to all of its non-U.S. accountholders that traded U.S. securities. The foreign financial institution is also allowed to remit the withheld taxes in aggregated amounts to the IRS, with no breakdown for individual clients. For example, in the case of U.S. stock dividends, the QI participant would report the total amount of dividend payments made to all of its non-U.S. accountholders during the year on a single 1042 Form, and would remit 30 percent of that total to the IRS, without providing any client-specific information. The practical effect, in the words of one Liechtenstein bank, was to preserve bank secrecy for non-U.S. accountholders, since the foreign financial institution was under no obligation to disclose any client names.[51]

Because U.S. securities transactions are configured, bought, and sold in U.S. dollars, foreign financial institutions are required to execute U.S. securities transactions through dollar accounts at U.S. financial institutions. If a foreign financial institution participates in the QI Program, it can designate these accounts as "QI Accounts." If the foreign financial institution does not participate in the program, it has only "Non-QI" or "NQI Accounts." Foreign financial institutions are required to designate each securities account they maintain with a U.S. financial institution as either a QI or NQI Account. With both types of accounts, the foreign financial institution internally tracks the dividends derived from U.S. securities and other U.S. source income paid to individual client accounts. With an NQI Account, the foreign financial institution must provide those individual client names to the U.S. financial institution, which in turn reports and remits withholding taxes to the IRS. But with a QI Account, the foreign financial institution may submit to the IRS forms using pooled reporting and aggregate withholdings, without disclosing the names of any non-U.S. persons holding U.S. securities. These financial institutions are thus allowed to withhold their client names from the IRS (and their American competitors) while maintaining the same access to the U.S. securities market – one of the world's most lucrative – as U.S. financial institutions.

To ensure that the program is operating as intended, QI participants agree to an auditing regime. Generally, audits under the QI Program are conducted by external auditors chosen by the QI participant. Audits are intended to ensure that QI participants adhere to the standards and procedures set forth in the QI agreement. So that QIs are able to maintain client secrecy, the IRS does not have access to the raw information reviewed by the external auditor, although the IRS sets the audit parameters, reviews the qualifications of the external auditor, and determines whether the auditor faces any impediments such that they cannot accurately review the QI participant's performance. Audits are conducted in the second and fifth years of the QI agreement, with audit reports remitted to the IRS. If an audit report raises concerns within the IRS, a second phase audit is ordered, focusing on the areas of concern. Should the concerns continue, a third phase is ordered. According to a December 2007 review of the QI Program by the U.S. Government Accountability Office ("GAO"), "high rates of documentation failure, underreporting of U.S. source income, and underwithholding" are the three most common reasons for third phase reviews.[52] Failure to satisfactorily resolve the concerns -- or submit timely-filed audit reports – results in termination of the relevant QI Agreement.

In its review of the QI Program, GAO found that the QI agreement is silent on whether external auditors must perform additional procedures "if information indicating that fraud or illegal acts that could materially affect the results of the [audit] come to their attention."[53] GAO's analysis indicates that, under the current QI agreement, auditors are not required to, and generally do not, follow-up on indications of fraud or illegal acts by the QI participant.[54]

Since the inception of the QI program, about 7,000 foreign financial institutions have signed QI agreements and participated in the program.[55] Due to mergers, withdrawals, and terminations, the IRS estimates that about 5,500 QI agreements are now active. The IRS estimates that about 100 foreign financial institutions have been involuntarily terminated from the QI program since its inception, for inadequate compliance, failed audits, or similar problems.[56] In Liechtenstein, 13 of its 15 banks have signed QI agreements; in Switzerland, virtually all major banks are QI signatories.

The QI Program has now been in effect for seven years, and evidence is emerging that some foreign financial institutions have been manipulating their QI reporting obligations to avoid reporting U.S. client accounts to the IRS. In its December 2007 study, for example, GAO discusses foreign accounts held in the name of foreign corporations, noting that "establishing a foreign corporation provides a mechanism for shielding the identity of the owner."[57] GAO explains further:

> "U.S. tax law enables the owners of offshore corporations to shield their identities from IRS scrutiny, thereby providing U.S. persons a mechanism to exploit for sheltering their income from U.S. taxation. Under current U.S. tax law, corporations, including foreign corporations, are treated as the taxpayers and the owners of assets of their assets and income. Because the owners of the corporation are not known to [the] IRS, individuals are able to hide behind the corporate structure."[58]

GAO warns that the consequence under the QI Program is that "U.S. persons may evade taxes by masquerading as foreign corporations."[59]

GAO states: "Even if withholding agents learn the identities of the owners of foreign corporations while carrying out their due diligence responsibilities, they do not have a responsibility to report that information to IRS."[60] To the contrary, GAO observes that "IRS regulations permit withholding agents (domestic and QIs) to accept documentation declaring corporations' ownership of income at face value, unless they have 'a reason to know' that the documentation is invalid."[61] GAO observes that the QI agreement "implicitly" requires foreign financial institutions to use their know-your-customer documentation to assess the validity of a W8 certificate, but concludes there is no requirement that foreign corporations beneficially owned by U.S. persons be treated as U.S. accountholders that have to be disclosed to the IRS.[62]

GAO notes that where a foreign corporation is owned by a U.S. person, the U.S person has the legal obligation to report the corporate ownership and any taxable income to the IRS on their personal tax returns. GAO also notes that "compliance in reporting income to IRS is poor when there is no third party reporting to IRS."[63] The GAO report determines that, in 2003, foreign corporations received roughly $200 billion in U.S. source income, representing nearly 70% of all U.S. source income reported that year. GAO calculates that only about $3 billion in tax revenue was paid on that income, reflecting a withholding rate of 1.4% and treaty benefits of $57 billion.[64] GAO concludes that it is unclear what proportion of the beneficial owners of these foreign corporations were U.S. persons who had failed to report their income.

These and other QI abuses[65] have led the IRS to consider strengthening the QI agreement to ensure that more foreign accounts beneficially owned by U.S. persons are disclosed to the IRS.

OECD Uncooperative Tax Haven Initiative. The United States has used tax treaties, TIEAs, and the QI Program to improve tax enforcement outside of the United States. A number of multilateral initiatives to curb international tax evasion have also been undertaken over the past ten years.

One of the most visible of recent international efforts to curb international tax evasion has been led by the Organization for Economic Cooperation and Development (OECD), a coalition of 30 nations, including the United States, committed to democratic governments and market economies. In 1996, in part at the urging of the United States, the OECD formed a working group called the Forum on Harmful Tax Competition to curb "harmful preferential tax regimes" and "harmful tax practices" that hurt efforts by individual countries to enforce their tax laws.

In 1998, the OECD issued a report which, among other matters, criticized tax havens that failed to cooperate with international tax enforcement efforts by refusing to provide requested information.[66] In 2000, the OECD published a second report focused in particular on how bank secrecy laws in many tax havens impeded their cooperation with international tax information requests. The report stated that all OECD countries should "permit tax authorities to have access to bank information, directly or indirectly, for all tax purposes so that tax authorities can fully discharge their revenue raising responsibilities and engage in effective exchange of information."[67]

As a result of these two reports, in mid-2000, the OECD published a list of 35 offshore jurisdictions that it planned to include in a subsequent list of "uncooperative tax havens," unless the countries made written commitments to exchange information in international criminal tax matters by December 2003, and in international civil tax matters by December 2005.[68] The OECD defined a "tax haven" as a country with no or nominal taxation, ineffective tax information exchange with other countries, and a lack of transparency in its tax or regulatory regime, including excessive bank or beneficial ownership secrecy.[69]

Many countries did not want to appear on either the OECD's list of 35 offshore jurisdictions or its subsequent list of uncooperative tax havens. To avoid being included on the list of 35 offshore jurisdictions, six countries, Bermuda, the Cayman Islands, Cyprus, Malta, Mauritius, and San Marino, gave the OECD signed commitment letters in early 2000, promising to provide effective tax information exchange in criminal and civil matters by the specified deadlines.[70] In response, the OECD omitted these countries from the list of 35. To avoid appearing on the list of uncooperative tax havens, other countries provided similar commitment letters to the OECD in 2000 and 2001, and the OECD agreed to omit them from the list of uncooperative tax havens being prepared.

Despite wavering support from the United States for the OECD effort,[71] by 2002, 28 of the original 35 offshore jurisdictions identified by the OECD had committed to providing effective information exchange in criminal and civil tax matters by the specified dates.[72] The result was that only seven countries were actually named on the OECD's official list of uncooperative tax havens made public in mid-2002.[73] Over time, four of the seven countries made the required commitments, so that, by 2008, the OECD list had shrunk to just three countries, Liechtenstein, Monaco, and Andorra. To date, these three countries have continued to refuse to agree to provide tax exchange information with other countries in civil and criminal matters.[74]

Over the same period it was developing the lists of offshore jurisdictions and uncooperative tax havens, the OECD took a number of steps to advance global tax information exchange. In 2000, it established the Global Forum on Taxation, with participants drawn from OECD member countries and non-member offshore jurisdictions, to discuss transparency and tax information exchange issues. In 2002, the OECD issued a model tax information exchange agreement that countries could sign on a bilateral or multilateral basis to meet their commitments to tax information exchange.[75] In 2004, to further promote the OECD's work, the G20 Finance Ministers issued a communiqué supporting the OECD's tax information exchange initiative and model agreement.[76]

In 2006, the OECD issued a new report assessing the legal and administrative frameworks for tax transparency and tax information exchange in 82 countries.[77] The purpose of this assessment was to help the OECD determine "what is required to achieve a global level playing field in the areas of transparency and effect exchange of information for tax purposes."[78] In October 2007, the OECD updated its 82-country assessment.[79] The OECD wrote:

> "Significant restrictions on access to bank [information] for tax purposes remain in three OECD countries (Austria, Luxembourg, Switzerland) and in a number of offshore financial centres (e.g. Cyprus, Liechtenstein, Panama and Singapore). Moreover, a number of offshore financial centres that committed to implement

standards on transparency and the effective exchange of information standards developed by the OECD's Global Forum on Taxation have failed to do so."[80]

OECD-led efforts to promote tax information exchange are ongoing. In March 2007, the OECD sponsored a series of meetings among more than 100 tax inspectors from 36 countries to discuss aggressive tax planning schemes seen within their jurisdictions. According to top OECD officials, the meetings indicated that key elements in most of these tax dodges could be traced to tax havens.[81] In January 2008, the OECD held discussions among its members on taking "defensive measures" against tax havens that refuse to cooperate with tax information requests.[82] Some OECD members have also recently called for a reinvigorated list of uncooperative tax havens to include countries that, despite a written commitment, have failed to provide tax information upon request in criminal and civil matters.[83]

EU Savings Directive. In addition to the OECD initiative, another highly visible multinational effort to promote tax information exchange and international tax enforcement cooperation is the European Union Savings Directive. This Directive focuses on the problem of European Union (EU) residents who open up a savings account in an EU country other than their home jurisdiction, in an attempt to hide assets and dodge taxes.

In essence, the EU Directive establishes a legal framework for EU countries to participate in automatic exchanges of information to identify EU residents with savings accounts in EU countries other than their home jurisdiction and to disclose the amount of interest payments made to those savings accounts. The aim of the Directive is to implement a European Commission principle that "all citizens resident in a Member State of the European Union should pay the tax due on all their savings income."[84]

The EU Savings Directive was formally adopted by the European Commission in 2003, took effect on July 1, 2005, and sponsored the first automated exchange of information among EU countries in 2006.[85] Of the 27 EU Member States, 24 participate in the automatic exchanges of information, which take place at least once per year.[86] Information is exchanged in a standardized format that specifies the identity and country of residence of the individual who received the interest payments, the amount of interest paid, and the types of debt claims that gave rise to the interest. Reportable payments include interest paid on cash deposits, corporate or government bonds, negotiable debt securities, and investment funds. Other types of payments are not covered, such as stock dividend payments, income paid from insurance or pension products, or interest payments from certain bonds.[87] In addition, the Directive applies only to savings accounts held by individuals; it does not apply to accounts held by corporations, trusts, foundations, or other legal entities.

Three EU members, Austria, Belgium, and Luxembourg, currently do not participate in the Directive's automatic information exchanges. Instead, under a special arrangement approved as part of the Directive, these three EU countries levy a withholding tax on the interest payments made to nonresident individuals and, once per year, remit 75% of the amounts withheld to the individuals' reported State of residence.[88] The three countries are allowed to retain 25% of the amount withheld to cover their administrative costs of applying the withholding tax.[89] The three countries are not required to provide client-specific information to any other country, such as the names of the individuals who received the interest payments or the amounts of interest paid; they are thereby able to preserve bank secrecy.

The option provided to these three countries of providing withheld taxes instead of information about the nonresident individuals who received interest payments is described in EU materials as a temporary arrangement during a "transitional period."[90] During the transitional period, the three countries are supposed to impose a 15% withholding tax on the interest payments for the first three years the Directive is in effect, a period that ended on June 30, 2008. For the next three years, until June 30, 2011, the three countries are supposed to impose a 20% withholding tax. Thereafter, they are supposed to impose a 35% withholding tax which is intended to be sufficiently high to discourage international tax evasion.[91]

The transitional period does not have a specified ending date, but is designed to continue until the three EU countries, Austria, Belgium, and Luxembourg, as well as six other countries, Andorra, Liechtenstein, Monaco, San Marino, Switzerland, and the United States, agree to exchange tax information upon request, as set out in the OECD Model Agreement for exchanging information in tax matters.[92]

The EU Savings Directive applies to all 27 countries in the European Union. By agreement, it also applies to a number of countries outside the European Union, including ten overseas dependent territories associated with the United Kingdom and the Netherlands,[93] as well as Andorra, Liechtenstein, Monaco, San Marino, and Switzerland. Four of these non-EU countries, Anguilla, Aruba, the Cayman Islands, and Montserrat, have agreed to participate in the Directive's automatic information exchanges.[94] The rest, however, comply with the EU Savings Directive in the same manner as Austria, Belgium, and Luxembourg, by applying a withholding tax during the specified transitional period rather than by supplying information about nonresident individuals who received interest payments on savings accounts within their jurisdictions.

The EU is currently in discussions to extend the Savings Directive to Hong Kong, Macao, and Singapore as well.[95]

The EU Savings Directive is required to be reviewed every three years. After the Liechtenstein tax scandal erupted, Germany requested that the review examine whether the Directive should be expanded to cover more types of payments, such as stock dividends and capital gains; and more types of accountholders such as shell companies, trusts, foundations, and other legal entities being used by individuals to hide assets and dodge taxes.[96] This discussion is ongoing.

Joint International Tax Enforcement Efforts. A final set of international tax initiatives that have intensified in recent years involve joint initiatives among various groups of countries to coordinate and enhance their tax enforcement efforts.

In 2004, for example, four countries, Australia, Canada, the United Kingdom, and the United States, established a Joint International Tax Shelter Information Centre (JIT SIC) to identify, develop, and share information on a real-time basis about cross-border abusive tax schemes. A Washington, D.C. office was established to house tax personnel from all four countries. In May 2007, Japan accepted an invitation to become the fifth member of JITSIC, and a second JITSIC office was opened in London. JITSIC personnel exchange information on an ongoing basis about abusive tax schemes, their promoters, and participants. Among other actions, JITSIC has tackled abusive tax schemes involving retirement account withdrawals, highly structured financing transactions designed to generate inappropriate foreign tax credit benefits, and futures and options transactions designed to generate phony tax losses.[97] The IRS has testified that JIT SIC has "sharply improved" IRS knowledge and understanding of these complex crossborder tax schemes.[98]

In 2006, the tax administrators of ten countries formed the "Leeds Castle Group" to meet regularly and discuss issues of global and national tax administration, including mutual compliance challenges. The countries participating in this effort are Australia, Canada, China, France, Germany, India, Japan, South Korea, the United Kingdom, and the United States. This group is actively promoting international tax cooperation.

In addition, since 2002, the OECD has sponsored the Forum on Tax Administration, a group consisting of the tax administrators from its 30 member nations and several other countries. This Forum has promoted dialogue between tax administrators to identify good tax administration practices and promote tax enforcement. The Forum has focused to date on: (1) developing a directory of aggressive tax planning schemes to help identify trends and countermeasures; (2) examining the role of tax intermediaries, such as lawyers and accountants, in facilitating tax evasion; (3) expanding 2004 Corporate Governance Guidelines to encourage companies to issue a set of tax principles to guide their tax activities; and (4) improving the training of tax officials, especially on international tax matters.

C. Tax Haven Banks and Offshore Tax Abuse

Over the past 30 years, dozens of countries have declared themselves tax havens and have authorized nominal or no taxation of assets transferred to their financial institutions by residents of other countries. These countries have enacted laws enabling nonresidents to form at minimal cost companies, trusts, foundations, and other legal entities to hold their assets in financial accounts protected by secrecy laws and practices enforced with criminal and civil penalties. Trillions of dollars in individual and corporate assets have since been deposited at financial institutions within these tax havens, too often as part of an effort by the beneficial owner to hide assets and dodge taxes in their home jurisdictions.

Increasingly, countries facing substantial tax evasion have taken actions to protect themselves from tax haven financial institutions that, knowingly or unknowingly, are facilitating tax dodging by nonresidents. These actions include participation in a wide range of international tax initiatives, from tax information exchange agreements, to the QI Program for foreign financial institutions, the OECD uncooperative tax haven initiative, the European Union Savings Directive, and various cooperative multinational tax enforcement initiatives.

The Liechtenstein tax scandal and the recent U.S. indictment of a Swiss banker and a Liechtenstein trust officer illustrate the scope of the problems facing by countries trying to enforce their tax laws. They also demonstrate the need to strengthen existing international tax initiatives.

III. LGT Bank Case History

The first case history examined in the Subcommittee investigation involves LGT Bank, a leading Liechtenstein financial institution that is owned by and financially benefits the Liechtenstein royal family. The evidence indicates that from at least 1998 to 2007, LGT has established practices and financial structures that could facilitate, and in some instances have resulted in, tax evasion by U.S. clients. These LGT practices include allowing U.S. citizens to maintain billions of dollars in assets in accounts not disclosed to U.S. tax authorities; advising U.S. clients on the use of complex offshore structures to hide their ownership of assets, and arranging client accounts and assets to avoid reporting requirements under the QI Program that would otherwise disclose the accounts and assets to U.S. authorities.

A. LGT Bank Profile

LGT Bank in Liechtenstein Ltd. ("LGT Bank") is the largest indigenous bank in Liechtenstein.[99] It specializes in providing wealth management services to high net worth individuals and families, and currently manages about €63 billion in client assets.[100] It has subsidiaries and affiliates in about a dozen countries, including Austria, the Cayman Islands, Germany, Ireland, Singapore, and Switzerland. The Chief Executive Officer of the bank is Prince Max von und zu Liechtenstein, the second son of Prince Hans-Adam II, current reigning sovereign of Liechtenstein.[101]

LGT Bank is part of the LGT Group Foundation ("LGT Group"), which is the "Wealth & Asset Management Group of the Princely House of Liechtenstein."[102] LGT Group is owned and controlled by the royal family in Liechtenstein, which has managed it for more than 70 years as a family business.[103] The LGT Group currently administers assets valued at about 100 billion Swiss francs.[104]

LGT Group offers a wide range of banking, investment, and trust services. Its primary components include LGT Bank, LGT Treuhand AG, LGT Trust Management Company, LGT Capital Management Ltd., LGT Capital Partners Ltd., LGT Private Equity Advisers Ltd., and LGT Financial Services Ltd.[105] LGT Capital Management, LGT Capital Partners, and LGT Private Equity Advisers offer investment services. LGT Treuhand AG and LGT Trust Management Company, along with multiple subsidiaries and affiliates, offer formation and management services such as establishing trusts, companies, or foundations; providing trustees, trust protectors, company officers and directors, or foundation board members; and administering the structures set up by LGT clients.[106]

Altogether, LGT Group has more than 1,600 employees at 29 locations in Europe, Asia, the Middle East, and the United States.[107] In the United States, its key financial institution is LGT Capital Partners (USA) Inc. located in New York City. LGT Capital Partners (USA) Inc. is characterized in the LGT Group Annual Report as offering "research services," and is not registered with the U.S. Securities and Exchange Commission ("SEC") as either a broker-dealer or investment advisor.[108]

In a recent brochure entitled "The Liechtenstein Trust Enterprise," apparently issued by members of the LGT Group, one page near the end of the brochure lists "Arguments in favour of Liechtenstein and the Liechtenstein Trust Enterprise."[109] The page states that the Principality of Liechtenstein has "[e]conomic and political stability," "[h]igh-quality financial services," "[d]ecades of tradition in asset management and asset structuring," "a liberal legal framework," and "[s]trict laws on professional secrecy for banks and trustees." It also notes that the Liechtenstein trust enterprise is an "[e]fficient instrument for protecting assets from undesirable access" while offering "[d]iscretion and anonymity."

B. LGT Accounts with U.S. Clients

The Liechtenstein tax scandal became public after a former LGT employee provided tax authorities around the world with data on about 1,400 persons with accounts at LGT Bank in Liechtenstein. The Subcommittee was able to obtain copies of more than 12,000 pages of internal LGT documents, dated from the mid-1990s to 2002, relating to clients connected to the United States. Some of these clients were U.S. citizens or permanent residents; some lived or worked in the United States; some owned real estate or a business in the United States; and some had children or close relatives who were U.S. citizens or residents and were also beneficial owners or beneficiaries of LGT account assets. While some of these clients appear to have opened LGT accounts that served a legitimate purpose, others appear to have used the accounts to hide assets and dodge U.S. taxes.

The Subcommittee investigated a number of LGT accounts with U.S. beneficial owners or beneficiaries. To investigate these accounts, the Subcommittee reviewed the internal LGT documentation it had obtained, and spoke with the former LGT employee who had released the documentation. The Subcommittee also contacted some of the U.S. clients named in the documents, and asked them to supply additional documentation and information. While some clients cooperated with the Subcommittee's inquiries, supplying documents and submitting to interviews or depositions, others asserted their Constitutional rights under the Fifth Amendment, and declined to provide any information. In addition, LGT informed the Subcommittee that it was unable to provide specific information about any of its clients, citing Liechtenstein laws prohibiting the disclosure of financial information about individuals.

LGT also declined to provide general information about accounts opened for U.S. clients, advising the Subcommittee that such disclosures, even if they did not reference specific clients, would violate Liechtenstein secrecy laws.[110] For example, LGT declined to disclose the total number of accounts it had opened for U.S. clients, the total amount of assets in those accounts, or the total amount of revenues produced by those accounts for LGT. It also declined to disclose how many LGT private bankers or trust officers work with U.S. clients, what percentage of their accounts are for U.S. clients versus clients from other countries, or what percentage of the accounts opened for U.S. clients had been disclosed to the United States.

LGT did, however, provide the Subcommittee with sample forms it requires new account holders to complete (such asW-8BEN certificates), a memorandum detailing its obligations under the QI Program, a copy of the External Auditor's Report on LGT's compliance with its QI obligations, and copies of some of its marketing and promotional materials. LGT also made its Head of Group Compliance, Mr. Ivo Klein, available for an interview a few days before the Subcommittee's scheduled hearing on this matter. LGT took the position that Mr. Klein could discuss only matters associated with LGT's actions under the QI Program and that disclosures on any other matters were prohibited by Liechtenstein law.[111] This restriction greatly limited the issues that Mr. Klein could address.

LGT's limited cooperation with the Subcommittee's inquiries impeded the Subcommittee's efforts to gain a full understanding of LGT's activities and practices regarding accounts opened for U.S. clients. The internal LGT documentation provided to the Subcommittee, however, and the information obtained from several LGT clients and others were sufficient to develop a partial picture of LGT's administration of accounts with U.S. clients.

The Subcommittee's investigation identified numerous LGT accounts with U.S. beneficial owners or beneficiaries with substantial assets. From at least 1998 to 2007, LGT employed practices that could facilitate, and in some instances have resulted in, tax evasion by U.S. clients. These LGT practices have included maintaining U.S. client accounts which are not disclosed to U.S. tax authorities; advising U.S. clients to open accounts in the name of Liechtenstein foundations to hide their beneficial ownership of the account assets; advising clients on the use of complex offshore structures to hide ownership of assets outside of Liechtenstein; and establishing "transfer corporations" to disguise asset transfers to and from LGT accounts. It was also not unusual for LGT to assign its U.S. clients code words that they or LGT could invoke to confirm their respective identities. LGT also advised clients on how to structure their investments to avoid disclosure to the IRS under the QI Program. Of the accounts examined by the Subcommittee, none had been disclosed by LGT to the IRS. These and other LGT practices contributed to a culture of secrecy and deception that enabled LGT clients to use the bank's services to evade U.S. taxes, dodge creditors, and ignore court orders.

LGT's trust office in Liechtenstein managed an estimated $7 billion in assets and more than 3,000 offshore entities for clients during the years 2001 to 2002. It is unclear what percentage of these assets and offshore entities was attributable to U.S. clients at that time, or what the comparable figures are for 2008.

For many of its U.S. clients, LGT helped establish one or more Liechtenstein foundations, a type of legal entity that is roughly equivalent to a trust formed under U.S. law.[112] Liechtenstein foundations are set up at the request of a "founder" who provides the initial assets and designates the beneficiaries. The legal document establishing the foundation is typically called the Foundation's "Statutes" or "Articles." Beneficiaries are often named in a separate document called the "By-Laws," which can also contain foundation directives or restrictions. The foundation is typically run by a "Foundation Council" or "Foundation Board," composed of one or more individuals or legal entities, who administer the assets and direct the foundation's activities. Founders can also appoint "Protectors" to oversee the foundation, replace Council or Board members, and add or remove beneficiaries. These functions are sometimes performed instead by a "Board of Curators."

LGT typically used its trust company, LGT Treuhand, to help a U.S. client establish a Liechtenstein foundation, identify individuals to serve as the Council or Board members needed to administer the foundation, arrange for the initial transfer assets, and open one or more LGT accounts in the foundation's name. LGT Treuhand would also, on occasion, help LGT foundations open accounts at other financial institutions. LGT appeared to treat these accounts as beneficially owned by the Liechtenstein foundation, a non-U.S. entity, rather than as beneficially owned by the U.S. persons who established them. As non-U.S. persons, the foundations were not required to submit W-9 Forms to LGT, and LGT did not file 1099 Forms disclosing the accounts to the IRS. Of the accounts examined by the Subcommittee in connection with U.S. clients, none had been disclosed by LGT to the IRS.

Under U.S. tax law, the IRS generally views Liechtenstein foundations as foreign trusts. U.S. persons with an interest in a foreign trust, including a Liechtenstein foundation, are required to disclose the existence of the trust to the IRS by filing Forms 3520 (Annual Return To Report Transactions With Foreign Trusts and Receipt of Certain Foreign Gifts) and 3520-A (Annual Information Return of Foreign Trust With a U.S. Owner). Form 3520 is due on or before the 90th day (or such later day as the Secretary may prescribe) after a reportable event.[113] Form 3520-A must be prepared by the trustee and provided to trust beneficiaries to be filed with their returns by March 15 of the following year (assuming the trust has a December 31 year-end). Trustees must supply copies of the Foreign Grantor Trust Owner Statement and the Foreign Grantor Trust Beneficiary Statement to the U.S. owners and U.S. beneficiaries by the same deadline. While the U.S. tax code requires the trust to file the form, it also makes the U.S. owner responsible for ensuring that the form is filed and the required information furnished to U.S. owners and U.S. beneficiaries.[114] The reporting obligations under Forms 3520 and 3520-A must be met even if a foreign government can impose penalties for disclosing financial information or foreign financial institutions or trust instruments prohibit disclosure of required information.[115]

In addition to disclosing any interest in a foreign trust, U.S. persons must also disclose to the United States all foreign bank accounts in which they have signatory authority or a financial interest. The TD F 90-22.1 Form, also known as the Foreign Bank Account Report or "FBAR," requires disclosure of all foreign accounts with at least $10,000. The form must be filed, not with the IRS, but with the U.S. Treasury Department. The civil penalty for failing to file the FBAR form is an automatic fine of $10,000. In the case of willful violations, the penalty can increase to the greater of $100,000 or 50% of the value of the account.[116]

The following descriptions of seven selected LGT accounts help illustrate the financial services offered by LGT to its U.S. clients, its efforts to ensure the secrecy of accounts opened for U.S. clients, and how LGT practices could facilitate, and have resulted in, tax evasion by U.S. clients.

(1) Marsh accounts: Hiding $49 million over twenty years

James Albright Marsh, Jr. ("Mr. Marsh") is a construction contractor who lived in Florida with his wife and six children, until he died in 2006.[117] He, his wife, and his children have always been U.S. citizens. In 1985, Mr. Marsh traveled to Liechtenstein, and LGT helped him establish two Liechtenstein foundations, the Chateau Foundation and Lincol Foundation, which then opened accounts at LGT Bank. Also during the 1980s, Mr. Marsh formed two more Liechtenstein foundations, called Topanga Foundation[118] and Largella Foundation,[119] apparently using two other financial institutions in Liechtenstein.[120] Over the years, these four Liechtenstein foundations opened accounts at five Liechtenstein banks.[121] By 2007, the Liechtenstein accounts had assets with a combined value in excess of $49 million.[122]

LGT supplied to the Marshes the instruments used to establish and administer the two foundations with LGT accounts, Chateau and Lincol.[123] These documents provided a large measure of control over the foundations to Mr. Marsh and his sons, and included strong secrecy protections. The Lincol documents, for example, stated that the Foundation's express "object" was to provide "economic support" for "members of certain families."[124] They provided that the Foundation would be administered by a Foundation Board, later called a Foundation Council.[125] In 2004, new By-Laws appointed Mr. Marsh and two of his sons, Kerry and Shannon, who were then 50 and 43 years old, as "Protectors" of the Lincol and Chateau Foundations.[126] As Protectors, they were authorized to remove any Member of the Foundation Council at will and replace that person with a new Member. In addition, the Council was required to obtain the consent of at least one Protector before distributing assets to a beneficiary, approving the Foundation's annual accounts, changing its rules, transferring the Foundation to a new domicile, converting it into a registered trust, or dissolving it. These provisions gave Mr. Marsh and his sons substantial control over the Foundation's administration, assets, and activities.

The documents also gave Mr. Marsh, as the Founder, authority to define a "Class of Beneficiaries" for the Foundation from which the Council had "absolute and complete discretion" to appoint the actual beneficiaries.[127] An earlier version of the document had authorized Mr. Marsh to name the actual beneficiaries instead of describing a class of beneficiaries.[128] The provision may have been refashioned to strengthen the claim that the Foundation had only contingent beneficiaries and therefore no U.S. beneficiaries and no obligation to file a tax return with the IRS. At the same time, five years earlier, Mr. March had separately executed a "letter of wishes" with respect to each of the two foundations, clearly indicating that he wished his wife and children – all U.S. citizens -- to be the beneficiaries.[129]

Secrecy provisions in the Foundation documents were also strengthened in 2005, perhaps to protect the Foundation against being compelled to disclose information. While earlier Foundation documents gave the Beneficiaries the right to demand information about the Foundation,[130] later versions, in a section entitled, "Information and Secrecy," provided that the Foundation Council was not obligated to disclose any information to the Class of Beneficiaries, and was "not entitled to disclose" such information if the Council concluded the information "may be used with an improper or unlawful intent or detrimental to the Foundation or the members of the Class of Beneficiaries."[131] The section also provided that the "any legal facts and aspects of the Foundation must not be drawn to the attention of outside parties, especially foreign authorities." These provisions apparently could have been used by the Foundation Council to refuse to produce information to a U.S. beneficiary being asked by the IRS to obtain information about the Foundation.

The documents also authorized the Foundation Council to take drastic action when pressed, including by transferring the Foundation to a different country, converting it into a registered trust, or dissolving it altogether. The Lincol Articles, for example, provided:

> "If as a result of certain events, such as economic or political measures, public or private law legislation or any other extraordinary events, the Foundation assets might be jeopardized or enjoyment of the beneficial interest rendered impossible, the Foundation Board shall be authorized to take appropriate defensive measures, including if necessary the transfer abroad of the domicile or the dissolution of the Foundation."[132]

Sometimes referred to as a "flee clause," these types of provisions could be used to avoid or frustrate an investigation into a Foundation's founder, assets, or beneficiaries. Counsel to LGT advised the Subcommittee that such clauses remain in use at LGT, though each foundation has different provisions, and flee clauses are not universally present.[133] The Lincol and Chateau Statutes also provided that revenues derived from the Foundation's assets "may not be withdrawn ... by creditors by way of injunction, levy of execution and writ, bankruptcy or probate proceedings."[134]

In addition to creating Foundation structures that empowered the Marshes and implemented strong secrecy protections, LGT took other steps to ensure the Marsh assets were not disclosed to U.S. tax authorities. Early on, for example, LGT instructed the Marshes to use the code, "Friends of J.N.," when they wished to "get in touch."[135] LGT also refrained from sending any mail about the accounts to the United States, instead keeping foundation records in Liechtenstein.

The documents obtained by the Subcommittee indicate that the Marshes traveled to Liechtenstein on a minimum of four occasions to handle matters related to the foundations. The first was in 1985, when the Lincol Foundation was established.[136] An LGT receipt shows a 1985 deposit of $3.3 million "in cash" for the Lincol Foundation,[137] and a letter of wishes signed by Shannon Marsh on the same day.[138] The second occasion was in 1989, when Mr. Marsh signed a new portfolio management agreement for the LGT trusts.[139] The third occasion was in 2000, when Mr. Marsh, accompanied by his son James, met with LGT personnel, terminated an LGT agency agreement,[140] agreed to sell the LGT foundations' U.S. securities,[141] and signed letters of wishes.[142] The fourth occasion was in 2004, when Mr. Marsh, accompanied by Shannon and Kerry, signed a document approving Chateau asset inventories from 2000 through 2003, and ratifying past investment decisions.[143] Shannon and Kerry signed documents on the same day agreeing to serve as "Protectors" of the LGT foundations.[144] In addition to these documents memoralizing the four trips to Liechtenstein, the records show multiple occasions on which Mr. Marsh provided instructions or signed documents authorizing assets to be bought or sold and addressing other foundation issues.[145]

In 2000, the United States launched the QI Program, to take effect in 2001. LGT signed a QI agreement scheduled to become effective in 2001. According to an internal LGT document titled "Aktenvermerk" or "Memorandum to File" regarding the Lincol and Chateau Foundations, Mr. Marsh and one of his sons, James, visited the bank in October 2000. The LGT document states: "[T]he QI situation was discussed. Both men gave the order to get out of all U.S. securities and to invest in the Euro area. The U.S. tax exempt bonds should be left alone. ... As usual the discussion was very hurried and a bit shallow. So the situation will be discussed at the next meeting."[146] This document, together with other records obtained by the Subcommittee, show that the two LGT foundations, which had a number of U.S. securities, sold those securities in 2000, and invested the proceeds in non-U.S. currencies and stocks. After steering the foundations into making this change in their investment portfolios, LGT appears to have treated the account as falling outside the QI reporting requirements.[147] Despite LGT's subsequent, six- year participation in the QI Program, none of the Marsh accounts was ever reported to the IRS.

It appears that the IRS finally learned of the Marsh accounts from the documents provided by the former LGT employee, and initiated an investigation in 2007. In May 2008, the Marshes filed overdue 3520 and 3520A Forms with the IRS disclosing the existence of the foreign foundations; filed overdue Foreign Bank Account Reports (FBARs) with the Treasury Department disclosing the foreign accounts; and filed with the IRS amended income tax returns from 2002 to 2006, disclosing the income from the Liechtenstein accounts that should have been reported earlier as taxable income.[148] The Marshes have apparently paid back taxes and interest owed on this offshore income for the period, 2002 to 2006, in an amount totaling about $2.9 million.[149] They have also requested a waiver of any penalties on the ground that Mr. Marsh's wife had no knowledge of the foundations until after his death and the IRS inquiry, and his sons claimed they did not know that they were beneficiaries or that the foundations had to be reported to the IRS.

The LGT documents reviewed by the Subcommittee show, however, that Mr. Marsh's sons were aware of and had participated in the affairs of the LGT foundations. For example, a 1985 letter of wishes was signed by Shannon when the Lincol Foundation was first created in

1985.[150] Shannon was 24 years old at the time. A 1992 handwritten letter by Shannon instructed LGT that another brother, Kerry, had "permission to review all documents and receipts pertaining to Lincol Foundation and Chateau Foundation. Please group our investments so that we pay as little as possible in commissions as you discussed last year with my brother Kerry."[151] At the time of this letter, Shannon was 30 years old and Kerry was 37. A 1993 document signed by Shannon informs LGT that two additional Marsh relatives were to be treated as principals with respect to the Lincol Foundation.[152] A 2000 internal LGT memorandum states: "On October 11, 2000 Mr. James G. Marsh, along with his father, Mr. James Albright Marsh visited me very briefly. Mr. Knecht presented the performance of both foundations, with the corresponding explanations. The men were basically satisfied."[153] In 2004, as mentioned earlier, Shannon and Kerry, who were then 43 and 50 years old respectively, were appointed "Protectors" of the Lincol and Chateau Foundations[154] and signed official acceptances of their appointments in Vaduz.[155]

The 2008 letters to the IRS prepared by legal counsel for the Marshes had this to say about Mr. Marsh:

> "Mr. Marsh, a construction contractor, was unsophisticated in the area of U.S. tax reporting requirements. It is believed that he did not know that the passive income earned in the Foundations was taxable in the United States. We believe that Mr. Marsh was under the erroneous belief that his income from the Foundations was not required to be reported until such time as the funds were repatriated to the United States. This may explain why he apparently did not spend any of the money in the Foundations for over twenty years."[156]

Mr. Marsh was apparently sophisticated enough to set up four foundations in Liechtenstein, amass at least $49 million in multiple accounts at five Liechtenstein banks, and avoid all QI reporting of his accounts. Assertions that he was not sophisticated enough to inquire about the tax consequences of these actions are not credible in the face of the evidence.

(2) Wu accounts: Hiding ownership of assets

William S. Wu is a U.S. citizen who was born in China and has lived for many years with his family in Forest Hills, New York. His sister, Veronica Wu, is a U.S. citizen who lives in Hong Kong.[157] In 1996, LGT helped Mr. Wu establish a Liechtenstein foundation called the JCMA Foundation; in 1997, LGT helped Ms. Wu establish a second Liechtenstein foundation called the Veline Foundation. The JCMA Foundation opened LGT accounts with assets that, by 2001, had a combined value of $4.3 million. The Veline Foundation opened LGT accounts with assets that appear to have peaked at a value of about $922,000; those accounts were closed by Ms. Wu in 2001, and the assets transferred to the Palone Foundation in Hong Kong.

The JCMA and Veline Foundations were established using LGT-supplied documents that provided a large measure of control over the foundations to their founders, and strong secrecy protections.[158] Because the provisions are similar to those described above in connection with the Marsh accounts, the same analysis will not be repeated here. The beneficiaries of the Foundations were Wu family members.

The original purpose of the JCMA Foundation ("JCMA") appears to have been to help conceal Mr. Wu's ownership of his personal residence in New York. Three months after

JCMA was formed, it was used in a complex arrangement to make it appear that Mr. Wu had sold his house to an independent third party that, in fact, he secretly controlled. To carry out this arrangement, JCMA acquired a wholly owned corporation in the Bahamas called Sandalwood International Ltd. ("Sandalwood"), and asked a Hong Kong company, Cobyrne Ltd., to hold the Sandalwood shares in trust for JCMA.[159] An internal LGT memorandum on JCMA states that the "sole purpose of Sandalwood is the holding of Tai Lung Worldwide Ltd. BVI."[160] Tai Lung Worldwide Ltd. is apparently a corporation formed in the British Virgin Islands.[161]

New York State property records show that, on Feb. 14, 1997, Mr. Wu sold his house in New York to Tai Lung Worldwide Ltd. ("Tai Lung") for an undisclosed sum.[162] In the New York property records, Tai Lung provides the same Hong Kong address used by Cobyrne in the trust agreement with JCMA. These documents suggest that Mr. Wu "sold" his house to what appeared to be an unrelated party from Hong Kong. In fact, the buyer, Tai Lung, was wholly owned by Sandalwood which, in turn, was owned by JCMA, Mr. Wu's Liechtenstein foundation. After the sale, Mr. Wu and his family continued to live in the same house, but apparently made monthly "rental" payments to a Tai Lung account at Standard Chartered Bank. [163]These rental payments may have served as a mechanism for Mr. Wu to move funds out of the United States without alerting U.S. authorities.

The LGT memorandum on JCMA notes briefly the arrangement whereby Sandalwood owns Tai Lung which maintains the house in New York. There is no indication that LGT expressed any concern about this arrangement, despite the fact that it involved multiple jurisdictions -- a house in New York owned by a BVI company (with a Hong Kong address), owned by a Bahamas company, owned by a Liechtenstein foundation with a founder from New York – and appeared to serve no purpose other than concealment. At the bottom of the LGT report on JCMA is the following notation: "ATTENTION US-Citizen."

Although JCMA was apparently originally established to assume ownership of Mr. Wu's New York residence, the documents suggest that it was soon used for other purposes as well, becoming a repository for substantial funds. Financial records produced to the Subcommittee by Mr. Wu show, for example, that by 2001, JCMA had cash and securities with a combined value of nearly $4.3 million.[164] The source of the funds for these assets is unclear. One explanation contained in the records obtained by the Subcommittee is a brief notation in an internal 2001 LGT profile of JCMA stating that its funds came from "inheritance as well as from real estate holdings in the USA."[165]

Mr. Wu provided the Subcommittee with formal Statements of Assets for JCMA for the years 2001 to 2006. These statements show a steady stream of withdrawals from the JCMA account at LGT: $300,000 during 2001; $840,000 in 2002; $1.5 million in 2003; $1.2 million in 2004; $500,000 in 2005; and $300,000 in 2006.[166] The Statements of Assets generally characterize these withdrawals as "distributions" from the Foundation, and occasionally specify they are distributions to the "first beneficiary," which is Mr. Wu.[167] The documents do not indicate, in most cases, how the funds were withdrawn or how they were used.

One instance in 2002, however, may be illustrative. On June 25, 2002, Mr. Wu met with LGT officials at its Hong Kong office to discuss the JCMA account. In connection with this visit, Mr. Wu instructed LGT to withdraw $100,000 from the JCMA account and place the funds in a "bank draft" – a cheque drawn directly from a bank's own funds – which he could take with him. [168]The JCMA Foundation Board approved the withdrawal, demonstrating Mr. Wu's control over the Foundation and its funds. To provide Mr. Wu with a U.S. dollar cheque, LGT contacted HSBC Bank in Hong Kong, where LGT maintained a correspondent account. On June 26, 2002, HSBC Hong Kong provided LGT with a bank cheque for $100,000 in U.S. dollars, "[p]ayable at any branch of HSBC Bank USA in the USA."[169] Mr. Wu signed the receipt for the cheque.[170] It is not clear from the records obtained by the Subcommittee when or where he cashed the check or how he spent the $100,000. Since the funds were provided via an HSBC bank cheque drawn on LGT's account, and likely cashed at an HSBC branch, the funds may be difficult to trace.

During his meeting with LGT officials in Hong Kong in 2002, Mr. Wu met at length with two LGT trust officers, Beat Muller and Kim Choy. After Mr. Wu confirmed that he and all family members named in the JCMA By-laws held U.S. passports, other than his wife who held a Singapore passport, the LGT officials advised him that U.S. tax laws required disclosure of JCMA to U.S. authorities unless the foundation was restructured:

> "[Kim Choy] explained the reporting requirements imposed on a US grantor, e.g. creation of the foundation, ensuring the Board Members file annual returns with the IRS. Also, as the income of the Foundation is taxed to the grantor, further annual filing of income of the foundation and payment of income tax on worldwide income of the foundation. Furthermore, if US beneficiaries have received distributions from the Foundation, the Board Members must provide a Beneficiary Statement to each recipient which should be attach[ed] to his/her income tax return to the IRS. Upon the death of the US grantor, the Board Members may be considered the statutory executor of his estate and will bear liability and exposure for any non-compliance by the grantor during his lifetime of reporting and other requirements to the IRS, the filing of the deceased's US estate tax return and payment of estate taxes on the assets of the Foundation at the date of his death.
>
> KC informed Mr. Wu that the JCMA Foundation must be re-structured and that LGT & Treuhand were looking at formulating solutions. We raised the possibility of an insurance product which Mr Wu didn't seem interested in. Other possibilities included:
>
> - lifetime transfers to his beneficiaries;
> - making use of Mr Wu's non-US siblings to restructure the Foundation;
> - private/corporate account.
>
> Mr. Wu acknowledged the need to restructure the Foundation and was receptive to any ideas we could come up with. Similarly, we would welcome any solutions from him or his advisers. Mr Wu has interests in other ventures/companies unconnected with LGT which require restructuring to address US tax/reporting requirements."[171]

This LGT memorandum demonstrates LGT's knowledge and understanding of U.S. tax laws, and its willingness to advise its U.S. clients on how to structure their accounts to avoid U.S. reporting obligations.

In response to the concerns expressed by LGT, it appears that JCMA Foundation wound down its activities, transferred its assets, dissolved, and was replaced by another Liechtenstein foundation called the Desert Rose Foundation. As part of this process, in July 2004, JCMA acquired a second British Virgin Islands corporation called Dickinson Holding & Finance, Ltd. ("Dickinson").[172] A month later, in August 2004, JCMA transferred nearly $1.2 million to Dickinson, characterizing the asset transfer as an "interest-free loan ... for an indefinite period of time."[173] Dickinson opened an account at LGT, deposited the funds, and began receiving and sending funds on behalf of JCMA.[174] Over time, JCMA transferred additional assets to Dickinson, characterizing the transfers as additional loans to the company. [175]In 2006, the Desert Rose Foundation ("Desert Rose") was formed and opened an account at LGT.[176] JCMA transferred its key remaining assets to Desert Rose, including its share certificate for Dickinson and its share certificate for Sandalwood.[177] The financial records show that Dickinson made "distributions" of $500,000 in 2005, and $300,000 in 2006, ; the distribution in 2005 was to the "first beneficiary," Mr. Wu, as was presumably the 2006 distribution.[178] Nevertheless, at the end of 2006, Dickinson Holding & Finance showed a balance of about $4.2 million, while Desert Rose showed an account balance of about $422,000, for a grand total of about $4.6 million.

These figures suggest that, while JCMA Foundation has been dissolved and its LGT accounts closed, Mr. Wu continues to control more than $4.6 million in assets at LGT accounts held in the name of Desert Rose Foundation and its wholly owned corporation, Dickinson Holding & Finance Ltd.

Mr. Wu utilized JCMA for nearly 10 years, and it is possible that he is still using the Desert Rose Foundation. In contrast, Mr. Wu' s sister, Veronica Wu, utilized her Liechtenstein foundation for only a four-year period, from 1997 until 2001, after which she directed LGT to dissolve Veline and transfer its assets to a Hong Kong foundation called the Palone Foundation with accounts at Credit Suisse Private Bank in Zurich.[179] While active, the Veline Foundation kept cash and securities in its LGT accounts, with a total asset value ranging as high as $922,000.[180]

Like JCMA, the Veline Foundation also appears to have been used to conceal Ms. Wu's ownership interests. The records show that soon after the foundation was established it acquired a bearer share certificate giving it 100% ownership of Manta Company Ltd. ("Manta"), a corporation formed in Western Samoa.[181] While many financial institutions refuse to handle bearer shares, since they can be used to hide the ownership of a company and are known instruments of money laundering,[182] LGT appears to have expressed no concern about this bearer share certificate which was kept in Veline's "deposit box" at LGT.[183] While the documents obtained by the Subcommittee are unclear as to the activities engaged in by Manta, one handwritten chart indicates that it functioned as a holding company for a Hong Kong corporation called Bowfin Co. Ltd. which, in turn, held real estate, a vehicle, a mobile telephone, and accounts at two banks, Standard Chartered Bank and Swiss Bank Corporation (now merged into UBS).[184] The document shows that these assets were owned by Bowfin, which was in turned owned by Manta, a bearer share corporation that was owned by Ms. Wu's Veline officers, further obscuring their ownership. The chart depicts, in short, a complex multi-tiered ownership chain using Liechtenstein, Samoan, and Hong Kong nominee entities designed to conceal the ultimate ownership interests of M s. Wu.[185]

LGT signed a QI Agreement with the United States in 2001. Ms. Wu's foundation was dissolved in April 2001, but Mr. Wu's foundation continued operating until at least 2004, and perhaps to the present time. Despite the concerns expressed by LGT personnel in 2002 regarding the bank's "exposure for any non-compliance" by Mr. Wu regarding his tax obligations, LGT does not appear to have reported his Foundation or the Foundation's accounts to the IRS under the QI Program at any time.

It is the Subcommittee's understanding that Mr. Wu is now in negotiation with the IRS over tax liability issues related to his Liechtenstein foundations.

(3) Lowy account: Using a U.S. corporation to hide ownership

Frank Lowy ("Mr. Lowy") is an Australian citizen and the main shareholder and Chairman of the Westfield Group.[186] His three sons, David, Peter and Stefen, hold high positions in the Westfield organization. Peter Lowy, a U.S. citizen living in California, is Chief Executive Officer of Westfield Group United States. Internal LGT documents obtained by the Subcommittee indicate that the Lowys maintained a longterm relationship with LGT, utilizing multiple Liechtenstein-related entities and transactions, including entities known as the Crofton Foundation, Jelnav, Yelnarf, and the Luperla Foundation.[187] An LGT memorandum notes that, in 1998, the Lowy account was one of the largest relationships at LGT Bank.[188] This analysis concentrates on the Luperla Foundation, because of its unique use of a U.S. corporation in Delaware to hide the identities of the Foundation beneficiaries. In 2001, Luperla assets had a combined value of about $68 million.

Formation of Luperla. Discussions regarding the formation of Luperla extended over a six-month period from November 1996 to April 1997. Although LGT generally requires clients LGT memorandum explained: "The Lowys have decided that they never want to travel to Liechtenstein or Switzerland in connection with these companies again."[189]

The records obtained by the Subcommittee show at least three meetings between LGT personnel and the Lowys on the formation of Luperla. The first was in November 1996, in Sydney, Australia, attended by Peter Widmer, the LGT relationship manager handling the Lowy account, meeting with Mr. Lowy, his son David, longtime family attorney Joshua Gelbard, and David Gonski.[190] At that meeting the participants discussed the creation of a new foundation. According to a later LGT memorandum, the Lowys expressed their intent to establish a large foundation with conservative investments that would serve as "insurance" for the Lowy family.[191] In January 1997, a second meeting took place in Los Angeles, California attended by Mr. Lowy, his sons, Peter and David, and two LGT employees. According to an LGT memorandum, this meeting was intended to discuss Luperla's "portfolio strategy" and "cost structure," and introduce Mr. Lowy to "the person who will also be responsible for 'his establishment.'"[192] Six weeks later, a meeting took place in London, in March 1997, attended by three LGT employees, Mr. Lowy, and his attorney Mr. Gelbard. This meeting discussed the transfer of assets to Luperla and LGT fees. An LGT memorandum summarizing the London meeting was copied to Liechtenstein Prince Philipp.[193]

LGT memoranda following these meetings note that Mr. Lowy had reached a settlement with the Australian Tax Office, did not want to bring new funds into Australia, and was concerned that if the Australian tax authorities learned of his having additional assets, the government might try to subject them to additional claims. As one LGT memorandum put it: "Special caution is to be used, however, since he doesn't believe the Australian tax authorities that the case with the payment of the 25 M is settled for good. ... The entire documentation and assembly is to be done in such a manner that [Mr. Lowy] and his attorneys can testify before court in Australia without hesitation."[194] These statements make it clear that LGT was aware that Mr. Lowy and his sons were hiding assets in the new foundation from Australian tax authorities.

LGT and the Lowys took a number of measures to keep secret Luperla's existence and the Lowy relationship at LGT, and to distance the Lowys and other entities they controlled from the new foundation. At the Lowy's request, for example, LGT agreed that, once the new foundation was established, to remove evidence of old LGT accounts and transactions.[195] In preparation for the January 1997 meeting with the Lowys in Los Angeles, an LGT trust officer wrote the following message to his associates:

> "Before the meeting in LA we should prepare our first proposals in writing. These should be written on neutral paper and without reference to any person or corporation in the Lowy field."[196]

LGT established Peter Widmer as its exclusive point of contact at LGT for the Lowys during the establishment of the new foundation, and subsequently limited the number of LGT personnel involved in the relationship.[197] The Lowys, in turn, made Mr. Gelbard their exclusive contact for matters related to Luperla,[198] and LGT agreed to accept his name on key documents. It was Mr. Gelbard, for example, who sent a letter requesting the creation of Luperla,[199] signed the Foundation's formation documents,[200] and signed Luperla's omitting any mention of the Lowys.[201] LGT also convinced the Lowys not to co-manage the assets in the foundation, on the ground that such direct involvement on their part would connect them to the entity.[202]

In addition, to disguise the transfer of assets from other Lowy-related entities, LGT proposed and the Lowys agreed to transfer the assets through a shell corporation especially set up for that purpose.[203] The primary source of assets for the new foundation had been described as proceeds from a complex securities transaction.[204] In early 1997, LGT acquired a British Virgin Islands corporation, Sewell Services Ltd., to serve as the intermediary for the asset transfers into Luperla from other Lowy related entities.[205] An account in the name of Sewell was opened at LGT Bank in Liechtenstein. Assets destined for the Luperla account were transferred into the Sewell account and then transferred internally, within the bank, from the Sewell to the Luperla account. Such intra-bank transfers make it extremely difficult to trace the flow of assets, because no documentation outside of the bank shows that the funds transferred into the bank were destined for or actually deposited into the Luperla account.

On May 2, 1997, the LGT relationship manager for the Luperla account outlined the complex series of transaction that were going to be used to move Lowy assets into Luperla:

(a) Around USD 54 million (balance Crofton with us) are going to the Sewell account with us (assignment from Sinitus); subsequently Sewell pays (assignment from LGT T) the amount to Luperla.

(b) An additional roughly USD 3 million will go to Sewell (account LGT) through third-bank payments, which are likewise to be paid to account Luperla at LGT (assignment LGT T). [by hand:] CHF 3.6 million according to K. Ulrich

(c) Crofton will close its account with Union Bank of Israel, Tel Aviv and send balance (around USD 0.2 million) to account Sewell; Sewell also pays this amount to Luperla at LGT (assignment LGT T). Luperla is then to remunerate USD 250,000.00 to its account (already opened by LGT T) with Union Bank of Israel.[206]

On March 12, 1997, Mr. Gelbard, the Lowy family attorney, sent a letter to LGT Treuhand, officially requesting establishment of the Luperla Foundation and detailing its structure.[207] The "Regulations" governing the operation of Luperla Foundation were signed by Mr. Gelbard on April 30, 1997.[208] On May 14, 1997, an LGT memorandum reported the transfer of assets to Luperla had been completed.[209] At its inception, the foundation held assets of $54.7 million in U.S. dollars and 3.6 million in Swiss francs.[210]

Naming Beneficiaries Through a U.S. Corporation. LGT internal memoranda are clear that Luperla's "'financial beneficiaries' are the father and the three sons David, Peter, and Stefen."[211] In keeping with the Lowys' desire for secrecy, however, the Luperla Foundation did not simply name them as beneficiaries in its documentation. Instead, LGT and the Lowys devised a mechanism that the Subcommittee has not seen before, directing a U.S. corporation to name the beneficiaries of the Liechtenstein foundation.

The key U.S. corporation is identified in the Luperla "Regulations." The first paragraph states, in essence, that the latest subsidiary of Beverly Park Corp., a Delaware corporation owned by another Lowy trust, would name the beneficiaries of the Luperla Foundation:

> "The persons, companies or other entities from time to time notified in writing to the [Luperla] Board of Foundation by the company (Company) in which Beverly Park Corporation, a company formed in Delaware, United States of America, on 3 January 1997, (Corporation) for the time being holds any share and if there is more than one such company, then the company in which the Corporation last became a shareholder before the notification (a certificate to that effect from any office bearer for the time being of the Corporation may be relied upon by the Board of Foundation) shall be within the class of distributees of the Foundation assets and the income therefrom, provided that the Company for the time being or its legal successor may revoke any such notification at any time by a further notice in writing to the Board of Foundation, and provided further that no Company shall directly or indirectly become a distributee or benefit therefrom.[212]

Beverly Park Corporation was, in fact, incorporated in Delaware on February 4, 1997, by a registered Delaware agent, Corporation Trust Company. Beverly Park is wholly owned by Cordera Holdings Pty Ltd., which is owned by Franley Holdings Pty Ltd., which is owned by LGF Holdings Pty Ltd., which is, in turn, owned by the Frank Lowy Family Trust.[213] Beverly Park's listed address is 11601 Wilshire Blvd., 11th floor, Los Angeles, CA, which is also the address of the Westfield Group United States. Since Beverly Park's incorporation, Peter Lowy has served as its President and as a Director.[214]

By delegating the authority to name beneficiaries to the last subsidiary of Beverly Park, the Luperla Foundation ceded authority to an entity under the ultimate control of the Frank Lowy Family Trust. In addition, this structure served to keep the ownership of the Luperla assets out of Luperla records and deepened the secrecy surrounding the identity of its beneficiaries.

LGT Trust's own internal memoranda indicate that LGT viewed the arrangement as a way to ensure that Mr. Lowy and his sons would be the financial beneficiaries of Luperla Foundation, without having to include their names in the Foundation documents. For example, a June 2001 LGT memorandum first discusses the role of Beverly Park: "I assume that instructions regarding the nomination of beneficiaries will be made by the 'Company' listed in the by-laws ... the company from which Beverley [sic] Park Corp. last acquired shares."[215] It goes on to state: "It is explicitly apparent from the memorandums for the file that, in accordance with the intention of the founder, the father [Frank Lowy] and his three sons DL [David Lowy], PL [Peter Lowy] and SL [Stephen Lowy] are to be financial beneficiaries."[216] A July 2001 LGT memorandum discusses when the Luperla Board is authorized to make disbursements of assets to Foundation beneficiaries. It states that the Luperla board "must categorically be notified of the identities of possible beneficiaries ('members of the class of distributees'[English]) through a corporation ... of which the Beverly Park Corporation ... has shares ... If the 'Corporation' holds several 'Companies,' then the capacity to designate falls to that company of which the 'Corporation' most recently took up shares before the notification."[217] The memorandum goes on to say: "The records document the intent of the benefactor to the effect that the economic benefactor and his three sons shall be financial beneficiaries ...."

Dissolving Luperla. On June 25, 2001, Luperla's board apparently approved a resolution for the "complete and final disbursement" of the Foundation's assets and to place the Foundation itself "in liquidation (since it can no longer fulfill the purpose of the foundation after this)."[218] Documents available to the Subcommittee do not explain what triggered this resolution.

To disburse its assets, LGT required a list of Luperla's beneficiaries from the last subsidiary of Beverly Park. To obtain this information, an LGT memorandum states: "The telephone conversation in this regard will be taken up with the economic benefactor and one or his sons and/or Joshua H. Gelbard."[219] The memorandum indicates that a telephone conversation was held with David Lowy that same day, and that LGT learned the key Beverly Park subsidiary was Lonas Ltd., incorporated in the British Virgin Islands on July 24, 2001.[220] By December 20, 2001, LGT had obtained numerous documents related to Beverly Park and Lonas.[221] Included were documents showing that Beverly Park held "a share" in Lonas, that Mr . Gelbard had been appointed the "first sole director" of Lonas, and that Luperla had received a "Mandate from Lonas Ltd. (notification letter) dated 12.13.2001, signed by Joshua H. Gelbard , sole director, regarding the disbursement of all assets of the fou ndation."[222]

An LGT memorandum shows that, even after receiving the notification letter from Lonas, signed by Mr. Gelb, regarding disbursement of the Luperla assets, the bank decided to check the information in that letter by telephoning David Lowy and recording the conversation. The memorandum states:

> "In closing, Dr. Konrad Bächinger brings up the order from Joshua Gelbard for the payment/disbursement of the foundation assets to two separate bank connections in Geneva in the ratio of 60:40. Besides verbal attestation to the accuracy of the order, David Lowy gives his consent that the Lowy family itself not be directly benefited in the framework of the commissioned transactions."[223]

LGT obtained David Lowy's authorization for the final Luperla disbursement a second time in a telephone call on December 20, 2001, demonstrating anew that LGT considered the Lowys to be the key decisionmakers behind Lonas, Beverly Park, and Luperla.[224] LGT memos and LGT bank records show that, on December 20, 2001, over $68 million in assets were moved in two tranches from the Luperla account at LGT bank to an account at Bank Jacob Safra in Geneva.

Answering IRS Inquiries. In 2007, the Lowys were contacted by the IRS with inquiries about Beverly Park. In submissions to the IRS, the Lowys and Beverly Park officers stated that there was no connection between Beverly Park and any foreign accounts and entities, including Luperla. Beverly Park claimed it "has no records demonstrating ownership of stock in any other entity, including Lonas Limited BVI."[225] Mr. Janks, Secretary and Director to Beverly Park, represented to the IRS that Beverly Park, its subsidiaries, officers, employees, and agents have no "legal or beneficial interest in ... or any direct or indirect signature, management, investment, or other authority over any foreign entities, trusts, corporations, partnerships, or foundations."[226] Peter Lowy, President and Director of Beverly Park, told the IRS he "do[es] not have sufficient personal knowledge" regarding Beverly Park's relationship with any foreign accounts or entities, but has "no reason to doubt the accuracy" of Mr. Janks' statements.[227] It is the Subcommittee's understanding that the IRS inquiry is ongoing.

(4) Greenfield accounts: Pitching a transfer to liechtenstein

Harvey and Steven Greenfield, father and son, are longtime participants in the U.S. toy industry.[228] Both are U.S. citizens from New York. In 1992, LGT helped Harvey Greenfield establish a Liechtenstein foundation, called Maverick Foundation, of which he is the sole primary beneficiary and for which his son holds a power of attorney. Two days later, two corporations were formed in the British Virgin Islands ("BVI") called Chiu Fu (Far East) Ltd. and TSF Company Ltd., both of which are wholly owned by the Maverick Foundation. The two BVI corporations apparently served as conduits to transfer funds to Maverick which, as of the end of 2001, had assets at LGT valued at about $2.2 million.[229]

Harvey Greenfield is Chairman and Chief Executive Officer of Commonwealth Toy and Novelty Company, Inc., which is a leading manufacturer of stuffed dolls and animals, is headquartered in New York, and has offices in seven countries. Steven Greenfield served as President of that company for 15 years, and has also worked with a number of startup companies primarily in the toy industry. LGT records show that Maverick was formed on January 22, 1992, and its two subsidiaries incorporated on January 24, 1992.[230] Maverick apparently maintained the stock certificates for both companies at LGT.[231] An internal LGT document profiling Maverick states that the origins of the funds in the Maverick account at LGT were "[e]arnings from commercial activity in the toy business. The client's sources toys from across Asia (but primarily China and Hong Kong) for distribution overseas."[232] Another internal LGT document regarding Maverick states that "Steven Greenfield is the holder of the power of attorney to give instructions."[233]

The documentation obtained by the Subcommittee regarding the Greenfields' Liechtenstein accounts and entities is limited. The documents do not provide much information about activities related to Maverick, Chiu Fu, or TSF Company for the first ten years of their existence, other than cryptic notes about a 1993 "[a]greement re. acquisition of special assets"; a 1996 "mandate" to LGT's banking operations in Hong Kong regarding "administration of the [Bank in Liechtenstein] account"; and "[c]ontracts of engagement with Chiu Fu and TSF."[234] There are also a few bank statements showing that Chiu Fu had an account at HSBC in Hong Kong and TSF had an account at Standard Chartered Bank in Hong Kong.[235]

In 2001, however, a detailed internal LGT memorandum opens a window on the Greenfield accounts with a vivid description of a meeting that took place in Liechtenstein, at the bank, on March 23, 2001. The meeting was attended by Harvey and Steven Greenfield, three LGT private bankers, and Prince Philipp von und zu Liechtenstein, Chairman of the Board of the LGT Group and brother to the reigning sovereign. According to LGT records, the meeting lasted over five hours, from 10:00 a.m. until 3:30 p.m., with the Prince in "partial attendance."

The meeting centered on an apparent sales pitch by LGT to convince the Greenfields to transfer an offshore trust with assets valued at "around U.S. $30 million" from a Bank of Bermuda branch in Hong Kong to LGT in Liechtenstein.[236] The memorandum explains:

> The Bank of Bermuda has indicated to the client that it would like to end the business relationship with him as a U.S. citizen. Due to these circumstances, the client is now on the search for a safe haven for his offshore assets. Next to the bankable assets, this Trust [at Bank of Bermuda] also still holds operating companies. It is, however, planned, to close these companies in the near future.
>
> There follows a long discussion about the banking location Liechtenstein, the banking privacy law as well as the security and stability, that Liechtenstein, as a banking location and sovereign nation, can guarantee its clients. The Bank ... indicate[s] strong interest in receiving the U.S. $30 million. Investment issues do not seem to be clarified completely. It is explained to the client that as a U.S. citizen he cannot invest in U.S. securities directly, but the possibility of investing in funds is not ruled out.[237]

The memorandum does not explain why the Bank of Bermuda wishes to end the relationship with the Greenfields, nor does LGT appear to ask. Instead, LGT presses the Greenfields to direct their offshore business to LGT.

The memorandum states that an LGT private banker offered to meet in Hong Kong at the end of April 2002, to determine if the transfer from Bank of Bermuda will take place. Two alternatives are suggested to arrange the transfer: (1) "[d]isbursement of the assets from the [Bank of Bermuda] Trust and subsequent dedication to the Maverick Foundation (under interposition of the BVI companies)" or (2) "[t]akeover of the Trust through LGT Trust Management Ltd. as new trustee." The memorandum also states: "The clients are very careful and eager to dissolve the Trust with the Bank of Bermuda leaving behind as few traces as possible."[238] LGT not only does not express any concern about the Greenfields' desire for secrecy, it offers concrete suggestions to disguise the transfer of assets and minimize the change, such as by recommending use of the BVI companies as conduits for the transferred funds from Bank of Bermuda or simply taking control of the existing Trust.

In addition to making the sales pitch, the meeting took care of some administrative matters regarding the Greenfields' existing LGT account. The memorandum notes, for example, that the Greenfields "sign[ed] off on the asset status of December 31, 1999 and December 31, 2000" for Maverick, which suggests that the Greenfields had not traveled to Liechtenstein in two years to review the account documentation. The LGT private bankers apparently also asked for signatures on "file copies" related to the Maverick account, but "[h]e refuses ... with the reasoning that they are already taken care of anyway through his signing off on the asset statuses.

I point out that due to the engagement contract, we merely carry out his instructions, and that he needs to document this for us with his signatures on the file copies. Nevertheless, the client does not sign the file copies."[239] These statements suggest that the Greenfields were responsible for directing the Maverick account investments, using LGT simply to carry out their directions.

The memorandum also discusses the two BVI corporations owned by Maverick. It states that they "were established in January 1992 with the purpose of channeling the assets into the Maverick Foundation," that they had not been closed as planned, and that they "are to continue to exist until further notice. Possibly, they could be used again to channel assets into the Maverick Foundation."[240] These statements show that LGT was comfortable with "channeling assets" through shell corporations to disguise the identity of the ultimate recipient.

Although the memorandum never mentions the Qualified Intermediary Program, many financial institutions had signed QI agreements for the first time in 2001, including LGT. Those agreements may have been responsible for the memorandum's comment that a number of financial institutions had told the Greenfields "that U.S. citizens are not those clients that one wishes for in offshore business."[241] LGT, however, appears to have been more than willing to retain and expand the business it had with the Greenfields.

The Subcommittee was unable to ascertain from LGT or the Greenfields whether the $30 million transfer took place or whether their LGT accounts were still open. The Subcommittee was told by the Greenfields' legal counsel, however, that the Greenfields are currently in negotiation with the IRS and Department of Justice over tax liability issues related to Liechtenstein.

(5) Gonzalez accounts: Inflating prices and frustrating creditors

Jorge and Conchita Gonzalez, and their son Ricardo, operated a car dealership in the United States for many years.[242] Beginning in 1986, LGT helped them acquire two Liechtenstein foundations and two Liechtenstein corporations to assist their car dealership which was located in Puerto Rico and specialized in selling Volvos, among other cars. The foundations were the Tragunda Foundation and Fondation Tragique; the companies were Auto und Motoren AG and Asmeral Investment Anstalt. LGT also helped them form a third Liechtenstein company, Tierzucht Investierungs Anstalt, which served as a holding company for a Spanish corporation, Ganadera, which owned a ranch in Spain. The foundations and companies each opened LGT accounts whose assets fluctuated over time. The latest LGT bank statement obtained by the Subcommittee indicates that, at the end of 2001, the accounts held assets with a combined value of about 7.4 million Swiss francs or about $4.5 million.[243]

This analysis concentrates on the Liechtenstein foundations and companies connected to the car dealership in the United States. The car dealership was associated with two corporations: Trebol Motors Corporation which actually sold the cars in Puerto Rico, and Trebol Motors Distributor Corporation which imported the cars from Volvo.[244] Both corporations ("Trebol") were owned by Jorge Gonzalez and, after his death, by Conchita and Ricardo Gonzalez.[245] Ricardo Gonzalez served as the general manager of both companies beginning in 1988.[246] Trebol was apparently the only Volvo dealership in Puerto Rico.[247]

Tragunda Foundation ("Tragunda"), established in 1986, owned 100 percent of the shares of the two Liechtenstein companies, Auto und Motoren AG ("AUM") and Asmeral Investment Anstalt ("Asmeral"). All three assisted Trebol. Tragunda appears to have provided substantial financing, at one point making a $6 million loan to AUM, which in turn loaned funds to Trebol.[248] Asmeral apparently acted as an intermediary for loans to Trebol from an LGT-related investment company known as FIWA AG.[249]

AUM played an even more central role. AUM represented itself to Volvo as a "guarantor" of Trebol's debts,[250] apparently without ever revealing that the companies shared common ownership.[251] As a result, Volvo sent AUM copies of the invoices it sent to Trebol for the inventory of cars Trebol purchased for sale in Puerto Rico, in order to keep AUM "informed of its potential liability."[252] AUM did not merely take receipt of the Volvo invoices; as described in later court proceedings, AUM sent additional invoices to Trebol for selected cars, specifying a higher cost for the cars than Volvo had actually charged. The First Circuit described this "double invoicing scheme" as follows:

> Plaintiffs showed that, between 1986 and 1989, AUM sent Trebol additional invoices for the same vehicles but with different purported prices. AUM's invoices sometimes overstated the vehicles' cost relative to the actual price in the authentic Volvo invoice by as much as $3000; not all AUM invoices contained inflated prices and some of the inflated ones involved small amounts (e.g., $50). In any case, Trebol used these inflated invoices to obtain higher inventory financing from Puerto Rican banks and Trebol also calculated its retail prices using the inflated cost as a starting point. Trebol also remitted the higher invoice amount to AUM, resulting in the accumulation of a pool of excess funds in Liechtenstein. ... Since Trebol was sent copies of the original Volvo-prepared invoices, a rational jury could conclude that Trebol knew of the actual prices and was defrauding Puerto Rican banks by means of the double invoicing scheme. If Trebol used the inflated invoice prices on its tax returns, tax authorities may also have been defrauded.[253]

These facts came to light in a civil lawsuit filed against Trebol challenging its pricing practices. In 1992, a group of individuals and corporations filed a federal class action lawsuit alleging that Volvo, Trebol, and Jorge, Conchita and Ricardo Gonzelez had engaged in a conspiracy to violate the Racketeering Influenced and Corrupt Organizations ("RICO") Act "by engaging in hundreds of predicate acts of mail and wire fraud" which were part of a complex "scheme to defraud Puerto Rican purchasers by overcharging them" for certain Volvo cars.[254] This litigation resulted in four years of pre-trial discovery, a three-week trial in 1996, multiple appeals decided in 1998, and additional damage proceedings finally resolved years later.

In June 1996, three days before the primary trial in the litigation was to start, Trebol and the Gonzalezes admitted that the facts alleged in the third amended Complaint filed in the case were true, and the district court entered a judgment against them on the issue of liability, reserving the question of damages for later.[255] Volvo went to trial, lost, and was found liable by a jury for damages of about $43 million, which the court then trebled under RICO to about $130 million.[256] Because Trebol and the Gonzalezes had admitted being engaged in a conspiracy with Volvo to violate the RICO Act, the district court ruled, in October 1996, that the $130 million damage award applied to them as well.[257] Volvo, Trebol, and the Gonzalezes appealed. In 19 98, the First Circuit reversed the judgment against Volvo entirely because it found that the facts did not sustain a finding of liability. The First Circuit allowed the judgment to stand against Trebol and the Gonzalezes, however, due to their factual admissions and remanded the case to the district court for a new hearing on damages.[258]

As a result of the litigation, Trebol declared bankruptcy in September 1996.[259] Since the district court decision applying the $130 million damage award to Trebol had been issued about a week later, in October 1996, the First Circuit ruled that the damage award could not be applied to Trebol due to the automatic stay that protects companies in bankruptcy, and vacated the judgment pending a lifting of the stay.[260] The end result was that, by 1998, Volvo was relieved of all RICO liability, Trebol was protected from any judgment while in bankruptcy, and the Gonzalezes faced new proceedings on their liability for RICO damages, attorney fees, and costs.

In 1997, after the initial damage award of $130 million and before the appeals court required the damage awards to be re-evaluated, the Gonzalezes acted on the advice of LGT to acquire a new Liechtenstein foundation called Fondation Tragique and transfer their Liechtenstein assets to that new entity. As an LGT internal document explained later: "For the purpose of protection from creditors, who are litigating the family in Puerto Rico, the assets already being held by the Tragunda Foundation were transferred to the Fondation Tragique."[261] This statement indicates that LGT was aware of the ongoing litigation, and fully prepared to help the Gonzalezes hide their assets from the "creditors" engaged in litigation against them.

In 1999, the district court drastically reduced the $130 million damage award against the Gonzalezes, finding them liable for only $200,000.[262] The Gonzalezes apparently paid this judgment in 2000.[263]

A 2001 internal LGT memorandum, prepared after several members of the Gonzalez family met with an LGT private banker in Zurich, Switzerland, indicates that LGT had been kept informed of these developments.[264] The memorandum also indicates that Tragique's initial beneficiaries, from 1997 until 2001, had consisted of one or more of the Gonzalez children, presumably to ensure that the assets transferred to Tragique could not be attached in connection with a judgment against Conchita or Ricardo Gonzalez in the Puerto Rican litigation. After the threat of litigation had passed, however, the Tragique beneficiaries were changed. The LGT memorandum put it this way:

> Now that the problems in Puerto Rico are resolved and a tax investigation is no longer to be presumed, we discuss the situation concerning the bylaws of the Foundation Tragique. In these regards, Conchita, as protector, signs an order to change the bylaws so that she appears as primary beneficiary, and that after her death the children – who are the current primary beneficiaries – appear as secondary beneficiaries with equal proportions.[265]

This memorandum suggests that LGT had no qualms about changing the beneficiaries of a foundation to prevent a creditor from attaching assets. It also shows that Ms. Gonzalez exercised significant control over Tragique, serving as the Foundation Protector, with authority to name the Foundation's beneficiaries.[266]

The memorandum also recounts other actions taken by Ms. Gonzalez, demonstrating her control over the range of Liechtenstein assets and entities associated with her family. The memorandum notes, for example, that, "Conchita signs the order to dissolve the Tragunda Foundation and to transfer the proceeds from liquidation ... to the Foundation Tragique"; she signed the "mandate" transferring "monies, including $550,000," from AUM to Tragique; and she approved transferring Tierzucht Investierungs, the Liechtenstein company once owned by Tragunda, to the new foundation.[267] The memorandum states: "Conchita signs the Status of Assets of the Foundation Tragique 2000." It also recounts that the LGT private banker discussed "the investment of Trangique's assets," and that Ms. Gonzalez approved investing "$1 million in cash" in fixed term deposits and "the rest in LGT Strategy Class Funds 5 years!"[268] In addition, the memorandum notes that the LGT private banker had carried $10,000 in cash to give to Ms. Gonzalez while in Zurich: "I deliver the amount of US$10,000.—to Conchita; the cash withdrawal receipt, to be debited to the Foundation Trangique, is initialed."[269] These actions show Ms. Gonzalez in control of the administration and assets of Tragique, Tragunda, and AUM.

By 2002, the three Liechtenstein companies controlled by Tragunda were gone. Asmeral had been dissolved;[270] AUM had been placed in liquidation;[271] and Tierzucht Investierungs had been transferred to Fondation Tragique. LGT records show that Tragunda had also been dissolved, and only about $2,000 remained in its LGT account.[272] Tragique, in contrast, held assets valued at about 7.4 million Swiss francs or about $4.5 million.[273]

The documents obtained by the Subcommittee do not indicate what happened after 2002.

(6) Chong accounts: Moving funds through hidden accounts

Richard M. Chong ("Mr. Chong") was born in the United States, lives in California, is a U.S. citizen, and specializes in venture capitalist projects involving China.[274] His father, Antonio T. Chong, founded the Yue Shing Tong Foundation at LGT in 1988, endowing it with funds allegedly from a chemical business he had developed in Taiwan and China.[275] Antonio Chong died in 1998, and his foundation passed onto to his wife Fanny L. Chong, a U.S. citizen and California resident who was the sole beneficiary.[276] Ms. Chong added her three children as beneficiaries and reorganized the foundation by creating four funds, one for herself called "Fund Mother"; one for Richard called "Fund Son R"; one called "Fund Daughter T" and one called "Fund Son C."[277] In 2002, the four funds in the Yue Shing Tong Foundation had assets with a combined value of about $9.4 million.[278]

In 1999, Ms. Chong gave her son, Richard Chong, power of attorney to "exercise [her] beneficial rights of the [Yue Shing Tong] Foundation on my behalf."[279] The documents obtained by the Subcommittee show that, for the next six years, the foundation accounts saw activity every few months, often involving large sums. Financial documents produced to the Subcommittee include lists of incoming and outgoing transfers from the Yue Shing Tong Foundation's four funds from 1992 to mid-2007.[280] These documents show such transactions as a $1.5 million incoming transfer from "one of our clients"; a $1.3 million incoming transfer from "UBS"; incoming transfers over six years from one source exceeding $7 million; $450,000 in incoming transfers from "Acme Components," company for which Mr. Chong once served as the managing director;[281] and outgoing transfers over six years to another source exceeding $1.3 million. The LGT records also show occasional cash withdrawals in Hong Kong that over the six-year period totaled $200,000. These and other documents obtained by the Subcommittee indicate that, unlike many of the reviewed accounts at LGT which saw only occasional activity, the Yue Shing Tong Foundation funds appear to have been used for a variety of business and personal transactions.

Another key development took place in 2004. That year, LGT helped the Foundation set up what LGT has sometimes referred to as a "transfer corporation" to help disguise asset flows into and out of a foundation's accounts.[282] A transfer corporation acts as a pass-through entity that breaks the direct link between the foundation and other persons with whom it is exchanging funds or assets, making it harder to trace the origin and ultimate recipient of those funds and assets.

In this case, LGT's office in Hong Kong helped Mr. Chong establish Apex Assets Ltd., using a Hong Kong corporate service provider called KCS Ltd.[283] The documentation reviewed by the Subcommittee is unclear as to whether LGT or Mr. Chong's foundation owned Apex. In any event, LGT opened a new account for Apex at the bank. Financial documents show that, after Apex was established, virtually all funds deposited into or withdrawn from the Yue Shing Tong accounts were routed through Apex.[284] A series of four letters sent by Mr. Chong to LGT from 2002 to 2006, for example, directed LGT to route a total of about $200,000 in Foundation funds, through Apex, to Dynamic Travel Service, allegedly to pay for "travel expenses to be incurred by Apex."[285] LGT also recommended Apex's use in other aspects of Mr. Chong's business. On one occasion, for example, when goods had been delivered to the wrong address in one of Mr. Chong's business ventures and had to be returned, his LGT contact sent Mr. Chong an email: "Can you ask your sender to ship them to Apex instead? This would also be better from a safety point of view."[286]

Because of the sums funneled through the foundation accounts, Mr. Chong routinely communicated with LGT personnel in Hong Kong, exchanging correspondence and emails most often with an LGT representative named Silvan Colani.[287] The Chong account was the only LGT account reviewed by the Subcommittee that made common use of emails. The communications dealt with a variety of issues that appear related to Mr. Chong's business ventures including securities transactions;[288] payments to Dynamic Travel; and transfers of funds to Sycamore Venture Capital L.P., a Silicon Valley venture capital business where Mr. Chong was a partner.[289] Other communications forwarded documents received from KCS related to Apex, including invoices[290] and even a Schedule K-1 Form from a corporate U.S. tax return listing Apex as a partner in a U.S. partnership.[291] On one occasion, LGT sent an email to Mr. Chong stating: "We have received your delivery of 63,303 units to Apex."[292] A letter from Mr. Chong the next day instructed LGT "to wire US$63,303 ... from the account number 32.8 to account number 32. 1 ," indicating that the "units" that had arrived the day before referred to dollars in an incoming wire transfer.[293]

Throughout the documentation, LGT personnel never appeared to question the large sums moving through the foundation accounts and willingly worked to keep the transactions secret through use of Apex, allowing transfers without identifying information for the originating or recipient parties, and even using code phrases to describe funding transfers.

On February 20, 2008, LGT's representative, Mr. Colani, sent Mr. Chong an email stating: "There is some important news that you should be aware of. Please have a look at www.lgt.com."[294] A historical review of the LGT website shows that was the day LGT issued a news announcement about the fact that a former LGT employee had released information on LGT accounts. Mr. Chong wrote: "Is this disclosure possibly affecting me?"[295] Mr. Colani responded: "Yes. I'm afraid we have to assume the possibility." Later he wrote to Mr. Chong: "Suggest you urgently seek local advice. Worst case, we must assume that all files up to 2002 are out. I'm very sorry."[296] LGT later gave Mr. Chong the name of several lawyers in California.[297]

The Subcommittee understands that Mr. Chong is now responding to IRS inquiries related to Liechtenstein.

(7) Miskin accounts: Hiding assets from courts and a spouse

Michael Miskin is a citizen of the United Kingdom, has claimed residency in Bermuda, but also lived in California for a decade, from 1991 to 2002.[298] In 2003, after his wife of nearly 40 years, Stephanie Miskin, filed for divorce, he ignored court orders to transfer California real estate and £3 million in alimony to his ex-wife, hid assets in offshore jurisdictions around the world, and effectively disappeared. In the early 1 990s, LGT helped Mr. Miskin open an account in Liechtenstein and transfer millions of Swiss francs to LGT, apparently from another Liechtenstein bank that had been disclosed to his wife's legal counsel. In 1998, LGT helped him form a Liechtenstein foundation, called the Micronesia Foundation, and transferred his LGT funds, then valued at nearly 10 million Swiss francs or $6.6 million, into the foundation's account, even though LGT believed Mr. Miskin had earned the money, "under the table."[299] In 2001, Micronesia's assets were valued by LGT at about 9.8 million Swiss francs which, due to a relative decline in the value of the dollar, was then equivalent to about $9.6 million.

U.S. Residency. Mr. Miskin has spent substantial time in the United States, but has denied being a U.S. resident subject to U.S. taxes. In a 2003 sworn statement submitted to a U.S. court, Mr. Miskin declared that he was a U.K. citizen and resident of Bermuda.[300] His then ex- wife disagreed, asserting in pleadings filed in the United States and the United Kingdom that he had resided in California from about 1991 until 2002.[301] Ms. Miskin indicated that Mr. Miskin had claimed Bermudan residency in an effort to avoid having to admit U.S. residency which, among other consequences, would have rendered him liable for U.S. taxes. She offered the following explanation to the court:

> "[P]erhaps ten years ago Defendant [Mr. Miskin] and I were granted Bermudan residency by obtaining a residential address and depositing a substantial sum of money with, I believe, the Bank of Bermuda. The advantage of Bermudan residency to the Defendant is that it provided him with a means to enter the United States without being obliged to go through any registration process. Defendant explained to me that all he needed to do was to have with him, at any time when he entered the United States, a return flight to Bermuda. Once his entry had been secured, it was simply a matter, so the Defendant told me, of cancelling the return ticket to Bermuda and securing a refund. This arrangement had the added advantage to Defendant that by virtue of his entry into the United States not being registered, his presence did not come to the attention of any of the US authorities and particularly the Internal Revenue Service. To minimize the risk of his presence as a "permanent resident" becoming known to the IRS, Defendant was scrupulous to ensure that he did not own any real estate, motor vehicle or indeed even hold bank accounts in his own name. This was achieved through the employment of nominee accounts and trust companies."[302]

Mr. Miskin admitted in his sworn statement to the court that he had lived at various times in California, but denied that his stays had been sufficient to make him a U.S. resident: "I have visited Santa Barbara [in California] in the past on a tourist visa permitting me to stay for only 90 days in the United States at any one time."[303] He also declared, "Although I have visited Santa Barbara in past years, I have stayed for less than 90 days and have never been a resident. On occasion, when I have stayed in the Seaview property [in California], my name has been put on the mailbox. I understood that my name was removed on my departure or shortly thereafter."[304] Ms. Miskin, in contrast, told the court that Mr. Miskin had lived in Santa Barbara "for many years," received mail there, was well-known by his neighbors and a local art center, and had purchased a $700,000 condominium, the Seaview property, which she helped remodel.[305]

Internal LGT documents produced to the Subcommittee indicate that, from 1998 to 2001, Mr. Miskin provided the bank with contact information, not in Bermuda, but in California, listing the address and telephone number for the Seaview property,[306] a Post Office Box address in Santa Barbara,[307] and a business card bearing a Santa Barbara telephone number.[308] Other LGT documents indicate that the bank was well aware of the fact that, while Mr. Miskin claimed Bermuda residency, he often lived in the United States: "Mr. Mistin's [sic] registered place of residence is in Bermuda. In the U.S., he is a 'visitor' and lives most of the time in Santa Barbara. As a resident of Bermuda, he has unrestricted entry and exit to and from the U.S."[309] LGT expressed no concern about Mr. Miskin's conduct. To the contrary, another LGT internal document suggests that LGT viewed Mr. Miskin's residency claim as a successful ploy to avoid U.S. taxation: "IMPORTANT: The financial beneficiary has his PLACE OF RESIDENCE IN BERMUDA and not in the U.S. Hence, he pays no taxes in the U.S.!!!!! !"[310]

California Realty. In 1998, Mr. Miskin acquired U.S. real estate but used offshore entities to hide his beneficial ownership interest in the property. The property is a condominium in Montecito, California, bearing the address of 68 Seaview Drive ("Seaview Property").[311] Mr. Miskin has admitted in court that the Seaview Property was purchased in April 1998, by Belmont Assets Ltd., a shell corporation formed in Guersey, and that Belmont Assets Ltd. is wholly owned by a Guernsey trust called Bonnymede Trust.[312] Mr. Miskin has denied, however, that he was the settlor, trustee, officer, or beneficiary of the Guernsey entities:

> "I do not now, nor have I ever, owned the property in Santa Barbara commonly known as 68 Seaview Drive. I understand that the property is owned by Belmont Assets Ltd. Although I have in the past acted as an advisor and consultant to Belmont Assets Ltd., I do not now, nor have I ever owned any interest in that entity. ... I believe that Belmont Assets Ltd. is owned by the Bonnymede Trust which was established in Guernsey. That is an irrevocable trust. The sole beneficiary is 'The Royal Masonic Benevolent Institution,' a charitable institution for the benefit of poor and distressed free masons. I was not the settlor of the Bonnymede Trust, nor to the best of my knowledge have I ever been either a trustee or a beneficiary of the Bonnymede Trust."[313]

Mr. Miskin claims he was not the settlor, trustee, or a beneficiary of the Bonnymede Trust, yet there is ample evidence that he controlled it. He admits having been "an advisor and consultant to Belmont Assets," which is a common means for beneficial owners to assert control over a company that they do not ostensibly own.[314] Moreover, in 2002, his granddaughter was added as a beneficiary of the trust,[315] a fact omitted from his court pleading. In addition, the Subcommittee contacted an employee of Anfossi Management in Bermuda, Douglas M. Tufts, who was a trustee of the Bonnymede Trust and a shareholder and director of Belmont Assets Ltd. Mr. Tufts stated that there is "no doubt" that Mr. Miskin initiated, controlled and benefitted from Bonnymede and Belmont.[316]

Mr. Tufts says he believes that Mr. Miskin paid Anfossi Management a retainer in late 2002, to provide trustees to Bonnymede and directors to Belmont. He said that expenses relating to Bonnymede, Belmont, and the Seaview property were paid from an Anfossi escrow account funded with the retainer. After the retainer was depleted, he said that Anfossi Management began billing Mr. Miskin. He said that the bills were sent to the Seaview Property – the same property Mr. Miskin denied owning or living at -- despite the fact that Mr. Miskin was ostensibly a resident of Bermuda, and Anfossi Management is located in Bermuda. Mr. Tufts said that Mr. Miskin did not pay all of his bills to Anfossi Management, and estimated that $15,000 to $20,000 remains outstanding.

In 2003, a U.K. court adjudicating the Miskin divorce proceedings found that Bonnymead Trust and Belmont Assets Ltd. were held "on a bare trust for, and for the exclusive benefit of" Mr. Miskin, and ordered the trust to transfer its assets to Ms. Miskin, including the Seaview Property.[317] After Ms. Miskin brought proceedings in California to enforce the U.K. court order and obtained a second court decision in her favor, the Guernsey entities complied, transferring the property to her in late 2003.[318]

If Mr. Miskin had admitted to being the owner of the California property from 1998 until 2003, this ownership interest would have strengthened arguments that he was, in fact, a U.S. resident subject to U.S. taxation.

LGT Accounts. An internal LGT memorandum obtained by the Subcommittee shows that, during the 1 990s, LGT helped Mr. Miskin hide millions of dollars in Liechtenstein from his wife and tax authorities. The memorandum, dated June 30, 1998, provides the bank's initial analysis of Mr. Miskin's request for a "New Establishment."[319]

> Mr. Alois Beck (LGT) asks me to call Mr. Mistin in Santa Barbara, CA (USA), because Mr. Mistin would like to have some information about a foundation or a trust in FL.[320]
>
> Mr. Mistin's registered place of residence is in Bermuda. In the U.S., he is a 'visitor' and lives most of the time in Santa Barbara. As a resident of Bermuda, he has unrestricted entry and exit to and from the U.S.
>
> About a few years ago, he made a rather large profit from the sale of his company[321] the Credit Bank in Belgium. Back then he still lived in England, as a nonresident. For tax reasons (I did not understand how that works), the accounting firm [Touche] & Ross recommended that he deposit annually the positive balance, for the time period in which £25,000.00 net gets credited in interest, into the account of his wife. The account was opened, and he had the signature as well (but he's not completely sure anymore). Eight years ago, he and his wife came to a clash, and since then he has been separated from her. Chagrined, he left England, and instructed the bank to transfer the money to UBS in Geneva.[322] That is when it was noticed that the amount is still in his wife's account. The bank had not carried out his instruction to transfer the principal back to his account after the interest was credited. His wife was aware of these tax-related transactions, as well as of the fact that the bank had

not carried out her husband's instructions. She took advantage of this opportunity and charged Mr. Mistin with having stolen the money from her and having hastily fled the country!!! Thereupon he had the money transferred from Geneva to the FL Landesbank. But after the Geneva bank disclosed information to the English attorneys (!!! !!) he brought the money from to the BIL in cash - that was 8 years ago. In the meantime, the charge has been withdrawn by his wife.

His wife is still keen on the money, however, and hence does not want to get divorced. The older son, very successful in business himself, is more on his mother's side; the younger son is more on his father's, but maintains good relations with the mother as well. In order to make sure that his wife never finds out about the foundation, the amounts are to be paid to his son 'anonymously.' The older son has several million himself and will for this reason not benefit from the foundation.

The assets, currently around 10 million Swiss francs, were earned 'under the table' and were always separate from the official, so he is not expecting to encounter problems related to the breach of the disclosure."

The LGT memo ends with the note: "We agreed that he will fax us three name suggestions. We will send him the prepared STOM [foundation without a mandate] documents via DHL tomorrow, July 1, 1998 to the following address: Michael Mistin, 68 Seaview Drive, Montecato, CA 93108 USA."

The LGT memorandum indicates that, eight years earlier, in or around 1991, Mr. Miskin transferred funds from "FL Landesbank," a reference to another Liechtenstein bank, to "the BIL," an abbreviation for the LGT "Bank in Liechtenstein." It is unclear whether Mr. Miskin transferred these funds to an LGT account in his own name or in the name of another person. In either event, the memorandum clearly portrays the funds as beneficially owned by Mr. Miskin. The memorandum states that the assets that had been deposited with LGT eight years earlier were "currently around 10 million Swiss francs."

The memorandum describes actions taken by Mr. Miskin over the years to hide his funds from tax authorities and his wife, including depositing funds from the sale of his business in his wife's bank account, transferring funds to a new bank to avoid his wife's "English attorneys,"[323] and depositing additional funds that had been "earned 'under the table.'" The memorandum also describes steps that will be taken "to make sure that his wife never finds out about the [new] foundation." The author of the memorandum expresses no reservations about Mr. Miskin's conduct or forming a new "Establishment" for him. Instead, the memorandum offers to act quickly by sending him an overnight package with account opening documentation. The address to be used is the very Seaview property that Mr. Miskin will later claim he never resided in.

LGT actually formed the Micronesia Foundation for Mr. Miskin on September 17, 1998, and opened an LGT account for the foundation with the nearly 10 million in Swiss francs transferred from Mr. Miskin's other accounts at the bank.[324]

In 2000, Mr. Miskin gave LGT a letter of wishes detailing how the Micronesia assets should be distributed upon his demise, further demonstrating his control over the foundation.[325] The letter lists his wife, son, and grandchildren as primary beneficiaries. The letter specifies:

> The foundation board shall advise beneficiaries to treat sums due to them with the utmost caution in respect of local taxes. The board shall seek out and advise, the best

possible way for beneficiaries to receive monies either by debit card or by loan or any other suitable method that should seek to avoid such local taxes. Leaving principle sums allotted to each beneficiary in a company or foundation in Liechtenstein should be recommended. Any beneficiary who takes legal action against the foundation will be automatically excluded from being a beneficiary.

Other LGT documents reviewed by the Subcommittee also demonstrate Mr. Miskin's control over Micronesia. On one occasion in 2000, for example, Mr. Miskin sent an email to his LGT contact after an apparent discussion of inheritance taxes on trust beneficiaries and Mr. Miskin's desire to ensure "my beneficiaries do not suffer taxes of 40 % and very possibly greater amounts." He closes with the line, "I will be sending you new instructions as soon as I have figured it out."[326] A 2001 fax from Mr. Miskin to LGT directs the transfer of £1 11,106 from Micronesia to a Barclays Bank in England "ASAP [as soon as possible]" for "the purchase price of my sons [sic] new house." The same fax directs a transfer of £15,000 from Micronesia to an account in Mr. Miskin's name at a Lloyds TSB Bank branch in Jersey.[327]

A 2002 letter to Mr. Miskin from his LGT account manager shows that LGT provided him with advice on offshore structures and how to continue to shield his assets from U.S. taxes:

Dear Mr. Miskin,

Thank you very much for your fax of February 23, 2002 and for the patience you had.

In the meantime I have spoken with an expert for structures of the area of G.[328] It turned out that with respect to the tax situation in the US-area a re-domicilization of the company to another jurisdiction would not be advisable and would additionally take a very long time. Therefore at least the company's seat has top remain in G. But it is possible to transfer the domicile of the trust as well as the representative office. In that case our suggestion would be to transfer the whole structure including the holding to a much more co-operative trust company [at] a representative office on the Isle of Man. This office being an office of high reputation would provide us with a nominee shareholder for the shares of the company and also will support us in taking over and administering the company as new trust officers in direct co-operation with us.... I would like to inform you that after you having decided to execute the transfer all the necessary details will be arranged by us.[329]

This letter, faxed to Mr. Miskin at a Santa Barbara, California number, demonstrates LGT's ongoing willingness to help him place assets in offshore structures.

Hiding Assets from the Courts. In 2003, Ms. Miskin filed for divorce in London.[330] Mr. Miskin did not appear at the divorce proceedings, and the divorce was finalized in July.[331] The U.K. court ordered Mr. Miskin to make a lump sum alimony payment to Ms. Miskin of £3 million. Mr. Miskin did not acknowledge the court order or provide the funds.[332] The documents reviewed by the Subcommittee indicate that the Micronesia Foundation was still active at LGT as of December 31, 2001, about 18 months before the court judgment,[333] so it is possible that these funds could have been used to satisfy the alimony payment. However, neither the court nor Ms. Miskin knew of the existence of the LGT foundation and account.

The U.K. court also awarded ownership of the Seaview Property to Ms. Miskin.[334] Real estate is not as easily hidden as funds, and Mrs. Miskin initiated action in the Superior Court of California, to enforce the British court order and take possession of the property. Mr. Miskin, through legal counsel, filed pleadings in opposition, contending among other arguments that the court had no personal jurisdiction over him and he did not own the property being transferred. Like the London court before it, however, the California court rejected his arguments and awarded the property to Ms. Miskin.

The documents reviewed by the Subcommittee do not indicate whether the Micronesia Foundation's assets, including the $9.6 million identified in 2001, remain at LGT.

(8) Other LGT practices

Internal LGT documentation obtained by the Subcommittee provides additional information about LGT practices that could be used to facilitate tax evasion.

Gap Between KYC and QI Obligations. In response to Subcommittee questions, LGT's most senior compliance officer, Mr. Klein, stated that LGT principally relied on the declarations of their clients to determine if they had U.S. or non-U.S. status for the purpose of QI reporting.[335] Mr. Klein also stated that since QI rules are distinct from Know-Your-Customer (KYC) due diligence rules, if LGT determined during a KYC evaluation that the beneficial owner of a trust or a company was a U.S. person, that information did not necessarily impact on the client's status for QI purposes.

This discrepancy is highlighted by LGT Bank's approach to the QI Audit Program. For example, LGT provided to the Subcommittee a copy of the 2006 QI External Auditor's Report, which was submitted by PriceWaterhouseCoopers AG to the IRS on June 26, 2007.[336] This chapter notes that the auditors had concluded that at least one accountholder originally listed as a non-U.S. person may be a U.S. person with tax liability. A letter from LGT Bank to the auditors states that the bank will take corrective measures, including soliciting an appropriate W-9 from the client.[337] LGT confirmed to the Subcommittee that should questions arise during the QI audits about the reliability of its information on the U.S. status of one of its clients, the bank will rectify the matter and solicit appropriate documentation. Thus, the contradiction between the QI and the KYC rules is clear: if the bank is advised through a QI audit that one of its account holders may be a U.S. person, it will actively seek to bring itself into compliance with the QI program. However, if the bank itself learns, through its KYC obligations, that the beneficial owner of an account holder is a U.S. person, it will not apply that knowledge to its QI reporting obligations.

This situation appears to demonstrate a gap in the QI Program. A condition precedent to becoming a QI is that the bank must apply appropriate KYC rules, which includes looking through a corporate entity or trust to determine the ultimate beneficial owner, or, as Mr. Klein described it, a "warm human body." So even though a bank is required to know the identity of the person behind a corporate account holder, the QI Program does not require the bank to look beyond a properly filed W8BEN. Thus, consistent with the QI Program, LGT Bank must document the beneficial owner of a corporation, but LGT Bank need not look through the nonU.S. status of the corporation that in fact holds an account for a U.S. beneficial owner.

Using Transfer Corporations to "Cover Up the Tracks" of Client Funds. As indicated in some of the case histories described earlier, LGT documents obtained by the Subcommittee show that it was not uncommon for LGT to set up intermediary, pass-through corporations that were used by the bank, in the words of an LGT employee, "to cover up the tracks" of funds moving into LGT client accounts. When asked about these corporations, the head of compliance Officer for LGT Group confirmed their existence, explaining that these "auxiliary services corporations" served several functions, including the transmission of funds "confidentially."[338]

The documents show that LGT used BTS Management Ltd., formed in the British Virgin Islands (BVI), to establish a number of the transfer corporations. The documents indicate that LGT typically asked BTS Management to form a BVI corporation which then opened an account at LGT or another bank, such as Bank du Gothard in Luxembourg. The transfer corporation then received funds or securities from an LGT client and immediately transferred those funds or securities to LGT, if its account was at an outside bank. In some instances the transfer corporation was then dissolved; in other instances, it continued in existence. Once the funds or securities were delivered to LGT bank, they were moved internally within the bank, using a mechanism called "journaling" to transfer them from one LGT account to another, here from the transfer corporation's LGT account to the client's LGT account. This internal transfer mechanism makes it much more difficult to trace the movement of funds and securities, since it leaves no record outside of the bank showing that the assets were transferred to the ultimate recipient, the LGT client.

The Subcommittee investigation uncovered several examples of LGT engaging in this practice. For example, Sera Financial Corporation is a BVI corporation that appears to have functioned as an LGT transfer corporation. An internal LGT document describes Sera Financial as a "[s]pecial purpose company (indirect subsidiary of LTV) for portfolio transfers for assets which are to be brought into an LTV structure."[339] The document shows, by account number, that Sera Financial held one account at Banque du Gothard and eleven separate accounts at LGT Bank in Liechtenstein.[340] The document explains this unusual account structure as follows:

> For each customer, a sub-account or deposit facility is opened under a reference at BdG [Banque du Gothard] and at LGT .... Funds transfers as well as securities deliveries to BdG are in favor of SERA .... BdG is instructed to forward cash values and securities without delay to LGT BIL [Bank in Liechtenstein] in favor of Sera Financial Corp. with specification of the reference. ... As soon as the assets are credited at BIL, they are transferred to the destination account ....[341]

One example of how Sera Financial was used involves a new trust set up for a U.S. client in 2000. A LGT memorandum to the file discussing the transfer of assets to the new trust states: "The trust shall open an account in the LGT Bank in Liechtenstein. The transfer of assets should take place using this account. To cover up the tracks from UBS Zurich to the trust in Liechtenstein, I recommend an intermediary Single Purpose Company."[342] LGT decided to use Sera Financial as the transfer corporation. A wire transfer instruction from Gotthard Bank shows how the transfer operation worked.[343] It shows that on October 31, 2000, after $1.2 million had been credited to the Sera Financial account at Banque du

Gothard: "BTS Management Limited, Tortola, as Managing Director of the company Sera Financial Corporation, Tortola, B.V.I. [h]ereby declares: ... that the following beneficiary(ies) is/are entitled to the above-referenced transaction," naming the U.S. citizen from Florida, known to the Subcommittee as a U.S. client of LGT at that time. The $1.2 million was then transferred to his account.

A second example involves Jaffra Development Inc., a BVI corporation that appears to have been used by LGT as a transfer corporation on a single occasion. An agreement in LGT files between Jaffra and a named LGT client describes Jaffra as "an indirect subsidiary of the LGT Trust Corporation," solely administered by BTS Management Ltd. [344]In the agreement, the "contractor," which is Jaffra, agrees not to "effect any transaction" or provide services to any "third party," except as set out in the agreement. The agreement then describes Jaffra' s contractual obligations as follows:

> The contractor [Jaffra] undertakes to open a separate account at the LGT Bank in Liechtenstein Corp., Vaduz, for the present transactions, and after completion of the transactions, at the latest by 01.01.2001, to liquidate this corporation. ... The client will transfer to account no. 0166153 of the contractor at the LGT Bank ... an amount of approximately CHF 6 million (six million 0/00 Swiss francs) in one or more installments after notice by telephone to the administrative board. ... The contractor will, in each case after receipt of a credit voucher, transfer the total value of assets, or the total value of assets less commission, fees (including account cancellation costs) as well as compensation, from account no. 0166153 of the contractor to the account no. 0165779, under the name of CHARIVARI FOUNDATION, Vaduz ("Recipient"), at the LGT Bank in Liechtenstein, in cash.

The contract states further: "BTS Management Ltd. receives a flat fee of CHF 5,000.00 for the completion of all transactions, as well as receiving outside costs, each of which is assessed on the day of deposit to the account of the contractor. The founding and liquidation costs for the JAFFRA DEVELOPMENT INC. are included in this compensation."

A third example involves Sewell Services Ltd., a BVI corporation which, like Jaffra, appears to have been used for a single client, in this case the Lowys, discussed earlier. A 1997 internal LGT memorandum described plans to move assets into a new foundation set up for the Lowys called Luperla Foundation. [345]The memorandum states that $54 million "are going to the Sewell account with us ... subsequently Sewell pays ... the amount to Luperla." It states that an "additional roughly $3 million will go to Sewell (account LGT)" from outside banks which Sewell is then to pay "to account Luperla at LGT." The memorandum states that after the transactions, "The Sewell account is to be closed on May 31, 1997, and the company [is] to be dissolved." As indicated in the earlier discussion of the Lowy accounts, over $54 million was, in fact, passed through the Sewell LGT account into the Luperla Foundation account at LGT.[346]

A final example involves Apex Assets Ltd., a corporation set up for Mr. Chong by LGT in 2004, as described earlier. It is unclear from the documentation reviewed by the Subcommittee whether Apex was owned by LGT or Mr. Chong's foundation. What the documents do show is that, from 2004 into 2007, virtually all funds transferred to or from Mr. Chong's foundation were routed through Apex.

Hiding Telephone Communications. Another strategy employed by LGT to enhance secrecy and client anonymity was to limit the ability of outside parties to trace client communications back to Liechtenstein. To achieve this objective, LGT not only instituted a policy of retaining client mail at the bank in Liechtenstein, or sending mail to locations outside of a client's home jurisdiction, but also undertook efforts to minimize the ability of outside parties to trace telephone calls back to the bank and even the country itself. One LGT document obtained by the Subcommittee, for example, providing information on how to contact a client, contained the following instruction:

> "CAUTION: Calls may be made only from public phone booths, preferably not from a FL [Liechtenstein] phone booth ! !!"[347]

A second, similar instruction was included later in the same document:

> "CAUTION: Calls may be made only from public phone booths abroad (Switzerland, Austria, etc.) !!!"[348]

In addition, the Subcommittee learned from a former LGT employee that after the country of Liechtenstein received its own area code for its telephones, LGT employees began using cell phones with the Liechtenstein area code to contact clients. However, shortly thereafter, tax authorities in another country began to conduct tax audits of individuals who had made calls to, or received calls from, telephone numbers with the Liechtenstein area code. The Subcommittee was told that, after learning of these audits, LGT employees abandoned use of telephone numbers with the Liechtenstein area code and instead used numbers with Swiss or Austrian area codes.

Enabling Bribery in the United States and Elsewhere. Perhaps one of the most disturbing documents reviewed by the Subcommittee involves an LGT analysis of a request to establish a new foundation and LGT account for an existing client which LGT states may be used, in part, to facilitate the payment of bribes in the United States. The key LGT memorandum follows a meeting that took place in September 2002, with the client, one or two LGT trust officers, and an LGT compliance officer regarding the client's request to establish LRAB Foundation to receive funds from transactions involving Glencore International, an oil trading firm founded by Marc Rich.[349] The memorandum states the following:

> 1. Private Account with LGT BIL, Vaduz
> Relatively large sums will be transferred into the existing account with LGT BIL [Bank in Liechtenstein]. For this reason, Mr. Skwaric has called on Mr. Karl Frick from Compliance for a client meeting. The assessment from Karl Frick is attached as a copy.
>
> 2. Marc Rich
> Marc Rich was the proprietor of a network of firms in Switzerland which were primarily active in merchandising. At times, over 1,500 persons in Switzerland alone were employed by him and a turnover of over USD 44.5 billion (2001, see copy) was achieved. He sold his portion to an employee, who continued to run the business as a

firm under the name Glencore International. Marc Rich is a controversial person and very questionable with his methods. On the other side, in this year, one can see that subsequent deposits from Glencore were made into the private account of the [client] couple and therefore confirm the information of the clients.

3. Evaluation of Compliance LGT BIL
The good impression which I have from the clients is also confirmed in the attached email from Karl Frick of the bank. I would like to add the following. The out-going transfers from the private account with LGT BIL have an amount of ca. USD 1 Million/per year. These are the office costs, carrying costs and payments in the realm of their commercial activity. **A small portion of the payments go however to the USA and Panama and may be classified as bribes.** Glencore International asked its largest
partner in Ecuador to pass these payments on to third parties. This system was first established in 2002 and, for this reason, the clients are very unlucky. Previously, the payments from Glencore International were made directly to said persons. [The client] declares that he will speak with Glencore again, but is also afraid that they could lose Glencore as clients.

4. Panama Corporation
I have discussed the possibility of a Panama Corporation as account holder and "transit account" with the clients. I have however, in agreement with SPR, dismissed our acting as director of such a corporation. My impression is that the clients know their situation very well; they can also asses the risks very well, but cannot change any part of their situation at the moment. The payments are however discussed with Karl Frick and can occur further.

The memorandum seems to indicate that the clients already had LGT accounts and already conducted substantial business with Glencore International through those accounts, but were interested in setting up a new foundation and Panama corporation to channel business- related transactions through their accounts. The memorandum states that "[a] small portion of the payments" that already went through the clients' LGT accounts and which would go through the proposed accounts "may be classified as bribes." Rather than object to these payments or bar them or the clients from the bank, however, the LGT trust officer states that he has a "good impression ... from the clients" which is "confirmed in the attached email" from the LGT compliance officer. When asked about this memorandum, the head of compliance for LGT Group would not discuss any client-specific information, but commented that, prior to 2002, LGT, like all banks in Liechtenstein, were "not as diligent as we should have been."[350] He declined to disclose whether the LRAB foundation or Panama corporation had been formed in response to the clients' request.

C. Analysis

The LGT information reviewed by the Subcommittee investigation indicates that, too often, LGT personnel viewed the bank's role to be, not just as a guardian of client assets or trusted financial advisor to investors, but also a willing partner to clients wishing to hide their assets from tax authorities, creditors, and courts. In that context, bank secrecy laws begin to serve as a cloak not only for client misconduct, but also for banks colluding with clients to evade taxes, dodge creditors, and defy court orders.

It is also instructive that when the LGT tax scandal broke in February 2008, the immediate reaction of the Liechtenstein government was not to condemn the taxpayers who misused the jurisdiction, promise tough action against LGT if it knowingly assisted tax fraud, or pledge to disclosure relevant information. Instead, the Liechtenstein government deplored the breach of its secrecy laws, expressed indignation that any country would purchase Liechtenstein financial data from a private individual, and issued an arrest warrant for the former LGT employee who allegedly disclosed the information.[351] In June 2008, an Internet website offered a $7 million reward for information leading to the arrest of the former LGT employee; the Subcommittee traced this reward offer to a web hosting company in Liechtenstein.[352]

In July, the Liechtenstein government advised the Subcommittee that it had initiated a special investigation into the conduct of LGT Bank and Mario Staggl, and established a commission to examine Liechtenstein laws, including the question of whether it does or should violate Liechtenstein law if a Liechtenstein financial institution were to aid or abet tax evasion or tax fraud by a U.S. client. When the Subcommittee asked Mr. Klein about the status of this investigation, he replied that he was not aware of it, despite his position as head of compliance for LGT Group. Liechtenstein is also considering entering into a tax information exchange agreement with the United States to provide wider cooperation in tax enforcement matters.

IV. UBS AG Case History

UBS AG of Switzerland is one of the largest financial institutions in the world, and has one of the world's largest private banks catering to wealthy individuals. From at least 2000 to 2007, UBS made a concerted effort to open accounts in Switzerland for wealthy U.S. clients, employing practices that could facilitate, and have resulted in, tax evasion by U.S. clients. These UBS practices included maintaining for an estimated 19,000 U.S. clients "undeclared" accounts in Switzerland with billions of dollars in assets that have not been disclosed to U.S. tax authorities; assisting U.S. clients in structuring their accounts to avoid QI reporting requirements; and allowing its Swiss bankers to market securities and banking services on U.S. soil without an appropriate license in apparent violation of U.S. law and UBS policy. In 2007, after its activities within the United States came to the attention of U.S. authorities, UBS banned its Swiss bankers from traveling to the United States and took action to revamp its practices. UBS is now under investigation by the IRS, SEC, and U.S Department of Justice.

A. UBS Bank Profile

UBS AG ("UBS") is one of the largest banks in the world, currently managing client assets in excess of $2.8 trillion.[353] UBS is the product of a 1998 merger between two leading Swiss banks, Union Bank of Switzerland and Swiss Bank Corporation. In 2000, it grew even larger after merging with PaineWebber Inc., a U.S. securities firm with more than 8,000 brokers, nearly $500 billion in client assets, and a substantial U.S. clientele.[354]

Today, UBS is incorporated and domiciled in Switzerland, but operates in 50 countries with more than 80,000 employees, of which about 38% work in the Americas, 33% in Switzerland, 17% in the rest of Europe, and 12% in Asia Pacific.[355] UBS shares are listed on the Swiss Exchange, New York Stock Exchange, and Tokyo Stock Exchange.[356]

UBS AG is the parent company of the UBS Group which includes numerous subsidiaries and affiliates.[357] UBS Group is managed by a Board of Directors, which oversees a Group Executive Board. The Chairman of the Board of Directors is Peter Kurer; the Group CEO is Marcel Rohner.[358]

UBS Group is organized into three major business lines: Global Wealth Management & Business Banking, Global Asset Management, and an Investment Bank. UBS has one of the largest private banking operations in the world, with hundreds of private bankers dedicated to providing financial services to wealthy individuals and their families around the world. UBS also maintains a Corporate Center that provides group-wide policies, financial reporting, marketing, information technology infrastructure, and service centers, and an Industrial Holdings segment which includes UBS' own holdings and non-financial businesses.[359]

UBS' private banking operations are included within the Global Wealth Management & Business Banking division, whose Chairman and CEO is Raoul Weil. That division is further divided into five regional segments: Wealth Management Americas; Wealth Management Asia Pacific; Wealth Management & Business Banking Switzerland; Wealth Management North, East & Central Europe; and Wealth Management Western Europe, Mediterranean, Middle East & Africa.[360]

In the United States, UBS maintains a large banking and securities presence, operating dozens of subsidiaries and affiliates. Its operations include a UBS AG branch office headquartered in Stamford, Connecticut; UBS Bank USA, a federally regulated bank chartered in Utah; three broker-dealers registered with the SEC, UBS International Inc., UBS Financial Services, Inc., and UBS Services LLC; and a variety of other businesses including UBS Fiduciary Trust Company in New Jersey; UBS Real Estate Securities Inc. in Delaware; UBS Trust Company National Association in New York; and UBS Life Insurance Company USA in California.[361] In 2007, UBS described its U.S. banking operations as follows: "Wealth Management US is a US financial services firm providing sophisticated wealth management services to affluent US clients through a highly trained financial advisor network."[362]

In addition to its U.S.-based operations, UBS services U.S. clients through business units based in Switzerland and other countries. For example, beginning in about 2003, UBS established "U.S. International Desks" in three of its Swiss locations, Geneva, Lugano, and Zurich. These desks, staffed with private bankers known as Client Advisors, deal exclusively with U.S. clients.[363] The U.S. International Desks originally categorized their U.S. clients according to the U.S. region where they lived, but in 2004, re-classified them according to the magnitude of their assets. "Core Affluent" clients were defined as those with assets ranging from 250 to 2 million Swiss Francs; "High Net Worth Individuals" (HNWI) had assets ranging from 2 million to 50 million Swiss Francs; and "Key Clients" have assets worth more than 50 million Swiss Francs.[364] In 2005, UBS formed a new Swiss subsidiary, called "Swiss Financial Advisors," which is a broker-dealer registered with the SEC. SFA is tasked with "serving US clients outside of Switzerland." All U.S. clients of SFA are required to file W-9

Forms. UBS AG's North American International Wealth Management Division also noted that "[a]ssets of clients [in SFA are] under Swiss law," meaning that creditors seeking to attach the assets would be required to file in Swiss courts.[365] U.S. clients who are unwilling to declare their accounts to the United States are not permitted by UBS to hold U.S. securities in their Swiss accounts, but can be serviced by Client Advisors in the Geneva, Lugano, and Zurich offices.[366]

B. UBS Swiss Accounts for U.S. Clients

Although UBS has extensive banking and securities operations in the United States that could accommodate its U.S. clients, from at least 2000 to 2007, UBS directed its Swiss bankers to target U.S. clients willing to open bank accounts in Switzerland. UBS told the Subcommittee it now has 19,000 Swiss accounts for U.S. clients with in the range of $18 billion in undeclared assets. In 2002, UBS assured its U.S. clients with undeclared accounts that U.S. authorities would not learn of them, because the bank is not required to disclose them; UBS procedures, practices and services protect against disclosure; and the account information is further shielded by Swiss bank secrecy laws. Until recently, UBS encouraged its Swiss bankers to travel to the United States to recruit new U.S. clients, organized events to help them meet wealthy U.S. individuals, and set annual performance goals for obtaining new U.S. business. It also encouraged its Swiss bankers to service U.S. client accounts in ways that would minimize notice to U.S. authorities. The evidence suggest that UBS Swiss bankers marketed securities and banking products and services in the United States without an appropriate license to do so and in apparent violation of U.S. law and the bank's own policies.

Information obtained by the Subcommittee about UBS Swiss accounts opened for U.S. citizens came in part from former UBS employee, Bradley Birkenfeld. Mr. Birkenfeld is a U.S. citizen who worked as a private banker in Switzerland from 1996 until his arrest in the United States in 2008. He worked for UBS in its private banking operations in Geneva from 2001 to 2005, until he resigned from the bank.[367] In 2007, while in the United States, Mr. Birkenfeld was subpoenaed by the Subcommittee to provide documentation and testimony related to his employment as a private banker. In a sworn deposition before Subcommittee staff, Mr. Birkenfeld provided detailed information about a wide range of issues related to UBS business dealings with U.S. clients. In 2008, Mr. Birkenfeld was arrested, indicted, and pled guilty to conspiring with a U.S. taxpayer, Igor Olenicoff, to hide $200 million in assets in Switzerland and Liechtenstein, to evade $7.2 million in U.S. taxes.[368]

(1) Opening undeclared accounts with billions in assets

From at least 2000 to 2007, UBS has opened thousands of accounts in Switzerland that are beneficially owned by U.S. clients, hold billions of dollars in assets, and have not been reported to U.S. tax authorities. These Swiss accounts were opened by U.S. clients, but, for a variety of reasons, the clients did not file W-9 Forms with UBS for the accounts. Because the clients did not file W-9 reports with the bank, UBS did not file 1099 Forms with the IRS reporting the account information. UBS refers to these accounts internally as "undeclared accounts."

In response to Subcommittee inquiries, UBS has estimated that it today has about 20,000 accounts in Switzerland for U.S. clients, of which roughly 1,000 are declared accounts and 19,000 are undeclared accounts that have not been disclosed to the IRS.[369] UBS also estimated that those accounts contain assets with a combined value of about 18.2 billion in Swiss francs or about $17.9 billion. UBS was unable to specify the breakdown in assets between the undeclared and declared accounts, except to note that the amount of assets in the undeclared accounts would be much greater.

These figures suggest that the number of U.S. client accounts in Switzerland and the amount of assets contained in those accounts have nearly doubled since 2002, when a UBS document reported that the Swiss private banking operation then had more than 11,000 accounts for clients in "North America," meaning the United States and Canada, with combined assets in excess of 21 billion Swiss francs or about $13.3 billion.[370] The UBS document also calculates that, in 2002, these accounts had earned the bank "net revenues" of about 150 million Swiss francs.[371] Since then, the Swiss private banking operations have reported opening many more U.S. client accounts in Switzerland with additional billions of dollars in assets.[372]

The UBS figures for 2008 also appear consistent with internal UBS documents from 2004 and 2005, which suggest that a substantial portion of the UBS Swiss accounts opened for U.S. clients at that time were undeclared. This information is contained in a set of monthly reports for select months in 2004 and 2005, which tracked key information for Swiss accounts opened for North American clients, meaning clients from the United States and Canada.[373]

These reports also break down the data for both declared and undeclared accounts.[374] The data suggests that the undeclared accounts not only held more assets, but also brought in more new money and were more profitable for the bank than the declared accounts.

The first data element in the reports is the total amount of assets in the specified accounts. Each month shows substantially greater assets in the undeclared accounts for U.S. clients than in the declared accounts. In October 2005, for example, the data shows a total of about 18 billion Swiss francs of assets in the undeclared accounts for U.S. clients[375] and 2.6 billion Swiss francs in the declared accounts.[376] Clearly, the assets in the undeclared accounts vastly outweigh the assets in the declared accounts for U.S. clients.

The monthly reports also track the extent to which the accounts brought in new money to UBS, referred to as "net new money" or NNM. The October 2005 report appears to show that, for the year to date, the undeclared accounts for U.S. clients had brought in more than 1.3 billion Swiss francs in net new money for UBS,[377] while the declared accounts had collectively lost about 333 million Swiss francs over the same time period.[378] These figures indicate that, in 2004 and 2005, the undeclared account assets were growing, while the declared account assets were shrinking.

The last data element in the monthly reports tracks the revenue generated by the accounts for UBS. Each month shows that UBS earned significantly more in revenues from the undeclared accounts for U.S. clients than from the declared accounts. For example, the October 2005 report shows that UBS obtained year-to-date revenues of about 180.9 million Swiss francs from the undeclared accounts[379] versus 22.1 million Swiss francs from the declared accounts.[380] By every measure employed by UBS in these monthly reports, the undeclared U.S. client accounts were more popular and more lucrative for the bank.

Still another UBS document, prepared in 2004 for a meeting of Swiss private banking officials in Geneva, to reach an "Executive Board Decision" on several matters, shows the banks awareness of the undeclared and declared accounts opened for U.S. clients. [381]About mid-way through, this document includes two flow charts showing how a UBS client advisor should handle an account with a "U.S. person." The first flow chart shows that accounts for U.S. persons domiciled in the United States should go to certain offices if a W-9 is filed, and to the North American desk in Zurich if "no W9 form" is filed. The second flow chart shows that, for U.S. persons domiciled outside of the United States, accounts with a W-9 form should go to WBS in Zurich to the "W9 Team," while accounts with "no W9 form signed" should go to the "Country team" in the country where the U.S. person was domiciled. These two flow charts provide additional evidence that the top management of UBS in Switzerland was well aware of the bank's practice of maintaining declared and undeclared accounts for U.S. clients, and had even institutionalized the administration of these accounts in different offices.

In his deposition before the Subcommittee, Mr. Birkenfeld indicated that, while he was employed at UBS from 2001 to 2005, it was his understanding that UBS had thousands of Swiss accounts opened by U.S. clients, the majority of which were undeclared and never disclosed to the IRS. He stated that, "I didn't see anyone declare any of those [Swiss] accounts in my entire career."[382]

In the recent U.S. criminal case involving Mr. Birkenfeld, the U.S. government filed a Statement of Facts, signed by Mr. Birkenfeld, stating that UBS Switzerland had "$20 billion of assets under management in the United States undeclared business, which earned the bank approximately $200 million per year in revenues."[383]

(2) Ensuring bank secrecy

UBS has not only maintained undeclared Swiss accounts for U.S. clients containing billions of dollars in assets, it has also adopted practices to ensure that, in keeping with Swiss bank secrecy laws, those undeclared accounts would not be disclosed to U.S. authorities.

Promising Bank Secrecy. UBS has assured its U.S. clients in writing that UBS will take steps to protect their undeclared accounts from disclosure to U.S. tax authorities. In November 2002, for example, senior officials in the UBS private banking operations in Switzerland sent the following letter to its U.S. clients about their Swiss accounts:

> Dear client:
>
> From our recent conversations we understand that you are concerned that UBS' stance on keeping its U.S. customers' information strictly confidential may have changed especially as a result of the acquisition of Paine Webber. We are writing to reassure you that your fear is unjustified and wish to outline only some of the reasons why the protection of client data can not possibly be compromised upon:
>
> --The sharing of customer data with a UBS unit/affiliate located abroad without sufficient customer consent constitutes a violation of Swiss banking secrecy provisions and exposes the bank employee concerned to severe criminal sanctions. Further, we should like to underscore that a Swiss bank which runs afoul of Swiss privacy laws will face sanctions by its Swiss regulator ... up to the revocation of the bank's charter. Already against this background, it must be clear that information relative to your Swiss banking relationship is as safe as ever and that the possibility

> of putting pressure on our U.S. units does not change anything. Our bank has had offices in the United States as early as 1939 and has therefore been exposed to the risk of US authorities asserting jurisdiction over assets booked abroad since decades. Please note that our bank has a successful track record of challenging such attempts.
>
> --As you are aware of, UBS (as all other major Swiss banks) has asked for and obtained the status of a Qualified Intermediary under U.S. tax laws. The QI regime fully respects client confidentiality as customer information are only disclosed to U.S. tax authorities based on the provision of a W-9 form. Should a customer choose not to execute such a form, the client is barred from investments in US securities but under no circumstances will his/her identity be revealed. Consequently, UBS's entire compliance with its QI obligations does not create the risk that his/her identity be shared with U.S. authorities.[384]

This letter plainly asserts that UBS will not disclose to the IRS a Swiss account opened by a U.S. client, so long as that account contains no U.S. securities, even if UBS knows the accountholder is a U.S. taxpayer obligated under U.S. tax law to report the account and its contents to the U.S. government.

UBS told the Subcommittee that it has no legal obligation to report such undeclared accounts to the IRS, provided that UBS ensures that the accounts do not contain U.S. securities and, thus, are not subject to reporting under the QI Program. UBS also told the Subcommittee that it recognizes that a U.S. accountholder may have a legal obligation to report a foreign trust, foreign bank account, or foreign income to the IRS. UBS pointed out, however, that those reporting obligations apply to the accountholder personally and not to UBS. UBS, thus, asserts that it has broken no law or QI obligation by allowing U.S. clients to open and maintain undeclared accounts in Switzerland, if those accounts do not contain U.S. securities.[385]

Helping U.S. Clients Avoid QI Disclosure. UBS has not only maintained undeclared accounts in Switzerland for numerous U.S. clients, it took steps to assist its U.S. clients to structure their Swiss accounts in ways that avoided U.S. reporting rules under the QI Program.

UBS informed the Subcommittee that, after it joined the QI Program in 2001, and informed its U.S. clients about its QI disclosure obligations, many of its U.S. clients elected to sell U.S. securities or open new accounts to avoid the QI reporting obligations attached.[386] UBS told the Subcommittee, for example, that in 2001, hundreds of its U.S. clients sold their U.S. securities so that their Swiss accounts would not be covered by the QI Program. UBS told the Subcommittee that it estimates that, in 2001, its U.S. clients sold over $2 billion in U.S. securities from their Swiss accounts. UBS allowed these U.S. clients to continue to maintain accounts in Switzerland, and helped them reinvest in other types of securities that did not trigger reporting obligations to the IRS, despite evidence that these U.S. clients were using their Swiss accounts to hide assets from the IRS.

UBS also told the Subcommittee that, in 2001, it helped about 250 U.S. clients with Swiss accounts to establish corporations, trusts, foundations, or other entities in non-U.S. countries, open new UBS accounts in the names of those foreign entities, and then, in a number of instances, transfer U.S. securities from the client's personal accounts to those new accounts. The offshore entities included corporations, trusts, and foundations set up in the British Virgin Islands, Hong Kong, Liechtenstein, Panama, and Switzerland.[387] UBS then accepted W8BEN Forms from these offshore entities in which they claimed ownership of the assets had been transferred from the U.S. clients' personal accounts. UBS treated the new accounts as held by non-U.S. persons whose identities did not have to be disclosed to the IRS, even though UBS knew that the true beneficial owners were U.S. persons.

These facts indicate that, soon after it joined the QI Program, UBS helped its U.S. clients structure their Swiss accounts to avoid reporting billions of dollars in assets to the IRS. Among other actions, UBS helped some of its U.S. clients to establish offshore structures to assume nominal ownership of assets, and allowed U.S. clients to continue to hold undisclosed accounts that were not reported to the IRS. Such actions, while not violations of the QI agreements per se, clearly undermined the program's effectiveness and led to the formation of offshore structures and undeclared accounts that could facilitate, and have resulted in, tax evasion by U.S. clients.

The actions taken by UBS, in many ways, matched LGT's response to the QI Program. Both UBS and LGT advised the Subcommittee that most of their U.S. clients engaged in a massive sell-off of U.S. securities after the banks signed QI agreements in 2001. In addition, both UBS and LGT provided assistance to a number of U.S. clients in establishing offshore corporations to hold U.S. securities. It appears that UBS exploited the gap between KYC rules and the QI Program in the same manner as LGT, by treating offshore corporations as non-U.S. persons for QI reporting purposes, despite knowing for KYC purposes that the offshore corporations and their assets were beneficially owned by U.S. persons. Both banks continued to maintain accounts for their U.S. clients, despite evidence that the clients were hiding their assets and accounts from the IRS. In this way, both UBS and LGT employed QI practices that kept the U.S. clients' accounts secret from the IRS and thereby facilitated tax evasion by the U.S. clients holding undeclared accounts.

The Statement of Facts in the Birkenfeld criminal case characterizes these actions as follows: "By concealing the U.S. clients' ownership and control in the assets held offshore, defendant Birkenfeld, the Swiss Bank, its managers and bankers evaded the requirements of the Q.I. program, defrauded the IRS and evaded United States income taxes."[388]

(3) Targeting U.S. clients

In addition to discovering that UBS maintained billions of dollars in undeclared accounts in Switzerland for U.S. clients and took steps to help U.S. client circumvent QI reporting requirements, the Subcommittee discovered that, from at least 2000 to 2007, UBS Swiss bankers engaged in an intensive effort to target U.S. clients to open Swiss accounts. UBS repeatedly sent its Swiss bankers onto U.S. soil to recruit new clients, expand existing accounts, and meet increasing business demands to bring new client money from the United States into Switzerland.

Legal and Policy Restrictions on U.S. Activities. U.S. securities law prohibits non-U.S. persons from advertising securities products or services or executing securities transactions within the United States, unless registered with the Securities and Exchange Commission (SEC).[389] In addition, securities products offered to U.S. persons must comply with U.S. securities laws, which generally means they must be registered with the SEC, a condition that may not be met by non-U.S. securities, mutual funds, and other investment products. In addition, although UBS AG is licensed to operate as a bank and broker-dealer in the United

States, those licenses do not extend to its non-U.S. offices or affiliates providing banking or securities services to U.S. residents.[390] Similar prohibitions may appear in State securities and banking laws. Moreover, in provisions known as "deemed sales" rules, U.S. tax laws and the standard QI agreement require sales of non-U.S. securities to be reported by foreign financial institutions on 1099 Forms sent to the IRS, if those sales were effected in the United States, such as arranged by a broker physically in the United States or through telephone calls or emails originating in the United States.[391]

To avoid violating U.S. law, exceeding its SEC and banking licenses, or triggering 1099 reporting requirements for deemed sales, since at least 2002, UBS has maintained written policies restricting the marketing and client-related activities that may be undertaken in the United States by UBS employees from outside of the country.

2002 UBS Restrictions on U.S. Activities. In 2002, for example, UBS issued a set of guidelines for its Swiss bankers administering securities accounts for U.S. clients.[392] These guidelines stated that, under U.S. tax regulations, securities trades in non-U.S. securities on behalf of a U.S. person trigger reporting requirements to the IRS under QI or IRS deemed sales rules, unless the trades are effected "by a UBS portfolio manager with discretion from a bank office of a non-US bank outside the territory of the US." To qualify for the exception and avoid reporting any securities trades or accounts to the IRS, the guidelines provide a long list of actions that UBS Swiss bankers cannot undertake with respect to their U.S. clients. Essentially, the guidelines instruct the Swiss bankers to persuade their U.S. clients to enter into a "discretionary asset management relationship" with the bank and then to "[c]ease to accept customer instructions from US territory" so that no securities trades are effected within the United States that might require reporting to the IRS.

The 2002 UBS guidelines tell the Swiss bankers, for example, to ensure that there is "no use of US mails, e-mail, courier delivery or facsimile regarding the client's securities portfolio;" "no use of telephone calls into the US regarding the client's securities portfolio;" "no account statements, confirmations, performance reports or any other communications" while in the United States; "no further instructions ... from ... clients while they are in the US;" "no marketing of advisory or brokerage services regarding securities;" "no discussion of or delivery of documents concerning the client's securities portfolio while on visits in the US:" "no discussion of performance, securities purchased or sold or changes in the investment mandate for the client" while in the United States; and "no delivery of documents regarding performance, securities purchased or sold or changes in the investment mandate for the client."

2004 Restatement of U.S. Restrictions. A 2004 UBS policy statement on "Cross-Border Banking Activities into the United States," replaced the 2002 guidelines, while repeating most of the prohibitions. This policy statement informed UBS non-U.S. bankers, for example, that U.S. federal and state laws restrict the actions that they can take while in the United States.[393] It states:

> "UBS AG has several U.S. branches and agencies and various non-banking subsidiaries all properly licensed, but these licenses **do not** encompass cross-border services provided to U.S. residents by UBS AG offices or affiliates outside of the United States. ... Some state laws prohibit banks without a banking license from that

state from soliciting deposits from that state's residents. States also may prohibit non-licensed lenders from making certain loans to consumers in such states. Any entity outside of the United States that is not registered with the SEC ... may not advertise securities services or products in the United States."[394]

The 2004 UBS policy statement goes on to list specific restrictions on activities that may be undertaken by its non-U.S. personnel while in the United States. These restrictions include the following:

UBS will not advertise and market for its services with material going beyond generic information relating to the image of UBS AG and its brand in the U.S. UBS AG may not organize, absent an opinion from Legal, events in the U.S.[395]

UBS AG may not establish relationships for securities products or services with new clients resident in the United States with the use of U.S. jurisdictional means. Thus, it must ensure that it does not contact securities clients in the United States through telephone, mail, e-mail, advertising, the internet or personal visits.[396]

UBS AG should ensure that:

- No marketing or advertising activity targeted to U.S. persons takes place in the United States;
- No solicitation of account opening takes place in the United States;
- No cold calling or prospecting into the United States takes place;
- No negotiating or concluding of contracts takes place in the United States;
- No carrying or transmitting of cash or other valuables of whatever nature out of the United States takes place; ...
- No routine certification of signatures, transmission of completed account documentation, or related administrative activity on behalf of UBS AG takes place;
- Employees do not carry on substantial activities at fixed location(s) while in the United States thereby establishing on office or maintaining a place of business.[397]

In his deposition before the Subcommittee, Mr. Birkenfeld claimed to have been unaware of these types of restrictions on his conduct until a colleague brought them to his attention in May 2005, by showing him the 2004 policy statement on UBS' internal computer system.[398] He told the Subcommittee, "When I read it, I was very concerned about what was going on in the bank, because this contradicted entirely what my job description was."[399] UBS has countered that its Swiss personnel were informed about the restrictions shortly after they were re-issued, in training sessions held during September 2004, which Mr. Birkenfeld attended.[400]

Sponsoring Travel to the United States. Despite the explicit and extensive restrictions on allowable U.S. activities set out in its policy statements, in interviews with the Subcommittee, UBS confirmed that, from at least 2000 to 2007, it routinely authorized and paid for its Swiss bankers to travel to the United States to develop new business and service existing clients.[401] Documents obtained by the Subcommittee related to UBS Swiss bankers also frequently reference travel to the United States. A 2003 "Action Plan" for the UBS private banking operation in Switzerland, for example, called for increased client contact "through business trips" to the United States and directed Swiss private bankers to seek "active referrals from existing clients for new relationships."[402] A 2005 document called for "frequent travelling" and "selective travelling" by UBS Swiss bankers to the United States as part of the services to be provided to U.S. clientele.[403]

During his deposition, Mr. Birkenfeld told the Subcommittee that, during his years at UBS, the private bankers from Switzerland who dealt with U.S. clients typically traveled to the United States four to six times per year, using their trips to search for new clients and provide financial services to existing clients.

> [W]e had a very large group of people in Lugano, Geneva, and Zurich that marketed directly into the U.S. market. The private bankers would travel anywhere between four and six times a year to the U.S., spend anywhere from one to two weeks in the U.S., prospecting, visiting existing clients, so on and so forth. ... As I remember, there [were] around 25 people in Geneva, 50 people in Zurich, and five to ten in Lugano. This is a formidable force.[404]

Mr. Birkenfeld testified that UBS not only authorized and paid for the business trips to the United States, but also provided the Swiss bankers with tickets and funds to go to events attended by wealthy U.S. individuals, so that they could solicit new business for the bank in Switzerland. He said that UBS sponsored U.S. events likely to attract wealthy clients, such as the Art Basel Air Fair in Miami; performances in major U.S. cities by the UBS Vervier Orchestra featuring talented young musicians; and U.S. yachting events attended by the elite Swiss yachting team, Alinghi, which was also sponsored by UBS. An internal UBS document laying out marketing strategies to attract U.S. and Canadian clients confirms that the bank "organized VIP events" and engaged in the "Sponsorship of Major Events" such as "Golf, Tennis Tournaments, Art, Special Events."[405] This document even identified the 25 most affluent housing areas in the United States to provide "targeted locations where to organize events."[406]

Mr. Birkenfeld described to the Subcommittee how Swiss private bankers used these events and other means to find new U.S. clients during their trips to the United States:

> You might go to sporting events. You might go to car shows, wine tastings. You might deal with real estate agents. You might deal with attorneys. ... It's really where do the rich people hang out, go and talk to them. ... [I]t wasn't difficult to walk into a party with a ... business card, and then someone ask[s] you, 'What do you do?' and you say, 'Well, I work for a bank in Switzerland, and we manage money there and open accounts.' And people immediately would recognize, oh, this is someone who could open new business by opening accounts.[407]

While travel by Swiss bankers to the United States was generally, not only allowed, but encouraged, UBS told the Subcommittee that, on four occasions since 2000, for a variety of reasons, it had imposed temporary bans on Swiss travel to the United States.[408] These short-term travel bans were imposed: (1) in 2001, following the 9/11 attack on the United States; (2) in 2003, coinciding with an IRS announcement of an Offshore Voluntary Compliance Initiative encouraging U.S. taxpayers with offshore credit cards to disclose their offshore accounts in exchange for avoiding certain penalties;[409] (3) in 2003 again, following the SARS epidemic outbreak; and (4) in September 2004, in response to the questioning of a UBS private banker by the IRS. Each of these travel bans was lifted shortly after it was imposed. In November 2007, however, UBS fundamentally changed its travel policy, instituting for the first time a prohibition on business travel by its Swiss private bankers to the United States, examined further below.[410]

To gain a better understanding of the extent to which UBS Swiss private bankers traveled to the United States in recent years, the Subcommittee conducted an analysis of over 500 travel records compiled by the Department of Homeland Security, at the Subcommittee's request, of persons traveling from Switzerland to the United States from 2001 to 2008, to identify UBS Swiss employees known to have provided banking and securities services to U.S. clients.[411] The Subcommittee determined that, from 2001 to 2008, roughly twenty UBS client advisors made an aggregate total of over 300 visits to the United States. Only two of these visits took place from 2001 to 2002; the rest occurred from 2003 to 2008. On several occasions, the visits appear to have involved multiple UBS client advisors traveling together to UBS-sponsored events in the United States. Some of these client advisors designated their visits as travel for a non-business purpose on the I-94 Customs declaration forms that all visitors must complete prior to entry into the United States.[412] Closer analysis, however, reveals that the dates and ports of entry for such trips coincided with the UBS-sponsored events, suggesting the visits were, in fact, business- related.

For example, the Subcommittee found that at least five UBS client advisors travelled to the United States for trips coinciding with the Art Basel Art Fair, an annual UBS-sponsored event held in early December in Miami Beach since 2002. The data shows that, over the years, several UBS Swiss client advisors were in Miami during the art show, including three in 2007. On the customs forms completed over the years by UBS travelers prior to landing at Miami International airport, only one client advisor stated that the purpose of the trip was for business, while five described the visit as for pleasure. These client advisors' trips, however, coincided closely with the dates of the Art Basel event, including an invitation-only private showing. Moreover, the Subcommittee's analysis of the customs and travel records obtained from the Department of Homeland Security show that a Swiss-based UBS client advisor traveled to New England from June 20-25, 2004, a trip coinciding with the UBS Regatta Cup, held in Newport, RI from June 19-26, 2004.

The Subcommittee's analysis also showed patterns of travel by Swiss-based UBS client advisors who made regular U.S. visits. One UBS employee, for example, travelled to the United States three times per year, at roughly four-month intervals, from 2003 to 2007. A senior UBS Swiss private bank official – Michel Guignard – visited the United States nearly every other month for a significant portion of the period examined by the Subcommittee. Martin Liechti, an even more senior Swiss private banking official, visited the United States up to eight times in a year.

This travel data provides additional evidence regarding the personnel and resources that have been dedicated by UBS to recruiting and servicing U.S. clients with Swiss accounts.

Assigning NNM Targets. UBS not only paid for its Swiss bankers to travel to the United States and helped them attend U.S. events to prospect for new U.S. clients, it also gave its Swiss bankers specific performance goals for bringing new money into the bank from the United States. These performance goals may have intensified the efforts of UBS Swiss bankers to recruit U.S. clients.

Mr. Birkenfeld told the Subcommittee that, during his tenure at UBS, his superiors at UBS gave him a specific, annual monetary goal, referred to as a "net new money" or "NNM" target that he was expected to bring into the bank by the end of the year from U.S. clients. He said that it was his understanding that an NNM target was established for each Swiss Client Advisor who dealt with U.S. clients. He indicated that the amount varied according to the seniority and track record of the particular client advisor. He told the Subcommittee: "So my job as a private banker predominantly was to bring in net new money, and then on top of it create return on assets, ROA. ... A rough estimate would be probably to bring in probably $50 million a year or $40 million."[413]

Mr. Birkenfeld explained that the NNM target could be met by securing additional assets from existing clients or by securing one or more new clients.

> [O]ne client could make your numbers or 10 or 25 could make your numbers. It's very hard to gauge that. And, again, when people aren't paying tax in the three areas I told you – inheritance, income, and capital gains – it's quite easy for people to bring money to you. They're very interested to bring as much money to the bank as possible.[414]

Internal UBS documents confirm that the bank carefully tracked annual figures for net new money and return on assets, among other performance measures for its Swiss private banking operations targeting clients in North America.[415] The documents also show that UBS took a variety of steps to encourage its bankers to meet their NNM goals. In 2003, for example, the head of the Wealth Management Americas division in Switzerland, Martin Liechti, sent a letter to his colleagues, urging each of them to refer at least five clients to Switzerland and promising to award the person with the most referrals with an expensive Swiss watch:

> Net New Money is, as you know a key element for our success. This means that we all have to work hard to achieve our NNM goals for 2003 and the years to come. In order to reach this goal, two main initiatives have been launched: The KeyClient initiative and the Referral Program within UBS. ...
>
> Each Country Team making a referral will get 0.3 3% of the revenues generated by the Financial Advisor over a time period of four years. As you know, we set, at the beginning of the year, a target of 5 referrals per CA [Client Advisor] to be made. I am aware that it is a challenge to reach this goal. In acknowledgement of your effort and commitment, I would like to award the Client Advisor in each Country Team who achieves, until the 31st of December 2003, the most referrals (amount of money and number of referrals), but at least the 5 referrals set as target, with a Breitling wristwatch. The same will be valid for the Rep Officer (including all Rep Offices in Latin America) who achieves this goal. Since 2003 will be a unique 'brand year' in UBS' history, each Breitling watch we award will be 'customized' with the UBS logo.[416]

In early 2007, Mr. Liechti sent an email setting a new NNM goal for all of UBS Swiss bankers with clients in the "Americas," including the United States. His email states:

> Welcome to the new year! I hope you enjoyed the holidays with your family and friends and took the opportunity to relax and 'recharge your batteries'.

> We achieved much in 2006 and I thank you for your huge efforts and dedication to the Americas.
>
> The markets are growing fast, and our competition is catching up. ... The answer to guarantee our future is GROWTH. We have grown from CHF 4 million per Client Advisor in 2004 to 17 million in 2006. We need to keep up with our ambitions and go to 60 million per Client Advisor! ...
>
> Our ambitions:
>
> 100 RoA [Return on Assets]
> 60 NNM per CA [Client Advisor]
> 100% Satisfied Clients ...
>
> In the Chinese Horoscope, 2007 is the year of the pig. In many cultures, the pig is a symbol for 'luck'. While it's always good to have [a] bit of luck, it is not luck that leads to success. Success is the result of vision and purpose, hard work and passion. ... Together as a team I am convinced we will succeed![417]

This email indicates that in two years, from 2004 to 2006, UBS Swiss bankers had quadrupled the amount of net new money being drawn into UBS from the "Americas," and that the bank's management sought to quadruple that figure again in a single year, 2007. This email helps to convey the pressure that UBS placed on its Swiss private bankers to bring in new money from the United States into Switzerland.

Another UBS document entitled, "KeyClients in NAM: Business Case 2003-2005," provides context for the Swiss private banking operations' focus on obtaining U.S. clients. This document observes that "3 1% of World's UHNWIs [Ultra High Net Worth Individuals] are in North America (USA + Canada)."[418] It also observes that the United States has 222 billionaires with a combined net worth of $706 billion.[419] This type of information helps explain why UBS dedicated significant resources to obtaining U.S. clients for its private banking operations in Switzerland.

Massive Machine. Mr. Birkenfeld told the Subcommittee that the overall effort of the UBS Swiss private banking operation to secure U.S. clients was the most extensive he had observed in his 12 years working in Swiss private banking. He stated:

> This was a massive machine. I had never seen such a large bank making such a dedicated effort to market to the U.S. market. And from my understanding and my work experience in Switzerland, it was the largest bank with the largest number of clients and assets under management of U.S. clients.[420]

He said that the Swiss bankers he worked with typically had an "existing book of business," that included numerous U.S. clients and had "a very regimented cycle of going out and acquiring new clients, taking care of your existing clients, make sure the revenue was there."[421] He described one private banker who saw as many as 30 or 40 existing clients on a single trip.[422] He estimated that the UBS Swiss bankers in the Geneva office where he worked maintained thousands of Swiss accounts for U. S. clients.[423]

When asked what motivated U.S. clients to open accounts in Switzerland instead of banking with UBS in their home country, Mr. Birkenfeld gave two reasons: "Tax evasion. ... And most of the time, people always liked the idea that they could hide some from their spouse or maybe a business partner or what have you, because the secrecy of having a bank account in Switzerland gave them anonymity and discretion."[424] When asked whether he ever said to his U.S. clients, "You don't have to pay taxes," or whether that was just understood, Mr. Birkenfeld responded, "It was clearly understood. Clearly understood."[425]

(4) Servicing U.S. clients with swiss accounts

UBS not only allowed U.S. clients to open undeclared accounts in Switzerland and assured them it would not disclose these accounts unless compelled by law, UBS also took steps to ensure that its Swiss bankers serviced their U.S. clients in ways that minimized disclosure of information to U.S. authorities. These measures included refraining from mailing Swiss account information into the United States, ensuring Swiss bankers traveling to the United States carried minimal or encrypted client account information, and providing training to help its bankers avoid surveillance by U.S. authorities.

In his deposition, Mr. Birkenfeld indicated that, during his tenure at UBS from 2001 to 2005, he worked closely with Swiss bankers who were servicing U.S. clients in the United States. He said the Swiss bankers he worked with typically had an "existing book of business," with numerous U.S. clients, and had "a very regimented cycle of ... taking care of your existing clients, mak[ing] sure the revenue was there."[426] He said: "So getting out into the field as we called it, was very, very important. You had to travel. Traveling was critical; otherwise the client would say, 'What do you mean you're not coming to visit me? What's wrong?' So, you know, you don't want to upset the client."[427]

Mr. Birkenfeld told the Subcommittee that, to his knowledge, almost all U.S. clients with Swiss accounts declined to have their account statements mailed to them in the United States.[428] Instead, UBS held client mail in Switzerland until the client was able to view the account documentation in person, after which the information was shredded. He explained:

> You paid 500 francs a year to have all of the statements and all of the transactions held in their folder, sealed, so when they came to the bank, 6 months, a year later, they could come and look at it, go through it, and then we would shred it .... So I've had some clients who would sit there for an hour or two hours, and then they come back and say, 'Okay. Everything's fine.' And they'd give the documents and say, 'You can shred them.' And we'd go and take it in the big shredding room and just shred everything. And then you'd start from zero again.[429]

Mr. Birkenfeld said that, in between visits to Switzerland to review their account information, many U.S. clients expected their Swiss banker to visit them in the United States and provide updated information about their accounts. He said that, prior to a business trip in which they planned to meet with specific clients, UBS Swiss private bankers typically collected and reviewed the relevant client account information. He said that the Swiss bankers did not normally bring the actual account statements with them into the United States, but took elaborate measures to disguise or encrypt client information to prevent it from falling into the wrong hands. He said, for example, some bankers kept "cryptic notes" on each account and took only those notes into the United States.[430] He described one Swiss banker who directed his assistant to transcribe by hand the information in his clients' account statements onto spreadsheets, omitting any identifying information other than a code name, and then sent the handwritten spreadsheets by overnight mail to his hotel in the United States, after which he would provide the spreadsheets to his U.S. clients in individual meetings.[431] Mr. Birkenfeld described other Swiss private bankers who brought into the United States UBS-supplied laptop computers, referred to as TAS computers, programmed to receive only highly encrypted information that, allegedly, [e]ven if the [U.S.] Customs opened it, for instance, they wouldn't see anything."[432] He said that the TAS computers could be used to "access the client's private bank statements from America and print them out, as well as view and print out product offerings."[433]

UBS cautioned its bankers, when traveling to the United States, to take measures to safeguard client information and supplied the TAS computers that some Swiss bankers used. A 2004 UBS policy statement provides: "When traveling cross-border, UBS AG employees always must remember that all clients of UBS AG expect us to take all necessary steps to safeguard confidentiality. Client advisors are referred to separate guidance on the protection of confidential information and other available resources that may assist."[434] Mr. Birkenfeld told the Subcommittee that UBS also cautioned its Swiss bankers to keep a low profile during their business trips to the United States so they would not attract attention from U.S. authorities. He noted, for example, that UBS business cards did not include a reference to a private banker's involvement in "wealth management."[435] He also said that some UBS Swiss private bankers who visited the United States on business told U.S. customs officials that they were instead in the country for "pleasure."[436]

Documentation obtained by the Subcommittee indicates that UBS also provided training to its client advisors on how to detect -- and avoid – surveillance by U.S. customs agents and law enforcement officers. An undated UBS training document entitled, "Case Studies Cross-Border Workshop NAM" provides a series of scenarios designed to train its personnel.[437] An excerpt from one of the scenarios is as follows:

> After passing immigration desk during your trip to USA/Canada, you are intercepted by the authorities. By checking your Palm, they find all your client meetings. Fortunately you stored only very short remarks of the different meetings and no names, As you spend around one week in the same hotel, the longer you stay there, the more you get the feeling of being observed. Sometimes you even doubt if all of the hotel employees are working for the hotel. A lot of client meetings are held in the suite of your hotel.
>
> One morning you are intercepted by an FBI-agent. He looks for some information about one of your clients and explains to you, that your client is involved in illegal activities.
>
> **Question 1: What would you do in such a situation?**
> **Question 2: What are the signs indicating that something is going on?**
>
> The document does not indicate UBS' preferred responses to these questions.

Mr. Birkenfeld told the Subcommittee that the UBS Swiss offices also employed techniques to help existing U.S. clients transfer money into and out of their accounts without identifying documentation. He noted, for example, that while he was at UBS, the bank typically wired funds and engaged in securities transactions without including client-specific information; instead the bank typically stated on the required documentation that the transaction was "on behalf of UBS for one of our clients."[438] He indicated that as the European Union tightened the rules for wire transfers, requiring the originating bank to identify the beneficial owner of the assets involved in a transaction, UB S increasingly restricted its Swiss bankers' use of wire transfers.[439] He said that UBS began to require clients to fly to Switzerland to withdraw cash from an account.

The Statement of Facts in the Birkenfeld criminal case describes additional actions taken by UBS bankers to help U.S. clients manage their Swiss accounts without alerting U.S. authorities. It states, for example, that UBS bankers advised U.S. clients to withdraw funds from their accounts using Swiss credit cards that "could not be discovered by United States authorities"; to "destroy all off-shore banking records existing in the United States"; and to "misrepresent the receipt of funds from the Swiss bank account in the United States as loans from the Swiss Bank."[440] The Statement of Facts also discloses that, on one occasion, "at the request of a U.S. client, defendant Birkenfeld purchased diamonds using that U.S. client's Swiss bank account funds and smuggled the diamonds into the United States in a toothpaste tube," presumably so that the U.S. client could obtain possession of his Swiss assets without alerting U.S. authorities.[441] It also states that Mr. Birkenfeld and his business associate Mario Staggl "accepted bundles of checks from U.S. clients and facilitated the deposit of those checks into accounts at the Swiss bank" and elsewhere, presumably to assist the clients in making transfers to their Swiss accounts, again without alerting U.S. authorities.[442]

Hold mail accounts, encrypted computers, wire transfers without client names, Swiss credit cards, requirements that clients travel outside of the United States to get information about their accounts – the consistent element in all of these UB S techniques is the effort to help U.S. clients hide assets sent to Switzerland. These UBS procedures, practices, and policies can also facilitate, and in some cases have resulted in, tax evasion by the bank's U.S. clients.

(5) Violating restrictions on U.S. activities

The UBS practices just described, related to Swiss banker activities undertaken in the United States to recruit and service U.S. clients, may have violated U.S. law as well as UBS policy. As explained earlier, U.S. securities and banking laws prohibit non-U.S. persons from advertising securities services or products, executing securities transactions, or performing banking services within the United States, without an appropriate license. Moreover, U.S. tax laws may require a foreign financial institution to report to the IRS on 1099 Forms sales of nonU.S. securities effected in the United States, such as by executing a transaction by a broker physically in the United States or ordering the completion of a transaction through telephone calls or emails originating from the United States.

It was to avoid violating U.S. law, exceeding its licensed activities, or triggering 1099 reporting requirements, that caused UBS to issue policy statements restricting the activities that its non-U.S. bankers could undertake while in the United States. Its 2002 and 2004 policy statements, for example, prohibited UBS Swiss bankers, while in the United States, from advertising securities products to their clients, informing clients of how their security portfolios were performing, providing copies of account statements, or using U.S. mails, faxes, telephone calls or email to discuss a client's securities portfolio.[443] UBS also prohibited its Swiss bankers from prospecting for new clients while in the United States, soliciting new accounts, or obtaining signatures on account opening documentation.

Despite these prohibitions, it appears that UBS Swiss bankers in the United States servicing U.S. clients routinely undertook actions that contravened the UBS restrictions. Mr. Birkenfeld described, for example, an art festival sponsored by UBS in Miami each year, which he attended with other Swiss bankers for the express purpose of soliciting new accounts. "We went to these events. We went to dinners, we went to art exhibitions, we went to private homes as private bankers, knowingly by management that they were paying for our hotel, paying for our airfare, paying us our salary, and getting us tickets to the UBS VIP tent to drink champagne with clients."[444] He testified that he witnessed Swiss bankers soliciting new accounts and completing account opening documentation while in the United States. He testified that in some cases, "instead of saying, 'I signed it in New York,' they brought the forms back to Geneva and they put in 'Geneva.'"[445] When asked whether he had promoted securities products during his trips to the United States, he responded, "We were promoting anything."[446]

Mr. Birkenfeld also told the Subcommittee that UBS Swiss bankers routinely communicated with their U.S. clients about the status of their accounts, including their securities portfolios. He said that some Swiss private bankers communicated with their U.S. clients by telephone or fax, or by sending occasional documents to them in the United States by overnight mail.[447] He said the bankers sometimes used code names during the telephone calls, so that the U.S. client would not have to identify themselves by name, in case anyone was listening.[448] He said that U.S. clients generally did not like sending or receiving emails via computer, "because they didn't want that link, for obvious reasons."[449] Nevertheless, some clients did use email, as shown in the case involving Mr. Birkenfeld and Mr. Olenicoff, examined further below. Mr. Birkenfeld also described how Swiss bankers brought into the United States information about clients' accounts and securities portfolios. He told the Subcommittee that his day-to-day interactions with clients were in direct contradiction to the restrictions set out in UBS' policy statements. He indicated those policies simply were not enforced while he was at the bank.[450]

2007 UBS Restrictions on U.S. Activities. In June 2007, UBS issued a new version of its policy statement restricting activities in the United States by its non-U.S. bankers.[451] This document repeated the prohibitions in the 2004 policy statement, while adding extensive new restrictions. For example, the 2007 policy statement states that, while non-U.S. UBS bankers could continue to travel to the United States, "[t]ravels must be kept to a minimum," and each traveling officer must be trained in and sign a certificate confirming compliance with the travel restrictions, inform his or her superior prior to a trip of planned events and clients to be visited, and report after the trip to the supervisor about all trip developments.[452] The policy statement goes on to state that "UBS will abstain from any active prospecting of any U.S. based persons," although it would continue to accept referrals from existing clients or "U.S. Licensed Officers."[453] In addition, it states that non-U.S. UBS bankers "must abstain from any activity that could be construed as soliciting securities or banking business from persons located in the United States," and "*must* not give any advice to prospective or existing clients on how to evade taxes or circumvent any other relevant restrictions."[454]

2007 Travel Ban to the United States. In November 2007, UBS went further, essentially ending all travel by its Swiss bankers to the United States to solicit new business.[455] UBS stated in an internal memorandum that it had decided "to realign the business model for U.S. clients by focusing our resources on our wealth management operations based in the United States ... and UBS Swiss Financial Advisors in Zurich."[456] UBS materials stated that UBS would permit "new account opening for securities related services only within those units"[457] and would service existing U.S. clients only when those clients were outside of the United State s and, for example, visiting Switzerland or utilizing telephone calls, faxes or other communication systems from outside the United States.[458] A document providing talking points to UBS bankers on how to inform their U.S. clients about the new policy suggests telling them: "Client advisors, including myself, will no longer be traveling outside of Switzerland to meet you .... [W]e will not be able to communicate with you about your securities account when you are in the United States. ... [W]e will not be able to execute your securities instructions if we are not satisfied that you are outside the U.S. when giving such orders."[459]

The talking points also indicate, that for a client who asked: "If I decide to transfer my assets to SFA [Swiss Financial Advisors], will Swiss client confidentiality still apply?," the recommended response was: "An SFA representative would be the best person to answer that question, but my understanding is that, although your information would be reported to the IRS and potentially available to the SEC, it otherwise generally would be covered by Swiss financial privacy protections."[460] For a client who asked: "What if I do not want U.S. tax reporting services or to supply a W-9?," the recommended response was: "Then you may retain your current account subject to the modifications I just described."[461] Those modifications included keeping all communications about the account outside of the United States.

According to UBS, the new policy, including the travel ban, became effective in November 2007, although a few previously planned business trips to the United States were allowed in December. UBS informed the Committee that, since January 2008, none of its Swiss private bankers has made a business trip to the United States.[462]

Contrary to this representation by UBS, however, a Subcommittee review of the relevant travel data for the Swiss bankers determined that, from January to April 2008, UBS client advisors made twelve trips to the United States, travelling from Switzerland to New York, Miami, San Francisco, and Las Vegas. The Customs I-94 Forms indicate that, on half of these trips, the Swiss bankers indicated they were travelling for business purposes, while on the other half, the Swiss bankers indicated they were travelling to the United States for non-business purposes. With respect to Mr. Liechti, head of the UBS Wealth Management Americas division, the I-94 Form shows that he arrived in the United States on April 20, 2008, on business. There is no record of his departure to date.

The clear contrast between the UBS policy restrictions dating back to at least 2002, and the activities undertaken by UBS Swiss bankers while traveling in the United States, as described by Mr. Birkenfeld in his deposition, in connection with his recent indictment, and in internal UBS documents, suggests that until recently, the UBS restrictions were not being enforced. This lack of enforcement, in turn, raises concerns that UBS Swiss bankers with U.S. clients may have been routinely violating not only the bank's internal policies, but also U.S. law. UBS is currently under investigation by the SEC, IRS, and Department of Justice regarding the activities of its Swiss bankers in the United States.

C. Olenicoff Accounts

Concerns raised by the activities of UBS Swiss bankers servicing accounts for U.S. clients are further illustrated by the UBS accounts opened in Switzerland by Mr. Birkenfeld for Igor Olenicoff.

Mr. Olenicoff is a billionaire real estate developer, U.S. citizen, and resident of California. [463]He is President and owner of Olen Properties Corporation. From 1992 until 2005, Mr. Olenicoff opened multiple accounts at banks in the Bahamas, England, Liechtenstein, and Switzerland. These accounts were opened in the name of multiple offshore corporations he controlled, including Guardian Guarantee Co., Ltd., New Guardian Bancorp ApS, Continental Realty Funding Corp., National Depository Corp., Sovereign Bancorp Ltd., and Swiss Finance Corp.[464] Some of his accounts were opened at UBS in Switzerland, and for a time, Mr. Olenicoff was Mr. Birkenfeld's largest private banking client.

In 2007, Mr. Olenicoff pled guilty to one criminal count of filing a false income tax return by failing to disclose the foreign bank accounts he controlled.[465] He was sentenced to two years probation and 120 hours of community service, and paid about $52 million to the IRS for six years of back taxes, interest, and penalties owed on assets and income hidden in foreign bank accounts.[466] In 2008, Mr. Birkenfeld pled guilty to conspiring with Mr. Olenicoff to defraud the IRS and avoid payment of taxes owed on about $200 million in assets transferred to accounts in Switzerland and Liechtenstein.[467]

The Subcommittee obtained a number of documents related to the Olenicoff and Birkenfeld matters which help illustrate the actions taken by UBS private bankers and others to help U.S. clients conceal their assets and evade U.S. taxes.

Account Opening. Mr. Birkenfeld told the Subcommittee that he first heard Mr. Olenicoff's name while working at Barclays Bank.[468] In 2001, soon after he began working for UBS, he contacted Mr. Olenicoff in California, flew to California for a meeting with Mr. Olenicoff and his son, and persuaded them to move their account to UBS in Switzerland.[469]

Mr. Olenicoff told Mr. Birkenfeld that he would like to open the UBS account in the name of Guardian Guarantee Corp. ("GGC"), one of the Bahamas corporations he controlled.[470] Mr. Birkenfeld provided the account opening documentation to Mr. Olenicoff in California, and to a Bahamas firm that administered GGC.[471] Mr. Olenicoff returned the completed forms.[472] On a UBS form that asked for the identity of the "beneficial owner of the assets" to be deposited into the account, Mr. Olenicoff identified GGC as the beneficial owner and listed himself and his son as the "contracting partners" who would inform UBS of any ownership change.[473] Mr. Olenicoff also made himself and other family members account signatories.[474] Mr. Birkenfeld agreed to open the account on those terms, even though he knew Mr. Olenicoff was the true beneficial owner of the assets, and the Bahamas corporation was being used to conceal that ownership.

As part of the account opening process, Mr. Olenicoff and his son signed a UBS form that "instruct[ed] UBS AG with respect to the above mentioned account not to invest in or hold US securities within the meaning of the relevant Qualified Intermediary Agreement."[475] By ruling out U.S. security investments, the Olenicoffs ensured that the account would not be reported to the IRS under the QI Program. In December 2001, Mr. Olenicoff transferred about $89 million from Barclays Bank in the Bahamas to the new GGC account at UBS in Switzerland.[476]

Restructuring Olenicoff Assets. To help develop the Olenicoff account, Mr. Birkenfeld enlisted the services of Mario Staggl, part owner of a Liechtenstein trust company, New Haven Treuhand AG. In November 2001, Mr. Olenicoff and his son travelled to Liechtenstein and met with Mr. Staggl and his partner, Klaus Biedermann.[477] During that meeting and in subsequent discussions, Mr. Olenicoff sought advice on how to restructure his offshore assets, taking into consideration the twin goals of avoiding taxes and maintaining "anonymity."

The documents show that a number of proposals were considered. In one email, Mr. Staggl stated: "The shares in OLEN US are 'owned' by the Bahamian Company. In order to avoid any potential exposure in a tax point of view we would recommend to transfer the Bahamian company shares into a Danish Holding Company. The Danish Holding Company would be owned by the first of the Liechtenstein Trusts."[478] He also wrote:

> "The cash available for UBS and Neue Bank can basically be held by the second Liechtenstein Trust. ... There is an easy way to get around [VAT taxes] by interposing an 'off-shore' jurisdiction since services rendered and charged to non Swiss or non Liechtenstein entities are not liable to VAT. We would recommend the second Liechtenstein Trust being the shareholder of the investment 'off-shore' vehicle. The jurisdiction could be the British Virgin Islands (BVI), Panama, Gibraltar. ... The administration would be looked after by New Haven in Liechtenstein. The second advantage of interposing the 'off-shore' vehicle would lead to another 'saf[e]ty-break' in a tax and anonymity aspect."[479]

Mr. Olenicoff responded in part by stating: "It is the preference of the current holder of the stock, a Bahamian Corporation to move the ownership to an onshore entity, but one which provided complete anonymity as to the beneficial owners."[480] In a later email, Mr. Staggl observed: "Subsequent to our telephone discussion of last week your most recent e-mail made it very clear to me – you want to become on-shore – but still maintain an off-shore status in tax and protection point of view."[481]

In late 2001, Mr. Olenicoff authorized Mr. Staggl's trust company, New Haven, to establish a Liechtenstein trust, The Landmark Settlement, and a Danish corporation, New Guardian Bancorp, on his behalf. Mr. Staggl caused to be executed a "Letter of Intent" which stated that New Haven would hold the trust property for the benefit of Mr. Olenicoff and, after his demise, for his children.[482] Mr. Staggl wrote to Mr. Olenicoff:

> "First, we will establish the Liechtenstein Trust to be known as 'The Landmark Settlement'. All the information we need in order to proceed are available at our offices. New Haven will be the trustee. Sheltons, our correspondent in Danemark, agreed to incorporate 'New Guardian Bancorp' wholly owned by the Liechtenstein 'The Landmark Settlement'."[483]

At Mr. Olenicoff's direction, Mr. Birkenfeld arranged a transfer of $40,000 from the GGC account at UBS to finance the set up of the two new entities.[484] Mr. Olenicoff then opened accounts in the name of New Guardian Bancorp ("NBG") at UBS in Switzerland and in the name of NBG and Landmark Settlement at Neue Bank in Liechtenstein.

In January 2002, Mr. Olenicoff's companion, Jeanette Bullington, opened a personal account at UBS in Switzerland.[485] As part of the account opening documentation, she signed one document instructing UBS not to invest her funds in U.S. securities "within the meaning of the relevant Qualified Intermediary Agreement."[486] She signed another stating: "I am aware of the new tax regulations. To this end, I declare that I expressly agree that my account shall be frozen for all investments in US securities."[487] These documents appear designed to ensure her account would not be disclosed to the IRS under the QI Program.

Transferring U.S. Securities Portfolio. In March 2002, Mr. Birkenfeld and Mr. Staggl helped Mr. Olenicoff transfer $60 million in U.S. securities from a "Smith Barney portfolio" to the NGB account at Neue Bank in Liechtenstein. Mr. Staggl explained that the transfer could go directly to NGB or, alternatively, to Landmark Settlement which owned NGB, but advised against sending the securities to an account opened in Mr. Olenicoff's personal name, since that could "jeopardize" the structure by exposing his association with the assets:

> "[T]he transfer of the Smith Barney portfolio to Neue Bank ... would be [in] no danger or exposure whatsoever. ... [T]o put your mind at rest, the portfolio arriving from Smith Barney will be put into Landmark Settlement account held with Neue Bank for the time being. ... I would not recommend to open a personal account in your name since this could potentially jeopardize the structure. For the time being you and Andrei are signatories on Landmark Settlement's bank account with Neue Bank. You may remember that you signed blank account signature cards for Neue Bank at the occasion of our meeting in Liechtenstein and one card has been used for New Guardian Bancorp and the other for Landmark Settlement."[488]

In April 2002, Mr. Staggl provided Mr. Olenicoff with wire transfer instructions to move the $60 million in U.S. securities directly to the NGB account at Neue Bank. The wire transfer instructions specified, however, that Smith Barney send the securities to "Neue Bank" without specifying the ultimate recipient of the securities. Mr. Staggl's email explained: "For secrecy purpose, there is no need to mention 'New Guardian Bancorp. Aps', but, if you prefer to do so the name of the beneficiary can be mentioned."[489] The transfer took place in April.[490] Although the Neue account afterwards contained substantial U.S. securities, the account was apparently never disclosed to the IRS under the QI Program.

Many other documents reviewed by the Subcommittee demonstrate Mr. Olenicoff's direct control of the UBS accounts opened in the names of GCC and NBC and the millions of dollars in assets held within those accounts. For example, on several occasions Mr. Olenicoff directed Mr. Birkenfeld to open new accounts for the corporate entities, move substantial funds from one UBS account to another, and close two of the accounts after a new one had been opened.[491] On another occasion, Mr. Olenicoff appears to have transferred substantial real estate assets in the United States from an entity he controlled in the Bahamas, National Depository Company, Ltd., to the Landmark Settlement in Liechtenstein.[492] On still another occasion, Mr. Olenicoff authorized Mr. Birkenfeld to issue five UBS credit cards for one of the UBS corporate accounts, and then appears to have cancelled those cards two weeks later.[493]

By 2005, Mr. Olenicoff had transferred a total of about $200 million in assets into the Swiss and Liechtenstein accounts opened in the name of entities that he controlled. Although Mr. Olenicoff clearly exercised control over the UBS accounts and assets, Mr. Olenicoff never submitted a W-9 Form to UBS admitting he was the beneficial owner, and UBS never filed a 1099 Form with the IRS reporting the accounts. As Mr. Birkenfeld put it, when asked if the accounts were undeclared, he responded, "Yes. Every bit."[494]

In 2005, after Mr. Birkenfeld left UBS, he and Mr. Staggl met with Mr. Olenicoff in Liechtenstein and advised him to transfer his assets from UBS to Neue Bank in Liechtenstein, "because Liechtenstein had better bank secrecy laws than Switzerland." Mr. Olenicoff agreed, and transferred his assets from UBS to Neue Bank that year.[495]

By 2007, Mr. Olenicoff's offshore assets had been discovered by the IRS. By the end of the year, he had pled guilty; Mr. Birkenfeld pled guilty by mid-2008. Mr. Staggl, who is under indictment for his role in managing the Olenicoff assets, remains at large in Liechtenstein and has been declared by the U.S. government to be a fugitive.

The Olenicoff accounts at UBS were open for about four years, from 2001 until 2005. During that time, Mr. Birkenfeld has admitted that he conspired with Mr. Olenicoff to help him evade U.S. taxes by hiding his assets in Switzerland and Liechtenstein. To accomplish that end, Mr. Birkenfeld assisted Mr. Olenicoff in forming a Liechtenstein trust and Danish corporation by directing him to a Liechtenstein trust company that offered formation services, opening UBS accounts in the names of those entities, allowing Mr. Olenicoff to omit his beneficial ownership of the account assets on internal UBS forms, and helping him circumvent disclosure of the accounts to the IRS under the QI Program by signing forms instructing UBS not to purchase U.S. securities for those accounts. Mr. Birkenfeld allowed Mr. Olenicoff to transfer tens of millions of dollars from other offshore accounts into the new UBS accounts, with no apparent questions about the source of the funds. He took instructions from Mr. Olenicoff about how to invest the funds in the UBS accounts, using email, letters, and faxes to and from the United States, even though Mr. Birkenfeld was not licensed to handle securities in the United States.

The Subcommittee does not know the extent to which Mr. Birkenfeld's actions were typical of UBS Swiss bankers; it has been unable to obtain internal UBS account documentation comparable to the documentation obtained from LGT. Mr. Birkenfeld told the Subcommittee that he did not view his actions as out of the ordinary. If true, the Olenicoff case history may be one of many within UBS Swiss operations that raise concerns.

D. Analysis

Unlike LGT, UBS did not generally refrain from conducting banking operations within the United States. UBS Swiss bankers targeted U.S. clients, traveled across the country in search of wealthy individuals, and aggressively marketed their services to U.S. taxpayers who might otherwise never have opened Swiss accounts. UBS practices resulted in its U.S. clients maintaining undeclared Swiss accounts that collectively held billions of dollars in assets that were not disclosed to the IRS. UBS serviced these accounts, in part, by offering banking and securities products and services within the United States that UBS Swiss bankers were not licensed to provide. Swiss bank secrecy laws hid not only the misconduct of U.S. taxpayers hiding assets at UBS in Switzerland, but also the actions taken by UBS bankers to assist those U.S. clients.

UBS has now stopped all travel by its Swiss bankers to the United States, issued more restrictive policies, and is conducting an internal review to gauge the nature and extent of the problem. UBS also cooperated with this Subcommittee in its efforts to gain a full understanding of the facts and issues.

ENDNOTES

[1] This $100 billion estimate is derived from studies conducted by a variety of tax experts. See, e.g., Joseph Guttentag and Reuven Avi-Yonah, "Closing the International Tax Gap," in Max B. Sawicky, ed., Bridging the Tax Gap: Addressing the Crisis in Federal Tax Administration (2006) (estimating offshore tax evasion by individuals at $40-$70 billion annually in lost U.S. tax revenues); Kimberly A. Clausing, "Multinational Firm Tax Avoidance and U.S. Government Revenue" (Aug. 2007) (estimating corporate offshore transfer pricing abuses resulted in $60 billion in lost U.S. tax revenues in 2004); John Zdanowics, "Who's watching our back door?" Business Accents magazine, Volume 1, No.1, Florida International University (Fall 2004) (estimating offshore corporate transfer pricing abuses resulted in $53 billion in lost U.S. tax revenues in 2001); "The Price of Offshore," Tax Justice Network briefing paper (3/05) (estimating that, worldwide, individuals have offshore assets totaling $11.5 trillion, resulting in $255 billion in annual lost tax revenues worldwide); "Governments and Multinational Corporations in the Race to the Bottom," *Tax Notes* (2/27/06); "Data Show Dramatic Shift of Profits to Tax Havens," *Tax Notes* (9/13/04). See also series of 2007 articles authored by Martin Sullivan in *Tax Notes* (estimating over $1.5 trillion in hidden assets in four tax havens, Guernsey, Jersey, Isle of Man, and Switzerland, beneficially owned by nonresident individuals likely avoiding tax in their home jurisdictions), infra footnote 3.

[2] See, e.g., "Tax Co-operation: Towards a Level Playing Field – 2007 Assessment by the Global Forum on Taxation," issued by the OECD (October 2007) (estimating a minimum of $5-7 trillion held offshore); "The Price of Offshore," Tax Justice Network briefing paper (March 2005) (estimating offshore assets of high net worth individuals at a total of $11.5 trillion); "International Narcotics Control Strategy Report," U.S. Department of State Bureau for International Narcotics and Law Enforcement Affairs (March 2000), at 565-66 (identifying nearly 60 offshore jurisdictions with assets totaling $4.8 trillion).

[3] See, e.g., "Tax Analysts Offshore Project: Offshore Explorations: Guernsey," *Tax Notes* (10/8/07) at 93 (estimating Guernsey has $293 billion in assets beneficially owned by nonresident individuals who were likely avoiding tax in their home jurisdictions); "Tax Analysts Offshore Project: Offshore Explorations: Jersey," Tax *Notes* (10/22/07) at 294 (estimating Jersey has $491 billion in assets beneficially owned by nonresident individuals who were likely avoiding tax in their home jurisdictions); "Tax Analysts Offshore Project: Offshore Explorations: Isle of Man," *Tax Notes* (11/5/07) at 560 (estimating Isle of Man has $150 billion in assets beneficially owned by nonresident individuals who were likely avoiding tax in their home jurisdictions); "Tax Analysts Offshore Project: Offshore Explorations: Switzerland," *Tax Notes* (12/10/07) (estimating Switzerland has $607 billion in assets beneficially owned by nonresident individuals who were likely avoiding tax in their home jurisdictions).

[4] See, e.g., "LGT: Illegally disclosed data material limited to the client data stolen from LGT Treuhand in 2002," LGT Group press release (2/24/08) at 1 (disclosing that 600 of the 1,400 named persons were from Germany); "Tax Scandal in Germany Fans Complaints of Inequity," *New York Times* (2/18/08).

[5] IRS News Release, "IRS and Tax Treaty Partners Target Liechtenstein Accounts," IR-2008-26 (2/26/08) at 1.

[6] See, e.g., HM Revenue & Customs Press Release, "Tax Commissioners battle against tax evasion," Nat 09/08 (2/26/08); Agenzia Entrate media release, >>Agenzia Entrate ha ricevuto informazione su italiani con depositi in Liechtenstein >> (2/26/08) ; Ministère du Budget, des comptes publics et de la fonction publique, « Lutte contre la fraude et l'évasion fiscale >> (2/26/08) ; La Agencia Tributaria media release, La Agencia Tributaria analiza información sobre ciudadanos españoles incluidos en las cuentas y depósitos bancarios de Liechtenstein" (2/26/08); Australian Taxation Office Media Release, "Tax Commissioners battle against tax evasion," No. 2008/08 (2/26/08).

[7] See IRS News Release, "IRS and Tax Treaty Partners Target Liechtenstein Accounts," IR-2008-26 (2/26/08) at 1 ("The national tax administrations of Australia, Canada, France, Italy, New Zealand, Sweden, United Kingdom, and the United States of America, all member countries of the OECD's Forum on Tax Administration (FTA), are working together following revelations that Liechtenstein accounts are being used for tax avoidance and evasion."); Organization for Economic Cooperation and Development (OECD) press release, "Tax disclosures in Germany part of a broader challenge, says OECD Secretary-General," (2/19/08).

[8] *United States v. Birkenfeld,* Case No. 08-CR-60099-ZLOCH (S.D.Fla) (hereinafter *"United States v. Birkenfeld"),* Statement of Facts, (6/19/08). The U.S. citizen had earlier pled guilty to one count of filing a false tax return and agreed to pay back taxes, interest and penalties totaling $52 million. See pleadings in *United States v. Olenicoff,,* Case No. SA CR No. 07-227-CJC (C.D.Cal.).

[9] In the mid-1990s, the IRS arrested John Mathewson, the owner and president of an offshore bank in the Cayman Islands, on tax-related charges. Mr. Mathewson agreed to cooperate with U.S. tax investigations of his clients. In 2001 testimony before this Subcommittee, Mr. Mathewson stated that, of the 2,000 clients at his Cayman bank, he estimated that 95% were Americans and virtually all were engaged in tax evasion. "Role of U.S. Correspondent Banking in International Money Laundering," before the Permanent Subcommittee on Investigations, S.Hrg. 107-84 (March 1, 2 and 6, 2001) at 13.

[10] Ex Parte Petition for Leave to Serve "John Doe" Summons, Case No. 08-2 1 864-MC-LENARD/GARBER (USDC SDFL)(6/30/08) (The IRS stated that the summons would ask UBS for the names of U.S. clients for whom UBS: "(1) did not have in its possession Forms W-9 executed by such United States taxpayers, and (2) had not filed timely and accurate Forms 1099 naming such United States taxpayers and reporting to United States taxing authorities all reportable payments made to such United States taxpayers."). This petition was filed under 26 USC 7609(f), which requires court approval of any IRS administrative summons that does not identify by name the persons for whom tax liability may attach.

[11] Id., Order, (7/1/08) (court order approving petition to serve John Doe summons on UBS).

[12] Subcommittee meeting with Swiss Embassy (7/10/08).

[13] See, e.g., the following hearings before the Permanent Subcommittee on Investigations: "Tax Haven Abuses: The Enablers, The Tools and Secrecy," S.Hrg. 109-797 (8/1/06) (hereinafter "Subcommittee 2006 Tax Haven Abuse Hearing"); "U.S. Tax Shelter Industry: The Role of Accountants, Lawyers, and Financial Professionals," S.Hrg. 108-473 (November 18, 20, 2003) (hereinafter "Subcommittee 2003 Tax Shelter Industry Hearing"); "What is the U.S. Position on Offshore Tax Havens?" S.Hrg. 107-1 52 (7/18/01) (hereinafter "Subcommittee 2001 Offshore Tax Haven Hearing"); "Crime and Secrecy: the Use of Offshore Banks and Companies," S.Hrg. 98-1 51 (March 15, 16 and May 24, 1983).

[14] The fraud charges against Volvo were later dismissed in their entirety by the appellate court.

[15] *United States v. Birkenfeld,"* Statement of Facts, (6/19/08).

[16] Email from Martin Liechti re "Happy New Year"; addressees not specified (undated).

[17] See footnote 1, *supra,* explaining the basis for this $100 billion estimate.

[18] "Using Data from the Internal Revenue Service's National Research Program to Identify Potential Opportunities to Reduce the Tax Gap," Government Accountability Office, Report No. GAO-07-423R (3/15/07) at 1 (conveying the IRS estimate of the annual U.S. tax gap at $345 billion).

[19] See Subcommittee 2006 Tax Haven Abuse Hearing.

[20] Id. (see case history involving Sam and Charles Wyly).

[21] Id. (see case histories involving Robert Holliday, Kurt Greaves, and Walter Anderson).

[22] Id. (see case histories involving the Equity Development Group and the POINT Strategy).

[23] "Crime and Secrecy: the Use of Offshore Banks and Companies," hearing before the U.S. Senate Permanent Subcommittee on Investigations, S.Hrg. 98-15 1 (March 15, 16 and May 24, 1983).

[24] The United States generally enters into a tax treaty with a country to establish maximum rates of tax for certain types of income, protect persons from double taxation, arrange for tax information exchange, and resolve other tax issues. In the case of a country with nominal or no taxes, however, the United States may forego addressing a full range of tax issues and instead seek to enter into simply a tax information exchange agreement. See "Offshore Tax Evasion: Stashing Cash Overseas," hearing before the Senate Committee on Finance (5/3/07) (hereinafter "Finance 2007 Hearing on Offshore Tax Evasion"), prepared testimony of Treasury Acting International Tax Counsel John Harrington, at 3.

[25] The United States has identified three primary forms of information exchange: (1) exchange of information on request, in which the tax authorities of one country request specific information about specific taxpayers from the tax authorities of the second country; (2) automatic exchange of information, in which the tax authorities of one country routinely provide detailed information about a class of taxpayers, such as information detailing the interest,

dividends, or royalties payments made to those taxpayers during a specified period; and (3) spontaneous exchange of information, in which the tax authorities of one country pass on information obtained in the course of administering its own tax laws to the tax authorities of another country without having been asked. Id. U.S. tax treaties typically encompass all three types of information exchange. Id.

[26] See list of tax treaties on IRS website at www.irs.gov (viewed 6/17/08).

[27] See copy of this Model Convention on IRS website (viewed 6/17/08).

[28] See Caribbean Basin Initiative of 1983, 98 P.L. 67, 97 Stat. 396, at § 222. See also 26 U.S.C. §§ 274(h)(6)(C) and 927(e). This statutory framework initially authorized the Treasury Secretary to conclude agreements with countries in the Caribbean Basin (thereby qualifying such countries for certain benefits under the Caribbean Basin Initiative) but later expanded this authority to conclude TIEAs with any country.

[29] See discussion of OECD initiative on uncooperative tax havens, infra.

[30] For example, the OECD noted last year that some tax havens that made written commitments to enter into TIEAs have not done so and that countries that signed a TIEA have sometimes refused or delayed producing requested information. Finance 2007 Hearing on Offshore Tax Evasion, prepared testimony of OECD Center for Tax Policy Director Jeffrey Owens, at 9; "OECD Signals Plan to Renew Efforts Against Non-Cooperative Jurisdictions," BNA Report on International Tax & Accounting, No. ISSN 1522-8800 (10/15/07).

[31] Some countries have both an MLAT and a tax treaty or tax information exchange agreement with the United States.

[32] A 2007 assessment by the OECD of 82 countries found that 17 countries, all known tax havens, have limited their participation in tax information exchanges to criminal tax matters. See "Tax Co-operation: Towards a Level Playing Field – 2007 Assessment by the Global Forum on Taxation," Report No. ISBN-978-92-64-03902-5 (October 2007).

[33] Liechtenstein is currently in negotiation with the United States regarding a possible tax treaty or tax information exchange agreement.

[34] "Treaty between the United States of America and the Principality of Liechtenstein on Mutual Leal Assistance in Criminal Matters," (signed 7/8/02) (hereinafter "United States-Liechtenstein MLAT"), reprinted in a Message from the President of the United States to the U.S. Senate transmitting the MLAT, Treaty Doc. 107-16 (9/5/02). Prior to the MLAT, Liechtenstein had provided legal assistance to the United States in criminal matters on the basis of a diplomatic agreement. After the attack on the United States on 9/11/01, however, the United States made a concerted effort to obtain formal MLAT agreements with a number of countries, including Liechtenstein.

[35] Letter of Submittal by the U.S. Secretary of State to the President regarding the United States-Liechtenstein MLAT (8/14/02), reprinted in Treaty Doc. 107-16 (9/5/02), at VI.

[36] Id.

[37] In addition to this tax treaty, in 1973, Switzerland entered into a Mutual Legal Assistance Treaty with the United States. That MLAT, however, by its terms, generally excludes "violations with respect to taxes," and so is not used for assistance in tax matters. Treaty between the United States of America and the Swiss Confederation on Mutual Assistance in Criminal Matters, (1/23/77), 273 UST 2019, at Article 2. Switzerland also has a 1981 domestic law allowing "International Mutual Assistance in Criminal Matters," but that law is difficult to use since it is confined to criminal cases, is limited to document and testimony requests, and allows multiple appeals within Switzerland. Subcommittee meeting with the Embassy of Switzerland (7/10/08).

[38] See, e.g., J. Springer, "An Overview of International Evidence and Asset Gathering in Civil and Criminal Tax Cases," 22 Geo. Wash. J. Int'l L. & Econ. 277, 303-08 (1988); Aubert, "The Limits of Swiss Banking Secrecy under Domestic and International Law," 273 Int'l Tax & Bus. Law. 273, 286-288 (1984); J. Knapp, "Mutual Legal Assistance Treaties as a Way to Pierce Bank Secrecy," Case W. Res. J. Int'l L. 405-08, 418-20 (1988). Tax evasion is an administrative offense, not a criminal offense in Switzerland. The only tax-related crime in Switzerland is for "tax fraud," which is difficult to establish.

[39] See "Convention between the United States of America and the Swiss Confederation for the Avoidance of Double Taxation with respect to Taxes on Income," (signed 10/2/96) (hereinafter "United States-Switzerland Tax Convention"), reprinted in a Message from the President of the United States to the U.S. Senate transmitting the Convention and a related Protocol, Treaty Doc. 105-8 (1/1/98).

[40] Id., Article 26(1).

[41] Id., Protocol (10).

[42] Letter of Submittal by the U.S. Secretary of State to the President regarding the United States-Switzerland Tax Convention (5/29/97), reprinted in Treaty Doc. 105-8 (6/25/97), at VII.

[43] For more information about the QI Program, see 26 USC §§1441-43; Treasury Regulation § 1.1441-1 (e)(5); Revenue Procedure 2000-12, 2000-4 I.R.B. 387.

[44] IRS briefing on the QI Program provided to the Subcommittee (5/9/08).

[45] The QI Agreement also requires the reporting of two other categories of income: (1) proceeds from the sale of non-U.S. securities if the sale was effected by a broker within the United States; and (2) foreign source income, such as dividends, interest, rents, royalties or other fixed, determinable, annual, or periodic income, if that foreign income is paid in the United States. See Treas. Reg. §§ 1.6045-1(a)(1), 1.6042-3(b), 1.6049-5(b)(6); "U.S. Tax and Reporting Obligations for Foreign Intermediaries' Non-U.S. Securities," 47 Tax Notes Int'l 913 (9/3/07).

[46] See, e.g., Treas. Reg. § 1.6042-3(a) and (b) on dividends, Treas. Reg. §§1.6049-1(a)(1) and 1.6049-5(b)(6) on interest payments.

[47] Treasury Regulations 1.1441-1, et seq., adopted in T.D. 8881, 2000-1 C.B. 1158 (5/15/2000).

[48] For a copy of the standardized agreement and country-specific forms, see the IRS website at ww.irs.gov; or Rev. Proc. 2000-12, 200-4 IRB 387, which includes a model QI agreement.

[49] W-9 Forms must be filed for "U.S. persons," defined as U.S. citizens and U.S. resident aliens; corporations, partnerships, and associations organized under U.S. law; domestic estates; and domestic trusts. See W-9 Form, Request for Taxpayer Identification Number and Certification (Rev. 10-2007), General Instructions. W-9 Forms ask an accountholder to provide their name, address, account numbers, and taxpayer identification number ("TIN"). W8 Forms are filed for non-U.S. persons. W8BEN forms are filed for non-U.S. persons who beneficially own an account opened in the name of an intermediary, such as a bank, attorney, trustee, corporation, trust, or foundation. See W8BEN Form, Certificate of Foreign Status of Beneficial Owner for United States Tax Withholding (Rev. 2- 2006). These forms ask the accountholder to provide their name, address, and the country where they reside.

[50] "Reportable payments" include several categories of income: (1) "reportable amounts," which are U.S. source payments such as interest, dividends, rents, royalties and other fixed, determinable, annual, or periodic income; (2) sales of foreign securities if effected in the United States; and (3) foreign-source interest, dividends, rents, royalties, or other fixed, determinable, annual, or periodic income, if paid in the United States. See, e.g., "U.S. Tax and Reporting Obligations for Foreign Intermediaries' Non-U.S. Securities," 47 Tax Notes Int'l 913 (9/3/07).

[51] See "Qualified Intermediary (QI)" presentation prepared by Brigitte Arnold of LGT Bank of Liechtenstein, (September 14-15, 2001) at 11 ("Conclusion[:] The application of the QI Rules from the banking perspective; was it worth it? Yes, because there is No Banking Secrecy without QI Status.").

[52] "Tax Compliance: Qualified Intermediary Program Provides Some Assurance That Taxes on Foreign Investors are Withheld and Reported, but Can Be Improved," (December 2007), GAO Report No. GAO-08-99 (hereinafter "2007 GAO Report on QI Program") at 26.

[53] Id. at 27.

[54] Last week, the IRS held a teleconference with major accounting firms to discuss the QI Program and QI audits. The IRS spokesperson was quoted as saying IRS officials, including the IRS Commissioner, "had a good discussion about the role the accounting community plays with qualified intermediaries." "IRS Commissioner Shulman, LMSB Officials Discuss QI Program with Accounting Firms," Daily Report for Executives, BNA (7/9/08), No. ISSN 1523-567X, at 1.

[55] IRS briefing on the QI Program provided to the Subcommittee (5/9/08).

[56] Id.

[57] 2007 GAO Report on QI Program, at 21 (initial caps removed).

[58] Id. at 3.

[59] Id. in "Highlights" section summarizing report.

[60] Id. at 22.

[61] Id.

[62] Id. at 12, 22.

[63] Id. at 22.

[64] Id. at 23-24.

[65] See, e.g., id. at 20 (identifying additional QI abuses such as $11 billion in payments made to accounts in "undisclosed jurisdictions" and $7 billion in payments to "unknown recipients" that should have led to 30% withholding, but actually resulted in withholding rates of about 3%).

[66] "Harmful Tax Competition: An Emerging Global Issue," issued by the OECD (1998).

[67] "Improving Access to Bank Information for Tax Purposes," issued by the OECD (2000), at ¶ 20. In 2004, this standard was incorporated into paragraph 5 of Article 26 of the OECD Model Tax Convention on Income and on Capital.

[68] See OECD report, "Towards Global Tax Co-operation: Progress in Identifying and Eliminating Harmful Tax Practices," (June 2000), reprinted in the Subcommittee 2001 Offshore Tax Haven Hearing record, 125-152, at 140; and chart prepared by the Subcommittee entitled, "2000 OECD List of Offshore Tax Havens," at 91.

[69] Finance 2007 Hearing on Offshore Tax Evasion, prepared testimony of OECD Center for Tax Policy Director Jeffrey Owens, at 5.

[70] Id.

[71] See Subcommittee 2001 Offshore Tax Haven Hearing.

[72] These 28 countries were in addition to the 6 countries that, in early 2000, had committed to tax information exchange in civil and criminal matters to avoid being included in the list of 35 offshore jurisdictions.

[73] "List of Unco-operative Tax Havens," issued by OECD (April 2002).

[74] In June 2008, however, Liechtenstein announced that it had concluded negotiation on an anti-fraud agreement with the European Union and its member states. The agreement would strengthen information exchange related to tax offenses. See press release, "Liechtenstein Strengthens European Tax Cooperation with Anti-Fraud Agreement," Liechtenstein Government Press Office (6/27/08).

[75] See OECD Model Agreement on Exchange of Information on Tax Matters (April 2002), text available at www.oecd.org/ctp/htp. This model agreement, with revisions adopted in 2004, is also included in Article 26 of the OECD Model Tax Convention on Income and on Capital, which is similar to the U.S. Model Income Tax Convention.

[76] G20 Communique (October 2005) issued in association with November 2004 meeting of G20 Finance Ministers. See also Gleneagles Communique, paragraph 14(i), issued by the G/8 Heads of Government at the Gleneagles Summit (July 2005); communiqué issued in association with the Saint Petersburg Summit (July 2006).

[77] "Tax Co-operation: Towards a Level Playing Field – 2006 Assessment by the OECD Global Forum on Taxation," Report No. ISBN-92-64-024077 (May 2006).

[78] Id. at 7.

[79] "Tax Co-operation: Towards a Level Playing Field – 2007 Assessment by the Global Forum on Taxation," Report No.ISBN-978-92-64-03902-5, issued by the OECD (October 2007).

[80] Id.

[81] See, e.g., "Offshore Financial Centers Playing Key Role In Aggressive Tax Plans, OECD Official Says," BNA Daily Report for Executives (3/27/07).

[82] "OECD Signals Plan to Renew Efforts Against Non-Cooperative Jurisdictions," BNA Report on International Tax & Accounting, No. ISSN 1522-8800 (10/15/07).

[83] See id.; Finance 2007 Hearing on Offshore Tax Evasion, prepared testimony of OECD Center for Tax Policy Director Jeffrey Owens, at 9.

[84] Rules applicable to the EU Savings Directive, European Commission Taxation and Customs Union Directorate website, http://ec.europa.eu/taxation_customs/taxation/personal_tax/savings_tax/rules_applicable/index_en.htm referencing 1999 European Council meeting in Helsinki (viewed 6/1 1/08)(hereinafter "ECTCU Website").

[85] See Council Directive 2003/48/EC (adopting the Savings Directive); Council Decision 2004/587/EC (setting a July 1, 2005 deadline for compliance).

[86] "Savings Taxation: frequently asked questions," MEMO/05/228 (6/30/05), ECTCU Website (viewed 6/11/08).

[87] Id.

[88] Council Directive 2003/48/EC.

[89] "Savings Taxation: frequently asked questions," MEMO/05/228 (6/30/05), ECTCU Website (viewed 6/11/08).

[90] Id.

[91] Id.

[92] Id.

[93] These countries are Anguilla, Aruba, the British Virgin Islands, the Cayman Islands, Guernsey, the Isle of Man, Jersey, Montserrat, the Netherlands Antilles, and the Turks & Caicos Islands. Id.

[94] Id.

[95] Id. In 2001 and 2002, the United States proposed regulations to require U.S. financial institutions to report to the IRS payments made to accounts held by residents of other countries in the same manner they report payments made to accounts held by U.S. persons. Treasury Proposed Rule No. 126100-00, "Guidance on Reporting of Deposit Interest Paid to Nonresident Aliens," 66 Fed. Reg. 3925 (2001); corrected by 66 Fed. Reg. 15820 and 66 Fed. Reg. 16019; withdrawn and replaced by Treasury Proposed Rule No. 133254-02, "Guidance on Reporting of Deposit Interest Paid to Nonresident Aliens," 67 Fed. Reg. 50386 (2002). These regulations, if

finalized, would have enabled the IRS to participate in automatic exchanges of information with 16 countries to identify accounts held by U.S. citizens in those countries for tax purposes, including a number of EU countries. The proposed regulations, however, have never been finalized. At the current time, the only country with which the United States engages in routine, automatic information exchanges on financial accounts for tax purposes is Canada. 26 CFR § 1.6049-8(a).

[96] See, e.g., Bertrand Benoit, "Germany seeks EU tax haven crackdown," Financial Times, (3/2/08).

[97] See, e.g., "Joint International Tax Shelter Information Centre Expands and Opens a Second Office in the United Kingdom," IRS Press Release No. IR-2007-104, (5/23/07).

[98] Finance 2007 Hearing on Offshore Tax Evasion, prepared statement of IRS Commissioner Mark Everson, at 9.

[99] LGT Bank was formerly known as the Liechtenstein Global Trust Bank.

[100] "Tax Haven Liechtenstein," public television documentary produced by Frontal 21 in Germany (3/25/08).

[101] The full name of Prince Max is His Serene Highness Maximilian Nikolaus Maria von und zu Liechtenstein. The full name of Prince Hans-Adam is His Serene Highness Johannes Adam Ferdinand Alois Josef Maria Marko d'Aviano Pius von und zu Liechtenstein.

[102] LGT Group Annual Report 2007.

[103] Id. at 5, 7. LGT Group is wholly owned by the Prince of Liechtenstein Foundation, whose beneficiaries are members of the royal family, primarily Prince Hans-Adams. Id. at 7. The Chairman of the Board of Trustees of the LGT Group is Prince Philipp von und zu Liechtenstein, brother of Prince Hans-Adam II, the current reigning sovereign of Liechtenstein. The Chief Executive Officer of LGT Group is Prince Max von und zu Liechtenstein, the second son of Prince Hans-Adam II.

[104] Id. at 3; www.lgt.com, "Business performance and strategic outlook," "LGT Group: key data as at 31 December 2007"(viewed 5/27/08).

[105] LGT Group Annual Report 2007, at 44-45, 78-79.

[106] LGT Group Portrait brochure (2007) at 15.

[107] LGT Group Annual Report 2007, at 5; www.lgt.com, "Business performance and strategic outlook," "LGT Group: key data as at 31 December 2007" (viewed 5/27/08).

[108] LGT Group Annual Report 2007, at 45.

[109] "The Liechtenstein Trust Enterprise," issued by LGT Treuhand AG and LGT Trust Management AG (undated), at 11.

[110] LGT cited the following laws as the basis for their refusal to provide the information requested by the Subcommittee: Article 14 of the Banking Act ("The members of the organs of banks and their employees as well as other persons acting on behalf of such banks shall be obliged to maintain the secrecy of facts that they have been entrusted to or have been made available to them pursuant to their business relationships with clients. The obligation to maintain secrecy shall not be limited in time."); Article 11 of the Trustee Act ("Trustees are obliged to secrecy on the matters entrusted to them and on the facts which they have learned in the course of their professional capacity and whose confidentiality is in the best interest of their client. They shall have the right to such secrecy subject to the applicable rules of procedure in court proceedings and other proceedings before Government authorities."); Processing of Personal Data - § 1 173a, Art. 28a ABGB (General Civil Code) ("The employer may not process data relating to the employee unless such data concern his or her qualification for the employment or are indispensable for the performance of the employment contract. In addition, the provisions of the Data Protection Act shall apply."); Article 10 – Data Confidentiality ("Whoever processes data or has data processed must keep data from applications entrusted to him or made accessible to him based on his professional activities secret, notwithstanding other legal confidentiality obligations, unless lawful grounds exist for the transmission of the data entrusted or made accessible to him."); Article 8 – Transborder Data Flows ("No personal data may be transferred abroad if the personal privacy of the persons affected could be seriously endangered, in particular where there is a failure to provide protection equivalent to that provided under Liechtenstein law. This shall not apply to states which are party to the EEA Agreement.; Whoever wishes to transmit data abroad must notify the Data Protection Commissioner beforehand in cases where: a) there is no legal obligation to disclose the data and b) the persons affected have no knowledge of the transmission."); Prohibited Acts of a Foreign State - Art. 2 of the Liechtenstein State Security law ("b) Prohibited Acts for a Foreign State: Whoever, without being authorized, performs acts for a foreign state on Liechtenstein territory that are reserved to an authority or an official, whoever aids and abets such acts, shall be punished by the Liechtenstein court (Landgericht) with imprisonment up to three years.); Prohibited Acts for a Foreign State – Art. 271 of the Swiss Penal Code ("1. Whoever, without being authorized, performs acts for a foreign state on Swiss territory that are reserved to an authority or an official,

whoever performs such acts for a foreign party or another foreign organization, whoever aids and abets such acts, shall be punished with imprisonment up to three years or a fine, in serious cases with imprisonment of no less than one year."); Economic Intelligence Service (Art. 273 SPC) ("Whoever seeks out a manufacturing or business secret in order to make it accessible to a foreign official agency, a foreign organization, a private enterprise, or their agents, whoever makes a manufacturing or business secret accessible to a foreign official agency, a foreign organization, a private enterprise, or their agents, shall be punished with imprisonment up to three years or a fine, in serious cases with imprisonment of no less than one year. Imprisonment and fine can be combined.")

111 LGT cited § 124 Penal Code, Liechtenstein.

112 For more information about how Liechtenstein foundations are structured and function, see, e.g., untitled and undated document by New Haven Trust Company of Liechtenstein describing Liechtenstein foundations, Bates Nos. SW 67796-99.

113 See 26 USC § 6048. Penalties for not filing Form 3520 in a timely manner, or if the information provided is incomplete or incorrect, are assessed at 35 percent of the gross value of the "reportable event." The reportable event could be a distribution from the trust or a transfer of property to the trust. The beneficiary must file the form if there has been a distribution from a trust or estate.

114 Penalties for failure to file Form 3520-A, or for not furnishing the information required, are 5 percent of the gross value of the portion of the trust's assets treated as owned by the U.S. person at the close of the year. The owner is subject to these penalties.

115 See Internal Revenue Code, § 6677(d) (imposing tax penalties for failure to file a form 3520 or 3520-A even if a foreign jurisdiction would impose a civil or criminal penalty for disclosure).

116 31 U.S.C. § 5321(a)(5).

117 The information about the Marsh account is derived from internal LGT documents produced to the Subcommittee and documents provided by the Marshes in response to a Subcommittee subpoena. The Marshes did not provide an interview or deposition to the Subcommittee, instead asserting their Constitutional rights under the Fifth Amendment.

118 See Topanga Foundation Statutes (9/10/98), Bates Nos. MAR-1534-44.

119 See Statutes of Largella Stiftung (11/4/04); Bye-Laws to the Statutes of Largella Stiftung, Vaduz (11/4/04); By-Laws to the Statutes of Largella Foundation, Vaduz (9/11/07), Bates Nos. MAR-1548-72.

120 See letter from Baker & McKenzie, legal counsel to the Marshes, sent to an IRS Revenue Agent in Georgia, (5/12/08), Bates No. MAR-1189-92, at 1189 ("[t]he Taxpayer, a U.S. citizen, opened several foreign bank accounts in the mid-1980s via the establishment of several foundations in Liechtenstein ....").

121 According to a letter sent to the IRS by legal counsel to the Marshes, at various points during the period 2002 to 2006, four foundations had accounts at five Liechtenstein banks: (1) the Chateau Foundation maintained one account at LGT Bank and three accounts at Centrum Bank; (2) the Lincol Foundation maintained one account at LGT Bank; (3) the Largella Foundation maintained ten accounts at Liechtensteinische Landesbank, and (4) the Topanga Foundation maintained one account at the Verwaltungs und Privatbank AG and four accounts at Privatbank von Graffenreid AG. Id. at 1190.

122 See, e.g., "Estate of James A. Marsh, 2006 Income Tax Returns," Bates Nos. MAR-1442-1465, at 1451-1452 (reporting that, at the time of Mr. Marsh's death on June 16, 2006, the Chateau Foundation accounts held a total of about $11.3 million; the Lincol Foundation account held a total of about $13 million; the Topanga Foundation accounts held a total of about $8.9 million; and the Largella Foundation accounts held a total of about $11.8 million in assets, for a combined total in June 2006 of about $45 million); "Fondation Chateau: Accounts for the year ended December 31, 2007," (4/28/08) Bates Nos. MAR-93 11-9335, at 9315 (showing Chateau accounts with an increased 2007 value of about $12.5 million); "Lincol Foundation: Accounts for the year ended December 31, 2007," (4/28/08) Bates Nos. MAR-91 50-9 173, at 9152 (showing Lincol accounts with an increased 2007 value of about $15.7 million); producing a 2007 combined total for all four foundations (assuming the Topanga and Largella accounts had not lost value since June 2006) of at least $49 million.

123 See, e.g., "Articles: Lincol Foundation, Vaduz," (10/19/00), Bates Nos. MAR-20-27 (hereinafter Lincol Articles"); "Statutes of Lincol Foundation," (6/7/05), Bates Nos. MAR-40-48 (hereinafter "Lincol Statutes"); "Bye- Laws to the Statutes of Lincol Foundation, Vaduz," (11/4/04), Bates Nos. MAR-35-38; "Bye-Laws to the Statues of Lincol Foundation, Vaduz," (6/9/05), Bates Nos. MAR-59-62; "By-Laws to the Statutes of Lincol Foundation, Vaduz," (9/11/07), Bates Nos. MAR-63-67; "Articles: Chateau Foundation, Vaduz" (10/19/00), Bates Nos. MAR- 574-581 (hereinafter Chateau Articles"); "Statutes of Chateau Foundation,"

(6/7/05), Bates Nos. MAR-595-603 (hereinafter "Chateau Statutes"); "Bye-Laws to the Statutes of Chateau Foundation, Vaduz," (11/4/04), Bates Nos. MAR-589-592; "Bye-Laws to the Statutes of Chateau Foundation, Vaduz," (6/9/05), Bates Nos. MAR-614-617; "By-Laws to the Statutes of Chateau Foundation, Vaduz," (9/11/07), Bates Nos. MAR-61 8-622.

124 See Lincol Statutes at 41; Lincol Articles at 21. See also Chateau Statutes at 596; Chateau Articles at 575.

125 Lincol Articles at 22; Lincol Statutes at 43. See also Chateau Articles at 576; Chateau Statutes at 598.

126 "Bye-Laws to the Statutes of Lincol Foundation, Vaduz," (11/4/04), Bates Nos. MAR-35-38; "Bye-laws to the Statutes of Chateau Foundation, Vaduz," (11/4/04), Bates Nos. MAR-5 89-592.

127 Lincol Statutes at 42. See also Chateau Statutes at 597.

128 Lincol Articles at 24. See also Chateau Articles at 578.

129 "Letter of wishes" for the Lincol Foundation (10/11/00), Bates No. MAR-19; "Letter of wishes" for the Chateau Foundation (10/11/00), Bates No. MAR-573.

130 Lincol Articles at 24-25; Chateau Articles at 578-579.

131 Lincol Statutes at 46; Chateau Statutes at 601.

132 Lincol Articles at 26. See also Chateau Articles at 580.

133 Subcommittee interview of Ivo Klein, head of compliance for LGT Group (7/11/08).

134 Lincol Statutes at 41; Chateau Statutes at 596.

135 LGT report on Fondation Chateau, (undated but including a 2002 valuation of foundation assets), PSI-USMSTR237.

136 LGT's internal records show that the Lincol Foundation was established on 10/17/85. LGT report on Lincol Foundation, (undated but subsequent to a client visit on October 11, 2000 and including a 2000 valuation of foundation assets), Bates No. PSI-USMSTR-613. LGT records show that the Chateau Foundation was established four months earlier, on June 26, 1985, but the Subcommittee did not locate documents showing that the Marshes traveled to Liechtenstein in June. LGT report on Fondation Chateau (undated but includes 2002 valuation of foundation assets), Bates No. PSI-USMSTR-237.

137 Bank in Liechtenstein receipt showing deposit of $3,320,700 "in cash" for the Lincol Foundation, (10/15/85), Bates No. PSI-USMSTR-607.

138 Letter of Wishes signed by Shannon Neal Marsh (10/15/85), Bates No. PSI-USMSTR - 605. The Subcommittee did not locate any 1985 document signed by James Albright Marsh.

139 Portfolio Management Agreement, signed by James Albright Marsh (12/5/89), Bates No. MAR-9505-9506.

140 Agreement concerning the Termination of the Agency Agreement (10/11/00), Bates No. MAR-9508-9509 (signed by James Albright Marsh).

141 LGT Memorandum to File about Lincol and Chateau Foundations (2/7/02, though the actual date is likely earlier), Bates No. PSI-USMSTR-614.

142 See Letters of Wishes signed by James Albright Marsh for the Chateau and Lincol Foundations (10/11/00), Bates Nos. MAR-19, 573.

143 Resolutions re Chateau Foundation, signed by James A. Marsh Jr. (11/10/04), Bates Nos. MAR-623, 642, 657, 672.

144 Deed of Signature (11/10/04), Bates No. MAR-95 18 (signed by Kerry Marsh); Deed of Signature (undated), Bates No. MAR-95 19 (signed by Shannon Marsh).

145 See, e.g., letter from Mr. Marsh to LGT trust officer Peter Meier (10/4/94), Bates No. MAR-9507 (instructing LGT to change the management of the Lincol Foundation from the Zurich to the Vaduz office of LGT); LGT report on Chateau and Lincol Foundations following a client visit on 10/11/00, Bates Nos. PSI_USMSTR-237, 613 (noting client instructions in 1994 and 1998). The Marshes may have also traveled to Liechtenstein in 1998, when new Topanga Statutes were issued. Mr. Marsh's initials appear on the Topanga Statutes, which were signed in Vaduz in 1998, but it is unclear whether he initialed the document then or at a later time.

146 Memorandum for File re Lincol and Chateau Foundations (2/7/02, though the actual date is likely earlier), Bates No. PSI-USMSTR-614.

147 The U.S. securities had been held by the Foundations which, under U.S. law, would likely be treated as grantor trusts, and should have resulted in the account being treated as held by a U.S. person and, under the QI Program, being reported on a 1099 Form to the IRS. See Model Qualified Intermediary Withholding Agreement, published in Revenue Procedure 2000-12, (1/24/00), 2000-1 C.B. 387.

148 See five letters from the Marshes' legal counsel, Baker & McKenzie, to an IRS Revenue Agent in Georgia (5/12/08), Bates No. MAR-1 176-92.

[149] See Marsh amended income tax returns for 2002 to 2006, Bates Nos. MAR 1193, 1221, 1259, 1340, 1394. The Subcommittee does not know whether the IRS has accepted this offer or has determined that additional taxes and interest are due. The 2006 Marsh estate tax return estimated having to pay back taxes, interest and penalties in an amount totaling $5.5 million. See Estate of James A Marsh 2006 Income Tax Returns (9/14/07), Bates Nos. MAR- 1442-1466, at 1455.

[150] Letter of Wishes signed by Shannon Neal Marsh (10/1 5/85), Bates Nos. MAR-9598-9599.

[151] Handwritten letter signed by Shannon N. Marsh to Mr. Alvate (5/23/92), Bates No. PSI-USMSTR-23 1.

[152] Document entitled, "Instruction," (11/17/93), Bates No. PSI-USMSTR-612 (signed by Shannon Neal Marsh).

[153] Memorandum for file re Lincol and Chateau Foundations (2/7/02, though the actual date is likely earlier), Bates No. PSI-USMSTR-614.

[154] Bye-Laws to the Statutes of Lincol Foundation (11/4/04), Bates Nos. MAR-35-38. Bye-laws to the Statutes of Chateau Foundation (11/4/04), Bates Nos. MAR-589-592.

[155] Deed of Signature (11/10/2004), Bates No. MAR-95 18 (signed by Kerry Marsh); Deed of Signature (undated), Bates No. MAR-95 19 (signed by Shannon Marsh).

[156] See letter from the Marshes' legal counsel, Baker & McKenzie, to an IRS Revenue Agent in Georgia regarding "Failure to timely report foreign income on Forms 1040," (5/12/08), Bates No. MAR-1 185-88, at 1186.

[157] Information about the Wu accounts is derived from internal LGT documents produced to the Subcommittee and from limited documentation supplied by Mr. Wu. Mr. Wu declined to provide either an interview or deposition to the Subcommittee, instead asserting his Constitutional rights under the Fifth Amendment.

[158] See, e.g., Articles of the JCMA Foundation, Vaduz (6/20/96), Bates Nos. WWU-PSI 1-8; By-Laws of the JCMA Foundation, Vaduz (6/25/96), Bates Nos. WWU-PSI 9-13; By-Laws of the Veline Foundation, Vaduz (8/21/97), Bates Nos. PSI-USMSTR-5873-75.

[159] See Declaration of Trust, signed by Cobyrne Ltd. and JCMA Foundation (10/1/96), Bates Nos. WWU-PSI 14-15. A few months later, the Sandalwood share certificate was moved to JCMA's "deposit box" at LGT. LGT report on JCMA Foundation (subsequent to 6/27/02), Bates No. PSI-USMSTR-4988.

[160] See LGT report on JCMA Foundation (subsequent to 6/27/02), Bates No. PSI-USMSTR-4988.

[161] The Subcommittee identified a second corporation, Tai Lung Company, Inc., now inactive, that was formed in New York State on the same day that JCMA was formed in Liechtenstein (June 20, 1996). The registered agent for this corporation is a Dr. Er Ke Yu who appears to operate an acupuncture and Chinese herbal center near Mr. Wu's personal residence in Forest Hills, New York. See NYS Department of State, Division of Corporations, Entity Information for Tai Lung Co., Inc. It is unclear what role, if any, this second corporation may have played in Mr. Wu's affairs.

[162] See New York City Department of Finance, Office of the City Register, Document No. FT-4380005495638 (2/14/97).

[163] See LGT report on JCMA Foundation (subsequent to 6/27/02), Bates No. PSI-USMSTR-4988.

[164] See Resolution of the Foundation Board of JCMA Foundation, Vaduz (2/7/02), Bates No. WWU-PSI 27.

[165] LGT report on JCMA Foundation (subsequent to 6/27/02), Bates No. PSI-USMSTR-4988.

See Resolution of the Foundation Board of JCMA Foundation, Vaduz (2/7/02), Bates No. WWU-PSI 27.

LGT "Background Information/Profile" of JCMA Foundation (12/20/01), Bates No. PSI-USMSTR-4990.

[166] See 2001 "Performance" statement, JCMA Foundation (1/1/02), Bates Nos. WWU-PSI 33-34; 2002 "Performance" statement, JCMA Foundation, (1/1/03), Bates Nos. WWU-PSI 52-53; 2003 "Performance" statement, JCMA Foundation, (1/2/04), Bates Nos. WWU-PSI 61-62; 2004 "Performance" statement, JCMA Foundation, (1/2/05), Bates Nos. WWU-PSI 75-77; 2005 "Performance" statement, JCMA, (1/1/06), Bates Nos. WWU-PSI 78, 85 (explaining in the notes that the 2005 withdrawals from JCMA were actually withdrawals from an LGT account opened for Dickinson and had been "entered in the Statement of Assets as ... additions to the loan of Dickinson Holding & Finance Ltd., BWI"); 2006 "Statement of Assets, Desert Rose Foundation," (4/17/07), Bates Nos. WWU-PSI 92, 97 (Desert Rose is a successor foundation to JCMA that began operation in 2006 and assumed ownership of Dickinson; its Statement of Assets states: "During the course of 2005 and 2006 DICKINSON HOLDING & FINANCE LTD., BVI, received monies and effected payments for and on behalf of the Foundation. These payments are registered in the books as additions/redemptions of the principal loan amount.").

[167] See, e.g., the 2004 and 2005 Statement of Assets, Bates Nos. WWU-PSI 65-71, 79-85.

[168] See letter to LGT signed by Mr. Wu (6/27/02), Bates No. PSI-USMSTR-4980. It is possible that LGT prepared this letter during his visit and presented it to Mr. Wu for signature, since the letter requesting the bank cheque

is dated one day after the bank cheque itself. See also Resolution by the JCMA Foundation Board (6/26/02), Bates No. PSI-USMSTR-4983 (approving the $100,000 withdrawal from its account).

[169] Receipt for HSBC demand cheque for $100,000, Cheque No. K93 9026 (6/26/02), Bates No. PSI-USMSTR 4981. See also HSBC On-Line Remittances Advice, (6/26/02), Bates No. PSI-USMSTR-4982 (notifying LGT of the $100,000 debit to its account and listing William Wu as the "beneficiary").

[170] Receipt for HSBC demand cheque for $100,000, Cheque No. K939026 (6/26/02), Bates No. PSI-USMSTR-4981.

[171] LGT Memorandum by Kim Choy regarding JCMA Foundation (6/26/02), Bates No. PSI-USMSTR-4989.

[172] See Resolution of the Board of Directors of Dickinson Holding & Finance Ltd. (4/17/07), Bates Nos. WWU-PSI 16-26, at 16 (showing company was incorporated on July 12, 2004).

[173] See 2004 Statement of Assets, JCMA Foundation (2/13/06), Bates No. WWU-PSI 64-71, at 69. This loan was apparently not reduced to writing until February 2006. Id.

[174] See 2006 "Statement of Assets, Desert Rose Foundation," (4/18/07), Bates Nos. WWU-PSI 92-107, at 97 ("During the course of 2005 and 2006 DICKINSON HOLDING & FINANCE LTD., BVI, received monies and effected payments for and on behalf of the Foundation. These payments are registered in the books as additions/redemptions of the principal loan amount.").

[175] See, e.g., 2005 "Performance" statement, JCMA (1/1/06), Bates Nos. WWU-PSI 78, 85 (noting that the 2005 endowment to and withdrawals from JCMA were "entered in the Statement of Assets as redemption/additions to the loan of Dickinson Holding & Finance Ltd., BWI").

[176] See 2006 "Statement of Assets, Desert Rose Foundation," (4/18/07), Bates Nos. WWU-PSI 92-107, at 95. The Subcommittee does not have the formation documents for Desert Rose, but the fact that Mr. Wu had possession of the 2006 Desert Rose financial statement suggests he is the founder of that foundation as well.

[177] Id. at 96-97. The document also states: "Sandalwood is the shareholder of a company called Tai Lung Worldwide Ltd., which owns a property in New York. ... During the course of 2006 it was resolved to distribute the shares to the first Beneficiary, however, the planned share transfer has not yet been completed." Id. at 96.

[178] Resolution of the Foundation Board of JCMA Foundation (12/31/05), Bates Nos. WWU-PSI-78; Resolution of the Foundation Board of JCMA Foundation, (4/18/07), Bates No. WWU-PSI-92.

[179] See, e.g., letter from Ms. Wu to LGT Bank's Representative Office in Hong Kong (3/27/01), Bates No. PSIUSMSTR-5877 (providing instructions to LGT to "wind up" Veline Foundation); LGT report on Veline Foundation after a 3/27/00 client visit (date of report preparation unclear), Bates No. PSI-USMSTR-5887 (containing notation that the Foundation was stricken from the Register on April 19, 2001). It is possible that Ms. Wu controls the Palone Foundation and, thus, was simply transferring her assets from one foundation she controlled to another.

[180] See, e.g., Statement of assets as per 31.12.2000 for Veline Foundation, Vaduz (2/5/01), Bates No. PSI-USMSTR5885.

[181] See "Bearer Share Certificate Transferable by Delivery" for Manta Co. Ltd. (issued 9/3/97 and provided to Ms. Wu on 4/18/01), Bates No. PSI-USMSTR 5878.

[182] See, e.g., "Vulnerability of private banking to money laundering activities," S.Hrg. 106-428 (11/10/99), testimony of Federal Reserve Board:

"A variant of personal investment corporation accounts that could increase the risk of the accounts being used for money laundering purposes are personal investment corporations that are owned through bearer shares. Bearer shares are negotiable instruments with no record of ownership so that title of the underlying entity is held essentially by anyone who possesses the bearer shares. Historically, bearer shares were used as a vehicle for estate planning in that at death the shares would be passed on to the deceased beneficiaries without the need for probate of the estate. However, in the context of potential illicit activity being conducted through an entity whose ownership is identified by bearer shares, it is virtually impossible for a banking organization to apply sound risk management procedures, including identifying the beneficial owner of the account, unless the banking organization physically holds the bearer shares in custody for the beneficial owner, which of course we encourage."

[183] See LGT report on Veline Foundation (subsequent to a 3/27/00 client visit), Bates No. PSI-USMSTR-5887 ("Single owner share certificate in LGT deposit box of Veline").

[184] See handwritten organizational chart showing Veline Foundation ownership of corporations and property (undated), Bates No. PSI-USMSTR-5889.

[185] In reviewing LGT documentation, the Subcommittee came across many other examples of complex structures used to hide ownership of assets. See, e.g., Chart entitled, "Purchase of an Apartment in London," (4/3/02), Bates No. PSI-USMSTR-6608; charts for entities related to Sunar Trust, Lovelight Foundation, Ramsar Foundation, and Bosham Foundation, (2/19/02 and 12/12/01), Bates Nos. PSI-USMSTR-6644-6674, 6573-6576.

[186] The information about the Lowy account is derived from internal LGT documents produced to the Subcommittee and documents provided by the Lowys in response to a Subcommittee subpoena.

[187] See, e.g., LGT Memorandum about Luperla (6/26/01), Bates No. PSI-USMSTR-8897 ("The memorandums for the file also mention the 'Yelnarf' structure which we've been conducting for years."); LGT Memorandum about Luperla (5/2/97), Bates Nos. PSI-USMSTR-8864-8865 (regarding Crofton" and Jelnav); LGT memorandum, subject "Westfields, Adelphi, Crofton," (11/26/96), Bates Nos. PSI-USMSTR-8773-8774 (Crofton); LGT memorandum "New Establishment Westfields/Lowy," (11/27/96), Bates No. PSI-USMSTR-8775 ("Get copy of Crofton Foundation laws" from another LGT employee); LGT Memorandum, subject "Frank Lowy," (3/13/97), Bates Nos. PSI-USMSTR - 8767-8768 ("After the transfer of the assets, Crofton will be closed.").

[188] "The mandate is to be classified as one of the largest business affairs of the LGT BIL [Bank in Liechtenstein]." LGT memorandum about Luperla (1/29/98), Bates No. PSI-USMSTR-8901.

[189] LGT memorandum, subject "Westfields, Adelphi, Crofton," (11/26/96), Bates Nos. PSI-USMSTR-8773-8774.

[190] Mr. Gonski's relationship to Mr. Lowy is not described in the material available to the Subcommittee. According to Westfield Group's website, Mr. Gonski has served as non-executive director of Westfield Holdings Ltd. since 1985. See http://westfield.com/ corporate//about-westfield-group/board-of-directors/ (viewed 7/7/08).

[191] "The Lowys view these monies as "insurance," i.e., they will be invested very long-term and rather conservatively." LGT memorandum, subject "Westfield/ Lowy Family," (1/23/97), Bates Nos. PSI-USMSTR-8771- 8772.

[192] LGT memorandum, subject "Westfields, Adelphi, Crofton," (12/17/96), Bates Nos. PSI-USMSTR-8760-8770 ("Regarding the composition of the portfolio strategy and the cost structure, Lowy insists on a meeting in Los Angeles, in which his sons David and Peter as well as possibly Stephen should take part. ... He would like that I meet with him in Los Angeles with the person who will also be responsible for 'his establishment.'"). See also LGT memorandum, subject "Westfield/ Lowy Family," (1/23/97), Bates Nos. PSI-USMSTR 8771-8772.

[193] LGT Memorandum, subject "Frank Lowy," (3/13/97), Bates Nos. PSI-USMSTR-8767-8768 ("Lowy seems to have been very pleased with our service and would like to invite S.D. Prince Philipp ... to London this summer for a special occasion."). H.S.H. Prince Philipp von und zu Liechtenstein was at the time a Member of the Board of Directors of LGT Bank and Chairman of the Board of Directors of LGT. See http://www.lgt.com/export/ sites/inta_lgtcom/de/wir_ueber_uns/lgt_portrait/publikationen/ $verwaltung_publikationen/cv/cv_s_d_prinz_philipp _von_und_zu_liechtenstein_en.pdf (viewed 7/7/08).

[194] LGT memorandum about Luperla (3/16/97), Bates Nos. PSI-USMSTR-8902-8903; LGT memorandum about Luperla (1/29/98), Bates No. PSI-USMSTR-8901 ("The substance of this meeting is that the client cannot officially bring these funds back into his Australian assets. Therefore they remain in the foundation.").

[195] See, e.g., LGT memorandum, subject "Westfield/ Lowy Family," by Peter Widmer, (1/23/97), Bates Nos. PSIUSMSTR-8771-8772 ("When everything is completed, one wants LGTT to destroy all files on the old structures, insofar as they don't have to be kept for legal reasons. Regarding this matter, I will specifically get in touch with LGTT after the transfer into this new structure."); LGT Memorandum, subject "Frank Lowy," (3/13/97), Bates Nos. PSI-USMSTR-8767-8768 ("We have promised once again, that all documents of Crofton will be destroyed, as long as will not have to be protected for legal reasons."); LGT Memorandum about Luperla (5/2/97), Bates Nos. PSIUSMSTR-8864-8865 ("After completion of these transactions, all documents from "Crofton" and "Jelnav" are definitely to be destroyed, insofar as this is legally possible. I ask Dr. Iob for confirmation of completion by June 30, 1997.").

[196] LGT Memorandum, Subject: "Westfields, Adelphi, Crofton," (12/17/96), Bates Nos. PSI-USMSTR-8769-8770.

[197] "We promised that the total relationship will remain under my control (key account) and that Wilfried Ospelt will personally take over the depot in an investment-strategic manner. For the short-term, the contacts should go exclusively through me." LGT memorandum, subject "Westfield/ Lowy Family," (1/23/97), Bates Nos. PSIUSMSTR-8771-8772.

[198] "Contact person will be in the future exclusively Joshua Gelbard." LGT memorandum, subject "Westfields, Adelphi, Crofton," (11/26/96), Bates Nos. PSI-USMSTR-8773-8774.

[199] Letter from J.H. Gelbard to LGT (3/12/97), Bates Nos. PSI-USMSTR-8860-61.

[200] Regulations Luperla Foundation, Vaduz (4/30/97), Bates Nos. PSI-USMSTR-8838-40.

[201] "Luperla is a foundation without engagement contract. Client is J. Gelbart [sic]." LGT memorandum about Luperla (3/16/97), Bates Nos. PSI-USMSTR-8902-8903. See also "Identification File" for Luperla Foundation (10/31/97), Bates No. US-MSTR-8905.

[202] "We were able to talk them out of the desire for co-management of the investment process by pointing out that every direct influence on the foundation can have disadvantages." LGT memorandum, subject "Westfield/ Lowy Family," (1/23/97), Bates Nos. PSI-USMSTR-8771-8772.

[203] LGT has employed similar tactics on other occasions to help clients disguise the flow of assets into their LGT accounts, as examined below.

[204] See, e.g., LGT memorandum about Luperla (1/29/98), Bates No. PSI-USMSTR-8901 ("The foundation assets shall come to the amount of approximately USD 100 million and originate from a relatively complex transaction, with the goal of bringing shares listed in the stock market back into the family's possession, which was successfully completed."); LGT memorandum about Luperla (6/26/01), Bates No. PSI-USMSTR-8897. ("The result from these memorandums for the file as well as from my memory is that the funds of the Luperla Foundation stem from a credit financing of the LGT Bank in Liechtenstein that at the time was carried out through a company Crofton. The result from the attached memorandums for the file is that the instructions regarding Crofton were issued by Sinus Treuhand, Zürich."). Several LGT documents also refer to an entity called Adelphi, but it is not clear that it was used in the final transaction. Compare LGT memorandum, subject "Westfields, Adelphi, Crofton," (11/26/96), Bates Nos. PSI-USMSTR-8773-8774 (the first order of business was to "settle the credit repayment formalities at Adelphia") and LGT Memorandum, Subject: "Westfields, Adelphi, Crofton," (12/17/96), Bates Nos. PSI-USMSTR8769-8770 ("the free funds in the amount of rd. USD 53 million from the Adelphi - Credit Repayment and their insertion into a new structure") with LGT Memorandum, subject "Frank Lowy," (3/13/97), Bates Nos. PSIUSMSTR-8767-8768 ("The Adelphi - assets will not be included in the new structure.").

[205] In a March 1997 letter to LGT requesting establishment of the Luperla Foundation, Mr. Gelbard agreed to a fee which included, among other things, "the formation and administration of a transfer company (with legal situs in the British Virgin Islands) and its bank accounts." Letter to LGT regarding formation of Luperla Foundation, (3/12/97), Bates No. PSI-USMSTR-8860-61. See also LGT memorandum about Luperla (3/16/97), Bates Nos. PSI-USMSTR8902-8903. ("The monies are to be transferred from Crofton via a specially taken-over BVI company (name: Sewell [name inserted by handwriting]).").

[206] LGT Memorandum about Luperla (5/2/97), Bates Nos. PSI-USMSTR-8864-8865. LGT had originally instructed that Sewell be dissolved after the Lowy funds were transferred into the Luperla account. Id. The order for dissolution was apparently not given, however, as indicated by an October 1997 LGT memorandum stating that another $30,000 was going to be transferred into the Luperla account at LGT, from the Crofton company, via the Sewell account at LGT bank. Moreover, the memorandum notes that a U.S. dollar account had been opened in the name of Sewell for this purpose, and "This has apparently already been done on many occasions." LGT memorandum, subject "Luperla Stiftung / Sewell Services Ltd. B.V.I.," (10/23/97), Bates No. PSI-USMSTR-8896.

[207] Letter from J.H. Gelbard to LGT regarding formation of Luperla Foundation (3/12/97), Bates Nos. PSIUSMSTR-8860-61.

[208] Regulations Luperla Foundation, Vaduz (4/30/97), Bates Nos. PSI-USMSTR-8838-40 (hereinafter "Luperla Regulations").

[209] LGT memorandum about Luperla Foundation (5/14/97), Bates No. PSI-USMSTR-8883.

[210] Id.

[211] LGT memorandum, subject "Westfield/ Lowy Family," (1/23/97), Bates Nos. PSI-USMSTR-8771-8772. See also LGT memorandum about Luperla by Werner Orvati, (6/26/01), Bates No. PSI-USMSTR-8897 ("It is explicitly apparent from the memorandums for the file that, in accordance with the intention of the founder, FL and his three sons DL, PL and SL are to be financial beneficiaries."); LGT memorandum about Luperla (7/16/01), Bates Nos. PSI-USMSTR-8867-8870 ("The records document the intent of the benefactor to the effect that the economic benefactor and his three sons shall be financial beneficiaries.").

[212] Luperla Regulations.

[213] See Organization Chart, provided by Beverly Park in response to an IRS request, Bates No. LOWY-PSI-36; Correspondence from P.S. Seddon, Secretary, Cordera Holdings Pty Limited to Mr. Peter Lowy (3/21/97), Bates No. LOWY-PSI-3714.

[214] In 1999, the other Beverly Park officers and directors were: Richard E. Green, Vice President and Director; Mark Stefanek, Treasurer and Secretary; Leon Janks, Assistant Secretary; and Arthur E. Schramm, Director. See "List of Officers/Directors" for Beverly Park Corp. (8/26/99), Bates No. LOWY-PSI-3 743. Beverly Park also appears to serve as a holding company for two properties purchased from other Westfield and Lowy affiliated entities. These properties, purchased on March 25, 1997, include a two-unit Park Avenue, Manhattan condominium for $4.9 million purchased from Westland Park Avenue Corporation (another Delaware corporation using the Westfield Group United States' office address); and a 7,000 square foot Beverly Hills home for $5.75 million purchased from Clareville, Ltd., a Bermuda corporation. See "Contract for the Purchase and Sale of Real Estate," (3/24/97), Bates Nos. LOWY-PSI-3868-3871 (Manhattan condominium); "Change of Ownership Statement," (5/13/97), Bates Nos. LOWY-PSI-3764-65 (Beverly Hills house). These properties were apparently used to house Westfield officers and directors as well as Lowy family members for business and leisure; Beverly Park charged Westfield substantial fees for some of these guest stays. See, e.g., "Beverly Park Corporation: Guest Log -Beverly Hills," and "Beverly Park Corporation: Guest Log -New York Condo," (monthly, July 1999 to May 2000), Bates No. LOWY-PSI-3914-3931.

[215] LGT Memorandum about Luperla (6/26/01), Bates No. PSI-USMSTR-8897.

[216] Id.

[217] LGT memorandum about Luperla (7/16/01), Bates Nos. PSI-USMSTR-8867-8870.

[218] Id. at 8870.

[219] LGT memorandum about Luperla (12/17/01), Bates Nos. PSI-USMSTR-8879-8880.

[220] Id.

[221] See id.; LGT memorandum about Luperla (12/18/01), Bates Nos. PSI-USMSTR-8873-8874; LGT memorandum about Luperla (12/20/01), Bates Nos. PSI-USMSTR-8875-8877. With respect to some documents, LGT was not satisfied with copies and requested originals. David Lowy, in a telephone conversation on December 17, 2001, assured LGT he would provide the original documents. These documents were then "personally delivered to Dr. Konrad Bächinger [of LGT] at his private address" the next day. Id.

[222] LGT memorandum about Luperla (12/17/01), Bates Nos. PSI-USMSTR-8879-8880.

[223] Id. at 8880.

[224] LGT memorandum about Luperla (12/20/01), Bates Nos. PSI-USMSTR-8875-8877 at 8877.

[225] "Beverly Park Response to IDR 1," (2/21/08), Bates No. LOWY-PSI-1980-1990, at 1985. See also id. at 1989.

[226] "IDR 23-1," (1/28/08), Bates No. LOWY-PSI-1976.

[227] "IDR 22-1," (1/28/08), Bates No. LOWY-PSI-1975.

[228] The information about the Greenfield accounts is derived from internal LGT documents produced to the Subcommittee. The Greenfields did not provide any documents or oral testimony to the Subcommittee, instead asserting their Constitutional rights under the Fifth Amendment.

[229] LGT Bank in Liechtenstein bank statement for Maverick Foundation (1/1/02) (showing a balance of $2,198,167.72); LGT Treuhand Memorandum regarding Maverick Foundation (3/27/0 1).

[230] LGT report on Maverick Foundation (subsequent to 3/23/0 1 client meeting) ; LGT report on Chiu Fu (Far East) Ltd. (undated), Bates No. PSI-USMSTR-3205; LGT report on TSF Company Ltd. (undated), Bates No. PSIUSMSTR-3 193.

[231] LGT report on Maverick Foundation (undated).

[232] LGT Background Information/Profile- Existing Customers for Maverick Foundation (10/12/01).

[233] LGT report on Maverick Foundation (undated).

[234] LGT report on Maverick Foundation (undated).

[235] See 1992 and 2001 bank statements, Bates Nos. PSI-USMSTR-3190-91, 3201-03.

[236] LGT Memorandum regarding Maverick Foundation (3/27/0 1), at 1.

[237] Id.

[238] Id.

[239] Id. at 2.

[240] Id. at 1, 2.

[241] Id. at 1.

[242] Information about the Gonzalez accounts is derived from internal LGT documents produced to the Subcommittee and numerous court pleadings, orders, and opinions. Jorge Gonzalez died in 1988.

[243] LGT Bank account summary for Fondation Tragique as of 12/31/2001, (1/1/2002), Bates No. PSI-USMSTR8700.

[244] See *Bonilla v. Volvo Car Corp.*, 150 F.3d 62, 65 (1st Cir. 1998) (hereinafter *"Bonilla v. Volvo").*

[245] Id.
[246] Sworn Statement of Ricardo Gonzalez (hereinafter "Gonzalez Sworn Statement"), appendix to *Perez v. Volvo,* 247 F.3d 303 (1st Cir. 2001) (hereinafter *"Perez v. Volvo").*
[247] *Bonilla v. Trebol Motors Corp.,* 150 F.3d 77, 85 (1st Cir. 1998) (hereinafter *"Bonilla v. Trebol").*
[248] See untitled chart (undated), Bates No. PSI-USMSTR-8762 ("Loan to Auto und Motoren US$6 Mio").
[249] See untitled chart (undated), Bates No. PSI-USMSTR-8762 ("Fid. Loan FIWA to Trebol"); LGT Background Information/Profile – Existing/Clients regarding FIWA AG, Vaduz (12/10/01), Bates No. PSI-USMSTR-954 (describing FIWA as an "LGT- group company" that holds shares).
[250] See *Bonilla v. Volvo* at 72; Gonzalez Sworn Statement at ¶ 7 ("On or about July 1985, Trebol and Volvo arranged for a Liechtenstein company named Auto Und Motoren ('AUM') to serve as a 'guarantor' of Trebol's payment obligations for new cars purchased by Trebol from Volvo for the 1986 model year and beyond.").
[251] The First Circuit notes that Volvo also loaned AUM $2.7 million in 1993, "to cover Trebol's debts," and Volvo later "authorized a transaction in which AUM swapped Trebol's debt to it for equity in Trebol." *Bonilla v. Volvo* at 72. See also Gonzalez Sworn Statement at ¶¶ 10-11. Both transactions offer added evidence that Volvo was unaware that AUM and Trebol were commonly owned. See also *Perez v. Volvo* at 317 ("If the [1993] transaction proves anything, it tends to prove that Volvo did not know, even at that late date, that AUM was a dummy corporation. Elsewise, why would Volvo lend AUM so large a sum?"). See also Gonzalez Sworn Statement at ¶ 15 (discussing relationship between AUM and Trebol, but failing to mention their common ownership and asserting: "I know that my family and company derived no benefit from AUM commensurate with the extremely high guarantee cost per car.").
[252] *Bonilla v. Volvo* at 72.
[253] Id. See also discussion in *Bonilla v. Volvo,* 150 F.3d 88, 90 (1st Cir. 1998) (hereinafter *"Bonilla v. Volvo* II")("A number of these invoices, as we now know, included inflated figures significantly exceeding the original invoice prices."); *Perez v. Volvo* at 308-09.
[254] *Bonilla v. Volvo,* at 65.
[255] Id. at 65.
[256] Id. at 62.
[257] See *Bonilla v. Trebol* at 80.
[258] *Bonilla v. Trebol* at 85. The First Circuit also vacated an award of $3.5 million against Volvo, Trebol and the Gonzalezes for attorney fees and costs related to improper conduct during the litigation, and remanded the issue to the district court for a new hearing on the amount of attorney fees and costs owed by the defendants. *Bonilla v. Volvo II* at 90, 95.
[259] *Bonilla v. Trebol* at 80.
[260] *Bonilla v. Trebol* at 87.
[261] LGT Background Information/Profile for Fondation Tragique, Vaduz (12/18/01), Bates No. PSI-USMSTR-871 1.
[262] Subcommittee telephone conversation with Conlee Whiteley, Kanner & Whiteley, LLC, legal counsel to the plaintiffs in the RICO suit (7/9/08).
[263] Id.
[264] LGT Memorandum for the File (11/9/01), Bates No. PSI-USMSTR-8704-05. According to the LGT memorandum, the meeting took place in Zurich, Switzerland, and was attended by an LGT private banker, Ms. Gonzalez, her daughter, her son Ricardo, and his wife.
[265] Id. The "tax investigation" referred to in the memorandum may refer to an inquiry that was apparently initiated by Puerto Rican tax authorities but did not result in any tax assessment.
[266] Id. See also untitled chart depicting Fondation Tragique (undated), Bates No. PSI-USMSTR-8763. This chart shows that Tragique is administered by a "Foundation Board" and "Protector." It states that "All resolutions of the Foundation Board require the consent of the Protector." It also states "The Protector can appoint and remove the beneficiaries" and "has all acces[s] on the assets of the Foundation." The chart also refers to the Foundation's By Laws, where the Foundation's beneficiaries are named, as a "Last Will" which can be used by the Foundation Protector to name the Foundation beneficiaries. The Foundation Protector for Tragique was Ms. Gonzalez.
[267] Id.
[268] Id.
[269] Id.

[270] LGT report onAsmeral Investment Anstalt (undated), Bates No. PSI-USMSTR 966 ("Status: Dissolved").

[271] LGT Background Information/Profile-Existing Customer for Auto and Motoren AG (3/10/01), Bates No. PSIUSMSTR-8729 ("Auto und Motoren AG in Liquidation ... The corporation does not conduct commercial activity anymore. It will be dissolved in the foreseeable future.").

[272] LGT Bank account summary for Tragunda Foundation for the period 1/1/2002-9/30/2002 (10/2/2002), Bates No. PSI-USMSTR-871 9.

[273] LGT Bank account summary for Fondation Tragique as of 12/31/2001, (1/1/2002), Bates No. PSI-USMSTR8700.

[274] The information about the Chong account is derived from internal LGT documents produced to the Subcommittee and documents provided by Mr. Chong in response to a Subcommittee subpoena. Mr. Chong did not provide an interview or deposition to the Subcommittee, instead asserting his Constitutional rights under the Fifth Amendment.

[275] LGT report on Yue Shing Tong Foundation (undated), Bates No. PSI-USMSTR-2206; LGT Background Information/Profile for Yue Shing Tong Foundation (2/6/02), Bates Nos. PSI-USMSTR-21 89-90 ("The original founder (father) built up a large and successful chemical business in Taiwan and China. The assets originally deposited were profits generated out of this business activity.").

[276] See LGT Background Information/Profile for Yue Shing Tong Foundation, (10/9/0 1), Bates No. PSI-USMSTR 2207; By-Laws Yue Shing Tong Foundation, Vaduz (2/15/02), Bates Nos. PSI-USMSTR-21 91-98, at 2192.

[277] See By-Laws Yue Shing Tong Foundation, Vaduz (2/15/02), Bates Nos. PSI-USMSTR-2191-98; Designation of Beneficiaries for Yue Sing Tong Foundation (6/27/0 1), Bates Nos. PSI-USMSTR-21 86-8 8.

[278] See LGT bank summary (6/29/02), Bates No. PSI-USMSTR-2203 (showing Mother account with $5.2 million); (6/29/02), Bates No. PSI-USMSTR-2204 (showing Son R account with $1.8 million); (1/1/02), Bates No. PSIUSMSTR-2202 (showing Daughter T account with $892,000); (1/1/02), Bates No. PSI-USMSTR-2205 (showing Son C account with $1.7 million).

[279] See handwritten document by Ms. Chong giving Power of Attorney to her son, Richard Chong (4/24/1998), Bates No. PSI-USMSTR-2199.

[280] See documents entitled, "Yue Shing Tong Foundation ('mother')", "Yue Shing Tong Foundation ('SUN R' a/c)," "Yue Shing Tong Foundation (Daughter Account)," "Yue Shing Tong C Foundation," (all undated), Bates Nos. CH- PSI 47-52. Other documents reviewed by the Subcommittee indicate that these lists were not comprehensive, however, and did not include all of the wire transfers into or out of the Foundation's funds.

[281] See, e.g., biography of Mr. Chong on website of Sycamore Ventures, www.sycamorevc.com (viewed 7/14/08).

[282] For more information about LGT's use of transfer corporations, see section 8 below, and discussion of the Sewell transfer corporation used in connection with the Lowy accounts and Luperla Foundation.

[283] See KCS Ltd. invoice to Apex, c/o LGT Bank in Liechtenstein AG, Representative Office Hong Kong (4/27/07), Bates No. CH-PSI 25. Other documents reviewed by the Subcommittee, including wire transfers at other financial institutions referring to Apex, indicate that it had a post office box address in Samoa.

[284] See documents entitled, "Yue Shing Tong Foundation ('mother')", "Yue Shing Tong Foundation ('SUN R' a/c)," "Yue Shing Tong Foundation (Daughter Account)," "Yue Shing Tong C Foundation," (all undated), Bates Nos. CH- PSI 47-52.

[285] Compare letters from Mr. Chong to LGT contact Silvan Colani (9/12/06 regarding $30,000), (3/7/06 regarding $60,000), (6/1/04 regarding $50,000), and (5/18/04 regarding $70,000), Bates Nos. CH-PSI 59, 60, 94, 107 with letter from Mr. Chong to LGT contact Silvan Colani (5/30/02 regarding $85,000 sent directly from Fund Mother to Dynamic Travel, prior to the formation of Apex).

[286] Email from LGT contact Silvan Colani to Mr. Chong (2/14/07), Bates No. CH-PSI 3. LGT has employed similar tactics on other occasions to help clients disguise the flow of assets into their LGT accounts, as examined below in Section 8.

[287] See, e.g., letter from Mr. Chong to Silvan Colani, Representative of LGT in Hong Kong (3/7/06), Bates No. CH-PSI 59.

[288] See, e.g., email from Mr. Chong to LGT contact Silvan Colani (3/20/07), Bates No. CH-PSI 8.

[289] Letter from Mr. Chong to LGT (undated), Bates No. CH-PSI 65.

[290] See, e.g., email from LGT contact Silvan Colani to Mr. Chong (12/26/06), Bates No. CH-PSI 1.

[291] See email from LGT contact Silvan Colani to Mr. Chong (4/18/07), Bates No. CH-PSI 16.

[292] Email from LGT contact Silvan Colani to Mr. Chong (2/28/07), Bates No. CH-PSI 5.

[293] Letter from Mr. Chong to LGT contact Silvan Colani (3/1/06), Bates No. CH-PSI 66. A handwritten note on this letter indicates that the $63,303 may have been "Acme dividends."

294 Email from LGT contact Silvan Colani to Mr. Chong (2/20/08), Bates No. CH-PSI 35.

295 Email from Mr. Chong to LGT contact Silvan Colani (2/21/08), Bates No. CH-PSI 37.

296 Email from LGT contact Silvan Colani to Mr. Chong (2/21/08), Bates No. CH-PSI 38.

297 Email from LGT contact Sonja Sprenger to Mr. Chong (2/21/08), Bates No. CH-PSI 39.

298 The information about the Miskin accounts is derived from internal LGT documents produced to the Subcommittee and pleadings filed in court cases in Switzerland, the United Kingdom, and United States. The Subcommittee was unable to contact Mr. Miskin despite extensive efforts.

299 LGT memorandum regarding a new establishment for Mr. Miskin (6/30/98), Bates Nos. PSI-USMSTR-6663-64.

300 See *Miskin v. Miskin,* Case No. 01111516, (Cal. Super. Ct. Anacapa Div. 2003) (hereinafter "Miskin Property Dispute in California"), Declaration of Michael Miskin in Support of Motion to Quash Service of Summons and Dismiss Action (8/1/03), at ¶ 1; Declaration of Michael Miskin (9/4/03), at ¶ 1.

301 See, e.g., Miskin Property Dispute in California, Opposition to Motion to Quash; Objections to Evidence; Request for Judicial notice; Declaration of Judith Ilene Bloom (8/29/03) at 3-4; *Miskin v. Miskin,* High Court of Justice, Family Division, Witness Statement of Stephanie Avril Miskin (1/23/03) at ¶¶ 6-16.

302 Miskin Property Dispute in California, Declaration of Stephanie Avril Miskin in Opposition to Motion to Expunge Lis Pendens (4/4/2003), at ¶ 6.

303 Miskin Property Dispute in California, Declaration of Michael Miskin in Support of Motion to Quash Service of Summons and Dismiss Action (8/1/03), at ¶ 3.

304 Miskin Property Dispute in California, Declaration of Michael Miskin (9/4/03), at ¶ 3.

305 Miskin Property Dispute in California, Opposition to Motion to Quash; Objections to Evidence; Request for Judicial notice; Declaration of Judith Ilene Bloom, legal counsel to Ms. Miskin (8/29/03) at 3-4; *Miskin v. Miskin,* High Court of Justice, Family Division, Witness Statement of Stephanie Avril Miskin (1/23/03) at ¶ 13.

306 See LGT Memorandum regarding a new establishment for Mr. Miskin (6/30/98), Bates Nos. PSI-USMSTR6663-64.

307 See, e.g., Letter of Wishes (7/28/00), Bates Nos. PSI-USMSTR-6653-54; Feststellung der wirtschaftlich berechtigten Person (Establishment of Economically Entitled Persons) (7/18/01), Bates No. PSI-USMSTR 6652.

308 Copy of business card for "Michael Miskin Ceramics" in "Santa Barbara, CA" (displaying a California telephone number), Bates No. PSI-MSMSTR-6665.

309 LGT Memorandum regarding a new establishment for Mr. Miskin (6/30/98), Bates Nos. PSI-USMSTR-6663-64. The 1998 memorandum mistakenly misspells Mr. Miskin's name as "Misten" and "Mistin."

310 LGT report on Micronesia Foundation subsequent to 9/17/98, Bates No. PSI-USMSTR-6660.

311 Montecito is a city in Santa Barbara County, California. The property is referred to in various documents as located in Montecito or Santa Barbara.

312 See Miskin Property Dispute in California, Supporting Declaration of David Anfossi (3/6/03) (stating that Mr. Anfossi and Douglas M. Tufts are the trustees of the Bonnymead Trust, sole shareholders and directors of Belmont Assets Ltd., and confirming the facts related to the purchase of the Seaview Property).

313 Miskin Property Dispute in California, Declaration of Michael Miskin in Support of Motion to Quash Service of Summons and Dismiss Action (8/1/03), at ¶¶ 4-5.

314 See, e.g., "Tax Haven Abuses: The Enablers, the Tools and Secrecy," before the Permanent Subcommittee on Investigations (8/1/06), S. Hrg. 109-797, at 218 (case history involving Kurt Greaves who was made a "business consultant" to companies he secretly controlled).

315 See "Deed of Appointment of Beneficiary" for the Bonnymead Trust (11/5/02).

316 Subcommittee interview of Douglas M. Tufts (7/7/08).

317 Order, *Miskin v. Miskin,* High Court of Justice, Family Division (7/31/03).

318 Subcommittee interview with Douglas M. Tufts (7/7/08).

319 LGT memorandum regarding a new establishment for Mr. Miskin (6/30/98), Bates Nos. PSI-USMSTR-6663-64.

320 LGT documents often refer to Liechtenstein as "FL," an abbreviation of the nation's local name "Fuerstentum Liechtenstein."

321 A later LGT document describes it as a "real-estate company (England)." LGT Background Information/Profile for Micronesia Foundation (12/13/01), Bates No. PSI-USMSTR-6666.

322 While this LGT memo indicates the funds were transferred through UBS Geneva, documents obtained by the Subcommittee appear to show that funds were transferred through Citibank Geneva.

[323] The Subcommittee reviewed documents which independently confirm Mr. Miskin' s transfer of $1 million from his wife's account to Citibank in Geneva and from there to Liechtensteinische Landesbank in Vaduz. These documents were made part of a court filing in London. They include a 1991 letter from Mr. Miskin's personal secretary to a private banker at Brown Shipley & Co. Ltd. in London, where the Miskins held accounts:
"Following your telephone conversation with Mr. Miskin today, I would confirm that the deposit in the sum of £1,000,000.00 deposited in Mrs S.A. Miskin's name for tax purposes, should have reverted to the name of Mr M Miskin on 30th November 1990. This, obviously, has not taken place due to an oversight and I would confirm that this deposit should have been changed into the name of Mr M Miskin as of today."
Letter to Brown Shipley & Co. Ltd. (5/13/91), Bates No. 51 (handwritten). A Brown Shipley letter stated that it had dealt only with Mr. Miskin, believed that he was the "ultimate beneficiary of all funds placed with us," and transferred the funds at his request to Citibank. Letter from Brown Shipley to Forsyte Kerman Solicitors (7/29/9 1), Bates No. 57 (handwritten). On June 27, 1991, Mr. Miskin transferred more than £3.7 million from Brown Shipley, including the funds formerly held in Mrs. Miskin's name, to Citibank (Switzerland), Geneva Branch. On July 30, 1991, Citibank (Switzerland) transferred more than £3.4 million and $400,000 to Liechtensteinische Landesbank in Vaduz. See letter from Citibank (Switzerland) to Lenz & Staehelin (8/28/91), Bates Nos. 62-64 (handwritten). This series of funding transfers came to light after a U.K. court had issued an "Injunction Prohibiting Disposal of Assets Worldwide," (1/24/03), to prevent Mr. Miskin from disposing of the marital assets. In response to a request from the U.K. court, the District Court of Zurich ordered Citibank to provide Mrs. Miskin with information about the transfers, resulting in the August 1991 letter by Citibank.

[324] See LGT receipt for deposit of about £3.65 million or about $6.2 million, (10/21/98), Bates No. PSI-USMSTR6656 (showing Mr. Miskin with a California address).

[325] Letter of Wishes for the Micronesia Foundation, (7/28/00), Bates Nos. PSI-USMSTR-6653-54.

[326] Email from Mr. Miskin to Peter Meier of LGT regarding "That Taxing Problem," (1/19/00), Bates No. PSIUSMSTR-6658.

[327] Fax from Mr. Miskin to LGT contact Alouis Beck (7/25/01), Bates No. PSI-USMSTR-6655.

[328] "G"may refer to Guernsey where the trust and corporation holding the Seaview Property were domiciled.

[329] Fax from "MMMag. Thomas Lungkofler" to Mr. Miskin (2/27/02), Bates No. PSI-USMSTR-6657.

[330] Ms. Miskin had first initiated divorce proceedings in 1991, but then reconciled with Mr. Miskin. On this occasion, she filed for divorce on January 13, 2003. See Miskin Property Dispute in California, Declaration of Stephanie Avril Miskin in Opposition to Motion to Expunge Lis Pendens (4/4/03), at ¶ 1.

[331] ee Order, *Miskin v. Miskin,* High Court of Justice, Family Division (7/31/03).

[332] See id.; Subcommittee interview with Judith Bloom (5/5/08).

[333] See LGT Background Information/Profile for Micronesia Foundation, (12/13/01), Bates No. PSI-USMSTR-6666.

[334] "Order," *Miskin v. Miskin,* High Court of Justice, Family Division (7/31/03). See also Miskin Property Dispute in California, Opposition to Motion to Quash (8/29/03), at 2.

[335] See also LGT documents, "Impact of new US withholding tax regulations on non-US entities," Bates Nos. LGT 1-4; "Declaration of Non-US Status," Bates Nos. LGT 5-8; "Tax form US withholding tax/private individuals," Bates No. LGT 9-10.

[336] "Qualified Intermediary External Auditor's Report for the Year 2006," Bates No. LGT 136-187, at 136.

[337] Id. at LGT 179.

[338] Subcommittee interview of Ivo Klein, Head of LGT Group Compliance (7/11/08).

[339] LGT report on Sera Financial Corporation (undated), Bates Nos. PSI-USMSTR-6553-4. The document notes that Sera Financial was established on December 15, 1997, and that the "share certificate" for Sera Financial was held "in the depository account of BTS Management Ltd. at LGT Bank in Lichetenstein AG, Vaduz (since Apr 9, 1999)."

[340] Id.

[341] Id.

[342] LGT Memorandum "New Registration," (11/2/00), Bates Nos. PSI-USMSTR-7696-97, at 7697.

[343] Gotthard Bank wire transfer instruction for $1.2 million transaction (10/31/00), Bates No. PSI-USMSTR 7680.

[344] "Vereinbarung [Agreement]," (6/21/00), Bates Nos. PSI-USMSTR-7935-36. See also LGT account summary, "Jaffra Development Inc.," Bates No. PSI-USMSTR-7934 (describing Jaffra as a "single purpose corporation").

[345] "Aktenvermerk [Memorandum for the Record], Luperla Foundation, (5/2/97), Bates Nos. PSI-USMSTR-5293-94. See also letter from J.H. Gelbard to LGT re "Formation of a Foundation by the name Luperla Foundation," (3/12/97), Bates No. PSI-USMSTR-8860-61 (describing the corporation to be established as a "transfer company").

[346] Sewell, however, was not immediately dissolved, but was apparently used for additional pass-through transactions for Luperla in October 1997. It was apparently dissolved in 1998. See LGT memorandum re "Luperla Stiftung / Sewell Services Ltd. B.V.I.," (10/23/97), Bates No. PSI-USMSTR-8896; see also LGT report on Luperla Foundation (undated, subsequent to 4/2/0 1) (noting that Sewell was deleted from the registry in the British Virgin Islands on 11/1/98).

[347] LGT report on Tissit Invest and Trade Inc. (undated, subsequent to its establishment in January 2001), Bates Nos. PSI-USMSTR-8004-8005.

[348] Id.

[349] LGT Note re "New Establishment of LRAB Foundation, Vaduz," (9/13/02), Bates No. PSI-USMSTR 8555 (emphasis added).

[350] Subcommittee interview of Ivo Klein, head of LGT Group Compliance (7/11/08).

[351] See "Press Release from the (Liechtenstein) Office of the Public Prosecutor," (2/27/08), available at www.liechtenstein.li/en/pdf-fl-med-aktuell-staatsanwaltschaft1.pdf (viewed 7/14/08); Press Release by the Liechteinstein Police, (3/11/08), available at http://www. landespolizei.li/News/Pressemitteilungen/tabid/850/articleType/ArticleView/articleId/263/ffentlicheFahndung-nach-Heinrich-KIEBER.aspx (viewed 7/14/08); "Liechtenstein Prince Defends Bank Secrecy as Scandal Threatens Country's Haven Status," Daily Tax Report, International Tax and Accounting (2/22/08), No. ISSN 0092- 6884, at 1; Mark Landler, "Liechtenstein issues international arrest warrant for tax informant," (3/12/08), International Herald Tribune.

[352] See www.eugen-von-hoffen.com (viewed 7/13/08).

[353] "Facts&Figures," (undated) available at www.ubs.com (viewed 5/28/08).

[354] "The Making of UBS," (undated) at 16, available at www.ubs.com (viewed 5/28/08).

[355] "Facts&Figures," (undated) available at www.ubs.com (viewed 5/28/08).

[356] UBS Annual Report 2007, Financial Statements, at 167.

[357] Id. at 25, 96-99.

[358] "Organizational Structure," (undated) available at www.ubs.com (viewed 5/28/08).

[359] UBS Annual Report 2007, Financial Statements, at 41.

[360] "Global Wealth Management & Business Banking," (undated), organizational chart available at www.ubs.com (viewed 5/28/08). These five regional segments were established in a reorganization that took effect in 2007. Prior to that reorganization, the Global Wealth Management & Business Banking division had just three segments: Wealth Management US, Wealth Management International & Switzerland, and Business Banking Switzerland. UBS Annual Report 2007, Financial Statements, at 41.

[361] UBS Annual Report 2007, Financial Statements, at 96-99; Strategy, Performance and Responsibility, at 104.

[362] UBS Annual Report 2007, Financial Statements, at 41. Wealth Management US is now included within Wealth Management Americas.

[363] Subcommittee interview of UBS, represented by outside legal counsel (6/19/08).

[364] Id.; "Organizational changes NAM," powerpoint presentation by Michel Guignard, of UBS private banking in Switzerland (5/10/05), at 4-6.

[365] Bates No. UPSI 49952.

[366] Subcommittee interview of UBS, represented by outside legal counsel (6/19/08).

[367] Birkenfeld deposition (10/11/07), at 14. Prior to UBS, he worked for private banking operations in Geneva at Credit Suisse and Barclays Bank.

[368] *United States v. Birkenfeld.*

[369] Subcommittee interview with UBS (7/14/08).

[370] Key Clients in NAM [North America]: Business Case 2003-2005, (undated), at 26 (chart entitled, "Assessment of Current KC [Key Client] Base).

[371] Id.

[372] See, e.g., email from Martin Liechti re "Happy New Year" (undated) (stating UBS Swiss client advisors had quadrupled their intake of net new money into Switzerland from 4 million Swiss francs per client advisor in 2004 to 16 million Swiss francs per client advisor in 2006).

[373] See "BS North America Report: Overview Figures North America," prepared in July, August, September, October, November, and December 2004, and January, February, March, August, September, and October 2005. These reports appear to be excerpts from larger reports. These documents, on their face, present data for Swiss accounts opened for U.S. and Canadian clients. According to UBS, however, it is possible that the data may include some Swiss accounts opened for persons from other countries.

[374] The 2004 monthly reports, for example, show data for "W9" accounts and "NON W9" accounts, which correspond to declared and undeclared accounts. The March 2005 report provides data for "W9" accounts and "SFA" accounts, which at that time corresponded to the declared accounts, as well as data for "NON W9" accounts, which corresponded to the undeclared accounts. "SFA" refers to Swiss Financial Advisors, the UBS subsidiary in Switzerland that is a registered U.S. broker-dealer, opens securities accounts only for U.S. clients who submit W-9 forms, and reports all such accounts to the IRS. Mr. Birkenfeld told the Subcommittee that SFA was referred to within UBS as "'the declared desk.'" Birkenfeld deposition at 84. He also explained that all Swiss bankers who formerly had declared accounts had been required to transfer them to SFA. Id. at 85. That meant U.S. clients in Switzerland with accounts outside of SFA were necessarily undeclared accounts. Reports later in 2005 use different terminology again, providing data for "US International" accounts, which correspond to the undeclared accounts, and data for a "W9 Business Row" and SFA accounts, which correspond to the declared accounts.

[375] Id. The 18 billion figure is derived from the amount shown for "US International" (18.5 billion) after subtracting the amount shown for "W9 Business Row" (0.5 billion). The Subcommittee also asked UBS to produce similar data for 2006 and 2007, but has yet to receive it.

[376] Id. The 2.6 billion figure is derived from adding together the figures shown for "W9 Business Row" (0.5 billion) and "SFA" (2.1 billion).

[377] The 1 billion figure is derived from the amount shown for "US International" (1.054 billion) after eliminating the loss shown for "W9 Business Row" (loss of 309.8 million), resulting in NNM of about 1.364 billion.

[378] The 333 million figure is derived from adding together the figures shown for "W9 Business Row" (loss of 309.8 million) and "SFA" (loss of 23.8 million).

[379] The 180.9 million figure is derived from the amount shown for "US International" (194.3 million) after subtracting the amount shown for "W9 Business Row" (13.4 million).

[380] The 22.1 million figure is reached by adding together the figures shown for "W9 Business Row" (13.4 million) and "SFA" (8.7 million).

[381] LGT presentation entitled, "North America Meeting[:] Update U.S. NewCo (W9)," (9/15/04), Bates Nos. UPSI 49907-27, at 17-18.

[382] Birkenfeld deposition (10/11/07), at 28.

[383] *United States v. Birkenfeld,* Statement of Facts, at 3.

[384] UBS letter addressed to "Dear client" (11/4/02).

[385] Subcommittee interview of UBS, represented by outside legal counsel (6/19/08).

[386] Subcommittee interview of UBS, represented by outside legal counsel (6/19/08).

[387] *United States v. Birkenfeld,* Statement of Facts, at 3.

[388] Id.

[389] See, e.g., Section 15(a)(1) of the Exchange Act, 15 U.S.C. § 78o(a)(1):

"(a) Registration of all persons utilizing exchange facilities to effect transactions; exemptions.

(1) It shall be unlawful for any broker or dealer which is either a person other than a natural person or a natural person not associated with a broker or dealer which is a person other than a natural person (other than such a broker or dealer whose business is exclusively intrastate and who does not make use of any facility of a national securities exchange) to make use of the mails or any means or instrumentality of interstate commerce to effect any transactions in, or to induce or attempt to induce the purchase or sale of, any security (other than an exempted security or commercial paper, bankers' acceptances, or commercial bills) unless such broker or dealer is registered in accordance with subsection (b) of this section."

[390] UBS makes this statement in its 2004 policy statement. See "Cross-Border Banking Activities into the United States **(version November 2004)**," prepared by UBS, Bates Nos. PSI-OPB 103-105, at 103 (emphasis in original).

[391] See, e.g., "U.S. Tax and Reporting Obligations for Foreign Intermediaries' Non-U.S. Securities," 47 Tax Notes Int'l 913 (9/3/07).

[392] See "Wealth Management and Business Banking Client Advisor's Guidelines for Implementation and Management of Discretionary Asset Management Relationship with U.S. Clients," (undated but likely late

2001). See also UBS letter to Mr. Birkenfeld (3/17/06), Bates Nos. PSI-OPB 84-85, at 1 ("[T]he rules which set forth UBS approach to servicing US resident clients have been posted on the UBS-intranet already since early 2002.").

[393] See "Cross-Border Banking Activities into the United States **(version November 2004)**," prepared by UBS, Bates Nos. PSI-OPB, at 103-105 (emphasis in original).

[394] Id.

[395] Id.

[396] Id.

[397] Id. at 103-104.

[398] Birkenfeld deposition, (10/11/07), at 105.

[399] Id. at 106.

[400] See UBS letter to Mr. Birkenfeld (3/17/06), Bates Nos. PSI-OPB 84-85, at 84 (stating Mr. Birkenfeld had been informed of the restrictions during two training sessions in September 2004).

[401] Subcommittee interview of UBS, represented by outside legal counsel (6/19/08).

[402] Chart entitled, "Action Plan 2003 for Country Team," (undated).

[403] "Organizational changes NAM," Powerpoint presentation by Michel Guignard of UBS private banking in Switzerland (5/10/05), at 7.

[404] Birkenfeld deposition (10/11/07), at 46, 47-48. Mr. Birkenfeld clarified during the deposition that the numbers he gave referred to "just the bankers" at the three Swiss offices.

[405] "KeyClients in NAM: Business Case 2003-2005," prepared by UBS Wealth Management (undated), at 38-39. "NAM" refers to UBS' North American division within its private banking operations in Switzerland.

[406] Id. at 40.

[407] Id. at 36-37.

[408] Subcommittee interview of UBS, represented by outside legal counsel (6/19/08).

[409] Id. See also Birkenfeld deposition before the Subcommittee (10/11/07), at 157. For more information about this IRS initiative, see the IRS website at www.irs.gov.

[410] See, e.g., UBS internal memorandum addressed to "Colleagues" regarding "Changes in business model for U.S. private clients," (11/15/08).

[411] To find likely UBS client advisors – as opposed to persons whose names coincidentally matched those persons identified to the Subcommittee as UBS personnel – the analysis eliminated all persons from the sample born after a given date who would be too young to be likely candidates. The data was then sorted by date traveled and the ports of entry used, to identify persons traveling at the same time to the same location. This data enabled the Subcommittee to identify UBS client advisors who, for example, made visits to Miami during the dates of the Art Basel event. The Subcommittee chose to eliminate from the analysis persons who did not appear to have a traveling correlation with other known UBS bankers or a link to a UBS event such as Art Basel, as well as persons with similar names to known UBS personnel but who reported different birthdays. The resulting figures, thus, represent a conservative analysis of the number of trips made by UBS Swiss personnel to the United States over the last seven years. The Subcommittee would like to express its appreciation for the assistance rendered by the U.S. Department of Homeland Security in securing, compiling, and analyzing this travel data.

[412] See Arrival-Departure Record, CBP Form I-94, for Nonimmigrant Visitors with a Visa for the United States, discussed in the website of the Customs and Border Patrol, at www.cbp.gov.

[413] Birkenfeld deposition at 20, 23.

[414] Id. at 22.

[415] See, e.g., "BS North America Report: Overview Figures North America," prepared by UBS (July 2004) (providing data on NNM, ROA, and other performance measures for 2004 and 2005); "UBS Management Summary Report-Graphs" (YTD [Year To Date] October 2002) (providing ROA and NNM data for Swiss offices dealing with U.S. clients).

[416] Letter entitled, "Referral Campain BU Americas," from UBS private banking head Martin Liechti to his "Colleagues," (6/2/03), apparently printed in an internal UBS publication, "PB Americas International News."

[417] Email from Martin Liechti re "Happy New Year" (undated).

[418] "KeyClients in NAM: Business Case 2003-2005," at 4.

[419] Id. at 5.

[420] Birkenfeld deposition at 46.

[421] Id. at 76.

[422] Id. at 121.
[423] Id. at 71.
[424] Id. at 33.
[425] Id. at 151.
[426] Birkenfeld deposition at 76.
[427] Id. at 76-77.
[428] Id. at 61.
[429] Id. at 61.
[430] Id. at 55.
[431] Id. at 121-122.
[432] Id. at 56-57.
[433] Id. at 55. See also reference to TAS in UBS Minutes of a May 2003 meeting of the Geneva Private Bank North America International group (5/14/03) at 1.
[434] "Cross-Border Banking Activities into the United States (version November 2004)" at 104.
[435] Birkenfeld deposition, at 158. See also UBS Minutes of a May 2003 meeting of the Geneva Private Bank North America International group (5/14/03) at 2 ("Do not indicate Wealth Management but only UBS AG on the new business cards").
[436] Birkenfeld deposition, at 166.
[437] Case Studies Cross-Border Workshop NAM, (undated) (emphasis in original).
[438] Birkenfeld deposition, at 247.
[439] Id. at 251.
[440] Birkenfeld Statement of Facts, at 3.
[441] Id. at 4.
[442] Id.
[443] See "Wealth Management and Business Banking Client Advisor's Guidelines for Implementation and Management of Discretionary Asset Management Relationship with U.S. Clients," (undated but likely late 2001); "Cross-Border Banking Activities into the United States **(version November 2004)**," prepared by UBS, Bates Nos. PSI-OPB, at 103-105 (emphasis in original).
[444] Birkenfeld deposition at 114.
[445] Id. at 115, 125.
[446] Id. at 111.
[447] Id. at 60.
[448] Id. at 63-64.
[449] Id. at 61.
[450] Mr. Birkenfeld told the Subcommittee that he was not even aware of the restrictions until May 2005, when a colleague showed him the 2004 policy statement on an internal UBS computer system. He said that after being shown the 2004 policy statement, he sent emails, in June 2005, to the UBS legal and compliance divisions asking about the contradiction between the policy statement and his day-to-day activities. He provided copies of these emails, which he said were never responded to in writing. Birkenfeld deposition, at 108-109, 125-26. He told the Subcommittee that he also brought the issue to the attention of his immediate supervisor whom he said, "yelled at me and said, 'Why are you getting everyone riled up?'" Id. at 126-127. He testified that he then brought the 2004 policy statement to two outside law firms, both of which advised him to resign. Id. at 127. Mr. Birkenfeld resigned from UBS in October 2005.
[451] See "Restrictions on Cross-Border Banking and Financial Services Activities: Country Paper USA (Effective Date June, 1st, 2007)," (otherwise undated).
[452] Id. at 4.
[453] Id. at 8.
[454] Id. at 5, 6 (emphasis in original).
[455] See, e.g., UBS internal memorandum addressed to "Colleagues" regarding "Changes in business model for U.S. private clients," (11/15/08).
[456] Id. at 1.
[457] Id.
[458] UBS prepared document with the heading, "Privileged and Confidential: Letters to Existing U.S. Clients with More than CHF 50,000 Who have Not been Informed Orally either to Retained Mail or Send to Non-U.S.

Address," (undated but likely in or after November 2007) (heading using all capital letters converted to initial capital format) (apparent form letter providing guidance to U.S. clients on the November 2007 policy).

[459] UBS prepared document with the heading, "Talking Points for Informing U.S. Private Clients with Securities Holdings about the Realignment of our Business Model Plus Q&A," (undated but likely in or after November 2007)(heading using all capital letters converted to initial capital format).

[460] Id. at 3.

[461] Id. at 1-2.

[462] Subcommittee interview of UBS, represented by outside legal counsel (6/19/08).

[463] See pleadings in *United States v. Olenicoff,* Case No. SA CR No. 07-227-CJC (C.D. Cal.) (hereinafter *"United States v. Olenicoff");* and *United States v. Birkenfeld.*

[464] *United States v. Olenicoff,* Plea Agreement for Defendant Igor M. Olenicoff (12/10/07) (hereinafter Olenicoff Plea Agreement), at 4.

[465] Id.

[466] See "California Real Estate Developer Sentenced for Filing a False Tax Return and Failure to Disclose Foreign Bank Accounts to IRS," in "Examples of General Tax Fraud Investigations FY2008," Internal Revenue Service, http://www.irs.gov/compliance/ enforcement/article/0,,id=174630,00.html (viewed 7/14/08).

[467] Birkenfeld Statement of Facts.

[468] According to Mr. Birkenfeld, Mr. Olenicoff had been a client at Barclays Bank in the Bahamas. Mr. Birkenfeld was then working for Barclays Bank in Switzerland. He said that, after joining the QI Program in 2001, Barclays decided to close all of its Bahamas accounts with U.S. clients, including Mr. Olenicoff. Mr. Birkenfeld said that the Barclays account manager in the Bahamas telephoned him to see if the Swiss office could accept the Olenicoff account. Mr. Birkenfeld said that he was then in the process of changing jobs from Barclays to UBS. Birkenfeld Deposition at 206-209.

[469] Birkenfeld deposition at 206-209; email from Mr. Birkenld to Mr. Olenicoff and his son (7/26/01), Bates No. SW 67087.

[470] See, e.g., email from Mr. Olenicoff to Mr. Birkenfeld (10/11/01), Bates Nos. SW 66660-61.

[471] Olenicoff Plea Agreement, at 4; Birkenfeld Statement of Facts, at 5; handwritten note from Mr. Birkenfeld (undated), Bates No. SW 67527; letter from McKinney, Bancroft & Hughes of the Bahamas to Mr. Olenicoff (10/17/01), Bates No. SW 17013.

[472] Letter from Mr. Olenicoff to Mr. Birkenfeld, (10/23/01), Bates No. SW 66645.

[473] UBS Verification of the beneficial owner's identity, signed by Mr. Olenicoff and his son, (10/23/01), Bates No. SW66648. Another document identified Mr. Olenicoff as GGC's president and his son as GGC's secretary. UBS Authorized signatories (10/23/0 1), Bates No. SW 66649.

[474] UBS Authorized signatories (10/23/01), Bates No. SW 66649.

[475] UBS waiver of right to invest in U.S. securities, signed by Mr. Olenicoff and his son (10/23/01), Bates No. SW 66652.

[476] Olenicoff Plea Agreement, at 4.

[477] See email from Mr. Olenicoff to Mr. Staggl, (12/1/01), Bates No. SW 65109 ("we all enjoyed our stay in your beautiful country").

[478] Email from Mr. Staggle to Mr. Olenicoff re "Various," (12/4/01), Bates No. SW 65110.

[479] Id. See also Birkenfeld Statement of Facts, at 5.

[480] Email from Mr. Olenicoff to Mr. Staggl re "Structure Discussion," (12/8/0 1), Bates No. SW 65111.

[481] Email from Mr. Staggl to Mr. Olenicoff re "Structure," (Jan. 2002), Bates No. SW 67200.

[482] Birkenfeld Statement of Facts at 5.

[483] Email from Mr. Olenicoff to Mr. Staggl re "Structure," (1/8/02), Bates No. SW 65103. See also Danish Commerce and Companies Agency Extract for New Guardian Bancorp ApS, (1/18/02), Bates No. SW66922.

[484] See, e.g., email from Mr. Olenicoff to Mr. Birkenfeld authorizing transfer, (12/27/0 1), Bates No. SW 67081.

[485] UBS Verification of beneficial owner's identity, (1/22/02), Bates No. SW 66974.

[486] UBS Waiver of right to invest in US securities, (1/22/02), Bates No. SW 66977.

[487] UBS Supplement for new Account US Status: Assets and Income/Declaration for US Taxable Persons, (undated but likely 1/22/02), Bates No. SW 66982.

[488] Email from Mr. Staggl to Mr. Birkenfeld and Mr. Olenicoff re "New Guardian – Status," (3/7/02), Bates No. SW 67196.

[489] Email from Mr. Staggl to Mr. Olenicoff re "Smith Barney Transfer," (4/23/02), Bates No. SW 65120; Email from Mr. Olenicoff to Mr. Staggle re "Smith Barney Transfer," (4/25/02); Bates No. SW 67331.

[490] Olenicoff Plea Agreement, at 4-5.

[491] See, e.g., letter from Mr. Olenicoff to Mr. Birkenfeld, (4/6/02), Bates No. SW 66782; Letter from Andrei Olenicoff to Mr. Birkenfeld, (9/3/02), Bates No. SW 67659.

[492] See, e.g., email from Mr. Staggl to Mr. Olenicoff, with copy to Mr. Birkenfeld, (6/8/04), Bates No. SW 16153; letter from Andrei Olenicoff to Mr. Staggl, (undated), Bates Nos. 67934-37).

[493] Birkenfeld Statement of Facts, at 5; Letter from Mr. Olenicoff to Mr. Birkenfeld, (3/25/02), Bates No. SW 66783 (authorizing $100,000 to be transferred to a new UBS account to allow "issuance of the five credit cards we discussed"); letter from Mr. Olenicoff to Mr. Birkenfeld, (4/6/02), Bates No. SW 66782 (cancelling the five credit cards two weeks later).

[494] Birkenfeld Deposition, at 209.

[495] Birkenfeld Statement of Facts at 6; Birkenfeld deposition at 209-210.

In: Tax Haven Banks
Editor: Wade D. Brookins

ISBN: 978-1-60692-283-5

Chapter 2

PERMANENT SUBCOMMITTEE ON INVESTIGATIONS ISSUES REPORT ON TAX HAVEN BANKS HIDING BILLIONS FROM THE IRS

Carl Levin

REPORT: TAX HAVEN BANKS AND U.S. TAX COMPLIANCE

WASHINGTON – At a Thursday hearing entitled, **Tax Haven Banks and U.S. Tax Compliance**, the latest in a series of hearings with insider information about the workings of the offshore industry, the Senate Permanent Subcommittee on Investigations will examine how tax haven banks facilitate tax evasion by U.S. clients, hide client and bank misconduct behind the cloak of bank secrecy laws, and add to the offshore abuses that cost U.S. taxpayers an estimated $100 billion dollars each year.

A six month-long bipartisan Subcommittee investigation examined LGT Bank in Liechtenstein and UBS in Switzerland to expose how tax haven banks are assisting U.S. taxpayers to evade taxes, in particular by urging U.S. clients to open accounts in their offshore jurisdictions, assisting them in structuring those accounts to avoid disclosure to U. S. authorities, and providing financial services in ways that do not alert U.S. authorities to the existence of the foreign accounts. Subcommittee Chairman Sen. Carl Levin (D-Mich.) and Ranking Minority Member Norm Coleman (R-Minn.) will release a **115-page joint staff report [PDF]** detailing the findings of the investigation in conjunction with the hearing.

"Tax havens are engaged in economic warfare against the United States, and the honest, hardworking American taxpayer is losing," said Levin. "The iron ring of secrecy around tax haven banks and their deceptive banking practices enable and encourage tax cheats to hide assets from the United States. Congress needs to enact strong penalties on tax haven banks that help U.S. taxpayers avoid paying taxes to Uncle Sam."

Senator Coleman said, "It is simply unacceptable that some individuals are using offshore tax havens and secrecy jurisdictions to shelter trillions of dollars from taxation, forcing working families to shoulder the tax burden. By exploiting gaping loopholes, these foreign banks are enabling felony tax evasion. Simply put, foreign banks should not be Al Capone safe-houses for evading taxes. Closing these loopholes means we must strengthen reporting requirements, broaden the scope of the audit program, and extend the amount of time the IRS has to investigate cases involving an offshore tax haven."

Exposing a trove of internal bank documents and interviews with bank insiders, the Subcommittee report shines a spotlight into the murky operations of two high-profile tax haven banks. Eight case studies expose bank practices that could facilitate, and have resulted in, tax evasion by U.S. clients:

1. **Marsh.** The Marshes of Ft. Lauderdale, Florida, hid $49 million in four Liechtenstein foundations over 20 years.
2. Wu. LGT helped William Wu hide ownership of assets, including his house in Forest Hills, New York, using an elaborate offshore structure.
3. **Lowy.** LGT used transfer companies and a foundation with a Delaware corporation to help the Lowys hide their beneficial interest in a foundation with $68 million in assets.
4. **Greenfield.** LGT private bankers, including Prince Philipp of Liechtenstein, met with Mr. Greenfield and his father to pitch the transfer of $30 million from Bank of Bermuda to LGT.
5. **Gonzalez.** LGT helped a Gonzalez car dealership inflate invoices, move funds offshore and, after getting sued for their pricing practices, hide assets in case of a court judgment.
6. **Chong.** LGT helped Richard Chong use hidden accounts to move millions of dollars related to his business ventures, routing them through an offshore corporation to avoid scrutiny.
7. **Miskin.** LGT helped Michael Miskin hide assets from courts, tax authorities, and his wife.
8. **Olenicoff.** Bradley Birkenfeld, a private banker employed by UBS AG, pleaded guilty last month to conspiring with a U.S. citizen, Igor Olenicoff, to defraud the IRS of $7.2 million in taxes owed on $200 million of assets hidden in Switzerland and Liechtenstein.

In reviewing these case histories, the investigation found: (1) bank secrecy laws and practices are serving as a cloak, not only for client misconduct, but also for misconduct by banks colluding with clients to evade taxes, dodge creditors, and defy court orders; (2) from at least 2000 to 2007, LGT and UBS employed banking practices that could facilitate, and have resulted in, tax evasion by their U.S. clients, including assisting clients to open accounts in the names of offshore entities; advising clients on complex offshore structures to hide ownership of assets; using client code names; and disguising asset transfers into and from accounts; (3) since 2001, LGT and UBS have collectively maintained thousands of U.S. client accounts with billions of dollars in assets that have not been disclosed to the IRS; UBS alone has an estimated 19,000 accounts in Switzerland for U.S. clients with assets valued at $18 billion, and the IRS has identified at least 100 U.S. taxpayers with accounts at LGT; and (4) LGT and UBS have assisted their U.S. clients in structuring their foreign accounts to avoid QI reporting to the IRS, including by allowing U.S. clients who sold their U.S. securities to continue to hold undisclosed accounts, and by opening accounts in the name of non-U.S. entities beneficially owned by U.S. clients; while these banking practices did not technically violate the banks' Qualified Intermediaryagreements with the IRS, the result is that the banks helped keep accounts secret from the IRS and thereby facilitated tax evasion by their U.S. clients.

Reforms recommended by the Levin-Coleman report to reign in tax haven abuses include the following:

1. **Strengthen QI Reporting of Foreign Accounts Held by U.S. Persons.** In addition to prosecuting misconduct under existing law, the Administration should strengthen the Qualified Intermediary Agreements by requiring QI participants to file 1099 forms for: (1) all U.S. persons who are clients (whether or not the client has U.S. securities or receives U. S. source income); and (2) accounts beneficially owned by U.S. persons, even if the accounts are held in the name of a foreign corporation, trust, foundation, or other entity. The IRS should also close the "QI-KYC Gap" by expressly requiring QI participants to apply to their QI reporting obligations all information obtained through their Know-YourCustomer procedures to identify the beneficial owners of accounts.
2. **Strengthen 1099 Reporting.** Congress should strengthen the statutory 1099 reporting requirements by requiring any domestic or foreign financial institution that obtains information that the beneficial owner of a foreign-owned financial account is a U.S. taxpayer to file a 1099 form reporting that account to the IRS.
3. **Strengthen QI Audits.** The IRS should broaden QI audits to require bank auditors to report evidence of fraudulent or illegal activity.
4. **Penalize Tax Haven Banks that Impede U.S. Tax Enforcement.** Treasury should penalize tax haven banks that impede U.S. tax enforcement or fail to disclose accounts held directly or indirectly by U.S. clients by terminating their QI status, and Congress should amend Section 311 of the Patriot Act to allow Treasury to bar such banks from doing business with U.S. financial institutions.

This hearing and report follow other investigations into offshore abuses by the Subcommittee. Hearings held by the Subcommittee in 2001 examined the historic and ongoing lack of cooperation by some offshore tax havens with international tax enforcement efforts and their resistance to divulging information needed to detect, stop and prosecute U.S. tax evasion. A hearing held in December 2002 and report issued in January 2003 provided an in-depth examination of an abusive tax shelter used by Enron. Two days of hearings in November 2003, and a bipartisan report issued in 2005, provided an inside look at how some respected accounting firms, banks, investment advisors, and lawyers had become engines pushing the design, sale, and implementation of abusive tax shelters to corporations and individuals across the country. In August 2006, a hearing and report examined six case studies illustrating the operation of the offshore tax industry, its service providers and clients, and how tax haven abuses are undermining, circumventing, or violating U.S. tax, securities, and anti-money laundering laws.

In: Tax Haven Banks
Editor: Wade D. Brookins

ISBN: 978-1-60692-283-5

Chapter 3

WRITTEN TESTIMONY OF DOUGLAS SHULMAN (INTERNAL REVENUE) BEFORE THE SENATE COMMITTEE ON HOMELAND SECURITY AND GOVERNMENTAL AFFAIRS' PERMANENT SUBCOMMITTEE ON INVESTIGATIONS HEARING ON TAX HAVEN FINANCIAL INSTITUTIONS: THEIR FORMATION AND ADMINISTRATION OF OFFSHORE ENTITIES AND ACCOUNTS FOR USE BY U.S. CLIENTS

JULY 17, 2008

Good morning Chairman Levin, Ranking Member Coleman and members of the Subcommittee. Thank you for the opportunity to appear before you today to discuss an issue of critical importance to tax administration in this country – the practice of sheltering U.S. earned income in foreign jurisdictions as a means of avoiding U.S. taxation.

This is my first opportunity to appear before the Subcommittee, but I have met with many of you privately. Let me reiterate to the entire Subcommittee what I have told those of you with whom I have met. This Subcommittee has a long and impressive history of investigating tax havens and offshore abuses that undermine the integrity of the Federal tax system and potentially divert billions of dollars from the United States Treasury. I am pleased to be here this morning to assist you in your latest efforts to examine offshore abuses.

I have made international issues a top priority for the IRS for my five-year tenure as Commissioner. There are a number of activities and initiatives underway, and more in the works, at the IRS to help ensure that we are adapting to the global economy. In some cases, this involves proactive dialogue with foreign tax administrators and multinational enterprises.

But the focus of my testimony today will be on some broader themes and more specific examples of the IRS' investigative activities where U.S. citizens are unlawfully hiding assets and associated income overseas. As you will hear, the IRS has significantly stepped up its efforts in this area, both in civil and criminal investigations. We are using a number of innovative techniques to root out noncompliance, as I will explain further. And, while I am limited in the detail that I can share about ongoing investigations, I am pleased with the early successes that we are having at systematically pursuing unlawful off-shore schemes.

ONGOING IRS INVESTIGATIONS

Let me start by laying out some of the facts that I am able to discuss regarding a specific case, because the case that I am about to describe is a matter of public record. It involves a major Swiss bank.

In 2001, the bank signed a disclosure agreement with the U.S. to become a qualified intermediary (QI). This, among other things, required the bank to report on the income of U.S. taxpayers that were clients of the bank. However, a former employee of the bank, as part of his June 19, 2008 guilty plea to assisting a wealthy real estate developer in evading $7.2 million in Federal income taxes by concealing $200 million of assets in Switzerland and Liechtenstein, stated that a number of the bank's clients objected to such reporting.

The IRS has since requested, via a so-called John Doe summons, that a Swiss bank turn over account information on any U.S. clients who may have used Swiss bank accounts to avoid U.S. income taxes. The summons directs the bank to produce records identifying U.S. taxpayers who had accounts with the bank in Switzerland between 2002 and 2007 and elected to have their accounts remain hidden from the IRS.

On July 1st a federal judge in Miami approved a Justice Department request to enable the IRS to serve the summons. We are working closely with the Justice Department to ensure that we get the information requested in the summons.

Accordingly, the IRS is exploring our options on how to bring a potentially large number of U.S. taxpayer cases to resolution.

Another recent example relates to U.S. citizens with accounts in Liechtenstein. To date, the IRS has initiated enforcement action involving close to 200 taxpayers with accounts in this jurisdiction. Because these are ongoing investigations that are not a matter of public record, I cannot go into great detail on these matters. At the highest level, we are again looking at circumstances where U.S. citizens have systematically avoided reporting income from foreign trusts.

PATTERNS OF EVASIVE ACTIVITIES

In the cases that we have seen around the world, I want to highlight a few patterns of behavior that we have uncovered in our investigations. Some of the activities I will describe are not, on their own, illegal. Taken together, though, they help paint a picture of the complexity these investigations present.

First, we have seen financial institutions avoiding wire transfers from U.S. banks. In some cases, funds are diverted through a series of wire transfers using tax secrecy jurisdiction banks to disguise the identity of the true owners.

In some cases, discreet communications are stressed to the client. Phone calls are discouraged in favor of private visits. E-mail is not permitted, and code words are used to communicate. Clients have been advised not to carry documents related to accounts into the U.S.

Another method observed in examinations involves individuals physically carrying large amounts of cash from U.S. sources to tax secrecy jurisdiction banks. In some cases, taxpayers were advised to physically transport millions of dollars to an overseas bank.

We have also observed a number of techniques using off-shore accounts to effect a form of estate planning. For example, there are cases where decedents who have an undisclosed foreign trust will leave an account to one or more heirs, but outside of the reported, taxed estate. The heirs may leave their inherited balance in the foreign trust unreported in the U.S. tax system.

These cases often involve sovereign jurisdictions where we have little legal authority and taxpayers that are often difficult to identify. As I will discuss later in my remarks, the United States has agreements to obtain and share tax information with many jurisdictions, but there are limits on our ability to use those agreements. And success in obtaining information can be short-lived. If we are successful in our enforcement strategies in one jurisdiction, the promoters and the schemers often simply move to another.

What I would like to do this morning is offer a little background about these issues and explain why they are so difficult for us. I then want to explain how we are dealing with these challenges, as well as lessons learned. Finally, I will discuss what we think needs to be done moving forward.

BACKGROUND

U.S. tax administration is complicated by the rapid pace at which our overall economy is globalizing. A growing percentage of large and mid-size business tax filings are from multinational businesses that include a variety of subsidiaries and partnerships operating within an enterprise structure where the ultimate parent is as likely to be foreign as domestic. In addition, a growing number of U.S. businesses acquire capital, raw materials, inventory, and other products and services from foreign businesses.

These events are natural outcomes of an increasingly global economy, and businesses have every right to optimize their global structures. Nonetheless, the complexities of globalization and cross-border activity continue to challenge U.S. tax administration. With multiple domestic and global tiered entities, it is often difficult to determine the full scope and resulting tax impact of a single transaction or series of transactions. Moreover, different jurisdictions impose a variety of different legal requirements and tax and accounting rules on multinational enterprises, leading to complex business structures. These factors create opportunities for aggressive tax planning.

It is not just large corporations that are taking advantage of globalization to engage in aggressive tax planning. Wealthy individuals are seeking ways to shelter income by moving it offshore or by participating in tax shelters organized by unscrupulous promoters who move in the shadows of the global economy.

Discovering and addressing these activities are complicated by the relative lack of transparency in the transactions that individuals and entities can conduct offshore. Not only are transactions themselves often intentionally designed, or carried out in a manner, to obscure the existence of assets or income, but the individuals engaging in the transaction, and their roles, are often intentionally difficult to identify.

I realize that the Subcommittee requested that I quantify the level of evasion through the use of offshore entities and accounts. Unfortunately, the IRS does not have data that will allow us to make a reliable estimate. The National Research Program study of individual taxpayers for Tax Year 2001, which is our best measure of the nation's tax gap, did not estimate the extent of offshore tax evasion.

IRS Approach to Combating Off-Shore Tax Evasion

Information Reporting

The IRS attempts to use an array of tools in attacking offshore noncompliance. The first of these is tax return information reporting. Most U.S. tax returns require that the filer provide information about foreign financial accounts, ownership in foreign entities, and financial statement data. For individuals, ownership of a foreign account is entered in Part III of Schedule B of the 1040, for partnerships in Schedule B on Form 1065, and for organizations exempt from income tax in Part VI on Form 990.

The Form 1120 and Form 3520 have financial statement and foreign ownership informational requirements. Individuals who have created controlled foreign corporations (CFC) are required to file information returns annually on Form 5471 for each CFC. The monetary penalty for failure to file a timely and substantially complete Form 5471 is $10,000, up to a maximum of $60,000 for continued failure. Failure to file can also result in a reduction of foreign tax credits.

Any U.S. person (including citizens, residents, domestic partnerships, corporations, estates or trusts) with offshore accounts in excess of $10,000 during the course of the calendar year must file a foreign bank and financial account (FBAR) report. This includes anyone who has a financial interest in or signature or other authority over any foreign financial account, including bank, brokerage, or other types of financial accounts, in a foreign country. FBAR forms are due on June 30 of each year.

There are severe civil and criminal penalties for non-compliance with the FBAR filing requirements. Civil penalties for a non-willful violation can range up to $10,000 per violation. Civil penalties for a willful violation can range up to the greater of $100,000 or 50 percent of the amount in the account at the time of the violation. Criminal penalties for violating the FBAR requirements while also violating certain other laws can range up to a $500,000 fine or 10 years imprisonment or both. Civil and criminal penalties may be imposed together.

We also get information reporting about transactions with, and the ownership of, foreign trusts. U.S. persons are generally required to report transfers to foreign trusts and distributions from foreign trusts on Form 3520. In addition, a U.S. person who is treated as the owner of a foreign trust under the grantor trust rules is required to ensure that the foreign trust files a Form 3520-A to provide a full accounting of the trust activities for the tax year. There are significant civil penalties (up to 100 percent of the gross reportable amount) for failure to comply with the reporting requirements.

It is important to note that there are legitimate reasons for a U.S. taxpayer to have an offshore account. As with all information reporting to the IRS, we use this information as part of a broader risk analysis before reaching any conclusions about whether a taxpayer is engaged in aggressive tax planning.

The obvious downside to these types of information reporting is that they are dependent on the willingness of the taxpayer to be compliant. That is why we have looked for means of third-party reporting that often gives us a better view of what is taking place and thus encourages better compliance by the taxpayer.

Qualified Intermediary Program

In 2001 new regulations that completely overhauled the system for withholding and reporting on foreign persons took effect. An essential component of the new system is the QI program.

Under the program, foreign financial institutions voluntarily agree by contract directly with the IRS to operate under a simplified set of the withholding and reporting rules that U.S. financial institutions must follow. This means that the foreign financial institution agrees to collect identifying documentation from its customers, withhold U.S. tax based on that documentation, deposit the withheld tax with the IRS, file withholding tax returns on a Form 1042, file information returns on Form 1042-S and 1099, and submit to periodic audits performed by external auditors supervised by IRS examiners.

Prior to the 2001 regulations, dividends paid to a foreign address was treated as paid to a foreign person, and if the address were in a treaty country, the dividends were treated as paid to a resident of that country. For certain portfolio interest, entitled to a zero rate under the Code, foreign intermediaries were required to forward documentation identifying foreign beneficial owners to U.S. financial institutions. There was widespread non-compliance with this rule, in part due to the impracticality of requiring vast amounts of paper containing customer identification to be transferred and shared among competing financial institutions. Prior to 2001, foreign financial institutions abroad did not generally collect U.S. tax documentation, did not withhold U.S. tax, did not file information returns with IRS, and did not submit to IRS oversight.

Under the 2001 regulations, foreign financial institutions are required to forward beneficial owner documentation to U.S. financial institutions only if the foreign financial institutions are not qualified intermediaries. If they are qualified intermediaries, they are required to make all withholding decisions based on documentation collected from beneficial owners, withhold and deposit tax with IRS, file withholding tax returns and information returns with IRS, and submit to IRS oversight.

To date, 7,007 QI agreements have been signed. There are currently 5,660 active QI agreements. The difference between signed agreements and active agreements is due to mergers, acquisitions and terminations. For example the QI team has issued 600 default letters and has terminated 100 QI agreements. Currently, the QI program exists in 60 countries.

In layman's terms, the QI program gives the IRS an important line of sight to the activities of foreign banks and other financial institutions. It also provides detailed information reporting that the IRS did not previously receive.

However, the success of the program is dependent on the foreign bank being in compliance with its QI requirements. When a foreign bank explicitly takes on those obligations under a QI agreement with IRS, the IRS is in a much better position to hold the bank responsible for living up to those obligations.

I believe the QI program is critical to sound tax administration in a global economy. By bringing foreign financial institutions more directly into the U.S. tax system, we can better ensure that U.S. persons are properly paying tax on foreign account activity, and that foreign persons are subject to the proper withholding rates. The QI program is relatively new, and as with any new and complex program, there will be flaws that must be addressed. In my view, we need to shore up the QI program and continuously enhance it.

Accordingly, the IRS is taking a number of steps to enhance the QI program.

First, because accounting firms perform audits of QIs according to detailed procedures prescribed by IRS regulations, we have reached out to the major accounting firms that engage in this business. We advised these firms of our concerns about activity that we are seeing in some QIs. We engaged in a discussion about the role of the accounting community in conducting the audits of QIs, and what can be done to enhance the detection and reporting of violations of the QI agreement. The discussion was positive, and I am confident the firms understand our concerns.

Pursuant to a 2007 Government Accountability Office report, we are working on an enhancement to our regulations that would require audit firms to specifically report indications of fraud or illegal acts.

Finally, we are working on enhancements to the program to increase the level and quality of information reporting coming through the program. Specifically, we are considering changes to the regulations to require QIs to look through certain foreign entities – such as trusts – to determine whether any U.S. taxpayers are beneficial owners. We are also considering a regulation to have QIs report U.S. taxpayers' worldwide income to the IRS in certain cases– not just U.S. source income.

Tax treaties, information exchange agreements, and international cooperation

The third tool in our arsenal is international agreements such as tax treaties and tax information exchange agreements (TIEAs), under which other countries agree to obtain information on behalf of the United States for use in U.S. tax matters. Tax treaties and TIEAs provide the authority for the IRS to request and obtain information from foreign sources that may not be available to the IRS. However, a request for information under a tax treaty or TIEA must generally specify certain information, such as the identity of the account holder. Without that information in the request, the other country would normally consider the request invalid.

We currently have agreements for information exchange with over 70 jurisdictions and have expanded the program in recent years to include offshore jurisdictions such as the Cayman Islands and the Bahamas. We continue to expand the number of countries with which we have agreements as well as to renegotiate some agreements, such as the U.S. - Belgium tax treaty, to improve information exchange. However, we are still significantly limited by bank secrecy laws or lack of beneficial ownership information in some jurisdictions.

Using the bi-lateral agreements that we have with individual countries, in 2004 we worked with the Tax Commissioners of Australia, Canada, and the United Kingdom to form the Joint International Tax Shelter Information Center (JITSIC). JIT SIC was created to combat abusive international tax shelter activity on a real-time basis. The JITSIC office was based in Washington, DC, but in September, 2007, JITSIC expanded to a second office in London, England. Along with the expansion to London, JITSIC welcomed Japan as a new member.

JITSIC's primary focus has been on the bilateral exchange of specific abusive transactions and their promoters and investors. The results, to date, have been promising. The U.S. has received information regarding some transactions of which it had not been previously aware. In light of the complexity of the transactions, and considering the inherent difficulty normally associated with obtaining taxpayer-specific shelter information from foreign countries, it is unlikely that these transactions would have been uncovered and understood, but for JIT SIC.

The U.S. has also received information regarding transactions of which it has been aware but may not have fully understood. Frequently, the information exchanged has provided additional facts and a better understanding of the transaction from the perspectives of two tax regimes. Without JITSIC, this type of exchange and accompanying dialogue would not take place.

In addition to JITSIC, the IRS and the tax administrations of nine other countries agreed to the establishment of the so-called "Leeds Castle" Group. Under this arrangement, the commissioners of the revenue bodies China, India, and South Korea agreed to meet regularly with their counterparts from the US, the UK, Japan, Australia, Canada, France and Germany to consider and discuss issues of global and national tax administration in their respective countries.

We also continue to work closely with our tax treaty partners in multi-lateral compliance activities using the relevant Exchange of Information articles in our tax treaties. We have also been an active participant of the Organization for Economic Cooperation and Development (OECD), in which we have worked to improve and strengthen worldwide standards for information exchange.

Informants

Informants have been valuable sources of information for IRS civil and criminal investigations into offshore tax evasion.

With the new "whistleblower" standards that reward informants, we are hopeful that we will get additional input on other potential violations.

Criminal investigations

The IRS is increasing our resources devoted to enforcing the failure to report foreign bank accounts and is currently pursuing dozens of criminal investigations of US taxpayers for offshore tax evasion. Many of these investigations are a result of the IRS' stepped up enforcement actions. In addition, the IRS receives information from many other sources that can result in enforcement actions to ensure taxpayer compliance with the tax laws.

The primary focus on these investigations is on US taxpayers who fail to file the FBAR. U.S. persons are required to file a Report of Foreign Bank and Financial Accounts (FBAR), Form TD F 90-22.1, each year if they have a financial interest in or signature authority or other authority over any financial accounts, including bank, securities or other types of financial accounts, in a foreign country, if the aggregate value of these financial accounts exceeds $10,000 at any time during the calendar year. The IRS is increasing our resources devoted to enforcing the failure to report foreign bank accounts.

John doe summons

The final tool I will mention to fight offshore evasion is the use of information received from the use of John Doe summonses. The IRS generally uses the John Doe summons authority to identify individuals, groups or classes of U.S. taxpayers whose member identities are unknown, who are involved in specific areas of tax noncompliance and who cannot be identified through other means. For example, we would use this type of summons when we know that taxpayers use offshore bank accounts to avoid paying taxes, but we do not know their identities. A John Doe summons served on a domestic processor of offshore bank records would give us their names, addresses and other identifying information.

The IRS requested and received court approval to serve 153 John Doe summonses in connection with its Offshore Credit Card Project. The IRS received court approval from multiple US District Courts on every John Doe summons request made.

And, as I have already explained, we continue to use the John Doe Summons in furtherance of our off-shore investigations.

How Congress Can Help

The first thing that Congress can do to assist us in these areas is to fully fund the Administration's request for the IRS' FY 2009 budget. We need sufficient resources to continue to address many of the issues that I have discussed. Grappling with complex international tax issues requires a top-notch workforce and technological tools. The President's FY 2009 Budget provides key resources to the IRS, and we urge your support.

The Budget also includes a collection of legislative proposals designed to enhance third-party reporting and, thereby, reduce the tax gap. The most significant of these proposals would require merchant card issuers to report annually on reimbursements to business entities. This legislation would help the IRS match taxpayer data with business activity and mitigate opportunities for noncompliance.

The President's budget has legislative proposals that would also be particularly helpful in the international area. The most significant of these would increase the foreign trust reporting penalty. The penalty provision would be amended to impose an initial penalty of the greater of $10,000 or 35 percent of the gross reportable amount (if the gross reportable amount is known). The additional $10,000 penalty for continued failure to report would remain unchanged. Thus, even if the gross reportable amount is not known, the IRS may impose a $10,000 penalty on a person who fails to report timely or correctly as required and may impose a $10,000 penalty for each 30-day period (or fraction thereof) that the failure to report continues.

Another area where Congress can help is to allow more time in which to conclude these civil audits where taxpayers have used foreign entities and bank accounts to avoid or evade federal taxes. Currently the statute of limitations is 3 years. However, because of the complexity of many of these cases, we often need additional time. We are currently reviewing the extension of the statute of limitations included in the Levin-Coleman (S. 681) bill and look forward to working with your staff, along with the staff and Members of the Senate Finance and House Ways and Means Committee, to find an acceptable approach.

Finally, it is important that Congress continue to support our effort to strengthen our network of tax treaties. They provide a basis for exchanging information.

Both Congress and the IRS are limited when dealing with individuals and businesses that hide their assets in foreign jurisdictions that use financial secrecy as a tool to attract commerce to their country. Thus, we must search for ways to reduce the incentive for taxpayers to seek out such offshore financial arrangements.

Deterrence is one of our most powerful weapons. In this regard, I am proud of the hard work the IRS and Justice Department investigators have put into these cases. As a result of their continuing work, I am confident that those who engage in these types of deliberate offshore tax evasion are very concerned right now. I believe that we owe it to the vast majority of honest taxpayers to pursue these cases aggressively, and I am committed to doing so.

CONCLUSIONS

Mr. Chairman, let me repeat what I said earlier about you and this Subcommittee. You have been at the forefront in investigating important areas of Federal tax non-compliance.

The subject of the hearing this morning is no exception. Offshore tax shelters are robbing the American treasury of billions of dollars each year.

I have attempted to bring you up to date on many of the things we are doing in the offshore arena, and I hope this has been beneficial. I look forward to your continuing investigations into these areas and your assistance in halting abusive offshore tax shelters.

I appreciate the opportunity to be here this morning, and I will be happy to respond to any questions.

In: Tax Haven Banks
Editor: Wade D. Brookins

ISBN: 978-1-60692-283-5

Chapter 4

STATEMENT OF KEVIN J. O'CONNOR (UNITED STATES DEPT. OF JUSTICE) BEFORE THE UNITED STATES SENATE COMMITTEE ON HOMELAND SECURITY AND GOVERNMENTAL AFFAIRS PERMANENT SUBCOMMITTEE ON INVESTIGATIONS HEARING ENTITLED "TAX HAVEN BANKS AND U.S. TAX COMPLIANCE"

Chairman Levin, Ranking Member Coleman, and Members of the Subcommittee, thank you for the opportunity to appear before you this morning to discuss the Department of Justice's (the Department) efforts to combat the use of tax haven banks by U.S. taxpayers and offshore entities to evade income taxes. Let me begin by commending the Chairman and the Subcommittee for your longstanding commitment to investigating and publicizing abuses of our federal tax system. Your work has brought attention to serious misconduct that threatens to undermine the fundamental integrity of our tax system. As a result, taxpayers have a greater understanding of their obligations and the consequences of noncompliance, and tax professionals are on notice that their efforts to design, market, and facilitate tax evasion schemes will not be tolerated.

Today I would like to focus my remarks on the Department's Tax Division's role in combating the continuing problem of offshore tax evasion. Since the adoption of the Sixteenth Amendment in 1913 the application of the individual income tax has been routinely debated, litigated, and amended. Over the years, Congress has made numerous changes to our tax laws to reflect advances in business, communication, and technology. One fundamental concept has, however, remained constant: U.S. taxpayers are subject to taxation on their worldwide income from whatever source that income is derived. The use of tax haven banks and offshore nominee accounts to evade tax is a direct assault on this basic principle and cannot be tolerated.

It is important to note that the overwhelming majority of Americans understand their tax obligations and pay their taxes in full and on time. It is also important to keep in mind that offshore entities conduct a wide variety of legitimate commercial activities. Thus, the mere fact that a U.S. taxpayer holds assets offshore or in a foreign bank is not inappropriate, provided that the information relating to the assets and the income generated by the assets are properly reported for U.S tax purposes. Consequently, our attention is focused on U.S. taxpayers who utilize nominee or shell entities and offshore bank accounts to conceal assets and income. These offshore schemes are often used by high wealth individuals and potentially result in the loss of billions of dollars a year in U.S. taxes. In these cases the Department, along with our counterparts at the Internal Revenue Service (IRS), has used, and will continue to use all of the tools at our disposal to ensure that noncompliance is detected, and, where appropriate, prosecuted.

While taxpayers who engage in tax evasion are subject to civil and criminal liability for their conduct, we are equally concerned about the role played by tax professionals in designing and implementing these schemes. The title of the Subcommittee's 2006 Report, "Tax Haven Abuses: The Enablers, The Tools, and the Secrecy" succinctly captures the essential nature of the participation by professionals in these schemes. As the report notes:

> A sophisticated offshore industry, composed of a cadre of international professionals including tax attorneys, accountants, bankers, brokers, corporate service providers, and trust administrators, aggressively promotes offshore jurisdictions to U.S. citizens as a means to avoid taxes and creditors in their home jurisdictions. These professionals, many of whom are located or do business in the United States, advise and assist U.S. citizens on the opening of offshore accounts, establishing sham trusts, and shell corporations, hiding assets offshore, and making secret use of their offshore assets here at home.

Tax Haven Abuses: The Enablers, The Tools and Secrecy, STAFF OF SENATE PERMANENT SUBCOMM. ON INVESTIGATIONS, COMM. ON HOMELAND SECURITY AND GOVERNMENTAL AFFAIRS, 1 (Aug. 1, 2006).

It is discouraging to see that some professionals continue to violate their legal and ethical responsibilities by facilitating these illegal schemes. While some simply turn a blind eye to misconduct, others actively market their tax evasion programs on U.S. soil. Holding these professionals accountable for their misconduct is a high priority, and we are not reluctant to seek injunctive relief and criminal sanctions where appropriate.

The Department has successfully prosecuted a number of taxpayers as well as tax professionals and institutions who assist them in using offshore accounts and entities to evade U.S. taxation. Recent prosecutions include:

- David Alan Struckman, co-founder of the Institute of Global Prosperity, an organization that promoted offshore "wealth-building" seminars, was convicted of tax evasion and conspiracy to defraud the United States. The bogus wealth- building methods marketed to clients included placing assets in purported foreign "common law" trusts to evade detection by the IRS. Struckman concealed more than $45 million earned from the sale of these products through the use of bogus trusts, nominee entities, and related offshore bank accounts in the Turks and Caicos and Eastern Europe. Struckman is currently in prison awaiting sentencing. The IRS and Tax Division continue to pursue enforcement activity against individuals who engaged in the scheme.

- Walter Anderson, a telecommunications entrepreneur, crafted an elaborate scheme using offshore trusts, shell entities and nominees in multiple tax haven jurisdictions, including the British Virgin Islands, Panama, and the Cayman Islands, for the purpose of evading more than $200 million of his federal income taxes. For his malfeasance, Mr. Anderson is currently serving nine years in federal prison for tax fraud.
- Bruce Cohen, a financial planner, was sentenced to 37 months in prison for his role in conspiring to defraud the United States. Along with his associates, Cohen developed and marketed sham "Loss of Income" trust policies to assist taxpayers in their attempt to evade income tax. Offshore accounts and nominee entities in the Bahamas and Bermuda were part of the scheme. Mr. Cohen's associates, Leif Rozen, a business owner, and Alan Hoehler, former in-house counsel, were also found guilty of conspiracy and federal tax charges and await sentencing.
- In addition to these cases the Tax Division and the IRS continue to actively pursue those who misuse offshore accounts and institutions for the purpose of evading U.S. taxation.

Our success in prosecuting these and other cases is a direct result of the close cooperation between the civil and criminal personnel of the Tax Division and the IRS. For example, lawyers in the Tax Division have worked with the IRS to investigate offshore tax evasion by bringing civil suits to obtain authority to serve John Doe summonses. A John Doe Summons enables the IRS, with court approval, to obtain information about possible fraud by taxpayers whose identities are unknown. These efforts yielded hundreds of thousands of documents and identified thousands of people that are now being investigated by the IRS for unreported and unpaid federal income taxes. The government's efforts in these cases not only helped gather necessary documents to identify taxpayers seeking to hide behind a veil of secrecy, but reassured law-abiding taxpayers that the tax laws are being enforced.

On the criminal side, the Tax Division serves as the nerve center for all federal tax prosecutions. Tax Division attorneys work closely with IRS Criminal Investigation Special Agents to develop and prosecute a wide array of tax crimes, including offshore evasion schemes. Tax Division attorneys also routinely provide tax expertise to United States Attorneys' offices across the country and work closely with Assistant United States Attorneys in prosecuting tax fraud complex cases.

Offshore tax evasion cases are, by their nature, international in scope. Investigations requiring international cooperation are time consuming and expensive and often raise complex legal issues such as national sovereignty and bank secrecy laws. Despite the challenges, United States law enforcement agencies and our foreign counterparts are fully engaged in a variety of information sharing arrangements designed to aid in shutting down illegal and abusive activity.

Critical to every investigation of offshore activity is the ability to obtain evidence from a foreign country. Depending on the scope of the investigation and the type of conduct at issue, Department attorneys and prosecutors use a variety of measures in attempting to secure both documentary and testimonial evidence. In addition to traditional letters rogatory, information can be requested, for example, pursuant to tax treaties or tax information exchange agreements (TIEAs) in both civil and criminal cases; pursuant to Mutual Legal Assistance

Treaties (MLATs) in criminal cases; or pursuant to the Hague Evidence Convention in civil cases. Unfortunately, we do not have such agreements – which can be faster and more effective than letters rogatory – with every country. Moreover, as noted, not all such agreements cover both civil and criminal matters; on occasion MLATs exclude tax crimes altogether, while other MLATs and tax treaties are limited to instances in which we can allege specific kinds of tax fraud. As a consequence, the Tax Division regularly works with the Criminal Division's Office of International Affairs (OIA) to negotiate more favorable MLATs covering all tax crimes and with the Treasury Department in attempting to negotiate the broadest possible information exchange provisions in our TIEAs and tax treaties.

In the case of MLATs, prosecutors in the Tax Division and the United States Attorneys' offices work closely with OIA, which has been delegated as the United States Central Authority for implementing mutual assistance. These requests seek specific types of evidence, frequently bank records, and OIA makes the request on behalf of the prosecutors. OIA works with foreign authorities to obtain as much evidence as possible in a timely manner. In the case of tax treaties and TIEAs, requests are made through the Deputy Commissioner (International) of the Large & Mid-Size Business Division of the IRS, who has been delegated as the United States Competent Authority for the exchange of information. In general, the level of cooperation under these agreements has been positive, and the continued development of our information sharing relationships is a high priority for the Department.

Tax evasion is a chronic drain on the public fisc and is a pernicious obstacle to effective tax administration. If not vigorously investigated and addressed it threatens to undermine confidence in our system of voluntary compliance and self-assessment. Although successful offshore tax enforcement is costly and time consuming, it is essential to the mission of the Tax Division. We are dedicated to ensuring that law abiding taxpayers have confidence that the tax laws are being fairly and equally applied, and that those who attempt to engage in tax evasion know that we will detect their schemes and hold them accountable for their misconduct.

Thank you for inviting me to discuss the Department's efforts to combat offshore tax evasion. I would be happy to answer questions that you may have.

In: Tax Haven Banks
Editor: Wade D. Brookins

ISBN: 978-1-60692-283-5

Chapter 5

OPENING STATEMENT OF SENATOR CARL LEVIN BEFORE U.S. SENATE PERMANENT SUBCOMMITTEE ON INVESTIGATIONS ON TAX HAVEN BANKS AND U.S. TAX COMPLIANCE

JULY 17, 2008

About 50 tax havens operate in the world today. Their twin hallmarks are secrecy and tax avoidance. Some tax havens are little known places like Andorra and Vanuatu that few Americans have heard of. Others, like Switzerland and Liechtenstein, are notorious for operating behind an iron ring of secrecy. Billions and billions of dollars worth of U.S. assets find their way into these secrecy tax havens, aided by banks, trust companies, accountants, lawyers, and others. Each year, the United States Treasury loses an estimated $100 billion in tax revenues from offshore tax abuses. Tax havens are engaged in economic warfare against the United States and honest, hardworking American taxpayers.

Today we will look at two banks that relied on secrecy and deception to hide, not just the tax avoidance schemes of their clients, but the actions they themselves took to facilitate U.S. tax evasion. First is LGT, a private bank owned by the royal family of Liechtenstein. Lichtenstein is a tiny alpine nation whose 35,000 citizens would fill one-third of the University of Michigan football stadium. It has no airport, but supports 15 banks that together boast of holding more than $200 billion in assets. Lichtenstein also boasts of secrecy laws that are more stringent than even those that have made Switzerland synonymous with hidden bank accounts.

The second bank is UBS, a Swiss bank. It is one of the world's largest financial institutions, the world's largest manager of private wealth, and a public company of international renown. Yet, as we will hear today, UBS has an estimated 19,000 so-called "undeclared accounts" for U.S. citizens with an estimated $18 billion in assets that have been kept secret from the IRS.

Both LGT and UBS operate behind a wall of secrecy that this hearing and our report will show needs to come down. The evidence we have been able to obtain breaks through some of that wall of secrecy to show how these two banks have employed banking practices that facilitate, and have resulted in, tax evasion by U.S. clients.

I initiated this investigation into tax haven banks in February 2008, as a global tax scandal erupted after a former employee of LGT provided tax authorities around the world with data on about 1,400 people with accounts at LGT Bank in Liechtenstein. On February 14, 2008, German tax authorities, having obtained the names of 600-700 German taxpayers with LGT accounts, executed multiple search warrants and arrested a prominent businessman for allegedly using LGT accounts to evade $1.5 million in taxes. Soon after, the IRS announced it had initiated enforcement action against 100 U.S. taxpayers in connection with accounts in Liechtenstein. The United Kingdom, Italy, France, Spain, and Australia made similar announcements on the same day. Altogether since February, nearly a dozen countries have announced plans to investigate taxpayers with Liechtenstein accounts, demonstrating not only the worldwide scope of the tax scandal, but also a newfound international determination to fight against tax evasion facilitated by tax haven banks.

The former LGT employee who exposed LGT's dirty laundry had to go into hiding to avoid arrest by Liechtenstein which has listed him as its Number 1 target for arrest. A $10 million reward has been placed on his head by unknown parties on the Internet. The Subcommittee obtained about 12,000 pages of LGT documents related to U.S. clients from this former LGT employee. We also interviewed him, and took his statement by videoconference, a tape of which, with precautions taken to obscure identifying details, will be presented during this hearing. His revelations are explosive.

The documents and information he provided depict a bank that is a willing partner, and an aider and bettor, to clients trying to evade taxes, dodge creditors, or defy court orders.

Internal LGT documents and other information show secrecy was a deeply embedded way of life at the bank. LGT used code names for its clients and directed its bankers to use pay phones when contacting them. A LGT document instructed bankers trying to contact a client as follows: "CAUTION: Calls may be made only from public phone booths, preferably not from a FL [Liechtenstein] phone booth ! ! !" LGT set up secret, shell transfer corporations which clients could use to route money into and out of their LGT accounts, in order to, in the words of LGT "cover the tracks." LGT created elaborate, deceptive offshore structures, using foundations, trusts or corporations, to hide a client's ownership of assets from tax authorities in other countries.

Our report presents seven case studies of U.S. clients using LGT services. Due to time constraints, we will discuss only four today. In preparation for this hearing, the Subcommittee served subpoenas on three of the four LGT clients seeking their personal appearance: Shannon Marsh, William Wu, and Steven Greenfield. Two of those individuals, Mr. Marsh and Mr. Wu are here today. The third, Mr. Greenfield, has refused to appear after a subpoena was served on him, and we will be seeking enforcement of our subpoena. The fourth, Peter Lowy, left the country despite our request that he appear today. The Subcommittee notified his legal counsel that he would be subpoenaed to appear, if necessary. He has now agreed to appear before the Subcommittee at a continuation of this hearing a week from tomorrow.

Later in the hearing, when these individuals are called to give testimony, I will describe in more detail what we've learned about their Liechtenstein accounts, but for now I will mention each case history only briefly.

Shannon Marsh. Shannon Marsh is a son of the late James Albright Marsh, a U.S. citizen from Florida in the construction business who formed four Liechtenstein foundations in the 1 980s, and transferred substantial funds to them. Two of these foundations were formed for him by LGT. By 2007, the assets in the four foundations had a combined value of $49 million. LGT instructed the Marshes to use the code, "Friends of J.N.," when they wished to "get in touch." The Marsh accounts were never disclosed to the IRS by LGT.

William Wu. William Wu is a U.S. citizen who has lived for many years with his family in New York. LGT helped Mr. Wu hide ownership of his house in New York by helping him arrange a fake sale to an offshore company he secretly controlled. LGT also helped him withdraw substantial funds from his Liechtenstein account, ranging from $100,000 to $1.5 million at a time, in ways that made the funds difficult to trace.

Steven Greenfield. Harvey and Steven Greenfield, father and son, are New York businessmen who specialize in importing toys. In March 2001, in Liechtenstein, LGT held a five-hour meeting with the Greenfields attended by three LGT private bankers and Prince Philipp, Chairman of the LGT Board of Directors and brother to the sovereign of Liechtenstein. The meeting was primarily a sales pitch to convince the Greenfields to transfer to LGT about $30 million from a Hong Kong bank after "leaving behind as few traces as possible." Again, Mr. Greenfield has refused to appear despite service of a subpoena, so we will be pursuing this matter.

Peter Lowy. Peter Lowy lives in California. His father, with his sons' help, set up an LGT foundation in 1998, after telling the bank that he did not want Australian tax authorities to know about the assets. LGT took measures to hide the Lowys' ownership of the assets, including by keeping their name off the formation documents for the new foundation, routing incoming assets through an offshore transfer corporation to prevent a direct link to the new foundation, and using a Delaware corporation headed by Peter Lowy to name the beneficiaries. In 2001, the Lowys dissolved the foundation and moved to Switzerland assets totalling about $68 million. Mr. Lowy will appear next week, on Friday, to answer questions about these matters.

The importance of these case studies is that they provide an inside look at what goes on behind the wall of secrecy that surrounds this Liechtenstein bank. And what does go on behind that wall? Banking practices that facilitate tax evasion – conduct that angers every honest American who pays taxes.

We have also managed to pierce some of the layers of Swiss secrecy that for too long have made Switzerland the place to bank for people with something to hide.

In late 2007, the Subcommittee took the deposition of Bradley Birkenfeld, who worked for more than 12 years as a private banker in Switzerland, including four years at the Geneva office of UBS. In 2008, Mr. Birkenfeld was charged and pled guilty to conspiring with a U.S. citizen, Igor Olenicoff, to defraud the IRS of $7.2 million in taxes owed on $200 million of assets hidden in secret accounts in Switzerland and Liechtenstein. In connection with this prosecution, the United States also detained as a material witness a senior UBS private banking official from Switzerland, Martin Liechti, then traveling on business in Florida. These enforcement actions appear to represent the first time that the United States has criminally prosecuted a Swiss banker for helping a U.S. taxpayer evade U.S. taxes. Mr. Liechti is here today, and I want to express my appreciation to the Justice Department and the U.S. Attorney for the Southern District of Florida for making him available.

Our report describes how Mr. Birkenfeld signed up Mr. Olenicoff as a client, in part by traveling to California from Switzerland to meet him, and opened UBS accounts for him in Switzerland in the name of offshore corporations Mr. Olenicoff controlled to hide his ownership of the assets. For a time, Mr. Olenicoff was Mr. Birkenfeld' s largest client.

The details of their tax evasion scheme are sordid enough. But what Mr. Birkenfeld told the Subcommittee was that what he did as a private banker at UBS was ordinary practice. He told us about the thousands of Swiss accounts at UBS for U.S. clients holding billions in assets, all undeclared. He also described the pressure placed on the Swiss private bankers to bring new money into the bank from the United States, called "net new money." His deposition and other documents show that each year, UBS assigns each private banker an annual net new money target. A January 2007 email sent out by Mr. Liechti to the Swiss bankers in the Americas division wished them a happy new year, recounted how, in 2002, they had brought in 4 million Swiss francs per banker, how that number had quadrupled in two years to 17 million Swiss francs per banker in 2006, and then urged them to quadruple their efforts again in 2007 to bring in 60 million Swiss francs per banker in net new money from the United States.

Mr. Birkenfeld told us that Swiss bankers regularly traveled to the United States to target U.S. citizens for net new money. He told us how these Swiss bankers maintained a low profile, using business cards that did not mention "wealth management," sometimes declaring they were in the United States for non-business purposes, and carrying encrypted computers that, allegedly, even U.S. Customs agents couldn't read. A Subcommittee analysis of travel records supplied by Customs corroborate his testimony. The travel records show that about 20 UBS Swiss bankers made about 300 trips to the United States since 2003, often traveling together to UBS-sponsored functions designed to attract wealthy potential clients. These travel records also showed that some UBS private banking officials made regular U.S. visits, including Mr. Liechti who traveled to the United States up to eight times in a year. He described one Swiss banker who saw 30 to 40 clients on each U.S. visit. All this to sell Swiss secrecy on U.S. soil.

He also described UBS Swiss bankers who presented their clients with securities products and helped execute securities transactions here in the United States, without a broker-dealer license from the Securities and Exchange Commission. In response to Subcommittee inquiries, UBS also admitted that, like LGT, its bankers had set up foreign corporations to disguise the ownership of accounts by U.S. clients.

The Subcommittee even obtained a document showing that UBS provided its Swiss private bankers with training on how to detect surveillance by U.S. customs agents and law enforcement officers while traveling here. Think about that – a major international bank is training its bankers to detect surveillance by U.S. authorities.

UBS efforts targeting U.S. clients to open Swiss accounts were, in the words of Mr. Birkenfeld, a "massive machine." And the push to open Swiss accounts took place even though UBS had branch banking and securities operations in the United States that were large enough to accommodate all of its U.S. clients.

Which brings up a fundamental question. Why would a U.S. taxpayer open a UBS account in Switzerland, when it could bank with UBS right here in the United States? Why would 19,000 U.S. clients with nearly $18 billion in assets choose to open Swiss accounts? It seems plain that part of the answer is that they wanted to open undeclared accounts that the IRS didn't know about. They wanted secrecy.

And UBS gave them secrecy. In November 2002, UBS sent a letter to all of its U.S. clients to reassure them that their secret Swiss accounts were still safely hidden, despite the Qualified Intermediary Program's going into effect. Here's what that letter said in part:

> "Dear client:
> From our recent conversations we understand that you are concerned that UBS' stance on keeping its U.S. customers' information strictly confidential may have changed.... We are writing to reassure you that your fear is unjustified and wish to outline only some of the reasons why the protection of client data can not possibly be compromised ...."

We all know what is going on here. U.S. clients who don't bank with UBS in the United States and instead bank with UBS in Switzerland are buying secrecy. And folks who buy secrecy have secrets they don't want to reveal, such as evasion of taxes, the ducking of creditors, or defiance of court orders. But those clients aren't the only ones relying on secrecy to cloak their actions. Banks in tax havens, including the two banks under examination today, are also covering up their own actions – actions they presumably didn't want to see exposed by media around the world.

This chart summarizes the Tax Haven Bank Secrecy Tricks we've uncovered during this investigation. Banks using code names for clients to disguise their identities; telling their bankers to use pay phones instead of business phones so authorities can't trace a call back to the bank; giving their bankers encrypted computers when they travel so tax authorities can't read any client information; funnelling money through so-called transfer companies to cover the tracks of the funds and make audits difficult; opening accounts in the names of foreign shell companies to hide the real owners; setting up fake charitable trusts for the same reason; providing bankers with counter-surveillance training – the list goes on. These tricks are all about deception, all about making it impossible for the IRS to follow the money, bring tax cheats to justice, and bring back into the U.S. treasury the tens of billions of dollars owed to Uncle Sam.

UBS has told the Subcommittee that it is changing its ways. It has banned travel by its Swiss bankers to the United States. It is encouraging U.S. clients to bank with UBS in the United States or at a subsidiary in Switzerland called Swiss Financial Advisors that requires all U.S. clients to disclose their accounts to the IRS. Liechtenstein tells us they are in negotiations with the United States to enter into a tax information exchange agreement and with its European neighbours to expand tax cooperation in connection with an anti-fraud agreement.

I hope it is true, but count me skeptical for a number of reasons. First, we haven't heard anything from LGT about reforms; it is not even here today, in contrast to UBS. Second, evading U.S. taxes is a billion dollar industry; it's gone on for decades; and the profits are huge, both for the tax cheats and for the banks holding their assets. The documents and testimony that we are releasing today disclose a culture of secrecy and deception that we are determined to end, despite its being strongly entrenched.

Tax evasion eats at the fabric of society, not only by starving health care, education, and other needed government services of resources, but also by undermining trust – making honest folks feel like they are being taken advantage of when they pay their fair share.

Our report outlines a number of ways we can fight back to end tax haven abuses. Here are a few.

First, we should support the recent innovative enforcement actions taken by the Justice Department and IRS to prosecute foreign bankers who help U.S. taxpayers cheat Uncle Sam and to compel foreign banks to disclose the names of their U.S. clients.

Second, we ought to enact new tools to penalize tax haven banks that impede U.S. tax enforcement. Congress should give the Treasury Department authority to bar U.S. financial institutions from doing business with those banks, and the IRS should remove those banks from the Qualified Intermediary program that allows them to avoid disclosing the names of their nonU.S. clients to U.S. authorities.

Third, Congress should create a rebuttable presumption in enforcement proceedings that U.S. taxpayers who form, send assets to, or receive assets from a legal entity in an offshore secrecy jurisdiction controls that entity and is liable for taxation on its assets and income.

Fourth, Congress ought to change the law to require banks who know U.S. clients are behind accounts opened in the name of offshore entities to treat those accounts as U.S. accounts that have to be disclosed to the IRS.

And we can do all that and more by enacting the Stop Tax Haven Abuse Act, a bill that I and Senator Coleman introduced last year.

Right now, tax haven banks and tax haven governments dress up their secrecy laws and banking practices with phrases like "financial privacy" and "wealth management." But secrecy breeds tax evasion. And secrecy hides, not only the wrongdoers, but also those who aid and abet the wrongdoing. We are determined to tear down those secrecy walls in favor of transparency, cooperation, and tax compliance.

I want to thank my Ranking Member, Senator Coleman, and his staff for their support of this investigation and the legislation to stop tax haven abuses.

TAX HAVEN BANK SECRECY TRICKS

- Code Names for Clients
- Pay Phones, not Business Phones
- Foreign Area Codes
- Undeclared Accounts
- Encrypted Computers
- Transfer Companies to Cover Tracks
- Foreign Shell Companies
- Fake Charitable Trusts
- Straw Man Settlors
- Captive Trustees
- Anonymous Wire Transfers
- Disguised Business Trips
- Counter-Surveillance Training
- Foreign Credit Cards
- Hold Mail
- Shred Files

In: Tax Haven Banks
Editor: Wade D. Brookins

ISBN: 978-1-60692-283-5

Chapter 6

OPENING STATEMENT SENATOR NORM COLEMAN: TAX HAVEN BANKS AND U.S. TAX COMPLIANCE

JULY 17, 2008

This morning, we return to a matter that is important to all American taxpayers: the role of foreign banks – particularly those in off-shore tax havens – in helping a disturbing number of wealthy Americans cheat on their taxes. At the outset, I want to express my appreciation to Senator Levin for his unwavering commitment throughout this effort. This has been a truly bipartisan investigation in every sense of the word. It would not have been possible to bring these important problems to light without your leadership, Mr. Chairman, and I thank you.

The problem we are confronting today is simple: tens of thousands of America's wealthiest citizens are using offshore secrecy jurisdictions to hide trillions of dollars and avoid paying their fair share of taxes. The offshore problem remains one of staggering proportions. These tax havens hold an estimated $1.5 trillion in American assets, resulting in lost taxes of roughly $100 billion. That's three times the size of the Minnesota state budget general fund – lost because of dishonest individuals and entities exploiting the secrecy of certain foreign countries.

In doing so, these privileged few are forcing honest American taxpayers to bear a disproportionate burden of investing in crucial areas like healthcare, homeland security, and education. That tax-loss sits like a millstone around the neck of honest American taxpayers, who are struggling with high taxes, ever- increasing gas prices, and rising healthcare costs.

But these crooked tax-cheats are not acting alone. Foreign banks in these offshore havens are enthusiastic partners in this deception. Hiding behind an impregnable fortress of secrecy laws, these banks have partnered with American tax-cheats to use offshore tax and secrecy havens to conceal ownership of assets and make sham transactions seem legitimate, while staying one step ahead of U.S. law enforcement and the IRS.

Over the course of the last year, the Subcommittee has engaged in a broad investigation into two of these banks: LGT Bank in Liechtenstein, and UBS AG in Switzerland. Both banks operate under strict secrecy laws, yet both banks enabled and promoted felony tax evasion, and sometimes even worse misconduct, like the bribery of American officials and others. The audacity and cleverness of the bankers we have examined are matched only by the zeal with which their American clients used their services.

Before we turn to the evidence, it's worthwhile to take a moment and review the relevant laws and rules to understand how the banks eagerly manipulated the regulatory and legal landscape to assist their tax-cheating clients. The key rules governing these foreign banks is called the Qualified Intermediary Program, or QI Program for short. The QI Program is intended to encourage foreign banks to assist the IRS collect taxes from overseas accounts by calling for contracts with the individual foreign banks. In short, contracts executed under the QI Program require the banks to report to the IRS when the accounts held by Americans have income derived from U.S. securities, and withhold the proper amount of taxes, sending that amount back to the United States.

In one sense, the QI Program has been quite effective: the IRS has been able to collect substantial taxes that it previously could not. But there was a loophole in these QI agreements, and these foreign banks drove a Mack truck right through it. Basically, while the QI agreements require the banks to reveal American accountholders with U.S. securities investments, the agreements do not require the reporting of accounts that are held by non-US citizens or entities.

So what did the banks do? They encouraged their American clients to form shell companies and trusts in jurisdictions with strict secrecy laws, helped them open accounts in the names of those trusts and companies, and then assisted them in shifting millions of dollars from accounts in their names to accounts in the names of the foreign entities. In doing so, these banks turned a blind eye to the fact that there was no legitimate reason for these maneuvers.

In his opening statement, Senator Levin highlighted the findings of our Subcommittee, as set forth in the bipartisan staff report we've issued to accompany this hearing. The case studies related to LGT are as appalling in their brazenness as they are disturbing in their commonality:

- A family falsely hiding nearly $50 million in trusts for decades.
- Another family moving funds from one shell corporation to another to yet another in a chain of transfers that was clearly designed for one reason: to avoid paying taxes.
- A family meeting with the royal family of Liechtenstein with the express purpose – in their words – of hiding the traces.
- The brazen facilitation of bribery here in the United States by Marc Rich and his affiliates.

Sadly, the list goes on, and on, and on. What's worse, LGT was not alone. UBS engaged in parallel misconduct. In short, soon after joining the QI Program, UBS undertook a systematic, wide- ranging effort to harvest tax cheats from the United States, help them restructure their Swiss accounts to avoid paying taxes on billions of dollars, and surreptitiously evade the attention of federal law enforcement agencies.

To be clear, our focus is on UBS' operations out of Switzerland. UBS has a large number of personnel based here in the United States, including in Minnesota, and they, like us, are surely appalled at what the Subcommittee has uncovered. Those people are not part of the misconduct we examine here today, nor do we suggest in any way that they are involved in these activities.

Moreover, we should note that UBS has been cooperative with the Subcommittee's investigation and has been responsive to its requests. UBS is also appearing today voluntarily, and not under compulsion of subpoena. I find it significant that, while UBS did not necessarily have to send a knowledgeable witness from Switzerland, it chose to do so, which stands in stark contrast to LGT's refusal to appear before us today.

The results of the Subcommittee's investigation are striking. The evidence reveals that the banks engaged in highly suspicious activities designed to hide the identities of their clients, including using code words, encrypted computers designed to thwart U.S. Customs officials, shell companies and trusts strewn around the world, and techniques to avoid surveillance by law enforcement. Some of the activities sound like the cloak-and-dagger deception in a James Bond movie.

It's bad enough if the banks were simply enabling tax crimes. But the problem is far worse and more pervasive than a mere see-no-evil acceptance of tax fraud. Our investigation has found that the banks have left their secrecy fortresses and furtively entered the United States to recruit and service thousands upon thousands of tax-cheats. Driven by a desire to service their clients' desires, regardless of legality, these banks actively promote and cultivate this conduct day after day. They didn't just facilitate this misconduct, they *orchestrated* it. That must stop and it must stop now.

So, the question is how do we fix this problem? The Subcommittee has offered a number of recommendations. First, Congress should pass the Stop Tax Haven Abuse Act, which is comprehensive legislation that Senator Levin and I introduced, along with Senator Obama. It would go far to stop offshore tax haven and tax shelter abuses by shining a light in the dark world of secrecy jurisdictions. We must also change the laws and regulations, which permit banks in tax havens to fulfill their contractual obligations to the IRS, even though they are facilitating criminal conduct. We must also improve the QI Program, by strengthening reporting requirements for those QI banks and expanding the audit process. We must also bolster our law enforcement activities and increase the statute of limitations for activities involving tax havens.

To be clear, foreign investment is vitally important to the United States. Such investments are critical to job growth and opportunity expansion, and are undeniably necessary for the economic wellbeing of our citizens. Nor is our focus here today on U.S. companies investing abroad, which bolsters our competitiveness in the increasingly global economy. To the contrary, our inquiry is focused on individual U.S. taxpayers who cheated the system with the active assistance of offshore banks.

There may indeed be valid reasons for holding accounts off shore, such as Americans living and working abroad, or those with families in other countries with political or economic instability. These persons, when they file the appropriate documents with the IRS and pay their fair share of taxes, have nothing to fear from this inquiry.

I want to close, however, by speaking directly to those who *should* be worried: those Americans, and their attorneys and financial enablers, who have gone offshore to dodge their taxes, escape our courts, or worse. Our message is simple: you are hurting this country. Millions of Americans struggle with bills and mortgages, pay for gas and health care, educate their children, and care for their loved ones. Hundreds of thousands of your fellow Americans protect us – both here and at war abroad – making unimaginable sacrifices on behalf of their country. By cheating on your taxes, you are forcing those people to carry even more weight on their sagging shoulders. You, the tax cheats, are not being asked to suffer as they are. You, the tax cheat, are not being asked to struggle with your daily bills and mortgages and gas prices and medical bills. You are simply being asked to pay your fair share to the country whose freedoms you enjoy so richly.

Listen closely to what we have uncovered in this investigation. Come forward and stop hiding. In one document, a foreign banker advised his American client to stop engaging in certain transactions, so that the American authorities would not catch him. He said boldly – and I quote – "let sleeping dogs lie." Well, the dogs are no longer sleeping.

In: Tax Haven Banks
Editor: Wade D. Brookins
ISBN: 978-1-60692-283-5

Chapter 7

EXHIBIT LIST: HEARING ON TAX HAVEN BANKS AND U.S. TAX COMPLIANCE

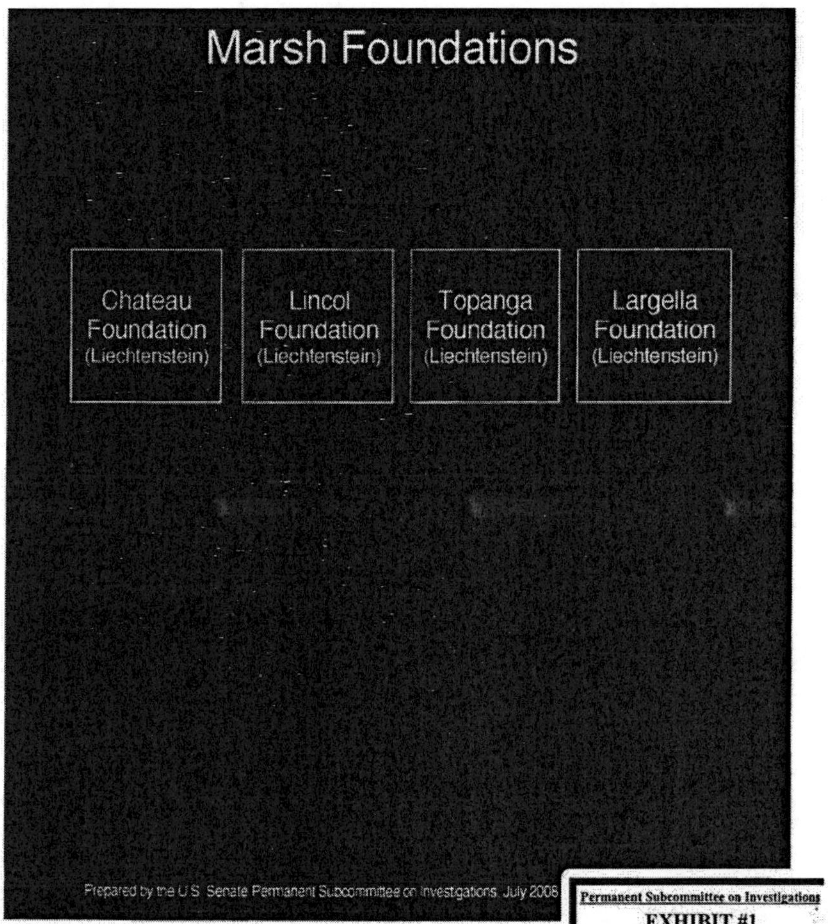

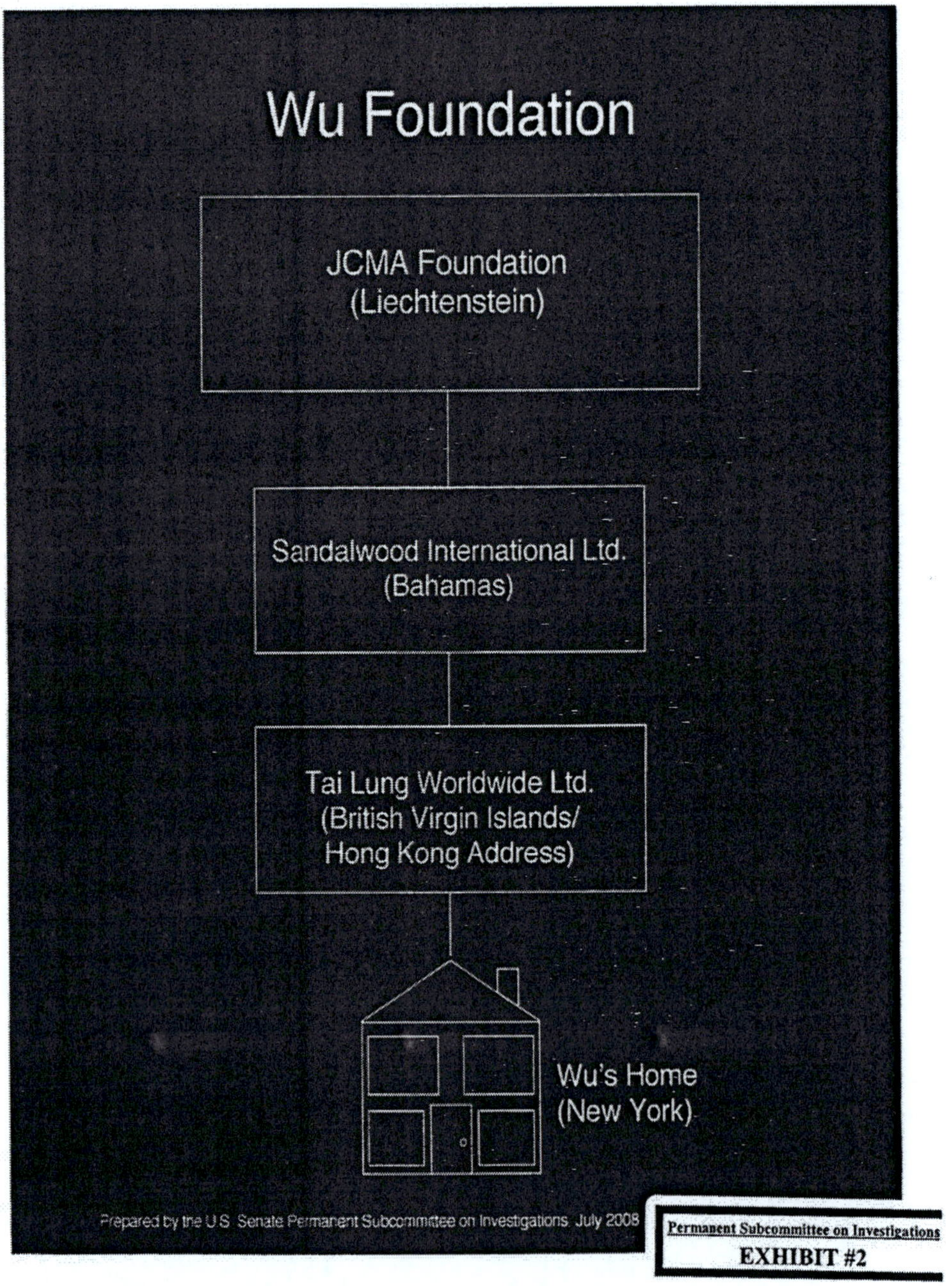
Wu Foundation
JCMA Foundation
(Liechtenstein)
Sandalwood International Ltd.
(Bahamas)
Tai Lung Worldwide Ltd.
(British Virgin Islands/
Hong Kong Address)
Wu's Home
(New York)
Prepared by the U.S. Senate Permanent Subcommittee on Investigations July 2008
Permanent Subcommittee on Investigations
EXHIBIT #2

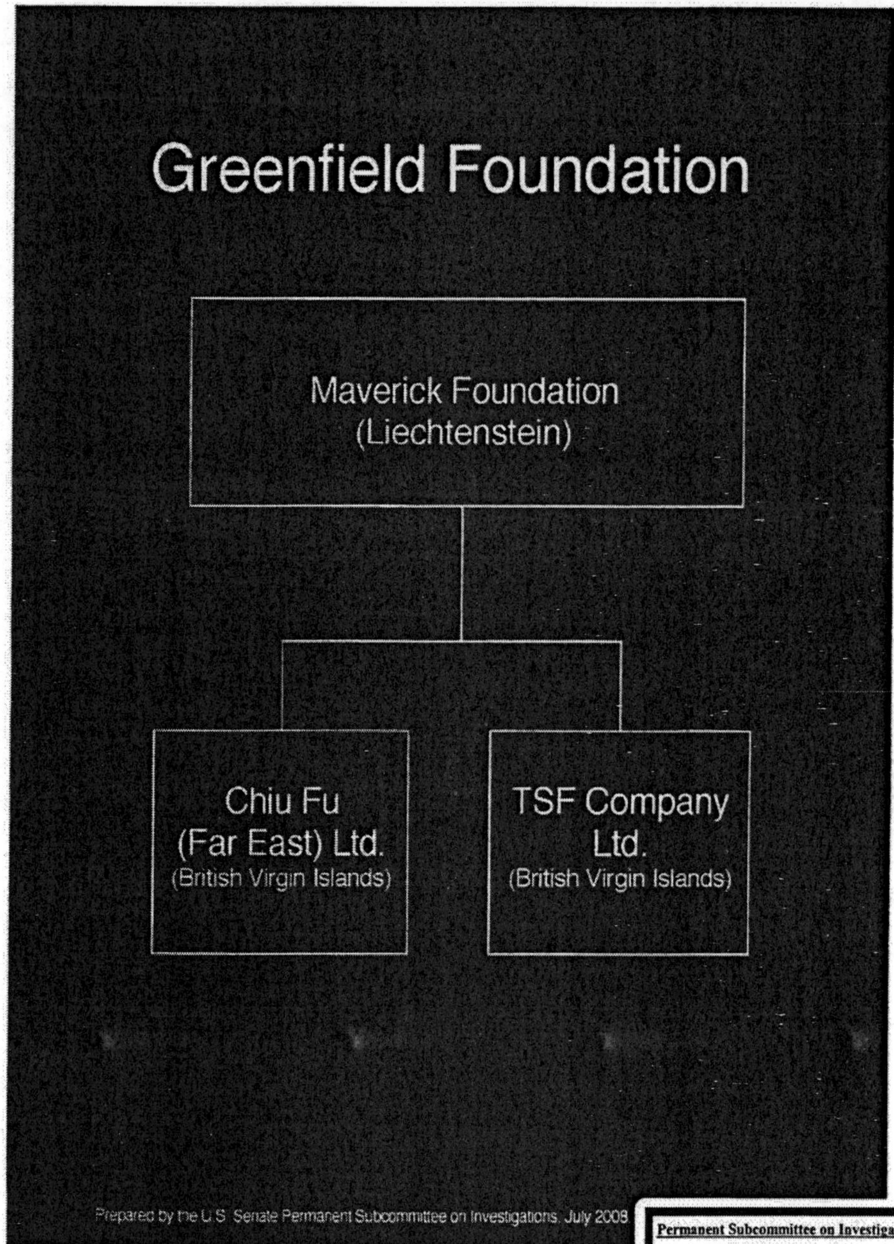

Permanent Subcommittee on Investigations

EXHIBIT #3

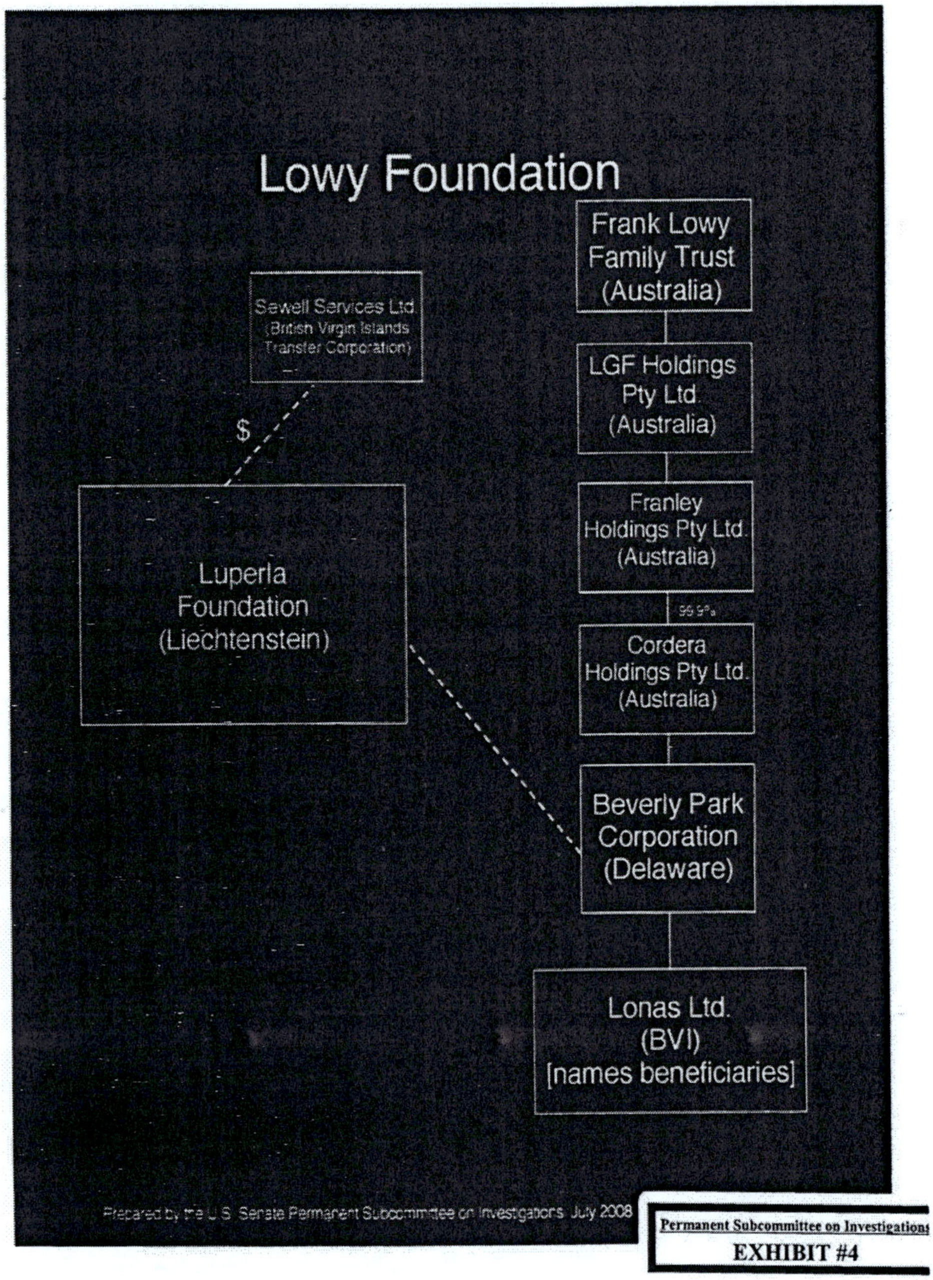
Lowy Foundation
Frank Lowy Family Trust (Australia)
Sewell Services Ltd. (British Virgin Islands Transfer Corporation)
LGF Holdings Pty Ltd. (Australia)
$
Luperla Foundation (Liechtenstein)
Franley Holdings Pty Ltd. (Australia)
99.9%
Cordera Holdings Pty Ltd. (Australia)
Beverly Park Corporation (Delaware)
Lonas Ltd. (BVI) [names beneficiaries]
Prepared by the U.S. Senate Permanent Subcommittee on Investigations July 2008
Permanent Subcommittee on Investigations
EXHIBIT #4

STATEMENT OF FORMER LGT TREUHAND EMPLOYEE, FORMERLY KNOWN AS HENRICH KIEBER

Permanent Subcommittee on Investigations
EXHIBIT #5

UNITED STATES SENATE PERMANENT SUBCOMMITTEE ON INVESTIGATIONS COMMITTEE ON HOMELAND SECURITY AND GOVERNMENTAL AFFAIRS

Statement of Former LGT Treuhand Employee

Washington, D.C.

Appearances:

On behalf of the Committee on Governmental Affairs:
ROBERT L. ROACH, ESQ.
Counsel and Chief Investigator
MICHAEL P. FLOWERS, ESQ. Counsel to the Minority 199 Russell Building
United States Senate
Permanent Subcommittee on Investigations
Committee on Homeland Security and
Governmental Affairs Washington, D.C. 20510

MR. ROACH: Good morning, sir. My name is Bob Roach. I am counsel for the Democratic staff of the Permanent Subcommittee on Investigations. With me is my colleague, Mike Flowers, who is counsel for the Republican staff of the Subcommittee.

MR. FLOWERS: Good morning, sir. CONFIDENTIAL INFORMANT: Good morning.

MR. ROACH: Thank you for joining us.

I understand you have a statement to make after which we will ask you a few questions about the banking and trust operations of the LGT Group. Please proceed.

CONFIDENTIAL INFORMANT: Good morning.

I swear that the testimony I am about to give will be the truth, the whole truth, and nothing but the truth so help me God.

In 2000, the LGT Trust was evaluating the so-called "paperless office." A project to scan every document of each client's legal entity and index them electronically, encoding an internal "bak track" code, a b-a-k. The project requires to hire over 20 new staff members. Based on my education and skills, I, then named Heinrich Kieber, worked--started to work at the LGT Trust in Vaduz in October 2000, and I worked there for more than 2 years until the date 2002.

The LGT Group in Liechtenstein is a provider of a vast range of financial services. The key business of the LGT Group consists of the LGT Bank and the LGT Trust services. Both are independent, commercial companies, and both use autonomous computer data storage systems.

The core trade of the LGT Trust, with head office in Vaduz and several branches in Switzerland, is selling and managing Liechtenstein legal entities such as foundations or establishments. They cater for clients from many different countries including the USA.

Generally, the client transfers his/her bank assets, such as securities and cash accounts and often also the nonbank assets, such as real estate, expensive paintings, patents, rights, et cetera, into the ownership of a selected one or more legal entity.

The client becomes then the beneficial owner of the legal entity.

Every single legal entity from Liechtenstein has to pay on average a worldwide matchless flat tax rate of only $1000 Swiss francs per year, regardless of the millions of different type of assets they own and income they gain.

The LGT Trust, back in the year 2002, had over 3,500 active legal entities under management, with the combined total bank assets of around 7.2 billion Swiss francs of which about 6 were invested at the LGT Bank and the rest in other Liechtenstein banks or Swiss banks. Back then, the LGT Bank had around 50 to 60 billion Swiss francs in their books. Today they hold over 100 billion Swiss francs. The real value of the nonbank assets are never recorded in the books.

The first couple of months I was in charge of the correct handling of all clients' legal entities' files to make sure that they are scanned properly and that not one of the very sensitive documents where all the data concerning the beneficial owners are recorded is lost in the process. Because of the nature of my job, I had access to all documents of all legal entities, active ones and the inactive ones.

The biggest task of the second stage was the proper indexing of all scanned documents. To be able to index the documents, we had to read every single one on our screens. It was then when I began to realize the very questionable business the LGT was often involved in and the dubious clients they were serving, the kind of business that goes beyond just facilitating massive tax evasion. Going through thousands of documents, I got very--I got the very clear picture of the highly sophisticated and sometimes surprisingly simple tricks and methods used to (a) help any clients to bring his or her bank assets to Liechtenstein and nonbank assets under the control of the one or more selective legal entity; (b) help any clients to keep his or her assets out of the reach of the taxman and people who may have a legal right to it or interest in it; (c) get around the laws of Liechtenstein and other countries; (d)--and (d)--avoid the attention of international law enforcement agencies and the international media.

Liechtenstein has implemented real tough new compliance laws in January 2001. In addition, in July 2002, they signed a mutual assistance treaty with the United States of America. This treaty was designed to protect the international financial markets against terror, organized and economic crimes. However, the business practices of LGT undermines those reforms that Liechtenstein enacted.

The LGT deliberately ignores the basic principles of the know-yourcustomer rules. For sure, I can frankly declare that in the vast majority of all legal entities, LGT does not have a clue about the real sources of their clients' huge wealth they manage, as it has been verified in the files I delivered to the U.S. Government.

The final part of my job was to conduct training programs for all of the 85 staff members of the LGT Trust, including CEO, members of the company's board--and members of the company's board. When I was teaching the CEO or a member of the board or a trust client advisor, I confronted them about the LGT's questionable practices that I have seen in many files. Sometimes I always raised this topic with foundations' bank account managers from the LGT Bank. All these discussions were about files with strong indication to corruption, links to dictators, or business deals to avoid a U.S. embargo, for example. The answer was always the same: None of your business.

Just stick to your designated job.

I obtained copies of the data of every legal entity and, furthermore, copies of vast internal documents before I left the company. All documents provided are authentic, original copies and have not been in any way changed or manipulated.

MR. ROACH: Thank you, sir.

CONFIDENTIAL INFORMANT: That's my statement.

MR. ROACH: Thank you, sir. I'd now like to ask you a few questions. First of all, in your statement you referred to tricks that LGT used to help clients bring their assets into the bank, including--would you mind commenting on that, including the use of shell companies to move funds internationally.

CONFIDENTIAL INFORMANT: Yes. There are several methods in use, depending on the type of assets the client wants to transfer into his or her legal entity in Liechtenstein. For bank assets, the LGT Group establishes, indirectly manages, and ultimately owns a number of legal entities, so called "special purpose vehicles," SPV. For the purpose of high-grade camouflage, there are two types of SPVs. Type A: big bank accounts around the world; and Type B: which do not have any bank accounts but own and control Type A. To protect the LGT Group, those types used are never from Liechtenstein. The LGT uses only SPV registered in Panama, in the British Virgin Islands, or sometimes even in Nigeria.

In practical terms, for a U.S. client, the LGT will transfer the bank's assets out of the United States through a chain of several Type A SPVs. Firstly, always into a country, for example, Canada, which from the IRS point of view is not suspicious. Next, through a series of other countries and therefore different jurisdictions. Preferably countries with very weak or, better, non-existing compliance laws. Before reaching Liechtenstein, it will run through a Swiss bank, for example the Banca del Gottardo in Lugano. This bank, in turn, has reciprocal rights to use the LGT Bank for its own customers.

For an additional layer of concealment, either the Swiss bank or the LGT Bank often perform a fake cash-out transaction to make it look like the monies have been paid out in cash over the counter where in fact they have been transferred into the concentration account of the LGT Bank and, at the same time, an equal amount has been credited into the client's legal entity's bank account. After one or two years in use, the SPVs are put into liquidation, then deleted, and new ones established.

The only purpose of all this is to make it extremely complicated for law enforcement agencies to follow the trail, as each step serves as a filter to hide the track of the client's money. For any bank or trust company in Liechtenstein, the matter of SPVs is commercially very sensitive material. The better sys--sorry. The better the system put in place, actually the less it will be detected. There's a lot of effort put into general research and checks of any possible legal implications, so that the LGT Group can always be many steps ahead of the tax authorities.

All of the clients' trust advisors and bank account managers of the LGT Group get regular in-house training in relation to the latest tricks and methods used so they can keep their knowledge up to date and can offer it to any existing or future customers.

MR. FLOWERS: Thank you, sir.

Sir, you mentioned during your statement that LGT helped clients to keep their assets out of reach of tax agencies or persons with legal claims on those assets. Could you please explain how that was accomplished?

CONFIDENTIAL WITNESS: Yes. What happens, the LGT strongly recommends to all clients to follow instructions such as, firstly, not to tell anybody concerning the legal entity to their lawyers, to other family members or relatives who are not part of the pool of beneficial owners, to friends or business partners. The reason is, any human relationship can go wrong and the client may end up in a situation where blackmailing is possible. Secondly, not to call the LGT Group from home--not from home, not from work. Use public phones instead. As Liechtenstein has an own country code number, the IRS may use the same plan as the Italian tax police did some years ago. They ordered the state-run phone company to record over a certain period the caller's i.d.; the time, date, and number dialed from a big city in Italy to Liechtenstein, to a Liechtenstein number. When the number called did not match a phone number--sorry--did match a phone number registered to a bank, trust company, or a lawyer, the tax police of Italy conducted a special assessment of the Italian callers. Thirdly, a third recommendation, only make calls in emergency to the nominated cell phone numbers of the clients' trust advisors. The LGT Trust only uses cell phone numbers from Switzerland or Austria. Again, because of the existence of a Liechtenstein-own country code number. When calling, the clients should always use the code words agreed and never state their own names or name of the legal entities. In addition, the LGT Group itself does not send any mail to their customers out of-- from Liechtenstein. If at all, mail gets sent out via Swiss or Austrian post office to avoid the attention of any tax enforcement agency around the world looking for mail coming from Liechtenstein.

In addition, any documents sent out are specially prepared in the way that the name of the bank, the client's name, or the legal entities' name is not revealed. The LGT Group does not call the clients at home or at work or on her or his phone--cell phones and does not communicate with their clients via email. The fact that all the LGT Trust's clients do not need their assets hidden in legal entities for their daily living helps very much to avoid detection and to keep the personal contact between the parties to a minimum, on average once per year.

MR. ROACH: Thank you.

You said that LGT used methods to allow it to get around compliance with the laws of Liechtenstein and other countries. How did LGT do that?

CONFIDENTIAL WITNESS: Yes, they're very sophisticated in that way. The know-your-customer rules necessitate a lot of up-to-date documentation concerning the client's identity and the true source of assets. In addition, a profile of every client has to be created, and any movement outside the set profile has to be reported to a preferably independent government entity, for example, to the financial intelligence unit. The LGT not only fails to keep the basic documentation up to date, often there is no clear indication of the beneficial owner or the source of the monies at all. Furthermore, they, the LGT Trust, predetermine the threshold of a client's profile in such an unrealistic way that it would--that it will not trigger the compulsive report even so when according to compliance law, the transaction is regarded as more than suspicious.

MR. FLOWERS: Thank you, sir.

Sir, based on your experiences while working at LGT, did LGT ever assist U.S. persons in repatriating their assets back to the United States in a manner that would have reduced the attentions of the United States Government?

CONFIDENTIAL WITNESS: Yes, there are several tricks in use, and I recall one. Then, at times, actually the LGT Trust would adjust the legal entities' documents to designate a new beneficial owner who will cause or result in the lowest tax obligation or, if possible, a zero tax obligation. Often this means creating a--new trust documents and changing the name of the real beneficial owner into the name of a person or relative who has recently died or, in some cases, is unfortunately in the process of dying. When the assets are transferred back to the United States, the real beneficial owners explain to the IRS that they have just inherited a large amount which was only discovered in recent times.

MR. ROACH: Now, in your statement, you also said that LGT sought to avoid the attention of international law enforcement and the media. How did LGT do that?

CONFIDENTIAL WITNESS: After some major scandals in the past 15 years, in an effort to avoid bad and further damage to their reputation, many powerful financial key players in Liechtenstein established smaller banks or trust companies whose names nobody recognizes. They have transferred their risky group of clients into those new banks or trust companies. In that way, if the risky clients are exposed in a scandal overseas, the larger well-known banks or trust companies are out of trouble and the media spotlight. The LGT Trust, but not so much the LGT Bank, did not accept new clients from Russia, for example, but would refer them to such smaller trust companies.

MR. FLOWERS: Sir, you made references in your statement to LGT's role in assisting in corruptive--or corruption, acts of corruption including breaking embargoes, for example. Could you please elaborate on that?

CONFIDENTIAL WITNESS: Yeah. The words I say here is that one set of documents indicate its pride in government officials in another country--in other countries including the United States. The LGT Bank introduced the client to the LGT Trust. The LGT Trust did accept the client but refused to nominate staff onto a new Panama company where such payments should be done in the future. At the end, in this file, the payments continued to be facilitated through the LGT Bank.

And there's another file which has a very strong indication to-- of corruption in a third world country. A head of a social government department owns over $5 million U.S. dollars with no explanation in the files whatever in regard to the source of the vast amount.

MR. ROACH: In an answer to a previous question, you identified some problems with LGT's know-your-customer program. What about LGT's compliance with the qualified intermediary program?

CONFIDENTIAL WITNESS: Yeah, I strongly believe that they are violating this one too. The IRS implemented the qualified intermediary stages QI to be able to collect the withholding tax on interest and dividends on U.S. securities through foreign intermediaries. The LGT Group realized quickly that without the QI stages, the banking secrecy for their U.S. clients cannot be sustained, because only as a QI the LGT Group can avoid having to report the underlying beneficial owners to the IRS. The IRS approved the QI stages to Liechtenstein as a country and to the LGT Group as a foreign intermediary in early 2001, as both were able to persuade the IRS that Liechtenstein's know-your-customer rules were top standard. All U.S. clients from the LGT Group with U.S. securities in the bank portfolios have been informed about the QI regulations. These clients had two options: Get out of the U.S. security--sell them or keep them. The clients wanting to keep the U.S. securities had great fears that the IRS may eventually find out who the ultimate beneficial owners are, for instance, through the external auditors' working paper the IRS can request to examine.

To reduce the panic, the LGT came up with the solutions: (a) to transfer all U.S. securities held by a legal entity of a U.S. tax person into a newly established Panama corporation. To add a further layer of secrecy between the foundation and that Panama corporation, another offshore company will own the Panama corporation. The LGT's argument for the Panama corporation solution was that the IRS regards it as a per se corporation; (b) having added enough offshore companies in between the U.S. client as a beneficial owner and the entity holding the U.S. securities, the LGT Trust declares the whole structure as being a non-U.S. status. This should keep the client out of trouble and taxes.

MR. ROACH: Thank you very much, sir. We appreciate your comments.

This concludes our questions. MR. FLOWERS: Thank you, sir. CONFIDENTIAL WITNESS: Thank you very much.

━━ = Redacted by the Permanent Subcommittee on Investigations

Shannon Neal Marsh

LETTER OF WISHES

I, the undersigned, Shannon Neal Marsh, born [redacted],
being Principal of

LINCOL FOUNDATION, VADUZ

hereby express my wish that:

In case of my death or incapacity and in case of death of all the Principals of LINCOL FOUNDATION, VADUZ, the right to give instructions shall pass to

- James Genery Marsh, born [redacted]
  and/or
- [redacted] Marsh, born [redacted]

Vaduz, October 15, 1985

(Shannon Neal Marsh)

Shannon Neal Marsh

Permanent Subcommittee on Investigations
EXHIBIT #6

PSI-USMSTR - 000605

BANK IN LIECHTENSTEIN
Aktiengesellschaft
FL-9490 Vaduz · Postfach 85 · Tel. 075/5 11 22 · Telex 77865

Vaduz, den 15. Oktober 1985 pb

LINCOL FOUNDATION, VADUZ

Wir haben heute von Ihnen erhalten:

US$ 2'629'700.-- Noten
" 691'000.-- "

US$ 3'320'700.-- ~~in cash /(./. Agio ca. $ 3'800.--)~~
===============

Gutschrift auf
☐ Konto US$-Konto
☐ Depot
erhalten Sie separat.

BANK IN LIECHTENSTEIN
Aktiengesellschaft

AF-1302 0984 10T SVD

Permanent Subcommittee on Investigations
EXHIBIT #7

PSI-USMSTR - 000607

BANK IN LIECHTENSTEIN
AG
(Address, Phone, fax)

Vaduz, October 15, 1985 pb

LINCOL FOFUNDATION, VADUZ

Today we received from you:

US$ 2,629,700.00	Notes	
" 691,000.00	"	
US$ 3,320,700	in cash / (./. Agio about $3,800.00)	

US Dollar account

BANK IN LIECHTENSTEIN
AG
(Two illegible signatures)

5/23/92

Belegexemplar

To Mr. Alvote

I SHANNON N. MARSH give
KERRY M. MARSH permission to review
all document's and reciept's
pertaining to Lincul Foundation and
25.6.85 Chateau Foundation. Please group our
investment's so that we pay as
little as possible in commision's as
you discussed last year with my
brother Kerry M. Marsh.

Thank You
Shannon N. Marsh
Shannon N. Marsh

KONTR. 635

Permanent Subcommittee on Investigations
EXHIBIT #8

PSI-USMSTR - 000231

Zusatz zum Mandatsvertrag

Belegexemplar

Instruction

[redacted] = Redacted by the Permanent Subcommittee on Investigations

In addition to the principals as per today Mrs. [redacted] Marsh, born on [redacted], is also empowered to act as a principal with individual signing power according to the Agency Agreement of LINCOL FOUNDATION, VADUZ, dated October 15, 1985.

The following two persons are also empowered to act as a principal with individual signing power after reaching the age of 25 according to the Agency Agreement of LINCOL FOUNDATION, VADUZ, dated October 15, 1985:

- Miss [redacted] Marsh, born [redacted]
- Mr. Michael Kerry Marsh, born [redacted]

Vaduz, 17th November 1993

Shannon Neal Marsh

KONTR. 635

Permanent Subcommittee on Investigations
EXHIBIT #9

PSI-USMSTR - 000612

Belegexemplar

635

635 SD. ... wp/ORV/RT

18. OKT 1994

KD : ERLEDIGT

Mr. Peter Meier:

Please change the management of LINCOL from Zurich to Vaduz as we discussed on October 4,1994

In addition please change LINCOL and CHATEAU so that they are gross oriented as per our discussion on October 4, 1994.

(3)

4/10/1994

Thank You

James A. Marsh Jr.

James A. Marsh Jr.

KONTR. 635

mit Ovali besprochen
Herr Zeiny per Tel
erledigt
27-11-94

Permanent Subcommittee on Investigations
EXHIBIT #10

MAR 09507

[redacted] = Redacted by the Permanent Subcommittee on Investigations

Letter of wishes

I, the undersigned, James Albright MARSH, born [redacted] being primary Beneficiary of

Lincol Foundation, Vaduz

I hereby express my wish that:

1 JAM any
- ~~Mr. James Albright MARSH, born on the~~ [redacted]
- Mr. Shannon Neal MARSH, born on the [redacted]
- Mrs. [redacted] MASH, born on the [redacted]
- Mss. [redacted] MARSH, born on the [redacted]
- Mr. Michael Kerry MARSH, born on the [redacted]

Mr. [redacted] MARSH born [redacted]

JAM

shall be ~~primary~~ second Beneficiaries for life. The beneficial interest shall be undivided; within the framework of the Articles each primary Beneficiary may dispose freely of the entire beneficial interest (100%).

In case of death or incapacity of all the primary Beneficiaries, the sole second Beneficiary shall be Mr. James Genery Marsh, born on the [redacted]

Beneficiaries' rights shall remain quiescent until the completion of their 18 year of life. Separated, the quiescent share of the beneficial interest shall be administered by the Foundation Board with the care of a pater familias. Upon the age limit being reached, the Foundation Board shall on the Beneficiaries' request submit accounts for the entire period of quiescence.

Notwithstanding the provisions in the above paragraph, the Foundation Board may unanimously resolve to grant benefits even before the age limit has been reached, if this is deemed necessary in order to safeguard the interests of the Beneficiaries concerned.

Before the age limit has been reached, neither the Beneficiaries concerned nor the natural or juridical persons entrusted with their legal representation shall be entitled to inspect, or to receive information or statements of account.

Date / place: Vaduz 11. Oct. 2000

James A Marsh 10/11/00

....

Mr. Marsh James Albright MARSH

Permanent Subcommittee on Investigations

EXHIBIT #11

MAR-00019

21.9.06

Letter of wishes

[redacted] = Redacted by the Permanent Subcommittee on Investigations

I, the undersigned, James Albright Marsh, born [redacted] being primary Beneficiary of

Fondation Chateau, Vaduz

hereby express my wish that:

JGAM

~~- Mr. James Albright MARSH, born on the~~ [redacted]
- Mr. Shannon Neal MARSH, born on the [redacted]
- Mrs. [redacted] MASH, born on the [redacted]
- Mss. [redacted] MARSH, born on the [redacted]
- Mr. Michael Kerry MARSH, born on the [redacted]

Mr. [redacted] born on [redacted]

shall be ~~primary~~ second Beneficiaries for life. The beneficial interest shall be undivided; within the framework of the Articles each primary Beneficiary may dispose freely of the entire beneficial interest (100%).

In case of death or incapacity of all the primary Beneficiaries, the sole second Beneficiary shall be Mr. James Genery Marsh, born on the [redacted].

Beneficiaries' rights shall remain quiescent until the completion of their 18 year of life. Separated, the quiescent share of the beneficial interest shall be administered by the Foundation Board with the care of a pater familias. Upon the age limit being reached, the Foundation Board shall on the Beneficiaries' request submit accounts for the entire period of quiescence.

Notwithstanding the provisions in the above paragraph, the Foundation Board may unanimously resolve to grant benefits even before the age limit has been reached, if this is deemed necessary in order to safeguard the interests of the Beneficiaries concerned.

Before the age limit has been reached, neither the Beneficiaries concerned nor the natural or juridical persons entrusted with their legal representation shall be entitled to inspect, or to receive information or statements of account.

Date / place: Vaduz 11. Oct. 2000

James A. Marsh 10/11/00

Mr. Marsh James Albright Marsh

Aktenvermerk

Betr.	LINCOL FOUNDATION / CHATEAU FOUNDATION
zur Erl.	
zur. Kennt	LGT Treuhand
Datum	Donnerstag, 7. Februar 2002

Erinnerungs- - Aktenvermerk

Am 11. Oktober 2000 besuchte mich auf sehr kurzfristige Vereinbarung Herr James G. Marsh zusammen mit seinem Vater, James Albright Marsh.

Herr Knecht LGT unterbreitete die Performance der beiden Stiftungen mit den entsprechenden Erläuterungen. Die Herren waren grundsätzlich zufrieden. Die Situation am Markt war ihnen auch bekannt.

Als weiteres Thema wurde die Situation wegen QI besprochen. Beide Herren gaben den Auftrag, aus allen US Titeln auszusteigen und im Euro Gebiet zu investieren. Die US steuerbefreiten Obligationen sind zu belassen.

Ich erkläre den Herren die STOM im Vergleich mit dem amerikanischen Trust. Sie sind damit einverstanden, die Akten in eine Discretionary Stiftung umzurüsten. Leider war nicht genügend Zeit, um die Unterlagen konform vorzubereiten. Wir erstellen in der Eile einen Letter of wishes, worin der Wunsch geäussert wird, dass James Albright Marsh als Erstbegünstigte bestellt werden sollte. Die Liste der Zweitbegünstigten wird auf der Vorlage etwas korrigiert und dann unterzeichnet. Nachdem bisher keine Beistatuten bestanden haben, sind die Akten für den nächsten Besuch entsprechend vorzubereiten. Ich habe den Herren den Mindestsatz von 0.2 0/00 angeboten.

Wie üblich war die Diskussion sehr hastig und etwas oberflächlich. Deshalb ist die Situation auch beim nächsten Besuch erneut zu erläutern.

Permanent Subcommittee on Investigations
EXHIBIT #12

PSI-USMSTR - 000614

Note to the File

Subject: LINCOL FOUNDATION/ CHATEAU FOUNDATION

Information copy: LFT Treuhand

Date: Thursday, February 7, 2002

Reminder – Note to file

On October 11, 2000, Mr. James G. Marsh, along with his father, Mr. James Albright Marsh visited me very briefly.

Mr. Knecht LGT, presented the performance of both foundations with the corresponding explanations. The men were basically satisfied. The market status was also made known to them.

As a further topic, the QI situation was discussed. Both men gave the order to get out of all US securities and to invest in the Euro area. The US tax exempt bonds should be left alone.

I explained the STOM to the men along with American trusts. They understand that the shares must be converted into a discretionary foundation. Unfortunately, there was not enough time to prepare the concurring documents. We quickly prepared a letter of wishes in which the wish was expressed that James Albright Marsh should be named as first beneficiary. The list of second beneficiaries will be corrected before the presentation and then signed. The documents for the next meeting will be prepared since there are no by-laws to date. I offered the men a minimal rate of 0.2 0/00.

As usual the discussion was very hurried and a bit shallow. So the situation will also be discussed at the next meeting.

(Illegible signature)

DEED OF SIGNATURE

I, the undersigned

Mr Kerry Michael Marsh

hereby accept my appointment as Protector of the

CHATEAU FOUNDATION, Vaduz

and shall sign in this capacity by affixing my signature as follows:

Kerry Michael Marsh

Vaduz, the 10th November 2004

Permanent Subcommittee on Investigations
EXHIBIT #13

DEED OF SIGNATURE

I, the undersigned

Mr Shannon Neal Marsh

hereby accept my appointment as Protector of the

CHATEAU FOUNDATION, Vaduz

and shall sign in this capacity by affixing my signature as follows:

Shannon Neal Marsh

Vaduz,

DEED OF SIGNATURE

I, the undersigned

Mr James Albright Marsh jun.

hereby accept my appointment as Protector of the

CHATEAU FOUNDATION, Vaduz

and shall sign in this capacity by affixing my signature as follows:

James Albright Marsh jun.

Vaduz,

DEED OF APPOINTMENT OF SUCCESSORS

▬ = Redacted by the Permanent Subcommittee on Investigations

I, the undersigned, Mr James Albright Marsh jun.

in my capacity as Protector of

CHATEAU FOUNDATION,

pursuant to the provisions of the pertinent By-Laws hereby revocably appoint as my successor as Protector:

Mrs [redacted] Marsh.

If Mrs Michelle Corinne Marsh does not become Successor Protector on the occasion of my ceasing to be a Protector, I herewith appoint revocably as her substitute to become Successor Protector:

Miss [redacted] Marsh.

If Miss Courtney Nichole Marsh does not become Successor Protector on the occasion of my ceasing to be a Protector, I herewith appoint revocably as her substitute to become Successor Protector:

Master Michael Kerry Marsh.

If Master Michael Kerry Marsh does not become Successor Protector on the occasion of my ceasing to be a Protector, I herewith appoint revocably as his substitute to become Successor Protector:

Master [redacted] Marsh.

Vaduz,

James Albright Marsh jun.

Resolution

The Foundation Board of the

Fondation CHATEAU, Vaduz

hereby resolves:

1. The inventory of assets and liabilities at 31. December 2000 showing a total of USD 10'015'623,50, which is attached to this resolution as Schedule 1, is hereby approved and adopted.

2. The investments made in 2000 according to Schedule 2 are hereby approved and adopted.

3. No distributions have been made in 2000.

4. LGT Treuhand AG, Vaduz, is entrusted with drawing up the inventory of assets and liabilities for the next business year.

Vaduz, 12. September 2003

The Foundation Board:

lic. iur. Marcel Telser

Profile Management Trust reg.

Anna-Marie Rapuser

Margit Böckle

The undersigned beneficiary/beneficiaries has/have taken due note of this resolution.

Vaduz, 10-11. 2004

MAR-00623

Permanent Subcommittee on Investigations

EXHIBIT #14

Marsh James Albright jun., Florida

LGT Treuhand
Aktiengesellschaft
Städtle 28
FL-9490 Vaduz

Vaduz, November 10, 2004 ANA/mvg

Fondation Chateau, Vaduz

Dear Sirs

In my capacity as economic founder and primary beneficiary of the above mentioned foundation, I hereby irrevocably grant formal approval and release to any and all administrational and management activities as well as any and all actions of LGT Treuhand AG as representative and the relevant employees of LGT Treuhand AG as Members of the Board of Directors during the entire mandate period.

I further declare that I will arrange for settlement of the final note of LGT Treuhand AG.

Yours sincerely,

James A. Marsh Jr.

Permanent Subcommittee on Investigations
EXHIBIT #15

MAR 09509

Shannon Neal Marsh
703 Harrison St., Hollywood , Florida

To the Members of the Foundation Council of
CHATEAU Foundation
P.O. Box 129
9490 Vaduz

Date: Vaduz, November 4, 2004

Dear Sirs

Upon my request you have agreed to be appointed members of the Foundation Council of CHATEAU Foundation.

I herewith declare to hold you harmless and to indemnify you against any and all charges, expenses, claims, demands, procedures, costs, damages or liabilities whatsoever direct or consequential arising out of or in connection with your duties as Members of the Foundation Council of the above mentioned Foundation except for gross negligent acts (which term does not include omissions).

In case that your acts or omissions are in conformity with any of the wishes or recommendations of the Protector (if any) of the above mentioned Foundation or with the provisions of the letter of wishes (if any) I shall hold you harmless and indemnify you as declared above but without any reservations or exceptions.

May I kindly ask you to declare your approval of the above by countersigning and returning a copy of this letter to me.

Yours sincerely,

Shannon Neal Marsh

Permanent Subcommittee on Investigations
EXHIBIT #16

MAR 09517

ESTATE OF JAMES A. MARSH

2006
INCOME TAX RETURNS

MORRISON, BROWN, ARGIZ
Certified Public Accountants + COMPANY, LLP

MAR-01442

Permanent Subcommittee on Investigations
EXHIBIT #17

Form 706 (Rev. 10-2006)

Estate of: JAMES A MARSH

SCHEDULE G - Transfers During Decedent's Life

(If you elect section 2032A valuation, you must complete Schedule G and Schedule A-1.)

Item number	Description. For securities, give CUSIP number. If trust, partnership, or closely held entity, give EIN	Alternate valuation date	Alternate value	Value at date of death
A.	Gift tax paid or payable by the decedent or the estate for all gifts made by the decedent or his or her spouse within 3 years before the decedent's death (section 2035(b))	XXXX		
B.	Transfers includible under section 2035(a), 2036, 2037, or 2038:			
1	LINCOL FOUNDATION - VALUE IS BASED ON MARKET VALUE OF UNDERLYING INVESTMENTS, WHICH ARE PRINCIPALLY MARKETABLE SECURITIES. (SEE ATTACHED STATUTES OF LINCOL FOUNDATION, SEE ATTACHED FINANCIAL STATEMENTS) (SEE ATTACHED STATEMENT FOR SCHEDULE M)			13,029,701.
2	FOUNDATION CHATEAU - VALUE IS BASED ON MARKET VALUE OF UNDERLYING INVESTMENTS, WHICH ARE PRINCIPALLY MARKETABLE SECURITIES. (SEE ATTACHED STATUTES OF			
	Total from continuation schedules (or additional sheets) attached to this schedule			32,027,702.
	TOTAL. (Also enter on Part 5 - Recapitulation, page 3, at item 7.)			45,057,403.

SCHEDULE H - Powers of Appointment

(Include "5 and 5 lapsing" powers (section 2041(b)(2)) held by the decedent.)

(If you elect section 2032A valuation, you must complete Schedule H and Schedule A-1.)

Item number	Description	Alternate valuation date	Alternate value	Value at date of death
				MAR-01451
	Total from continuation schedules (or additional sheets) attached to this schedule			
	TOTAL. (Also enter on Part 5 - Recapitulation, page 3, at item 8.)			

(If more space is needed, attach the continuation schedule from the end of this package or additional sheets of the same size.)
(The instructions to Schedules G and H are in the separate instructions.)

Schedules G and H - Page 21

605181
10-13-06

Redacted by the Permanent Subcommittee on Investigations

6

2006.06000 MARSH, JAMES A MARSH__1

Estate of: JAMES A MARSH

CONTINUATION SCHEDULE

Continuation of Schedule G
(Enter letter of schedule you are continuing.)

Item number	Description	Alternate valuation date	Alternate value	Value at date of death
	FOUNDATION CHATEAU, SEE ATTACHED FINANCIAL STATEMENTS)(SEE ATTACHED STATEMENT FOR SCHEDULE M)			11,295,644.
3	TOPANGA FOUNDATION (JMLPM)- VALUE IS BASED ON MARKET VALUE OF UNDERLYING INVESTMENTS, WHICH ARE PRINCIPALLY MARKETABLE SECURITIES. (SEE ATTACHED STATUTES OF TOPANGA FOUNDATION)			8,893,712.
4	LARGELLA FOUNDATION (LANDERT), - VALUE IS BASED ON MARKET VALUE OF UNDERLYING INVESTMENTS, WHICH ARE PRINCIPALLY MARKETABLE SECURITIES. (SEE ATTACHED STATUTES OF LARGELLA FOUNDATION, SEE ATTACHED FINANCIAL STATEMENTS)(SEE ATTACHED STATEMENT FOR SCHEDULE M)			11,838,346.
				MAR-01452
	TOTAL. (Carry forward to main schedule.)			32,027,702.

005031
05-01-08

7

2006.06000 MARSH, JAMES A MARSH__1

Redacted by the Permanent Subcommittee on Investigations

Form 706 (Rev. 10-2006)

Estate of: JAMES A MARSH

SCHEDULE K - Debts of the Decedent, and Mortgages and Liens

Item number	Debts of the Decedent - Creditor and nature of claim, and allowable death taxes	Amount unpaid to date	Amount in contest	Amount claimed as a deduction
1	ESTIMATE OF U.S. INCOME TAX, INTEREST AND PENALTIES ON INCOME NOT PREVIOUSLY REPORTED FOR ASSETS LISTED ON SCHEDULE G			5,500,000.
	Total from continuation schedules (or additional sheets) attached to this schedule			
	TOTAL. (Also enter on Part 5 - Recapitulation, page 3, at item 14.)			5,500,000.

Item number	Mortgages and Liens - Description	Amount
		MAR-01455
	Total from continuation schedules (or additional sheets) attached to this schedule	
	TOTAL. (Also enter on Part 5 - Recapitulation, page 3, at item 15.)	

(If more space is needed, attach the continuation schedule from the end of this package or additional sheets of the same size.)
(The instructions to Schedule K are in the separate instructions.)

Schedule K - Page 25

005241
10-13-06

10
2006.06000 MARSH, JAMES A MARSH__1

Redacted by the Permanent Subcommittee on Investigations

BAKER & McKENZIE

Baker & McKenzie LLP
Mellon Financial Center
1111 Brickell Avenue, Suite 1700
Miami, Florida 33131, USA

Tel: +1 305 789 8900
Fax: +1 305 789 8953
www.bakernet.com

May 12, 2008

▬▬ = Redacted by the Permanent Subcommittee on Investigations

Bill Everett, Revenue Agent
SB/SE Division
Stop 662-D
2888 Woodcock Blvd.
Atlanta, Georgia 30341

RE: Anna Marsh (SSN [redacted]) and
James A. Marsh, deceased (SS# [redacted])
Reasonable Cause Statement
Failure to timely report foreign income on Forms 1040
Calendar Years: 2002 - 2006

Dear Mr. Everett:

As you know, the undersigned represent Anna Marsh, a U.S. citizen taxpayer with SS# [redacted] (**"Mrs. Marsh"**) and the Estate of James A. Marsh, a deceased U.S. citizen taxpayer with SS# [redacted] (**"Mr. Marsh"**, and together with Mrs. Marsh, the **"Taxpayers"**) and have previously filed Forms 2848, Power of Attorney.

Enclosed please find completed and executed amended Forms 1040X, Amended U.S. Individual Income Tax Return, for calendar years 2002 through 2006 (collectively referred to as **"Forms"**), filed on behalf of the Taxpayers. Form 1040 for 2007 is currently under extension. The Taxpayers' failure to timely report certain foreign income on their Forms 1040 for the years specified was due to reasonable cause, and not any willful act or specific intent on the part of the Taxpayers, as explained herein below.

Many years ago, Mr. Marsh funded several foundations in Liechtenstein, called Foundation Chateau, Lincol Foundation, Largella Foundation and Topanga Foundation (collectively, the **"Foundations"**).

Over the years and prior to the death of Mr. Marsh in June 2006, neither Mr. Marsh nor Mrs. Marsh received any distributions from the Foundations.

Permanent Subcommittee on Investigations
EXHIBIT #18

MAR-01185

BAKER & MCKENZIE

= Redacted by the Permanent Subcommittee on Investigations

As a U.S. person under IRC § 7701(a)(30), and the substantive settler of the Foundations, Mr. Marsh was required to report income earned from the Foundations pursuant to IRC § 641(a)(4).

Mr. Marsh, a construction contractor, was unsophisticated in the area of U.S. tax reporting requirements. It is believed that he did not know that the passive income earned in the Foundations was taxable in the United States. We believe that Mr. Marsh was under the erroneous belief that his income from the Foundations was not required to be reported until such time as the funds were repatriated to the United States. This may explain why he apparently did not spend any of the money in the Foundations for over twenty years.

Mr. Marsh relied on his U.S.-based accountant(s) to handle all of his IRS filings. The U.S. accountant(s) apparently did not advise Mr. Marsh regarding his U.S. tax reporting obligations with respect to the Foundations, nor was Mr. Marsh aware of the necessity to disclose the passive income in the Foundations to his U.S. accountant(s). As a consequence, the passive income earned from the Foundations was never reported, and Mr. Marsh remained unaware of his U.S. tax reporting obligations under IRC § 641(a)(4) to the IRS.

Mrs. Marsh, who will be 85 years old on [redacted] 2008, was not aware of the existence of the Foundations until the commencement of an IRS examination after her husband's death. Her husband was extremely private and did not discuss financial issues with her. He was the one in their relationship who took care of business and financial matters, paying the bills and dealing with the tax return preparer so that even if Mrs. Marsh had been aware of the Foundations, she would have assumed that her husband had taken care of any reporting requirements.

Recently, while assisting Mrs. Marsh and her sons with the IRS examination, we brought to her attention that her husband's passive income in respect to the Foundations needed to be reported. Mrs. Marsh agreed without any hesitation to do everything that was required to meet her tax reporting requirements. She requested that we assist her in seeking the financial data necessary to meet the tax filing requirements. Pursuant thereto, after many months of dogged effort, all of the necessary financial information was finally obtained from Liechtenstein and carefully analyzed by U.S. tax accountants (particularly because the Foundations had many mutual fund/PFIC

BAKER & MCKENZIE

investments). This financial data collection and complicated tax analysis was done at great expense in professional fees, both legal and accounting, in Liechtenstein and in the United States.

The facts above clearly demonstrate that Mrs. Marsh has acted in a responsible manner, exercising business care and prudence, and making more than reasonable efforts to determine the Taxpayers' tax reporting obligations as quickly as possible. Promptly upon being notified of their U.S. tax reporting obligations, Mrs. Marsh has cooperated fully with counsel to assist in filing these tax returns.

This letter and the enclosed Forms are intended to satisfy all of the Taxpayers' U.S. tax reporting obligations and any tax liability owed for calendar years 2002 through 2006.

We believe the facts, circumstances and reasons set forth above demonstrate an affirmative showing that the Taxpayers' failure to report the Foundation income in a timely manner was due to reasonable cause, and not willful neglect. We respectfully request that any possible penalties which otherwise could be imposed for the Taxpayer's failure to report timely income for calendar years 2002 through 2006 be waived.

Please note that Mrs. Marsh has attested below to the facts stated above under penalties of perjury. If you require any further information, we request that you contact Alan L. Weisberg, Esq. at (305) 374-5544. Thank you for your understanding and consideration of this matter.

Very truly yours,

Weisberg and Kainen

By: Alan L. Weisberg

Baker & McKenzie LLP

By: Robert F. Hudson, Jr.

BAKER & MCKENZIE

***

Attestation

Under penalties of perjury, I, Anna Marsh, individually and as Personal Representative for the Estate of James A. Marsh, do hereby declare that I have examined the above reasonable cause statement, and to the best of my knowledge and belief, it is true, correct and complete.

By: Anna S. Marsh Date: 5/12/08
Anna A. Marsh

By: Anna S. Marsh Date: 5/12/08
Anna A. Marsh, as Personal Representative for the Estate of James A. Marsh

BAKER & McKENZIE

Baker & McKenzie LLP
Mellon Financial Center
1111 Brickell Avenue, Suite 1700
Miami, Florida 33131, USA

Tel: +1 305 789 8900
Fax: +1 305 789 8953
www.bakernet.com

May 12, 2008

Bill Everett, Revenue Agent
SB/SE Division
Stop 662-D
2888 Woodcock Blvd.
Atlanta, Georgia 30341

[redacted] = Redacted by the Permanent Subcommittee on Investigations

RE: **Anna Marsh (SSN[redacted] and**
James A. Marsh, deceased (SS#[redacted])
Reasonable Cause Statement
[redacted]
Failure to timely report foreign bank and financial accounts
Calendar Years: 2002 - 2006

Dear Mr. Everett:

As you know, the undersigned represent Anna Marsh, a U.S. citizen taxpayer with SS#[redacted] (**"Mrs. Marsh"**) and the Estate of James A. Marsh, a deceased U.S. citizen taxpayer with SS#[redacted] (**"Mr. Marsh"** or the **"Taxpayer"**) and have previously filed Forms 2848, Power of Attorney.

Enclosed please find completed and executed Forms TD F 90-22.1, Report of Foreign Bank and Financial Accounts, for calendar years 2002 through 2006 (collectively referred to as "**Forms**"), filed on behalf of the Taxpayer. The Taxpayer's failure to timely report certain foreign bank and account information for the years specified was due to reasonable cause, and not any willful act or specific intent on the part of the Taxpayer, as explained herein below.

The Taxpayer, a U.S. citizen, opened several foreign bank accounts in the mid-1980s via the establishment of several foundations in Liechtenstein, called Foundation Chateau, Lincol Foundation, Largella Foundation and Topanga Foundation (collectively, the "**Foundations**"). Those accounts that were open at any time during the period from January 1, 2002 through December 31, 2006 are listed in the chart below (collectively, the "**Accounts**"):

Bank	Foundation	Account No.	Relevant Years
Centrum Bank	Chateau		2006
			2006
			2006
LGT Bank	Chateau	Redacted by Permanent Subcommittee on Investigations	2002 – 2006
LGT Bank	Lincol		2002 – 2006
Liechtensteinische Landesbank	Largella		2002- 2006
			2002- 2006
			2002- 2006
			2002- 2006
			2002- 2006
			2002, 2003
			2002
			2002- 2006
			2003 – 2005
			2003, 2004
Verwaltungs und Privatbank AG	Topanga		2002 - 2006
Privatbank von Graffenreid AG	Topanga		2002 - 2006
			2002 – 2006
			2002 – 2006
			2002 - 2004

The Taxpayer, a construction contractor, was unsophisticated in the area of U.S. tax and reporting requirements. It is believed that he did not know that the existence of these Foundations or the passive income in the Accounts was required to be reported to the U.S. Department of Treasury. We believe that The Taxpayer was under the erroneous belief that his interest in the Accounts was not required to be reported until such time as the funds in the Accounts were repatriated to the United States. This seemingly may explain why he apparently did not spend any of the money in the Accounts for over twenty years.

The Taxpayer relied on his U.S. accountant(s) to handle all of his IRS filings. The U.S. accountant(s) apparently never advised the Taxpayer regarding his U.S. reporting obligations with respect to non-U.S. bank accounts, nor was the Taxpayer aware of the necessity to disclose his passive income in the Accounts to his U.S. accountant(s). As a consequence, the Accounts were never reported, and the Taxpayer apparently remained unaware of his reporting obligations under 31 USC §5314.

Mrs. Marsh, who will be 85 years old on [redacted] 2008, was not aware of the existence of the Accounts until the commencement of an IRS examination after her husband's death. Her husband was extremely private and did not discuss financial issues with her. He was the one in their relationship who took care of business and financial matters, paying the bills and dealing with the tax return preparer so that even if Mrs. Marsh had been aware of the Foundations, she would have assumed that her husband had taken care of any reporting requirements.

Recently, while assisting Mrs. Marsh and her sons with the IRS examination, we brought to her attention that her husband's interest in the Accounts needed to be properly reported. Mrs. Marsh agreed without any hesitation to do everything that was required to meet her tax reporting requirements. She requested that we assist her in seeking the financial data necessary to meet the filing requirements. Pursuant thereto, after many months of dogged effort, all of the necessary financial information was finally obtained from Liechtenstein and carefully analyzed by U.S. tax accountants. This financial data collection and complicated tax analysis was done at great expense in professional fees, both legal and accounting, in Liechtenstein and in the United States.

The facts above clearly demonstrate that Mrs. Marsh, individually and on behalf of her deceased husband as Personal Representative of the Estate of James A. Marsh, has acted in a responsible manner, exercising business care and prudence, and making more than reasonable efforts to determine the Taxpayer's tax and information reporting obligations as quickly as possible. Promptly upon being notified of the Taxpayer's U.S. tax reporting obligations, Mrs. Marsh cooperated fully with counsel to assist in filing these reporting forms.

This letter and the enclosed Forms are intended to satisfy the Taxpayer's 31 U.S.C. §5314 reporting obligations for calendar years 2002 through 2006. We believe the acts, circumstances and reasons set forth above demonstrate an affirmative showing that the Taxpayer's failure to report the Accounts in a timely manner was due to reasonable cause, and not willful neglect. We respectfully request that, pursuant to 31 U.S.C. §5321(a)(5)(B)(ii), any and all possible penalties which otherwise could be imposed for the Taxpayer's failure to report timely the Accounts for calendar years 2002 through 2006 be waived.

▬ = Redacted by the Permanent Subcommittee on Investigations

Please note that Mrs. Marsh, individually and on behalf of her deceased husband as Personal Representative of the Estate of James A. Marsh, has attested below to the facts stated above under penalties of perjury. If you require any further information, we request that you contact Alan L. Weisberg, Esq. at (305) 374-5544. Thank you for your understanding and consideration of this matter.

Very truly yours,

Weisberg and Kainen

By: Alan L. Weisberg

Alan L. Weisberg

Baker & McKenzie LLP

By: R. F. Hudson, Jr.

Robert F. Hudson, Jr.

***

Attestation

Under penalties of perjury, I, Anna Marsh, individually and as Personal Representative for the Estate of James A. Marsh, do hereby declare that I have examined the above reasonable cause statement and, to the best of my knowledge and belief, it is true, correct and complete.

By: Anna A. Marsh Date: 5/12/08

Anna A. Marsh

By: Anna A. Marsh Date: 5/12/08

Anna A. Marsh, as Personal Representative for the Estate of James A. Marsh

[redacted]

Mellon Financial Center
1111 Brickell Avenue, Suite 1700
Miami, Florida 33131, USA

Tel: +1 305 789 8900
Fax: +1 305 789 8953
www.bakernet.com

Asia Pacific
Bangkok
Beijing
Hanoi
Ho Chi Minh City
Hong Kong
Jakarta
Kuala Lumpur
Manila
Melbourne
Shanghai
Singapore
Sydney
Taipei
Tokyo

Europe & Middle East
Almaty
Amsterdam
Antwerp
Bahrain
Baku
Barcelona
Berlin
Bologna
Brussels
Budapest
Cairo
Dusseldorf
Frankfurt / Main
Geneva
Kyiv
London
Madrid
Milan
Moscow
Munich
Paris
Prague
Riyadh
Rome
St. Petersburg
Stockholm
Vienna
Warsaw
Zurich

North & South America
Bogota
Brasilia
Buenos Aires
Caracas
Chicago
Chihuahua
Dallas
Guadalajara
Houston
Juarez
Mexico City
Miami
Monterrey
New York
Palo Alto
Porto Alegre
Rio de Janeiro
San Diego
San Francisco
Santiago
Sao Paulo
Tijuana
Toronto
Valencia
Washington, DC

May 12, 2008

Bill Everett, Revenue Agent
SB/SE Division
Stop 662-D
2888 Woodcock Blvd.
Atlanta, Georgia 30341

[redacted] = Redacted by the Permanent Subcommittee on Investigations

RE: Kerry Marsh (SSN [redacted])
Shannon Marsh (SSN [redacted])
Reasonable Cause Statement
Failure to Timely File Form 3520
Calendar Year: 2006

Dear Mr. Everett:

As you know, the undersigned represent Kerry Marsh, a U.S. citizen taxpayer with SS# [redacted] ("**Kerry Marsh**") and Shannon Marsh, a U.S. citizen taxpayer with SS# [redacted] ("**Shannon Marsh**") and have previously filed Forms 2848, Power of Attorney.

Enclosed please find the following completed and executed Forms 3520, Annual Return to Report Transactions With Foreign Trusts and Receipt of Certain Foreign Gifts, for calendar year 2006 (the "**Forms**"), filed on behalf of Kerry Marsh; Shannon Marsh; [redacted] Marsh, a U.S. taxpayer with SS# [redacted] ("[redacted]"); [redacted] Marsh, a U.S. taxpayer with SS# [redacted] ("[redacted]"); [redacted] Marsh, a U.S. taxpayer with SS# [redacted] ("[redacted]"); [redacted] Marsh, a U.S. taxpayer with SS# [redacted] ("[redacted]"; Kerry Marsh, Shannon Marsh, [redacted], [redacted] are referred to herein as the "**Taxpayers**").

The Taxpayers' failure to file these Forms in a timely manner was due to reasonable cause, and not any willful act or specific intent on the part of the Taxpayers, as explained herein below.

Many years ago, James A. Marsh, the father of Kerry Marsh and Shannon Marsh, funded several foundations in Liechtenstein, including one called Topanga Foundation (the "**Foundation**").

MIADMS/336548.2

BAKER & MCKENZIE

After the death of James A. Marsh and the commencement of an IRS examination, Kerry Marsh and Shannon Marsh learned that each of the Taxpayers was a beneficiary of the Foundation, and that such Foundation is a simple trust whose income is required to be distributed to each of the Taxpayers as a beneficiary. As such, we informed Kerry Marsh and Shannon Marsh that under IRC §6048(b), each of the Taxpayers is required to file Form 3520 with respect to the Foundation because they are each deemed to receive annual distributions despite the fact that they did not actually receive any income (or other) distributions in 2006 from the Foundation. Kerry Marsh and Shannon Marsh agreed without any hesitation to do everything that was required to meet the Taxpayers' tax reporting requirements. They requested that we assist them in seeking the financial data necessary to meet the filing requirement. Pursuant thereto, after many months of dogged effort, all of the necessary financial information was finally obtained from Liechtenstein and carefully analyzed by U.S. tax accountants. However, such financial and tax data was only received well after the last filing deadline for 2006 and only just now completed to be able to file the enclosed Forms. This financial data collection and complicated tax analysis (due principally to the substantial number of PFIC investments involved) was done at great expense in professional fees, both legal and accounting, in Liechtenstein and in the United States.

The facts above clearly demonstrate that Kerry Marsh and Shannon Marsh, on behalf of all of the Taxpayers, have acted in a responsible manner, exercising business care and prudence, and making more than reasonable efforts to determine their tax and information reporting obligations as quickly as possible. Promptly upon being notified of their U.S. tax reporting obligations, they cooperated fully with counsel to assist in filing the enclosed Forms.

We believe the foregoing facts, circumstances and reasons set forth above demonstrate an affirmative showing that the Taxpayers' failure to file the enclosed Forms in a timely manner was due to reasonable cause, and not willful neglect. Accordingly, we respectfully request that any and all possible penalties which otherwise could be imposed pursuant to IRC § 6677(a) and (b) be waived.

Please note that Kerry Marsh and Shannon Marsh have attested below to the facts stated above under penalties of perjury. If you require any further information, we request that you contact Alan L. Weisberg,

BAKER & MCKENZIE

Esq. at (305) 374-5544. Thank you for your understanding and consideration of this matter.

Very truly yours,

Weisberg and Kainen

By: Alan L. Weisberg

Baker & McKenzie LLP

By: Robert F. Hudson, Jr.

***

Attestation

Under penalties of perjury, I, Kerry Marsh, do hereby declare that I have examined the above reasonable cause statement, and to the best of my knowledge and belief, it is true, correct and complete.

By: Kerry Marsh

Date: 5/12/08

Under penalties of perjury, I, Shannon Marsh, do hereby declare that I have examined the above reasonable cause statement, and to the best of my knowledge and belief, it is true, correct and complete.

By: Shannon Marsh

Date: 5/12/2008

JCMA Foundation , 9490 Vaduz
SB: Gächter Dagmar **KB: Sprenger Sonja**

Mand.Nr.: [redacted]
L. Kundenbesuch: 27.06.2002

Gründungsdatum: 20.06.1996 Status: Aktiv

[redacted] = Redacted by the Permanent Subcommittee on Investigations

Verwaltungs- / Stiftungsräte

Profile Management Trust reg., Vad Zeichnungsrecht: Einzeln
Feuerstein Nicola Dr., Triesenberg Zeichnungsrecht: Kollektiv

Banken

LGT Bank in Liechtenstein AG, Vaduz AB: Müller Beat Tel. [redacted] Zlg-Kto: [redacted]

Diverses

Anlageberater:	Müller Beat,
Protektor:	WU Veronica,
Protektor:	WU Margaret S.B.,
Repräsentant:	LGT Treuhand AG, Vaduz
Vermittler:	LGT Investment Management, Hong Kon
Auftraggeber:	Privater Auftraggeber

Fix-Honorare

Domizilhonorar	800.00	20.06.2003	LGT Treuhand AG, Vaduz
Kapitalsteuer	1'000.00	20.06.2003	Liechtensteinische Steuerverwaltung, Vaduz
Stiftungsratshonorar	3'000.00	20.06.2003	LGT Treuhand AG, Vaduz

Pauschal-Honorare

0.00 fällig am:
Vermögenswert per: 0.00 Fakturierbares Pauschalhonorar: 0.00

Zweck

- 100%ige Beteiligung: - Sandalwood International Limited, Bahamas
- Verwaltung durch Byrne (T. Corkhill), Hong Kong
* - Aktienzertifikat --> ins Depot JCMA 14.1.97
- einziger Zweck von von Sandalwood ist das Halten der Tai Lung Worldwide Ltd., BVI

Tai Lung hält ein Haus in New York, das vermietet ist.
Die Mieteinkünfte werden auf das Konto der Standard Chartered Bank überwiesen.

* Cobyrne Ltd. + Declare Limited sind Directors / beides nominee company von Byrne, welche Sandalwood treuhänderisch für die JCMA halten (siehe diesbezüglich auch Declaration of Trust und Service Agreement)

Besitznachweis, Verträge, Vollmachten

- die zwei Schwestern des Kunden, Mrs [redacted] Wu und Mrs [redacted] Wu haben auf dem LGT-Konto seit 1.8.96 bzw. 25.7.97 Einzelzeichnungsrecht

Weisungen (Verwaltung, Buchhaltung, Beistatut usw.)

- Statuten und Beistatuten mit Protektor

Pendenzen / Geschichte

- LTV hat Auftraggeber noch nie getroffen

- Privatadresse von [redacted] Wu erhalten (s. Schr. Ph. Jehle vom 21.7.97): bei der nächsten Beistatuten-Aenderung berücksichtigen; Mrs WU=Protektor

- die 3 Töchter des 1B leben an der selben Adresse wie der 1B (Brief PJ 10.8.99) Adresse des Sohnes fehlt --> Beistatuten

- Annahmeerklärung mit Nachfolgeregelung i.S. Protektor unterzeichnen (s. Schreiben HK 27.06.2002 - wird erfolgen)

ACHTUNG US-Citizen

Permanent Subcommittee on Investigations
EXHIBIT #19

PSI-USMSTR - 004988

01-16-2006 14:11

▬ = Redacted by the Permanent Subcommittee on Investigations

JCMA Foundation 9490 **Vaduz** **Client No.:** [redacted]
SB: Dagmar Gächter **KB: Sonja Sprenger** Client Request: 6/27/2002

Founding date: 6/20/1996 Status: Active

Management/ Foundation Board
Profile Management Trust re., Vaduz Signature right: Individual
Dr. Nicola Feuerstein, Triesenberg Signature right: Joint

Banks
LGT Bank in Liechtenstein AG, Vaduz AB: Beat Müller Tel. [redacted] ZigAcct: [redacted]

Miscellaneous

Investment Adviser:	Beat Müller
Protector:	Veronica WU
Protector:	Margaret S.B. WU
Representative:	LGT Treuhand AG, Vaduz
Agent:	LGT Investment Management, Hong Kong
Client:	Private Client

Fixed Fees

Domicile fee	800.00	6/20/2003	LGT Treuhand AG, Vaduz
Capital Tax	1,000.00	6/20/2003	Liechtenstein Tax Authority, Vaduz
Foundation Board Fee	3,000.00	6/20/2003	LGT Treuhand AG. Vaduz

Lump Sum Fee
{no entry}

Purpose
- 100% Share: - Sandalwood International limited, Bahamas
- Managed by Byrne (T. Corkholl), Hong Kong
- Stock certificate -- on deposit JCMA 1/14/97
- sole purpose of Sandalwood is the holding of Tai Lung Worldwide, ltd., BVI

Tai Lung has a house in New York that is rented.
The rental income is transferred to the account of Standard Chartered Bank.

Cobyrne Ltd. + Declare Limited are directors / both nominee companies of Byrne, which Sandalwood holds in trust for JCMA (Also see Declaration of Trust and Service Agreement concerning this.)

Proof of Ownership, Contracts, Powers of Attorney
- from 8/1/96 to 7/25/97 the two sisters of the client, Mrs. [redacted] Wu and Mrs. [redacted] Wu, had individual signature rights to the LGT account.

Instructions (Management, accounting, by-laws, etc.)
- statutes and by-laws with Protector.

Pending/History
- LTV has never met the client.
- The private address for [redacted] Wu maintained (See 7/21/97 Ph. Jehle document): Allowed for in the next by-laws alteration; Mrs. WU = Protector
- the 3 daughters in 1B live at the same address as 1B (8/10/99 PJ letter) son's address is missing -- by-laws
- signed explanation with succession regulations according to Protector (See HK 6/27/2002 document.)

ATTENTION US citizen

DECLARATION OF TRUST

THIS TRUST DEED is made **1 October 1996** between **Cobyrne Limited** of **37/F., Wu Chung House, 213 Queen's Road East, Wanchai, Hong Kong** (hereinafter called the trustee) of the one part and JCMA Foundation, p.o. box 683, FL-9490 Vaduz/Principality of Liechtenstein ——— (hereinafter called the beneficiary) of the other part.

WHEREAS the beneficiary is the beneficial owner of the following shares:

Name of Company:	**Sandalwood International Limited**
Address:	**Providence House, East Hill Street, P O Box N-3944, Nassau, Bahamas**
Number of shares:	**1**
Share Number:	**1**

AND WHEREAS the beneficiary has requested the trustee to register the said shares in the trustee's name, and it was agreed that the trustee should execute such declaration of trust as is hereinafter contained.

NOW THIS DEED WITNESSETH as follows:

1. The trustee hereby declares that it holds the shares specified as aforesaid and all dividends and interest accrued or to accrue upon the same or any of them upon trust for the beneficiary and its successors in title and agrees to transfer pay and deal with the said shares and the dividends and interest payable in respect of the same in such manner as the beneficiary shall from time to time direct in writing subject to the following terms and conditions:

   Directions to transfer shares from one beneficiary to another will be subject to the Articles of Association of the company concerned and the trustee reserves the right to notify the company concerned of changes in the beneficial ownership where it is considered necessary. In cases where notification is given and where under the Articles of Association of the company concerned the directors indicate an unwillingness to accept the transfer of beneficial interest the trustee will be under no obligation to accept the instructions given to him.

2. The trustee will at the request of the beneficiary or its successors in title attend all meetings of shareholders or otherwise which it shall be entitled to attend by virtue of being the registered proprietor of the said shares or any of them and will vote at every such meeting in such manner as the beneficiary or its successors in title shall have previously directed in writing and in default of and subject to any such direction at the discretion of the trustee and further will if so required by the beneficiary or its successors in title execute all proxies or other documents which shall be necessary or proper to enable the beneficiary, its personal representatives or assigns or its or their nominees to vote at any such meeting in the place of the trustee. The trustee reserves the right to give notice to the company when voting on any resolution that he is acting on specific instructions from the beneficiary.

../2

Permanent Subcommittee on Investigations

EXHIBIT #20

3. The trustee shall keep the beneficiary or its successors in title reasonably informed of the operations of the aforesaid company. Failure to notify the beneficiary of any specific matter will not be construed as a breach of this trust.

4. The trustee shall render debit notes for services rendered through Byrne Corporate Services Limited of 37th Floor, Wu Chung House, 213 Queen's Road East, Wanchai, Hong Kong as their agents and Byrne Corporate Services Limited shall have a lien on the shares the subject of the trust to the extent of any unpaid fees due to them so rendered. Should fees properly rendered by Byrne Corporate Services Limited remain outstanding for more than three (3) consecutive months after the date of the rendering of the debit note concerned the trustee is hereby empowered by the beneficiary to transfer all or such part of the shares held under this trust to his own name and to sell same or to dispose of them according to his best advantage and the trustee shall be under no further obligation to the beneficiary. Provided however that the right to transfer and sell shall not be acted upon until fourteen days (14) after a final reminder requesting payment has been sent by registered post to the beneficiary at his last known address.

5. The beneficiary hereby undertakes to indemnify the trustee to the full extent of any and all obligations which arises out of the trustee holding the said shares on behalf of the beneficiary.

IN WITNESS WHEREOF the parties hereto have now set their signatures on the day and in the year beforementioned.

WITNESSED BY:

For and on behalf of
COBYRNE LIMITED

Cobyrne Limited
Trustee

WITNESSED BY:

JOMA Foundation

Martina Toggenburg

Peter Schmid
Beneficiary

Vaduz, 21st November 1996 mto

ACRIS Detailed Document Information Page 1 of 1

▬ = Redacted by the Permanent Subcommittee on Investigations

New York City Department of Finance
Office of the City Register

HELP
[Click help for additional instructions]
Selecting a help option will open new window

Current Search Criteria:
Name: TAI LUNG*
Date: To Current Date
Party Type: All Parties
Borough/County: All Boroughs/Counties
Document Class: All Document Classes

Detailed Document Information

DOCUMENT ID:	FT_4380005495638	CRFN:	N/A	COLLATERAL:	N/A
# of PAGES:	5	REEL-PAGE:	4524-2412	EXPIRATION DATE:	N/A
DOC. TYPE:	DEED	FILE NUMBER:	N/A	ASSESSMENT DATE:	2/18/1997
DOC. DATE:	1/21/1997	RECORDED / FILED:	2/14/1997	SLID #:	N/A
		BOROUGH:	QUEENS		
DOC. AMOUNT:	$0.00	RPTT #:	03384	MAP SEQUENCE #:	0
MESSAGE:	N/A				

PARTY 1

NAME	ADDRESS 1	ADDRESS 2	CITY	STATE	ZIP	COUNTRY
WU, WILLIAM S	[redacted]		FOREST HILLS	NY		US

PARTY 2

NAME	ADDRESS 1	ADDRESS 2	CITY	STATE	ZIP	COUNTRY
TAI LUNG WORLDWIDE LTD	213 QNS ROAD EAST WU CHUNG HOUSE		WAN CHAI			HK

PARTY 3/Other

NAME	ADDRESS 1	ADDRESS 2	CITY	STATE	ZIP	COUNTRY

PARCELS

BOROUGH	BLOCK	LOT	PARTIAL	PROPERTY TYPE	EASEMENT	AIR RIGHTS	SUBTERRANEAN RIGHTS	PROPERTY ADDRESS	UNIT	REMARKS
QUEENS	3251	70	ENTIRE LOT	PRE-ACRIS	N	N	N			

REFERENCES

CRFN	DOCUMENT ID	BOROUGH	YEAR	REEL	PAGE	FILE NBR

REMARKS

Print | View Document | Search Results | Search Options | Main Options

Go To: Finance Home Page | NYC.gov Home Page | Contact NYC.gov | FAQs | Privacy Statement | Site Map

Permanent Subcommittee on Investigations
EXHIBIT #21

REEL 4 5 2 4 PG 2 4 1 2

CONSULT YOUR LAWYER BEFORE SIGNING THIS INSTRUMENT – THIS INSTRUMENT SHOULD BE USED BY LAWYERS ONLY

THIS INDENTURE, made the 21st day of January, nineteen hundred and ninety-seven

BETWEEN

ORIGINAL

WILLIAM S. WU, residing at [redacted] Forest Hills, NY

= Redacted by the Permanent Subcommittee on Investigations

party of the first part, and

TAI LUNG WORLDWIDE, LTD., having its principal place of business at 213 Queens Road East, 37th Floor, Wu Chung House, Wan Chai, Hong Kong

party of the second part,

WITNESSETH, that the party of the first part, in consideration of Ten Dollars and other valuable consideration paid by the party of the second part, does hereby grant and release unto the party of the second part, the heirs or successors and assigns of the party of the second part forever,

ALL that certain plot, piece or parcel of land, with the buildings and improvements thereon erected, situate, lying and being in the

See annexed Schedule A

TOGETHER with all right, title and interest, if any, of the party of the first part in and to any streets and roads abutting the above described premises to the center lines thereof; TOGETHER with the appurtenances and all the estate and rights of the party of the first part in and to said premises; TO HAVE AND TO HOLD the premises herein granted unto the party of the second part, the heirs or successors and assigns of the party of the second part forever.

AND the party of the first part covenants that the party of the first part has not done or suffered anything whereby the said premises have been encumbered in any way whatever, except as aforesaid.

AND the party of the first part, in compliance with Section 13 of the Lien Law, covenants that the party of the first part will receive the consideration for this conveyance and will hold the right to receive such consideration as a trust fund to be applied first for the purpose of paying the cost of the improvement and will apply the same first to the payment of the cost of the improvement before using any part of the total of the same for any other purpose.

The word "party" shall be construed as if it read "parties" whenever the sense of this indenture so requires.

IN WITNESS WHEREOF, the party of the first part has duly executed this deed the day and year first above written.

IN PRESENCE OF:

WILLIAM S. WU

REEL4524 PG2413

▬ = Redacted by the Permanent Subcommittee on Investigations

SCHEDULE A

ALL that certain plot, parcel of land, with the buildings and improvements thereon erected, situate lying and being in the Second Ward, Borough and County of Queens, City and State of New York, being shown as a part of Block 4 on a certain map entitled, "Map No. 3 of Forest Hills Gardens, situated at Forest Hills, Borough of Queens, City of New York, surveyed for Sage Foundation Homes Company, dated April, 1913 by C.B. Fancy, C.E." and filed in the office of the clerk, now Register, of Queens County on 7/15/13 as map No. 97 bounded and described as follows:

BEGINNING at a point on the westerly side of street known as [redacted], as laid down on said map distant 279.94 feet measured along said side of [redacted] southerly form the corner formed by the intersection of the said westerly side of [redacted] with the southerly side of [redacted] as now laid out 50 feet wide; and

RUNNING THENCE southerly along the westerly side of [redacted] on an arc of a circle bearing to the right and at a radius of 888.26 feet a distance of 30.06 feet;

THENCE South 71 degrees 29 minutes 13 seconds West and part of the distance through a party wall 78.50 feet;

THENCE south 26 degrees 29 minutes 13 seconds west 6.36 feet;

THENCE south 71 degrees 29 minutes 13 seconds west 17.73 feet;

THENCE north 63 degrees 30 minutes 47 seconds west 6.36 feet;

THENCE north 18 degrees 30 minutes 47 seconds west 16.03;

THENCE south 71 degrees 29 minutes 13 seconds west 5.50 feet to the east side of a private lane hereinafter described;

THENCE along said lane north 18 degrees 30 minutes 47 seconds west 13.97 feet;

▬ = Redacted by the Permanent Subcommittee on Investigations

REEL 4 5 2 4 PG 2 4 1 4

THENCE north 71 degrees 29 minutes 13 seconds east and part of the distance through a party wall 112.73 feet to the westerly side of [redacted], to the point or place of beginning.

TOGETHER with an undivided interest of, in and to the rear service lane or driveway which lane or driveway is bounded and described as follows:

BEGINNING at a point on the southerly side of [redacted] as now laid out, 50 feet wide distant 127.30 feet westerly measured along said side of [redacted] on a course running south 48 degrees 34 minutes 35 seconds west from the corner formed by the intersection of said southerly side of said place with the westerly side of said street known as [redacted] and

RUNNING THENCE south 41 degrees 4 minutes 28 seconds, east 52.42 feet;

THENCE south 74 degrees 47 minutes 37 seconds east 16.75 feet;

THENCE south 15 degrees 11 minutes 19 seconds east 48.03 feet;

THENCE south 18 degrees 30 minutes 47 seconds east 120 feet;

THENCE north 71 degrees 29 minutes 13 seconds east 11.10 feet;

THENCE south 18 degrees 30 minutes 47 seconds east 21.97 feet;

THENCE south 71 degrees 29 minutes 13 seconds west 23.60 feet;

THENCE north 18 degrees 30 minutes 47 seconds west 176.40 feet;

THENCE north 41 degrees 4 minutes 28 seconds west 72.92 feet to the said southerly side of Middlemay Place and

THENCE north 48 degrees 34 minutes 35 seconds east along said side of said place 10 feet to the point or place of beginning.

SAID PREMISES being known as and by street address 81 [redacted], Forest Hills, New York.

STATE OF NEW YORK, COUNTY OF QUEENS ss:

On the 21st day of January 1997, before me personally came WILLIAM S. WU

to me known to be the individual described in and who executed the foregoing instrument, and acknowledged that he executed the same.

SO IN ORIGINAL

Antonia Trupiano
Notary Public

SO IN ORIGINAL

~~ANTONIA TRUPIANO
Notary Public, State of New York
Qualified in Queens County
Commission Expires August 8, 19~~

ANTONIA TRUPIANO
Notary Public, State of New York
No. 01TR5031060
Qualified in Queens County
Commission Expires August 8, 1998

STATE OF NEW YORK, COUNTY OF ss:

On the day of 19 , before me personally came

to me known to be the individual described in and who executed the foregoing instrument, and acknowledged that executed the same.

= Redacted by the Permanent Subcommittee on Investigations

STATE OF NEW YORK, COUNTY OF ss:

On the day of 19 , before me personally came to me known, who, being by me duly sworn, did depose and say that he resides at No. ; that he is the of , the corporation described in and which executed the foregoing instrument; that he knows the seal of said corporation; that the seal affixed to said instrument is such corporate seal; that it was so affixed by order of the board of directors of said corporation, and that he signed h name thereto by like order.

STATE OF NEW YORK, COUNTY OF ss:

On the day of 19 , before me personally came the subscribing witness to the foregoing instrument, with whom I am personally acquainted, who, being by me duly sworn, did depose and say that he resides at No. ; that he knows to be the individual described in and who executed the foregoing instrument; that he, said subscribing witness, was present and saw execute the same; and that he, said witness, at the same time subscribed h name as witness thereto.

REEL 4524 PG 2415

Bargain and Sale Deed
WITH COVENANT AGAINST GRANTOR'S ACTS

TITLE No. CR2440

WILLIAM S. WU
TO
TAI LUNG WORLDWIDE, LTD

SECTION
BLOCK 3251
LOT 70
COUNTY OR TOWN QUEENS
premises known as:
[redacted]
Forest Hills, N.Y.

RETURN BY MAIL TO:

TAI LUNG WORLDWIDE, LTD.
C/O FRANK J. DIDERO, ESQ.
47-14 158th Street
Flushing, New York
Zip No. 11358

Reserve this space for use of Recording Office.

▬▬▬ = Redacted by the Permanent Subcommittee on Investigations

CITY REGISTER RECORDING AND ENDORSEMENT PAGE
- QUEENS COUNTY -
(This page forms part of the instrument)

Block(s) 3251
Lot(s) 70
[redacted], Forzay Hills

Record & Return to: Frank J. Didio, Esq. 47-14 158th St, Flushing, N.Y. 11358
Title/Agent Company name: Pioneer Land Title Corp.
Title Company number: QR 2190

OFFICE USE ONLY - DO NOT WRITE BELOW THIS LINE

THE FOREGOING INSTRUMENT WAS ENDORSED FOR THE RECORD AS FOLLOWS:

Examined by (✓):

Mtge Tax Serial No.	
Mtge Amount	$
Taxable Amount	$
Exemption (✓)	YES ☐ NO ☐
Type:	[339EE] [255] [OTHER ___]
Dwelling Type:	[1 or 2] [3] [4 to 6] [over 6]

TAX RECEIVED ON ABOVE MORTGAGE ▼

County (basic)	$
City (Addt'l)	$
Spec Addt'l	$
TASF	$
MTA	$
NYCTA	$
TOTAL TAX	$

Apportionment Mortgage (✓) YES ☐ NO ☐

Joy A. Bobrow, City Register

City Register Serial Number ➡ 010725

Indexed By (✓): B
Verified By (✓):

Block(s) and Lot(s) verified by (✓) PS
Address ☑ Tax Map ☐
Extra Block(s) Lot(s)

Recording Fee	A	$ 42
Affidavit Fee	(C)	$
TP-584/582 Fee	(Y)	$
RPTT Fee	(R)	$ 25

HPD-A ☑ HPD-C ☐

New York State Real Estate Transfer Tax ▼
$ 1520—

Serial Number ➡

New York City Real Property Transfer Tax Serial Number ➡ 003384

New York State Gains Tax Serial Number ➡

REEL 4524 PG 2416

RECORDED IN QUEENS COUNTY
OFFICE OF THE CITY REGISTER

1997 FEB 14 P 3:11

Witness My Hand and Official Seal

Joy A. Bobrow

City Register

CRGFM490.BPG 1-93

LGT Bank in Liechtenstein
A Member of Liechtenstein Global Trust

LGT Bank in Liechtenstein AG
Representative Office Hong Kong
Suite 2908
Two Exchange Square
8 Connaught Place Central
GPO Box 13398 Hong Kong

Telephone (852) 2523 6180
Telefax (852) 2868 0059
Internet www.lgt.com
E-Mail lgthk@lgt.com

Memorandum

1/1

Subject	**JCMA Foundation**
Author/dept./tel.	Kim Choy
Date	June 26, 2002
For action by	
For information	BM, PW, Sonja Sprenger

Meeting held on 25 June 2002.

Attendees : Mr William Wu
LGT – Beat Muller, Kim Choy

KC joined the meeting following BM's presentation of Mr Wu's account(s) with LGT Bank to discuss the JCMA Foundation.

Mr Wu confirmed that he and all family members named in the By-laws except his wife hold US passports and all live in the US. His wife has retained her Singapore passport (N.B. Singapore does not permit dual nationality).

The JCMA Foundation's assets consist of an account with LGT Bank and shares in a BVI company (Sandalwood) which in turns owns the family home in the US.

KC explained the reporting requirements imposed on a US grantor, e.g. creation of the foundation, ensuring the Board Members file annual returns with the IRS. Also, as the income of the Foundation is taxed to the grantor, further annual filing of income of the foundation and payment of income tax on worldwide income of the foundation. Furthermore, if US beneficiaries have received distributions from the Foundation, the Board Members must provide a Beneficiary Statement to each recipient which should be attach to his/her income tax return to the IRS. Upon the death of the US grantor, the Board Members may be considered the statutory executor of his estate and will bear liability and exposure for any non-compliance by the grantor during his lifetime of reporting and other requirements to the IRS, the filing of the deceased's US estate tax return and payment of estate taxes on the assets of the Foundation at the date of his death.

KC informed Mr Wu that the JCMA Foundation must be re-structured and that LGT & Treuhand were looking at formulating solutions. We raised the possibility of an insurance product which Mr Wu didn't seem interested in. Other possibilities included:

- lifetime transfers to his beneficiaries;
- making use of Mr Wu's non-US siblings to restructure the Foundation ;
- private/corporate account.

Mr Wu acknowledged the need to restructure the Foundation and was receptive to any ideas we could come up with. Similarly, we would welcome any solutions from him or his advisers. Mr Wu has interests in other ventures/companies unconnected with LGT which require restructuring to address US tax/reporting requirements.

Fehler! AutoText-Eintrag nicht definiert.

Permanent Subcommittee on Investigations
EXHIBIT #22

PSI-USMSTR - 004989

LGT Treuhand AG
18 Städtle
FL-9490 Vaduz
Liechtenstein

Dear Sirs,

Re: JCMA Foundation, Ref. no. 328.1

Please arrange to buy a bank draft for USD100,000.00 in favour of William WU by debiting the above account. The undersigned will collect the bank draft in person.

Thank you for your attention.

Yours truly,

Kontr. 2635 /pi

....

Date: 27 June, 2002

Permanent Subcommittee on Investigations
EXHIBIT #23

PSI-USMSTR - 004980

[redacted] = Redacted by the Permanent Subcommittee on Investigations

HSBC K939026 1-108/210

Issuing Office HKH HONG KONG Date 26 JUN 2002 Ref DD [redacted]

On demand pay to the order of WILLIAM WUXXXXXX

Amount USD ONE HUNDRED THOUSAND ONLY USD100,000.00*

To HSBC Bank USA
140 Broadway
New York
NY 10005 USA
Payable at any branch of HSBC Bank USA in the USA

For The Hongkong and Shanghai Banking Corporation Limited
Incorporated in the Hong Kong SAR with limited liability

CHIN KWAN YUET WAH ROSANNA 7606

LAI KWOK KAI ARNO 6649

Please DO NOT Write Below This Line

[redacted]

Acknowledge receipt of cheque [redacted]

PSI-USMSTR - 004981

Member HSBC Group

ON-LINE REMITTANCES ADVICE

Branch HONG KONG OFFICE
Date 26 JUN 2002

= Redacted by the Permanent Subcommittee on Investigations

REFERENCE DD [redacted]

Drawn On / To / From
HSBC BANK USA
NEW YORK

WE HAVE DEBITED YOUR ACCOUNT
[redacted] ON 26 JUN 2002 WITH
THE AMOUNT OF A DEMAND DRAFT

REMITTANCE AMOUNT USD***100,000.00
COMMISSION HKD *976.38
TOTAL CHARGES USD*******125.00

DR AMOUNT USD***100,125.00

Beneficiary
WILLIAM WU

By order of
LGT BANK IN L AKT

Payment Details

Bk to Bk Infor

To ~~LGT BANK IN LIECHTENSTEIN AG~~
P O BOX 85 9490 VADUZ
LIECHTENSTEIN

REMFORM4 (1599)

Note: 1. For inward remittance transactions, amount credited is subject to final settlement and any additional charges will be debited to your account under advice to you.
2. For clean cheque transactions, the interest charged represents the interim cost to the bank between the immediate crediting of your account and the receipt of the cleared funds.

PSI-USMSTR - 004982

Resolution

The Foundation Board of the

JCMA Foundation, Vaduz

pursuant to Art. 8 and 10 of the Articles and to Art. 1 of the By-Laws as well as in accordance to the request of the first beneficiary hereby resolves to carry out the following distribution:

Amount	USD*100'000.--* by cheque
Beneficiary	William WU
Bank	HSBC Hong Kong and Shanghai Banking Corp. Hong Kong
Date	26 June 2002

Vaduz, 26 June 2002 SSP/dgc

The Foundation Board

Profile Management Trust reg.

Sonja Sprenger

Dr Nicola Feuerstein

PSI-USMSTR - 004983

Resolution

The Foundation Board of

JCMA FOUNDATION, Vaduz

has passed the following resolution:

1. The statement of assets as per 31 t December 2001 in the total amount of USD*4'283'473.49* to enclosure ./1 is herewith approved.
2. All investments carried out in 2001 according to enclosures ./2 are herewith approved.
3. All distributions carried out in 2001 according to enclosures ./2 are herewith approved.
4. LGT Treuhand Aktiengesellschaft, Vaduz, will be instructed to establish the statement of assets for the next year.

Vaduz, 07 February 2002 / dgc

The Foundation Board:

Profile Management Trust reg.

ppa. D. Gächter

Dagmar Gächter

Sonja Sprenger

Dr. Nicola Feuerstein

Permanent Subcommittee on Investigations
EXHIBIT #24

WWU-PSI-00027

LGT Bank in Liechtenstein
A Member of Liechtenstein Global Trust

LGT Bank in Liechtenstein
Aktiengesellschaft
Herrengasse 12
FL-9490 Vaduz

Telefon +423 235 11 22
Telefax +423 235 15 22
Internet www.lgt.com
E-Mail info@lgt.com
MWST-Nr. 50 119

JCMA Foundation
9490 Vaduz

Vaduz, January 1, 2002 1/3
BML / BHK / 20:22:38 ECopy

▬ = Redacted by the Permanent Subcommittee on Investigations

Performance [redacted]

Period 01.01.2001 - 31.12.2001			ref. currency: USD
Assets as of 31.12.2000	including accr. interests (	8,642.11)	4,666,442.19
Deposits			0.00
Withdrawals			304,086.86-
Balance transfer from/to another account			0.00
Balance deliveries of securities	including accr. interests (	0.00)	0.00
			4,362,355.33
Assets as of 31.12.2001	including accr. interests (	921.52)	4,283,472.49
Performance			78,882.84-

Details of performance	
Profit or loss	130,864.45-
Dividends / credit interests	56,379.10
Debit interests	453.17-
Expenses and commissions	3,944.32-
Performance	78,882.84-

Average capital	100.00 %	4,438,475.83
Performance	1.78- %	78,882.84-

We do not accept responsibility for the accuracy or completeness of the information provided above.

Resolution

The Foundation Board of the

JCMA Foundation, Vaduz

hereby resolves:

1. The inventory of assets and liabilities at 31 December 2003 showing a total of USD*2'172'145.97*, which is attached to this resolution as Schedule 1, is hereby approved and adopted.

2. The investments made in 2003 according to Schedule 2 are hereby approved and adopted.

3. The distributions and payments made in 2003 according to Schedule 2 are hereby approved and adopted.

4. LGT Treuhand AG, Vaduz, is entrusted with drawing up the inventory of assets and liabilities for the next business year.

Vaduz, 10 March 2004 / dgc

The Foundation Board

Profile Management Trust reg.

ppa. D. Gächter
Dagmar Gächter

lic.iur. Marco Sacchet

Dr Nicola Feuerstein

Permanent Subcommittee on Investigations
EXHIBIT #25

WWU-PSI-00055

FL-9490 Vaduz MWST-Nr. 50 119

JCMA Foundation
9490 Vaduz

Vaduz, January 2, 2004 1/3
BML / BHX / 01:25:14 E

▬▬▬ = Redacted by the Permanent Subcommittee on Investigations

Performance [redacted]

Period 01.01.2003 - 31.12.2003			ref. currency: USD
Assets as of 31.12.2002	including accr. interests (	0.00)	3,233,227.78
Deposits			525,000.00 (P)
Withdrawals			4,680,795.10-
Balance transfer from/to another account			0.00
Balance deliveries of securities	including accr. interests (	0.00)	2,650,000.00
			1,727,432.68
Assets as of 31.12.2003	including accr. interests (	5,491.85-)	2,172,144.97
Performance			444,712.29

Details of performance

Profit or loss	464,967.46
Dividends / credit interests	6,491.85-
Debit interests	11,527.28-
Expenses and commissions	2,236.04-
Performance	444,712.29

Average capital	100.00 %	2,067,800.55
Performance	21.51 %	444,712.29

Only the Banks official account and safe custody advices are binding.

WWU-PSI-00061

Resolution

of the Foundation Board of

JCMA Foundation, Vaduz

The Foundation Board takes note of the Statements of Assets as per 31 December 2004 together with its notes and schedules which shall form an integral part of this resolution. After due consideration the Foundation Board states:

1. The Foundation's net assets as per 31 December 2004 amount to USD 1'202'636.25.
2. During the course the business year 2004 an amount of USD 1'026'250.00 was distributed to the first beneficiary.
3. The investments are in line with the statutory object of the Foundation and the declaration of intent of the founder.
4. In compliance with its statutory object the Foundation has not pursued any commercial activities in the business year 2004.

Based on these facts the Foundation Board herewith unanimously approves and adopts the said Statement of Assets and resolves to entrust the Legal Representative with the drawing up of the Statements of Assets for the business year to come.

Vaduz, 13 February 2006/SSP/xpt

The Foundation Board

Profile Management Trust reg. Sonja Sprenger

Daniela Greuig lic. iur. Marco Sacchet

Permanent Subcommittee on Investigations
EXHIBIT #26

WWU-PSI-00064

JCMA Foundation, Vaduz

Notes to the Statement of Assets as per 31 December 2004

4. Participations	**2004 USD**	**2003 USD**
Sandalwood International Limited, B.V.I. 100% owned by the Foundation		
Authorized Capital: USD 50'000.00 divided into 50'000 shares of USD 1.– each Issued Capital: 1 share of USD 1.– each	1.00	1.00
Dickinson Holding & Finance Ltd., B.V.I. 100% owned and controlled by the Foundation		
Authorized Capital: USD 50'000.00 divided into 50'000 shares of USD 1.– each Issued Capital: 1'000 shares of USD 1.– each	1'000.00	0.00
A statement of assets as of 31 December 2004 was provided by the directors on 15 September 2004, it shows a total of fair market value of USD 1'349'698.71	1'001.00	1.00

5. Loans		**2005 USD**	**2004 USD**
August 2004	Principal loan amount paid	1'178'515.46	0.00
		1'178'515.46	**0.00**

In August 2004 an interest free loan in the amount of USD 1'179'515.46 was granted to DICKINSON HOLDING & FINANCE LTD, BVI, for an indefinite period of time. A loan agreement was made in writing on 13 February 2006.

WWU-PSI-00069

JCMA Foundation, Vaduz

Notes to the Statement of Assets as per 31 December 2004

	2004 USD	2003 USD
6. Liabilities		
Lombard Loan		
On 31 May 1999 the Foundation entered into a lombard loan contract with LGT Bank in Liechtenstein AG, Vaduz. In this respect a general deed of pledge and of assignment was signed.	0.00	-1'522'690.18

The Foundation Board has no notice of any other liabilities, commitments or obligations the effect of which should be considered for disclosure in the Statement of Assets or as a basis for recording a contingency or making adjustment or provision. To-date there are neither annuities nor titles nor enforceable legal claims against the Foundation.

JCMA Foundation, Vaduz

Endowments and Distributions in 2004

	USD
Endowments	
none	0.00

	USD
Distributions	
To the first beneficiary according to a board resolution dated 12 February 2004	525'000.00
To the first beneficiary according to a board resolution dated 24 May 2004	200'500.00
To the first beneficiary according to a board resolution dated 10 August 2004	300'750.00
	1'026'250.00

WWU-PSI-00071

LGT Bank

Herrengasse 12, FL-9490 Vaduz
Tel. +423 235 11 22 · Fax +423 235 15 22
info@lgt.com · www.lgt.com
ÖR H. 842/97, Sitz: 9490 Vaduz · MWSt-Nr. 50119

JCMA Foundation
9490 Vaduz

Vaduz, January 2, 2005 1/3
BML / BHK / 04:54:45 E

▬ = Redacted by the Permanent Subcommittee on Investigations

Performance [redacted]

Period 01.01.2004 - 31.12.2004			ref. currency: USD
Assets as of 31.12.2003	including accr. interests (	5,491.85-)	2,172,144.97
Deposits			4,967,938.95
Withdrawals			1,242,355.13-
Balance transfer from/to another account			0.00
Balance deliveries of securities	including accr. interests (	1,850.00-)	5,903,506.84-
			5,778.05-
Assets as of 31.12.2004	including accr. interests (	0.00)	23,119.79
Performance			28,897.84

Details of performance	
Profit or loss	15,002.86
Dividends / credit interests	13,358.52
Debit interests	22.53-
Expenses and commissions	558.99
Performance	28,897.84

Average capital	100.00 %	1,061,926.94
Performance	2.72 %	28,897.84

This performance statement is meant only for information purposes and is not legally binding.

WWU-PSI-00075

Resolution

of the Foundation Board of

JCMA Foundation, Vaduz

The Foundation Board takes note of the Statements of Assets as per 31 December 2005 together with its notes and schedules which shall form an integral part of this resolution. After due consideration the Foundation Board states:

1. The Foundation's net assets as per 31 December 2005 amount to USD 1'188'957.64.
2. The assets development for the business year 2005 shows a decrease in Foundation's assets of USD 463'754.13.
3. During the course the business year 2005 an amount of USD 49'939.93 (equivalent of HKD 387'600.--) was endowed to the Foundation and an amount of USD 500'000.-- was distributed to the first beneficiary. The endowment and distributions were entered in the Statement of Assets as redemption/additions to the loan of Dickinson Holding & Finance Ltd., BVI.
4. The investments are in line with the statutory object of the Foundation and the declaration of intent of the founder.
5. In compliance with its statutory object the Foundation has not pursued any commercial activities in the business year 2005.

Based on these facts the Foundation Board herewith unanimously approves and adopts the said Statement of Assets and resolves to entrust the Legal Representative with the drawing up of the Statements of Assets for the business year to come.

Vaduz, 30 March 2006/SSP/xpt

The Foundation Board

Profile Management Trust reg.

Daniela Gredig   lic. iur. Marco Sacchet   Sonja Sprenger

Permanent Subcommittee on Investigations

EXHIBIT #27

WWU-PSI-00078

JCMA Foundation, Vaduz

▬ = Redacted by the Permanent Subcommittee on Investigations

Notes to the Statement of Assets as per 31 December 2005

1. General Information on the Foundation

The formation documents of JCMA Foundation were deposited with the public registry in Vaduz on 20 June 1996.

The currently valid Articles of the Foundation date back to 20 June 1996. In compliance with the said Articles, Beneficiaries of the Foundation were appointed in separate By-Laws on 25 June 1996.

As from 18 October 2004 the Foundation Board consists of two members, namely Sonja Sprenger (PGR Art. 180a) and Profile Management Trust reg., Vaduz. While Sonja Sprenger has joint signatory power, Profile Management Trust reg., Vaduz is entitled to represent and bind the Foundation by its sole signature.

The statutory minimum Foundation Fund amounts to CHF 30'000.--.

2. Cash at banks

			2005 USD	2004 USD
LGT Bank in Liechtenstein AG, Vaduz Account No. [redacted]				
USD Account			328.35	550.63
SGD Account	SGD	11.33	6.82	6.93
HKD Account	HKD	798.52	103.03	37.75
Total LGT Bank in Liechtenstein AG, Vaduz			438.20	595.31
Total Cash at banks			**438.20**	**595.31**

Please refer to the attached bank statements for details.

Profile Management Trust reg. is the sole authorized signatory on the bank accounts of the Foundation.

3. Securities

	2005 USD	2004 USD
LGT Bank in Liechtenstein AG, Vaduz Safe Custody Account No. [redacted]		
Money Market Funds	9'002.98	22'524.48
Total Securities	9'002.98	22'524.48
Total Securities	**9'002.98**	**22'524.48**

WWU-PSI-00081

JCMA Foundation, Vaduz

Notes to the Statement of Assets as per 31 December 2005

Generally the valuation of the above securities is made on a market value basis (daily rates) as of the end of the year in accordance with the information provided by the bank. Please note that the total includes unrealized profits and losses.

When managing the assets the Foundation Board takes into consideration the recommendations coming from LGT Bank in Liechtenstein AG, Vaduz. All securities transactions are detailled in the Schedules.

For further details on the asset and currency allocation, security transactions and the performance please refer to the Schedules.

4. Participations	**2005 USD**	**2004 USD**
SANDALWOOD INTERNATIONAL LIMITED, BVI 100% owned by the Foundation		
Authorized Capital: USD 50'000.00 divided into 50'000 shares of USD 1.-- each Issued Capital: 1 share of USD 1.-- each	1.00	1.00
Sandalwood is the shareholder of a company called Tai Lung Worldwide Ltd., which owns a property in New York. Financial Statements were not provided by the directors.		
DICKINSON HOLDING & FINANCE LTD. 100% owned and controlled by the Foundation		
Authorized Capital: USD 50'000.00 divided into 50'000 shares of USD 1.-- each Issued Capital: 1'000 shares of USD 1.-- each	1'000.00	1'000.00
The Foundation granted a loan to DICKINSON, which is operating a bank account with LGT Bank in Liechtenstein AG. The attached statement of assets as of the year-end show a market value of USD 3'443'753.94 (2004) and USD 3'774'387.02 (2005).		
	1'001.00	1'001.00

JCMA Foundation, Vaduz

Notes to the Statement of Assets as per 31 December 2005

5. Loans	**2005 USD**	**2004 USD**
DICKINSON HOLDING & FINANCE LTD.		
Principal loan amount paid	1'178'515.46	1'178'515.46
Additions during the year	49'939.93	0.00
Redemptions during the year	-500'015.45	0.00
	728'439.94	**1'178'515.46**

In August 2004 an interest free loan in the amount of USD 1'178'515.46 was granted to DICKINSON HOLDING & FINANCE LTD, BVI, for an indefinite period of time. A loan agreement was made in writing on 13 February 2006.

During the course of 2005 DICKINSON HOLDING & FINANCE LTD, BVI, received monies and effected payments for and on behalf of the Foundation. These payments are registered in the books as additions/redemptions of the principal loan amount.

6. Liabilities	**2005 USD**	**2004 USD**
Lombard Loan		
On 31 May 1999 the Foundation entered into a lombard loan contract with LGT Bank in Liechtenstein AG, Vaduz. In this respect a general deed of pledge and of assignment was signed.	**0.00**	**0.00**

The Foundation Board has no notice of any other liabilities, commitments or obligations the effect of which should be considered for disclosure in the Statement of Assets or as a basis for recording a contingency or making adjustment or provision. To-date there are neither annuities nor titles nor enforceable legal claims against the Foundation.

JCMA Foundation, Vaduz

Endowments and Distributions in 2005

		USD
Endowments		
- according to a declaration of endowment dated 13 September 2005		49'939.93
transferred to Dickinson Holding & Finance Ltd, BVI	*HKD 387'600.00*	
Total		49'939.93

	USD
Distributions	
- according to a board resolution dated 27 May 2005 *transferred from the bank account of Dickinson Holding & Finance Ltd, BVI*	200'007.72 *)
- according to a board resolution dated 17 August 2005 *transferred from the bank account of Dickinson Holding & Finance Ltd, BVI*	300'007.73 *)
Total	500'015.45

*) incl. charges, fees & commissions

WWU-PSI-00084

Resolution

of the Foundation Board of

Desert Rose Foundation, Vaduz

The Foundation Board takes note of the Statement of Assets as per 31 December 2006 together with its notes and schedules which shall form an integral part of this resolution. After due consideration the Foundation Board states:

1. The Foundation's net assets as per 31 December 2006 amount to USD 422'249.10.

2. The Cash Flow Statement for the business year 2006 shows a decrease in Foundation's assets of USD 316'633.02.

3. During the course of the said business year no endowments were made and a total of USD 300'000.00 was distributed.

4. The investments of assets are in line with the statutory object of the Foundation and the declaration of intent of the founder.

5. In compliance with its statutory object the Foundation has not pursued any commercial activities in the business year 2006.

Based on these facts the Foundation Board herewith unanimously approves and adopts the said Statement of Assets and resolves to entrust the Legal Representative with the drawing up of the Statement of Assets for the business year to come.

Vaduz, 18 April 2007/SSP/rwe

The Foundation Board

Profile Management Trust reg.

Xenia Hostettler | lic. iur. Andrea Brüllmann | Sonja Sprenger

Permanent Subcommittee on Investigations
EXHIBIT #28

WWU-PSI-00092

22. AUG. 2007 18:53 NR. 2062 S. 5/16

Desert Rose Foundation, Vaduz

Notes to the Statement of Assets as per 31 December 2006

Generally the valuation of the above securities is made on a market value basis (daily rates as per 31 December) in accordance with the information provided by the bank. Please note that the total includes unrealized profits and losses on exchange rates and currency exchange.

When managing the assets the Foundation Board takes into consideration the recommendations coming from LGT Bank in Liechtenstein AG, Vaduz. All securities transactions are detailed in the Schedules.

For further details on the asset and currency allocation, securities transactions and the performance please refer to the Schedules.

4. Participations	**2006 USD**	**2005 USD**
SANDALWOOD INTERNATIONAL LIMITED, BVI 100% beneficially owned by the Foundation		
Authorized Capital: USD 5'000.00 divided into 5000 shares of USD 1.– each Issued Capital: 1 share of USD 1.– each	1.00	1.00
Sandalwood is the shareholder of a company called Tai Lung Worldwide Ltd., which owns a property in New York. Financial Statements have not been provided by the directors. During the course of 2006 it was resolved to distribute the shares to the first Beneficiary, however, the planned share transfer has not yet been completed.		
DICKINSON HOLDING & FINANCE LTD. 100% owned and controlled by the Foundation		
Authorized Capital: USD 50'000.00 divided into 50'000 shares of USD 1.– each Issued Capital: 1'000 shares of USD 1.– each	1'000.00	1'000.00
The Foundation granted a loan to DICKINSON, which is operating a bank account with LGT Bank in Liechtenstein AG. The attached statement of assets as of the year-end show a market value of USD 3'774'387.02 (2005) and USD 4'250'013.53 (2006).		
Total Participations	**1'001.00**	**1'001.00**

WWU-PSI-00096

Desert Rose Foundation, Vaduz

Notes to the Statement of Assets as per 31 December 2006

5. Loans

	2006 USD	2005 USD
DICKINSON HOLDING & FINANCE LTD.		
Principal loan amount paid	728'439.94	1'178'515.46
Additions in 2005	0.00	49'939.93
Redemptions in 2005	0.00	-500'015.45
Redemptions during the year	-324'311.87	0.00
	404'128.07	728'439.94

In August 2004 an interest free loan in the amount of USD 1'178'515.46 was granted to DICKINSON HOLDING & FINANCE LTD., BVI, for an indefinite period of time. A loan agreement was made in writing on 13 February 2006.

During the course of 2005 and 2006 DICKINSON HOLDING & FINANCE LTD., BVI, received monies and effected payments for and on behalf of the Foundation. These payments are registered in the books as additions/redemptions of the principal loan amount.

6. Liabilities

The Foundation Board has no notice of liabilities, commitments or obligations the effect of which should be considered for disclosure in the Statement of Assets or as a basis for recording a contingency or making adjustment or provision. To-date there are neither annuities nor titles nor enforceable legal claims against the Foundation.

22. AUG. 2007 18:33 NR. 2062 S. 7/16

Desert Rose Foundation, Vaduz

Endowments and Distributions in 2006

	USD
Endowments	
none	0.00
	0.00

	USD
Distributions	
- according to a Board Resolution dated 20 November 2006 *transferred from the bank account of Dickinson Holding & Finance Ltd.*	300'000.00 *)
	300'000.00

*) *Includes bank charges paid by Dickinson Holding & Finance Ltd.*

WWU-PSI-00098

Veline Foundation - gelöscht am 19.04.2001 , 9490 Vaduz Mand.Nr.: [redacted]
SB: Gächter Dagmar KB: Sprenger Sonja L. Kundenbesuch: 27.03.2000

Gründungsdatum: 21.08.1997 Status: Gelöscht

[redacted] = Redacted by the Permanent Subcommittee on Investigations

Verwaltungs- / Stiftungsräte
Profile Management Trust reg., Vad Zeichnungsrecht: Einzeln
Feuerstein Nicola Dr., Vaduz Zeichnungsrecht: Kollektiv

Banken
LGT Bank in Liechtenstein AG, Vaduz AB: Jehle Philip / LGT HK ZR-Nr.: [redacted] Zlg-Kto: [redacted]

Diverses

Anlageberater:	Jehle Philip / LGT HK,
Aktien / Zessionen:	LGT Bank Depot Ordinario,
Repräsentant:	LGT Treuhand AG, Vaduz
Vermittler:	LGT Investment Management, Hong Kon
Auftraggeber:	Privater Auftraggeber

Fix-Honorare

Domizilhonorar	800.00	21.08.2001	LGT Treuhand AG, Vaduz
Kapitalsteuer	1'000.00	21.08.2001	Liechtensteinische Steuerverwaltung, Vaduz
Stiftungsratshonorar	3'000.00	21.08.2001	LGT Treuhand AG, Vaduz

Pauschal-Honorare
0.00 fällig am:
Vermögenswert per: 0.00 Fakturierbares Pauschalhonorar: 0.00

Zweck
- 100%ige Beteiligung: - Manta Company Limited, Western Samoa ??
  - Zweck: s. Organigramm mit div. Angaben
  - 1 Inhaber-Aktienzertifikat im LGT-Depot der Veline
  --> siehe auch Pendenzen!

AKTIE am 12.04.2001 nach Hong Kong /Rep. Office per UPS gesandt zur Weiterleitung an Kunde

Besitznachweis, Verträge, Vollmachten

Weisungen (Verwaltung, Buchhaltung, Beistatut usw.)
- unsere Kontaktperson für sämtliche Pendenzen Mrs Ann Mary Pak, KK Young & Co., Hong Kong (siehe AV psc vom 14.6.99)

Pendenzen / Geschichte
- Passkopien der Dritt- und Viertbegünstigten fehlen (vorläufig abgelehnt durch die Kundin am 11.12.97)
- siehe AV scp vom 11.12.97 und cc-mail scp an Ph. Jehle vom 18.2.98 betr. Manta bzw. Struktur:
  - sind alle Unterlagen ok, insbesondere das 'neue' eingelieferte Aktienzertifikat Manta? (Kopie beiliegend)
    Ist Manta 100%ige Beteiligung von Veline?

  --> scp mit Kundin und KK Young besprechen (siehe Schr. K.K. Young 30.7.98 und u/Fax an KK Young vom 13.8.98)
  (- SAB: M2 und Akt ev. anpassen)

- Financial Statements bei NALA MANAGEMENT am Jahresanfang anfordern.
- VS00 von Kunde unterzeichnen per Fax nach HK 05.02.00

Permanent Subcommittee on Investigations
EXHIBIT #29

PSI-USMSTR - 005887

OCT-16-2006 14:12

▬▬ = Redacted by the Permanent Subcommittee on Investigations

Veline Foundation – closed on 4/19/2001 9490 **Vaduz** Client No.: [redacted]
SB: Dagmar Gächter **KB: Sonja Sprenger** Client Request: 3/27/2000

Founding date: 8/21/1997 Status: closed

Management/ Foundation Board
Profile Management Trust re., Vaduz — Signature right: Individual
Dr. Nicola Feuerstein, Vaduz — Signature right: Joint

Banks
LGT Bank in Liechtenstein AG, Vaduz AB: Phillip Jehle / LGT Hong Kong ZR#[redacted] ZigAcct:[redacted]

Miscellaneous

Investment Adviser:	Phillip Jehle / LGT Hong Kong
Shares/Assignments:	LGT Bank Depot Ordinario
Representative:	LGT Truchand AG, Vaduz
Agent:	LGT Investment Management, Hong Kong
Client:	Private Client

Fixed Fees

Domicile fee	800.00	8/21/2001	LGT Treuhand AG, Vaduz
Capital Tax	1,000.00	8/21/2001	Liechtenstein Tax Authority, Vaduz
Foundation Board Fee	3,000.00	8/21/2001	LGT Treuhand AG. Vaduz

Lump Sum Fee
{no entry}

Purpose
- 100% Share:
  - Manta Company Limited, Western Samoa ??
  - Purpose: S. organization with miscellaneous assets
  - 1 bearer stock certificate in Veline LGT-Deposit
  - also see Pending

SHARE sent on 4/12/2001 to Hong Kong /Rep. Office by UPS to pass on to client

Proof of Ownership, Contracts, Powers of Attorney
{no entry}

Instructions (Management, accounting, by-laws, etc.)
- Our contact person for all pending matters, Mrs. Ann Mary Pak, KK Young & Co., Hong Kong (See AV psc of 6/14/99)

Pending/History
- pass copies of the third and fourth beneficiaries are missing (temporarily declined by the client on 12/11/97)
- see AV sep of 12/11/97 and cc mail sep to Ph. Jehle dated 2/18/98 concerning Manta and structure:
- are all documents ok, especially the new Manta stock certificate issued? (See attachment.) Is Manta owned 100% by Veline?

→ sep discussed with client and KK Young (See KK Young letter of 7/30/98 and our fax to KK Young of 8/13/98.)
(SAB: M2 and Akt will adapt)

- Financial Statements ordered from NALA MANAGEMENT at beginning of year.
- Client VSOO signed by fax per Hong Kong

Discussion with Ms. Ann Mary Pak (AMP) and PJ in Rep. Office, Hong Kong, on 6/14/1999

AMP is second generation accountant. She takes care of select customers. She only makes acquisitions based on world wide propaganda for her clients.

AMP is married and has two adult children. The family lives in the US; she has been in the US and Canada for about 4 years.

AMP is Chinese with Canadian residency. She inherited offshore assets from her deceased father, which she kept from her mother who was living in Hong Kong at the time.

I recommend establishing FL Foundation through the mother with corresponding beneficiary regulations. AMP is convinced of the foundation idea and will recommend it or introduce it to other clients. Since there are a lot of US citizens among the clients I point out our business policy with regard to US residents/citizens/green card holders. AMP shares our opinion. She has no problem with it.

Impression: Potential for LGT BIL and LTV. Agreeable and serious contact. Plan date for next Far East trip {two illegible handwritten words}

PS. Veline Foundation: all pending can be clarified directly with AMP. {initials}
6/16/99

6/30/99 {initials}

Statements of assets as per 31.12.2000

05.02.2001

▬ = Redacted by the Permanent Subcommittee on Investigations

Veline Foundation
Vaduz

USD

Assets

EUR ACCOUNT	[redacted]	EUR	13'624.37	12'704.94
EUR FIDUCIARY DEPOSIT		EUR	323'369.05	301'546.81
Total LGT Bank in Liechtenstein AG Vaduz				314'251.75
Total Cash in banks				314'251.75
SAFE CUSTODY ACCOUNT	[redacted]			574'570.07
Total LGT Bank in Liechtenstein AG Vaduz				574'570.07
Total Securities				574'570.07
Manta Company Limited				1.00
Total				1.00
Total Participations				1.00
				888'822.82

Liabilities

Capital	18'404.91
Remaining net worth	870'417.91
Total	888'822.82
Total Net worth	888'822.82
	888'822.82

Exchange rates LGT: EUR 0.932516

7.2.2001

Permanent Subcommittee on Investigations
EXHIBIT #30

PSI-USMSTR - 005885

BEARER SHARE CERTIFICATE

Transferable by Delivery

This Share Certificate is issued by

MANTA COMPANY LIMITED

pursuant to its Memorandum and Articles of Association and pursuant to the provisions of the International Companies Act 1987 of Western Samoa.

Registered office of the Company:
Level 2, Chandra House
Convent Street
Apia, Western Samoa

Shares covered by this Certificate total ONE (1)

and numbered from 1

Description of Shares: ORDINARY USD1.00 each

Certificate Number: 1

This is to certify that the Bearer of this Share Certificate is entitled to the shares described herein.

This Certificate was sealed by the Company on 3rd **day of** September, **19** 97

For and on behalf of
BROMUS LIMITED

SEAL

President

DIRECTOR
For and on behalf of
P H I [illegible] INC.

SECRETARY

I HEREBY ACKNOWLEDGE RECEIPT OF THE ORIGINAL OF THIS SHARE CERTIFICATE.

Control Number: 10

DATE: 18 April 2001

Dividend coupons issued in conjunction with this Share Certificate. 1 and 2

THIS SHARE CERTIFICATE IS ISSUED WITHOUT ALTERATION OR ERASURE

Permanent Subcommittee on Investigations
EXHIBIT #31

PSI-USMSTR - 005878

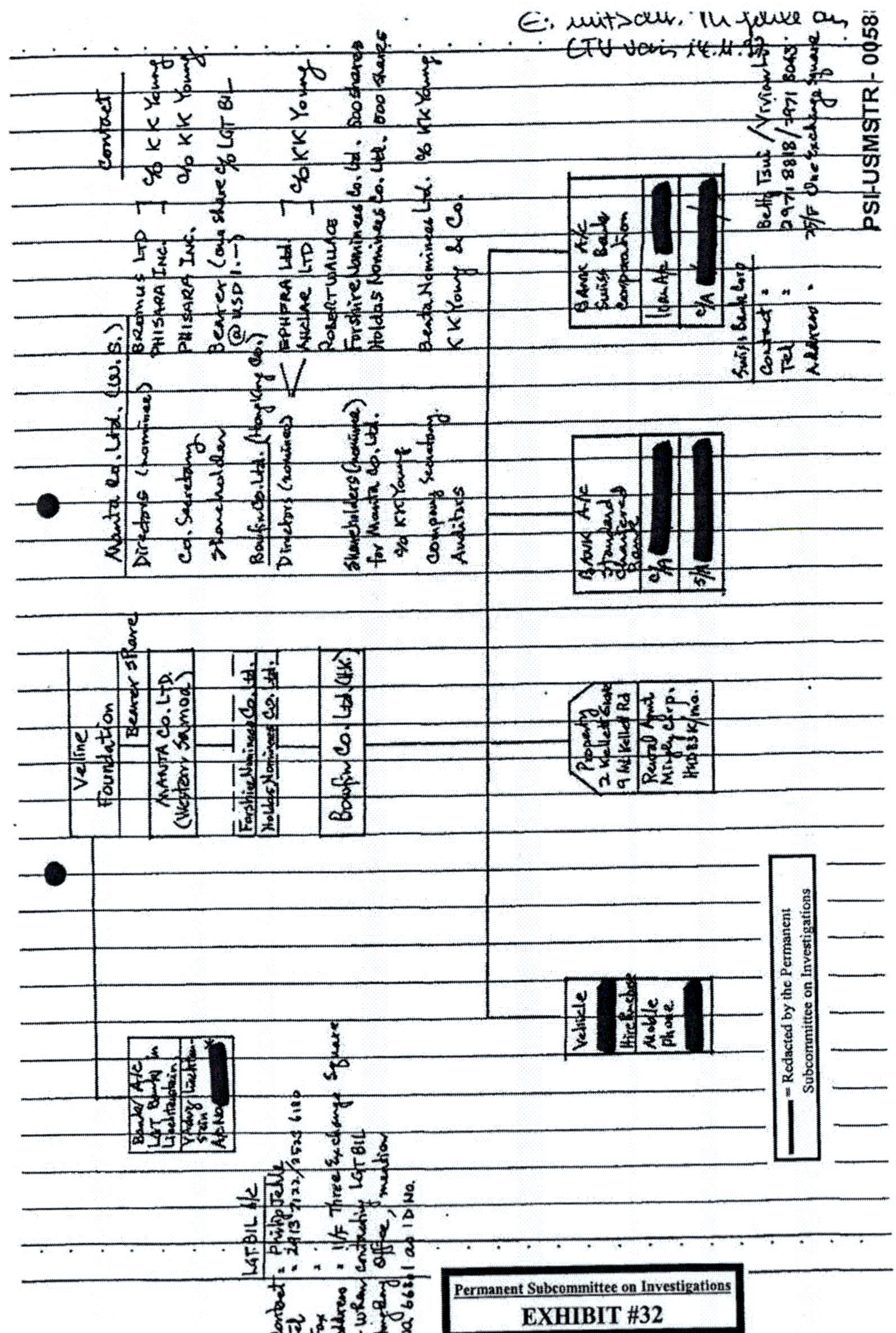
Velline Foundation
Bearer Share
MANTA Co. LTD. (Western Samoa)
Forshire Nominees Co. Ltd.
Holdas Nominees Co. Ltd.
Bowfin Co. Ltd. (HK)
Manta Co. Ltd. (W.S.)
Contact
Directors (nominee)
BROMUS LTD
PHISARA INC.
c/o K K Young
Co. Secretary
PHISARA INC.
c/o K K Young
Shareholder
Bearer (one share @ USD 1.–)
c/o LGT BIL
Bowfin Co. Ltd. (Hong Kong Co.)
Directors (nominee)
EPHPRA Ltd.
ANCLAE LTD
c/o KK Young
ROBERT WALLACE
Shareholders (nominee) for Manta Co. Ltd.
c/o KK Young
Forshire Nominees Co. Ltd. 500 shares
Holdas Nominees Co. Ltd. 500 shares
Company Secretary
Benta Nominees Ltd. c/o KK Young
Auditors
K K Young & Co.
Bank A/C LGT Bank in Liechtenstein
Vaduz Liechtenstein
A/c No [redacted]
LGT BIL A/c
Contact : Philipp Jehle
Tel : 2913 7122/2523 6180
Fax :
Address : 1/F Three Exchange Square
* When contacting LGT BIL Hong Kong Office, mention No. 66801 as ID No.
Vehicle
[redacted]
Hire Purchase
Mobile Phone
[redacted]
Property
2 Kellett Grove
9 Mt Kellett Rd
Rental Agent
Mingly Corp.
HKD 83K/mo.
Bank A/C Standard Chartered Bank
C/A [redacted]
S/A [redacted]
Bank A/C Swiss Bank Corporation
Loan A/c [redacted]
C/A [redacted]
Swiss Bank Corp
Contact : Betty Tsui / Vivian Lo
Tel : 2971 8818 / 2971 8043
Address : 25/F One Exchange Square
= Redacted by the Permanent Subcommittee on Investigations
Permanent Subcommittee on Investigations
EXHIBIT #32
PSI-USMSTR - 0058

LGT Bank in Liechtenstein
A Member of Liechtenstein Global Trust

LGT Bank in Liechtenstein
Aktiengesellschaft
Herrengasse 12
FL-9490 Vaduz

Telefon 075 235 11 22
Telefax 075 235 15 22
Telex 889 222

Aktenvermerk

1/2

Thema	**Westfields, Adelphi, Crofton**
VerfasserIn/Abt./Tel.	Peter Widmer / R22 / 1296
Datum	26. November 1996
Zur Erledigung	
Zur Kenntnisnahme	Dr. K. Bächinger E. Mattle W. Orvati, LGT Treuhand 27.11.96 → KD Westfields

Treffen mit:	- Frank Lowy - David Lowy - David Gonski - Joshua Gelbard
Datum:	21. November 1996 (in Sydney)
LGT Bank:	P. Widmer

1. Zuerst ist es darum gegangen, die Kreditrückzahlungsformalitäten bei Adelphi zu regeln. Dies ist erfolgt und im beiliegenden cc:mail an Elmar Mattle vom 21. November 1996 festgehalten. Beigeheftet sind für Elmar Mattle auch die Instruktionen der Crofton Foundation zur vorläufigen Anlage der Gelder bei LGT Bank für jeweils 1 Monat, visiert durch Joshua Gelbard.

2. Weiteres Vorgehen:

   a) Errichtung einer neuen Stiftung

   Namenswahl ist Sache von LGT; es gibt keine Preferenzen. Statuten können soweit als möglich jenen der Crofton Foundation entsprechen. (Falls diese bei LGT Treuhand nicht vorliegen, habe ich eine Kopie.)

   b) Protektor

   Eine weitere neu zu gründende Gesellschaft soll als Protektor auftreten; Joshua H. Gelbard soll wiederum deren Board angehören. Daneben werden 1 - 3 LGT-Leute gewünscht (P. Widmer und evtl. Dr. K. Bächinger, W. Orvati oder jemand von der Anlageseite).

   c) Überträge von Crofton auf neue Foundation

   Diese sollen über eine Zwischengesellschaft erfolgen, wobei wiederum Joshua Gelbard Ansprechpartner sein wird. Er wird hiefür nach Vaduz kommen.

R22/hg - WESTFIEL.DOC - 26.11.1996 - 12.39

Permanent Subcommittee on Investigations
EXHIBIT #33

PSI-USMSTR-008773

LGT Bank in Liechtenstein
A Member of Liechtenstein Global Trust

Aktenvermerk 2/2

d) Dokumentation

Die Draft-Dokumentation bezüglich neu zu gründender Gesellschaft sollte bis spätestens Ende Dezember an folgende Adresse gesandt werden:

Joshua H. Gelbard
Advocate
J.H. Gelbard & Co.
Law Office
5 Manne Street
Tel Aviv 64168
Israel

▬▬ = Redacted by the Permanent Subcommittee on Investigations

(Joshua möchte in dieser Sache im telefonischen Kontakt auf deutsch verkehren. Tel. [redacted] Schriftverkehr bleibt Englisch.

3. Die Lowys haben entschieden, dass sie im Zusammenhang mit diesen Gesellschaften nie mehr nach FL oder CH reisen möchten. Aus diesem Grund ist von einem Treffen in Los Angeles (anstelle des für den 17.12.1996 in Vaduz geplanten Meetings), an dem auch noch weitere Lowy-Familienmitglieder (u.a. Peter) teilnehmen sollen, gesprochen worden. Dieses Treffen sollte frühestens in der 2. Hälfte Januar stattfinden. Ich habe offen gelassen, wer und ob überhaupt jemand von der Bank daran teilnehmen wird. Eventuell gibt es auch die Möglichkeit einer Videokonferenz.

   Ansprechpartner wird in Zukunft ausschliesslich Joshua Gelbard sein.

4. Ich werde die Koordination der Aktivitäten nach meiner Rückkehr an die Hand nehmen. Für mögliche Vorarbeiten wäre ich aber schon jetzt dankbar.

i.A.

P. Widmer

PSI-USMSTR - 008774

[logo]LGT Treuhand
A Member of Liechtenstein Global Trust

LGT Trust
Corporation
Herrengasse 12
FL-9490 Vaduz

Telephone: 075 235 11 22
Telefax: 075 235 15 22
Telex: 889 222

1/2

Memorandum for the Record

Subject	**Westfields, Adelphi, Crofton**
Compiler / Tel.:	Peter Widmer / R22 / 1296
Date:	Nov. 26, 1996
For Follow up:	
cc:	Dr. K. Bächinger E. Mattle W. Orvati, LGT Treuhand Nov. 17, 1996 → [illegible] order KD Westfields [illegible]

Meeting with:	- Frank Lowy - David Lowy - David Gonski - Joshua Gelbard
Date:	Nov. 21, 1996 (in Sydney)
LGT Bank:	P. Widmer

1. The first issue at hand was to settle the credit repayment formalities at Adelphi. This was done, and recorded in the enclosed cc: e-mail to Elmar Mattle of Nov. 21, 1996. Attached for Elmar Mattle are also the instructions from the Crofton Foundation for the preliminary investment of the monies at LGT for one month each, signed off by Joshua Gelbard.

2. Future approach:

a) Establishment of a new foundation

Choice of name is a matter for LGT; there are no preferences. Insofar as possible, laws can correspond to those of the Crofton Foundation. (In case these are not available at LGT Treuhand, I have a copy.)

b) Protector

An additional newly to be established company is to act as protector; Joshua H. Gelbard, in turn, is to be a member of this new board. Additionally, 1 – 3 LGT people are desired (P. Widmer and possibly Dr. K. Bächinger, W. Orvati or someone from the investment side.)

[redacted] = Redacted by the Permanent Subcommittee on Investigations

[logo]LGT Treuhand
A Member of Liechtenstein Global Trust

Memorandum for the Record 2/2

c) Transfers from Crofton to new foundation

These are to be carried out by a holding company, whereby once again Joshua Gelbard will be contact person. He will come to Vaduz for this.

d) Documentation

The draft documentation regarding the newly to be established company should be sent no later than end of December to the following address:

Joshua H. Gelbard
Advocate
J. H. Gelbard & Co.
Law Office
5 Manne Street
Tel Aviv 64168
Israel

(In this matter, Joshua would like to correspond in German during phone conversations. Tel. [redacted] fax [redacted]; written communication remains in English.

3. The Lowys have decided that they never want to travel to Liechtenstein or Switzerland in connection with these companies again. For this reason, there was talk of a meeting in Los Angeles (instead of the one planned for Dec. 17, 1996 in Vaduz), at which other Lowy family members (Peter, among others) should participate. The earliest this meeting should take place is in the second half of January. I left open who and if someone from the bank will participate. Possibly there will also be the option of a video conference.

Contact person will be in the future exclusively Joshua Gelbard.

4. I will take on the details of the activities after my return. I'd be thankful already, however, for preparatory work, if possible.

on behalf of [illegible]

P. Widmer

LGT Treuhand
A Member of Liechtenstein Global Trust

LGT Treuhand
Aktiengesellschaft
Städtle 18-22
FL-9490 Vaduz

Telefon 41-75-235 27 27
Telefax 41-75-235 27 15
Telex 88 92 27 blt

Aktenvermerk

1/1

Thema	Neugründung Westfields / Lowy Gruppe (AUS)
Verfasser(in) / Tel.	Werner Orvati
Datum	27. November 1996 / pfi
Bestimmt für	Dr. P. Iob
Zur Kenntnisnahme	Dr. K. Bächinger, Dr. P. Schlachter, P. Widmer

Neugründung Westfields / Lowy

Beiliegender Aktenvermerk vom 26.November 1996 von Peter Widmer.

Vorgehen:

1. Kopie der Crofton Foundation Statuten von P. Widmer einholen.

2. Welche Bestimmungen befinden sich in den Statuten Crofton bzw. Beistatuten betreffend den Protektor?

3. Wer ist Aktionär der Protektor Gesellschaft und wo ist sie zu domizilieren?

4. Sorgfaltspflichtvereinbarung: Ist die LGT BIL genügend dokumentiert über die Vermögenswerte, die auf die neu zu errichtende Stiftung übertragen werden? Soll die Berufsgeheimnisträgererklärung überhaupt abgegeben werden?

5. Erstellung erster Entwürfe für die folgenden Unterlagen:

   ✓ - Errichtungsauftrag (ist Joshua H. Gelbard Auftraggeber?)
   ✓ - Statuten der neu zu errichtenden Stiftung
   ✓ - sofern möglich Beistatutenentwurf
   - Zusammenstellung der üblichen Angaben für die Protektorgesellschaft wie Jurisdiktion, Name, Kapital, Aktionäre, Verwaltungsratmitglieder, etc.

TERMIN: 13.12. 1996

AWWESTF.DOC - 28.11.1996 - 08,22

Permanent Subcommittee on Investigations
EXHIBIT #34

PSI-USMSTR - 008775

[logo]LGT Treuhand
A Member of Liechtenstein Global Trust

LGT Trust
Corporation
Städtle 18 - 22
FL-9490 Vaduz

Telephone: 41-75-235 27 27
Telefax: 41-75-235 27 15
Telex: 88 92 27 bilt

1/1

Memorandum for the Record

Subject	**New Establishment Westfields / Lowy** [by hand:] Group (AUS)
Compiler / Tel.:	Werner Orvati
Date:	Nov. 27, 1996 / pfi
For follow up:	Dr. P. Iob
cc:	Dr. K. Bächinger, Dr. P. Schlachter, P. Widmer

New establishment Westfields / Lowy

Enclosed memo of Nov. 26, 1996 from Peter Widmer.

Approach:

1. Get copy of the Crofton Foundation laws from P. Widmer.

2. Which rulings are in the Crofton laws and/or bylaws regarding the protector?

3. Who is stockholder of the protector company and where is it to be domiciled?

4. Due diligence agreement: Is LGT BIL sufficiently documented on the asset values that will be transferred to the newly to be established foundation?
Should the declaration of the job-secrecy carrier even be submitted?

5. Compilation of first drafts for the following documents:

√ - Establishment order (is Joshua H. Gelbard [sic] the client?)
√ - laws of the newly to be established foundation
√ - insofar as possible, bylaw draft
- listing of the usual data for the protector company like jurisdiction, name, capital, stockholders, members of the management board, etc.

[√ marks by hand]

APPOINTMENT: Dec. 13, 1996

[signed]

AVWESTF_DOC – NOV. 28, 1996 – 08,22

IDV 1403-C-019[illegible]

LGT Bank in Liechtenstein
A Member of Liechtenstein Global Trust

LGT Bank in Liechtenstein
Aktiengesellschaft
Herrengasse 12
FL-9490 Vaduz

Telefon 075 235 11 22
Telefax 075 235 15 22
Telex 889 222

Aktenvermerk

1/2

Thema	**Westfields, Adelphi, Crofton**
Verfasserin/Abt./Tel.	P. Widmer / R22 / 1296
Datum	17. Dezember 1996
Zur Erledigung	
Zur Kenntnisnahme	H. Nipp (Pt. 3) Dr. K. Bächinger W. Orvati → ?. lob KD Westfields

Telefon mit: - Frank Lowy (17.12.96)
- Joshua Gelbard (16.12.96)

Unter Bezugnahme auf meine beiden AV's vom 26.11. und 10.12.1996 bezüglich den aus der Adelphi-Kreditrückzahlung frei gewordenen Gelder in Höhe von rd. USD 53 Mio. und deren Einbringung in eine neue Struktur mit anschliessender Übergabe ins PM, möchte ich den letzten Stand der Verhandlungen festhalten.

1. Gelbard hat mir den Empfang der Entwürfe für die neue Stiftung und die Vorschläge bezüglich Protektor bestätigt. Lowy war zu jenem Zeitpunkt auch in Israel und hat die Unterlagen bereits eingesehen. Grundsätzlich sind diese in Ordnung. Die offenen Fragen, welche jetzt schon beantwortet werden können, werden direkt an LGT Treuhand (Dr. lob) gefaxt.

   Von der rechtlichen Seite werden die Abklärungen frühestens im Februar / März 1997 erledigt sein. Die Unterzeichnung der Dokumente kann dannzumal in London oder Amsterdam erfolgen.

2. Bezüglich Ausarbeitung von Anlagestrategie und Kostenstruktur insistiert Lowy auf einem Treffen in Los Angeles, an dem auch seine Söhne David und Peter sowie ev. Stephen teilnehmen sollen. Meinen Vorschlag für eine Videokonferenz hat er abgelehnt. Er möchte, dass ich ihn mit der Person, welche für "seine Anlagen" dann auch verantwortlich sein wird, in Los Angeles treffe.

   Der Grund hiefür sind Diskretionsüberlegungen sowie die Tatsache, dass er und seine Familie sich nach diesem entscheidenden Meeting weitestgehend von der Verwaltung dieser Vermögensteile zurückziehen möchten.

   Mit Lowy bin ich so verblieben, dass ich ihn nach dem 10.1.1997 in Los Angeles kontaktieren werde, um das Treffen von voraussichtlich 20. oder 21.1.1997 zu bestätigen.

   Vorgängig zum LA-Treffen sollten wir unsere ersten Vorschläge schriftlich unterbreiten, wobei diese auf neutralem Papier und ohne Bezug auf irgend eine Person oder Gesellschaft aus dem Lowy Umfeld erfolgen sollten. Die Übermittlung soll erst nach persönlicher Absprache durch mich mit Frank erfolgen.

Permanent Subcommittee on Investigations
EXHIBIT #35

LGT Bank in Liechtenstein
A Member of Liechtenstein Global Trust

Aktenvermerk 2/2

3. Darf ich Heinz Nipp ersuchen, die Person zu bestimmen, welche für den Besuch in Los Angeles in Frage kommt und mit mir die Ausarbeitung der ersten schriftlichen Vorschläge vornimmt.

4. Die Festgelder sind vorläufig auf 1-Monats-Rollover-Basis bei uns angelegt. Sofern die Bereinigung der Rechtsfragen länger als erwartet dauern würde, könnte sich Lowy vorstellen, dass der ~~PM-Auftrag auch bereits durch die "alten" Gesellschaften erteilt wird.~~

P. Widmer

A-WESX.DOC · 17.12.1996 · 15.26

PSI-USMSTR-008770

[Logo]
LGT Treuhand
A Member of Liechtenstein Global Trust

LGT Bank in Liechtenstein
Corporation
Staedtle 18+22
FL-9490 Vaduz
Principality of Liechtenstein
VAT-No. 50119

Telephone: +423 235 27 27
Telefax: +423 235 27 15
Internet: www.lgt.com
E-Mail info@lgt.com

Note for File 1/2

Subject:	**Westfields, Adelphi, Crofton**
Writer/ Tel.:	P. Widmer/R22/1296
Date:	17 December 1996
For follow up:	
To the attention of:	H. Nipp Dr. K. Baechinger W. Orvati → [SIGNED] KD Westfields

Telephone Conversations with: -Frank Lowy (12.17.96)
-Joshua Gelbard (12.16.96)

In reference to my two memos from 11.26 and 12.10.1996 regarding the free funds in the amount of rd. USD 53 million from the Adelphi-Credit Repayment and their insertion into a new structure with subsequent transfer in the PM, I would like to record the last condition of the proceedings.

1. Gelbard has confirmed to me the receipt of the designs/drafts for the new Foundation and the proposals regarding the protector. Lowy was also in Israel at that time and has already accepted the documents. In principle, they are in order. The open questions, which can now be answered, will be faxed directly to LGT Treuhand (Dr. Iob).

   On the legal side, the clarifications will be completed by February/March 1997 at the earliest. The signing of the documents can then occur in London or Amsterdam.

2. Regarding the composition of the portfolio strategy and the cost structure, Lowy insists on a meeting in Los Angeles, in which his sons David and Peter as well as possibly Stephen should take part. He refused my suggestion for a video conference. He would like that I meet with him in Los Angeles with the person who will also be responsible for "his establishment".

   The reason for this is considerations of discretion as well as the fact that he and his family would like to withdraw themselves as far as possible from the management following this scheduled meeting.

   I determine with Lowy that I will contact him in Los Angeles after the 1.10.1997 in order to confirm the meeting likely on the 20th or 21st of January 1997.

   Before the meeting in LA, we should prepare our first proposals in writing. These should be written on neutral paper and without reference to any person or corporation in the Lowy field. The forwarding should first occur via personal consultation with Frank through me.

[Logo]
LGT Treuhand
A Member of Liechtenstein Global Trust

Note for File 2/2

3. May I ask Heinz Nipp to certify the person who comes into question regarding the meeting in Los Angeles and to conduct the composition of the first written proposals.

4. The fixed deposits are applied by us preliminarily on a 1-month-rollover-basis. If the adjustment of the legal questions lasts longer than expected, Lowy can introduce that the PM-Order should also already be informed through the "old" corporations.

[SIGNED]
P. Widmer

R22mni – A-WEST.DOC – 12.18.1996 – 10,32 IDV 1403-C-0195

LGT Bank in Liechtenstein
A Member of Liechtenstein Global Trust

LGT Bank in Liechtenstein
Aktiengesellschaft
Herrengasse 12
FL-9490 Vaduz

Telefon 075 235 11 22
Telefax 075 235 15 22
Telex 889 222

Aktenvermerk

1/2

Thema	**Westfield / Lowy Family**
Verfasserin/Abt./Tel.	Peter Widmer / R22 / 1296
Datum	23. Januar 1997
Zur Erledigung	
Zur Kenntnisnahme	H. Nipp Dr. K. Bächinger Th. Piske W. Ospelt LGT T (Dr. P. Iob) KD Adelphi

Treffen mit:	- Frank Lowy - David Lowy - Peter Lowy
Ort/Datum:	Los Angeles, 20. Januar 1997
LGT Bank:	- Wilfried Ospelt - Peter Widmer

1. Beim Treffen ist es darum gegangen, die Anlagestrategie für aus einer Spezialfinanzierung stammende und bei uns angelegte Festgelder in Höhe von rund US$ 54,2 Mio. festzulegen und gleichzeitig die Überführung in eine neue Struktur zu diskutieren resp. festzulegen.

   Unsere Diskussion ist zu unserer vollen Zufriedenheit verlaufen. Wir konnten unsere Minimalziele mehr als erreichen: Das Geld bleibt bei uns resp. wird ins PM übergeführt. Bezüglich Fees haben wir eine All-In-Lösung (inkl. LGT Treuhand und Fremde) zu 70 bp (bei einem Minimalziel von 45 bp) durchgesetzt.

2. Anlagestrategie:

   - Strategie: Ertrag USD
   - Horizont: mind. 5 Jahre, eher aber 5 - 10 Jahre
   - Benchmark: Inflation USA + 2 %
   - Individuelles Mandat, Sondervermögen in Einzelfällen nicht ausgeschlossen
   - Beimischung spezieller Strategien: eher nicht erwünscht

Permanent Subcommittee on Investigations
EXHIBIT #36

R22Nip - LOWY.DOC - 23.01.1997 - 11.14

PSI-USMSTR - 008771

LGT Bank in Liechtenstein
A Member of Liechtenstein Global Trust

Aktenvermerk 2/2

3. Aus der Diskussion sind folgende weiteren Punkte festzuhalten:

- Die Lowys betrachten diese Gelder als "Versicherung", d.h. sie werden sehr langfristig und eher konservativ angelegt.

- "Wirtschaftlich Begünstigte" sind der Vater und die drei Söhne David, Peter und Stefen.

- Bis die Struktur definitiv feststeht, bleiben die Gelder bei uns als Festgeld angelegt und weiter jeweils 1 Monat verlängert.

- Die Lowys möchten ein- bis zweimal jährlich anhand einer Präsentation über die Zusammensetzung und Performance informiert werden. Eine dieser Präsentationen kann in Europa stattfinden.

- Sowohl mit dem Vater wie auch den Söhnen können wir einzeln und in mündlicher Form verkehren.

- Den Wunsch nach Mitbestimmung beim Anlageprozess konnten wir ihnen ausreden, mit dem Hinweis, dass jede direkte Einflussnahme auf die Stiftung Nachteile bringen kann.

- Wir haben zugesichert, dass die Gesamtbeziehung unter meiner Kontrolle (Key Account) bleiben wird und dass Wilfried Ospelt sich dem Depot "anlagestrategiemässig" persönlich annehmen wird. Die Kontakte sollen vorläufig ausschliesslich über mich laufen.

4. Bezüglich Struktur benötigen die Lowys noch 1 - 2 Monate, bis die Gründungen bei LGTT stattfinden können. Grund: Man möchte alle bisher involvierten Parteien ersetzen, d.h. Leute wie Gelbard, Leibler oder Sinitus Treuhand sollen nicht mehr in die neue Lösung einbezogen werden.

Mit Joshua Gelbard dürfen wir weiter offen sprechen. So wie es im Moment aussieht, wird auch auf den "Protector" verzichtet werden.

Wenn alles erledigt ist, möchte man, dass LGTT sämtliche Akten über die alten Strukturen vernichtet, soweit wir diese nicht aus rechtlichen Gründen aufbewahren müssen. Diesbezüglich werde ich mit LGTT nach Überführung in die neue Struktur speziell Kontakt aufnehmen.

Peter Widmer

PSI-USMSTR - 008772

[logo]LGT Treuhand
A Member of Liechtenstein Global Trust

LGT Trust
Corporation
Herrengasse 12
FL-9490 Vaduz

Telephone: 075 235 11 22
Telefax: 075 235 15 22
Telex: 889 222

Memorandum for the Record

Subject **Westfield / Lowy Family**

Compiler / Tel.: Peter Widmer / R22 / 1296

Date: Jan. 23, 1997

For follow up:

cc: H. Nipp
Dr. K. Bächinger
Th. Piske
W. Ospelt
LGT T (Dr. P. Iob)
KD Adelphi

Meeting with: - Frank Lowy
- David Lowy
- Peter Lowy

Place / Date: Los Angeles, Jan. 20, 1997

LGT Bank: - Wilfried Ospelt
- Peter Widmer

1. The meeting concerned determining the investment strategy for fixed deposits invested with us stemming from special financing in the amount of around US$ 54.2 million, and simultaneous discussion or determination of the transfer to a new structure.

Our discussion went to our complete satisfaction. We were able to more than reach our minimum goals: The money will stay with us, or be transferred into the PM. Regarding fees, we have pushed through an "all-in" solution (incl. LGT Trust and external people) at 70 bp (with a minimum goal of 45 bp).

2. Investment strategy:

- Strategy: proceeds USD
- Projected timeline: minimum 5 years, probably more around 5 – 10 years
- Benchmark: Inflation USA + 2 %
- Individual mandate, special assets possible in individual cases
- Add-in of special strategies: rather undesired

[logo]LGT Treuhand
A Member of Liechtenstein Global Trust

Memorandum for the Record 2/2

3. The following additional points from the discussion are to be recorded:

- The Lowys view these monies as "insurance," i.e., they will be invested very long-term and rather conservatively.

- "financial beneficiaries" are the father and the three sons David, Peter, and Stefen.

- Until the structure is determined definitively, the monies will remain invested as fixed deposits with us and continue to be extended 1 month at a time.

- The Lowys would like to be informed about the composition and performance once to twice a year by means of a presentation. One of these presentations can take place in Europe.

- We can communicate individually and verbally both with the father as well as with the sons.

- We were able to talk them out of the desire for co-management of the investment process by pointing out that every direct influence on the foundation can have disadvantages.

- We promised that the total relationship will remain under my control (key account) and that Wilfried Ospelt will personally take over the depot in an investment-strategic manner. For the short-term, the contacts should go exclusively through me.

4. Regarding structure, the Lowys still need 1 – 2 months until the establishments at LGTT can take place. Reason: One wants to replace all previously involved parties, i.e., people like Gelbard, Leibler, or Sinitus Trust should not be included in the new solution.

We are allowed to continue talking openly to Joshua Gelbard. The way it looks at the moment, one will also do without the "protector."

When everything is completed, one wants LGTT to destroy all files on the old structures, insofar as we don't have to keep them for legal reasons. Regarding this matter, I will specifically get in touch with LGTT after the transfer into the new structure.

[signed]

Peter Widmer

LGT Treuhand
A Member of Liechtenstein Global Trust

LGT Treuhand
Aktiengesellschaft
Städtle 18-22
FL-9490 Vaduz

Telefon 41-75-235 27 27
Telefax 41-75-235 27 15
Telex 88 92 27 blk

Aktenvermerk

1/1

Thema	**Termin London: 12.3.1997, 15.00 Uhr**
Verfasser(in) / Tel.	Werner Orvati
Datum	4. März 1997 / SKO
Zur Erledigung	Dr. P. Iob
Zur Kenntnisnahme	P.O. 6. März 1997

Telefon vom 3.3.1997 mit Peter Widmer.

Am 23.1.1997 haben P. Widmer und W. Ospelt die Familie L. in Los Angeles getroffen.

Grundsätzlich ist eine Vereinbarung betreffend die Vermögensverwaltung von zirka USD 54 Mio. erzielt worden.

Unsererseits wurde Ende 1996 an den Anwalt Joshua Gelbert in Israel ein Entwurf für Stiftungsunterlagen zugesandt.

Anlässlich der Besprechung vom 12.3.1997, 15.00 Uhr in London mit F.L. sowie J. Gelbert soll die definitive Struktur sowie die Vermögensübertragung besprochen werden.

P. Widmer sage ich bis zum 6.3.1997 die Namhaftmachung des LGTT Vertreters an dieser Besprechung zu (P. Schlachter oder P. Iob).

i.A. S.[signature]

W. Orvati

Permanent Subcommittee on Investigations
EXHIBIT #37

PSI-USMSTR - 008765

[logo]LGT Treuhand
A Member of Liechtenstein Global Trust

LGT Trust
Corporation
Städtle 18 - 22
FL-9490 Vaduz

Telephone: 41-75-235 27 27
Telefax: 41-75-235 27 15
Telex: 88 92 27 blit

1/1

Memorandum for the Record

Subject	**Appointment London: March 12, 1997, 3 p.m.**
Compiler / Tel.:	Werner Orvati
Date:	March 4, 1997 / SKO
For action:	Dr. P. Iob
cc:	P. O. March 6, 1997

Phone call of March 3, 1997 with Peter Widmer.

On Jan. 23, 1997, P. Widmer and W. Ospelt met the L. family in Los Angeles.

Fundamentally, an agreement was reached regarding the asset management of around USD 54 million.

From our side, a draft for foundation documents was sent to the attorney Joshua Gelbert in Israel at the end of 1996.

On the occasion of the discussion of March 12, 1997, 3 p.m. in London with F. L. and J. Gelbert, the definitive structure as well as the asset transfer is to be discussed.

I promise P. Widmer to name the LGTT representative at this discussion by March 6, 1997 (P. Schlachter or P. Iob).

[by hand:] on behalf of S. [illegible]

W. Orvati

- 1/2 -

J. H. Gelbard

LGT Treuhand Aktiengesellschaft
att. Werner Orvati / Dr. Paolo Iob
Städtle 18
FL-9490 Vaduz

London, 12 March 1997

Formation of a Foundation by the name Luperla Foundation

Dear Sirs,

I kindly request you to set up the Luperla Foundationaccording to the following enclosed documents

- Formation Deed in English (Appendix A)
- Statutes of Foundation (Appendix B)
- Regulation of Foundation (Appendix C)

The payment of the capital in the amount of sFr. 30'000.-- will be effected to the Foundation's account with LGT Bank in Liechtenstein AG, Vaduz.

As legal representative of the Foundation shall be appointed:

- LGT Treuhand Aktiengesellschaft

As Board Members of the Foundation with authority to sign any two jointly shall be appointed

- Dr. Konrad Bächinger, c/o LGT Bank in Liechtenstein
- Mr. Hans-Werner Ritter, Eichgasse 4a, FL-9490 Vaduz
- Mr. Peter Widmer, c/o LGT Bank in Liechtenstein AG, Vaduz
- Mr. Werner Orvati, c/o LGT Treuhand AG, Vaduz

Signatories on the account of the Foundation with LGT Bank in Liechtenstein shall be

- the Members of the Foundation Board according to their right to represent
- LGT Treuhand, singly

Permanent Subcommittee on Investigations
EXHIBIT #38

PSI-USMSTR - 008860

- 2/2 -

The Foundation is to enter into a Management Agreement with LGT Bank in Liechtenstein AG, Vaduz as set out in Appendix D.

I agree that an annual all-in-fee of 0.7 % of the average Foundations' assets shall be debited to the Foundation in accordance with the above referred Management Agreement. This fee includes

- the management of the Foundation's assets
- the formation and administration of the Foundation and its bank accounts
- the formation and administration of a transfer company (with legal situs in the British Virgin Islands) and its bank accounts
- the annual tax and registration payments for the Foundation and the transfer company in Liechtenstein and the British Virgin Islands

I also have taken note of the fact that LGT Treuhand AG and LGT Bank in Liechtenstein AG accepts liability for any damage suffered by ourselves and or the Foundation and its Beneficiaries due to any breach of duty of the members of the Foundation Board delegated by LGT Treuhand AG and LGT Bank in Liechtenstein AG.

Yours sincerely,

J.H Gelbard

PSI-USMSTR - 008861

LGT Bank in Liechtenstein
A Member of Liechtenstein Global Trust

LGT Bank in Liechtenstein
Aktiengesellschaft
Herrengasse 12
FL-9490 Vaduz

Telefon 075 235 11 22
Telefax 075 235 15 22
Telex 889 222

Aktenvermerk

1/2

Thema	**Frank Lowy**
Verfasserin/Abt./Tel.	Peter Widmer / R22 / 1296
Datum	13. März 1997
Zur Erledigung	W. Ospelt, PBA E. Mattle, SFI Dr. P. Iob, LGTT
Zur Kenntnisnahme	S.D. Prinz Philipp von und zu Liechtenstein (Pt 3) H. Nipp, GDV Dr. K. Bächinger, GB2 W. Orvati, LGTT H.W. Ritter, LGTT

Besuch bei:	- Frank Lowy - Josua Gelbard
Datum/Ort:	12. März 1997 in London
LGT:	- Dr. Paolo Iob - Wilfried Ospelt - Peter Widmer

1. Der Entscheid zur Überführung der Crofton Vermögenswerte von rund USD 55 Mio. (weitere Beträge, die bisher bei SBG waren, sollen folgen) ins PM ist definitiv gefallen. Die neue Struktur steht, Stiftungsunterlagen und Mandatsvertrag sind unterzeichnet, und die Zwischengesellschaft ist bestimmt (Stiftungsräte W. Orvati, H.W. Ritter, Dr. K. Bächinger, P. Widmer). Was wir jetzt noch benötigen, sind die Unterschriften der zeichnungsberechtigten Personen auf den Vergütungsaufträgen.

2. Die Überführung der Festgelder wird bei Fälligkeit stattfinden. Die Anlagen im PM werden im Laufe von 1 - 2 Monaten erfolgen. W. Ospelt wird dafür verantwortlich zeichnen.

   Ausgehandelt wurde eine All-in Fee von 0,7 %, wobei darin auch alle Kosten der LGT Treuhand eingeschlossen sind. M.E. kann LGTT für effektive Kosten plus einen Nominalbetrag für deren Bemühungen Rechnung an PM stellen.

3. Lowy scheint mit unserem Service sehr zufrieden gewesen zu sein und möchte diesen Sommer S.D. Prinz Philipp, Dr. K. Bächinger und P. Widmer zu einem speziellen Anlass nach London einladen.

4. Westfield International möchte wieder an die Börse und hat dafür in den USA per voraussichtlich 7. Mai 1997 ein IPO vorgesehen.

Permanent Subcommittee on Investigations
EXHIBIT #39

LGT Bank in Liechtenstein
A Member of Liechtenstein Global Trust

Aktenvermerk 2/2

5. Wir haben nochmals versprochen, dass alle Unterlagen von Crofton vernichtet werden, soweit diese aus rechtlichen Gründen nicht aufbewahrt werden müssen. Crofton wird nach Übertrag der Aktiven saldiert.

6. Die Adelphi-Aktiven werden nicht in die neue Struktur eingeschlossen.

7. Besten Dank an alle, die mit ihrer konstruktiven Mitarbeit diesen Abschluss ermöglicht haben.

Peter Widmer

822/wg - LOWY2.DOC - 13.03.1997 - 09.51

PSI-USMSTR-008768

[logo] LGT Trust
A Member of the Liechtenstein Global Trust

LGT Trust
Corporation
Staedtle 28
FL – 9490 Vaduz
Principality of Liechtenstein
VAT # 50119

Telephone + 423 235 27 27
Telefax + 423 235 27 15
Internet
www.lgt.com/lgttreuhand
Email lgttrust@lgt.com

Memorandum for the file 1 / 2

Subject	Frank Lowy
~~From / Tel.~~	~~Peter Widmer / R22 / 1296~~
Date	13 March 1997
For follow-up:	W. Ospelt, PBA E. Mattle, SFI Dr. P. Iob, LGTT
CC	S.D. Prince Philipp from and to Liechtenstein (Pt 3) H. Nipp, GDV Dr. K. Baechinger, GB2 W. Orvati, LGTT H.W. Ritter, LGTT

Visit by:	- Frank Lowy - Josua Gelbard
Date / Place:	12 March 1997 in London
LGT:	- Dr. Paolo Iob - Wilfried Ospelt - Peter Widmer

1. The decision of the transfer of the Crofton assets, worth around USD 55 million (further amounts, that were formerly with SBG, shall follow) is definitely cancelled in the PM. The new structure stands, foundation documents and engagement contracts are signed, and the mediating company is determined (board of directors W. Orvati, H.W. Ritter, Dr. K. Baechinger, P.Widmer). What we now will require, are the signature of the signatory beneficiary person on the payment contract.

2. The transfer of the fixed deposits will take place at the payment date. The arrangements in the PM will follow after a duration of 1 – 2 months. W. Ospelt will be responsible for showing this.

A Member of the Liechtenstein Global Trust

Memorandum for the file 2 / 2

An All-in Fee of 0,7 % was negotiated, where by all costs of the LGT Trust are included. M.E. can adjust for effective costs plus a nominal amount for their service bill.

3. Lowy seems to have been very pleased with our service and would like to invite S.D. Prince Philipp, Dr. K. Baechinger and P. Widmer to London this summer for a special occasion.

---

4. Westfield international would like to be listed on the stock exchange again and has scheduled in advance an IPO in the USA on 7 May 1997.

[end of page 1]

5. We have promised once again, that all documents of Crofton will be destroyed, as long as will not have to be protected for legal reasons. After the transfer of the assets, Crofton will be closed.

6. The Adelphi – assets will **not** be included in the new structure.

7. Many thanks to everyone, who with their constructive team work, have made this conclusion possible.

[signature]
Peter Widmer

R22 / nig – LOWY2.doc – 03.13.1997 – 09,51 IDV 1404 C 0196

LGT Treuhand
A Member of Liechtenstein Global Trust

LGT Treuhand
Aktiengesellschaft
Städtle 18-22
FL-9490 Vaduz

Telefon 41-75-235 27 27
Telefax 41-75-235 27 15
Telex 88 82 27 blk

Aktenvermerk

1/1

Thema **Luperla Foundation**

Verfasser(in) / Tel.	pio
Datum	16. März 1997 / pio
Zur Erledigung	pio
Zur Kenntnisnahme	pio

Neugründung Luperla Foundation / Meeting mit F.L. vom 12.3.97 / London

Das Meeting findet im Connaught Hotel, Mayfair, London statt. Anwesend sind F.L., dessen Anwalt Joshua Gelbart sowie unsererseits Peter Widmer, Wilfried Ospelt und pio. Es wird folgendes besprochen:

1. F.L. ist zur Gründung entschlossen. Es ist jedoch besondere Vorsicht anzuwenden, da er den australischen Steuerbehörden nicht abnimmt, dass der Fall mit der Bezahlung der 25M endgültig abgeschlossen ist. Die ganze Dokumentation und Aufbau ist so abzufassen, dass F.L. sowie dessen Anwälte in Australien vor Gericht bedenkenlos aussagen können.

2. Die Luperla ist eine Stiftung ohne Mandatsvertrag. Auftraggeber ist J. Gelbart.

3. Die Gründung soll anhand der durch F.L. vorgelegten Dokumente erfolgen, welche entsprechend mit den Anwälten in Australien abgesprochen sind. J. G. und ich machen verschiedene Vorschläge zur Ergänzung der Dokumente. Es sind dies:

   <u>Statuten:</u>
   Ermächtigungsnorm zur Zuwahl eines Protektors
   Arbitrage-Klausel

   <u>Beistatuten:</u>
   Nomination des Protektors sowie Festlegung von dessen Rechten und Pflichten
   Einführung eines Letztbegünstigten
   Einschränkung betreffend allfälliger Gesetzesänderungen in Liechtenstein hinsichtlich der Auskunftspflichten gegenüber Behörden oder Dritten

4. Es wird die Vergabe eines Vermögensverwaltungsauftrages verabredet. J. Gelbart als Auftraggeber unterzeichnet das Belegexemplar.

5. Die Gelder sollen von Crofton via eine extra übernommene BVI-Gesellschaft (Name: Sewell......) überwiesen werden. Der Auftrag an LGT BIL für Crofton muss von Sinitus Treuhand in Zürich erfolgen. Den Auftrag an Sinitus wird J. Gelbart veranlassen (Beilage: Entwurf eines Schreibens an Sinitus/am 12.3.97 an J.G. übergeben).

Permanent Subcommittee on Investigations
EXHIBIT #40

PSI-USMSTR - 008902

LGT Treuhand
A Member of Liechtenstein Global Trust

Aktenvermerk 2/2

Weiteres Vorgehen:

1. Gründung der Luperla Foundation veranlassen und Konti bei LGT BIL einrichten.

2. Übernahme der BVI-Gesellschaft veranlassen und Konti bei LGT BIL einrichten.

---

3. Kontonummern an J. Gelbard mitteilen (per Telefon, keine Schriftstücke)

4. VV-Auftrag an LGT-BIL vergeben

5. Geldtransfer überwachen

6. Instruktion von J. Gelbart betreffend Änderung/Ergänzung Statuten/Beistatuten abwarten

LTV/pio
16.3.97

Luperla Foundation / AV 16.3.97

PSI-USMSTR - 008903

[logo]LGT Treuhand
A Member of Liechtenstein Global Trust

LGT Trust
Corporation
Städtle 18 - 22
FL-9490 Vaduz

Telephone: 41-75-235 27 27
Telefax: 41-75-235 27 15
Telex: 88 92 27 blt

1/2

Memorandum for the Record

Subject	**Luperla Foundation**
Compiler / Tel.: Roger	pio
Date:	March 16, 1997 / pio
For action:	pio
cc:	pio

New Establishment Luperla Foundation / Meeting with F. L. of March 12, 1997 / London

The meeting takes place in the Connaught Hotel, Mayfair, London. In attendance are F. L., his attorney Joshua Gelbart [sic], as well as from our side Peter Widmer, Wilfried Ospelt, and pio. The following is discussed:

1. F. L. is resolute about the establishment. Special caution is to be used, however, since he doesn't believe the Australian tax authorities that the case with the payment of the 25 M is settled for good. The entire documentation and assembly is to be done in such a manner that F. L. and his attorneys can testify before court in Australia without hesitation.

2. Luperla is a foundation without engagement contract. Client is J. Gelbart.

3. The establishment is to be carried out by means of the documents presented by F. L., which have been discussed with the attorneys in Australia accordingly. J. G. and I make various suggestions for amendment of the documents. These are:

Laws:
Authorization standard for addition of a protector
Arbitrage clause

Bylaws:
Nomination of the protector as well as determination of his rights and duties
Introduction of a final beneficiary
Restriction regarding possible legal changes in Liechtenstein regarding the disclosure duties toward agencies or third parties

4. The assignment of an asset-management contract is agreed upon. J. Gelbart as client signs the file copy.

[initialed]

[logo]LGT Treuhand
A Member of Liechtenstein Global Trust

Memorandum for the Record 2/2

5. The monies are to be transferred from Crofton via a specially taken-over BVI company (name: Sewell [by hand]). The order to LGT BIL for Crofton has to come from Sinitus Trust in Zurich. J. Gelbart will request the order to Sinitus. (Enclosure: Draft of a letter to Sinitus / handed over to J. G. on March 12, 1997).

Further Approach:

1. Request establishment of Luperla Foundation and set up account at LGT BIL.

2. Request takeover of BVI company and set up accounts at LGT BIL.

3. Give account numbers to J. Gelbard [sic] (by phone, no papers).

4. Assign asset-management contract to LGT BIL.

5. Monitor money transfer.

6. Wait for instructions from J. Gelbart regarding change/amendment laws/bylaws.

LTV / pio
March 16, 1997

[initialed]

Luperla Foundation / Memo March 16, 1997

Belegexemplar

Regulations
Luperla Foundation, Vaduz

Permanent Subcommittee on Investigations
EXHIBIT #41

PSI-USMSTR - 008838

Based on the power contained in Art. 4 of the Statutes of Luperla Foundation with seat in Vaduz, Liechtenstein, and all other powers it enabling the Board of Foundation hereby issues the following as replacement of the Regulations issued on 20.III.97

REGULATIONS

1. The persons, companies or other entities from time to time notified in writing to the Board of Foundation by the company (Company) in which Beverly Park Corporation, a company formed in Delaware, United States of America on 3 January 1997, (Corporation) for the time being holds any share and if there is more than one such company, then the company in which the Corporation last became a shareholder before the notification (a certificate to that effect from any office bearer for the time being of the Corporation may be relied upon by the Board of the Foundation) shall be within the class of distributees of the Foundation assets and the income therefrom, provided that the Company for the time being or its legal successor may revoke any such notification at any time by a further notice in writing to the Board of Foundation, and provided further that no Company shall directly or indirectly become a distributee or benefit therefrom.

2. The Board of Foundation may pay to any one or more of the distributees appointed under 1. above, to the exclusion of any of the other distributees, such portions or all of the Foundation assets or the income therefrom at such time or times as the Board of Foundation shall think fit in its absolute and uncontrolled discretion.

3. Any expenses and costs including legal costs, if any, related to the maintenance and administration, the asset management, the execution of the present Regulations and the dissolution of the Foundation shall be charged to the income, if and when they become due, and only in the event that the income does not cover sufficiently the aforementioned expenses and costs, to the Foundation assets.

4. At present there is no public, governmental or other supervisory authority or agency or similar person or institution to supervise the Foundation except as expressly provided for in the Statutes or Regulations of the Foundation. If any such authority or agency is introduced in Liechtenstein, the Foundation Board is to immediately inform the Corporation accordingly.

5. The present Regulations shall have the same legal effects as the Statutes. In case of differences between the Statutes and the Regulations the provisions of the latter shall prevail provided they do not violate any compulsory provisions of the Statutes.

Regulations of Luperla Foundation, Vaduz dated April 30, 1997

PSI-USMSTR - 008839

6. **The Board of Foundation may change, alter, amend or revoke these Regulations at any time.**

Vaduz, April 30, 1997

EINVERSTANDEN:
Approuvé:
Approved:

The Foundation Board:

Dr. Konrad Bächinger	**Peter Widmer**
Hans-Werner Ritter	**Werner Orvati**

Regulations of Luperla Foundation, Vaduz dated April 30, 1997

PSI-USMSTR - 008840

LGT Bank in Liechtenstein
A Member of Liechtenstein Global Trust

LGT Bank in Liechtenstein
Aktiengesellschaft
Herrengasse 12
FL-9490 Vaduz

Telefon 075 235 11 22
Telefax 075 235 15 22
Telex 889 222

ERLEDIGT

Aktenvermerk

1/2

Thema	**Luperla Foundation, Vaduz**
Verfasserin/Abt./Tel.	Peter Widmer / R22 / 1296
Datum	2. Mai 1997
Zur Erledigung	Dr. P. Iob, LGT Treuhand Wilfried Ospelt E. Matt[illegible]
Zur Kenntnisnahme	H. [illegible]pp Dr. K. Bächinger
Treffen mit:	- David Lowy - J.H. Gelbard
Datum:	30. April 1997 im Hotel Savoy, Zürich
LGT Bank:	P. Widmer

uk → spr
zur Info
(und Ablage?)
ufe

1. Die Herren waren in Zürich um mit Sinitus Treuhand die Überträge der Vermögenswerte auf Luperla vorzubereiten. Ich bin mit Ihnen das Vorgehen nochmals durchgegangen:

   a) Ca. USD 54 Mio. (Saldi Crofton bei uns) gehen auf Konto Sewell bei uns (Auftrag kommt von Sinitus); anschliessend vergütet Sewell (Auftrag kommt von LGT T) den Betrag an Luperla. ✓

   b) Weitere rd. USD 3 Mio. werden durch Drittbankvergütung bei Sewell (Konto LGT) eingehen, welche ebenfalls auf Konto Luperla bei LGT zu vergüten sind (Auftrag LGT T). →OK 3.6 Mio. [illegible] K. Ulrich

   c) Crofton wird deren Konto bei Union Bank of Israel, Tel-Aviv schliessen lassen und Saldo (ca. USD 0.2 Mio.) auf Konto Sewell vergüten; Sewell zahlt auch diesen Betrag an Luperla bei LGT (Auftrag LGT T). ✓

      Luperla soll dann USD 250'000.– auf deren Konto (durch LGT T bereits eröffnet) bei Union Bank of Israel vergüten. ✓

   d) Das Konto Sewell ist am 31.5.1997 zu saldieren und die Gesellschaft zu löschen. Auftrag durch LGT T. ✓

2. Die Belegexemplare "Regulations" und "Statutes" der Luperla Foundation habe ich von J. Gelbard gegenzeichnen lassen, diese liegen diesem AV für P. Iob bei.

   Bezüglich der Stiftung ist somit alles i.O.

Permanent Subcommittee on Investigations
EXHIBIT #42

AF/ja - LUPERLA.DOC - 02.05.1997 - 10,01

PSI-USMSTR 008864

LGT Bank in Liechtenstein
A Member of Liechtenstein Global Trust

Aktenvermerk

2/2

3. Bezüglich Anlagestrategie und Fees bleibt alles beim alten: Ertrag USD, All-in 70bp (siehe AV vom 23.1.1997).

   Die neuen Investitionsvorschläge habe ich übergeben. Diese wurden geschätzt und als i.O. in Empfang genommen.

   Nach Eingang der Gelder, voraussichtlich ab nächster Woche, resp. nach Auslaufen der Festgelder kann mit dem Anlageprozess begonnen werden, wobei ich nochmals festgehalten habe, dass es bis zur vollen Investition 1-2 Monate dauern kann.

4. Ich bitte die Geldflüsse mit **E. Matfle** zu koordinieren.

5. Nach Abschluss dieser Transaktionen sollen dann definitiv alle Unterlagen von "Crofton" und "Jelnav" vernichtet werden, soweit dies aus rechtlichen Gründen möglich ist. Ich bitte Dr. Iob um Bestätigung der Erledigung bis 30.6.1997.

P. Widmer

Beilage für Dr. Iob

PSI-USMSTR-008865

[stamp:] **COMPLETED**

[logo]LGT Treuhand
A Member of Liechtenstein Global Trust

LGT Trust
Corporation
Herrengasse 12
FL-9490 Vaduz

Telephone: 075 235 11 22
Telefax: 075 235 15 22
Telex: 889 222

1/2

Memorandum for the Record

Subject	**Luperla Foundation, Vaduz**
Compiler / Tel.:	Peter Widmer / R22 / 1296 [by hand:] [illegible initials] → spr
Date:	May 2, 1997 FYI (and file?) [initialed]
For action:	Dr. P. Iob, LGT Trust Wilfried Ospelt E. Mattle
cc:	H. Nipp Dr. K. Bächinger

Meeting with:	- David Lowy - J. H. Gelbard
Date:	April 30, 1997 in the Hotel Savoy, Zurich
LGT Bank:	- Wilfried Ospelt - Peter Widmer

[The top half of this page is struck through by hand.]

1. The gentlemen were in Zurich to prepare with Sinitus Trust the asset transfers to Luperla. I reviewed the approach with them once more:

a) Around USD 54 million (balance Crofton with us) are going to the Sewell account with us (assignment from Sinitus); subsequently Sewell pays (assignment from LGT T) the amount to Luperla. √

b) An additional roughly USD 3 million will go to Sewell (account LGT) through third-bank payments, which are likewise to be paid to account Luperla at LGT (assignment LGT T).
[by hand:] → CHF 3.6 million according to K. Ulrich

c) Crofton will close its account with Union Bank of Israel, Tel Aviv and send balance (around USD 0.2 million) to account Sewell; Sewell also pays this amount to Luperla at LGT (assignment LGT T). √

ABT/kz LUPERTA[sic].doc- May 2, 1997 – 10,01

IDV 1403-C-0195

[logo]LGT Treuhand
A Member of Liechtenstein Global Trust

Memorandum for the Record 2/2

Luperla is then to remunerate USD 250,000.00 to its account (already opened by LGT T) with Union Bank of Israel. √

---

d) The Sewell account is to be closed on May 31, 1997 and the company to be dissolved. Assignment through LGT T. √

[all √ by hand]

2. I have had the file copies "Regulations" and "Statutes" of the Luperla Foundation countersigned by J. Gelbard; these are attached to this memo for P. Iob.

Regarding the foundation, everything is herewith in order.

3. Regarding investment strategy and fees everything remains the same: proceeds USD, all-in 70 bp (see memo of Jan. 23, 1997).

I have turned over the new investment suggestions. These were appreciated and received as in order.

After in payment of monies, probably starting next week, or after the fixed deposits run out, the investment process can be started, whereby I stated once more that it can take 1 – 2 months for full investment.

4. I request that the money flows be coordinated with **E. Mattle.**

5. After completion of these transactions, all documents from "Crofton" and "Jelnav" are definitely to be destroyed, insofar as this is legally possible. I ask Dr. Iob for confirmation of completion by June 30, 1997.

[signed]

P. Widmer

Enclosure for Dr. Iob
[not at hand for translation]

ERLEDIGT

LGT Bank in Liechtenstein
A Member of Liechtenstein Global Trust

LGT Bank in Liechtenstein
Aktiengesellschaft
Herrengasse 12
FL-9490 Vaduz

Telefon 075 235 11 22
Telefax 075 235 15 22
Telex 889 222

Aktenvermerk

1/1

Thema	**Luperla Foundation, Vaduz**
Verfasserin/Abt./Tel.	Peter Widmer / R22 / 1296
Datum	14. Mai 1997
Zur Erledigung	
Zur Kenntnisnahme	H. Nipp Dr. K. Bächinger Dr. P. Iob, LGT Treuhand Wilfried Ospelt KD

Im Anschluss an meinen AV vom 2. Mai 1997 möchte ich mitteilen, dass die Überträge der Vermögenswerte auf die Luperla Foundation abgewickelt wurden. Nach Abschluss dieser Transaktionen verfügt die Luperla Foundation über Guthaben von USD 54,7 Mio. und CHF 3,6 Mio.

Der Investitionsprozess hat bereits angefangen und wird bis zum Abschluss in bezug auf das richtige Timing der Anlagen noch eine geraume Zeit dauern.

Wie in obigem AV erwähnt, werden wir per Ende Mai veranlassen, dass die alten Konti geschlossen werden. Offen bleibt darum nur noch die Bestätigung von Dr. Iob, dass die alten "Crofton" und "Jelnav" Akten bei LGTT entfernt wurden.

P. Widmer

Permanent Subcommittee on Investigations
EXHIBIT #43

PSI-USMSTR - 008883

COMPLETED [stamped]

[logo] LGT Bank in Liechtenstein
A Member of Liechtenstein Global Trust

LGT Bank in Liechtenstein
Corporation
Herrengasse 12
FL-9490 Vaduz

Telephone 075 235 11 22
Fax 075 235 15 22
Telex 889 222

Memorandum for the File 1/1

Topic: **Luperla Foundation, Vaduz**

Author / Tel.: Peter Widmer / R22 / 1296

Date: 14 May 1997

For Follow-Up:

To the Attention of: H. Nipp
Dr. K. Bächinger
Dr. P. Iob, LGT Treuhand
Wilfried Ospelt
KD

I would like to disclose, in connection to my memorandum for the file from 2 May 1997 that the transfer of assets to the Luperla Foundation has been carried out. Upon completion of this the Luperla Foundation will have assets of USD 54.7 Mil. and CHF 3.6 Mil. at its disposal.

The investment process has already begun and, with reference to the right timing of the investments, will take a fairly long time until completion.

As mentioned in the above mentioned memorandum for the file, we will arrange as per the end of May for the old accounts to be closed. Therefore, all that remains outstanding is the confirmation from Dr. Iob that the old "Crofton" and "Jelnav" shares at LGTT have been removed.

[signature]

P. Widmer

LGT Treuhand
A Member of Liechtenstein Global Trust

LGT Treuhand
Aktiengesellschaft
Städtle 18-22
FL-9490 Vaduz
Fürstentum Liechtenstein

Telephone 41-75-235 27 27
Telefax 41-75-235 27 15
Telex 88 92 27 blt
E-Mail lgtt@lgttrust.lol.li
100653,2664 CompuServe

Aktenvermerk

1/1

Thema	**Luperla Stiftung / Sewell Services Ltd. B.V.I.**
Verfasser(in) / Tel.	NMU
Datum	23. Oktober 1997 / nmu
Zur Erledigung	
Zur Kenntnisnahme	RT, EVO

Herr Elmar Mattle (arbeitet bei Peter Widmer, welcher Stiftungsrat von Luperla Foundation und den Kontakt zum Auftraggeber hält) von der LGT BIL ruft an und teilt folgendes mit:

Von einer Gesellschaft namens Crofton, welche das Konto bei der LGT BIL hat werden ca. USD 30'000.-- auf das Konto der Sewell Services Ltd. transferiert (Sewell Services Ltd. ist die Tochtergesellschaft der Luperla Stiftung). Ich habe die Eröffnung eines USD-Kontos veranlasst => 0125926AC (USD). Von der Sewell soll dieser Betrag dann auf das Konto der Luperla vergütet werden. Dies wurde anscheinend schon öfters so gemacht.

Nach Durchsicht der Akten stelle ich fest, dass vom Konto der Sewell am 7.5.1997 USD 54.7 Mio. und CHF 3.6 Mio. sowie am 12.5.1997 USD 211'000.-- mittels Vergütungsaufträgen an die Luperla überwiesen wurden, ohne Nennung des Auftraggebers. Am 16.5.1997 wurde dann die Kontoverbindung bei der LGT BIL gelöscht.

EVO/RT bitte mit ORV Kontakt aufnehmen, um Hintergrundinformationen über die gesamte Struktur zu erfahren. Falls ORV nicht informiert sein sollte, an Peter Widmer gelangen.

Ferner sind noch folgende Pendenzen offen:

- Belegexemplare der Statuten und Beistatuten wurden noch nicht unterzeichnet (=> wurden am 25.4.97 an Herrn Widmer zur Weiterleitung an Kunden gesandt) Erledigt?
- Die schriftliche Bestätigung, betr. Aktenvernichtung der Unterlagen Crofton/Yelnarf der Rechtsabteilung LGT BIL ist noch hängig (s. Av PIO v. 3.7.97) P

Stiftungsräte der Luperla sind:	*Dr. Bächinger*
	Peter Widmer
	Werner Orvati
	Hans-Werner Ritter

[signature]
Natalie Müller

Permanent Subcommittee on Investigations
EXHIBIT #44

PSI-USMSTR - 008896

[logo]
LGT Trust
A Member of Liechtenstein Global Trust

LGT Treuhand
Corporation
Städtle 18-22
FL-9490 Vaduz
Principality of Liechtenstein

Telephone 41-75-235 27 27
Tefax 41-75-235 27 15
Telex 88 92 27 bilt
Email lgttrust@lgtt.lol.li
100653,2664 CompuServe

Memorandum for the File

1/1

Concerned Issues	**Luperla Foundation / Sewell Service Ltd. B.V.I.**
Author / Tel.	NMU
Date	10.23.1997 / nmu
For Follow-Up	
For the information of	RT, EVO

Mr. Elmar Mattle (who works with Peter Widmer, a member of the board of trustees of the Luperla Foundation, who maintains contact with the client), from the LGT BIL, calls and communicates the following:

Approximately 30,000.-- is being transferred from a corporation named Crofton, which has the account at the LGT BIL, to the account of the Sewell Services Ltd. (Sewell Services Ltd. is the subsidiary of the Luperla Foundation). I have brought about the opening of a USD account => 0125926AC (USD). This amount shall then be paid to the account of the Luperla from the Sewell. This has apparently already been done on many occasions.

After review of the files I establish that on 05.07.1997 USD 54.7 million and CHF 3.6 million, and on 05.12.1997 USD 211,000.--, was transferred from the account of the Sewell to the Luperla by means of authorized payment orders, without mention of the client. Then, on 05.16.1997, the account relationship at the LGT BIL was cancelled.

EVO/RT, please establishment contact with ORV to procure background information concerning the entire structure. If ORV does not have this information, make a request with Peter Widmer.

Furthermore, the following pending items are left open:

- File copies of the statutes and bylaws have still not been signed (=> were sent to Mr. Widmer on 04.25.1997 to be forwarded to the client). *completed*

- The written authorization regarding file destruction of the Crofton/Yelnarf documents of the LGT BIL legal department is still pending (see memo PIO dated 07.03.1997). *P*

Members of the board of trustees of the Luperla are: Dr. Bächinger
Peter Widmer
Werner Orvati
Hans-Werner Ritter

[signature]
Natalie Müller

LGT Treuhand
A Member of Liechtenstein Global Trust

LGT Treuhand
Aktiengesellschaft
Städtle 18-22
FL-9490 Vaduz
Fürstentum Liechtenstein

Telephone 41-75-235 27 27
Telefax 41-75-235 27 15
Telex 88 92 27 blt
E-Mail lgttrust@lgtt.lol.li
100653,2664 CompuServe

Aktenvermerk

1/1

Thema **Luperla Foundation, Vaduz ("Luperla")**

Verfasser(in) / Tel. erm / 2621

Datum 29. Januar 1998

Zur Erledigung

Zur Kenntnisnahme Mbd, pfr

Besprechung vom 28.01.1998 mit Herrn Peter Widmer (wp) in Bendern

Anlässlich unserer Besprechung erläutert wp im wesentlichen die Hintergründe der Luperla. Hinter dieser Stiftung steht Herr Frank P. Lowy, einer der reichsten Männer Australiens (Hauptaktionär und Chairman der Westfields Holdings, verdient ca. USD 5,5 Mio p.a.= Rang 2 in Australien), Privatvermögen über mehrere Milliarden USD). Seine drei Söhne, ebenfalls in der Westfields in Top-Positionen tätig, sind wp ebenso persönlich bekannt.
Das Stiftungsvermögen soll sich auf ca. 100 Mio. USD belaufen und stammt aus einer realtiv komplexen Transaktion, die zum Ziel hatte, die börsenkotierten Aktien der Westfields wieder in Famileinbesitz zurückzuführen, was schliesslich auch gelungen ist.
ORV hat angeblich mitgewirkt und ist im Detail darüber informiert. Es soll sich wp zufolge um keinerlei "Risikogelder" handeln.

Das Wesentliche unserer Besprechung ist, dass der Klient diese Gelder nicht offiziell in sein australisches Vermögen zurückführen kann. Es bleibt somit in der Stiftung und wp ist überzeugt, dass sich daran auch nichts ändern wird, solange das PM-Mandat ordentlich ausgeführt wird. Das Mandat ist als eines der grössten Geschäfte der LGT BIL einzustufen (hat bisher ca 7 Mio CHF gebracht!). Gerade deshalb ist darauf zu achten, dass keine Belastungen oder Transaktionen über das Luperla-Konto getätigt werden, die den Klienten grundsätzlich "nervös" machen.
Ich versichere wp, dass dies nicht mehr geschehen werde (s. VG über USD 600,-- unter namentlicher Anführung der Sewell). Ich werde veranlassen, dass **jede Transaktion vor Ausführung wp vorgelegt** wird. nochmals in F4 notiert /mml

Bezüglich der Sewell informiere ich wp, dass die Streichung veranlasst wurde.

Was die Rückvergütung der abgebuchten USD 600,-- Trident-fees betrifft, so wird wp diese bei Herr M. Knecht veranlassen. Die Rückvergütung seitens der Trident ist auf ein internes Treuhandkonto gutzuschreiben und nach Absprache mit M. Knecht an LGT BIL weiterzuleiten.

LTV/erm
29. Januar 1998

Permanent Subcommittee on Investigations
EXHIBIT #45

PSI-USMSTR - 008901

[logo]
LGT Trust
A Member of Liechtenstein Global Trust

LGT Treuhand
Corporation
Stadtle 18-22
FL-9490 Vaduz
Principality of Liechtenstein

Telephone 41-75-235 27 27
Tefax 41-75-235 27 15
Telex 88 92 27 bilt
Email lgttrust@lgtt.lol.li
100653,2664 CompuServe

Memorandum for the File

1/1

Concerned Issues **Luperla Foundation, Vaduz ("Luperla")**

Author / Tel. erm / 2621

Date 01.29.1998

For Follow-Up

For the information of nmu [initialed], pfr

Meeting on 01.28.1998 with Mr. Peter Widmer (wp) in Bendern

On the occasion of our meeting, wp provides basic background information of the Luperla. Behind this foundation is Mr. Frank P. Lowy, one of the richest men in Australia (primary shareholder and chairman of the Westfields Holdings, earning approximately USD 5.5 million annually = second place in Australia, with private assets of several billion USD). His three sons, likewise active in top positions of the Westfields, are just as well-known to wp.
The foundation assets shall come to the amount of approximately USD 100 million and originate from a relatively complex transaction, with the goal of bringing shares listed in the stock market back into the family's possession, which was successfully completed.
ORV apparently assisted in this and is informed of the details. According to wp, no activities involving "risk money" are to be involved.

The substance of this meeting is that the client cannot officially bring these funds back into his Australian assets. Therefore, they remain in the foundation and wp is convinced that nothing along these lines will change, so long as the PM-mandate is properly conducted. The mandate is to be classified as one of the largest business affairs of the LGT BIL (has up to this point brought in CHF 7 million!). For exactly this reason it must be ensured that no fees or transactions occur through the Luperla account that make the clients "nervous" in principle.
I reassure wp that this will no longer occur (see assets fee of USD 600.-- under quotation of the name "Sewell"). I will determine that **every transaction be presented to wp before being carried out.** *noted again in F4 /* [initialed]

As concerns the Sewell, I inform wp that the abatement has already been initiated.

Mr. M. Knecht will determine what the written-off USD 600.-- Trident fees concern (which are being repaid). The repayment is to be credited to an internal trust account on the part of the Trident and to be continued after consultation with M. Knecht.

LTV/erm
01.29.1998
[signature]

LGT Treuhand
A Member of Liechtenstein Global Trust

LGT Treuhand
Aktiengesellschaft
Städtle 28
FL-9490 Vaduz
Fürstentum Liechtenstein
MWST-Nr. 50119

Telefon +423 235 27 27
Telefax +423 235 27 15
Internet
www.lgt.com/lgttreuhand
E-Mail lgttrust@lgt.com

Aktenvermerk

1/1

Thema	**LUPERLA STIFTUNG**
Verfasser(in) / Tel.	Werner Orvati /ORV (Sandra Schneider /ssn/2640)
Datum	26. Juni 2001
Zur Erledigung	
Zur Kenntnisnahme an	Dr. K. Bächinger Dr. E. Müller

Beiliegend Kopien aus der Zeit der Errichtung von Luperla Foundation:

1. <u>Herkunft der Mittel</u>

   Aus diesen Aktenvermerken, wie auch aus meiner Erinnerung ergibt sich, dass die Mittel der Luperla Stiftung aus einer Kreditfinanzierung der LGT Bank in Liechtenstein stammen, die seinerzeit über eine Gesellschaft Crofton abgewickelt wurde. Aus den beiliegenden Aktenvermerken ergibt sich, dass die Instruktionen betreffend Crofton von Sinns Treuhand, Zürich, erteilt wurden. Ich bin davon ausgegangen, dass Crofton bei Dr. Karlheinz Ritter verwaltet worden sei.

2. <u>Begünstigung</u>

   Hinweise betreffend die Interpretation der Beistatuten betreffend Nomination von Begünstigten bei Vorliegen von Instruktionen durch die Company oder im Falle des Widerrufs solcher Instruktionen oder im Falle des Fehlens solcher Instruktionen, habe ich in den Akten nicht gefunden. Ich gehe davon aus, dass Instruktionen betreffend die Nomination von Begünstigten durch die in den Beistatuten aufgeführte "Company" gemacht werden, falls diese Instruktionen widerrufen werden oder nicht vorhanden wären, könnte sich der Stiftungsrat auf Instruktionen abstützen, welche durch diejenige Gesellschaft gegeben würde, von welcher Beverley Park Corp. zuletzt Aktien erworben hätte.

   Aus den Aktenvermerken ist eindeutig ersichtlich, dass gemäss Stifterwille FL und seine drei Söhne DL, PL und SL wirtschaftlich begünstigt werden sollen. AV von Peter Widmer vom 23.01.1997, S. 2, Linie 4.

   In den Aktenvermerken wird auch die bei uns über Jahre geführte Struktur "Yelnarf" erwähnt.

<u>Beilagen:</u>
Aktenvermerke vom 27.11.1996 - 29.01.1998

Permanent Subcommittee on Investigations
EXHIBIT #46

PSI-USMSTR - 008897

[logo]
LGT Trust
A Member of Liechtenstein Global Trust

LGT Trust
Corporation
Städtle 28
FL-9490 Vaduz
Principality of Liechtenstein
VAT-No. 50119

Telephone +423 235 27 27
Fax +423 235 27 15
Internet
www.lgt.com/lgttreuhand
E-Mail lgttrust@lgt.com

Memorandum for the File

1/1

Topic: **LUPERLA FOUNDATION**

Author / Tel.: Werner Orvati / ORV (Sandra Schneider / ssn/2640)

Date: 26 June 2001

For Follow-Up:

To the Attention of: Dr. K. Bächinger
Dr. E. Müller

Copies from the time of the Establishment of the Luperla Foundation attached:

1. Origin of Funds

The result from these memorandums for the file as well as from my memory is that the funds of the Luperla Foundation stem from a credit financing of the LGT Bank in Liechtenstein that at the time was carried out through a company Crofton. The result from the attached memorandums for the file is that the instructions regarding Crofton were issued by Sinus Treuhand, Zürich. I assumed that Crofton was being managed by Dr. Karlheinz Ritter.

2. Benefit

I didn't find information regarding the interpretation of the by-laws with regard to the nomination of beneficiaries upon presentation of instructions by the Company or in the case of revocation or absence of such instructions in the file. I assume that instructions regarding the nomination of beneficiaries will be made by the "Company" listed in the by-laws, if these instructions are revoked or don't exist, the foundation board can support itself on instructions that are given by the company from which Beverley Park Corp. last acquired shares.

It is explicitly apparent from the memorandums for the file that, in accordance with the intention of the founder, FL and his three sons DL, PL and SL are to be financial beneficiaries. Memorandum for the file from Peter Widmer from 01.23.1997, page 2, line 4.

The memorandums for the file also mention the "Yelnarf" structure which we've been conducting for years.

Attachments:
Memorandums for the file from 11.27.1996 - 01.29.1998

LGT Treuhand
A Member of Liechtenstein Global Trust

LGT Treuhand
Aktiengesellschaft
Städtle 28
FL-9490 Vaduz
Fürstentum Liechtenstein
MWST-Nr. 50119

Telefon +423 235 27 27
Telefax +423 235 27 15
Internet
www.lgt.com/lgttreuhand
E-Mail lgttrust@lgt.com

Aktenvermerk

1/4

Thema **LUPERLA FOUNDATION, VADUZ**

Verfasser(in) / Tel. Dr. Erik Müller

Datum 16. Juli 2001 / mmu

Zur Erledigung bereits zugestellt / 18.07.01

Zur Kenntnisnahme Dr. K. Bächinger, lic. oec. HSG W. Orvati, Dr. N. Feuerstein 20.7.01

Bestellung von möglichen Begünstigten bzw. Vornahme von Ausschüttungen an Begünstigte unter Berücksichtigung der geltenden Stiftungsstatuten und Regulations sowie des Stifterwillens:

1. Gesellschaftsrechtlich massgebende Bestimmungen

1.1. Gemäss Art. 5 der geltenden Statuten bestimmt der Stiftungsrat im Rahmen der Reglemente über Ausmass und Art von Ausschüttungen an die Stiftungsbegünstigten. Ferner werden "Begünstigte der Stiftung und der Inhalt der Begünstigung [...] vom Stiftungsrat bestimmt. Die nähere Regelung erfolgt in einem eigenen Beistatut." (Art. 4). Der Begriff des Beistatuts wird synonym mit dem des Reglements verwendet. Die Englischversion nennt "Regulations", welche rechtsgültig erlassen wurden.

1.2. Auch die statutarische Zweckdefinition unter Art. 3 sieht vor, dass die Stiftung (über den eigentlichen Stiftungszweck gemäss Abs. 1 hinaus) "in Auslegung der Reglemente auch Zuwendungen an natürliche oder juristische Personen sowie Institutionen etc. machen" kann.

1.3. Schliesslich ist gemäss Art. 11 der geltenden Statuten, welcher unter anderem die Stiftungsauflösung regelt, der Stiftungsrat "jederzeit berechtigt, durch einstimmigen Beschluss die Stiftung aufzulösen." Ferner ist bei der Auflösung der Stiftung "das Stiftungsvermögen nach Massgabe der Begünstigungsbestimmungen [in der Englischversion: Regulations] zu verwenden."

1.4. Damit kommt den Begünstigungsbestimmungen auf jeden Fall - sei es im Fall einer vollumfänglichen und endgültigen Ausschüttung des Stiftungsvermögens mit anschliessender Löschung der Stiftung oder im Zuge einer Verwendung des Stiftungsvermögens im Sinne des Art. 11 der Statuten - eine zentrale Bedeutung zu. Umso mehr als den Regulations unter Art. 5 derselben grundsätzlich dieselbe Rechtskraft wie den Statuten und im Fall entgegenlaufender Bestimmungen das grössere Gewicht beigemessen wird.

Permanent Subcommittee on Investigations
EXHIBIT #47

PSI-USMSTR - 008867
10.

LGT Treuhand

Aktenvermerk 2/4

2. Regulations

Die Begünstigungsbestimmungen sehen für die Vornahme von Ausschüttungen zwei zwingende Schritte vor:

2.1. Notifikation(en)

Grundsätzlich werden mögliche Begünstigte ("members of the class of distributees") durch eine Gesellschaft ("Company"), an welcher die am 3. Januar 1997 gegründete und in Delaware/USA domizilierte Beverly Park Corporation ("Corporation") beteiligt ist, dem Stiftungsrat bekanntgegeben/notifiziert. Ist die Corporation an mehreren Companies beteiligt, fällt diese Bestellungskompetenz jener Company zu, an welcher die Corporation vor der Notifikation zuletzt Beteiligung genommen hat.

Begünstigte können "persons, companies or other entities" sein.

Zwingende (kumulative) Voraussetzungen für die Aufnahme in den Kreis der Begünstigten sind, dass

- die Company selbst weder direkt noch indirekt begünstigt ist (somit kann sie gewissermassen als "excluded person" betrachtet werden) und dass
- eine (bereits erfolgte) Begünstigtenbestellung durch die Company oder deren Rechtsnachfolger jederzeit durch schriftliche Mitteilung an den Stiftungsrat widerrufen werden kann.

2.2. Ausschüttung(en)

Besteht ein nach den oben beschriebenen Bestimmungen bestellter Begünstigtenkreis, liegt es im uneingeschränkten Ermessen des Stiftungsrats ("absolute and uncontrolled discretion"), eine oder mehrere Ausschüttungen zu Gunsten eines oder mehrerer Begünstigten ("member of the class of distributees") zu tätigen.

3. Stifterwille

Die Aktenlage dokumentiert den Stifterwillen dahingehend, dass der wirtschaftliche Stifter und dessen drei Söhne wirtschaftlich begünstigt werden sollen (siehe auch Aktenvermerk von Herrn Orvati vom 26. Juni 2001). Zu einer erwünschten Begünstigungsreihenfolge, verschiedenen Begünstigtenquoten, zeitlichen Rahmen oder Begünstigungsumfang liegen - mit Ausnahme der Bestimmungen von Statuten und Regulations - keine Hinweise vor. Die Existenz eines schriftlich zum Ausdruck gebrachten Stifterwillens in der Form eines Letter of Wishes (Side Letter, Record of Intent) geht aus den Akten nicht hervor.

PSI-USMSTR - 008868

LGT Treuhand

Aktenvermerk 3/4

4. Conclusio

Die gegenständliche Stiftung wurde in der Form einer **"Discretionary Foundation"** ausgestaltet, wobei ein Letter of Wishes nicht vorliegt.
Die statutarischen Bestimmungen definieren einen sehr weitreichenden Zweck und sehen **keinen bestimmten Begünstigtenkreis** vor, sondern verweisen auf mögliche Reglemente bzw. Beistatuten, die die ordentliche Begünstigung regeln.
Die bestehenden **Regulations** schreiben eine klare Vorgehensweise mit zwei getrennten Kompetenzbereichen sowie bestimmte Voraussetzungen vor:

4.1. Die **Notifikationskompetenz** liegt bei der Company, wobei keine Kriterien zur Auswahl möglicher Begünstigter ("members of the class of distributees") festgelegt wurden. Hingegen gibt es zwingende Voraussetzungen für eine solche Notifikation:

- Schriftlichkeit;
- Adressat ist der Stiftungsrat;
- Company darf nicht direkt oder indirekt begünstigt sein;
- Notifikation muss (auf schriftlichem Wege) widerruflich sein;

Bezüglich der notifizierenden Company sind folgende Voraussetzungen gegeben:

- die Corporation muss an der Company beteiligt sein;
- falls mehrere solcher Beteiligungen bestehen, muss die notifizierende Company die vor der Notifikation zuletzt erworbene sein;

4.2. Die **Ausschüttungskompetenz** wurde uneingeschränkt und vollumfänglich dem Stiftungsrat zugewiesen ("absolute and uncontrolled discretion").

5. Massnahmen

5.1. Im vorliegenden Fall wurden bereits folgende Massnahmen gesetzt:

- Zirkularbeschluss vom 25. Juni 2001, die Stiftung im Hinblick auf eine endgültige und vollumfängliche Ausschüttung in Liquidation zu setzen, da diese danach den Stiftungszweck nicht mehr erfüllen kann sowie sämtliche Vermögensanlagen in liquide Form zu bringen;
- entsprechende Veranlassung bei der depotführenden und vermögensverwaltenden LGT Bank in Liechtenstein AG;
- entsprechende Benachrichtigung des ÖRA als Stiftungsregister.

5.2. Im Hinblick auf o.a. Ausschüttung sollte Folgendes schriftlich vorliegen:

- Notifikationsschreiben der Company wie oben ausgeführt;

LGT Treuhand

Aktenvermerk 4/4

- Rechtsgültiger Nachweis der Corporation darüber, dass sie an der Company beteiligt ist und dass die Company die vor dem Notifikationsdatum zuletzt erworbene Beteiligung ist;
- Geeigneter Nachweis darüber, dass die Company nicht direkt oder indirekt begünstigt ist;
- (Formeller) Stiftungsratsbeschluss über die Deutung des Stifterwillens;
- Stiftungsratsbeschluss über Umfang der Begünstigung und Ausschüttungsmodalitäten;
- Einverständnis des wirtschaftlichen Stifters, sofern er nicht selbst vollumfänglich in den Genuss der Stiftungsreinvermögens kommt;

Abschliessend und der Vollständigkeit halber sei darauf hingewiesen, dass keine Unabänderlichkeitsklausel in den geltenden Stiftungsbestimmungen vorgesehen ist, der Stiftungsrat gemäss Art. 11 der Statuten dieselben jederzeit abändern und gemäss Art. 6 der Regulations auch diese abändern, vervollständigen oder widerrufen kann, wobei gleichzeitig der Stifterwille grundsätzlich seine Berücksichtigung zu finden hat.

Dr. Erik Müller

PSI-USMSTR - 008869

[logo]
LGT Trust
A Member of Liechtenstein Global Trust

LGT Treuhand
Corporation
Städtle 28
FL-9490 Vaduz
Principality of Liechtenstein
VAT-Nr. 50119

Telephone +423 235 27 27
Fax +423 235 27 15
Internet www.lgt.com/lgttreuhand
Email lgttrust@lgt.com

Memorandum for the File

1/4

Concerned Issues	**LUPERLA FOUNDATION, VADUZ**
Author / Tel.	Dr. Erik Müller
Date	07.16.2001 / nmu
For Follow-Up	*already delivered / 07.18.2001*
For the information of	Dr. K. Bächinger, lic. oec. HSG W. Orvati, Dr. N. Feuerstein [initialed]

Specification of possible beneficiaries and initiation of disbursements to beneficiaries with regard to the effective statutes and regulations of the foundation as well as the intent of the benefactor;

1. **Authoritative stipulations under company law**

1.1. According to Article 5 of the effective statutes, the board of trustees determines the size and type of disbursement to the beneficiaries of the foundation in the framework of the regulations. Furthermore, the "beneficiaries of the foundation and the content of the benefit (...) are determined by the board of trustees. The more detailed specifications are to result from their own bylaw." (Article 4). The terms of the bylaw are synonymous with those used in the regulations. The English version names "regulations" [English], which were issued with legal force.

2.2. Also, the statutory definition of purpose under Article 3 specifies that the foundation (by virtue of its own foundation purpose, according to Paragraph 1 forward) can "also make donations to natural or juridical persons as well as institutions through the issue of regulations."

3.3. Finally, according to Article 11 of the effective statutes, which govern the dissolution of the foundation, among other things, the board of trustees of the foundation is "empowered at any time to dissolve the foundation by means of a unanimous resolution." Furthermore, upon the dissolution of the foundation, "the assets of the foundation are to be utilized under the authority of the regulations of benefit (in the English version: regulations)."

4.4. Thus the regulations of benefit assume a central meaning in any case - be it in the case of a complete and final disbursement of the assets of the foundation with the subsequent dissolution of the foundation or of the process of utilization of the assets of the foundation according to the terms of Article 11 of the statutes. The same legal force is imputed [to the above-mentioned regulations] as to the statutes, even more than to the regulations under Article 5 (of the regulations), and in the case of contradictory regulations, greater importance is imputed [to the above-regulations].

[logo]
LGT Trust

Memorandum for the File 2/4

2. Regulations

The regulations of benefit require two mandatory steps for the execution of disbursements:

2.1. Notification(s)

The board of trustees must categorically be notified of the identities of possible beneficiaries ("members of the class of distributees" [English]) through a corporation ("Company" [English]), of which the Beverly Park Corporation ("Corporation" [English]) has shares; the Beverly Park Corporation was founded on 01.03.1997 and is domiciled in Delaware / USA. If the "Corporation" holds several "Companies," then the capacity to designate falls to that company of which the "Corporation" most recently took up shares before the notification.

Beneficiaries can be "persons, companies, or other entities" [English].

Mandatory (cumulative) premises for entry into the exclusive group of beneficiaries are that

- the "Company" itself is neither directly nor indirectly benefited (therefore it can be specifically regarded as an "excluded person" [English]), and that
- an (already effective) designation of beneficiary can be revoked by the "Company" or its legal successors at any time by means of written message to the board of trustees.

2.2. Disbursement(s)

If there does exist an exclusive group of designated beneficiaries as described above, then it falls to the unrestricted discretion of the board of trustees ("absolute and uncontrolled discretion" [English]) whether to effect one or more disbursements in favor of one or more beneficiaries ("member of the class of distributees" [English]).

3. Intent of the benefactor

The records document the intent of the benefactor to the effect that the economic benefactor and his three sons shall be financial beneficiaries (see also memo from Mr. Orvati dated 06.26.2001). No directions exist pertaining to desired succession of beneficiaries, different beneficiary proportions, time frames, or extent of benefit - with the exception of the stipulations of statutes and regulations. The existence of the intent of the benefactor, brought to written expression in the form of a Letter of Wishes (Side Letter, Record of Intent), does not appear in the files.

[logo]
LGT Trust

Memorandum for the File 3/4

4. Conclusion

The above-described foundation was structured in the form of a **"Discretionary Foundation"**, whereupon a Letter of Wishes is not present.
The statutory stipulations define a very far-reaching purpose and specify **no certain group of beneficiaries**, but rather refer to possible regulations and/or bylaws that regulate the proper benefit.
The existing **Regulations** prescribe clear proceedings with two divided realms of competence as well as certain requirements:

4.1. The **capacity of notification** rests with the Company, whereby no criteria were established for the selection of possible beneficiaries ("members of the class of distributees"). On the other hand, there are mandatory requisites for such a notification:

- Written Form
- Addressee is the Board of Trustees
- Company may not be directly or indirectly benefited
- Notification must be revocable (by written means)

Concerning the notifying Company, the following requisites are given:

- the Corporation must be a shareholder of the Company
- if several such holdings exist, then the notifying Company must be the last acquired before the notification

4.2. The **capacity for disbursement** was allotted completely and without restriction to the board of trustees ("absolute and uncontrolled discretion").

5. Proceedings

5.1. In the case at hand, the following proceedings have already occurred:

- Circular resolution dated 06.25.2001, regarding a complete and final disbursement, to place the foundation in liquidation (since it can no longer fulfill the purpose of the foundation after this), and to bring all investments of assets into liquid form;
- Corresponding initiation at the custodial (for the depot) and asset-managing bank, the LGT Bank in Liechtenstein AG;
- Corresponding notice in writing from ÖRA as a foundation record

5.2. With regard to the above-listed disbursement, the following should be in our possession in writing:

- Letter of notification of the Company as listed above;

[logo]
LGT Trust

Memorandum for the File 4/4

- Legal verification from the Corporation attesting that it is a shareholder of the Company and that the Company is the holding last acquired before the date of notification;
- Proper verification attesting that the Company is neither directly nor indirectly benefited;
- (Formal) resolution of the board of trustees concerning the interpretation of the intent of the benefactor;
- Resolution of the board of trustees concerning the extent of the benefit and types of disbursement;
- Consent of the economic benefactor, inasmuch as he does not himself exclusively receive the complete benefit of the net assets of the foundation.

In conclusion and for the sake of completeness it is established that no immutable stipulation is specified in the effective regulations of the foundation, that that board of trustees can alter the statutes at any time according to Article 11 (of these statutes), and that it can alter, supplement, or revoke these according to Article 6 of the Regulations, whereby the intention of the benefactor as a rule must always be taken into consideration.

[signature]
Dr. Erik Müller

LGT Treuhand
A Member of Liechtenstein Global Trust

LGT Treuhand
Aktiengesellschaft
Städtle 28
FL-9490 Vaduz
Fürstentum Liechtenstein
MWST-Nr. 50119

Telefon +423 235 27 27
Telefax +423 235 27 15
Internet
www.lgt.com/lgttreuhand
E-Mail lgttrust@lgt.com

Aktenvermerk

1/3

Thema	**Luperla Foundation, Vaduz**
Verfasser(in) / Tel.	Dr. Erik Müller
Datum	17. Dezember 2001 / ssn
Zur Erledigung	
Zur Kenntnisnahme	Dr. K. Bächinger, Dr. N. Feuerstein

Im Hinblick auf die endgültige Ausschüttung des gesamten Stiftungsvermögens der Luperla Foundation sind folgende Voraussetzungen gemäss meinem Aktenvermerk vom 16.07.2001 zu erfüllen:

1. Notifikationsschreiben der Company;
2. Rechtsgültiger Nachweis der Corporation darüber, dass sie an der Company beteiligt ist und dass die Company die vor dem Notifikationsschreiben zuletzt erworbene Beteiligung ist;
3. **Geeigneter Nachweis darüber, dass die Company nicht direkt oder indirekt begünstigt ist;**
4. (Formeller) Stiftungsratsbeschluss über die Deutung des Stifterwillens;
5. Stiftungsratsbeschluss über Umfang der Begünstigung und Ausschüttungsmodalitäten;
6. Einverständnis des wirtschaftlichen Stifters, sofern er nicht selbst vollumfänglich in den Genuss des Stiftungsreinvermögens kommt.

Zu 6.: Das diesbezügliche Telefongespräch mit dem wirtschaftlichen Stifter und einem seiner Söhne geführt und /oder Joshua H. Gelbard, wird aufgenommen werden.

Zu 4. und 5.: Interne Dokumente, die noch erstellt werden.

Zu 1., 2. und 3.: Folgende Dokumente wurden am 14.12.2001 zur Prüfung vorgelegt:

<u>Zur Beverly Park Corporation:</u>

- Vollmacht vom 13.12.2001 von Beverly Park Corp. zu Gunsten von Joshua Gelbard im Namen derselben zu handeln, unterschrieben durch den Director Leon C. Janks **(Kopie)**; ***Original notwendig.***
- Notarielle Bestätigung vom 13.12.2001 über die Richtigkeit der Vollmacht vom 13.12.2001, wonach Leon C. Janks Director & Officer von Beverly Park Corp. ist (Kopie); ***Original notwendig.***
- Passkopie Joshua Gelbard: Kopie ab Original bestätigt durch Dr. K. Bächinger;
- Certificate of Qualification vom 04.02.1997 betreffend Beverly Park Corp., unterschrieben vom Secretary of State of California **(Kopie)**;

Permanent Subcommittee on Investigations
EXHIBIT #48

PSI-USMSTR - 008878

LGT Treuhand

Aktenvermerk

2/3

- Bestätigung des Secretary of State (datiert vom 04.01.1997) über die Echtheit des Certificate of Incorporation betreffend Beverly Park Corp., die am 03.01.1997 ausgestellt wurde **(Kopie)**;
- To whom it may concern, ausgestellt von Joshua Gelbard am 13.12.2001, wonach er bestätigt, dass sich die Beverly Park Corp. nach dem 24.07.2001 an keiner Gesellschaft beteiligt hat (Original; handschriftlich);
- ~~Certificate of Good Standing des Secretary of State vom 17.12.2001 zur Beverly Park~~ Corp. (Kopie); ***Original notwendig.***
- Opinion der Kanzlei Debevoise & Plimpton, New York, wonach Beverly Park Corp. "duly formed, validly existing and in good standing under the law of the states of Delaware" ist (Kopie); ***Original notwendig.***

Zur Lonas Ltd., B.V.I.:

- Aktienzertifikat der Lonas Limited, B.V.I. (incorporated on 24.07.2001) (über eine Aktie à USD 1,--, Aktienzertifikat Nr. 1) vom 06.08.2001: Kopie ab Original bestätigt durch Dr. K. Bächinger;
- Certificate of the Registered Agent of Lonas Ltd., datiert vom 06.08.2001, wonach die Beverly Park Corp. eine Aktie in der Form des Zertifikats Nr. 1, ausgestellt am 06.08.2001, hält (Original);
- Deed of Appointment von Lonas Ltd. vom 24.07.2001 und unterschrieben vom Registered Agent, wonach Joshua H. Gelbard zum first sole Director der Lonas bestellt wird (Original);
- Memorandum of matters resolved by the company's sole director on the 06.08.2001, unterschrieben von Joshua H. Gelbard **(Kopie)**;
- Certificate of Incorporation vom Gründungstag 24.07.2001 (Original);
- Memorandum and Articles of Association of Lonas Ltd., B.V.I., vom Gründungstag 24.07.2001 (Original).
- Auftrag von Lonas Ltd. (Notifikationsschreiben) vom 13.12.2001, unterschrieben von Joshua H. Gelbard, Sole Director bezüglich der Ausschüttung aller Stiftungsvermögenswerte (Original).

Aufgrund der oben beschriebenen Sachlage sind meines Erachtens folgende Dokumente im Original einzuholen, bevor die Ausschüttung vorgenommen wird:

- Certificate of Good Standing des Secretary of State vom 17.12.2001 zur Beverly Park Corp.;
- Opinion der Kanzlei Debevoise & Plimpton, New York, wonach Beverly Park Corp. "duly formed, validly existing and in good standing under the law of the states of Delaware" ist;
- Vollmacht vom 13.12.2001 von Beverly Park Corp. zu Gunsten von Joshua Gelbard im Namen derselben zu handeln, unterschrieben durch den Director Leon C. Janks;
- Notarielle Bestätigung vom 13.12.2001 über die Richtigkeit der Vollmacht vom 13.12.2001, wonach Leon C. Janks Director & Officer von Beverly Park Corp. ist;
- Geeigneter Nachweis darüber, dass die Company nicht direkt oder indirekt begünstigt ist; eine solche Bestätigung kann durch Joshua Gelbard in seiner Eigenschaft als Director der Lonas unter Verwendung des Firmenstempels ausgestellt werden.

PSI-USMSTR - 008879

LGT Treuhand

Aktenvermerk 3/3

Telefonat mit David Lowy vom 17.12.2001:

Ich informiere Herrn Lowy über die Notwendigkeit der oben aufgeführten Originaldokumente. Er teilt mir mit, dass er mit Ausnahme des ersterwähnten Certificate of Good Standing alle Dokumente Herrn Dr. Konrad Bächinger übermitteln werde. Die Notwendigkeit des besagten Certificate of Good Standing vom 17.12.2001 relativiert sich meines Erachtens, nachdem sich die zweitgenannte Legal Opinion auf dieses Certificate bezieht und das good standing der Beverly Park Corp. bestätigt.

Ich teile Herrn Lowy ferner mit, dass nach Erhalt der Originaldokumente die Ausschüttung vorgenommen werden könne. Die entsprechenden Beschlüsse werden unsererseits bereits vorbereitet.

Herr David Lowy ist unter der Nummer 0061/418227700 (Israel) erreichbar.

Telefonkonferenz mit Dr. Konrad Bächinger und David Lowy vom 18.12.2001:

Der Nachweis darüber, dass die Lonas Ltd. weder direkt nocht indirekt begünstigt ist, wurde uns per Fax (bestätigt und unterfertigt durch Joshua Gelbard in seiner Eigenschaft als Director) zugestellt und ist in Ordnung.

Zusätzlich zu den oben aufgeführten Dokumenten wird meinerseits ein Telefonat mit der Overseas Management Company (OMC) geführt und ein aktuelles Unterschriftenverzeichnis angefordert, aus dem die Unterschriftsberechtigung von Frau Geidis Dixon, die das Certificate of the Registered Agent und das Deed of Appointment von Joshua Gelbard als Director unterschrieben hat.

Abschliessend und im Hinblick auf die Ausführung des Vergütungsauftrags im Sinne des Notifikationsschreibens vom 13.12.2001 zeigt sich David Lowy damit einverstanden, sämtliche Fremdwährungskonten der Luperla in USD zu konvertieren und auf dem USD-Konto zusammenzuführen. Schliesslich zeigt er sich mit einer Pauschalfaktura der LGT Treuhand AG für alle Bemühungen im Zusammenhang mit der Liquidation, Endausschüttung und Löschung der Luperla Foundation in Höhe von CHF 25.000,-- zuzüglich MWSt einverstanden.

Dr. Erik Müller

PSI-USMSTR - 008880

[logo]
LGT Trust
A Member of Liechtenstein Global Trust

LGT Treuhand
Corporation
Städtle 28
FL-9490 Vaduz
Principality of Liechtenstein
VAT-Nr. 50119

Telephone +423 235 27 27
Fax +423 235 27 15
Internet www.lgt.com/lgttreuhand
Email lgttrust@lgt.com

Memorandum for the File

1/3

Concerned Issues	**Luperla Foundation, Vaduz**
Author / Tel.	Dr. Erik Müller
Date	12.17.2001 / ssn
For Follow-Up	
For the information of	Dr. K. Bächinger, Dr. N. Feuerstein

In consideration of the final disbursement of the total foundation assets of the Luperla Foundation, the following prerequisites must be fulfilled according to my memo for the file dated 07.16.2001:

1. Notification letter of the company;
2. Legally valid authorization of the corporation attesting that it holds the company and that the company is the holding last acquired before the notification letter;
3. **Proper authorization that the company is not directly or indirectly benefited;**
4. (Formal) resolution of the board of trustees concerning the interpretation of the founder's intention;
5. Resolution of the board of trustees concerning the extent of benefit and the form of disbursements;
6. Consent of the economic benefactor, insofar as he himself does not exclusively benefit from the net assets of the foundation.

Pertaining to 6.: The telephone conversation in this regard will be taken up with the economic benefactor and one of his sons and/or Joshua H. Gelbard.

Pertaining to 4. and 5.: Internal documents, which still must be issued.

Pertaining to 1., 2., and 3.: The following documents were presented for review on 12.14.2001:

<u>Pertaining to Beverly Park Corporation:</u>

- Power of attorney dated 12.13.2001 from Beverly Park Corp. in favor of Joshua Gelbard to act in his own name, signed by the director Leon C. Janks (copy); ***original is necessary.***
- Notarized certification dated 12.13.2001 attesting to the accuracy of the authorization dated 12.13.2001, which states that Leon C. Janks is director and officer of Beverly Park Corp. (copy); ***original is necessary.***
- Copy of the passport of Joshua Gelbard: copy from the original certified by Dr. K. Bächinger;
- Certificate of Qualification dated 02.04.1997 regarding Beverly Park Corp., signed by the Secretary of State of California (copy);

[logo]
LGT Trust

Memorandum for the File 2/3

- Certification of the Secretary of State (dated 01.04.1997) attesting to the authenticity of the Certificate of Incorporation regarding Beverly Park Corp., which was issued on 01.03.1997 (**copy**);
- "To whom it may concern," issued by Joshua Gelbard on 12.13.2001, in which he specifies that the Beverly Park Corp. does not hold shares of any corporation after 07.24.2001 (original, hand-written);
- Certificate of Good Standing of the Secretary of State dated 12.17.2001 regarding Beverly Park Corp. (copy); ***original is necessary.***
- Opinion of the office of Debeviose & Plimpton, New York, which states that Beverly Park Corp. is "duly formed, validly existing and in good standing under the law of the state of Delaware" (copy); ***original is necessary.***

Pertaining to the Lonas Ltd., B.V.I.:

- Shares certificate of the Lonas Limited, B.V.I. (incorporated on 07.24.2001) (of a share at USD 1.00, shares certificate No. 1) dated 08.06.2001: copy from the original certified by Dr. K Bächinger;
- Certificate of the Registered Agent of Lonas Ltd., dated 08.06.2001, in which is stated that the Beverly Park Corp. holds a share in the form of the certificate No. 1, issued on 08.06.2001 (original);
- Deed of Appointment from Lonas Ltd. dated 07.24.2001 and signed by the registered agent, which states that Joshua H. Gelbard is appointed as first sole director of the Lonas (original);
- Memorandum of matters resolved by the company's sole director on 08.06.2001, signed by Joshua H. Gelbard (copy);
- Certificate of Incorporation from the day of founding, 07.24.2001 (original);
- Memorandum and Articles of Association of the Lonas Ltd., B.V.I., from the day of founding, 07.24.2001 (original);
- Mandate from Lonas Ltd. (notification letter) dated 12.13.2001, signed by Joshua H. Gelbard, sole director, regarding the disbursement of all assets of the foundation (original).

On the basis of the state of affairs as described above, it is my consideration that the following documents must be obtained in original form before the disbursement can be initiated:

- Certificate of Good Standing of the Secretary of State dated 12.17.2001 regarding Beverly Park Corp.;
- Opinion of the office of Debeviose & Plimpton, New York, which states that Beverly Park Corp. is "duly formed, validly existing and in good standing under the law of the state of Delaware";
- Power of attorney dated 12.13.2001 from Beverly Park Corp. in favor of Joshua Gelbard to act in his own name, signed by the director Leon C. Janks;
- Notarized certification dated 12.13.2001 attesting to the accuracy of the authorization dated 12.13.2001, which states that Leon C. Janks is director and officer of Beverly Park Corp.;
- Proper authorization that the company is not directly or indirectly benefited; such certification can be issued by Joshua Gelbard in his capacity as director of the Lonas through utilization of the stamp of the firm.

[logo]
LGT Trust

Memorandum for the File 3/3

Telephone conversation with David Lowy dated 12.17.2001:

I inform Mr. Lowy of the importance of the above-listed documents in original form. He says to me that he will transmit all documents to Dr. Konrad Bächinger with the exception of the first Certificate of Good Standing. The necessity of the aforementioned Certificate of Good Standing dated 12.17.2001 becomes relative in my consideration, especially because the second-named legal opinion pertains to this certificate and \\certifies the good standing of the Beverly Park Corp.

I communicate to Mr. Lowy that the disbursement can be initiated after receipt of the original documents. The appropriate resolutions are already being prepared on our part.

Mr. David Lowy is attainable at the number 0061/418227700 (Israel).

Telephone conference with Dr. Konrad Bächinger and David Lowy dated 12.18.2001:

The verification that the Lonas Ltd. is neither directly nor indirectly benefited was delivered to us per fax (certified and signed by Joshua Gelbard in his capacity as director) and is satisfactory.

In addition to the documents listed above, a telephone conversation is taken up with the Overseas Management Company (OMC) on my part and a current list of authorized signatories is requested, on which [appears] the signatory rights of Ms. Geidis Dixon, who undersigned the Certificate of the Registered Agent and the Deed of Appointment of Joshua Gelbard as director.

Lastly, and in view of the execution of the authorized payment order along the terms of the notification letter from 12.13.2001, David Lowy states that he gives consent to convert all foreign-currency accounts of the Luperla to USD and to collect them in the USD account. Subsequently, he agrees to a flat fee of the LGT Trust Corp. for all endeavors associated with the liquidation, final disbursement, and dissolution of the Luperla Foundation in the amount of CHF 25,000.-- in addition to value-added tax.

[signature]
Dr. Erik Müller

LGT Treuhand
A Member of Liechtenstein Global Trust

LGT Treuhand
Aktiengesellschaft
Städtle 28
FL-9490 Vaduz
Fürstentum Liechtenstein
MWST-Nr. 50119

Telefon +423 235 27 27
Telefax +423 235 27 15
Internet
www.lgt.com/lgttreuhand
E-Mail lgttrust@lgt.com

Aktenvermerk

1/2

Thema	**Luperla Foundation, Vaduz**
Verfasser(in) / Tel.	Dr. Erik Müller
Datum	18. Dezember 2001 / ssn
Zur Erledigung	
Zur Kenntnisnahme	Dr. K. Bächinger, Dr. N. Feuerstein

Telefonat mit Dr. Konrad Bächinger und David Lowy vom 18.12.2001:

Der Nachweis darüber, dass die Lonas Ltd. weder direkt nocht indirekt begünstigt ist, wurde uns heute per Fax (bestätigt und unterfertigt durch Joshua Gelbard in seiner Eigenschaft als Director) zugestellt und ist in Ordnung.

Zusätzlich zu den in meinem gestrigen Aktenvermerk aufgeführten Dokumenten wird ein Telefonat mit der Overseas Management Company geführt und ein aktuelles Unterschriftenverzeichnis angefordert, aus dem die Unterschriftsberechtigung von Frau Geidis Dixon, die das Certificate of the Registered Agent und das Deed of Appointment von Joshua Gelbard als Director unterschrieben hat.

David Lowy wird über Joshua Gelbard OMC informieren lassen, dass wir mit ihnen in Kontakt treten werden, um die Frage der zeichnungsberechtigten Personen der OMC zu klären.

Am 18.12.2001 bei uns eingelangte Dokumente:

Faxmitteilung von Joshua Gelbard mit den Koordinaten von Frau Geidis Dixon (OMC) unter Beilage eines Faxes an Frau Dixon, wonach er sie über unsere bevorstehende Kontaktaufnahme informiert und diese beauftragt, uns umfassend Auskunft zu erteilen.

Telefonat mit Frau Geidis Dixon von OMC vom 18.12.2001 (ca. 15.00h MEZ):

Nach einem Telefonat mit Frau Dixon sendet übermittelt mir diese eine List of Authorized Signatories for Overseas Management Company Trust (B.V.I.) Ltd.

Ich stelle fest, dass diese lediglich vom Director der OMC unterschrieben ist, ohne Beglaubigung.

Permanent Subcommittee on Investigations
EXHIBIT #49

PSI-USMSTR - 008873

LGT Treuhand

Aktenvermerk

2/2

Telefonat mit Frau Dixon vom 18.12.2001 (ca 20.30h MEZ):

Ich teile Frau Dixon mit, dass wir eine beglaubigte Version des Unterschriftenverzeichnisses benötigen, verbunden mit dem Nachweis über ein öffentlich nachgewiesenes Zeichnungsrecht.

Sie wird uns diese per Fax zusenden; das Original soll per Kurier folgen.

Dr. Erik Müller

PSI-USMSTR - 008874

[logo]LGT Treuhand
A Member of Liechtenstein Global Trust

LGT Trust
Corporation
Städtle 28
FL-9490 Vaduz
Principality of Liechtenstein
VAT-No. 50119

Telephone: +423 235 27 27
Telefax: +423 235 27 15
Internet:
www.lgt.com/lgttreuhand
E-Mail lgttrust@lgt.com

Memorandum for the Record

1/2

Subject: **Luperla Foundation, Vaduz**

Compiler / Tel.: Dr. Erik Müller

Date: Dec. 18, 2001 / ssn

For action:

Cc: Dr. K. Bächinger, Dr. N. Feuerstein

Phone conversation with Dr. Konrad Bächinger and David Lowy of Dec. 18, 2001:

The confirmation that Lonas Ltd. is not benefited directly or indirectly was sent to us today by fax (confirmed and signed by Joshua Gelbard in his capacity as director) and deemed to be in order.

In addition to the documents listed in my memo of yesterday, a phone conversation is conducted with Overseas Management Company and a current signature directory requested, from which the signatory authorization of Ms. Geidis Dixon [word missing], who has signed the Certificate of the Registered Agent and the Deed of Appointment from Joshua Gelbard as director.

David Lowy will have OMC informed via Joshua Gelbard that we will get in touch with them in order to clarify the question of the persons who have signatory rights for OMC.

Documents received by us on Dec. 18, 2001:

Fax from Joshua Gelbard with information on Ms. Geidis Dixon (OMC) with enclosure of a fax to Ms. Dixon, in which he informs her of our upcoming approach and instructs her to give us comprehensive information.

Phone conversation with Ms. Geidis Dixon of OMC of Dec. 18, 2002 (around 3 p.m. Middle European Time):

After the phone call with Mr. Dixon, she sends me a List of Authorized Signatories for Overseas Management Company Trust (B. V. I.) Ltd.

I discover that it is signed merely by the OMC director, without notarization.

[logo]LGT Treuhand
A Member of Liechtenstein Global Trust

Memorandum for the Record

2/2

Phone conversation with Ms. Dixon of Dec. 18, 2001 (around 8:30 p.m. Middle European Time):

I inform Ms. Dixon that we need a notarized version of the signature directory, connected with confirmation of a publicly verified signatory right.

She will send us these by fax; the original is to follow by courier.

[signed]

Dr. Erik Müller

LGT Treuhand
A Member of Liechtenstein Global Trust

LGT Treuhand
Aktiengesellschaft
Städtle 28
FL-9490 Vaduz
Fürstentum Liechtenstein
MWST-Nr. 50119

Telefon +423 235 27 27
Telefax +423 235 27 15
Internet
www.lgt.com/lgttreuhand
E-Mail lgttrust@lgt.com

Aktenvermerk

Thema	**Luperla Foundation, Vaduz**
Verfasser(in) / Tel.	Dr. Erik Müller
Datum	20. Dezember 2001 / ssn
Zur Erledigung	
Zur Kenntnisnahme	Dr. K. Bächinger, Dr. N. Feuerstein

E-mail an Frau Dixon (OMC) vom 19.12.2001

zur Erinnerung, uns ehestmöglich das gewünschte Unterschriftenverzeichnis im voraus per Fax und anschliessend per Kurier zuzustellen (unter Angabe der Adresse).

Prüfung der am 18.12.2001 Herrn Dr. Konrad Bächinger an seine Privatadresse persönlich überbrachten (bei uns am 19.12. eingelangten) Origiginaldokumente:

Zur Beverly Park Corporation:

- Vollmacht vom 13.12.2001 von Beverly Park Corp. zu Gunsten von Joshua Gelbard im Namen derselben zu handeln, unterschrieben durch den Director Leon C. Janks (Kopie war bereits vorhanden; siehe AV vom 17.12.2001);
- Notarielle Bestätigung vom 13.12.2001 über die Richtigkeit der Vollmacht vom 13.12.2001, wonach Leon C. Janks Director & Officer von Beverly Park Corp. ist (Kopie war bereits voranden; siehe AV vom 17.12.2001);
- Certificate of Qualification vom 04.02.1997 betreffend Beverly Park Corp., unterschrieben vom Secretary of State of California (Kopie war bereits voranden; siehe AV vom 17.12.2001);
- Certificate of Good Standing des Secretary of State vom 24.03.1997 zur Beverly Park Corp. (die bereits vorhandene Kopie datiert zwar vom 17.12.2001, deren Richtigkeit wird jedoch von der Kanzlei Debevoise & Plimpton, N.Y. bestätigt: siehe unten);
- Opinion der Kanzlei Debevoise & Plimpton, New York, wonach Beverly Park Corp. "duly formed, validly existing and in good standing under the law of the states of Delaware" ist (Kopie war bereits voranden; siehe AV vom 17.12.2001);
- Certificate of Amendment of Beverly Park Corporation vom 19.03.1997 (betreffen Kapitalerhöhung) sowie Certificate of Incorporation vom 03.01.1997 in Kopie.

Zur Lonas Ltd., B.V.I.:

- der bereits per Fax übermittelte Nachweis darüber, dass die Lonas Ltd. weder direkt nocht indirekt begünstigt ist, (bestätigt und unterfertigt durch Joshua Gelbard in seiner Eigenschaft als Director).

Permanent Subcommittee on Investigations
EXHIBIT #50

PSI-USMSTR - 008875

LGT Treuhand

Aktenvermerk

2/3

Damit sind die im Original erforderlichen Dokumente, die gemäss AV vom 17.12.2001 einzuholen waren, bevor die Ausschüttung vorgenommen wird, eingelangt.

Telefonkonferenz mit Dr. Konrad Bächinger und David Lowy vom 19.12.2001:

Die Telefonkonferenz wird aufgenommen und anschliessend auf Band zur Aufbewahrung im Akt überspielt.

Wir informieren David Lowy über das Ergebnis unserer Prüfung obgenannter Dokumente:

Die Legal Opinion der Kanzlei Debevoise & Plimpton liegt zwar im Original vor, jedoch ist nicht ersichtlich, welche Person diese ausgestellt hat, da kein Kurzzeichen vorhanden und Unterschrift handschriftlich unter dem Titel "Debevoise & Plimpton" erfolgt ist.

David Lowy wird veranlassen, dass Kanzleipartner Peter R. Schwartz eine spezielle Bestätigung ausstellt, wonach er selbst die besagte Legal Opinion ausgefertigt hat.

Ferner teilen wir David Lowy mit, dass die List of Authorized Sigantories von OMC noch nicht eingetroffen ist. David Lowy wird sich darum kümmern.

Abschliessend wiederholt Dr. Konrad Bächinger den Auftrag von Joshua Gelbard zur Vergütung/Ausschüttung des Stiftungsvermögens auf zwei verschiedene Genfer Bankverbindungen im Verhältnis 60:40. Neben der mündlichen Bestätigung von David Lowy betreffend die Richtigkeit des Auftrags gibt David Lowy sein Einverständnis dazu, dass die Familie Lowy selbst im Rahmen der beauftragten Transaktion nicht direkt begünstigt wird.

Die aufgenommenen Bänder werden im Gesellschaftsakt aufbewahrt.

Am 19.12.2001 bei uns eingelangte Dokumente:

- Schriftliche Faxbestätigung von Peter R. Schwarz, wonach er Partner von Debevoise & Partner ist, die legal opinion selbst unterfertigt hat und dazu legitimiert ist;
- Faxbestätigung von J. Gelbard, wonach die Lonas Ltd. die jüngste Beteiligung der Beverly Park Corporation ist;
- List of Authorized Signatories legalized by Apostille per Fax (Original folgt per Kurier);

Telefonat mit Dr. Konrad Bächinger vom 19.12.2001:

Wir werden die Originalunterschriftenliste abwarten bevor wie die Vergütung veranlassen, was ich auch David Lowy mitteile. Die übrigen Unterlagen sind vollständig vorhanden; über Sabrina Venturi, Niederlassung Lugano, die mehrere Jahre bei Morgan & Morgan gearbeitet hat erfahre ich, das OMC eine effektiv tätige Treuhandgesellschaft ist.

PSI-USMSTR - 008876

LGT Treuhand

Aktenvermerk 3/3

Kurier vom 20.12.2001:

Wie vereinbart erhalten wir die Originalunterschriftenliste von OMC, notariell beglaubigt und apostilliert. Damit sind alle erforderlichen Dokumente im Original vorhanden.

Telefonat mit David Lowy vom 20.12.2001:

Ich bestätige den Erhalt der Dokumente und die Ausführung der Transaktion, die er mir nochmals bestätigt.

Dr. Erik Müller

PSI-USMSTR - 008877

[logo]
LGT Trust
A Member of Liechtenstein Global Trust

LGT Treuhand
Corporation
Städtle 28
FL-9490 Vaduz
Principality of Liechtenstein
VAT-No. 50119

Telephone +423 235 27 27
Fax +423 235 27 15
Internet www.lgt.com/lgttreuhand
Email lgttrust@lgt.com

Memorandum for the File

1/3

Concerned Issues	**Luperla Foundation, Vaduz**
Author / Tel.	Dr. Erik Müller
Date	12.20.2001 / ssn
For Follow-Up	
For the information of	Dr. K. Bächinger, Dr. N. Feuerstein

Email to Ms. Dixon (OMC) dated 12.19.2001

as a reminder to provide us with the requested list of authorized signatories as soon as possible per fax and subsequently per courier (under the address specified).

Review of the original documents personally delivered to Dr. Konrad Bächinger at his private address on 12.18.2001 (delivered to us 12.19):

Pertaining to the Beverly Park Corporation:

- Power of attorney dated 12.13.2001 from Beverly Park Corp. in favor of Joshua Gelbard to act under his own name, signed by the director, Leon C. Janks (copy was already available, see memo dated 12.18.2001);
- Notarized certification dated 12.13.2001 attesting to the accuracy of the authorization dated 12.13.2001, according to which Leon C. Janks is the director and officer of the Beverly Park Corp. (copy was already available, see memo dated 12.17.2001);
- Certificate of Qualification dated 02.04.1997 regarding Beverly Park Corp, signed by the Secretary of State of California (copy was already available, see memo dated 12.17.2001);
- Certificate of Good Standing of the Secretary of State dated 03.24.1997 regarding Beverly Park Corp. (the already available copy actually dates from 12.17.2001, but its accuracy is certified by the offices of Debevoise & Plimpton, N.Y.: see below);
- Opinion of the office of Debevoise & Plimpton, New York, which reads that Beverly Park Corp. is "duly formed, validly existing and in good standing under the law of the state of Delaware" (copy was already available, see memo dated 12.17.2001);
- Certificate of Amendment of Beverly Park Corporation dated 03.19.1998 (concerning increase in capital) as well as Certificate of Incorporation in copy form dated 01.03.1997.

Pertaining to the Lonas Ltd., B.V.I.:

- the already transmitted authentication that the Lonas Ltd. is neither directly nor indirectly benefited (certified and signed by Joshua Gelbard in his capacity as director).

[logo]
LGT Trust

Memorandum for the File 2/3

Hereby the originals of the required documents have arrived; they needed to be obtained according to the memo dated 12.17.2001 before the disbursement could be effected.

Telephone conference with Dr. Konrad Bächinger and David Lowy dated 12.19.2001:

The telephone conference commences and is subsequently stored by recording on electronic tape.

We inform David Lowy of the result of our review of the above-named documents.

The legal opinion of the office of Debevoise & Plimpton does appear in the original, but it is not apparent which person issued it since no department code can be seen, nor does there appear a hand-written signature under the title "Debevoise & Plimpton."

David Lowy will order that his colleague Peter R. Schwartz issue a special certificate in which he himself will sign the legal opinion in question.

Further, we tell David Lowy that we still do not have the List of Authorized Signatories from OMC in our possession. David Lowy will look into this.

In closing, Dr. Konrad Bächinger brings up the order from Joshua Gelbard for the payment/disbursement of the foundation assets to two separate bank connections in Geneva in the ratio of 60:40. Besides verbal attestation to the accuracy of the order, David Lowy gives his consent that the Lowy family itself not be directly benefited in the framework of the commissioned transactions.

The recorded electronic tape is stored in the corporation's file.

Documents arriving to us on 12.19.2001:

- Written fax certificate from Peter R. Schwarz which states that he is a partner of Debevoise & Plimpton; also included is the legal opinion that he has personally signed, which authorizes it;
- Fax certificate from J. Gelbard which states that the Lonas Ltd. is the most recently holding of the Beverly Park Corporation;
- List of Authorized Signatories legalized by apostille per fax (original arrives per courier).

Telephone conversation with Dr. Konrad Bächinger dated 12.19.2001:

We will wait for the original authorized signatory list before we initiate the payment, which I also say to David Lowy. The other documents are all available; I learn that OMC is an effective trust corporation from Sabrina Venturi, at the Lugano branch, who has worked for several years with Morgan & Morgan.

[logo]
LGT Trust

Memorandum for the File 3/3

Courier dated 12.20.2001:

As arranged, we receive the original list of authorized signatories from OMC, certified by notary and apostillized. Herewith all required documents are in our possession in original form.

Telephone conversation with David Lowy dated 12.20.2001:

I certify the receipt of the documents and the execution of the transactions, which he authorizes for me once more.

[signature]
Dr. Erik Müller

Form 4564	Department of the Treasury Internal Revenue Service Information Document Request	Request Number 1
To: (Name of Taxpayer and Company, Division or Branch)	Subject: Form 1120 - 200506	
Beverly Park Corporation	Submitted to: Beverly Park Corporation	
10990 Wilshire Blvd, Suite 1600 Los Angeles, CA 90024	Dates of Previous Requests: None	

Description of Documents Requested:

Background Information

1. A worldwide organization chart listing all related entities, including foreign and domestic, in existence in 2004 and 2005, where ownership of each entity is 5% or greater (directly and indirectly), including, but not limited to Cordera Holding (Sydney, Australia). This chart should include:
   - Entity name,
   - Entity address,
   - Entity type (i.e. partnership, sole proprietor, corporation, trust, joint venture, limited liability company, branches, etc.),
   - Percentage of ownership,
   - Date of formation,
   - Country of formation, and
   - Business activity.

   This chart should also indicate names and address of individual shareholders or owners which own at least 5% (directly and indirectly) of these related entities.
2. Corporate By-Law for Beverly Park Corp ✓
3. Articles of Incorporation for Beverly Park Corp ✓
4. Corporate minutes from date of inception 3/25/97 to fiscal year ended 200706. ✓
5. Copies of Beverly Park's Corp's Income tax return for 200406, 200606 and 200706. ✓
6. All loan agreements in existence in 200506 ✓
7. All bank statements, including but not limited to, checking and savings, from April 1, 2005 to July 31, 2006.
8. All brokerage statements, from April 1, 2005 to July 31, 2006.
9. Copies of resolution from Board of director naming the person authorized to draw checks on the bank account.

Please be advised that we may require additional information and documents as we determine necessary as the examination progresses.

▬ = Redacted by the Permanent Subcommittee on Investigations

Information Due By Nov. 26, 2007 At Next Appointment X Mail In

FROM

Name and Title of Requestor
[redacted]
Internal Revenue Agent

Employee ID: [redacted]

11/1/2007

Office Location:
[redacted]

Phone: [redacted]
Fax: [redacted]

Page 1

Form 4564 (Rev. 04/2004) Workpaper #: 610-

Permanent Subcommittee on Investigations

EXHIBIT #51

LOWY-PSI-000035
CONFIDENTIAL

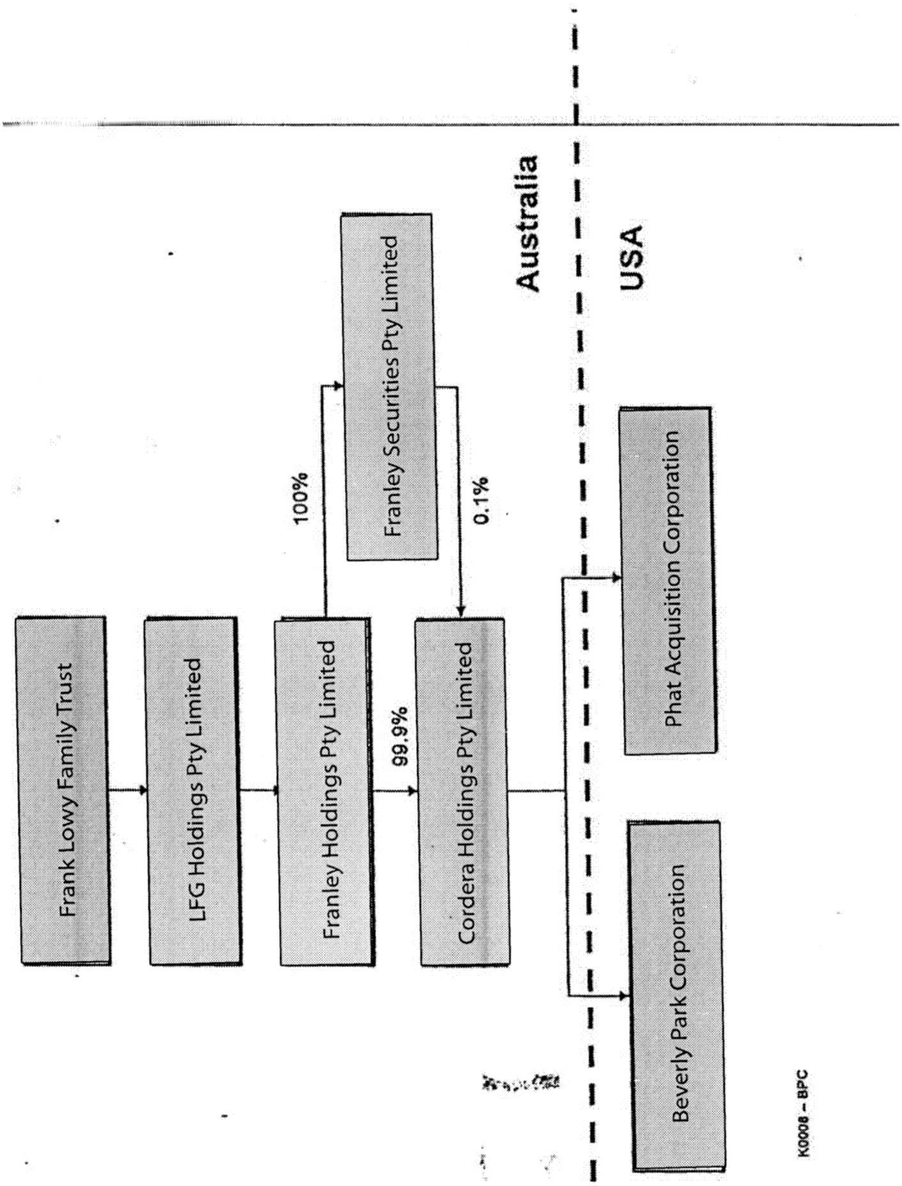

LOWY-PSI-000036
CONFIDENTIAL

CORDERA HOLDINGS PTY LIMITED
(Incorporated in New South Wales)
A.C.N. 000 699 249
24th Floor
100 William Street
SYDNEY NSW 2011
Tel: 61 2 9358 7180
Fax: 61 2 9358 7015

---

21 March 1997

Mr Peter Lowy
President
Beverly Park Corporation
12th Floor
11601 Wilshire Boulevard
Los Angeles CA 90025
USA

By Fax: 1 310 478 4519

Dear Mr Lowy

Cordera Holdings Pty Limited hereby offers to subscribe for 11,489 shares of the authorised common shares par value $0.01 each of Beverly Park Corporation for an issuance price of US$1,000 per share. Please advise if acceptable, and we will wire funds for value March 25, 1997.

Very truly yours
CORDERA HOLDINGS PTY LIMITED

by: [signature]
P S SEDDON
SECRETARY

MAR 21 '97 13:39 WESTFIELD DIRECTORS 612 93587015 P.1/1

LOWY-PSI-003714
CONFIDENTIAL

LIST OF OFFICERS/DIRECTORS

NOTE: DISTRIBUTION OF THIS PAGE TO THE FOLLOWING ONLY:
RICHARD GREEN, PETER LOWY, IRV HEPNER, MARK STEFANEK, ROGER PORTER, ARTHUR SCHRAMM

Beverly Park Corporation

Officers

Peter S. Lowy	*President*
Richard E. Green	*Vice President*
Mark A. Stefanek	*Treasurer and Secretary*
Leon Janks	*Assistant Secretary*

Directors

Peter S. Lowy
Richard E. Green
Arthur E. Schramm

Executive Committee

None

N:\CORPORATE\Lists of Officers and Directors\Officers and Directors - current.doc
08/26/1999

LOWY-PSI-003743
CONFIDENTIAL

IDR 22-1: Please have Peter Lowy, Director, complete the attached questionnaire regarding foreign bank accounts and foreign entities. Please have him sign the questionnaire and initial each page.

1. I was appointed President and a Director of Beverly Park Corporation (the "Company") on January 3, 1997.

2. I have not been personally involved with the Company's day-to-day operations.

3. I do not have sufficient personal knowledge to complete the questionnaire attached to this IDR and have asked Leon Janks, who has been the Secretary of the Company since November 30, 2001, to inquire into the matters raised.

4. Mr. Janks has done so, and the response to IDR 23-1 contains all relevant information he is able to provide to the questions presented.

5. I have reviewed Mr. Janks's response to IDR 23-1 and have no reason to doubt the accuracy of any of the facts stated therein.

Dated: January 28, 2008

Peter S. Lowy

LOWY-PSI-001975
CONFIDENTIAL

Permanent Subcommittee on Investigations
EXHIBIT #52

IDR 23-1: Please have Leon Janks, Director, complete the attached questionnaire regarding foreign bank accounts and foreign entities. Please have him sign the questionnaire and initial each page.

Since October 1, 1998, my firm, Green, Hasson & Janks LLP, has handled the books and records for Beverly Park Corporation (the "Company"). I became the Assistant Secretary of the Company on February 22, 1999, and I became a Director and Vice President, Treasurer, and Secretary on November 30, 2001. For the period of time beginning October 1, 1998, through the present, I have no recollection of the Company or its subsidiaries having any legal or beneficial interest in, or of the Company, its subsidiaries, officers, employees, or agents having any direct or indirect signature, management, investment, or other authority over any foreign bank accounts, brokerage accounts, or mutual funds as described in Part I or Part II of the questionnaire attached to this IDR. Similarly, for the period of time beginning October 1, 1998, through the present, I have no recollection of the Company or its subsidiaries having any legal or beneficial interest in, or of the Company, its subsidiaries, officers, employees, or agents having any direct or indirect signature, management, investment, or other authority over any foreign entities, trusts, corporations, partnerships, or foundations as described in Part III or Part IV of the questionnaire attached to this IDR.

In December 2001, the Company granted a power of attorney to an Israeli lawyer, Mr. Joshua Gelbard of Gelbard, Amit, Wexler, who I understand was completing certain formalities concerning the wind-up of an overseas entity associated with the parent of the Company. I was not directly involved in any of the activities undertaken by Mr. Gelbard, but it is my understanding that the Company was not associated with the overseas entity and had no financial interest in the wind-up.

For the period of time between January 3, 1997, when the Company was incorporated, and September 30, 1998, I have reviewed the books and records of the Company that are in the care, custody, and control of Green, Hasson & Janks LLP. From that review, I have found no indication of the Company or its subsidiaries having any legal or beneficial interest in, or of the Company, its subsidiaries, officers, employees, or agents having any direct or indirect signature, management, investment, or other authority over any foreign bank accounts, brokerage accounts, or mutual funds as described in Part I or Part II of the questionnaire attached to this IDR. Similarly, based upon my review of the books and records of the Company for that period of time, I have found no indication of the Company or its subsidiaries having any legal or beneficial interest in, or of the Company, its subsidiaries, officers, employees, or agents having any direct or indirect signature, management, investment, or other authority over any foreign entities, trusts, corporations, partnerships, or foundations as described in Part III or Part IV of the questionnaire attached to this IDR.

Leon Janks

Dated: January 28, 2008

LOWY-PSI-001976
CONFIDENTIAL

State of Delaware
The Official Website for the First State

Department of State: Division of Corporations

Entity Details

THIS IS NOT A STATEMENT OF GOOD STANDING

File Number:	2282071	Incorporation Date / Formation Date:	12/17/1991 (mm/dd/yyyy)
Entity Name:	BEVERLY PARK CORP.		
Entity Kind:	CORPORATION	Entity Type:	GENERAL
Residency:	DOMESTIC	State:	DE

REGISTERED AGENT INFORMATION

Name:	THE CORPORATION TRUST COMPANY		
Address:	CORPORATION TRUST CENTER 1209 ORANGE STREET		
City:	WILMINGTON	County:	NEW CASTLE
State:	DE	Postal Code:	19801
Phone:	(302)658-7581		

Additional Information is available for a fee. You can retrieve Status for a fee of $10.00 or more detailed information including current franchise tax assessment, current filing history and more for a fee of $20.00.

Would you like ○ Status ○ Status,Tax & History Information Submit

Back to Entity Search

To contact a Delaware Online Agent click here.

Permanent Subcommittee on Investigations
EXHIBIT #53

State of Delaware
The Official Website for the First State

Entity Details

THIS IS NOT A STATEMENT OF GOOD STANDING

File Number:	2702491	Incorporation Date / Formation Date:	01/03/1997 (mm/dd/yyyy)
Entity Name:	BEVERLY PARK CORPORATION		
Entity Kind:	CORPORATION	Entity Type:	GENERAL
Residency:	DOMESTIC	State:	DE

REGISTERED AGENT INFORMATION

Name:	THE CORPORATION TRUST COMPANY		
Address:	CORPORATION TRUST CENTER 1209 ORANGE STREET		
City:	WILMINGTON	County:	NEW CASTLE
State:	DE	Postal Code:	19801
Phone:	(302)658-7581		

Additional Information is available for a fee. You can retrieve Status for a fee of $10.00 or more detailed information including current franchise tax assessment, current filing history and more for a fee of $20.00.

Would you like ○ Status ○ Status,Tax & History Information Submit

Back to Entity Search

To contact a Delaware Online Agent click here.

LGT Treuhand
A Member of Liechtenstein Global Trust

LGT Treuhand
Aktiengesellschaft
Städtle 18+22
FL-9490 Vaduz
Fürstentum Liechtenstein
MWST-Nr. 50119

Telefon +423 235 27 27
Telefax +423 235 27 15
Internet
www.lgt.com/lgttreuhand
E-Mail lgttrust@lgt.com

Aktenvermerk

1/3

Thema	**MAVERICK FOUNDATION**
Verfasser(in) / Tel.	Christina Meusburger
Datum	27. März 2001
Zur Erledigung	Dagmar Gächter
Zur Kenntnisnahme	Dr. Pius Schlachter ll

Mit Tpi besprochen.
ll 28.3.01

Zeit und Ort der Besprechung

Freitag, 23 März 2001, 10:00 bis 15:30 Uhr, LGT Bank in Liechtenstein AG, Vaduz

Anwesende

Harvey Greenfield (Erstbegünstigter der Maverick Foundation)
Steven David Greenfield (Zweitbegünstigter und Instruktionsberechtigter der Maverick Foundation)
Dr. Henry Leimer (HL)
Gerhard Walch (GW)
S.D. Prinz Philip von und zu Liechtenstein (teilweise)
Christina Meusburger

BESPRECHUNGSPUNKTE

1. Allgemeines

Die Maverick Foundation wurde im Januar 1992 gegründet. Derzeit befinden sich in der Maverick Foundation rund USD 2.2 Mio. Weiters hält die Maverick Foundation zwei BVI Companies. Beide wurden im Januar 1992 mit dem Zweck gegründet, die Vermögenswerte in die Maverick Foundation einzuschleusen. Anschliessend sollten beide BVI Companies geschlossen werden, was bis heute nicht passiert ist.

Neben der Maverick Foundation verfügt der Kunde über einen Trust mit der Bank of Bermuda in Hong Kong. In diesem Trust befinden sich Vermögenswerte im Ausmass von rund USD 30 Mio. **Der Kunde als Erstbegünstigter und seine Kinder die Zweitbegünstigte der Maverick Foundation sind, sind US Passport Holders und leben zum Teil in New York.** Die Begünstigtenregelung für den Trust, den der Kunde mit der Bank of Bermuda hält, dürften ähnlich gelagert sein wie in der Maverick Foundation. Die Bank of Bermuda hat gegenüber dem Kunden signalisiert, dass sie die Geschäftsbeziehung mit ihm als US-Persons beenden möchte. Aufgrund dieser Umstände ist der Kunde nun auf der Suche nach einem Safe Heaven für sein Offshore Assets. Neben den bankable As … esellschaften gehalten, die

Permanent Subcommittee on Investigations
EXHIBIT #54

LGT Treuhand

Aktenvermerk

operativ tätig sind. Es ist jedoch beabsichtigt, diese Gesellschaften demnächst zu schliessen.

Es folgt eine lange Diskussion über den Bankplatz Liechtenstein, das Bankgeheimnis sowie die Sicherheit und Stabilität, die Liechtenstein als Bankplatz und souveräner Staat seinen Kunden gewährleisten kann. Von Seiten der Bank und insbesondere von HL wird grosser Interesse signalisiert, die 30 Mio USD entgegenzunehmen. Die Investitionsseite scheint nicht vollständig abgeklärt zu sein. Es wird gegenüber dem Kunden zwar klargestellt, dass er als US-Person nicht direkt in US-Securities investieren kann. Die Möglichkeit in Fonds zu investieren, wird jedoch nicht ausgeschlossen. Meines Wissens gibt es eine Entscheidung der Generaldirektion der LGT Bank in Liechtenstein AG, nach der LGT-in house Fonds US-Persons nicht angeboten werden. Damit bliebe die Möglichkeit in andere Offshore Fonds zu investieren, wobei diese grossteils für US-Persons nicht zugänglich sind.

2. Struktur

Die Maverick Foundation wurde seinerzeit als Stiftung mit Mandatsvertrag gegründet. Ich zeige die Nachteile, die der Mandatsvertrag für den Kunden bewirken kann auf. Der Kunde kann meiner Argumentation folgen und ist schliesslich der Meinung, dass wir diesen Mandatsvertrag auflösen müssten, wobei ich auch auf die mit der Auflösung des Mandatsvertrages verbundenen höheren Kosten für die Stiftung aufmerksam mache. Die beiden BVI-Gesellschaften sollen bis auf weiteres erhalten bleiben. Möglicherweise können sie wieder zur Einschleusung von Vermögenswerten in die Maverick Foundation Verwendung finden.

3. Vermögensstatus und Belegexemplare

Der Kunde zeichnet den Vermögensstatus per 31.12.1999 und 31.12.2000 ab. Weigert sich jedoch verschiedene Belegexemplare abzuzeichnen, da diese ja ohnehin durch die Abzeichnung der Vermögensstati erledigt seien. Ich gebe zu bedenken, dass wir aufgrund des Mandatsvertrages nur seine Weisungen ausführen und er uns dies durch seine Unterschrift auf den Belegexemplaren zu dokumentieren habe. Dennoch unterzeichnet der Kunde die Belegexemplare nicht.

4. Weiteres Vorgehen

Der Instruktionsberechtigte wird Ende April in Hong Kong sein. Ich biete an, dass ich ihn bei dieser Gelegenheit, da ich ja voraussichtlich Ende April ebenfalls in Hong Kong sein werde, treffen kann. Bis dann will sich der Instruktionsberechtigte entscheiden, ob und in welcher Form eine Übertragung des derzeit im Trust befindlichen Vermögens in die Maverick Foundation vor sich gehen soll. Als Alternativen habe ich folgendes aufgezeigt:

- Ausschüttung der Vermögenswerte aus dem Trust und anschliessende Widmung an die Maverick Foundation (unter Zwischenschaltung der BVI Companies)
- Übernahme des Trusts durch LGT Trust Management Ltd. als neuer Trustee

LGT Treuhand

Aktenvermerk 3/3

5. Schlussbemerkung
Die Kunden sind sehr vorsichtig und bestrebt den Trust mit der Bank of Bermuda unter Hinterlassung so weniger Spuren wie möglich aufzulösen. Auch von anderen Institutionen wurde ihnen signalisiert, dass US-Persons nicht die Kunden sind, die man sich in Offshore-Business wünscht.

Für mich war dieses Meeting ein anschauliches Beispiel dafür, dass Treuhandgeschäfte, wenn sie von Vertretern der Bankseite eingefädelt und gemanaged werden völlig nebensächlich betrachtet werden. Dieser Eindruck entstand vor allem dadurch, dass HL die Frage der Auflösung des Mandatsvertrages wörtlich als "Peanuts" bezeichnete, wobei ich der Meinung bin, dass diese Frage noch vor der Annahme zusätzlicher Vermögenswerte durch den Stiftungsrat zu lösen ist.

Ch. Meusburger

Christina Meusburger

[logo] LGT Trust
A Member of Liechtenstein Global

LGT Trust Corporation
Städtle 18+22
FL-9490 Vaduz
Fürstentum Liechtenstein
MWST-Nr. 50119

Tel.: +423 235 2727
Fax: +423 235 2772
Internet www.lgt.com/lgttreuhand
E-mail lgttrust@lgt.com

Memorandum for the Record

Subject	**MAVERICK FOUNDATION**
Author	Christina Meusburger (handwriting: discussed with (illegible), initial, March 3, 2001)
Date	March 27, 2001
For execution	Dagmar Gächter
Noted by	Dr. Pius Schlachter (initial)

Time and Place of Meeting

Friday, March 23, 2001, 10:00 a.m. to 3:30 p.m., LGT Bank at Liechtenstein corporation, Vaduz

Attendees

Harvey Greenfield	(sole beneficiary of the Maverick Foundation)
Steven David Greenfield	(second beneficiary and holder of power of attorney to give instructions of the Maverick Foundation)

Dr. Henry Leimer (HL)
Gerhard Walch (GW)
S.D. Prinz Philip von und zu Liechtenstein (partial attendance)
Christina Meusburger

TOPICS FOR DISCUSSION

1. Preface
The Maverick Foundation was established in January 1992. There are currently U.S.$ 2.2 million in the Maverick Foundation. In addition, the Maverick Foundation holds two BVI companies. Both were established in January 1992 with the purpose of channeling the assets into the Maverick Foundation. Afterwards, both BVI companies were to be closed, which has not happened to date.

In addition to the Maverick Foundation, the client has a Trust with the Bank of Bermuda in Hong Kong. This Trust has assets in the magnitude of around U.S. $ 30 million. **The client as sole beneficiary, and his children as secondary beneficiaries of the Maverick Foundation, hold U.S. passports and live partially in New York.** The beneficiary rules for the Trust, which the client has with the Bank of Bermuda, are likely stored similarly to how they are stored in the Maverick Foundation. The Bank of Bermuda has indicated to the client that it would like to end the business relationship with him as a U.S. citizen. Due to these circumstances, the client is now on the search for a safe haven for his offshore assets. Next to the bankable assets, this Trust also still holds operating companies. It is, however, planned, to close these companies in the near future.

There follows a long discussion about the banking location Liechtenstein, the banking privacy law as well as the security and stability, that Liechtenstein, as a banking location and sovereign nation, can guarantee its clients. The Bank, and especially HL, indicate strong interest in receiving the U.S.$30 million. Investment issues do not seem to be clarified completely. It is explained to the client that as a U.S. citizen he cannot invest in U.S. securities directly, but the possibility of investing in funds is not ruled out. To my knowledge, there is a decision by the directorate-general of the LGT Bank at Liechtenstein, Inc., according to which LGT in-house funds are not offered to U.S. citizens. Thus would remain the possibility to invest in other offshore funds, though these are largely not open to U.S. citizens.

2. Structure
The Maverick Foundation was established as a foundation with a contract of engagement. I present the disadvantages that this engagement contract can have for the client. The client is able to follow my arguments, and is ultimately of the opinion that we should dissolve this engagement contract, whereby I also draw attention to the increased costs for the foundation that will be associated with the dissolution of the contract. The two BVI companies are to continue to exist until further notice. Possibly, they could be used again to channel assets into the Maverick Foundation.

3. Asset Status and File Copies
The client signs off on the asset status of December 31, 1999 and December 31, 2000. He refuses, however, to sign off on various file copies, with the reasoning that they are already taken care of anyway through his signing off on the asset statuses. I point out that due to the engagement contract, we merely carry out his instructions, and that he needs to document this for us with his signature on the file copies. Nevertheless, the client does not sign the file copies.

4. Future Actions
The person who holds the power of attorney to give instructions will be in Hong Kong at the end of April. I offer to meet him there, since I expect to be in Hong Kong at the end of April myself. By then, the person who holds the power of attorney to give instructions intends to decide if, and in which form, a transfer of the current Trust assets to the Maverick Foundation should take place. I presented the following alternatives:

- Disbursement of the assets from the Trust and subsequent dedication to the Maverick Foundation (under interposition of the BVI companies)
- Takeover of the Trust through LGT Trust Management Ltd. as new trustee

5. Conclusion
The clients are very careful and eager to dissolve the Trust with the Bank of Bermuda leaving behind as few traces as possible. The clients received indications from other institutions as well that U.S. citizens are not those clients that one wishes for in offshore business.

For me, this meeting was an illustrative example of how trust business dealings, when initiated and managed by bank representatives, are seen as completely tangential. This impression was created especially by the fact that HL described the question of the dissolution of the engagement contract literally as "peanuts," whereas I am of the opinion that this question should be resolved by the foundation's board of trustees before accepting any additional assets.

(signature)
Christina Meusburger

LGT Bank in Liechtenstein
A Member of Liechtenstein Global Trust

LGT Bank in Liechtenstein
Aktiengesellschaft
Herrengasse 12
FL-9490 Vaduz

Telefon +423 235 11 22
Telefax +423 235 15 22
Internet www.lgt.com
E-Mail info@lgt.com
MWST-Nr. 50 119

Maverick Foundation
9490 Vaduz

Vaduz, January 1, 2002 1/1
HLE / BHK / 09:32:16 E

Redacted by the Permanent Subcommittee on Investigations

Summary

as of 31.12.2001

acc. no.	overview accounts/portfolios		cur.	amount	curr.rate	amount in USD
AA	USD ACCOUNT		USD	194.22		194.22
00	SAFE CUSTODY ACCOUNT	incl.acc.interest	USD (	0.00	)	2,197,973.50
					T O T A L	2,198,167.72

Permanent Subcommittee on Investigations
EXHIBIT #55

Maverick Foundation , 9490 Vaduz
SB: Gächter Dagmar **KB: Sprenger Sonja**

Mand.Nr.: [redacted]
L. Kundenbesuch: 23.03.2001

Gründungsdatum: 22.01.1992 Status: Aktiv

[redacted] = Redacted by the Permanent Subcommittee on Investigations

Verwaltungs- / Stiftungsräte

Profile Management Trust reg., Vad Zeichnungsrecht: Einzeln
Feuerstein Nicola Dr., Vaduz Zeichnungsrecht: Kollektiv

Banken

LGT Bank in Liechtenstein AG, Vaduz AB: Leimer Henry / LGT ZR-Nr.: [redacted] Zlg-Kto: [redacted]

Diverses

Anlageberater:	Leimer Henry / LGT HK,
Hauptgesellschaft:	Maverick Foundation, Vaduz
Repräsentant:	LGT Treuhand AG, Vaduz
Vermittler:	LGT Investment Management, Hong Kon
Auftraggeber:	Privater Auftraggeber

Fix-Honorare

Domizilhonorar	800.00	22.01.2003	LGT Treuhand AG, Vaduz
Kapitalsteuer	1'000.00	22.01.2003	Liechtensteinische Steuerverwaltung, Vaduz
Stiftungsratshonorar	3'000.00	22.01.2003	LGT Treuhand AG, Vaduz

Pauschal-Honorare

Vermögenswert per: 0.00 fällig am: 0.00 Fakturierbares Pauschalhonorar: 0.00

Zweck

Halten von 2 BVI Gesellschaften:
- CHIU FU (Far East) Limited
- TSF Company Limited

Beide Aktienzertifikate im Depot der Maverick Foundation

Besitznachweis, Verträge, Vollmachten

Vereinbarung betr. Erwerb Sondervermögen der BIL Vaduz vom 13.5.1993.

PM-Mandate der BIL Hong Kong betr. Verwaltung des BIL-Kontos am 7.2.1996
neu abgeschlossen
Mandatsverträge mit Chiu Fu und TSF

Instruktionsberechtigung f. Steven Greenfield

Weisungen (Verwaltung, Buchhaltung, Beistatut usw.)

Pendenzen / Geschichte

- siehe auch Pendenzen bei TSF und Chiu Fu!

- Passkopien der beiden zweitbegünstigten Frauen fehlen
- vorhandene Passkopien Vater + Sohn abgelaufen

- Umwandlung in STOM/Unterlagen in den Pendenzen

- BEX/ZLG/Inv. Chiu Fu + TSF

Permanent Subcommittee on Investigations
EXHIBIT #56

Maverick Foundation , 9490 Vaduz

Client Nr.: [redacted]

Assistant: Gächter, Dagmar **Account Manager: Sprenger, Sonja** Last Client Visit: 03.23.2001

Date Established: 01.22.1992 Status: Active

Management Board / Board of Advisors

[redacted] = Redacted by the Permanent Subcommittee on Investigations

Profile Management Trust reg., Vad Signatory Rights: Single

Feuerstein, Nicola Dr., Vaduz Signatory Rights: Collective

Banks

LGT Bank in Liechtenstein AG, Vaduz Investment advisor: Leimer, Henry/LGT Ref-No.: [redacted] Account: [redacted]

Miscellaneous

Investment Advisor:	Leimer, Henry / LGT HK
Head Corporation:	Maverick Foundation, Vaduz
Representative:	LGT Trust Inc., Vaduz
Broker:	LGT Investment Management, Hong Kong
Client:	Private Client

Fixed Fees

Domicile fees	800.00	Jan. 22, 2003	LGT Trust Inc., Vaduz
Capital taxes	1,000.00	Jan. 22, 2003	Tax Authority of Liechtenstein, Vaduz
Board of Trustees fees	3,000.00	Jan. 22, 2003	LGT Trust, Inc., Vaduz

Flat Fees

Value of Assets per: 0.00 Due on: 0.00 Billable Flat Fee: 0.00

Purpose

Holding 2 BVI companies:

- CHIU FU (Far East) Limited
- TSF Company Limited

Both stock certificates in the depot of the Maverick Foundation.

Proof of Ownership, Contracts, Powers of Attorney

Agreement re. acquisition of special assets of the BIL Vaduz on May 13, 1993.

PM-mandates of BIL Hong Kong re. administration of the BIL account newly determined on February 7, 1996.
Contracts of engagement with Chiu Fu and TSF

Steven Greenfield is the holder of the power of attorney to give instructions.

Special Instructions (Administration, Accounting, By-Laws etc.)

Comments / History

- see also comments for TSF and Chiu Fu!

- passport copies of both secondary-beneficiary women missing
- existing passport copies of father + son expired

- Conversion in STOM/documents in the comments

- BEX/ZLG/Inv. Chiu Fu + TSF

TSF Company Limited , Tortola / B.V.I.
SB: Gächter Dagmar KB: Sprenger Sonja

Mand.Nr.: [redacted]
L. Kundenbesuch:

Gründungsdatum: 24.01.1992 Status: Aktiv

[redacted] = Redacted by the Permanent Subcommittee on Investigations

Verwaltungs- / Stiftungsräte

IPC Management Trust reg., Vaduz Zeichnungsrecht: Einzeln

Banken

Standard and Chartered Bank, Hong Kong AB: ZR-Nr.: [redacted]:

Diverses

Hauptgesellschaft:	Maverick Foundation, Vaduz
Repräsentant:	HWR Services Limited, TORTOLA
Vermittler:	LGT Investment Management, Hong Kon
Auftraggeber:	Privater Auftraggeber

Fix-Honorare

VR-Honorar	3'000.00	24.01.2003	LGT Treuhand AG, Vaduz

Pauschal-Honorare

0.00 fällig am:

Vermögenswert per: 0.00 Fakturierbares Pauschalhonorar: 0.00

Zweck

Besitznachweis, Verträge, Vollmachten

- 100% Tochtergesellschaft der Maverick Foundation

Weisungen (Verwaltung, Buchhaltung, Beistatut usw.)

Pendenzen / Geschichte

- Zweck der TSF? --> Kunde fragen
- Konto bei Standard Chartered Bank noch sinnvoll, da kein Geld?

- Scheckbuch der Standard Chartered bank

Permanent Subcommittee on Investigations
EXHIBIT #57

PSI-USMSTR - 003193

TSF Company Limited, Tortola/ B.V.I. Client No.: [redacted]

Assistant: Gaechter Dagmar Account Manager: Sprenger Sonja

Last Client Visit:

Date Established: 01.24.1992 Status: Active

[redacted] = Redacted by the Permanent Subcommittee on Investigations

Management-/Board of Advisors

IPC Management Trust reg., Vaduz Signatory Rights: Individual

Banks

Standard Chartered Bank, Hong Kong Contact: Routing No.: [redacted]

Miscellaneous

Main Corporation:	Maverick Foundation, Vaduz
Representative:	HWR Services Limited, TORTOLA
Broker:	LGT Investment Management, Hong Kong
Client:	Private Client

Fixed Fees

[VR]- Fee	3,000.00	01.24.2003	LGT Trust AG, Vaduz

Flat Fees

	0.00	due on:	
Value of Assets per:		0.00	Billable Flat Fee: 0.00

Purpose

Proof of Ownership, Contracts, Powers of Attorney

-100% Daughter Corporation of the Maverick Foundation

Special Instructions (Administration, Accounting, Bylaws etc.)

Comments/ History

-Aim of the TSF? → ask client

-Account with Standard Chartered Bank still wise, because no money?

-Checkbook of the Standard Chartered bank

Chiu Fu (Far East) Limited , Tortola / B.V.I.
SB: Gächter Dagmar **KB: Sprenger Sonja**

Mand.Nr.: [redacted]
L. Kundenbesuch:

Gründungsdatum: 24.01.1992 Status: Aktiv

[redacted] = Redacted by the Permanent Subcommittee on Investigations

Verwaltungs- / Stiftungsräte
IPC Management Trust reg., Vaduz Zeichnungsrecht: Einzeln

Banken
The Hongkong and Shanghai, Hong Kong AB: ZR-Nr.: [redacted]

Diverses

Hauptgesellschaft:	Maverick Foundation, Vaduz
Repräsentant:	HWR Services Limited, TORTOLA
Vermittler:	LGT Investment Management, Hong Kon
Auftraggeber:	Privater Auftraggeber

Fix-Honorare

VR-Honorar	3'000.00	24.01.2003	LGT Treuhand AG, Vaduz

Pauschal-Honorare
0.00 fällig am:
Vermögenswert per: 0.00 Fakturierbares Pauschalhonorar: 0.00

Zweck

Besitznachweis, Verträge, Vollmachten
- Tochtergesellschaft der MAVERICK FOUNDATION
- Agency Agreement mit Maverick Foundation

Weisungen (Verwaltung, Buchhaltung, Beistatut usw.)

Pendenzen / Geschichte
- Zweck der Chiu Fu? - ev. Bankkto. bei HSBC schliessen? Zeichnungsrecht ändern/ bei nächstem Kundenbesuch wird HK die Instruktion des Kunden einholen, das Konto zu löschen, das seitens HSBC die Offenlegung des wirtschaftl. Begünstigten fordert (die Stiftung wird nicht anerkannt)

- Check-Buch im roten Akt

- Kontoauszüge bei HSBC einholen

Permanent Subcommittee on Investigations
EXHIBIT #58

PSI-USMSTR - 003205

Chiu Fu (Far East) Limited, Tortola/ B.V.I.

Client No.: [redacted]

Assistant: Gaechter Dagmar **Account Manager: Sprenger Sonja**

Last Client Visit:

Date Established: 01.24.1992 Status: Active

[redacted] = Redacted by the Permanent Subcommittee on Investigations

Management-/Board of Advisors

IPC Management Trust reg., Vaduz Signatory Rights: Individual

Banks

The Hongkong and Shanghai, Hong Kong Contact: Routing No.: [redacted] Account No.:

Miscellaneous

Main Corporation:	Maverick Foundation, Vaduz
Representative:	HWR Services Limited, TORTOLA
Broker:	LGT Investment Management, Hong Kong
Client:	Private Client

Fixed Fees

[VR]-Fee	3,000.00	01.24.2003	LGT Trust AG, Vaduz

Flat Fees

Value of Assets per: 0.00 due on: 0.00 Billable Flat Fee: 0.00

Purpose

Proof of Ownership, Contracts, Powers of Attorney

-Daughter corporation of the MAVERICK FOUNDATION

-Agency agreement with Maverick Foundation

Special Instructions (Administration, Accounting, Bylaws etc.)

Comments/ History

- Aim of the Chiu Fu? - ev. Bank account with HSBC closed?
  Signatory right change/ with next client visit HK will obtain the instructions from the client to terminate the account, that requires the disclosure of the financial beneficiary on the part of HSBC (the foundation not approved)

-Checkbook in the red file

-Obtain account statements from HSBC

LGT Bank in Liechtenstein
A Member of Liechtenstein Global Trust

LGT Bank in Liechtenstein
Aktiengesellschaft
Herrengasse 12
FL-9490 Vaduz

Telephone +423 235 11 22
Telefax +423 235 15 22
Internet www.lgt.com
E-mail info@lgt.com

▬ = Redacted by the Permanent Subcommittee on Investigations

Background Information/Profile – Existing Customers

(Legal entities/Companies)
(The German Version is binding)

Ref. CMU/dgc

Account/custody a/c no. [redacted]

Contracting partner / name MAVERICK FOUNDATION, Vaduz

Background Information/Profile

1. Contracting partner's details

1.1
☒ Non-operating company
- ☐ Company with commercial basis
- ☒ Foundation, trust, holding company, etc.

Principal purpose of company:
Investment of Assets

1.2
☐ Operating company
☐ Manufacturing ☐ Trading ☐ Services ☐ Holding company

Principal business activity of the company (including sector):

Range of products/services:

Principal markets and related sales (in CHF):

Own office premises: ☐ Yes ☐ No

Number of employees (approx.):

2. Commercial background/origin of assets

Origin of funds to be provided (earnings from commercial activity, inheritance, sale of participations, sale of property, etc.):
Earnings from commercial activity in the toy business. The client's sources toys from across Asia (but primarily China and Hong Kong) for distribution overseas.

3. Details of intended use

☒ Asset investment ☐ Business account
☐ Other purpose (please state):

4. Other information

4.1
Profession and business of commercial beneficiary/beneficiaries:
Businessman in the toy industry

4.2
Comments:

The contracting partner undertakes to notify the bank, on his own initiative, of any changes in writing.

4.3
Vaduz, 12. October 2001 — MAVERICK Foundation

Place/Date — Signature

Permanent Subcommittee on Investigations
EXHIBIT #59

Profile Management Trust reg.

/ - Maverick.doc - 12.10.2

ZRK 7845-C-05.01

[logo]
LGT Trust
A Member of Liechtenstein Global Trust

LGT Trust
Corporation
Städtle 28
FL-9490 Vaduz
Principality of Liechtenstein

Telephone +423 235 27 27
Telefax +423 235 27 15
Internet www.lgt.com/lgttreuhand
E-Mail lgttrust@lgt.com

Background Information/Profile
(Documentation of Existing Corporate Relationship(s) to 1.January.2001)

P-BG

Clients, Domicile TSF Company Ltd., BVI

1. Description of Entity

☐ Company with commercial basis
X Foundation, trust, holding company, etc.

Year Founded/Purchased: 1992

1.1 Primary Business
Asset Management, however currently no asset worth

1.2 Details of intended use of Assets:
currently no asset worth/ follow up regulation

2. Commercial background/origin of assets incl. detailed origin of funds to be provided (earnings from commercial activity, inheritance, sale of participations, sale of property, etc.):

Earnings from business activity/ business in the toy industry. sale of products in China/Hong Kong and export overseas.

3. Country Risk Category
X 1 ☐ 2 ☐ 3

Vaduz 12.20.2001
Place/Date

[SIGNED]
Signature – Client Advisor

X Power of Attorney per Separate Document
☐ This document replaces the previous version, dated:

Permanent Subcommittee on Investigations
EXHIBIT #60

TSF LTV/V.071001

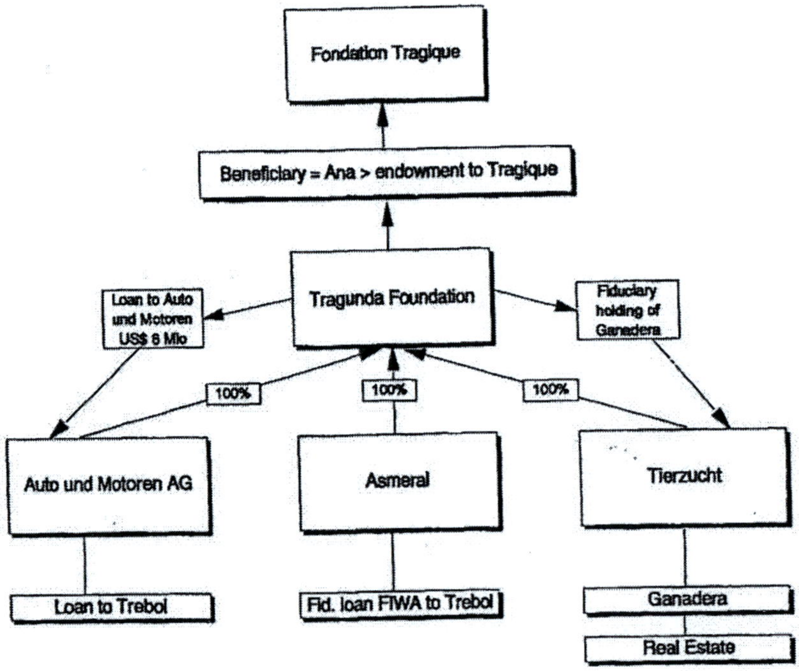

Permanent Subcommittee on Investigations
EXHIBIT #61

PSI-USMSTR - 008762

LGT Treuhand
A Member of Liechtenstein Global Trust

LGT Treuhand
Aktiengesellschaft
Städtle 28
FL-9490 Vaduz
Fürstentum Liechtenstein

Telefon +423 235 27 27
Telefax +423 235 27 15
Internet www.lgt.com/lgttreuhand
E-Mail lgttrust@lgt.com
MWSt-Nr. 50119

Hintergrundinformationen/Profil

P-BG

Formular für bestehende Geschäftsbeziehungen vor dem 1. Januar 2001

Rechtsträger, Sitz Fondation Tragique, Vaduz

☐ Gesellschaft mit kommerziellem Hintergrund
☒ Stiftung, Trust, Holding, usw.

Gründungs-/Übernahmejahr: 1979

1.1 Gewöhnliche Geschäftstätigkeit

Holdingfunktion, Asset Protection
Verwaltung des eigenen Vermögens
Ausschüttung an Begünstigte gemäss Beistatut

1.2 Verwendungszweck der Vermögenswerte

Vermögensanlage

Nachfolgemandat

Zwecks Schutz vor Gläubiger, welche in Puerto Rico gegen die Familie prozessierten, wurden die bereits in der Tragunda Foundation gehaltenen Vermögenswerte in die Fondation Tragique übertragen. Es handelt sich um Gesellschaften, die bereits durch die LGT betreut werden (Auto und Motoren AG in Liquidation, Tierzucht Investierungs-Anstalt).

☒ 1 ☐ 2 ☐ 3

Vaduz, 18. Dezember 2001
Ort, Datum

Unterschrift des Kundenberaters

☐ Bevollmächtigte gemäss separatem Formular
☐ Dieses Formular ersetzt das Formular vom:

Permanent Subcommittee on Investigations
EXHIBIT #62

PSI-USMSTR - 008711

[logo]
LGT Trust
A Member of Liechtenstein Global Trust

LGT Trust
Corporation
Städtle 28
FL-9490 Vaduz
Principality of Liechtenstein

Telephone +423 235 27 27
Telefax +423 235 27 15
Internet www.lgt.com/lgttreuhand
E-Mail lgttrust@lgt.com
VAT-No. 50119

Background Information/Profile **P-BG**
(Documentation of Existing Corporate Relationship(s) to 1.January.2001)

Clients, Domicile Tragunda Foundation, Vaduz

1. Description of Entity

☐ Company with commercial basis
X Foundation, trust, holding company, etc.

Year Founded/Purchased: 1986

1.1 Primary Business
Holding Function
Management of own assets, disbursements to beneficiaries in accordance with by-laws

1.2 Details of intended use of Assets:
Asset Investment

2. Commercial background/origin of assets incl. detailed origin of funds to be provided (earnings from commercial activity, inheritance, sale of participations, sale of property, etc.):

Disbursements from shares, which already represent Mandates looked after by LGT (Auto and Motors AG, Asmeral Investments Establishment, Animal Husbandry Investment Establishment, Vaduz)

3. Country Risk Category
X 1 ☐ 2 ☐ 3

Vaduz 3 December 2001
Place/Date

[SIGNED]
Signature – Client Advisor

☐ Power of Attorney per Separate Document
☐ This document replaces the previous version, dated:

Tragunda/V.071001

LGT Bank in Liechtenstein
A Member of Liechtenstein Global Trust

LGT Bank in Liechtenstein
Aktiengesellschaft
Herrengasse 12
FL-9490 Vaduz

Telefon +423 235 11
Telefax +423 235 15 22
Internet www.lgt.com
E-Mail info@lgt.com

Kopie

[redacted] = Redacted by the Permanent Subcommittee on Investigations

Hintergrundinformationen/Profil – Bestehende Kunden
(Juristische Personen/Gesellschaften)

Ref. LTV/MP/ci

Konto-/Depot-Nr. [redacted]

Vertragspartner/Name Auto und Motoren AG, in Liquidation, Vaduz

Hintergrundinformationen/Profil

1. Informationen zum Vertragspartner

erfasst	verifiziert
Vis.:	Vis.: ....

1.1 ☒ Nicht-Tätige Gesellschaft
- ☒ Gesellschaft mit kommerziellem Hintergrund
- ☐ Stiftung, Trust, Holding, usw.

Hauptzweck der Gesellschaft:
An- und Verkauf von Volvo-Automobilen

1.2 ☐ Tätige Gesellschaft
☐ Fabrikationsbetrieb ☐ Handelsgesellschaft ☐ Dienstleistungsbetrieb ☐ Holdinggesellschaft

Hauptgeschäftstätigkeit der Gesellschaft (inkl. Branche):

Produkte/Dienstleistungspalette:

Hauptmärkte und deren Umsätze (in CHF)

Eigene Büroräumlichkeiten: ☐ Ja ☐ Nein

Anzahl Mitarbeiter ca.):

2. Wirtschaftlicher Hintergrund/Herkunft der Vermögenswerte

Herkunft der einzubringenden Mittel (Erträge aus geschäftlicher Tätigkeit, Erbschaft, Verkauf von Beteiligungen, Liegenschaftsverkauf usw.):
Gewinnspanne aus der Geschäftstätigkeit

3. Informationen zum Verwendungszweck

☐ Vermögensanlage ☐ Geschäftskonto
☐ Sonstiger Zweck (bitte nennen):

4. Sonstige Angaben

4.1 Beruf und Geschäftstätigkeit der wirtschaftlich berechtigten Person/Personen:
~~Privatier~~ Witwe, die Import + Export von Automobilen (Volvo + Subaru) ~~[illegible]~~ (zs. mit ihrem Ehemann) gemacht hat. Heute ist sie pensioniert

4.2 Bemerkungen:
Die Gesellschaft hat keine kommerzielle Tätigkeit mehr. Sie wird in absehbarer Zeit gelöscht. 13.5.02

Der Vertragspartner verpflichtet sich, Änderungen von sich aus schriftlich der Bank mitzuteilen.

4.3 Vaduz 3. Oktober 2001
Ort/Datum

Auto und Motoren AG, in Liquidation
Unterschrift

Permanent Subcommittee on Investigations
EXHIBIT #63

Kontrolliert ....
KYC Team

PSI-USMSTR - 008729

[logo]**LGT Bank in Liechtenstein**
A Member of Liechtenstein Global

LGT Bank in Liechtenstein
Stock Corporation
Herrengasse 12
FL-9490 Vaduz

Telephone: +423 235 11 22
Telefax: +423 23[illegible]
Internet: www.lgt.com
E-Mail info@lgt.com

Copy

Background Information/Profile- Existing Customer
(Legal entities/Companies)

Ref. LTV/MP/ci

[redacted] = Redacted by the Permanent Subcommittee on Investigations

Account/custody a/c no. [redacted]

Contracting partner / Name Auto and Motoren [Motors] Corp., in liquidation, Vaduz

Background Information/Profile

composed	verified
Sig.: [signed]	Sig.: ______

1. Contracting partner's details

1.1

X Non-operating company

☐ Company with commercial basis

X Foundation, trust, holding company, etc.

Principal purpose of company:
Purchase and sale of Volvo automobiles

1.2

☐ Operating company

☐ Manufacturing ☐ Trading ☐ Services ☐ Holding Company

Principal business activity of the company (including sector):

Range of products/services:

Principal markets and related sales (in CHF):

Own office premises: ☐ Yes ☐ No

Number of employees (approx.):

2. Commercial background/origin of assets

Origin of funds to be provided (earnings from commercial activity, inheritance, sale of participations, sale of property, etc.):
Profit margin from professional activity

3. Details of intended use

☐ Asset investment ☐ Business account
☐ Other purpose (please state):

4. Other information

4.1
Profession and business of commercial beneficiary/beneficiaries:
Person of independent means; [hand-written] Widow who conducted the import and export of automobiles (Volvo and Subaru) with her husband. She is now retired. 05.13.2002 [initialed]

4.2
Comments:
The corporation does not conduct commercial activity anymore. It will be dissolved in the foreseeable future.

The contracting partner undertakes to notify the bank, on his own initiative, of any changes in writing.

4.3
Vaduz / 10.03.2001
Place/Date

Auto and Motors Corp., in liquidation
Signature
[signed]

Inspected [initialed]
KYC Team

Asmeral Investment Anstalt , 9490 Vaduz
SB: Prete Rosa **KB: Meier Peter**

Mand.Nr.: [redacted]
L. Kundenbesuch: 26.05.1997

Gründungsdatum: 02.07.1986 Status: Gelöscht

[redacted] – Redacted by the Permanent Subcommittee on Investigations

Verwaltungs- / Stiftungsräte
Peter Meier, Eschen Zeichnungsrecht: Einzeln LIQU. VR

Banken
LGT Bank in Liechtenstein AG, Vaduz AB: ZR-Nr.: [redacted] Zlg-Kto: [redacted]

Diverses

Aktien / Zessionen:	Dossier / Gesellschaftsakt,
Repräsentant:	LGT Treuhand AG, Vaduz
Auftraggeber:	Privater Auftraggeber

Fix-Honorare

Domizilhonorar	800.00	01.07.2000	LGT Treuhand AG, Vaduz
Kapitalsteuer	1'000.00	01.07.2000	Liechtensteinische Steuerverwaltung, Vaduz
VR-Honorar	3'000.00	01.07.2000	LGT Treuhand AG, Vaduz

Pauschal-Honorare
0.00 fällig am:
Vermögenswert per: 0.00 Fakturierbares Pauschalhonorar: 0.00

Zweck

Besitznachweis, Verträge, Vollmachten

Weisungen (Verwaltung, Buchhaltung, Beistatut usw.)

Pendenzen / Geschichte

→ 95053

Permanent Subcommittee on Investigations
EXHIBIT #64

PSI-USMSTR - 000966

Asmeral Investment Anstalt [Institution], **9490 Vaduz**
Assistant: Prete Rosa **Account Manager: Meier, Peter**

Client-No.: [redacted]
Last Client Visit: May 26. 1997

[redacted] = Redacted by the Permanent Subcommittee on Investigations

Date Established: July 2, 1986 Status: Dissolved

Management Board / Board of Advisors
Peter Meier, Eschen Signatory Rights: Individual LIQU. Management Board

Banks:
LGT Bank in Liechtenstein AG, Vaduz Investment advisor: Ref. No.: [redacted] Account: [redacted]

Miscellaneous:

Stocks / Transfers:	Dossier / company file
Representative:	LGT Treuhand AG [LGT Trust, Inc.], Vaduz
Client:	Private client

Fixed Fees:

Domicile fee	800.00	July 1, 2000	LGT Treuhand AG, Vaduz
Capital Tax:	1,000.00	July 1, 2000	Liechtensteinische Steuerverwaltung, Vaduz [Tax Authority of Liechtenstein]
Management Board fee	3,000.00	July 1, 2000	LGT Treuhand AG, Vaduz

Flat Fees:

0.00 Due on:

Value of assets as of: Billable Flat fee: 0.00

Purpose

Proof of Ownership, Contracts, Powers of Attorney

Special Instructions (Administration, Accounting, Bylaws, etc.)

Comments / History

[in handwriting:] → 95053

LGT Treuhand
A Member of Liechtenstein Global Trust

LGT Treuhand
Aktiengesellschaft
Städtle 28
FL-9490 Vaduz
Fürstentum Liechtenstein
MWST-Nr. 50119

Telefon +423 235 27 27
Telefax +423 235 27 15
Internet
www.lgt.com/lgttreuhand
E-Mail lgttrust@lgt.com

Aktenvermerk

1/2

[redacted] = Redacted by the Permanent Subcommittee on Investigations

Thema	**Foundation Tragique**
Verfasser(in) / Tel.	Peter Meier
Datum	11. September 2001 /
Zur Erledigung	Rosa Prete
Zur Kenntnisnahme	STR TL

Ricardo Gonzales war zusammen mit seiner Mutter Conchita, seiner Schwester [redacted] und seiner Gattin [redacted] beim Zwischenhalt von Madrid nach Moskau in Zürich, wo wir uns im Hotel Splügen zu dieser Besprechung der Pendenzen trafen.

[redacted] unterfertigt den Vergütungsauftrag und den Auftrag zur Löschung ihres Privatkontos [redacted] bei der LGT.

Ich übergebe an Conchita den Betrag von US$ 10.000.--, der Barbezugsbeleg zu Lasten Tragique wird abgezeichnet.

Conchita unterfertigt den Vermögensstatus der Tragique 2000.

Ich diskutiere die Vermögensanlage der Tragique und bespreche die Anlagevorschläge der LGT, von C. Wehinger vorbereitet. Conchita unterzeichnet den Auftrag, die Gelder, inkl. $ 550000.- welche von Auto und Motoren zu übertragen sind, wie folgt anzulegen: $ 1 Mio. in Cash = Festgelder und den Rest in LGT Strategy Class Funds 5 Jahre!

Nachdem die Probleme in Puerto Rico nun erledigt sind und eine Steueruntersuchung nicht mehr zu vermuten ist, besprechen wir die Situation im Beistatut der Tragique. Diesbezüglich unterzeichnet Conchita als Protektorin einen Auftrag, das Beistatut so zu ändern, dass sie als Erstbegünstigte aufscheint und nach ihrem Tode die Kinder - die jetzigen Erstbegünstigten - als Zweitbegünstigte zu gleichen Teilen.

Der Vermögensstatus 2000 der Tragunda Foundation wird unterfertigt.

Conchita unterzeichnet als betroffene Begünstigte den Auftrag, die Tragunda Foundation zu löschen und den Liquidationserlös - insbesondere das Treuhandverhältnis Ganadera bei Tierzucht Investierungs Anstalt - auf die Foundation Tragique zu übertragen.

Die Tierzucht Investierungs Anstalt hält nach wie vor die spanische Gesellschaft Ganadera, auf welche die Immobilien eingetragen sind. Derzeit ist das Geschäft mit der Vermietung der Liegenschaft für Hochzeiten ein voller Erfolg. Nächsten Monat findet die Hochzeit eines Schweizer Paares statt!!!! Auch während der Woche finden Firmen Events statt. Letztes Jahr war die Abrechnung Kos ... osten betragen p.a. ca. $ 150.000.--. In diesem Jah ... Dadurch lässt sich dann

Permanent Subcommittee on Investigations
EXHIBIT #65

PSI-USMSTR - 008704

LGT Treuhand

Aktenvermerk 2/2

eine klare Berechnung der Rendite feststellen. Die Immobilie ist immer noch zum Verkauf, der Verhandlungspreis ist um die US$ 25 Mio. (ESP 3 Mia.).

Die Auto und Motoren kann gelöscht werden. Der Betrag von ca. $ 550.000.– ist umgehend auf die Tragique zu übertragen, der Liquidationserlös nach Ablauf der 6 Monate. Ein entsprechender Auftrag wird unterfertigt. Die Probleme in Puerto Rico sind erledigt. Die Trebol kommt wieder in die Gewinnzone. Allerdings wird es noch einige Jahre dauern bis die Verlustvorträge abgebaut sind. In diesem Zusammenhang fällt auch das Problem der FIWA, welche noch ein Aktienpaket von ca. 3% hält. Dieses sollte nun übertragen werden, aber es dürfen keine "schlafenden Hunde" geweckt werden. Ich habe vorgeschlagen, dass die FIWA an die TREBOL einen Brief schreibt, dass sie die Beteiligung verkaufen wollen und der Trebol Realty ein Vorkaufsrecht - first choice - einräumen. Derzeit ist der effektive Wert noch nicht so hoch, so dass ein Verkauf in Höhe von ca. $ 2 - 300.000.– möglich wäre. Die vertragliche Vereinbarung ist zu berücksichtigen bzw. gegenseitig aufzuheben. Der Brief von FIWA darf nicht von Peter Meier unterzeichnet werden. Der Brief sollte nach dem 22.9. geschrieben werden. Grund ist der Abbau der Investments in USA.

Ich erkläre die Situation in FL und lasse in diesem Zusammenhang das Formular über die wirtschaftlich berechtigten Personen abzeichnen und bestätigen, dass die Adressen stimmen. Conchita ist als weitere Begünstigte aufzulisten.

Ich habe die Herrschaften darüber informiert, dass ich die LGT verlassen werde. Sie bedauern dies natürlich sehr. Um meinen Nachfolger vorzustellen., bietet sich ev. die Möglichkeit am 19. - 22. September in Madrid!! Ricardo wird mich diesbezüglich aber noch anrufen.

PSI-USMSTR - 008705

[logo]
LGT Bank in Liechtenstein
A Member of Liechtenstein Global Trust

LGT Treuhand
Aktiengesellschaft
Städtle 28
FL-9490 Vaduz
Principality of Liechtenstein
VAT-Nr. 50119

Telephone +423 235 27 27
Fax +423 235 27 15
Internet www.lgt.com/lgttreuhand
Email lgttrust@lgt.com

Memorandum for the File

1/2

[redacted] = Redacted by the Permanent Subcommittee on Investigations

Concerned Parties	**Foundation Tragique**
Author / Tel.	Peter Meier
Date	09.11.2001
For Follow-Up	Rosa Prete
To the Attention of	SPR TLU [initialed]

Ricardo Gonzales was with his mother Conchita, his sister [redacted] and his wif[redacted] on a stopover in Zürich between Madrid and Moscow, where we met in the Hotel Splügen for a meeting concerning pending issues.

[redacted] igns the authorized payment order and the mandate for the cancellation of her private accoun[redacted] LGT.

I deliver the amount of US$ 10,000.-- to Conchita; the cash withdrawal receipt, to be debited to the Foundation Tragique, is initialed.

Conchita signs the Status of Assets of the Foundation Tragique 2000.

I discuss the investment of Tragique's assets and discuss the investment advice of the LGT, prepared by C. Wehinger. Conchita signs the mandate; the monies, including $550,000.-- which are to be transferred from the Auto and Motors Foundation, are to be invested as follows: $1 million in cash = fixed term deposits, and the rest in LGT Strategy Class Funds 5 years!

Now that the problems in Puerto Rico are resolved and a tax investigation is no longer to be presumed, we discuss the situation concerning the bylaws of the Foundation Tragique. In these regards, Conchita, as protector, signs an order to change the bylaws so that she appears as primary beneficiary, and that after her death the children - who are the current primary beneficiaries - appear as secondary beneficiaries with equal proportions.

The Status of Assets 2000 of the Tragunda Foundation is signed.

As the concerned beneficiary, Conchita signs the order to dissolve the Tragunda Foundation and to transfer the proceeds from liquidation - especially the trust Ganadera with the Tierzucht Investierungs [Animal Husbandry Investment] Foundation - to the Foundation Tragique.

The Animal Husbandry Investment Foundation still holds the Spanish establishment Ganadera, under which the properties are registered. Currently, the operation of renting the property for weddings is a complete success. Next month the wedding of a Swiss couple is taking place!!!! Also, corporate events take place during the week. Last year, the accounting of the costs and revenues balanced out evenly. The costs come to the annual amount of approximately $150,000.--. This year, the property is almost completely booked. Because of this, a clear calculation of the returns can be made.

[logo]
LGT Treuhand

2/2

Memorandum for the File

The property is still up for sale; the negotiation price is around US$ 25 million (ESP 3 billion).

The Auto and Motors Foundation can be dissolved. The amount of approximately $550,000.-- is immediately to be transferred to the Foundation Tragique, the proceeds from liquidation after the course of six months. A corresponding mandate is signed. The problems in Puerto Rico are resolved. The Trebol is going into the black again. However, it will still take some years before the accumulated deficit is eliminated. The problem with the FIWA also falls in this context; FIWA still holds a block of shares of approximately 3%. This should be transferred, but we must "let sleeping dogs lie." I have suggested that the FIWA write a letter to the TREBOL, saying that it would like to sell the shares and grant the Trebol Realty a first choice purchase option. Currently, the effective value is still high enough so that a sale of the amount of approximately $2 - 300,000.-- would be possible. The contractual agreement is to be taken into consideration and respectively to be annulled. The letter from FIWA may not be signed by Peter Meier. The letter should be written after 09.22. The reason for this is the reduction of the investments in the USA.

I explain the situation in Liechtenstein, and in this context I have the form about the persons entitled to financial benefit signed and confirm that the addresses are correct. Conchita is to be added as another beneficiary.

I have informed the clients that I will leave the LGT. Naturally, they regret this very much. The possibility may present itself to introduce my successor from 09.19 to 09.22 in Madrid!! However, Ricardo must still call me in this regard.

[signed]

PSI-USMSTR - 00876

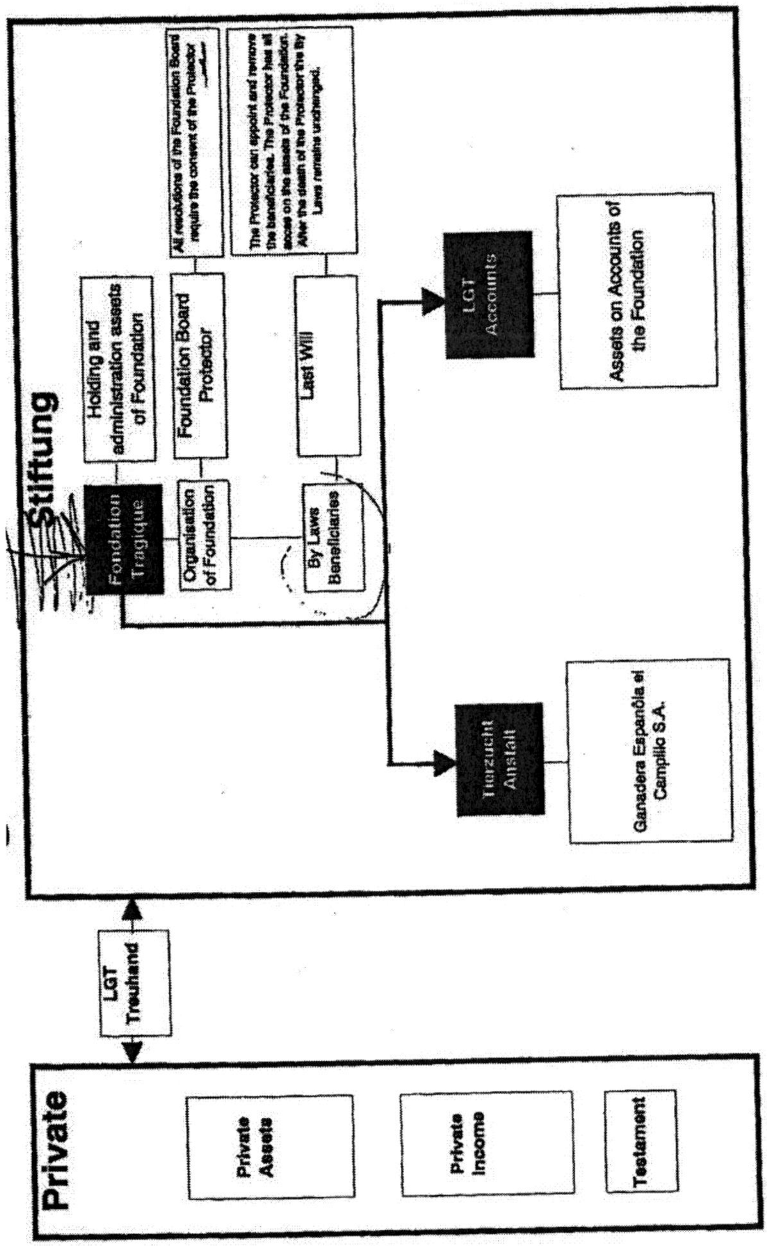

Permanent Subcommittee on Investigations

EXHIBIT #66

LGT Treuhand
A Member of Liechtenstein Global Trust

LGT Treuhand
Aktiengesellschaft
Städtle 28
FL-9490 Vaduz
Fürstentum Liechtenstein

Telefon +423 235 27 27
Telefax +423 235 27 15
Internet www.lgt.com/lgttreuhand
E-Mail lgttrust@lgt.com
MWSt-Nr. 50119

Hintergrundinformationen/Profil

P-BG

Formular für bestehende Geschäftsbeziehungen vor dem 1. Januar 2001

Rechtsträger, Sitz Fondation Tragique, Vaduz

1. Informationen zum Rechtsträger

☐ Gesellschaft mit kommerziellem Hintergrund
☒ Stiftung, Trust, Holding, usw.

Gründungs-/Übernahmejahr: 1979

1.1 Gewöhnliche Geschäftstätigkeit

Holdingfunktion, Asset Protection
Verwaltung des eigenen Vermögens
Ausschüttung an Begünstigte gemäss Beistatut

1.2 Verwendungszweck der Vermögenswerte

Vermögensanlage

2. Wirtschaftlicher Hintergrund und Herkunft der eingebrachten und einzubringenden Vermögenswerte (so genau als möglich); Angaben zum Herkunftsland

Nachfolgemandat

Zwecks Schutz vor Gläubiger, welche in Puerto Rico gegen die Familie prozessierten, wurden die bereits in der Tragunda Foundation gehaltenen Vermögenswerte in die Fondation Tragique übertragen. Es handelt sich um Gesellschaften, die bereits durch die LGT betreut werden (Auto und Motoren AG in Liquidation, Tierzucht Investierungs-Anstalt).

3. Länderrisikokategorisierung

☒ 1 ☐ 2 ☐ 3

Vaduz, 18. Dezember 2001
Ort, Datum

Unterschrift des Kundenberaters

☐ Bevollmächtigte gemäss separatem Formular
☐ Dieses Formular ersetzt das Formular vom:

Permanent Subcommittee on Investigations
EXHIBIT #67

Tragique 071…
PSI-USMSTR - 008711

[logo]
LGT Trust
A Member of Liechtenstein Global Trust

LGT Trust
Corporation
Städtle 28
FL-9490 Vaduz
Principality of Liechtenstein

Telephone +423 235 27 27
Telefax +423 235 27 15
Internet www.lgt.com/lgttreuhand
E-Mail lgttrust@lgt.com
VAT-No.: 50119

Background Information/Profile **P-BG**
(Documentation of Existing Corporate Relationship(s) to 1.January.2001)

Clients, Domicile Fondation Tragique, Vaduz

1. Description of Entity

☐ Company with commercial basis
X Foundation, trust, holding company, etc.

Year Founded/Purchased: 1979

1.1 Primary Business
Holding function, Asset Protection
Management of own Assets
Disbursements to Beneficiaries according to By-laws

1.2 Details of intended use of Assets:
Investment of assets

2. Commercial background/origin of assets incl. detailed origin of funds to be provided (earnings from commercial activity, inheritance, sale of participations, sale of property, etc.):

Successor Mandate
For the purpose of protection from creditors, who are litigating the family in Puerto Rico, the assets already being held by the Tragunda Foundation were transferred to the Fondation Tragique. This concerns companies, that were already being overseen by the LGT (Auto and Motors AG in Liquidation, Tierzucht Investierungs-Anstalt [Animal Husbandry Investment Establishment])

3. Country Risk Category
X 1 ☐ 2 ☐ 3

Vaduz 18 December 2001
Place/Date

[SIGNED]
Signature – Client Advisor

☐ Power of Attorney per Separate Document
☐ This document replaces the previous version, dated:

Tragique/V.071001

LGT Bank in Liechtenstein
A Member of Liechtenstein Global Trust

LGT Bank in Liechtenstein
Aktiengesellschaft
Herrengasse 12
FL-9490 Vaduz

Telefon +423 235 11 22
Telefax +423 235 15 22
Internet www.lgt.com
E-Mail info@lgt.com

▬ = Redacted by the Permanent Subcommittee on Investigations

Hintergrundinformationen/Profil – Bestehende Kunden
(Juristische Personen/Gesellschaften)

Ref. ____________

Konto-/Depot-Nr. [redacted]

Vertragspartner/Name FIWA AG, Vaduz

Hintergrundinformationen/Profil

1. Informationen zum Vertragspartner

1.1
☐ Nichttätige Gesellschaft
- ☐ Gesellschaft mit kommerziellem Hintergrund
- ☐ Stiftung, Trust, Holding, usw.

Hauptzweck der Gesellschaft:

1.2
☒ Tätige Gesellschaft
☐ Fabrikationsbetrieb ☐ Handelsgesellschaft ☒ Dienstleistungsbetrieb ☐ Holdinggesellschaft

Hauptgeschäftstätigkeit der Gesellschaft (inkl. Branche):

Halten von Beteiligungen

Produkte/Dienstleistungspalette: Hauptmärkte und deren Umsätze (in CHF):

Eigene Büroräumlichkeiten: ☐ Ja ☐ Nein Anzahl Mitarbeiter ca.: ____________

2. Wirtschaftlicher Hintergrund/Herkunft der Vermögenswerte

Herkunft der einzubringenden Mittel (Erträge aus geschäftlicher Tätigkeit, Erbschaft, Verkauf von Beteiligungen, Liegenschaftsverkauf usw.):

3. Informationen zum Verwendungszweck

☐ Vermögensanlage ☒ Geschäftskonto
☐ Sonstiger Zweck (bitte nennen): ____________

4. Sonstige Angaben

4.1
Beruf und Geschäftstätigkeit der wirtschaftlich berechtigten Person/Personen:

4.2
Bemerkungen:
LGT - Gruppengesellschaft

Der Vertragspartner verpflichtet sich, Änderungen von sich aus schriftlich der Bank mitzuteilen.

4.3
Vaduz, 10.12.2001

Ort/Datum

Permanent Subcommittee on Investigations
EXHIBIT #68

PSI-USMSTR-000954

[logo]**LGT Bank in Liechtenstein**
A Member of Liechtenstein Global

LGT Bank in Liechtenstein
Aktiengesellschaft
Herrengasse 12
FL-9490 Vaduz

Telephone: +423 235 11 22
Telefax: +423 235 15 22
Internet: www.lgt.com
E-Mail: info@lgt.com

Background Information / Profile – Existing /Clients
Judicial persons / Companies

[redacted] = Redacted by the Permanent Subcommittee on Investigations

Account No. / Depository No. [redacted]   Ref. ______

Contractual Partner / Name   FIWA AG [FIWA, Inc.], Vaduz

1. Background Information / Profile

1. Information on the Contractual Partner
1.1.

□ Non-active company
- □ Company with commercial background
- □ Foundation, trust, holding company, etc.

Principal purpose of company:

1.2.

X Active company
□ Manufacturing business □ Trading business X Service business □ Holding company

Principal business activity of company (incl. sector):

Holding of shares

Products / Range of Services   Main markets and their sales volume (in Swiss francs)

Own office space: □ yes □ no   Number of employees (roughly): ______

2. Commercial Background / Origin of Assets
Origin of funds to be paid in (earnings from business activity, inheritance, sale of shares, sale of real estate, etc.):

3. Information on Intended Usage

□ Asset investment X Business account
□ Other purpose (please state): ______

4. Other Information
4.1. Occupation and business activity of economic beneficiary / beneficiaries:

4.2.
Comments:
LGT - group company

The contractual partner commits himself to notify the bank of any changes in writing of his own accord.

4.3.
Vaduz, Dec. 10, 2001   [signed]   [signed]
Place / Date   Signature

ZRK 5351-C-03.01

LGT Treuhand
A Member of Liechtenstein Global Trust

LGT Treuhand
Aktiengesellschaft
Städtle 28
FL-9490 Vaduz
Fürstentum Liechtenstein

Telefon +423 235 27 27
Telefax +423 235 27 15
Internet www.lgt.com/lgttreuhand
E-Mail lgttrust@lgt.com
MWSt-Nr. 50119

Background Information/Profile

(The German Version is binding)

Form for existing business relationships before January 1, 2001

Mandate/domicile Yue Shing Tong Foundation

1. Informations concerning legal entity

☐ Company with commercial basis
☒ Foundation, trust, holding company, etc.

Year of foundation/take-over: 1988

1.1. Usual business activity

INVESTMENTS

1.2. Intended use of assets

SUCCESSOR ORGANIZATION

2. Commercial background and origin of provided assets and assets to provide and details to the country of origin.

The original founder (father) built up a large and successful chemical business in Taiwan and China. The assets originally deposited were profits generated out of this business activity. The father passed away in 1998 and additional assets were received from Mees Pierson at the time.

3. Profession and business of present commercial beneficiary/beneficiaries

Current beneficiaries are retired (mother) while Son R works for a venture capital firm and Daughter T is a house wife with three children.

Vaduz, 09 October 2001
Place/Date

Signature

☐ Power of attorney in pursuance of separate printed form

Permanent Subcommittee on Investigations
EXHIBIT #69

PSI-USMSTR - 002207

Richard M. Chong

From:	Rick [[redacted]
Sent:	Tuesday, January 02, 2007 12:00 AM
To:	'Chalet@hk.super.net'
Subject:	RE: Apex Assets
Attachments:	Apex Asset approved expenses - Dec 2006.pdf

▬ = Redacted by the Permanent Subcommittee on Investigations

-----Original Message-----
From: Chalet@hk.super.net [mailto:Chalet@hk.super.net]
Sent: Wednesday, December 27, 2006 8:55 PM
To: Richard Chong
Subject: Apex Assets

Dear Rick,

I hope you had a good Christmas.

Please find enclosed some invoices for Apex Assets from KCS. If you agree with them, could you kindly sign them and fax them over to us for settlement.
We have sufficient funds on Apex to cover them.

Let me take this opportunity to wish you all the very best for 2007.

Thanks & best regards,
Silvan

--
No virus found in this incoming message.
Checked by AVG Free Edition.
Version: 7.5.432 / Virus Database: 268.15.28/605 - Release Date: 12/27/2006 12:21 PM

--
No virus found in this outgoing message.
Checked by AVG Free Edition.
Version: 7.5.432 / Virus Database: 268.16.2/613 - Release Date: 1/1/2007 2:50 PM

Permanent Subcommittee on Investigations
EXHIBIT #70

CH-PSI-00001

Richard M. Chong

From: Rick [redacted]
Sent: Wednesday, February 14, 2007 6:38 PM
To: 'Chalet@hk.super.net'
Subject: RE: Delivery for 32.1

▬ = Redacted by the Permanent Subcommittee on Investigations

Will do. Rick

From: Chalet@hk.super.net [mailto:Chalet@hk.super.net]
Sent: Wednesday, February 14, 2007 6:16 PM
To: Rick
Subject: Re: Delivery for 32.1

Dear Rick,

I'm sorry, I've just been informed by our relevant department that they cannot deliver the goods to 32.1. The instruction was incomplete and did not correctly identify the final recipient. We will have to return them.

Can you ask your sender to ship them to Apex instead? This would also be better from a safety point of view.

Thanks & best regards,
Silvan

> ----- Original Message -----
> **From:** Rick
> **To:** Chalet@hk.super.net
> **Sent:** Tuesday, February 13, 2007 10:56 PM
> **Subject:** RE: Delivery for 32.1
>
> Yes. Expecting it. Thanks. Rick
>
> --
> No virus found in this incoming message.
> Checked by AVG Free Edition.
> Version: 7.5.441 / Virus Database: 268.17.37/682 - Release Date: 2/12/2007 1:23 PM
>
> --
> No virus found in this outgoing message.
> Checked by AVG Free Edition.
> Version: 7.5.441 / Virus Database: 268.17.37/682 - Release Date: 2/12/2007 1:23 PM

--
No virus found in this incoming message.
Checked by AVG Free Edition.
Version: 7.5.441 / Virus Database: 268.17.39/686 - Release Date: 2/14/2007 7:54 AM

1

CH-PSI-00003

RICHARD M. CHONG

1 March 2007

Mr. Henri Leimer
Mr. Silvan Colani
Representative
LGT
3 Exchange Square
11th Floor
Central, Hong Kong
Fax no : 852-2868-0059

▬ = Redacted by the Permanent Subcommittee on Investigations

Dear Henri & Silvan,

Please take this memo as instruction to wire US$63,303 (sixty three thousand three hundred and three United States dollars only) from the account number [redacted] to account number [redacted] immediately.

The transfer can begin as soon as possible. Please email me or fax me at 415-[redacted] as soon as this has been completed.

Sincerely,

Richard M. Chong

ACME DIVIDENDS.

176 JORDAN AVENUE • SAN FRANCISCO, CA • 94118
PHONE: 415-982-4910 • FAX: 415-840-0487

CH-PSI-00066

Richard M. Chong

From: Rick [redacted]]
Sent: Thursday, March 01, 2007 5:49 PM
To: 'Chalet@hk.super.net'
Subject: RE: delivery

[redacted] = Redacted by the Permanent Subcommittee on Investigations

Faxed to you today.

Rick

From: Chalet@hk.super.net [mailto:Chalet@hk.super.net]
Sent: Wednesday, February 28, 2007 3:42 AM
To: Richard Chong
Subject: delivery

Dear Rick,

We have received your delivery of 63,303 units to Apex. If you wish to move them to M or R, please fax us a brief instruction letter with your signature.

Thanks & best regards,
Silvan

--
No virus found in this incoming message.
Checked by AVG Free Edition.
Version: 7.5.446 / Virus Database: 268.18.4/703 - Release Date: 2/26/2007 2:56 PM

--
No virus found in this outgoing message.
Checked by AVG Free Edition.
Version: 7.5.446 / Virus Database: 268.18.5/707 - Release Date: 3/1/2007 2:43 PM

1

CH-PSI-00005

Richard M. Chong

From: Chalet@hk.super.net
Sent: Wednesday, April 18, 2007 10:06 PM
To: Rick
Subject: Fw: Apex Assets Limited
Attachments: Schedule K-1.pdf

Dear Rick

Enclosed for your information.

Regards,
Silvan

-----Original Message-----
From: Gloria Ma (KCS Ltd) [mailto:gloria.ma@kcs.com]
Sent: Thursday, April 19, 2007 10:46 AM
To: Colani, Silvan
Cc: Chris Ho (KCS Ltd)
Subject: Apex Assets Limited

Dear Silvan

I have received the Schedule K-1 (Form 1065) from Sycamore Venture Capital, LP for your attention.

<<Schedule K-1.pdf>>
Regards
Gloria Ma

Gloria Ma
Associate Director

KCS Limited
8th Floor, Gloucester Tower, The Landmark
15 Queen's Road Central, Hong Kong

Direct line +852 3589 8822
Direct Fax +852 3589 8522
General Line +852 3589 8899
gloria.ma@kcs.com
www.kcs.com

CH-PSI-00016

KCS

Since 1946

KCS Limited
8th Floor, Gloucester Tower, The Landmark
15 Queen's Road Central, Hong Kong

Tel +852 3689 8899
Fax +852 3689 8555
www.kcs.com

Apex Assets Limited
c/o LGT Bank in Liechtenstein AG
Representative Office Hong Kong
Suite 4203, Two Exchange Square
8 Connaught Place
Central, Hong Kong
Attn: Mr Silvan Colani

Our ref [redacted]

Fee note [redacted]

Date 27/4/2007

[redacted] = Redacted by the Permanent Subcommittee on Investigations

Time spent in liasing with Computershare – Australia regarding the procedures of share transfer and relaying same to the party concerned.

Arranging for the standard transfer form regarding the transfer of the shares of Arasor International Ltd to be signed by the director of the Company and forwarding the signed form to LGT Bank in Liechtenstein AG, Representative Office in Hong Kong, for action.

Updating the Company's record.

Fee for the above	HK$2,200
Disbursements:	
Telephone	2
Total	HK$2,202

PAYMENT METHOD

Direct payment
Send crossed cheque made payable to "KCS Limited" to 8th Floor, Gloucester Tower, The Landmark, 15 Queen's Road Central, Hong Kong together with the remittance advice below.

Direct transfer through bank accounts
Instruct your bank to remit funds by telegraphic transfer to either of our following bank accounts:

Bank: Standard Chartered Bank (Hong Kong) Limited, Shop 16, G/F & Lower G/F, New World Tower, Central, Hong Kong
Account name: KCS Limited
HK$ current a/c [redacted]
US$ savings a/c
Swift code
When making remittance to these accounts please indicate clearly whom the funds are from and our fee note number(s) to enable us to identify them.

Fees are payable on presentation.
KCS Limited is incorporated in the British Virgin Islands with limited liability.

•Hong Kong •Singapore •Shanghai •Beijing •Shenzhen •Jakarta

KCS

Since 1946

KCS Limited
8th Floor, Gloucester Tower, The Landmark
15 Queen's Road Central, Hong Kong

Tel +852 3689 8899
Fax +852 3689 8555
www.kcs.com

REMITTANCE ADVICE

Our ref [redacted]

Client Apex Assets Limited

Fee note number [redacted]

Date 27/4/2007

Amount HK$2,202

CH-PSI-00025

Richard M. Chong

From: Chalet@hk.super.net
Sent: Wednesday, March 21, 2007 11:34 PM
To: Rick
Subject: Re: Apex Assets

Hi Rick,

Gloria has confirmed the holding and is checking how we can transfer the shares into the account of Apex where it can be traded.

I will revert as soon as we know more.

Regards,
Silvan

----- Original Message -----
From: Rick
To: Silvan Colani
Sent: Tuesday, March 20, 2007 6:23 AM
Subject: Apex Assets

Silvan,

I believe that Apex Assets should be holding 214,145 shares of Arasor Intl which is now listed on the Australia stock exchange (symbol : ARR). I believe that these shares are registered and therefore eligible for trading. Can you check with the administrators of Apex Assets to find out about the procedures and costs of beginning to sell these shares?

Thanks,
Rick

--
No virus found in this outgoing message.
Checked by AVG Free Edition.
Version: 7.5.446 / Virus Database: 268.18.14/727 - Release Date: 3/19/2007 11:49 AM

--
No virus found in this incoming message.
Checked by AVG Free Edition.
Version: 7.5.446 / Virus Database: 268.18.16/729 - Release Date: 3/21/2007 7:52 AM

RICHARD M. CHONG

7 March 2006

Mr. Silvan Colani
Representative
LGT
3 Exchange Square
11th Floor
Central, Hong Kong
Fax no : 852-2868-0059

[redacted] = Redacted by the Permanent Subcommittee on Investigations

Dear Henri,

Please take this memo as instructions to transfer US$60,000 (sixty thousand United States dollars only) from the "M" account to Apex Assets and subsequently to the following recipient as soon as possible :

Dynamic Travel Service, Inc.
821 Sacramento Street
San Francisco, CA 94108

Dynamic Travel Service Inc
Bank of America
Chinatown Branch San Francisco
Acct #[redacted]
Routing Number [redacted]

This is payment for travel expenses to be incurred by Apex. Please email me or fax me at 415-[redacted]s soon as this has been completed.

Sincerely,

Richard M. Chong

176 JORDAN AVENUE • SAN FRANCISCO, CA • 94118
PHONE: 415-982-4910 • FAX: 415-840-0487

CH-PSI-00059

LGT Treuhand AG
28 Städtle
FL-9490 Vaduz
Liechtenstein

= Redacted by the Permanent Subcommittee on Investigations

Dear Sirs,

Re: account [redacted] / ref. [redacted]

Please take this letter as your authority to transfer USD 37,500.– from the above account as follows:

Beneficiary's bank: LGT Bank in Liechtenstein, Vaduz
Beneficiary: Apex Assets Ltd.
Account no.: [redacted] / ref. [redacted]

Thereafter, please transfer the funds as follows:

U.S. Trust Company of New York
New York, New York
ABA# [redacted]
For the account of Sycamore Venture Capital, L.P.
Account# [redacted]
Reference: Apex Assets

SVC capital call

Thank you for your attention to this matter.

Yours faithfully,

Date :

CH-PSI-00065

Richard M. Chong

From: Chalet@hk.super.net
Sent: Wednesday, February 20, 2008 9:45 PM
To: Richard Chong
Subject: Update

Dear Rick,

There is some important news that you should be aware of. Please have a look at www.lgt.com

Sonja is currently in Hong Kong. If you wish to discuss, please give me a call.

Best regards,
Silvan

Permanent Subcommittee on Investigations
EXHIBIT #71

CH-PSI-00035

Richard M. Chong

From: Richard Chong [[redacted]]
Sent: Thursday, February 21, 2008 7:12 AM
To: 'Chalet@hk.super.net'
Subject: RE: Update

▬▬ = Redacted by the Permanent Subcommittee on Investigations

Silvan,

Is this disclosure possibly affecting me?

Rick

CH-PSI-00036

GRIFFITH & THORNBURGH, LLP
ATTORNEYS AND COUNSELORS
8 EAST FIGUEROA STREET, SUITE 300
POST OFFICE BOX 9
SANTA BARBARA, CA 93102-0009
TELEPHONE: 805-965-5131
TELECOPIER: 805-965-6751

SUPERIOR COURT OF THE STATE OF CALIFORNIA

IN AND FOR THE COUNTY OF SANTA BARBARA

ANACAPA DIVISION

STEPHANIE MISKIN Plaintiff vs. MICHAEL MISKIN, an individual; BELMONT ASSETS LTD., a Guernsey Trust; and ALL PERSONS CLAIMING AN INTEREST IN THE PROPERTY NAMES AS DOES 1 through 25, incl. Defendants	CASE NO. 01111516 DECLARATION OF MICHAEL MISKIN IN SUPPORT OF MOTION TO QUASH SERVICE OF SUMMONS AND DISMISS ACTION

I, MICHAEL MISKIN, declare:

1. I am a citizen of the United Kingdom. I am a legal resident of Bermuda.

2. I have not been present in the United States, or in the State of California, at any time in calendar year 2003.

3. I have visited Santa Barbara in the past on a tourist visa permitting me to stay for only 90 days in the United States at any one time.

4. I do not now, nor have I ever, owned the property in Santa Barbara commonly known as 68 Seaview Drive. I understand that the property is owned by Belmont Assets Ltd. Although I have in the past acted as an advisor and consultant to Belmont Assets Ltd.. I do not now, nor have I ever owned any interest in that entity.

Permanent Subcommittee on Investigations
EXHIBIT #72

5. I believe that Belmont Assets Ltd. is owned by the Bonnymede Trust which was established in Guernsey. That is an irrevocable trust. The sole beneficiary is "The Royal Masonic Benevolent Institution", a charitable institution for the benefit of poor and distressed free masons. I was not the settlor of the Bonnymede Trust, nor to the best of my knowledge have I ever been either a trustee or a beneficiary of the Bonnymede Trust.

6. I never told Stephanie Miskin that I would acquire 68 Seaview Drive through my personal trust headquartered in Guernsey, or that I would be the beneficial owner of the property. Although Stephanie helped plan renovations to the property, these were undertaken with the permission of Belmont Assets, Ltd and ultimately paid for by Belmont Assets, Ltd.

I declare under penalty of perjury that the foregoing is true and correct. Executed on August 1, 2003 in Jalisco, Mexico.

Michael Miskin

GRIFFITH & THORNBURGH, LLP
ATTORNEYS AND COUNSELORS
8 EAST FIGUEROA STREET, SUITE 300
POST OFFICE BOX 9
SANTA BARBARA, CA 93102-0009
TELEPHONE: 805-965-5131
TELECOPIER: 805-965-6751

John R. Rydell II, 62606

ATTORNEYS FOR: Defendant, Michael Miskin

SUPERIOR COURT OF THE STATE OF CALIFORNIA

IN AND FOR THE COUNTY OF SANTA BARBARA

ANACAPA DIVISION

STEPHANIE MISKIN Plaintiff vs. MICHAEL MISKIN, an individual; BELMONT ASSETS LTD., a Guernsey Trust; and ALL PERSONS CLAIMING AN INTEREST IN THE PROPERTY NAMES AS DOES 1 through 25, incl. Defendants	CASE NO. 01111516 DECLARATION OF MICHAEL MISKIN

I, MICHAEL MISKIN, declare:

1. I am a citizen of the United Kingdom. I am a legal resident of Bermuda.

2. I make this declaration as part of a special appearance challenging the jurisdictin of this court.

3. I have not been present in the United States, or in the State of California, at any time in calendar year 2003. Although I have visited Santa Barbara in past years, I have stayed for less than 90 days and have never been a resident. On occasion, when I have stayed in the Seaview property, my name has been put on the mailbox. I understood that my name was removed on my departure, or shortly thereafter.

4. I thought that my prior declaration made it abundantly clear that I have never owned the property at 68 Seaview Drive in Santa Barbara.

5. I understand that Stephanie Miskin's counsel has stated that there is no reason for me to be a party to this case provided that I "disavow any claim to the real property." Based on the understanding that the court will quash the summons and dismiss me as a party with prejudice, I hereby disavow any claim to 68 Seaview Drive, Santa Barbara, California.

I declare under penalty of perjury that the foregoing is true and correct. Executed on September 4, 2003 in Jalisco, Mexico.

Michael Miskin

JUDITH ILENE BLOOM, SBN 65236
LESLIE R. HOROWITZ, SBN 97630
JAMES E. DANIELS II, SBN 205814
CLARK & TREVITHICK
A Professional Law Corporation
800 Wilshire Boulevard, Twelfth Floor
Los Angeles, California 90017
Telephone: (213) 629-5700
Facsimile: (213) 624-9441

Attorneys for Plaintiff Stephanie Miskin

FILED
SUPERIOR COURT of CALIFORNIA
COUNTY OF SANTA BARBARA
APR - 4 2003
GARY M. BLAIR, EXEC. OFFICER
By Jeff Hite, Deputy Clerk

CLARK & TREVITHICK
800 WILSHIRE BOULEVARD, TWELFTH FLOOR
LOS ANGELES, CA 90017
(213) 629-5700 TELEPHONE • (213) 624-9441 FACSIMILE

SUPERIOR COURT OF THE STATE OF CALIFORNIA

FOR THE COUNTY OF SANTA BARBARA

STEPHANIE MISKIN, Plaintiff, v. MICHAEL MISKIN, an individual; BELMONT ASSETS LTD., a Guernsey Trust; and ALL PERSONS CLAIMING AN INTEREST NAMED AS DOES 1 through 25, inclusive, Defendants.	CASE NO. 01111516 **Assigned to Hon. Thomas P. Anderle** **DECLARATION OF STEPHANIE AVRIL MISKIN IN OPPOSITION TO MOTION TO EXPUNGE LIS PENDENS** **Hearing: 4-15-03** **Dept: 3** **Time: 9:00 a.m.** **Filed: 1-31-03**

Stephanie Avril Miskin declares as follows:

1. I am the plaintiff in this action. I have personal knowledge of the facts stated here in and if called as a witness I am competent to testify thereto.

2. I married defendant Michael Miskin on June 21, 1964 in England. We have been married at all times since then. I filed a petition for divorce with the High Court of Justice Family Division in London, England on January 13, 2003. My petition was assigned case number FD03D00289.

///

Permanent Subcommittee on Investigations
EXHIBIT #73

[redacted] = Redacted by the Permanent Subcommittee on Investigations

3. Michael Miskin was in London in May and June, 2002 during which time he stayed at my house, the address of which is Belmont, [redacted] I have a personal computer at my home with e-mail capability. Michael used my computer for e-mail communications when he was in London. Attached hereto collectively as Exhibit "A" are various communications I was able to retrieve from the hard drive of the computer. I did not create any of these communications and they were clearly sent to and from Michael during his stay in London last year.

4. When Defendant and I married in June 1964, we purchased together our first home which was an apartment in Belmont Court, Whetstone, London, N20. When we sold that apartment and moved to my current home in 1969 Defendant suggested that we gave our new home the name of "Belmont". In 1991 or thereabouts Defendant rented an apartment for his occupation in Santa Barbara. Although I cannot remember its precise address, I do recall that it was within a complex of apartments known either as Montecito Shores or Bonnymead. I do not know if he was still living there when the Bonnymead Trust was formed in 1994.

5. Between 1994 and 1997 Defendant repeatedly expressed his desire to purchase a permanent home in the United States. Together we viewed a number of properties and in late 1997 we jointly selected a beachfront condominium at 68 Seaview Drive in Montecito, Santa Barbara. That is the property that is the subject of this action. The purchase price was about $700,000 although the apartment was in poor condition. Defendant told me he was buying the condominium through his personal trust based in Guernsey of which he was the beneficial owner. I agreed to and did supervise extensive renovations at the condominium. After returning to London in June, 1998 for our younger son's announcement of his engagement and subsequent wedding, I returned to Montecito for New Year's 1999. Defendant told me that once I saw how splendid the condomium looked after the renovations, I might want to stay. While the condomium did look wonderful, I found it necessary to return to London as our marital situation was causing me great distress

6. I have read the supporting declaration of David Anfossi dated 6 March 2003. I am interested that Mr Anfossi should make a declaration of this nature as he is a personal friend of

CLARK & TREVITHICK
800 WILSHIRE BOULEVARD, TWELFTH FLOOR
LOS ANGELES, CA 90017
(213) 629-5700 TELEPHONE • (213) 624-9441 FACSIMILE

Defendant and is a significant link between the Defendant and Bermuda. In recent years both Defendant and I have been entertained to dinner with Mr Anfossi and his wife both in London and in Bermuda. I should explain that perhaps ten years ago Defendant and I were granted Bermudan residency by obtaining a residential address and depositing a substantial sum of money with, I believe, the Bank of Bermuda. The advantage of Bermudan residency to Defendant is that it provided him with a means to enter the United States without being obliged to go through any registration process. Defendant explained to me that all he needed to do was to have with him, at any time when he entered the United States, a return flight to Bermuda. Once his entry had been secured, it was simply a matter, so the Defendant told me, of cancelling the return ticket to Bermuda and securing a refund. This arrangement had the added advantage to Defendant that by virtue of his entry into the United States not being registered, his presence did not come to the attention of any of the US authorities and particularly the Internal Revenue Service. To minimize the risk of his presence as a "permanent resident" becoming known to the IRS, Defendant was scrupulous to ensure that he did not own any real estate, motor vehicle or indeed even hold bank accounts in his own name. This was achieved through the employment of nominee accounts and trust companies.

CLARK & TREVITHICK
800 WILSHIRE BOULEVARD, TWELFTH FLOOR
LOS ANGELES, CA 90017
(213) 629-5700 TELEPHONE • (213) 624-9441 FACSIMILE

7. In our most recent meeting with David Anfossi in London in June 2002, a topic during dinner conversation was Defendant's dissatisfaction with the service which he was receiving from his Guernsey trustees. I specifically recall Mr Anfossi assuring Defendant that the service which would be supplied to him by the Bermudan trustees would be very much to his satisfaction.

8. Defendant claims to have obtained citizenship of Bermuda although I do not know if he still claims British citizenship.

I declare under penalty of perjury under the laws of the State of California that the foregoing is true and correct.

Date: April 1 2003

S. Miskin

Stephanie Avril Miskin

COPY

JUDITH ILENE BLOOM, SBN 65236
LESLIE R. HOROWITZ, SBN 97630
JAMES E. DANIELS II, SBN 205814
CLARK & TREVITHICK
A Professional Law Corporation
800 Wilshire Boulevard, Twelfth Floor
Los Angeles, California 90017
Telephone: (213) 629-5700
Facsimile: (213) 624-9441

Attorneys for Plaintiff Stephanie Miskin

FILED
SANTA BARBARA
SUPERIOR COURT
AUG 2 9 2003
GARY M. BLAIR, EXEC. OFFICER
By [signature]
KRISTI L. RUSSELL, Deputy Clerk

SUPERIOR COURT OF THE STATE OF CALIFORNIA

FOR THE COUNTY OF SANTA BARBARA

STEPHANIE MISKIN,

Plaintiff,

v.

MICHAEL MISKIN, an individual; BELMONT ASSET[...] and ALL PERSONS [...] INTEREST NAME[...] inclusive,

Defen[...]

CASE NO. 01111516
Assigned to Hon. Thomas P. Anderle

OPPOSITION TO MOTION TO QUASH; OBJECTIONS TO EVIDENCE; REQUEST FOR JUDICIAL NOTICE; DECLARATION OF JUDITH ILENE

[...]: **January 31, 2003**

[...] m.

12a.

73

Defendant Mi[...] the complaint because he claims there is no per[...]ggests that he makes no claim to the real property, but carefully stops short of giving a plain statement that eschews any claim to the real property. As the materials submitted in support of the application to serve defendant Miskin by publication shows, he has a significant presence in Santa Barbara, lives and receives mail in Santa Barbara, and it would not be unfair to compel him to respond to the complaint. Of course, if he will provide a plain statement that he makes no claim to the real property, he can be

CLARK & TREVITHICK
800 WILSHIRE BOULEVARD, TWELFTH FLOOR
LOS ANGELES, CA 90017
(213) 629-5700 TELEPHONE • (213) 624-9441 FACSIMILE

dismissed from the case and avoid the expense and trouble of providing a defense.

By way of update, plaintiff reports that the court in England with jurisdiction over the dissolution of marriage has entered an order confirming that plaintiff has full ownership and control of Bonnymead Trust, the sole owner of defendant Belmont. It enjoins defendant Miskin as well as David Anfossi and Douglas Tufts from interfering with her ownership and control. She is in the process of obtaining new management in place of the Anfossi entities. Once that has been completed and defendant Miskin disavows any claim to the real property and questions relating to the purported post-lis pendens deed of trust are resolved, this litigation can be ended. Interestingly, former management of Belmont has discharged counsel and purports to have Belmont appear in proper person. An entity like Belmont must appear through counsel, but new management will either appoint new counsel or the case will simply be dismissed since plaintiff now owns Belmont. A copy of the English order is attached to the Request for Judicial Notice.

Defendant's citation of case law that the burden of proof rests with the plaintiff (accounting for all of the citation of legal authority in the motion) is not meaningful if in fact defendant is a resident of California. Moreover, once plaintiff shows the existence of minimum contacts with California, the burden shifts back to defendant to show that the exercise of jurisdiction over him is unfair, *Integral Dev. Corp. v. Weissenbach*, 99 Cal. App. 4th 576 (2002); *Bridgestone Corp. v. Superior Court*, 99 Cal. App. 4th 767 (2002).

CLARK & TREVITHICK
800 WILSHIRE BOULEVARD, TWELFTH FLOOR
LOS ANGELES, CA 90017
(213) 629-5700 TELEPHONE • (213) 624-9441 FACSIMILE

2.

PLAINTIFF HAS ESTABLISHED GENERAL JURISDICTION OVER DEFENDANT

Defendant's initial claim, that he is a nonresident, has not been established. As the papers provided in support of the application for an order to serve by publication showed, defendant has been living in Santa Barbara for a number of years. His name is on the mailbox of the real property subject of the complaint and his neighbors and the guard at the condominium know him to live there. He had a regular relationship with the adult art center. His website has been full of pictures of Santa Barbara where he brags of his involvement with CHP charities. The fact that he is now visiting Costa Rica or Mexico (where he signed his declaration) does not change his actual residence. His divorce in England was precipitated by his meretricious relationship with California resident Joanna Middleton of Santa Barbara.

Defendant is a resident of Santa Barbara and as such, is subject to the general jurisdiction of the courts in California.

> "The first and most important basis for jurisdiction of the person of an individual is presence within the boundaries of the state. This is true of any person voluntarily within the state, whether he is a permanent resident or a temporary visitor; his presence gives the state power over him." 2 WITKIN, CALIFORNIA PROCEDURE 665 (4th ed. 1996) *citing* RESTATEMENT SECOND CONFLICT OF LAWS § 28.

The Judicial Council Report explained what residence means:

> "Residence is the place where the individual has an abode or where he has settled down to live for a period of time, but not necessarily with an intention of making a home there as to create a domicil.[sic]" Code of Civil Procedure § 410.10 Judicial Council Comment (Residence).

The Miskin declaration is carefully vague as to where he was living and when. His characterization of his presence in Santa Barbara for so many years as "visiting" is disingenuous at best. There are undoubtedly financial advantages, particularly under applicable tax laws, for maintaining a Bermuda residence and moving from country to country. But the plain facts show that Miskin has been living in Santa Barbara for many years. The fact that investigators were unable to find him to serve him personally only means he put more effort than most into hiding. That does not mean he was not living in California and is not subject to California's power.

The law provides that residence alone (residence short of formal domicile) is sufficient to establish jurisdiction. *Id.* at 676. Residence does not require proof of intent, *id.* The factors to consider include (1) amount of time defendant spends in the state; (2) nature of his place of abode in the state; (3) defendant's attitude toward the state; and (4) what defendant does in the state. JUDICIAL COUNCIL 1969 REPORT 73; SECOND RESTATEMENT CONFLICT OF LAWS §30 comment a.

Defendant has failed to provide details as to item (1). But the declarations previously submitted show that defendant Miskin has lived in Santa Barbara for a number of years. He receives mail in Santa Barbara and has his name posted on the mailbox at the real property at issue in the case. Neighbors and condominium guards know him as a resident. He is well-known at the

CLARK & TREVITHICK
800 WILSHIRE BOULEVARD, TWELFTH FLOOR
LOS ANGELES, CA 90017
(213) 629-5700 TELEPHONE • (213) 624-9441 FACSIMILE

art center where he throws pots. His website shows pictures of Santa Barbara and he donates proceeds from local art shows to CHP charities. He lived with the plaintiff in Santa Barbara despite maintaining a Bermuda "residence" for tax avoidance.

The nature of defendant's place of abode is the real property condominium purchased at about $700,000 in an exclusive Montecito development. It is not a motel or other pay-by-the-day temporary lodging.

Defendant's attitude toward the state is difficult to determine and there is nothing in his declaration to enlighten the court.

What defendant does in California is to live, enjoy his retirement, engage in an engrossing ceramics hobby, and control his remaining business affairs.

As a California resident, served (by publication) in California, defendant Miskin is subject to the power of this court and should be held to answer, in the absence of an unambiguous disavowal of any claim to the real property.

CLARK & TREVITHICK
800 WILSHIRE BOULEVARD, TWELFTH FLOOR
LOS ANGELES, CA 90017
(213) 629-5700 TELEPHONE • (213) 624-9441 FACSIMILE

3.

THE COURT HAS SPECIFIC JURISDICTION OVER DEFENDANT

Even if defendant were not a California resident, his activities in California relating to the real property where he lives justifies the assertion of jurisdiction over him in matters relating to that real property. By acting as the owner of the real property and by maintaining control over the real property, he has purposefully availed himself of the benefits of living and owning property in California and should be held to answer here when there is an adverse claim to the real property. It is fair that he be called to answer in California as to his claims to ownership of the real property which is located here and where he has lived for many years. His last minute decision to spend time in Costa Rica does not change the fairness of having him appear in California and prove what claim he may have to the real property. If he makes no claim, he can say so and avoid the litigation.

The ownership or use of property within a state is a basis for jurisdiction against an individual, Code of Civil Procedure §410.10 Judicial Council Comment (Ownership, Use or

Possession of Thing in State).

"A state has power to exercise judicial jurisdiction over an individual who has owned, used or possessed an immovable thing in the state with respect to any cause of action arising from the thing while it was owned, used or possessed by the defendant." *Id.*

The Comment cites the RESTATEMENT for the proposition that an "immovable thing" includes real property and its improvements, *id. citing* RESTATEMENT SECOND §38, Comments a and c. Since the claim arises from competing claims to real property in Santa Barbara and to which plaintiff alleges defendant makes a claim, jurisdiction is entirely proper.

The case law has expanded the scope of what constitutes purposeful availment and what is fair. For example, in *Cornelison v.Chaney*, 16 Cal. 3d 143 (1976), the court approved the exercise of jurisdiction over a nonresident trucker for an accident in Nevada while defendant was en route to California. Even in *Seagate Tech. v. A.J. Kogyo Co., Ltd.*, 219 Cal. App. 3d 696 (1990), a foreign national corporate CEO was found to have sufficient contacts with California because as CEO he caused the corporation to make a guaranty (written in Japanese) that was breached that caused the financial collapse of the trading partner. He never visited California and had nothing to do with the transaction other than authorize the guaranty letter.

Defendant has not provided the court with sufficient information as to his whereabouts and where he claims he has lived all these years. He cannot move for dismissal without explaining why the detailed information previously provided to the court is wrong. Surely he has the information easily available from the court file. In addition, defendant Belmont, who itself had no need for the information, subpoenaed the files of the investigators used by plaintiff. Plaintiff raised no privilege or other objection and the files were duly delivered to Belmont who asked for them only for the use of Miskin. Since there was nothing to challenge in the work done by the investigators, Miskin includes no specific challenge to the declaration provided in support of the application to serve by publication.

///

///

///

CLARK & TREVITHICK
800 WILSHIRE BOULEVARD, TWELFTH FLOOR
LOS ANGELES, CA 90017
(213) 629-5700 TELEPHONE • (213) 624-9441 FACSIMILE

4.

CONCLUSION

Defendant is subject to the jurisdiction of this court. He is a long-time resident of Santa Barbara and the suit involves defendant's rights, if any, to real property within the County where he has lived for many years. There is nothing unfair about compelling defendant either to disavow any claim to the real property or to present his claims here and now.

DATED: August 28, 2003

Respectfully submitted,

CLARK & TREVITHICK

By: ______________________

Judith Ilene Bloom
Attorneys for Plaintiff Stephanie Miskin

CLARK & TREVITHICK
800 WILSHIRE BOULEVARD, TWELFTH FLOOR
LOS ANGELES, CA 90017
(213) 629-5700 TELEPHONE • (213) 624-9441 FACSIMILE

LGT Treuhand
A Member of Liechtenstein Global Trust

LGT Treuhand
Aktiengesellschaft
Städtle 18-22
FL-9490 Vaduz
Fürstentum Liechtenstein

Telephone 41-75-235 27 27
Telefax 41-75-235 27 15
Telex 88 92 27 blt
E-Mail lgttrust@lgtt.lol.li
100653,2664 CompuServe

Aktenvermerk

1/2

Thema	**Neugründung Michel Mistin**
Verfasser(in) / Tel.	Peter Meier
Datum	30. Juni 1998
Zur Erledigung	Daniela Gstöhl
Zur Kenntnisnahme	Dr. Schlachter

GENEHMIGUNG ZUR GRUENDUNG:
Dr. Pius Schlachter

Herr Alois Beck (LGT) bittet mich, Herrn Mistin in Santa Barbara CA (USA) anzurufen, da dieser einige Informationen über eine Stiftung oder einen Trust in FL erfahren möchte.

Herr Mistin hat seinen registrierten Wohnsitz in Bermuda. In den USA ist er „Visitor" und lebt die meiste Zeit in Santa Barbara. Als Resident of Bermuda kann er unlimitiert in USA ein und aus reisen.

Vor ca. einigen Jahren hat er durch den Verkauf seiner Gesellschaft über die Kreditbank in Belgien einen grösseren Gewinn gemacht. Damals lebte er noch in England, als Non Resident. Aus steuerlichen Gründen (ich habe das System nicht verstanden) haben ihm die Buchhalter Tuch & Ross empfohlen, jährlich das Guthaben für die Dauer, dass Netto £ 25.000.-- an Zinsen gutgeschrieben werden, auf das Konto seiner Frau zu buchen. Das Konto wurde von ihm eröffnet und er hatte auch die Unterschrift (ist sich aber nicht mehr ganz sicher). Vor 8 Jahren kam es zu Streit mit seiner Frau und seit dem lebt er getrennt von ihr. Im Verdruss hat er England verlassen und dabei die Bank beauftragt, das Geld an die UBS in Genf zu überweisen. Da wurde festgestellt, dass der Betrag noch auf dem Konto seiner Frau lag. Die Bank hatte seinen Auftrag, nach Gutschrift der Zinsen das Kapital wieder auf sein Konto zu übertragen nicht ausgeführt. Seine Frau hatte Kenntnis von diesen steuerlichen Transaktionen und auch vom nicht ausgeführten Auftrag. Sie benutzte die Gelegenheit und hat Herrn Mistin angeklagt, ihr das Geld gestohlen und das Land fluchtartig verlassen zu haben!!! Daraufhin hat er das Geld von Genf auf die FL Landesbank überweisen lassen. Nachdem aber die Genfer Bank den englischen Anwälten Auskunft erteilten (!!!!!) hat er das Geld in Bar von der Landesbank zur BIL gebracht - das war vor 8 Jahren. Die Klage wurde mittlerweile von seiner Frau zurückgezogen.

Seine Frau ist aber immer noch auf das Geld scharf und möchte sich deshalb nicht scheiden lassen. Der ältere Sohn, selbst im Geschäft sehr erfolgreich, hält eher zur Mutter und der jüngere eher zu ihm, pflegt aber auch guten Kontakt zur Mutter. Damit seine Frau nie Kenntnis von der Stiftung erhält, sollen die Beträge an seinen jüngeren Sohn „anonym" ausgezahlt werden. Der ältere hat selbst etliche Millionen und soll deshalb von der Stiftung nicht begünstigt werden.

Permanent Subcommittee on Investigations
EXHIBIT #74

PSI-USMSTR - 006663

LGT Treuhand
A Member of Liechtenstein Global Trust

Aktenvermerk 2/2

Das Vermögen, derzeit ca. 10 Mio. CHF wurde „schwarz" erwirtschaftet und war immer vom offiziellen getrennt, er rechnet also nicht mit Problemen wegen Pflichtteilsverletzung!!

Ich habe mit Ihm vereinbart, dass er uns per Fax drei Namensvorschläge sendet. Wir senden ihm die vorbereiteten STOM Unterlagen per DHL morgen 1. Juli 1998 an folgende Adresse:
Michael Mistin
68 Seaview Drive
Montecato CA 93108
USA

Falls alle Namensvorschläge besetzt sind, senden wir die Unterlagen ohne Namen.

aqx

PSI-USMSTR - 006664

[logo] LGT Trust
A Member of Liechtenstein Global Trust LGT Trust Tel. 41-75-235 27 27
Corporation Fax 41-75-235 27 15
Städtle 18-22 Telex 88 92 27 bilt
FL-9490 Vaduz E-mail lgttrust@lgtt.lol.li
Fürstentum Liechtenstein 100653,2664 CompuServe

Memorandum for the Record 1 / 2

Subject **New Establishment Michel Misten**

Author Peter Meier (Stamp) APPROVAL FOR ESTABLISHMENT

Date June 30, 1998 (signature)

For action Daniela Gstöhl Dr. Pius Schlachter

Cc Dr. Schlachter (initialed)

Mr. Alois Beck (LGT) asks me to call Mr. Mistin in Santa Barbara, CA (USA), because Mr. Mistin would like to have some information about a foundation or a trust in FL.

Mr. Mistin's registered place of residence is in Bermuda. In the U.S., he is a "visitor" and lives most of the time in Santa Barbara. As a resident of Bermuda, he has unrestricted entry and exit to and from the U.S.

About a few years ago, he made a rather large profit from the sale of his company through the Credit Bank in Belgium. Back then he still lived in England, as a non-resident. For tax reasons (I did not understand how that works), the accounting firm Tuch & Ross recommended that he deposit annually the positive balance, for the time period in which £25,000.00 net gets credited in interest, into the account of his wife. The account was opened, and he had the signature as well (but he's not completely sure anymore). Eight years ago, he and his wife came to a clash, and since then he has been separated from her. Chagrined, he left England, and instructed the bank to transfer the money to UBS in Geneva. That is when it was noticed that the amount is still in his wife's account. The bank had not carried out his instruction to transfer the principal back to his account after the interest was credited. His wife was aware of these tax-related transactions, as well as of the fact that the bank had not carried out her husband's instructions. She took advantage of this opportunity and charged Mr. Mistin with having stolen the money from her and having hastily fled the country!!! Thereupon he had the money transferred from Geneva to the FL Landesbank. But after the Geneva bank disclosed information to the English attorneys (!!!!!) he brought the money from to the BIL in cash - that was 8 years ago. In the meantime, the charge has been withdrawn by his wife.

His wife is still keen on the money, however, and hence does not want to get divorced. The older son, very successful in business himself, is more on his mother's side; the younger son is more on his father's, but maintains good relations with the mother as well. In order to make sure that his wife never finds out about the foundation, the amounts are to be paid to his son "anonymously." The older son has several million himself and will for this reason not benefit from the foundation.

Memorandum for the Record 2 / 2

The assets, currently around 10 million Swiss francs, were earned "under the table" and were always separate from the official, so he is not expecting to encounter problems related to the breach of the disclosure [rules].

We agreed that he will fax us three name suggestions. We will send him the prepared STOM [foundation w/o a mandate] documents via DHL tomorrow, July 1, 1998 to the following address:

Michael Mistin
68 Seaview Drive
Montecato CA 93108
USA

If all suggested names are already taken, we will send the documents without a name.

(signature or initial)

= Redacted by the Permanent Subcommittee on Investigations

Michael Miskin
PO Box 5872 Santa Barbara CA 93150 USA

July 28th[th] 2000
My Ref: MM/MM/PM3

To: Micronesia Foundation
Vaduz, Liechtenstein.

Letter of Wishes

Dear Sirs,

The following is my latest letter of wishes and intentions with respect to the assets of Micronesia Foundation, without binding you to any commitments whatsoever towards myself nor influencing in any way the administration of the foundation. It is rather my attention to detail, my general intent and directives on how assets of the foundation can be best Administered and distributed to the advantage of the beneficiaries. If I should alter my opinion, I will inform you thereof in good time. However should circumstances arise whereby the carrying out of the intent expressed below, or in any later letter, should appear unreasonable, then you should desist from the realisation of such intent.

With consideration of the above, I declare: -

Primary, secondary and tertiary beneficiaries may hereinafter be referred to and are classified by quantum. No monies or assets are to be distributed by the foundation to any beneficiaries until after my demise. In the absence of direction for whatever reason, the cash assets of the foundation are to be invested as previously, in Sterling or US Dollar deposits on one to three month time deposits with prime triple "A" banks only. Following any capital distribution as specified herein, only the yield shall be distributed among the beneficiaries. Should the total sum of the yield to be distributed be greater or lesser than the sums specified below, then the amount allocated to each beneficiary should be treated as a percentage of the whole and thereby increased or decreased on a pro-rata basis. Any real property that may be an asset of the foundation should be liquidated at the discretion of the board of the foundation, having taken reliable advice from two reputable firms of Chartered Surveyors or Realtors, wherever this may apply. All monies that may derive from real estate liquidation must be applied to the cash assets of the foundation.

1st. Primary beneficiary, Stephanie Avril Miskin of "Belmont", [redacted] She shall receive the sum of Sixty Thousand pounds per annum with the first payment being made within thirty days of my demise. She shall not have any rights of inspection and must, for the safety of the foundation and its very existence, be kept totally at arms length. Her legacy shall no longer be paid, in the event that she either decease, re-marry, live with a person as a common law spouse or is considered to be living as such at the discretion of the board of the foundation, or she takes any threatening action against the foundation, or it's servants, agents, representatives or any of the other beneficiaries, for the purpose of challenging the foundation. On her demise, her legacy will pass to [redacted] hereinafter mentioned, in addition to any existing legacy he may have from the foundation at that time.

Page....2

Permanent Subcommittee on Investigations
EXHIBIT #75

[redacted]

PSI-USMSTR - 006653

2nd Primary Beneficiary, [redacted] shall receive the sum of one Hundred Thousand Pounds per annum In the unlikely event that he should not survive, his legacy shall be passed to his wife [redacted] of the same address, provided that they are still husband and wife at the time of his demise and thereafter in any event to his daughter [redacted] shall be allowed to be able to have full access to the affairs of the foundation in my stead, immediately following my demise and not before. He shall be allowed to revise only his subsequent letters of wishes and intentions and only after the specific wishes contained herein have been properly executed.

Secondary beneficiary, [redacted], will receive, upon my demise and before my son [redacted] is given this letter of wishes, the sum of one hundred thousand dollars.

The following tertiary beneficiaries, who like any secondary beneficiaries, have no rights, will receive the sums mentioned immediately upon my demise.

[redacted] will each receive a "One Time" amount in the sum of twenty Thousand Dollars.

The foundation board shall advise beneficiaries to treat sums due to them with the utmost caution in respect of local taxes. The board shall seek out and advise, the best possible way for beneficiaries to receive monies either by debit card or by loan or any other suitable method that should seek to avoid such local taxes. Leaving principle sums allotted to each beneficiary in a company or foundation in Liechtenstein should be recommended. Any beneficiary who takes legal action against the foundation will be automatically excluded from being a beneficiary.

This replaces my previous letter in its absolute entirety.

Yours Faithfully

Michael Miskin

LGT Bank in Liechtenstein
A Member of Liechtenstein Global Trust

LGT Bank in Liechtenstein
Aktiengesellschaft
Herrengasse 12
FL-9490 Vaduz

Telefon +423 235 11 22
Telefax +423 235 15 22
Internet www.lgt.com
E-Mail info@lgt.com

Feststellung der wirtschaftlich berechtigten Person

Ref. ____________

Konto-/Depot-Nr. [redacted]

Vertragspartner Micronesia Foundation, Vaduz

▬ = Redacted by the Permanent Subcommittee on Investigations

Der/Die Unterzeichnete erklärt hiermit,

☐ **dass er/sie selbst an den Vermögenswerten letztlich wirtschaftlich berechtigt ist:**

x **dass an den Vermögenswerten letztlich wirtschaftlich berechtigt ist/sind:**

1. Name(n) Miskin
   Vorname(n) Michael
   Geburtsdatum
   Wohnadresse P.O. Box 5872
   PLZ/Ort Santa Barbara, California 93150
   Domizilland USA
   Nationalität USA

2. Name(n)
   Vorname(n)
   Geburtsdatum
   Wohnadresse
   PLZ/Ort
   Domizilland
   Nationalität

3. Name(n)
   Vorname(n)
   Geburtsdatum
   Wohnadresse
   PLZ/Ort
   Domizilland
   Nationalität

Der Vertragspartner verpflichtet sich, Änderungen der Bank von sich aus umgehend schriftlich mitzuteilen.

Micronesia Foundation

Vaduz, 18. Juli 2001

Ort/Datum

Permanent Subcommittee on Investigations
EXHIBIT #76

PSI-USMSTR - 006652

/- Micronesia - 18.07.2001 - 11,43

For Peter Meyer
[illegible]

Michael Miskin
Ceramics
Santa Barbara, CA.
(805) 565-5672

PSI-USMSTR - 006665

Micronesia Foundation , 9490 Vaduz
SB: Juon Erin **KB: Lungkofler Thomas**

Mand.Nr.: [redacted]
L. Kundenbesuch:

Gründungsdatum: 17.09.1998 Status: Aktiv

[redacted] = Redacted by the Permanent Subcommittee on Investigations

Verwaltungs- / Stiftungsräte

Profile Management Trust reg., Vad	Zeichnungsrecht: Einzeln	einzeln
Telser Marcel, Triesen	Zeichnungsrecht: Kollektiv	koll. zu zweien

Banken

LGT Bank in Liechtenstein AG, Vaduz AB: Beck Alois Tel. 1753 ZR-Nr.: [redacted] Zlg-Kto: [redacted]

Diverses

Anlageberater:	Beck Alois,
Repräsentant:	LGT Treuhand AG, Vaduz
Auftraggeber:	Privater Auftraggeber

Fix-Honorare

Kapitalsteuer	1'000.00	17.09.2002	Liechtensteinische Steuerverwaltung, Vaduz

Pauschal-Honorare

Minimalhonorar	5'500.00	fällig am:	17.09.2002	
Vermögensabh. Hon.	0.00 -	2'500'000.00	0.3750 %	
Vermögensabh. Hon.	2'500'000.01 -	5'000'000.00	0.2500 %	
Vermögensabh. Hon.	5'000'000.01 -	99'999'999'999.0	0.2000 %	
Vermögenswert per:	30.06.2001	9'764'163.00		Fakturierbares Pauschalhonorar: 25'153.00

Zweck

Besitznachweis, Verträge, Vollmachten

Weisungen (Verwaltung, Buchhaltung, Beistatut usw.)

WICHTIG:

Der wirtschaftlich Berechtigte hat seinen WOHNSITZ IN BERMUDA und nicht in der USA. Er bezahlt also keine Steuern in der USA !!!!!!

Pendenzen / Geschichte

"Appointment of a Protector and his authority to act" in der Stellmappe zur Unterschrift vom Kunden und danach erlassen.

Widmungserklärungen in der Stellmappe müssen noch von Dr. Pius Schlachter unterzeichnet werden.

Gemäss Absprachde mit MP ist entgegen den Beistatuten, keine BUC zu führen. Den Kunden beim nächsten Besuch darauf aufmerksam machen und die BST entsprechend ändern.

SR wechsel?

By laws rechtsgültig erlassen? Wo abgelegt?

Passkopie fehlt

Terminvereinbarung für Kundenbesuch dringend

Pendenzen in Stellmappe

[redacted] = Redacted by the Permanent Subcommittee on Investigations

Management Board / Board of Advisors
Profile Management Trust reg., Vad Signatory Rights: Individual Individual
Telser, Marcel, Triesen Signatory Rights: Collective Collective for two

Banks
LGT Bank in Liechtenstein Corp., Vaduz Investment advisor: Beck, Alois Tel. 1753 Ref. No.:[redacted] Account: [redacted]

Miscellaneous
Investment Advisor: Beck, Alois
Representative: LGT Treuhand AG [LGT Trust Corp.], Vaduz
Client: Private Client

Fixed Fees
Capital Taxes: 1,000.00 Sept. 17, 2002 Liechtensteinische Steuerverwaltung, Vaduz
[Tax Authority of Liechtenstein]

Flat Fees
Minimum fee 5,500.00 due on: Sept. 17, 2002
Asset-related fees 0.00 - 2,500,000.00 0.3750%
Asset-related fees 2,500,000.01 - 5,000,000.00 0.2500%
Asset-related fee 5,000,000.01 - 99,999,999,999.00 0.2000%
Value of Assets as of: June 30, 2001 9,764,163.00 Billable Flat Fee: 25,153.00

Purpose

Proof of Ownership, Contracts, Powers of Attorney

Special Instructions (Administration, Accounting, By-laws, etc.)
IMPORTANT:

The financial beneficiary has his PLACE OF RESIDENCE IN BERMUDA and not in the U.S. Hence, he pays no taxes in the U.S. !!!!!!

Comments/History
"Appointment of a Protector and his authority to act" in the stand-up folder for client's signature, and subsequent authorization.

Dedication declarations in the stand-up folder still need to be signed by Dr. Pius Schlachter.

According to consultation with MP, contrary to the by-laws, no accounting is to be done. Alert the client to this during his next visit, and change the by-laws accordingly.

Board of trustee change?

By-laws legally enacted? Filed where?

Passport copy is missing

Date for client visit urgently needed

Comments in the stand-up folder

▬ = Redacted by the Permanent Subcommittee on Investigations

LGT Bank in Liechtenstein
A Member of Liechtenstein Global Trust

LGT Bank in Liechtenstein Aktiengesellschaft
Herrengasse 12 Telefon 075 235 11 22
FL-9490 Vaduz Telefax 075 235 15 22

Bitte mit Valuta 21. Oktober 1998 ausführen.
Bitte danach Konto löschen !!

Barbezug dgs 2649
[redacted] GBP-Konto
GBP ~~3'671'814.00~~ (gem. Tel. Mit J. Bühler)
3'650'314.- Franko

Vaduz, 21.10.1998 / 08.11

AUSZ[illegible]NG
FRANKO

Mr.
Michael Miskin

1155 Hill Road
Santa Barbara CA 93108

[redacted]
Kontokorrent GBP
GBP ACCOUNT

PFUND STERLING	GBP	3.650.314,00
WIR BELASTEN IHR KONTO MIT VALUTA 21.10.1998 per Saldo	GBP	3.650.314,00

UNTERSCHRIFT 0012 0005 01 01 D1

Michael Miskin

LGT Bank in Liechtenstein
Aktiengesellschaft
Moser Helene

KA 5196 0196 40T 00

Permanent Subcommittee on Investigations
EXHIBIT #77

PSI-USMSTR - 006656

MMMag. Thomas Lungkofler

Fax

Date	February 27, 2002 / TLU	Pages	1 (incl. cover sheet)
Subject			
From	MMMag. Thomas Lungkofler	Telefax	00423 235 27 15
		Telephone	00423 235 26 86
To	Mr. Michael Miskin	Telefax	001 805 969 6141

Dear Mr. Miskin,

Thank you very much for your fax of February 23, 2002 and for the patience you had.

In the meantime I have spoken with an expert for structures of the area of G. It turned out that with respect to the tax situation in the US-area a re-domiciliation of the company to another jurisdiction would not be advisable and would additionally take a very long time. Therefore at least the company's seat has to remain in G. But it is possible to transfer the domicile of the trust as well as the representative office. In that case our suggestion would be to transfer the whole structure including the holding to a much more co-operative trust company as a representative office on the Isle of Man. This office being an office of high reputation would provide us with a nominee shareholder for the shares of the company and also will support us in taking over and administrating the company as new trust officers in direct co-operation with us.

The holding (trust) would be transferred with the help of the corresponding office mentioned above to our company. Then either we administer the trust under our law for the future as it is or we even change the trust into a discretionary one with the foundation being the beneficiary. Doing so, the great advantages of a discretionary structure could be used. So from outside nothing really changes but the aim to implement the existing structure into the foundation would be reached as well as a better service could be provided to the client.

It would also be possible to transfer the ownership of the company from the trust directly to the foundation. Then the foundation would hold the company via the nominee shareholder provided by the corresponding office.

The remaining issue is to know if the trust settlement allows a transfer of the domicile. If not, the trust settlement has to be amended.

I would like to inform you that after you having decided to execute the transfer all the necessary details will be arranged by us. In case you have any further questions or comments, do not hesitate to contact me. I am looking forward to hearing from you and I would appreciate it if you could call me at your earliest convenience so that we can discuss some further details.

Yours sincerely

Thomas Lungkofler

Permanent Subcommittee on Investigations
EXHIBIT #78

PSI-USMSTR - 006657

Richard M. Chong

From: Chalet@hk.super.net
Sent: Thursday, February 21, 2008 7:41 PM
To: Richard Chong
Subject: Re: Update

Hi Rick,

Yes, I'm afraid we have to assume the possibility.

Silvan

----- Original Message -----
From: Richard Chong
To: Chalet@hk.super.net
Sent: Thursday, February 21, 2008 11:12 PM
Subject: RE: Update

Silvan,

Is this disclosure possibly affecting me?

Rick

CH-PSI-00037

Richard M. Chong

From: Chalet@hk.super.net
Sent: Thursday, February 21, 2008 8:16 PM
To: Richard Chong
Subject: Re: Update

Suggest you urgently seek local advice.

Worst case, we must assume that all files up to 2002 are out.

I'm very sorry. Sonja is here if you wish to discuss.

Silvan

CH-PSI-00038

= Redacted by the Permanent Subcommittee on Investigations

Richard M. Chong

From: Sprenger Sonja [sonja.sprenger@lgt.com]
Sent: Thursday, March 13, 2008 6:43 AM
To: [redacted]
Cc: Peter Xenia; Colani, Silvan
Subject: AW: Lawyer recommendation

Dear Richard

Following our yesterday's telephone conversation I have made enquines, and wish to inform you of the findings as follows:

After having consulted with Mr. Falk regarding conflict of interest issues we had put him on our list of counsels who we generally refer client isssues to, because we appreciate the quality of his advice. Mr. Falk was of the clear opinion that his representation of you would not conflict with advice he has given LGT group companies in US tax matters beforehand. Mr. Falk's law firm has now reviewed the situation in detail and came to the conclusion that Mr. Falk's representation of you in this matter could raise potential conflicts. Mr. Falk's office apologises for any inconvenience this may have caused to you.

I also want to emphasize that it is your free decision whether you want to keep Mr. Falk as your representative. Otherwise please feel free to contact the other counsel recommended to you below.

Please do not hesitate to contact me if you need more information in this respect.

Best regards
Sonja

-----Ursprüngliche Nachricht-----
Von: Sprenger Sonja
Gesendet: Donnerstag, 13. März 2008 13:13
An: 'rchong@[redacted]
Cc: Peter Xenia; Colani, Silvan
Betreff: Lawyer recommendation

Dear Richard

Following our telephone conversation, please find the name and contact details of a San Francisco based lawyer:

Heller Ehrman LLP
Brett R. Dick
333 Bush Street
San Francisco, CA 94104-2878
USA
Tel. +1 415 772 6394
Fax. +1 415 772 6268
E-Mail: brett.dick@hellerehrman.com

Please do not hesitate to contact me if you need more information in this respect.

Best regards
Sonja

LGT Treuhand AG
Stadtle 28

CH-PSI-00039

P.O. Box 683
FL-9490 Vaduz
Phone +423 235 27 27, Fax +423 235 27 15
Mail: lgt.trust@lgt.com
Web: http://www.lgt.com

Sera Financial Corporation Road Town , Tortola / B.V.I. Mand.Nr.: TH - 68062
SB: Bösch Wolfgang **KB: Bösch Wolfgang** L. Kundenbesuch:

Gründungsdatum: 15.12.1997 Status: Aktiv

[redacted] = Redacted by the Permanent Subcommittee on Investigations

Verwaltungs- / Stiftungsräte

BTS Management Ltd., Tortola / B. Zeichnungsrecht: Einzeln

Banken

LGT Bank in Liechtenstein AG, Vaduz	AB: Ritter Yvonne	ZR-Nr.: [redacted]	Zlg-Kto: [redacted]
Banque du Gothard, Luxembourg	AB: Horst Bartsch	ZR-Nr.: [redacted]	Zlg-Kto:
LGT Bank in Liechtenstein AG, Vaduz	AB: Ritter Yvonne	ZR-Nr.: [redacted]	Zlg-Kto:
~~LGT Bank in Liechtenstein AG, Vaduz~~	~~AB: Ritter Yvonne~~	~~ZR-Nr.:~~ [redacted]	~~Zlg-Kto:~~
LGT Bank in Liechtenstein AG, Vaduz	AB: Ritter Yvonne	ZR-Nr.: [redacted]	Zlg-Kto:
LGT Bank in Liechtenstein AG, Vaduz	AB: Ritter Yvonne	ZR-Nr.: [redacted]	Zlg-Kto:
LGT Bank in Liechtenstein AG, Vaduz	AB: Ritter Yvonne	ZR-Nr.: [redacted]	Zlg-Kto:
LGT Bank in Liechtenstein AG, Vaduz	AB: Ritter Yvonne	ZR-Nr.: [redacted]	Zlg-Kto:
LGT Bank in Liechtenstein AG, Vaduz	AB: Ritter Yvonne	ZR-Nr.: [redacted]	Zlg-Kto:
LGT Bank in Liechtenstein AG, Vaduz	AB: Ritter Yvonne	ZR-Nr.: [redacted]	Zlg-Kto:
LGT Bank in Liechtenstein AG, Vaduz	AB: Ritter Yvonne	ZR-Nr.: [redacted]	Zlg-Kto:
LGT Bank in Liechtenstein AG, Vaduz	AB: Ritter Yvonne	ZR-Nr.: [redacted]	Zlg-Kto:

Diverses

Anlageberater:	Ritter Yvonne,
Aktien / Zessionen:	Dossier / Gesellschaftsakt,
Repräsentant:	Trident Trust Comp. (BVI) Ltd., Tortola, B

Fix-Honorare

Pauschal-Honorare

0.00 fällig am:
Vermögenswert per: 0.00 Fakturierbares Pauschalhonorar: 0.00

Zweck

Spezialgesellschaft (indirekte Tochter der LTV) für Portfoliotransfers für Vermögenswerte, welche in eine LTV-Struktur eingebracht werden.

Besitznachweis, Verträge, Vollmachten

Weisungen (Verwaltung, Buchhaltung, Beistatut usw.)

Zuständige Personen bei der LTV sind MTE und SRE, bei der Banque du Gothard (BdG) Herr Germain Rubbini.

SEHR WICHTIG: LGT-BIL HAUPTNUMMER DARF NICHT FÜR TRANSAKTIONEN VERWENDET WERDEN; NUR FÜR UNTERSCHRIFTENREGELUNG ERÖFFNET.

Abwicklungsprozedere:

1. Es muss vorgängig eine Aufstellung der zu transferierenden Vermögenswerte sowie ein unterzeichneter und durch den KB visierter Vertrag vorliegen. Die Sorgfaltspflicht/Herkunft der Gelder wird vom entsprechenden KB wahrgenommen.

2. Für jeden Kunden wird ein unter einer Referenz ein Unterkonto bzw. Depot bei der BdG und bei der LGT BIL eröffnet- und zwar bei der LGT-BIL und bei BdG. Jedes Unterkonto den wir Horst Bartsch mitteilen müssen ('Referenz'); das LGT-BIL Konto ist wie 'üblich' (gemäss Muster) zu eröffnen.

3. Geldtransfers sowie Titellieferungen an dei BdG gehen z.G. SERA, Ref.... Die BdG wird angewiesen die Barwerte und Wertpapiere unverzüglich an LGT BIL weiterzuleiten, zu Gunsten Sera Financial Corp. unter Angabe der Referenz.

4. Sobald die Vermögenswerte bei der BIL gutgeschrieben sind, werden sie valutagerecht auf das Destinationskonto (siehe Vert[illegible] [illegible]r Regel über einen Barbezug. Auf dem Barbezug-/Bareinzahlu[illegible] Agio/Disagio verrechnet

Permanent Subcommittee on Investigations
EXHIBIT #79

PSI-USMSTR - 006553

Sera Financial Corporation Road Town , Tortola / B.V.I. Mand.Nr.: TH - 68062
SB: Bösch Wolfgang **KB: Bösch Wolfgang** L. Kundenbesuch:

Gründungsdatum: 15.12.1997 Status: Aktiv

werden
darf ('spesenfrei').

5. Ueberträge auf die BdG sind immer z.G. der Sera Financial unter Angabe der Referenz z.Hd. Hr. Germain Rubbini zu tätigen.

Das Aktienzertifikat befindet sich im Depot der BTS Management Ltd. bei der LGT Bank ~~in Liechtenstein AG, Vaduz (seit 9.4.1999).~~

Pendenzen / Geschichte
Pendenzen sind auf den jeweiligen Uebersichtslisten (im jeweiligen physichen Akt) ersichtlich.

PSI-USMSTR - 006554

[redacted] = Redacted by the Permanent Subcommittee on Investigations

Translation of German original. Translator comments in brackets < >.

Sera Financial Corporation Road Town, Tortola / B.V.I.

Mand.No.: TH -68062
L. customer visit:

SB: Bösch Wolfgang **KB: Bösch Wolfgang**
Establishment date: Dec 15, 1997 Status: Active

Administrative board / board of trustees

BTS Management Ltd., Tortola / B. Signature authority: individual

Banks

LGT Bank in Liechtenstein AG, Vaduz	AB: Ritter Yvonne	ZR-No.: [redacted]	Paymt. Acc.: [redacted]
Banque du Gothard, Luxembourg	AB: Horst Bartsch	ZR-No.: [redacted]	Paymt. Acc.:
LGT Bank in Liechtenstein AG, Vaduz	AB: Ritter Yvonne	ZR-No.: [redacted]	Paymt. Acc.:
LGT Bank in Liechtenstein AG, Vaduz	AB: Ritter Yvonne	ZR-No.: [redacted]	Paymt. Acc.:
LGT Bank in Liechtenstein AG, Vaduz	AB: Ritter Yvonne	ZR-No.: [redacted]	Paymt. Acc.:
LGT Bank in Liechtenstein AG, Vaduz	AB: Ritter Yvonne	ZR-No.: [redacted]	Paymt. Acc.:
LGT Bank in Liechtenstein AG, Vaduz	AB: Ritter Yvonne	ZR-No.: [redacted]	Paymt. Acc.:
LGT Bank in Liechtenstein AG, Vaduz	AB: Ritter Yvonne	ZR-No.: [redacted]	Paymt. Acc.:
LGT Bank in Liechtenstein AG, Vaduz	AB: Ritter Yvonne	ZR-No.: [redacted]	Paymt. Acc.:
LGT Bank in Liechtenstein AG, Vaduz	AB: Ritter Yvonne	ZR-No.: [redacted]	Paymt. Acc.:
LGT Bank in Liechtenstein AG, Vaduz	AB: Ritter Yvonne	ZR-No.: [redacted]	Paymt. Acc.:
LGT Bank in Liechtenstein AG, Vaduz	AB: Ritter Yvonne	ZR-No.: [redacted]	Paymt. Acc.:

Miscellaneous

Investment advisor <AB>: Ritter Yvonne,
Shares / assignments: dossier / company act,
Representative: Trident Trust Comp. (BVI) Ltd., Tortola, B

Fixed fees

Flat fees

Asset value per:	0.00	due on: 0.00	Billable flat fee: 0.00

Purpose

Special purpose company (indirect subsidiary of LTV) for portfolio transfers for assets which are to be brought into an LTV structure.

Proof of ownership, agreements, powers of attorney

Instructions (administration, accounting, bylaws, etc.)

Responsible persons at LTV are MTE and SRE, at Banque du Gothard (BdG) Mr. Germain Rubbini.

VERY IMPORTANT: LGT-BIL PRIMARY NUMBER MUST NOT BE USED FOR TRANSACTIONS; OPENED ONLY FOR SIGNATURE REGULATION.

Processing procedure:

1. A list of the assets to be transferred as well as a signed agreement approved by the KB must first be available. Due diligence/origin of the funds is administered by the respective KB.

2. For each customer, a sub-account or deposit facility is opened under a reference at BdG and at LGT <problem with sentence in German> BIL - namely, at LGT-BIL and at BdG. Each sub-account <problem with sentence in German> that we must communicate to Horst Bartsch ("reference"); the LGT-BIL account is to be opened as "usual" (according to model).

3. Funds transfers as well as security deliveries to BdG are in favor of SERA, Ref.... BdG is instructed to forward cash values and securities without delay to LGT BIL in favor of Sera Financial Corp. with specification of the reference.

4. As soon as the assets are credited at BIL, they are transferred to the destination account (see agreement) on value date. This occurs as a rule per cash withdrawal. On cash withdrawal/deposit slip, there should be a note that no agio/disagio may be calculated

<Alternate Translation, bullet #2, PSI-USMSTR-6553>

2. For each customer, a sub-account or deposit facility is opened under a reference at BdG and at LGT-BIL We must communicate each sub-account to Horst Bartsch ("reference"); the LGT-BIL account is to be opened as "usual" (according to model).

Sera Financial Corporation Road Town, Tortola / B.V.I. Mand.No.: TH -68062

SB: Bösch Wolfgang **KB: Bösch Wolfgang** L. customer visit:

Establishment date: Dec 15, 1997 Status: Active

("free of charge").

5. Balances to BdG are always to be transferred in favor of Sera Financial with specification of the reference addressed to Mr. Germain Rubbini.

The share certificate is held in the depository account of BTS Management Ltd. at LGT Bank in Liechtenstein AG, Vaduz (since Apr 9, 1999)

Tasks / history

Tasks can be seen in the respective overview lists (in each physical act).

LGT Treuhand
A Member of Liechtenstein Global Trust

LGT Treuhand
Aktiengesellschaft
Städtle 18+22
FL-9490 Vaduz
Fürstentum Liechtenstein
MWST-Nr. 50119

Telefon +423 235 27 27
Telefax +423 235 27 15
Internet
www.lgt.com/lgttreuhand
E-Mail lgttrust@lgt.com

Aktenvermerk

1/2

Thema	**NEUGRÜNDUNG**
Verfasser(in) / Tel.	Christina Meusburger
Datum	2. November 2000 / cho
Zur Erledigung	Rahel Kieber-Fuchs, Corina Hohl, Gruppe Support
Zur Kenntnisnahme	Dr. Pius Schlachter

1. Allgemeines

Der Neukunde Herr Burt Kroner besucht uns am 20. Oktober 2000. Der Kontakt zu Burt Kroner kam über Vermittlung eines langjährigen Kunden der LGT Treuhand, Herrn Anthony Mitchell, zustande. Herr Kroner ist US-Passport-Holder und wohnt in Florida. Herr Kroner möchte seine bei der UBS Zürich liegenden Vermögenswerte, zumindest teilweise, in einen Trust einbringen. Die Bankbeziehung zur UBS Zürich unterhält Herr Kroner seit ca. 3 Jahren.

2. Sorgfaltspflicht

Herr Kroner übermittelt eine umfangreiche Dokumentation aus der die Herkunft seiner Vermögenswerte erklärbar ist.

Zusammen mit Herrn Mitchell gründete Herr Kroner im April 1993 die Singer Assets Finance Corporation, deren Geschäftsgegenstand es ist, Lotterien anzukaufen und an eine AAA Rated Insurance Company weiterzuverkaufen. Diese AAA Rated Insurance Company, die unter dem Namen "Enhance Financial Services Group" betrieben wird, erwarb im Jahre 1995 einen 50% Anteil an der Singer Asstes Finance Corporation. Für diese 50% zahlte Enhance im Jahr 1995 4,25 Mio USD. Zwei Jahre später, 1997 erwarb Enhance weitere 37.5% an Singer. Diesmal für 16 Mio USD und 6 Monate später die restlichen 12.5% für 5.33 Mio USD. Zu diesen Vorgängen übergibt mir Burt Kroner folgende Unterlagen:

- einen Artikel aus dem WallStreet Journal vom 24.3.1997 in dem berichtet wird, dass Enhance weitere 37,5% an Singer erworben hat.
- Annual Report 1994 von Enhance Financial Services Group Incorp., von diesem Jahresbericht mache ich eine Kopie jener Seite auf der über den Ankauf von diskontierten Lotteriegewinnen berichtet wird.
- Annual Report der Enhance Financial Services Group aus dem Jahr 1996. Hier wird wiederum über Singer Assets Finance Company berichtet.

In Anbetracht der verfügbaren Informationen bestehen keine Bedenken gegen die Entgegennahme der Vermögenswerte.

PSI-USMSTR - 007696

LGT Treuhand

Aktenvermerk

2/2

3. Lösungsansatz

Ich erläutere eingehend Stiftung und Trust, wobei sich Herr Kroner schliesslich für einen liechtensteinischen Trust entscheidet. In diesen Trust wird Herr Kroner jene Vermögenswerte einbringen, die derzeit bei der UBS Zürich liegen und nicht in US-Securities investiert sind. Insgesamt handelt es sich dabei um ein Volumen von ca. 1.2 Mio USD.

Der Trust soll ein Konto bei der LGT Bank in Liechtenstein eröffnen. Auf dieses Konto soll der Übertrag des Vermögens stattfinden. Um die Spur von der UBS Zürich zum liechtensteinischen Trust abzuschneiden, empfehle ich die Zwischenschaltung einer Single Purpose Company. Herr Kroner scheint ein sehr vorsichtiger Mensch zu sein und ist auch in Anbetracht der relativ hohen Gebühren im Verhältnis zu den einzubringenden Vermögenswerten (CHF 10'000.–) damit einverstanden.

4. US-Person

Herr Kroner unterzeichnet den von Baker McKenzie entworfenen Indemnification Letter.

5. Details zum Trust

Weiters unterzeichnet Herr Kroner folgende Unterlagen:

- Auftrag an die LGT Trust Management Limited einen Trust zu errichten mit Gründungshonorar CHF 5'000.-- und jährlichem Honorar von 0.4% der Assets under Trust
- Declaration of Due Diligence
- Power of Attorney zu Gunsten von Herrn Anthony Mitchell, Herr Mitchell ist Instruktionsberechtigter des Trusts
- Letter of Wishes - solange Herr Kroner lebt, soll er am Trustgut begünstigt sein. Nach seinem Ableben soll sein Testament, das sich bei Herrn Mitchell befindet, Grundlage für die Begünstigung sein.

6. Antrag an die Geschäftsleitung

Ich ersuche die Geschäftsleitung um Genehmigung zur Gründung des beschriebenen Trusts.

1) Bankstatements UBS 31.12.99+98
2) Seriosität der Lotterie muss sich aus den Unterlagen ergeben
3) Freistellungserklärung Baker McKenzie für US-Steuer

Antrag bewilligt:

Dr. Pius Schlachter

15.11.00

PSI-USMSTR - 007697

[company logo] LGT Trust LGT Trust Telephone + 423 235 27 27
A member of Liechtenstein Global Trust Corporation Telefax + 423 235 27 15
Staedtle 18+22 Internet
Fl-9490 Vaduz www.lgt.com/lgttreuhand
Fuerstentum Liechtenstein Email lgttrust@lgt.com
MWST-Nr. 50119

Memorandum for the record 1/2

Subject New Registration

Sender/Tel. Christina Meusburger

Date 2.November 2000/ cho

To: Rahel Kieber-Fuchs, Corina Hohl, Group Support

CC: Dr. Pius Schlachter [initialed]

1. General

The new client, Mr. Burt Kroner, visits us on 20 October 2000. The contact with Burt Kroner was facilitated by a long time client of LGT Trust, Mr. Anthony Mitchell. Mr. Kroner is a US passport holder and lives in Florida. Mr. Kroner wishes to place his assets, currently with UBS Zurich, at least partially, in a trust fund in the. Mr. Kroner's has had a banking relationship to UBS Zurich for approximately three years.

2. Liabilities

Mr. Kroner hands over extensive documentation from which the origin of his assets can be traced.

Together with Mr. Mitchell, Mr. Kroner founded the Singer Assets Finance Corporation in April 1993, whose business purpose is to purchase lotteries and then resell them to an AAA Rated Insurance Companies. These AAA Rated Insurance Companies, which operate under the name "Enhance Financial Services Group," acquired a 50% share in the Singer Asstes [sic] Finance Corporation in the year 1995. In 1995, Enhance paid 4,25 million USD for this 50%. Two years later in 1997, Enhance acquired a further 37.5% in Singer. For this, Enhance paid 16 million USD and six months later acquired the remaining 12.5% for 5.33 million USD. Relative to this course of action, Burt Kroner hands over to me the following records:

- an Article from the Wall Street Journal dated 3.24.1997 reported that Enhance had acquired a further 37.5% in Singer.
- Enhance Financial Services Group Incorporated 1994 annual report, of which I am making a copy of every page on which the purchase of discontinued lottery winnings is discussed.
- Enhance Financial Services Group Annual Report from the year 1996 where, again, Singer Assets Finance Company is mentioned.

In consideration of the available information, there remain no concerns against the acceptance of the assets.

[logo] LGT Trust

Memorandum for the record 2/2

3. Solutions

I explain in detail foundation and trust, whereby Mr. Kroner decides on a Liechtenstein-based trust. Mr. Kroner will transfer all the assets currently held in the UBS Zurich and that are not invested in US securities, to this trust. Collectively, this amounts to approximately 1.2 million US dollars.

The trust shall open an account in the LGT Bank in Liechtenstein. The transfer of assets should take place using this account. To cover up the tracks from UBS Zurich to the trust in Liechtenstein, I recommend an intermediary Single Purpose Company. Mr. Kroner appears to be a very careful individual and seems to also be in agreement to the relatively high fees (CHF 10,000) related to the incoming assets.

4. US-Persons

Mr. Kroner undersigns Indemnification Letter drafted by Baker McKenzie.

5. Details of the Trust

Furthermore, Mr. Kroner undersigns the following records:

- Request to LGT Trust Management Limited to establish a trust with foundation fees of CHF 5,000,-- and annual fees of 0.4% of the Assets under Trust
- Declaration of due diligence
- Power of Attorney in support of Mr. Anthony Mitchell, Mr. Mitchell is individual holding power of attorney to give instructions of the trust.
- Letter of Wishes – as long as Mr. Kroner is alive, he shall be beneficiary of the trust. After his passing, his will, which Mr. Mitchell has, shall serve as the foundation for the nomination of beneficiaries.

6. Request to the General Management

I seek out approval of the general management to acceptance of the establishment of the aforementioned trust.

Contract agreed:
[handwriting/notes:]

1. Bankstatements UBS 12.31.99 + 98
2. [unable to decipher]
3. [unable to decipher]

[signature]

Dr. Pius Schlachter

Document Properties	

Gotthard Bank
Niederlassung Luxemburg
6, Avenue Maria-Thérèse
L-2132 Luxemburg

[redacted] = Redacted by the Permanent Subcommittee on Investigations

Feststellung des wirtschaftlich Berechtigten

Betreff: Überweisung/Einzahlung/Scheckeinreichung/WertschriftenÜbertrag

in Höhe von ca. USD 1'200'000.--

zu Gunsten Konto Nr. [redacted]

lautend auf Sera Financial Corporation, B.V.I.

Rubrik (falls gegeben) [redacted]

bei Banque du Gothard, Succursale de Luxembourg

Datum der Transaktion bis spätestens 31.12.2000

Der/die Unterzeichnete, BTS Management Limited, Tortola, als Direktor der Gesellschaft Sera Financial Corporation, Tortola, B.V.I.

erklärt hiermit:

☒ dass folgende Person(en) an der obengenannten Transaktion wirtschaftlich berechtigt ist/sind:

Name/Vorname: [redacted]

Geburtsdatum/-ort: [redacted]

wohnhaft in: Boca Raton, FL33496, USA

☐ dass die eingebrachten Werte rechtmässigen Ursprungs sind und weder aus Drogen - oder Waffenhandel stammen noch aus anderen Verbrechen oder Vergehen.

Der/Die Unterzeichnete nimmt davon Kenntnis, dass die Bank den Behörden gegenüber zum Zeugnis und zur Auskunft verpflichtet ist, soweit Bestimmungen der luxemburgischen Gesetzgebung dies vorsehen.

BTS MANAGEMENT LTD.

Ort und Datum: Vaduz, 31.10.00/soh

NFE
Unterschrift

Anlage: Kopie Ausweispapier des/der wirtschaftlich Berechtigten

PSI-USMSTR - 007680

[redacted] = Redacted by the Permanent Subcommittee on Investigations

Gotthard Bank
Luxemburg Branch Office
6, Avenue Maire-Therese
L-2131 Luxemberg

Statement of Beneficiary

~~Subject: e-transfer / deposit / check / transfer of securities~~
In the amount of: approx. USD 1,200,000
To account nr.[redacted]
Account holder: Sera Financial Corporation, B.V.I.
Rubric (if appl.) [redacted]
Bank du Gothard, Succursale de Luxembourg
Date of Transaction no later than 12/31/2000

The undersigned, BTS Management Limited, Tortola, as Managing Director of the company Sera Financial Corporation, Tortola, B.V.I

Hereby declares:

X that the following beneficiary(ies) is/are entitled to the above-referenced transaction:

Last name / First name: [redacted]
DOB: [redacted]
Resident in: Boca Raton, FL 33496, USA

☐ that the assets in question are of rightful origin and do not stem from illegal drug or weapons trade or other criminal activities.

The undersigned understands that the bank is obligated to provide the competent authorities with information upon request in so far as provided by Luxemburg legislation.

Place / Date: Vaduz, 10/31/00 / soh BTS Management LTD
NFE
Signature

Attachment: copy of beneficiary's personal ID

Jaffra Development Inc. --> gelöscht am 23.07.2001 , Tort Mand.Nr.: [redacted]
SB: Bösch Wolfgang **KB: Bösch Wolfgang** L. Kundenbesuch:

Gründungsdatum: 16.05.2000 Status: Gelöscht

[redacted] = Redacted by the Permanent Subcommittee on Investigations

Verwaltungs- / Stiftungsräte
BTS Management Ltd., Tortola / B. Zeichnungsrecht: Kollektiv

Banken
LGT Bank in Liechtenstein AG, Vaduz AB: Ritter Yvonne ZR-Nr.:[redacted]Zlg-Kto:

Diverses

Anlageberater:	Ritter Yvonne,
Aktien / Zessionen:	Dossier / Gesellschaftsakt,
Repräsentant:	Morgan & Morgan Trust, British Virgin Isl

Fix-Honorare

Pauschal-Honorare
0.00 fällig am:
Vermögenswert per: 0.00 Fakturierbares Pauschalhonorar: 0.00

Zweck
Single Purpose Gesellschaft

Besitznachweis, Verträge, Vollmachten

Weisungen (Verwaltung, Buchhaltung, Beistatut usw.)

Pendenzen / Geschichte

Permanent Subcommittee on Investigations
EXHIBIT #80

PSI-USMSTR - 007934

Jaffra Development Inc. > cancelled on 07.23.2001, Tort
Assistant: Bösch, Wolfgang **Account Manager: Bösch, Wolfgang**

Client Number: [redacted]
Last Client Visit:

Date Established: 05.16.2000 Status: Cancelled

[redacted] = Redacted by the Permanent Subcommittee on Investigations

Management / Board of Advisors
BTS Management Ltd., Tortola / B. Signatory Rights: Collective

Banks
LGT Bank in Liechtenstein Corp., Vaduz Contact: Ritter, Yvonne Ref. No.: [redacted] Account:

Miscellaneous

Investment Advisor:	Ritter, Yvonne
Shares / Transfers:	Dossier / Corporation File
Representative:	Morgan & Morgan Trust, British Virgin Islands

Fixed Fees

Flat Fees

Value of Assets per: 0.00 due on: 0.00 Billable Flat Fee: 0.00

Purpose
single purpose corporation

Proof of Ownership, Contracts, Powers of Attorney

Special Instructions (Administration, Accounting, Bylaws, etc.)

Comments/History

Vereinbarung

[redacted] = Redacted by the Permanent Subcommittee on Investigations

Dieter Noack, Via Moscia 61, 6612 Ascona / TI

als Auftraggeber

und

JAFFRA DEVELOPMENT INC., Road Town, Tortola, B.V.I.

als Auftragnehmerin

Präambel

Die Auftragnehmerin ist eine indirekte Tochtergesellschaft der LGT Treuhand Aktiengesellschaft, Städtle 18, FL-9490 Vaduz, welche ihrerseits eine 100%ige Tochtergesellschaft der LGT Bank in Liechtenstein AG, Vaduz, ist.

Einziger Verwaltungsrat der Auftragnehmerin ist die BTS Management Ltd., Tortola, B.V.I.

Die Auftragnehmerin verpflichtet sich, keine, ausser die in nachfolgender Ziffer 2 in Verbindung mit Ziffer 3 erwähnte Transaktion über die JAFFRA DEVELOPMENT INC., B.V.I., zu tätigen und diese Gesellschaft keinem Dritten zur Verfügung zu stellen. Die Auftragnehmerin verpflichtet sich, für die vorliegende Transaktionen ein separates Konto bei der LGT Bank in Liechtenstein AG, Vaduz, zu eröffnen und nach Abschluss der Transaktionen, spätestens am 1. Januar 2001, diese Gesellschaft zu liquidieren.

Auftrag

1. Der Auftraggeber ermächtigt und beauftragt die Auftragnehmerin wie folgt und die Auftragnehmerin nimmt diesen Auftrag an.

2. Der Auftraggeber wird auf Konto Nr. 0166153 der Auftragnehmerin bei der LGT Bank in Liechtenstein AG, Herrengasse 12, FL-94590 Vaduz

   einen Betrag von ca. CHF 6 Mio
   (Schweizer Franken sechs Millionen 0/00)

   in einer oder mehreren Tranchen nach telefonischem Voraviso an den Verwaltungsrat der Auftragnehmerin übertragen.

3. Die Auftragnehmerin wird - jeweils nach Erhalt einer Gutschrift - die gesamten Vermögenswerte oder die entsprechenden Vermögenswerte einer jeweiligen Tranchen, abzüglich Kommissionen, Spesen (inkl. Kontolöschungskosten) sowie Entschädigung, vom Konto Nr. [redacted] der Auf-

tragnehmerin auf das Konto Nr. [redacted] lautend auf CHARIVARI STIFTUNG, Vaduz ("Empfänger"), bei der LGT Bank in Liechtenstein, in bar übertragen.

4. Die Auftragnehmerin garantiert, die kontoführende Bank entsprechend dem erteilten Auftrag weiter zu beauftragen.

Im übrigen trifft die Auftragnehmerin keine wie immer geartete Haftung für die ordnungsgemässe Abwicklung der Übertragung, insbesondere übernimmt sie keine Garantie für die Abwicklung innerhalb bestimmter Fristen. Sämtliche aus der Abwicklung der Übertragung resultierenden Ansprüche hat der Auftraggeber direkt beim kontoführenden Institut geltend zu machen.

5. Für die Durchführung der gesamten Transaktion erhält die BTS Management Ltd. eine Pauschale von CHF 5'000.00, sowie zusätzlich Drittkosten, jeweils bewertet per Eingangstag auf dem Konto der Auftragnehmerin. Die Gründungs- sowie Liquidationskosten für die JAFFRA DEVELOPMENT INC. sind in dieser Entschädigung inbegriffen.

Diese Entschädigung ist auch geschuldet, wenn bis zum 31. Dezember 2000 keine Transaktion erfolgt. Diesfalls wird oben genannte Entschädigung am 1. Januar 2001 zur Zahlung fällig.

6. Änderungen und Ergänzungen dieser Vereinbarung bedürfen der Schriftform.

7. Dieses Vertragsverhältnis untersteht dem liechtensteinischen Recht. Für allfällige Streitigkeiten aus diesem Vertragsverhältnis vereinbaren alle Parteien die ausschliessliche Zuständigkeit des Fürstlich Liechtensteinischen Landgerichtes in Vaduz.

8. Der Unterfertigte bestätigt, dass er dieses Instrument nicht zur missbräuchlichen Inanspruchnahme des Bankgeheimnisses / Treuhändergeheimnisses verwenden wird und die Vermögenswerte nicht aus kriminellen Handlungen oder Unterlassungen herrühren.

Vaduz, 21. Juni 2000

= Redacted by the Permanent Subcommittee on Investigations

Dieter Noack, Auftraggeber

JAFFRA DEVELOPMENT INC., Auftragnehmerin

BTS Management Ltd.

PSI-USMSTR - 007936

Agreement

Dieter Noack, Via Moscia 61, 6612 Ascona / TI

▬▬ = Redacted by the Permanent Subcommittee on Investigations

as client

and

JAFFRA DEVELOPMENT INC., Road Town, Tortola, B.V.I.

as contractor

Preamble

The contractor is an indirect subsidiary of the LGT Trust Corporation , Städtle 18, FL-9490 Vaduz, which is for its part a 100% subsidiary of the LGT Bank in Liechtenstein Corp., Vaduz.

The sole entity of the administrative board of the contractor is BTS Management Ltd., Tortola, B.V.I.

The contractor undertakes that it will not effect any transaction through the JAFFRA DEVELOPMENT INC., B.V.I., except where mentioned in the following Item 2 in connection with Item 3, and that it will not place this corporation in the service of any third party. The contractor undertakes to open a separate account at the LGT Bank in Liechtenstein Corp., Vaduz, for the present transactions, and after completion of the transactions, at the latest by 01.01.2001, to liquidate this corporation.

Mandate

1. The client authorizes and instructs the contractor as follows and the contractor accepts this mandate.

2. The client will transfer to account no. [redacted] of the contractor at the LGT Bank in Liechtenstein Corp., Herrengasse 12, FL-94590 Vaduz

   an amount of approximately CHF 6 million
   (six million 0/00 Swiss francs)

   in one or more installments after notice by telephone to the administrative board.

3. The contractor will, in each case after receipt of a credit voucher, transfer the total value of assets, or the corresponding total value of assets less commission, fees (including account cancellation costs) as well as compensation, from account no. [redacted] of the

contractor to the account no.[redacted] under the name of CHARIVARI FOUNDATION, Vaduz ("Recipient"), at the LGT Bank in Liechtenstein, in cash.

4. The contractor guarantees to re-commission the custodian bank corresponding to the mandate issued.

   Incidentally, the contractor is not to be kept responsible in any way for the proper processing of the transfer, and it especially makes no guarantee to processing within a specified period of time. ~~The contractor must make a claim with the custodian institution for all claims resulting from the~~ processing of the transfer.

5. The BTS Management Ltd. receives a flat fee of CHF 5,000.00 for the completion of all transactions, as well as receiving additional outside costs, each of which is assessed on the day of deposit to the account of the contractor. The founding and liquidation costs for the JAFFRA DEVELOMENT INC. are included in this compensation.

   This compensation is still owed if no transaction occurs before 12.31.2000. In this case, the above-mentioned compensation is due for payment on 01.01.2001.

6. Changes and supplementation to this agreement must appear in writing.

7. This contract relation derives authority from the law of Liechtenstein. For possible disputes which arise from this contract relation, all parties agree to the exclusive jurisdiction of the royal district court of Liechtenstein in Vaduz.

8. The undersigned declares that he will not utilize this deed for improper usage of bank secrecy or trust secrecy, and that the values of assets do not originate from criminal activity or neglect.

Vaduz, 06.21.2000

[redacted] = Redacted by the Permanent Subcommittee on Investigations

[signature]
Dieter Noack, Client

JAFFRA DEVELOPMENT INC., Contractor

BTS Management Ltd.

[signature] [signature]

LGT Bank in Liechtenstein
A Member of Liechtenstein Global Trust

LGT Bank in Liechtenstein
Aktiengesellschaft
Herrengasse 12
FL-9490 Vaduz

ERLEDIGT

Telefax 075 235 15 22
Telex 889 222

Aktenvermerk

1/2

Thema	**Luperla Foundation, Vaduz**
Verfasserin/Abt./Tel.	Peter Widmer / R22 / 1296
Datum	2. Mai 1997
Zur Erledigung	Dr. P. Iob, LGT Treuhand Wilfried Ospelt E. Matfle
Zur Kenntnisnahme	H. Nipp Dr. K. Bächinger

wfe → spr
zur Info
(und Ablage?)
wfe

Treffen mit:	- David Lowy - J.H. Gelbard
Datum:	30. April 1997 im Hotel Savoy, Zürich
LGT Bank:	P. Widmer

1. Die Herren waren in Zürich um mit Sinitus Treuhand die Überträge der Vermögenswerte auf Luperla vorzubereiten. Ich bin mit Ihnen das Vorgehen nochmals durchgegangen:

   a) Ca. USD 54 Mio. (Saldi Crofton bei uns) gehen auf Konto Sewell bei uns (Auftrag kommt von Sinitus); anschliessend vergütet Sewell (Auftrag kommt von LGT T) den Betrag an Luperla. ✓

   b) Weitere rd. USD 3 Mio. werden durch Drittbankvergütung bei Sewell (Konto LGT) eingehen, welche ebenfalls auf Konto Luperla bei LGT zu vergüten sind (Auftrag LGT T). →CHF 3.6 Mio. gem. K. Ulrich

   c) Crofton wird deren Konto bei Union Bank of Israel, Tel-Aviv schliessen lassen und Saldo (ca. USD 0.2 Mio.) auf Konto Sewell vergüten; Sewell zahlt auch diesen Betrag an Luperla bei LGT (Auftrag LGT T). ✓

      Luperla soll dann USD 250'000.-- auf deren Konto (durch LGT T bereits eröffnet) bei Union Bank of Israel vergüten. ✓

   d) Das Konto Sewell ist am 31.5.1997 zu saldieren und die Gesellschaft zu löschen. Auftrag durch LGT T. ✓

2. Die Belegexemplare "Regulations" und "Statutes" der Luperla Foundation habe ich von J. Gelbard gegenzeichnen lassen, diese liegen diesem AV für P. Iob bei.

   Bezüglich der Stiftung ist somit alles i.O.

Permanent Subcommittee on Investigations
EXHIBIT #81

AV... - LUPERLA.DOC - 02.05.1997 - 13,01

PSI-USMSTR-008864

LGT Bank in Liechtenstein
A Member of Liechtenstein Global Trust

Aktenvermerk 2/2

3. Bezüglich Anlagestrategie und Fees bleibt alles beim alten: Ertrag USD, All-in 70bp (siehe AV vom 23.1.1997).

   Die neuen Investitionsvorschläge habe ich übergeben. Diese wurden geschätzt und als i.O. in Empfang genommen.

   Nach Eingang der Gelder, voraussichtlich ab nächster Woche, resp. nach Auslaufen der Festgelder kann mit dem Anlageprozess begonnen werden, wobei ich nochmals festgehalten habe, dass es bis zur vollen Investition 1-2 Monate dauern kann.

4. Ich bitte die Geldflüsse mit E. Matfle zu koordinieren.

5. Nach Abschluss dieser Transaktionen sollen dann definitiv alle Unterlagen von "Crofton" und "Jelnav" vernichtet werden, soweit dies aus rechtlichen Gründen möglich ist. Ich bitte Dr. Iob um Bestätigung der Erledigung bis 30.6.1997.

P. Widmer

Beilage für Dr. Iob

[illegible] PSI-USMSTR 008865

[stamp:] **COMPLETED**

[logo]LGT Treuhand
A Member of Liechtenstein Global Trust

LGT Trust
Corporation
Herrengasse 12
FL-9490 Vaduz

Telephone: 075 235 11 22
Telefax: 075 235 15 22
Telex: 889 222

1/2

Memorandum for the Record

Subject **Luperla Foundation, Vaduz**

Compiler / Tel.: Peter Widmer / R22 / 1296 [by hand:] [illegible initials] → spr

Date: May 2, 1997 FYI (and file?)
[initialed]

For action: Dr. P. Iob, LGT Trust
Wilfried Ospelt
E. Mattle

cc: H. Nipp
Dr. K. Bächinger

Meeting with: - David Lowy
- J. H. Gelbard

Date: April 30, 1997 in the Hotel Savoy, Zurich

LGT Bank: - Wilfried Ospelt
- Peter Widmer

[The top half of this page is struck through by hand.]

---

1. The gentlemen were in Zurich to prepare with Sinitus Trust the asset transfers to Luperla. I reviewed the approach with them once more:

a) Around USD 54 million (balance Crofton with us) are going to the Sewell account with us (assignment from Sinitus); subsequently Sewell pays (assignment from LGT T) the amount to Luperla. √

b) An additional roughly USD 3 million will go to Sewell (account LGT) through third-bank payments, which are likewise to be paid to account Luperla at LGT (assignment LGT T).
[by hand:] → CHF 3.6 million according to K. Ulrich

c) Crofton will close its account with Union Bank of Israel, Tel Aviv and send balance (around USD 0.2 million) to account Sewell; Sewell also pays this amount to Luperla at LGT (assignment LGT T). √

[logo]LGT Treuhand
A Member of Liechtenstein Global Trust

Memorandum for the Record 2/2

Luperla is then to remunerate USD 250,000.00 to its account (already opened by LGT T) with Union Bank of Israel. √

d) The Sewell account is to be closed on May 31, 1997 and the company to be dissolved. Assignment through LGT T. √

[all √by hand]

2. I have had the file copies "Regulations" and "Statutes" of the Luperla Foundation countersigned by J. Gelbard; these are attached to this memo for P. Iob.

Regarding the foundation, everything is herewith in order.

3. Regarding investment strategy and fees everything remains the same: proceeds USD, all-in 70 bp (see memo of Jan. 23, 1997).

I have turned over the new investment suggestions. These were appreciated and received as in order.

After in payment of monies, probably starting next week, or after the fixed deposits run out, the investment process can be started, whereby I stated once more that it can take 1 – 2 months for full investment.

4. I request that the money flows be coordinated with **E. Mattle.**

5. After completion of these transactions, all documents from "Crofton" and "Jelnav" are definitely to be destroyed, insofar as this is legally possible. I ask Dr. Iob for confirmation of completion by June 30, 1997.

[signed]

P. Widmer

Enclosure for Dr. Iob
[not at hand for translation]

- 1/2 -

J. H. Gelbard

~~LGT Treuhand Aktiengesellschaft~~
att. Werner Orvati / Dr. Paolo Iob
Städtle 18
FL-9490 Vaduz

London, 12 March 1997

Formation of a Foundation by the name Luperla Foundation

Dear Sirs,

I kindly request you to set up the Luperla Foundationaccording to the following enclosed documents

- Formation Deed in English (Appendix A)
- Statutes of Foundation (Appendix B)
- Regulation of Foundation (Appendix C)

The payment of the capital in the amount of sFr. 30'000,-- will be effected to the Foundation's account with LGT Bank in Liechtenstein AG, Vaduz.

As legal representative of the Foundation shall be appointed:

- LGT Treuhand Aktiengesellschaft

As Board Members of the Foundation with authority to sign any two jointly shall be appointed

- Dr. Konrad Bächinger, c/o LGT Bank in Liechtenstein
- Mr. Hans-Werner Ritter, Eichgasse 4a, FL-9490 Vaduz
- Mr. Peter Widmer, c/o LGT Bank in Liechtenstein AG, Vaduz
- Mr. Werner Orvati, c/o LGT Treuhand AG, Vaduz

Signatories on the account of the Foundation with LGT Bank in Liechtenstein shall be

- the Members of the Foundation Board according to their right to represent
- LGT Treuhand, singly

PSI-USMSTR - 008860

The Foundation is to enter into a Management Agreement with LGT Bank in Liechtenstein AG, Vaduz as set out in Appendix D.

I agree that an annual all-in-fee of 0.7 % of the average Foundations' assets shall be debited to the Foundation in accordance with the above referred Management ~~Agreement. This fee includes~~

- the management of the Foundation's assets
- the formation and administration of the Foundation and its bank accounts
- the formation and administration of a transfer company (with legal situs in the British Virgin Islands) and its bank accounts
- the annual tax and registration payments for the Foundation and the transfer company in Liechtenstein and the British Virgin Islands

I also have taken note of the fact that LGT Treuhand AG and LGT Bank in Liechtenstein AG accepts liability for any damage suffered by ourselves and or the Foundation and its Beneficiaries due to any breach of duty of the members of the Foundation Board delegated by LGT Treuhand AG and LGT Bank in Liechtenstein AG.

Yours sincerely,

J.H Gelbard

PSI-USMSTR - 008861

QUALIFIED INTERMEDIARY (QI)

STEP Event 2001 / September 14/15, 2001:
Presentation by Brigitte Arnold
LGT Bank in Liechtenstein Aktiengesellschaft, Vaduz

LGT Bank in Liechtenstein
A Member of Liechtenstein Global Trust

Permanent Subcommittee on Investigations
EXHIBIT #82

QUALIFIED INTERMEDIARY (QI)

NEW US WITHHOLDING TAX REGULATIONS FROM THE BANKING PERSPECTIVE

LGT Bank in Liechtenstein Aktiengesellschaft, Vaduz - QI - bra/mta/RE - 03.04.2002 7:57 Datei.ppt - Folie 2

LGT

New US Withholding Tax Regulations

- Withholding tax on interests and dividends on US securities
- Effective date - January 1, 2001
- Major Impacts
  - Documentation
  - Withholding
  - Reporting
  - Allocation
- Increased responsibilities for foreign intermediaries (QI vs. NQI)

LGT Bank in Liechtenstein Aktiengesellschaft, Vaduz - QI - bra/mta/RE - 03.04.2002 7:57 Datei.ppt - Folie 3

Disadvantages of being a NQI

- ◆ Extensive documentation requirements:
  - Full disclosure of beneficial owner to the IRS. Form W-8BEN or Form W-9 required for each account
- ◆ Full withholding of 30% on dividends and interests in case of non-disclosure
- ◆ Comprehensive reporting requirements
  - NQI must report taxable income for each underlying beneficial owner

  → Penalty of 20% of income in case of failure
- ◆ NQI liable for additional tax, interest and penalties

LGT Bank in Liechtenstein Aktiengesellschaft, Vaduz - QI - bra/mta/RE - 03.04.2002 7:57 Datei.ppt - Folie 4

Becoming a QI is a must

- Relief from beneficial owner disclosure requirements
- Use of local KYC documentation is acceptable; not required to pass W-8 documentation on to withholding agent or IRS
- Documentation remains with the QI
- QI files income reports by „reporting pools". No need for reporting by individual beneficial owners
- Simplified withholding and reporting requirements vs. a NQI

LGT Bank in Liechtenstein Aktiengesellschaft, Vaduz - QI - bra/mta/RE - 03.04.2002 7:57 Datei.ppt - Folie 5

Qualification as QI (general)

- Approved Country Know-Your-Customer Rules
- Agreement with IRS
- Auditing of procedure (no requirement to divulge identity of account holders to IRS)

US Accounts

- Generally QIs and NQIs must pass Forms W-9 up to the US paying agent (full disclosure of names of US customers)

→ Backup withholding tax of 31% (*) on all dividends, interest payments and sales proceeds in case of non-disclosure

(*) progressively reduced to 28% during the next 5 years

LGT Bank in Liechtenstein Aktiengesellschaft, Vaduz - QI - bra/mta/RE - 03.04.2002 7:57 Datei.ppt - Folie 7

QI Status of LGT Bank Vaduz

- Approval of Liechtenstein's KYCR by the IRS as per 28.02.2001
- Internal decision as per 01.03.2001 to become QI
- Application for QI status submitted to IRS as per 07.03.2001
- LGT Bank Vaduz permitted to act as a QI beginning 01.01.2001 (retroactive)

LGT Bank in Liechtenstein Aktiengesellschaft, Vaduz - QI - bra/mta/RE - 03.04.2002 7:57 Datei.ppt - Folie 8

Documentation Benefits for LGT

- ◆ Client confidentiality maintained
- ◆ KYC available
- ◆ Documentation transition rules available
- ◆ Relief for simple and grantor trusts available
- ◆ → All QI benefits available

LGT Bank in Liechtenstein Aktiengesellschaft, Vaduz - QI - bra/mta/RE - 03.04.2002 7:57 Datei.ppt - Folie 9

Simple and Grantor Trusts (FL Foundations etc.)

- ◆ LGT as QI bank avoids having to report underlying beneficial owners to IRS if
  - LGT as QI obtains documentation
  - LGT as QI additionally identifies beneficial owners (passport etc.)

otherwise

- ◆ Full disclosure of underlying beneficial owners to IRS (QI and NQI)

Conclusion

The application of the QI Rules from the banking perspective; was it worth it?

Yes, because there is

[redacted]

LGT Bank in Liechtenstein Aktiengesellschaft, Vaduz - QI - bra/mta/RE - 03.04.2002 7:57 Datei.ppt - Folie 11

LGT Bank in Liechtenstein
A Member of Liechtenstein Global Trust

LGT Bank in Liechtenstein
Aktiengesellschaft
Herrengasse 12
FL-9490 Vaduz

Telephone +423 235 11 22
Telefax +423 235 15 22
Internet www.lgt.com
E-Mail info@lgt.com

Impact of new US withholding tax regulations on non-US entities

1. Qualification of non-US entities under the US regulations

For the qualification of non-US entities, it has to be determined whether the entity itself can be regarded as the beneficial owner of the assets it holds, whether it is considered to be a US or a non-US person and whether it is a corporation (company) or a trust for tax purposes.

1.1. Beneficial ownership in general

US federal income tax law defines the beneficial owner as the person who, according to US tax law, is the owner of the relevant income for tax purposes and who beneficially owns the income. In general, a person is treated as the owner of the income, and thus as the beneficial owner, to the extent it is required under US tax principles to include the amount paid in gross income on a tax return. A person, who receives income as a nominee, asset manager or agent for another person or who has to be considered as a mere structure, can thus not be considered the beneficial owner under US tax principles.

1.2. US or non-US entity

Basically, an entity (corporation, company, partnership or other business entity) is regarded as being a non-US entity, if it is incorporated or created outside the territory of the United States.

Trusts (and foundations or similar vehicles without a commercial purpose) are regarded as being US trusts if a US court is able to exercise supervision over the administration of the trust (the so-called court test) and a US person has the authority to control all substantial decisions of the trust (the so-called control test). Both tests must be met at the same time in order for a trust to be qualified as a US person.

1.3. Business entity or trust

It is of importance for the classification of non-US entities, whether they were founded to pursue a commercial business activity (business entity) or not (trust).

1.3.1. Business entities

A business entity is a non-US business entity if the type of legal structure to which it belongs appears on the list of **„per se corporations“** (see the appendix) published by the US authorities. This list contains an overview of countries with specified legal entities, e.g. the Swiss and Luxembourg AG, the UK Public Limited Company etc.

Or, if they do not appear on the „per se corporations“ list, non-US business entities can be classified according to the **„check the box rules“**:

- If, under local law, none of the shareholders/owners/members have unlimited personal liability for the debts of or claims against the entity (i.e. all these persons bear only limited liability), then the entity automatically and without having to make any special declaration will be classified as a corporation for US income tax purposes. It also has the option under the check the box rules to explicitly elect to be treated as a partnership, e.g. as a transparent "flow through" entity. To do so, it must file a Form 8832 with the US tax authorities.

- If, under local law, any or only one shareholder/owner/member has unlimited liability for the debts of or claims against the entity, then the entity will basically be treated as a (transparent) partnership. Such an entity also has the possibility under the check the box rules to opt explicitly to be treated (if there is more than one member) as a corporation (by filing Form 8832) for US income tax purposes.

- The same rules apply to an entity which is owned by a sole owner. If this person does not bear unlimited liability, the entity will basically be treated as a corporation (unless an explicit election to the contrary has been made). In contrast, if the person does bear unlimited liability, the entity will be disregarded unless it has explicitly elected to be treated as a corporation (by filing Form 8832).

The above classification rules apply irrespective of whether the shareholders/owners/members are US persons or non-US persons.

US tax legislation contains special rules concerning Controlled Foreign Corporations, Personal Holding Companies, Passive Foreign Investment Companies etc., which cannot be dealt with within the scope of these explanations.

1.3.2. Trusts

According to US law, a trust exists if it was created by a will or by an inter vivos declaration whereby trustees take title to property for the purpose of protecting or conserving it for the beneficiaries. The persons who created such a trust might also be the beneficiaries. Generally speaking, a trust exists according to US law if the arrangement is to vest in trustees responsibility for the protection and conservation of beneficiaries who cannot share in the discharge of this responsibility. Trustees and beneficiaries do not therefore form a joint enterprise for the conduct of business, i.e. they do not form a business entity.

Trusts are further divided into grantor trusts, simple trusts and complex trusts.

<u>a. Grantor trusts</u>

The following trusts are grantor trusts according to US tax law if the grantor, the person who settled or funded the trust, is still alive:

- Any non-US trust established by a US person (citizen, resident alien) for the benefit or potential benefit of a US person. Normally, any non-US trust so established will be considered for the benefit of US persons, except if any such benefit to US persons is explicitly prohibited.

- Any non-US trust established by a non-US person, if such person within five years after establishing the trust becomes a US person (citizen, resident alien). This will lead to the trust being treated as if established by a US person.

- Any non-US trust established by a non-US person, if the trust is revocable.

- Any non-US trust established by a non-US person, whereby only the settlor or the settlor's spouse may benefit from distributions from the trust during the lifetime of the settlor.

- Any non-US trust established by a non-US person prior to September 19, 1995 and which is a "grandfathered" grantor trust according to US tax law.

<u>b. Simple trusts</u>

If a trust does not fulfil the criteria of a grantor trust, it is regarded as a simple trust, if it is required

- under the governing documents to distribute all the trust's income annually on a current basis to the beneficiaries, and

- the trust is not allowed to distribute or accumulate income or gains for charitable purposes, and

- the trust does not in fact distribute any capital or accumulated income in excess of current income.

c. Complex trusts

Trusts, which are neither grantor trusts nor simple trusts, are regarded as complex trusts.

d. Non-US foundations (e.g. Liechtensteiner foundations and similar entities)

Foundations and similar vehicles, which normally cannot be formed to pursue commercial objectives but have as their main objective the preservation of family wealth, will be treated as trusts under US tax principles. The basic rules described above for trusts are therefore applicable. The same could apply to similar entities (e.g. Liechtenstein trust enterprises (Trust Reg.), trusts and establishments). On the other hand, if such an entity does pursue commercial business purposes and activities, it should be classified in accordance with the check the box rules. Therefore, such entities always have to be examined to ascertain whether they are to be treated as transparent or non-transparent.

e. Trusts/foundations with underlying company

With these structures, the trust (or the foundation etc.) is not the entity which holds the investments but rather a business entity. This entity (and not the trust) is then the bank's regular client. The question of which structures are to be classified for tax purposes is determined according to the rules applying to business entities („per se corporations", „check the box rules").

2. Tax treatment of business entities and trusts under the withholding regulations

2.1. Business entity

Non-US business entities, which are either included on the list of „per se corporations" or classified as corporations according to the „check the box rules", are basically regarded as the beneficial owners of the securities and income which they hold. The restriction that a person, who receives income as a nominee, asset manager, or trustee or who serves purely as a conduit, is not recognized as the beneficial owner applies fully in this case.

In cases where the entity cannot be regarded as the beneficial owner, it is considered to be an intermediary for tax purposes.

2.2. Trusts

Grantor trusts and simple trusts are regarded as transparent entities for tax purposes. They are not recognized as being the beneficial owners of the assets they hold, but rather as intermediaries.

In contrast, complex trusts are regarded as beneficial owners.

3. Consequences of tax classification within the scope of the Qualified Intermediary regulations

In order for the banks with Qualified Intermediary (QI) status to meet the requirements of the QI Agreement they must be aware of the tax status of their custody account holders. An adequate approach to this problem is by asking the client to confirm his or her status either on a declaration statement or the official IRS forms provided for this purpose.

3.1. Entities which are recognised as beneficial owners

Non-US entities, which can be regarded as the beneficial owners of the assets they hold, are obligated to confirm these circumstances on the declaration of non-US status to be passed on to LGT Bank in Liechtenstein Aktiengesellschaft, Vaduz. This will enable LGT Bank in Liechtenstein Aktiengesellschaft, Vaduz, to treat the entity as a non-US person. The form with regard to non-US status will remain with the bank, i.e. neither the declaration nor the information it contains will be forwarded to the USA.

3.2. Entities which are regarded as intermediaries

3.2.1. General

If a non-US entity is not regarded as a beneficial owner but rather as an intermediary according to the US tax regulations, it is not entitled to submit a Form W-8BEN. It must inform LGT Bank in Liechtenstein Aktiengesellschaft, Vaduz, of its status on the Form W-8IMY and on the declaration regarding non-US status. The W-8BEN forms of the actual beneficial owners are to be attached to these forms. LGT Bank in Liechtenstein Aktiengesellschaft, Vaduz, is obligated to forward these forms to its US custodian, which will pass the information on to the US tax authorities (with the exception of the declaration regarding non-US status, which is kept solely at the bank).

LGT Bank in Liechtenstein Aktiengesellschaft, Vaduz, will only disclose the names of its custody account clients and the actual beneficial owners with the explicit consent of the custody account client concerned.

3.2.2. Special relief measures for grantor and simple trusts / Liechtenstein foundations and similar vehicles (which do not have US persons as the grantor or beneficiaries)

At the beginning of December 2000, the US tax authorities (IRS) issued supplementary regulations which provide a significant improvement with respect to non-US trusts and offshore foundations (e.g. Liechtenstein foundations), which are treated as equivalent to trusts according to US tax law, as well as to similar entities that are not themselves regarded as being the beneficial owners (i.e. grantor and simple trusts). A decisive point in this supplementary ruling is that in the case of these legal structures, the identity of the custody account client and the beneficial owner does not have to be disclosed to the US custodian and the US tax authorities if, in addition to the Forms W-8IMY for the trust (foundation) and W-8BEN for the beneficial owner (the grantor or beneficiary), the QI bank also receives from the beneficial owners those documents which identify them as the beneficial owners according to the valid know-your-customer rules.

Custody account clients of LGT Bank in Liechtenstein Aktiengesellschaft, Vaduz, can benefit directly from these relief measures. To do so, they must submit to LGT Bank in Liechtenstein Aktiengesellschaft, Vaduz, in addition to the declaration regarding non-US status, a legally signed Form W-8IMY for the trust concerned together with the Forms W-8BEN for the grantor and the beneficial owners, as well as a certified photocopy of the passports of these persons. Generally, the photocopies can be certified by a notary public, a court or another recognized certification authority. All the submitted forms (declaration regarding non-US status, W-8IMY, W-8BEN, photocopies of passports) will be kept exclusively at the bank and not forwarded to the US custodian or the US tax authorities.

In cases where US persons are involved as beneficial owners, these relief measures do not apply. In such instances, as was previously the case, the persons concerned must disclose their identity to the US tax authorities using Form W-9.

3.3. Responsibilities

The responsibility for the correct qualification of the entity as a beneficial owner or intermediary lies solely with the entity and/or with the persons which represent it. In cases of doubt, a tax expert should be consulted in view of the important consequences attached to an incorrect qualification as a beneficial owner (submission of a Form W-8IMY and disclosure of the beneficial owner on Form W-8BEN).

LGT Treuhand

▬▬ = Redacted by the Permanent Subcommittee on Investigations

LGT Treuhand Aktiengesellschaft
Städtle 28, FL-9490 Vaduz
Telefon +423 235 27 27 · Telefax +423 235 27 15
E-Mail lgt.trust@lgt.com
Internet www.lgt.com/lgttreuhand
FL-R H.702/63 · Sitz: 9490 Vaduz · MWSt-Nr. 50119

Aktenvermerk 1/1

LGT TREUHAND AG LEITSTELLE COMPLIANCE
Eingangsdatum: 18/09/02
GEPRÜFT IM SINNE DER BESTEHENDEN RICHTLINIEN
Visum CO: [signature]
Datum: 18/09/02

Thema	**Neugründung LRAB Foundation, Vaduz (Weitere Abklärungen)**
Verfasser(in) / Tel.	Mag. Hans-Jörg Gatt
Datum	13. September 2002 / HJG
Zur Erledigung	Barbara Gmeiner (BGI)
Zur Genehmigung	Compliance / Geschäftsleitung / Teamleitung Sonja Sprenger

1. Privatkonto bei LGT BIL, Vaduz
Auf dem bestehenden Konto bei LGT BIL werden relativ grosse Summen transferiert. Aus diesem Grund hat Herr Skwaric Herrn Karl Frick von der Compliance zur Kundenbesprechung hinzugezogen. Die Beurteilung von Karl Frick liegt als Kopie bei.

2. Marc Rich
Marc Rich war Inhaber eines Firmengeflechts in CH welches vornehmlich im Warenhandel tätig war. Zeitweise waren über 1'500 Personen alleine in CH für ihn tätig und ein Umsatz von über USD 44.5 Mia. (2001, siehe Kopie) wurde erzielt. Er hat seine Anteile an Angestellte verkauft, welche die Firma unter dem Namen Glencore International weiterführen. Marc Rich ist eine umstrittene Person und teilweise in seinen Methoden sehr fragwürdig. Andererseits sieht man, dass in diesem Jahr auf dem Privatkonto des [redacted] ausschliesslich Eingänge von Glencore waren und somit die Angaben der Kunden untermauert werden.

3. Einschätzung der Compliance LGT BIL
Der gute Eindruck den ich von den Kunden habe wird im beigelegten email auch von Karl Frick von der Bank bestätigt. Folgendes möchte ich aber anbringen. Die ausgehenden Transfers auf dem Privatkonto bei LGT BIL haben ein Volumen von ca. USD 1 Mio. / pro Jahr. Dies sind die Bürokosten, Frachtkosten und Zahlungen im Rahmen ihrer geschäftlichen Tätigkeit. Ein kleiner Teil der Zahlungen gehen aber in die USA und nach Panama und können als Schmiergeldzahlungen eingestuft werden. Glencore International hat sie als ihr grösster Partner in Ecuador ersucht, diese Zahlungen an Dritte weiterzugeben. Dieses System wurde erst 2002 errichtet und die Kunden sind damit sehr unglücklich. Früher wurden die Zahlungen von Glencore International direkt an besagte Personen geleistet. [redacted] gibt an, dass er nochmals mit Glencore sprechen wird, aber gleichzeitig Angst hat, dass sie Glencore als Kunden verlieren könnten.

4. Panamagesellschaft
Ich habe mit den Kunden die Möglichkeit einer Panamagesellschaft als Kontoinhaber und „Durchgangskonto" besprochen. Ich habe aber, in Absprache mit SPR, **abgelehnt**, dass wird als Direktoren einer solchen Gesellschaft agieren. Mein Eindruck ist, dass sich die Kunden ihrer Situation sehr bewusst sind, sie können auch das Risiko sehr gut abschätzen, können aber an der Situation momentan nichts ändern. Die Zahlungen sind jedenfalls mit Karl Frick besprochen und können auch weiterhin erfolgen.

[signature]
Mag. Hans-Jörg Gatt

Permanent Subcommittee on Investigations
EXHIBIT #83

PSI-USMSTR - 008555

▬▬ = Redacted by the Permanent Subcommittee on Investigations

[Logo]
LGT Treuhand
A Member of Liechtenstein Global Trust

LGT Treuhand Corporation
Staedtle 18, FL-9490 Vaduz
Telephone: +423 235 27 27 Telefax: +423 235 27 15
E-Mail Info@lgt.com
Internet: www.lgt.com
OR H. 702/63 – Location 9490 Vaduz - MWST-Nr. 50119

1/4

Note for File

Subject:	**New Establishment of LRAB Foundation, Vaduz [STAMPED]**
Writer/ Tel.:	Mag. Hans-Joerg Gatt
Date:	13 September 2002 / HJG
For Execution:	Barbara Gmeiner (BGI)
For Notice:	Compliance [INITIALED] / Executive [INITIALED] / Team Management Sonja Sprenger

1. Private Account with LGT BIL, Vaduz

Relatively large sums will be transferred into the existing account with LGT BIL. For this reason, Mr. Skwaric has called on Mr. Karl Frick from Compliance for a client meeting. The assessment from Karl Frick is attached as a copy.

2. Marc Rich

Marc Rich was the proprietor of a network of firms in Switzerland which were primarily active in merchandising. At times, over 1,500 persons in Switzerland alone were employed by him and a turnover of over USD 44.5 billion (2001, see copy) was achieved. He sold his portion to an employee, who continued to run the business as a firm under the name Glencore International. Marc Rich is a controversial person and very questionable with his methods. On the other side, in this year, one can see that subsequent deposits from Glencore were made into the private account of the [redacted] and therefore confirm the information of the clients.

3. Evaluation of Compliance LGT BIL

The good impression which I have from the clients is also confirmed in the attached email from Karl Frick of the bank. I would like to add the following. The out-going transfers from the private account with LGT BIL have an amount of ca. USD 1 Million/per year. These are the office costs, carrying costs and payments in the realm of their commercial activity. A small portion of the payments go however to the USA and Panama and may be classified as bribes. Glencore International asked its largest partner in Ecuador to pass these payments on to third parties. This system was first established in 2002 and, for this reason, the clients are very unlucky. Previously, the payments from Glencore International were made directly to said persons [redacted] declares that he will speak with Glencore again, but is also afraid that they could lose Glencore as clients.

4. Panama Corporation

I have discussed the possibility of a Panama Corporation as account holder and "transit account" with the clients. I have however, in agreement with SPR, dismissed our acting as director of such a corporation. My impression is that the clients know their situation very well; they can also asses the risks very well, but cannot change any part of their situation at the moment. The payments are however discussed with Karl Frick and can occur further.

[SIGNED]
Mag. Hans-Joerg Gatt

Wealth Management and Business Banking
CLIENT ADVISOR'S GUIDELINES FOR IMPLEMENTATION AND MANAGEMENT OF DISCRETIONARY ASSET MANAGEMENT RELATIONSHIP WITH U.S. CLIENTS

Introduction

As of January 2002, UBS has determined to serve its U.S. resident client base through their existing banking relationships, for clients with securities holdings ideally coupled with a discretionary asset management relationship. In no cases, will UBS entertain relationships with securities-related communication from or to the United States. Client Advisors have a significant role in implementing the discretionary asset management relationship and managing it for those clients that adopt it. They also must make sure that no securities-related communication from or to U.S. territory occurs. These guidelines set out the effect of adopting the discretionary asset management relationship, the process for implementing its adoption for clients and guidelines for managing the discretionary asset management relationship once it is adopted by the clients.

A. Effect of adopting the discretionary asset management relationship

Most importantly, UBS will have the duty to manage the client's discretionary account in accordance with the investment mandate selected by the client. However, because the client is granting UBS discretionary authority, UBS will make decisions concerning the trades in securities to be made in the discretionary account.

Under United States (US) tax regulations, trades in foreign (non-US) securities on behalf of a US person – effected by a UBS portfolio manager with discretion from a bank office of a non-US bank outside the territory of the US – will not be viewed as being done on US territory, and will therefore be considered to be effected outside of the US. Accordingly, such trades will not be subject to reporting under [the US Internal Revenue Service's (IRS) deemed sales rules or the QI Agreement, which UBS has entered into with the US IRS.

Under US securities regulations, trades effected in securities - by a UBS portfolio manager with discretion from a bank office of a non-US bank outside the territory of the US – should not trigger registration requirements under the US laws governing brokers and investment advisers (provided, in the case of the law governing investment advisers, the guidelines set out below for the management of the discretionary asset management relationship are carefully followed).

B. Process for implementing the discretionary asset management relationship

In summary, (and subject to special treatment for some non-standard clients discussed below), US client relationships will be restructured into discretionary asset management contracts (i.e., PM mandates or managed fund portfolios), (1) through a letter (and in some cases, a phone call) to the client alerting the client that no securities orders will be accepted from them, (2) oral agreement (by telephone) by the client to the discretionary asset management relationship and (3) follow-up as soon as possible to obtain a contract that must be concluded and signed outside the US at the next possible meeting.

<u>Immediate Action – As of 17 January 2002</u>

(1) Send letter to all PB and PCC clients (except APS/AFS and W-9 clients)
(2) Cease to accept customer instructions from US territory
(3) Ensure retained mail implemented for all PB and PCC clients
(4) Prepare for call to PB and PCC clients by: (a) identifying active traders, (b) determining the appropriate investment mandate and whether there are any special instructions, (c) determining standard pricing for asset size and investment mandate
(5) Start calling all PB and PCC clients that conduct active trading [visit key clients] to obtain the agreement of such clients to the discretionary asset management relationship: use attached Script, Question & Answer and Note to File which includes the details that must be covered in obtaining the client's agreement to the discretionary relationship

PSI-OBB-0008285

Permanent Subcommittee on Investigations
EXHIBIT #84

Follow up Action

(1) If client agrees, arrange and hold meeting with client outside of the U.S. for client to sign documents
(2) If client does not agree, complete asset transfer instructions

Ongoing Action for non-active Clients

When a trading instruction is received from clients, follow step (4)(b) and (c) and (5) above under Immediate Action and take appropriate step under Follow up Action

APSAFS Clients

Such contracts (note: **not** the entire relationship) have to be terminated immediately

W-9 Clients

W-9 clients have been centralized into a specialized unit to ensure appropriate handling. Please refer to the following link:

http://bw.ubs.com/page/0/36/0,1080,636-157251-1-0,00.shtml

C. Guidelines for managing the discretionary asset management relationship once it is adopted

It is critical that no further instructions are received from PB and PCC clients while they are in the US. In addition, Client Advisers are not permitted to communicate advice or information about the client's securities portfolio while the client is in the US. Set out below are the kinds of communications that are not permitted and the kinds of communications that are permitted.

Communications that are not permitted

No marketing of advisory or brokerage services regarding securities –

- No direct mailings
- No telemarketing
- No e-mail or other electronic communications
- No seminars

No use of US mails, e-mail, courier delivery or facsimile regarding the client's securities portfolio –

- All account documentation must be executed outside of the US
- No account statements, confirmations, performance reports or any other communications

No use of telephone calls into the US regarding the client's securities portfolio –

- No calls to client regarding performance, securities purchased or sold or changes in the investment mandate for the client
- No responding to inquiries regarding any of the same if the client calls from the US

No discussion of or delivery of documents concerning the client's securities portfolio while on visits in the US with the client –

- No discussion of performance, securities purchased or sold or changes in the investment mandate for the client
- No delivery of documents regarding performance, securities purchased or sold or changes in the investment mandate for the client

PSI-OBB-10-000286

Client Advisors may communicate with the clients regarding any aspect of the client's private banking relationship – except the securities portfolio – (in the case of PB clients) and banking (in the case of PCC clients) with UBS. These aspects could include information or discussion regarding, for example, the client's deposit account, non-securities holdings or loans. Communications regarding these aspects of the relationship can take place while the client is in the US through the telephone, mails, email, facsimile or while the Client Advisor is visiting in the US with the client.

Cross-Border Banking Activities into the United States (version November 2004)

1. Introduction; Regulated Activities in United States and Status of UBS Entities

The U.S. legal regulatory framework draws an important distinction between banking and securities activities:

Banking activities, most important cash and custody services, are governed by various federal and state laws and are regulated by various federal and state banking supervisors, including, in the case of UBS AG's branches, agencies, and bank depository subsidiaries, the Federal Reserve Board (the "Board"), the Office of the Comptroller of the Currency ("OCC"), the Federal Deposit Insurance Corporation ("FDIC") and the Connecticut, Illinois and Utah state banking departments.

Securities related activities (i.e., broker-dealer, investment advisor) are governed by various federal and state laws and are regulated by the Securities and Exchange Commission ("SEC") and state securities supervisors. Broker-dealers also are members of, and governed by, a self-regulatory organization ("SRO") known as the National Association of Securities Dealers ("NASD"). There is a separate regulator and regulatory scheme for providers of commodities services.

UBS AG has several U.S. branches and agencies and various non-banking subsidiaries all properly licensed, but these licenses **do not** encompass cross-border services provided to U.S. residents by UBS AG offices or affiliates outside of the United States. (Unless otherwise specified, all references herein to "UBS AG" refer to offices located, or employees based, outside of the United States).

2. Advertising & Events

Advertising: Some state laws prohibit banks without a banking license from that state from soliciting deposits from that state's residents. States also may prohibit non-licensed lenders from making certain loans to consumers in such states. Any entity outside of the United States that is not registered with the SEC (and, in the case of brokerage activities, with the NASD) may not advertise securities services or products in the United States. Therefore, UBS AG will not advertise and market for its services with material going beyond generic information relating to the image of UBS AG and its brand in the U.S.

Events. UBS AG may not organize, absent an opinion from Legal, events in the U.S.

3. Establishing Relationships with New Clients Resident in the United States

Securities services/products. UBS AG may not establish relationships for securities products or services with new clients resident in the United States with the use of U.S. jurisdictional means. Thus, it must ensure that it does not contact securities clients in the United States through telephone, mail, e-mail, advertising, the internet or personal visits.

Banking services/products. To avoid possible violations of state law and/or to avoid establishing and maintaining a place of business in the United States, UBS AG should ensure that:

- No marketing or advertising activity targeted to U.S. persons takes place in the United States;
- No solicitation of account opening takes place in the United States;
- No cold calling or prospecting into the United States takes place;

Permanent Subcommittee on Investigations
EXHIBIT #85

PSI-OPB - 0000103

- No negotiating or concluding of contracts takes place in the United States;
- No carrying or transmitting of cash or other valuables of whatever nature out of the United States takes place; The same applies to actively organizing such transfers or attempting to circumvent this prohibition through other means.
- No routine certification of signatures, transmission of completed account documentation, or related administrative activity on behalf of UBS AG takes place;
- Employees do not carry on substantial activities at fixed location(s) while in the United States thereby establishing an office or maintaining a place of business.

Outside the United States. Soliciting and accepting banking business from U.S. residents while they are outside of the United States generally is not problematic.

4. Maintaining Relationships with Clients Resident in the United States

Securities services/products. UBS AG may not maintain relationships for securities services or products with clients resident in the United States, unless the relationship is conducted without the use of U.S. means (e.g., telephone, mail, e-mail, advertising, the internet or personal visits into the United States) and consistent with procedures UBS AG has established in this regard.

Banking services/products. If UBS AG obtains a U.S. resident client for banking services without violating the restrictions set forth in section 3 above, it may service the account:

- UBS AG may provide statements, account information and transaction confirmations to the client, provided it does so in accordance with the terms agreed by the client and in compliance with all applicable internal procedures.
- UBS AG may provide product and service information subject to the points mentioned in section 6 below.
- UBS AG may certify signatures, transmit account documentation and conduct related administrative activity for existing clients.

Under no circumstances will UBS AG be carrying or transporting cash and other valuables of whatever nature on behalf of clients into or out of the United States. The same applies to actively organizing such transfers or attempting to circumvent the prohibition.

When traveling cross-border, UBS AG employees always must remember that all clients of UBS AG expect us to take all necessary steps to safeguard confidentiality. Client advisors are referred to separate guidance on the protection of confidential information and other available resources that may assist.

5. Dealing with Financial Intermediaries and other Non-Private Clients Resident in the United States

Securities services/products. UBS AG may not deal with financial intermediaries or other non-private clients resident in the United States in matters relating to securities services and products, except for registered broker-dealers and U.S. licensed banks, provided that it does not directly or indirectly deal with the private and non-private clients of such broker-dealers and banks.

Banking services/products. UBS AG may accept referrals from financial intermediaries in the United States, provided that the financial intermediaries (i) do not work for UBS AG, (ii) do not actively market UBS AG services and products, and (iii) make referrals only to accommodate client requests. In dealing with such intermediaries, UBS AG must comply with the restrictions set forth in sections 3 and 4 above.

6. Product Offering

Securities products. All securities products offered to U.S. persons must be compliant with U.S. laws, which generally means that they must be registered with the SEC. The purchase of securities may be exempt from registration if certain condition are met.

Lending products. It may be necessary to obtain a state license to offer lending products, depending on the purpose, amount, interest rate and borrower of the product. There is a reasonable argument that federal consumer protection laws do not apply to products offered by non-U.S. entities, but state consumer protection laws (*e.g.*, anti-usury) may apply.

Research. UBS AG research may not be distributed to clients in the United States, except in very limited circumstances.

E-Banking. UBS AG has implemented specific restrictions for e-banking for U.S. customers.

UBS

For Internal Use Only

Restrictions on Cross-Border Banking and Financial Services Activities

Country Paper USA[1]

(Effective Date June, 1st, 2007)

Permanent Subcommittee on Investigations
EXHIBIT #86

PSI-OPB - 0000268

[1] The terms "USA" or "United States" for the purposes of this paper also embraces all territories and dependencies of the United States, e.g., Puerto Rico.

UBS

For Internal Use Only

1. Introduction

1.1 **Overview of U.S. Regulatory Framework:** The United States has a comprehensive legal framework concerning the regulation of banking and securities services that generally requires a financial institution that provides banking or securities services to persons in the United States to be licensed by an appropriate federal regulator and/or one or more U.S. state regulators.. The U.S. legal regulatory framework distinguishes between *banking* and *securities* activities (and among particular securities activities, i.e., investment advice [including discretionary asset management], brokerage, and investment funds). As discussed below, in some cases the rules relating to securities services are more restrictive than the rules applicable to banking services.

1.2 **U.S. Presence of UBS Global WM&BB:** UBS AG has several U.S. offices and affiliates, each a "U.S. Licensed Office", that are licensed to provide banking services, securities services, or both in various U.S. states (such as UBS AG's branch offices in New York and UBS Financial Services Inc.). However, these licenses do not permit non-U.S. offices or affiliates of UBS AG to provide banking or securities services to U.S. residents.[2]

1.3 **Purpose of this Paper:** In addition to its U.S. Licensed Offices , UBS AG, through the employees of its non-U.S. offices and affiliates ("UBS Employees"), is interested in servicing U.S. residents, but only to the extent permitted by U.S. law. Failure to comply with U.S. rules and regulations may result in substantial civil, administrative and criminal sanctions against UBS AG and its employees and could have a substantial negative impact on UBS AG's reputation in the United States. Accordingly, all UBS non-U.S. offices and affiliates must conduct their business with U.S. residents in strict accordance with the rules and limitations set forth in this Country Paper.

This paper is intended for use by (i) any UBS Employee who has any contact with an existing or prospective client who is a resident of the United States, including but not limited to Traveling Officers, and (ii) any UBS Employee who has supervisory or compliance responsibilities with respect to such UBS Employees. All staff concerned must sign the certification mentioned in Section 2.1.3. to confirm compliance with this Country Paper.

1.4 **Definitions**

1.4.1 **UBS AG or UBS:** Unless stated otherwise, references to "UBS AG" or "UBS" refer to offices or affiliates of UBS AG located outside of the United States.

1.4.2 **UBS Employee:** Any employee or officer of a non-U.S. office or affiliate of UBS.

1.4.3 **Traveling Officer:** Any UBS Employee who travels to the United States and meets with a person resident in the United States who is either an existing or prospective client of UBS.

---

[2] UBS Swiss Financial Advisers AG ("UBS SFA"), a Swiss subsidiary of UBS AG registered with the U.S. Securities Exchange Commission ("SEC") as an investment adviser and with the Swiss Federal Banking Commission as a securities dealer is able to solicit U.S. resident prospects and service U.S. resident customers. As with U.S. Licensed Offices UBS SFA's licenses do not permit other non-U.S. offices or affiliates of UBS AG to provide banking or securities services to U.S. residents.

UBS

For Internal Use Only

1.4.4 **Communication Concerning Securities Services or Products:** Any communication to facilitate, induce or attempt to induce a securities transaction or any communication concerning the advisability of purchasing or selling a specific security or securities in general.

1.5. **More Information:** Questions concerning this paper or the obligations and limitations discussed in this paper should be directed to:

Franz Zimmermann, Legal, Global WM&BB

Thomas Christen, US Competence Center, Global WM&BB

UBS

For Internal Use Only

2. General Principles

2.1 **Travel to the United States:** UBS Employees may travel to the United States to meet with existing and prospective clients **so long as** all of the requirements and restrictions of this Country Paper are met.

2.1.1 Travels must be kept to a minimum.

2.1.2 Each Traveling Officer must be properly trained on the rules set forth in this Country Paper before traveling.

2.1.3 Each Traveling Officer must confirm compliance with the restrictions set forth in this Country Paper by signing a specific certification.

2.1.4 Before each trip to the United States, a Traveling Officer must obtain specific approval from his or her supervisor supported by submission of a travel plan listing those events the Traveling Officer intends to attend, and those existing and prospective clients the Traveling Officer intends to meet.

2.1.5 After returning from each trip to the United States, a Traveling Officer must report to his or her supervisor about all events attended and all existing and prospective clients visited, and to confirm that he or she complied with the provisions of this Country Paper.

2.2 **UBS Activities Outside of the United States:** The restrictions set forth in this Country Paper generally do not apply to communications or dealings between UBS and an existing or prospective client while that client is located outside of the United States.

2.3 **No Place of Business in the United States:** A UBS Employee may not engage in any activity that would result in UBS establishing a place of business in the United States.

2.3.1 A Traveling Officer must not carry on substantial activities at any fixed location in the United States thereby establishing an office or maintaining a place of business.

2.3.2 An existing or prospective client should not be able to predict or anticipate when or where a Traveling Officer will be in the United States without having made a specific appointment.

2.4 **No Communications Concerning Securities Services or Products via U.S. Jurisdictional Means**

2.4.1 A UBS Employee may not communicate concerning securities services or products with a person resident in the United States when such person is in the United States. This includes visits at a U.S. address and communications by mail, telephone, e-mail, facsimile, telex or otherwise to the United States.

2.4.2 A client relationship for a U.S. resident with securities holdings must either (i) be subject to a strictly enforced retained mail policy or (ii) have a correspondence address outside the United States.

2.4.3 Any client request to receive mail relating to a securities account at a U.S. address or otherwise receive information concerning securities services or products in the United States must be denied.

PSI-OPB - 0000271

UBS

For Internal Use Only

2.4.4 While in the United States a Traveling Officer must not discuss securities services or products with a client.

2.4.5 While in the United States, a Traveling Officer must not hand out to the client any document that relates to the client's securities holdings.

2.4.6 While in the United States, a Traveling Officer must not distribute to, collect from, or discuss with an existing or prospective client any contract, brochure or other document that relates to securities services or products

2.4.7 A UBS Employee, including a Traveling Officer, must respond to a U.S. resident client's inquiries concerning securities services or products that, if the client wishes to discuss these matters, he or she must do so when outside the United States.

2.5 **No Solicitations in the United States:** A UBS Employee must abstain from any activity that could be construed as soliciting securities or banking business from persons located in the United States. In this regard, the following general restrictions apply.

2.5.1 **Advertising:** UBS may not advertise UBS's banking and securities services in the United States other than with materials that provide generic information relating to the image of UBS and its brand in the United States. Such materials may not include information about any specific service or product offered by UBS and may not include references to banking, or securities products or services. Legal must approve an advertisement before it may be distributed in the United States.

2.5.2 **Events:** A Traveling Officer may only organize or participate in an event in the United States after receiving specific approval for that event from Legal. Any such event organized by UBS, its US-offices or affiliates, or third parties must be limited to discussing general information about UBS or banking services. Under no circumstances may a Traveling Officer solicit banking or securities business or discuss securities-related matters at such events.

2.5.3 **Dealing with Financial Intermediaries in the United States:** Any contractual arrangement with a U.S. based Financial Intermediary must be approved in advance by Legal. UBS may not enter into any arrangements with other UBS-units or third parties (e.g. Finders, Financial Intermediaries wherever located) specifically designed to refer U.S. resident persons to UBS.

2.5.4 **Cold Calls:** A UBS Employee may not make cold calls to any person located in the United States.

2.5.5 **Distributing Account Opening Documents:**

2.5.5.1 No person may distribute contractual documentation relating to securities services or products to any person located in the United States.

2.5.5.2 No person may distribute account opening documents as described in section 4.3.1 below unless the document is expressly requested by a client or prospective client.

2.6 **Accepting or Facilitating Transfers of Assets**

2.6.1 A Traveling Officer must not transport cash, bills, checks, securities or any other valuables into, out of or within the United States on behalf of an existing or prospective client.

PSI-OPB - 0000272

2.6.2 A Traveling Officer or other UBS Employee must not otherwise organize such transfers or take any other step to attempt to circumvent this prohibition through other means.

UBS

For Internal Use Only

2.7 **Executing Contracts:** A Traveling Officer may not execute any contract on behalf of UBS while in the United States

2.8 **Emergencies:**

The Security Risk Control Hotline +41 44 234 24 24 is always available (24 hours a day) for emergency calls regarding any urgent matter.

2.9 **Adherence to Law:** A UBS Employee may not take any step that would assist any person to violate or evade any applicable law.

2.9.1 A UBS Employee must not give any advice to prospective or existing clients on how to evade taxes or circumvent any other relevant restrictions applicable to them.

2.10 **Adherence to Relevant UBS Directives and Procedures:** In addition to the limitations discussed above, all client relationships remain subject to all relevant regulations set-forth in more detail by pertinent directives, policies and procedures. In particular, client relationships are subject to:

2.10.1 Relevant AML/KYC and related requirements which apply to the respective booking center.

2.10.2 All investment profiling and similar requirements relating to the products and services the client wishes to receive.

2.11 **Product-Specific Issues**

2.11.1 **Securities products.** All persons offering securities to U.S. persons must comply with U.S. laws which generally means that the securities offered must be registered with the SEC. The purchase of securities may however be exempt from registration if certain conditions are met. Legal will direct the business either by issuing general guidance or on a case-by-case basis.

2.11.2 **Lending products.** It may be necessary to obtain a state license to offer lending products, depending on the purpose, amount, interest rate and borrower of the product. Legal will direct the business either by issuing general guidance or on a case-by-case basis.

2.11.3 **Research.** UBS research may not be distributed to clients in the United States, except in very limited circumstances. Approval must be obtained from Legal before distributing any UBS research to a U.S. resident.

2.11.4 **E-Banking.** UBS has implemented specific restrictions for e-banking for U.S. customers.

UBS

For Internal Use Only

3. Servicing Existing Clients Located in the United States

3.1 **General Restrictions:** With respect to a U.S. resident who is already a client of UBS all of the restrictions outlined in Section 2 above continue to apply.

3.2 **Permissible Activities:** If UBS AG has obtained a U.S. resident client for banking services (e.g., the client is acquired on an unsolicited basis), UBS employees may take additional steps with respect to a banking account. The following applies to banking services not securities services.

3.2.1 A UBS Employee may provide statements, account information and transaction confirmations to the client in the United States, provided (i) such documents relate only to banking services and not to securities services or products; and (ii) the UBS Employee delivers the documents in accordance with the terms agreed by the client and in compliance with all applicable internal procedures.

3.2.2 A UBS Employee may provide banking services and product information subject to the product restrictions discussed in section 2.11 above.

3.2.3 While in the United States, a Traveling Officer may certify signatures, transmit (updated) account documentation and conduct related administrative activity for existing clients so long as such activities relate only to banking services or products.

3.3 **Activities with Existing Securities Client:** In any meeting, the Traveling Officer may not communicate with the client concerning securities services or products. If an existing securities client who has not entered into a discretionary mandate with UBS inquires whether a better structure for receiving services exists, the Traveling Officer may confirm that there is (*i.e.*, a discretionary mandate) but indicate that any other discussion would have to take place outside of the United States.

UBS

For Internal Use Only

4. Establishing Relationships with New Clients in the United States ("Prospecting")

4.1 **No Active Prospecting-Principle**

UBS will abstain from any active prospecting of any U.S. based persons. Further, a UBS Employee must adhere to all of the restrictions set forth in Section 2 above when communicating or dealing with a prospective client.

4.2 **Permissible Activities:** Traveling Officers and other UBS staff may however:

4.2.1 Contact prospects who have articulated an interest for banking services and are referred by existing clients or U.S. Licensed Offices .

4.2.2 Talk to prospects who have shown an interest for banking services about their personal circumstances, topics of general economic interest and UBS in general.

4.2.3 Under no circumstances may a UBS Employee who communicates with a prospective client concerning banking products or services communicate with that prospective client concerning securities services or products.

4.3 **Account Opening Process:** If a Traveling Officer meets with a prospective client (as described in Section 4.2 above) and the prospective client asks to open a banking account with UBS, the following process should be followed.

4.3.1 A Traveling Officer may distribute to an unsolicited banking services prospect the standard UBS account opening documentation in the United States. However, UBS forms that relate to securities business (e.g. an Asset Management Agreement) can only be offered to or discussed with the prospect when he or she is outside of the United States.

4.3.2 An unsolicited banking services prospect may execute the standard UBS account opening documentation in the United States. However, the prospective client must return the forms to the appropriate UBS booking center by mail.

4.3.3 Traveling Officers may not be directly involved in the execution of the account opening documentation while in the United States or in the mailing of the documentation from the prospective client to the booking center outside of the United States.

4.3.4 Further guidance with regard to the correct completion of contractual forms (client details, signatures, locations, dates) can be found in section 2.1.1 of the Compliance & Legal Manual.

4.3.5 Account openings generally will not occur by means of correspondence (*i.e.* no account opening documentation is sent to the United States).

UBS
Wealth Management

Strictly private and confidential

KeyClients in NAM
Business Case 2003-2005

PSI-OPB - 0000029

Permanent Subcommittee on Investigations
EXHIBIT #87

Table of Contents

- Market Assessment
- Restrictive Regulatory Environment
- Competitive Environment
- Assessment of current KeyClient base
- Key Success Factors
- Marketing Strategy
- Goals

UBS
Wealth Management

030

[redacted]

Restrictive Regulatory Environment

UBS
Wealth Management

Restrictive Regulatory Environment

- Main Restrictive Regulations
- Descriptions
- Implications

UBS
Wealth Management

0040

Restrictive Regulatory Environment

<u>Main Restrictive US Regulations</u> (Booking center CH)

- Qualified Intermediary Status (QI)
- Deemed Sales Requirements
- Voluntary Disclosure / I.R.S.
- Patriot Act I & II
- Broker Dealer Act
- Investment Advisor Act

<u>Main Restrictive Canadian Regulations</u>

- The Bank Act (s. 510)

UBS
Wealth Management

041

Restrictive Regulatory Environment

<u>Description of Main Restrictive US Regulations</u> (booking center CH)

- QI agreement covers US Securities. Clients who are liable to taxation in the US can hold US securities only if they are declared. US clients with undeclared accounts may no longer hold any US securities.

- The Deemed Sales Rules enlarge the scope of the QI agreement to cover non-US securities for US persons. It makes it necessary for UBS to cease to accept securities instructions from within the US.

- Voluntary Disclosure: the government encourages US tax payers to come forward to voluntarily register and pay prior tax obligations and penalties.

UBS
Wealth Management

13

042

Restrictive Regulatory Environment

- USA PATRIOT ACT: "Uniting and Strengthening of America by Providing Appropriate Tools Required to Intercept and Obstruct Terrorism". Imposition of strict Know Your Customer Regulations, and constant monitoring of money movements.

- Broker-Dealer and Investment Advisor Acts: Laws requiring broker/dealers, investment advisors and firms providing investment advice to register with the SEC and adhere to SEC regulations.

UBS
Wealth Management

[redacted]0043

[redacted]

Restrictive Regulatory Environment

Description of Main Restrictive Canada Domestic Regulations

- Section 510 is the key provision of the Bank Act with respect to proposed activities of a foreign bank. It is not permissible for non-Canadians banks outside of Canada to seek out banking relationships with Canadian residents while the residents are in Canada. Generally speaking, UBS AG would not be permitted to provide broker-dealer type services, investment management or advisory services in Canada without being registered to provide such services with the appropriate provincial regulatory body.

UBS
Wealth Management

15

0044

[redacted]

Restrictive Regulatory Environment

Implications for UBS (booking center CH)

- US Regulations: Decrease in traditional advantages, and existing loss of Simple Assets (US Offshore Voluntary Disclosure).
- Canadian Regulations: Closer attention is necessary in regard to giving domestic clients investment advice, and with marketing and promotional activities. Employees of UBS who are not registered in Canada also need to be careful not to negotiate or enter into contract within Canada.

Implications for UBS (Canada Domestic)

- Full registration of CA is required to proactively market own services in Canada.

UBS
Wealth Management

16

[redacted]0045

Assessment of Current KeyClient Base

UBS
Wealth Management

[redacted]

Assessment of Current KC Base

KCs Statistics

2002	Number of Clients	Total Assets*	Net New Money*	Net Revenues*	Return on Assets	Actively Managed Shares
Total KC	23	2'047'227	774'826	14'049	0.88	49.49%
Total NAM all segments	11'170	21'117'661	241'650	150'000	1.00	48.26%

* Numbers are listed in thousands of CHF

Comment:

The RoA is extremely high. Therefore, we anticipate a decrease due to an increasing competition.

UBS
Wealth Management

26

[redacted]

UBS

UBS AG
P.O. Box, 8098 Zurich
Tel. +41 1 234 11 11

Daniel H. Perron
Bärengasse 16
8001 Zürich

Tel. +41 1 237 70 70
Fax +41 1 237 70 77
daniel.perron@ubs.com

www.ubs.com

BB 8

November 4, 2002

Dear client

From our recent conversations we understand that you are concerned that UBS' stance on keeping its U.S. customers' information strictly confidential may have changed especially as a result of the acquisition of Paine Webber. We are writing to reassure you that your fear is unjustified and wish to outline only some of the reasons why the protection of client data can not possibly be compromised upon:

- The sharing of customer data with a UBS unit/affiliate located abroad without sufficient customer consent constitutes a violation of Swiss banking secrecy provisions and exposes the bank employee concerned to severe criminal sanctions. Further, we should like to underscore that a Swiss bank which runs afoul of Swiss privacy laws will face sanctions by its Swiss regulator, the Swiss Federal Banking Commission, which can amount up to the revocation of the bank's charter. Already against this background, it must be clear that information relative to your Swiss banking relationship is as safe as ever and that the possibility of putting pressure on our U.S. units does not change anything. Our bank has had offices in the United States as early as 1939 and has therefore been exposed to the risk of US authorities asserting jurisdiction over assets booked abroad since decades. Please note that our bank has a successful track record of challenging such attempts.

- As you are aware of, UBS (as all other major Swiss banks) has asked for and obtained the status of a Qualified Intermediary under U.S. tax laws. The QI regime fully respects client confidentiality as customer information are only disclosed to U.S. tax authorities based on the provision of a W-9 form. Should a customer choose not to execute such a form, the client is barred from investments in US securities but under no circumstances will his/her identity be revealed. Consequently, UBS's entire compliance with its QI obligations does not create the risk that his/her identity be shared with U.S. authorities.

We look forward to working with you.

Sincerely,
UBS AG

Michel P. Guignard
Executive Director

Daniel H. Perron
Executive Director

Permanent Subcommittee on Investigations
EXHIBIT #88

PSI-OPB - 0000022

From: Liechti, Martin

Subject: Happy New Year

Welcome to the new year! I hope you enjoyed the holidays with your family and friends and took the opportunity to relax and "recharge your batteries".

We achieved much in 2006 and I thank you for your huge efforts and dedication to the Americas.

The markets are growing fast, and our competition is catching up. Also, new competition, like Itau, is showing up on the radar. The answer to guarantee our future is GROWTH. We have grown from CHF 4 million per Client Advisor in 2004 to 17 million in 2006. We need to keep up with our ambitions and go to 60 million per Client Advisor! Best shift will have to be implemented to keep up and bring our RoA to 100 bp.

Our ambitions:

100 RoA
60 NNM per CA
100% Satisfied Clients
100% UBP

In the Chinese Horoscope, 2007 is the year of the pig. In many cultures, the pig is a symbol for "luck". While it's always good to have bit of luck, it is not luck that leads to success. Success is the result of vision and purpose, hard work and passion. We have to put ourselves into a position where "luck" can find us! That we can do by sharpening our focus on our priorities for this year, which are:

To reach our ambitions don't try the extraordinary, but do the ordinary in an extraordinary way!

Our Senior Managers and our Desk Heads must CREATE, CARE and COACH the A-TEAM!

Together as a team I am convinced we will succeed!

With best wishes for the New Year,

Martin Liecht

Permanent Subcommittee on Investigations
EXHIBIT #89

Referral Campaign BU Americas

http://bw.ubs.com/page/print/1,1209,636-142506-1-6526,00.

Page URL: http://bw.ubs.com/page/0/6/0,1080,636-142506-1-6526,00.shtml

PB Americas International News : Monday, 2 June 2003 - 14:23

Referral Campaign BU Americas

Dear Colleagues,

The first five months of this year have been very challenging for our industry. The decline in investor confidence, the military conflict in the Middle East, and the ever increasing regulatory scrutiny that has descended upon our business, continue to present difficult challenges. We are, however, convinced that even in this difficult environment, we are well-positioned to provide our clients with the best solutions for their financial needs.

Net New Money is, as you know, a key element for our success. This means that we all have to work hard to achieve our NNM goals for 2003 and the years to come. In order to reach this goal, two main initiatives have been launched: The KeyClient initiative and the Referral Program within UBS. These initiatives have two goals: On the one side they will, as I said, help us to achieve our NNM targets. On the other side, they should help us to increase co-operation between UBSI, the Private Bank and the other Business Groups of UBS and between the Client Advisors and the Product Specialists. The success of these initiatives is crucial for the success of the Integrated Business Model of UBS, thus crucial for our success.

The Referral Agreement, which we have been elaborating during the previous weeks, has been signed and contains the following key point: Each Country Team making a referral will get 0.33% of the revenues generated by the Financial Advisor over a time period of four years. As you know, we set, at the beginning of the year, a target of 5 referrals per CA to be made. I am aware that it is a challenge to reach this goal. In acknowledgement of your effort and commitment, I would like to award the Client Advisor in each Country Team who achieves, until the 31st of December 2003, the most referrals (amount of money and number of referrals), but at least the 5 referrals set as target, with a Breitling wristwatch. The same will be valid for the Rep Officer (including all Rep Offices in Latin America) who achieves this goal. Since 2003 will be a unique "brand year" in UBS' history, each Breitling watch we award will be "customized" with the UBS logo.

Although 2003 is likely to remain a challenging year for investors, we are well positioned to build on our strengths, capabilities and services. Our excellent reputation for client service combined with the continued 'flight to quality' will help us to gain more market share. We are committed to become the pre-eminent advisor to our clients' financial affairs. It is therefore imperative that you give this campaign the attention it deserves. I am already looking forward to awarding those of you who will achieve this goal!

Martin Liechti

Permanent Subcommittee on Investigations

EXHIBIT #90

http://bw.ubs.com/...

Referral Campaign BU Americas

- White dial with luminous hands and hour markers.
- Date display.
- Stainless steel case.
- Black leather strap.
- Water-resistant to 330 feet.
- Sapphire crystal.
- Automatic movement.

- Mother-of-pearl dial with luminous hour markers.
- Date display.
- Stainless steel case.
- Black leather diver strap.
- Water-resistant to 330 feet.
- Sapphire crystal.
- Superquartz movement.

UBS

BS North America Report
Overview Figures NAM
July 2004
Contact: Iana Kurth Tel. 1923 - 74795

Overview Figures North America

		YTD Jul 04 Assets (in CHFm)	YTD Jul 04 AMS	YTD Jul 04 ROA	July 2004 NNM (in CHFm)	July 2004 Revenue (in CHFm)
North America		**27'077**	**56.5%**	**1.13%**	**-97.7**	**23.7**
W9	[redacted]					
CAN DOM	[redacted]					
CAN INTL	[redacted]					
NON W9		**15'971**	**64.3%**	**1.23%**	**-72.9**	**15.7**
	KEY CLIENTS NAM (OGEC8QA)	**1'018**	**50.9%**	**1.03%**	**6.5**	**0.9**
	[redacted]					
	WM US NORTH EAST (OGEK5YA)	**5'460**	**61.4%**	**1.21%**	**-22.8**	**5.2**
	CD CORE AFFLUENT NE ZH (OGEAKKA)	917	74.1%	1.47%	-5.4	1.1
	CD US NE ZH (OGA8VCA)	1'548	63.6%	1.25%	-15.1	1.6
	CD US NE ZH HNWI (OGAHTQA)	1'837	58.2%	1.07%	2.2	1.6
	CD US NE LG (OGAZ4WA)	749	60.6%	1.17%	-5.8	0.7
	MGT CT US NE (AXTF) (OGAAXEA)	409	40.7%	0.79%	-1.2	0.2
	WM US MIDWEST/ SE/ WESTERN (OGE96JA	**4'349**	**67.7%**	**1.22%**	**-26.8**	**4.3**
	CD US MW ZH (OGAZAVA)	1'101	70.2%	1.18%	-0.1	1.1
	CD US SE ZH (OGAZSQA)	1'492	45.4%	1.00%	-21.3	1.2
	CD WESTERN ZH (OGAYHHA)	1'756	85.0%	1.46%	-5.8	2.0
	[redacted]					
LONDON	**NORTH AMERICA ADVISORS (OGEGAEA)**	**1'247**	**23.4%**	**0.40%**	**-27.3**	**0.0**
	[redacted]					

UPSI 00060246

UBS

BS North America Report
Overview Figures NAM
August 2004
Contact Jana Kurth Tel 1923 - 74795

Overview Figures North America

		Assets (in CHFm)	AMS (in %)	ROA (in %)	Aug 04 NNM* (in CHFm)	YTD Aug 04 NNM* (in CHFm)	Aug 04 Revenue (in CHFm)	YTD Aug 04 Revenue (in CHFm)
North America		**27'099**	**56.6**	**1.12**	**51.1**	**362.3**	**24.3**	**196.3**
W9	[redacted]							
CAN DOM	[redacted]							
CAN INTL	**WM CANADA INTERNATIONAL**	**5'621**	**54.8**	**1.24**	**-9.5**	**3.9**	**5.1**	**41.9**
	CANADA INTL NASSAU	802	53.7	0.80	-6.9	8.5	0.5	1.1
	CD CANADA INTERN. GENEVA	1'208	57.6	1.24	1.4	-12.9	1.2	10.1
	CD CANADA INTERN. ZURICH	3'611	54.2	1.27	-3.9	8.9	3.4	30.8
	CD CANADA EAST ZH	1'710	59.8	1.33	1.0	-32.7	1.6	15.6
	CD CANADA WEST/ONTARIO ZH	1'901	49.1	1.21	-4.9	41.6	1.7	15.2
NON W9		**15'911**	**64.7**	**1.23**	**53.7**	**221.5**	**15.7**	**130.0**
	[redacted]							
	[redacted]							
	WM US NORTH EAST	**5'533**	**61.9**	**1.21**	**71.0**	**123.3**	**5.4**	**44.3**
	CD CORE AFFLUENT NE ZH	915	74.1	1.46	-4.8	-23.3	1.1	9.1
	CD US NE ZH	1'593	64.9	1.25	62.7	96.1	1.6	18.9
	CD US NE ZH HNWI	1'851	59.2	1.09	13.9	49.9	1.8	8.3
	CD US NE LG	767	58.6	1.17	0.3	1.2	0.7	5.8
	MGT CT US NE (AXTF)	406	41.0	0.79	-1.0	-9.3	0.3	2.2
	WM US MIDWEST/ SE/ WESTERN	**4'282**	**68.2**	**1.21**	**6.4**	**105.6**	**4.1**	**34.9**
	CD US MW ZH	1'090	70.0	1.12	-7.3	-5.5	1.0	8.6
	CD US SE ZH	1'446	46.3	0.99	22.0	31.7	1.2	10.0
	CD WESTERN ZH	1'746	85.0	1.44	-8.3	79.3	1.9	16.2
	WM AFFLUENT CLIENTS AMERICAS	**963**	**51.1**	**1.88**	**5.9**	**-7.3**	**1.4**	**10.4**
	WM AFFLUENT CLIENTS AME LG	56	56.0	1.91	0.2	0.6	0.1	0.6
	WM AFFLUENT CLIENTS AME GE	254	50.0	2.33	-1.5	0.1	0.4	2.9
	WM AFFLUENT CLIENTS AME ZH	654	51.2	1.74	5.9	-5.6	0.9	6.8
LONDON	**NAM ADVISORS**	**1'260**	**24.0**	**0.45**	**-5.8**	**122.0**	**0.5**	**3.9**
	[redacted]							

[illegible]

UBS

BS North America Report
Overview Figures NAM
September 2004
Contact: Jana Kurth Tel 1923 - 74795

Overview Figures North America

		Assets (in CHFm)	AMS (in %)	ROA (in %)	Sep 04 NNM* (in CHFm)	YTD Sep 04 NNM* (in CHFm)	Sep 04 Revenue (in CHFm)	YTD Sep 04 Revenue (in CHFm)
North America		27'108	57.0	1.14	15.2	377.5	28.3	224.6
W9	[redacted]							
CAN DOM	[redacted]							
CAN INTL	WM CANADA INTERNATIONAL	5'652	56.5	1.26	23.3	27.3	6.6	48.6
	CANADA INTL NASSAU	808	58.5	0.83	0.1	8.6	0.6	1.7
	CD CANADA INTERN. GENEVA	1'209	57.3	1.25	-2.0	-14.9	1.4	11.5
	CD CANADA INTERN. ZURICH	3'635	55.8	1.30	24.4	33.3	4.6	35.4
	CD CANADA EAST ZH	1'711	60.4	1.37	8.6	-24.1	2.4	17.9
	CD CANADA WEST/ONTARIO ZH	1'924	51.8	1.23	15.8	57.4	2.2	17.4
NON W9		15'780	65.0	1.25	-82.0	139.5	18.3	148.3
	[redacted]							
	WM US NORTH EAST	5'488	61.7	1.23	-40.3	83.0	6.4	50.7
	CD CORE AFFLUENT NE ZH	933	74.7	1.50	-4.5	-27.8	1.4	10.5
	CD US NE ZH	1'433	63.8	1.26	-26.2	69.8	1.7	20.6
	CD US NE ZH HNWI	1'935	58.8	1.12	-2.3	47.6	2.0	10.3
	CD US NE LG	759	58.8	1.21	-8.9	-7.6	1.0	6.8
	MGT CT US NE (AXTF)	427	44.5	0.80	-0.1	-9.3	0.3	2.5
	WM US MIDWEST/ SE/ WESTERN	4'328	67.7	1.23	-24.9	80.8	5.0	39.9
	CD US MW ZH	1'104	70.6	1.20	-0.3	-5.9	1.4	10.0
	CD US SE ZH	1'486	44.5	1.00	-19.7	11.4	1.3	11.3
	CD WESTERN ZH	1'737	85.6	1.46	-6.4	71.9	2.4	18.6
	WM AFFLUENT CLIENTS AMERICAS	1'011	51.8	1.86	1.3	-5.9	1.4	11.8
	WM AFFLUENT CLIENTS AME LG	55	55.8	1.90	0.2	0.9	0.1	0.7
	WM AFFLUENT CLIENTS AME GE	259	49.5	2.29	0.2	0.3	0.4	3.4
	WM AFFLUENT CLIENTS AME ZH	697	52.3	1.72	-1.2	-6.8	0.9	7.7
LONDON	NAM ADVISORS	1'272	23.6	0.45	30.6	-152.6	0.5	4.3
	[redacted]							

[illegible]

UBS

BS North America Report
Overview Figures NAM
October 2004
Contact: Jana Korth Tel 1923 - 74795

Overview Figures North America

		Assets (in CHFm)	AMS (in %)	ROA (in %)	Oct 04 NNM* (in CHFm)	YTD Oct 04 NNM* (in CHFm)	Oct 04 Revenue (in CHFm)	YTD Oct 04 Revenue (in CHFm)
North America		26'429	56.4	1.13	-131.0	246.5	23.6	248.2
W9	[redacted]							
CAN DOM	[redacted]							
CAN INTL	WM CANADA INTERNATIONAL	5'482	54.7	1.25	-62.7	-35.5	5.4	54.0
	CANADA INTL NASSAU	754	50.6	0.82	-43.0	-34.4	0.5	2.2
	CD CANADA INTERN. GENEVA	1'180	56.4	1.25	-6.3	-21.2	1.2	12.7
	CD CANADA INTERN. ZURICH	3'549	55.1	1.29	-13.6	-19.7	3.8	39.1
	CD CANADA EAST ZH	1'674	60.1	1.37	0.9	-23.1	1.9	19.8
	CD CANADA WEST/ONTARIO ZH	1'875	50.5	1.22	-14.6	42.8	1.9	19.3
NON W9		15'375	64.9	1.25	-44.3	95.2	14.9	163.3
	[redacted]							
	[redacted]							
	WM US NORTH EAST	5'201	61.2	1.22	-13.0	69.9	4.8	55.5
	CD CORE AFFLUENT NE ZH	7	78.7	1.50	-1.7	-29.5	0.0	10.5
	CD US NE ZH	1'452	70.5	1.26	-17.9	51.9	1.5	22.2
	CD US NE ZH HNWI	2'364	57.5	1.10	-1.3	48.9	2.0	12.3
	CD US NE LG	751	59.1	1.21	10.2	3.0	0.8	7.6
	MGT CT US NE LAXTR	627	54.1	0.82	-7.1	-16.4	0.5	3.0
	WM US MIDWEST/ SE/ WESTERN	4'320	68.1	1.23	-35.5	45.3	4.2	44.1
	CD US MW ZH	1'071	70.9	1.18	-3.2	-9.1	0.9	10.8
	CD US SE ZH	1'437	44.6	1.01	-26.6	-15.2	1.3	12.6
	CD WESTERN ZH	1'812	85.0	1.45	-5.4	66.5	2.0	20.7
	WM AFFLUENT CLIENTS AMERICAS	1'009	51.2	1.85	-0.7	-6.6	1.5	13.3
	WM AFFLUENT CLIENTS AME LG	55	56.0	1.90	0.1	1.0	0.1	0.8
	WM AFFLUENT CLIENTS AME GE	253	47.9	2.26	-1.0	-0.6	0.4	3.8
	WM AFFLUENT CLIENTS AME ZH	701	52.0	1.71	-1.6	-8.4	1.0	8.7
LONDON	NAM ADVISORS	1'202	23.0	0.44	-15.2	137.4	0.4	4.7
	[redacted]							

UBS

BS North America Report
Overview Figures NAM
November 2004
Contact: [illegible] Kurth Tel. 1923 - 74795

Overview Figures North America

		Assets (in CHFm)	AMS (in %)	ROA (in %)	Nov 04 NNM* (in CHFm)	YTD Nov 04 NNM* (in CHFm)	Nov 04 Revenue (in CHFm)	YTD Nov 04 Revenue (in CHFm)
North America		**25'878**	**56.3**	**1.13**	**-21.3**	**225.2**	**24.6**	**272.9**
W9	[redacted]							
CAN DOM	**WM CANADA DOM**	1'912	24.1	0.99	-0.4	49.7	3.1	19.7
CAN INTL	**WM CANADA INTERNATIONAL**	5'354	54.7	1.25	24.1	-11.4	5.8	59.3
	CANADA INTL NASSAU	760	47.8	0.81	38.5	2.1	0.5	2.7
	CD CANADA INTERN GENEVA	1'152	57.2	1.25	5.1	-16.1	1.2	13.9
	CD CANADA INTERN ZURICH	2'442	55.4	1.29	-17.4	2.3	3.5	42.7
	CD CANADA EAST ZH	1'622	60.3	1.36	-2.9	-26.0	1.8	21.6
	CD CANADA WEST/ONTARIO ZH	1'820	51.2	1.22	-14.5	28.3	1.8	21.1
NON W9		**15'025**	**64.7**	**1.25**	**-52.5**	**42.8**	**15.7**	**179.0**
	KEY CLIENTS NAM	930	45.0	1.20	-2.9	41.5	0.8	9.2
	[redacted]							
	WM US NORTH EAST	5'032	61.2	1.21	-14.2	55.7	5.0	60.6
	CD CORE AFFLUENT NE ZH	-	0.0	1.50	-0.4	-29.9	0.0	10.5
	CD US NE ZH	1'371	71.7	1.26	-7.2	44.7	1.5	23.7
	CD US NE ZH HNWI	2'297	57.5	1.11	-14.8	34.0	2.3	14.6
	CD US NE LG	743	58.7	1.20	0.7	3.7	0.7	8.2
	MGT CT US NE (AXTF)	620	55.0	0.84	7.2	-8.2	0.5	3.5
	WM US MIDWEST/ SE/ WESTERN	4'207	68.7	1.22	-18.2	27.1	4.2	48.3
	CD US MW ZH	1'053	71.3	1.18	-4.8	-13.9	1.0	11.9
	CD US SE ZH	1'393	46.1	1.00	-8.6	-23.8	1.1	13.7
	CD WESTERN ZH	1'761	84.9	1.44	-4.8	61.8	2.0	22.7
	WM AFFLUENT CLIENTS AMERICAS	1'082	50.7	1.85	0.0	-6.6	1.7	15.0
	WM AFFLUENT CLIENTS AME LG	54	56.0	1.88	-0.0	1.0	0.1	0.9
	WM AFFLUENT CLIENTS AME GE	260	47.7	2.28	-1.8	-2.4	0.5	4.3
	WM AFFLUENT CLIENTS AME ZH	767	51.4	1.71	-0.2	8.9	1.1	9.8
LONDON	**NAM ADVISORS**	1'172	23.4	0.44	11.3	126.1	0.4	5.1
	ACQUISITION NAM	[illegible]	[illegible]	[illegible]	[illegible]	[illegible]	[illegible]	[illegible]

[illegible]

UBS

BS North America Report
Overview Figures NAM
December 2004
Contact: Jana Kurth Tel. 1923 - 74795

Overview Figures North America

		Assets [illegible]	AMS [illegible]	ROA [illegible]	Dec 04 NNM* [illegible]	YtD Dec 04 NNM* [illegible]	Dec 04 Revenue [illegible]	YtD Dec 04 Revenue [illegible]
North America		**26'060**	**55.1**	**1.14**	**-133.4**	**91.8**	**27.4**	**300.3**
W9	[redacted]							
CAN DOM	[redacted]							
CAN INTL	**WM CANADA INTERNATIONAL**	**5'386**	**55.7**	**1.26**	**37.2**	**25.8**	**6.0**	**65.3**
	CANADA INTL NASSAU	* 733	50.4	0.82	32.9	34.9	0.5	3.2
	CD CANADA INTERN. GENEVA	1'159	57.5	1.26	-5.3	-21.5	1.3	15.2
	CD CANADA INTERN. ZURICH	3'494	56.2	1.30	9.5	11.8	4.2	46.9
	CD CANADA EAST ZH	1'637	61.2	1.37	-8.1	-34.1	2.0	23.6
	CD CANADA WEST/ONTARIO ZH	1'857	51.8	1.24	17.6	45.9	2.1	23.3
NON W9		**15'066**	**62.7**	**1.25**	**-200.8**	**-158.1**	**17.6**	**196.6**
	VIPA ACQUISITION NAM GE	**524**	**48.8**	**0.99**	**-13.3**	**-18.7**	**0.2**	**9.9**
	[redacted]							
	WM US NORTH EAST	**5'105**	**61.2**	**1.22**	**9.8**	**65.5**	**5.3**	**65.8**
	CD CORE AFFLUENT NE ZH	-	0.0	1.50	-0.7	-30.0	-	10.5
	CD MILLIONAIRES US NE ZH	1'363	71.8	1.29	-7.3	37.4	2.0	25.7
	CD HNWI US NE ZH	2'322	57.8	1.10	-15.0	19.0	1.9	16.5
	CD US NE LG	765	57.1	1.21	2.0	5.7	0.8	9.1
	MGT CT US NE (AXTF)	655	55.4	0.86	26.1	16.9	0.5	4.1
	WM US MIDWEST/ SE/ WESTERN	**4'102**	**66.7**	**1.24**	**-179.9**	**-152.9**	**4.8**	**53.0**
	CD US MW ZH	1'069	58.7	1.18	-10.0	-23.9	1.1	13.0
	CD US SE ZH	1'416	45.6	1.01	-1.1	-24.9	1.3	15.1
	CD WESTERN ZH	1'618	83.7	1.47	-168.9	-107.1	2.3	25.0
	WM AFFLUENT CLIENTS AMERICAS	**1'118**	**52.5**	**1.92**	**-4.1**	**-10.7**	**2.3**	**17.3**
	WM AFFLUENT CLIENTS AME LG	56	57.6	1.95	0.2	1.2	0.1	1.0
	WM AFFLUENT CLIENTS AME GE	290	50.8	2.38	-1.1	-3.5	0.8	5.1
	WM AFFLUENT CLIENTS AME ZH	771	52.7	1.78	-3.6	-12.2	1.4	11.2
LONDON	**NAM ADVISORS**	**1'220**	**22.1**	**0.45**	**2.7**	**128.8**	**0.6**	**5.7**
	ACQUISITION NAM	[illegible]	**0.0**	**0.60**	[illegible]	**0.0**	[illegible]	**0.0**

* [illegible]

Overview Figures North America

January 2005

		Assets	AMS	ROA	Jan 05 NNM*	YTD Jan 05 NNM*	Jan 05 Revenue	YTD Jan 05 Revenue
North America		27'057	0.0	1.11	67.3	67.3	24.9	24.9
SFA	UBS SFA AG	427	-	0.32	1.5	1.5	0.114	0.1
W9	[redacted]							
CAN DOM	WM CANADA DOM	2'957	0.0	0.35	51.5	51.5	0.344	0.9
CAN INTL	WM CANADA INTERNATIONAL	5'309	0.0	1.31	-12.3	-12.3	5.6	5.6
	CANADA INTL NASSAU	759	0.0	0.78	3.9	3.9	0.5	0.5
	CD CANADA INTERN. GENEVA	1'186	0.0	1.19	-4.9	-4.9	1.2	1.2
	CD CANADA INTERN. ZURICH	3'570	0.0	1.81	-11.3	-11.3	3.9	3.5
	CD CANADA EAST ZH	1'678	0.0	1.35	-8.7	-8.7	1.9	1.9
	CD CANADA WEST/ONTARIO ZH	1'894	0.0	1.27	-2.5	-2.5	2.0	2.0
NON W9		15'515	0.0	1.21	-12.6	-12.6	15.7	15.7
	MPA ACQUISITION NAM GE	[illegible]	0.0	0.85	26.6	26.6	[illegible]	6.2
	[redacted]							
	WM US NORTH EAST (OGEKSYA)	5'189	0.0	1.15	-61.9	-61.9	5.0	5.0
	CD US NE ZH HNWI	2'339	0.0	1.11	-58.7	-58.7	2.2	2.2
	CD MILLIONAIRES US NE ZH	1'380	0.0	1.36	-5.4	-5.4	1.6	1.6
	CD US NE LG	792	0.0	1.11	1.1	1.1	0.7	0.7
	MGT CT US NE	678	0.0	0.91	2.7	2.7	0.5	0.5
	RETENTION CD US NE	-	0.0	0.0	-1.7	-1.7	-0.0	-0.0
	WM US MIDWEST/ SE/ WESTERN	4'243	0.0	1.23	6.6	6.6	4.3	4.3
	CD US MW ZH	1'095	0.0	1.26	2.9	2.9	1.2	1.2
	CD US SE ZH	1'467	0.0	0.98	5.7	5.7	1.2	1.2
	CD WESTERN ZH	1'681	0.0	1.42	-2.0	-2.0	2.0	2.0
	WM AFFLUENT CLIENTS AMERICAS	1'153	0.0	1.66	5.0	5.0	1.6	1.6
	WM AFFLUENT CLIENTS AME LG	57	0.0	1.85	0.2	0.2	0.1	0.1
	WM AFFLUENT CLIENTS AME GE	291	0.0	1.89	-0.0	-0.0	0.5	0.5
	WM AFFLUENT CLIENTS AME ZH	805	0.0	1.58	4.8	4.8	1.1	1.1
LONDON	NAM ADVISORS	1'285	0.0	0.51	31.0	31.0	0.5	0.5

Contact: [illegible] tel. 1922 - 74795

UBS

BS North America Report
Overview Figures NAM
February 2005
Contact: Jana Kurth Tel. 1923 - 74795

Overview Figures North America

		Assets (in CHFm)	AMS (in %)	ROA (in %)	Feb 05 NNM* (in CHFm)	YtD Feb 05 NNM* (in CHFm)	Feb 05 Revenue (in CHFm)	YtD Feb 05 Revenue (in CHFm)
North America		**26'922**	**53.9**	**1.13**	**20.5**	**88.9**	**25.6**	**50.6**
SFA	UBS SFA AG	556	n/a	0.43	0.7	2.2	0.2	0.4
W9	[redacted]							
CAN DOM	WM CANADA DOM	2'084	24.5	0.57	41.7	93.3	1.0	2.0
CAN INTL	WM CANADA INTERNATIONAL	5'461	56.7	1.21	-0.0	-12.3	5.5	11.0
	CANADA INTL NASSAU	743	50.5	0.87	4.3	-5.2	0.6	1.1
	CD CANADA INTERN. GENEVA	1'175	58.4	1.20	-2.2	-7.1	1.2	2.4
	CD CANADA INTERN. ZURICH	3'547	57.3	1.78	0.8	-10.4	3.7	7.6
	CD CANADA EAST ZH	1'665	62.2	1.32	5.0	-9.7	1.8	3.7
	CD CANADA WEST/ONTARIO ZH	1'877	53.0	1.24	-4.1	-6.8	1.9	3.9
NON W9		**15'413**	**63.2**	**1.25**	**-50.1**	**-63.2**	**16.5**	**32.2**
	VIPA ACQUISITION NAM GE	960	47.5	1.01	-16.9	3.7	0.8	1.6
	[redacted]							
	WM US NORTH EAST	5'192	61.1	1.21	16.4	-44.0	5.5	10.5
	CD US NE ZH HNWI	2'387	55.4	1.20	51.5	-7.2	2.6	4.7
	CD MILLIONAIRES US NE ZH	1'375	73.0	1.36	12.2	6.5	1.6	3.1
	CD US NE LG	790	59.3	1.14	-4.7	-3.6	0.8	1.5
	MGT CT US NE	638	59.3	1.00	-40.7	-38.0	0.6	1.1
	RETENTION CD US NE	2	32.9	2.62	-1.8	-1.8	0.0	0.0
	WM US MIDWEST/ SE/ WESTERN	4'196	67.8	1.23	-24.2	-17.6	4.3	8.7
	CD US MW ZH	1'092	72.3	1.20	-0.3	2.6	1.0	2.2
	CD US SE ZH	1'438	46.0	0.99	-19.3	-13.5	1.2	2.4
	CD WESTERN ZH	1'666	83.7	1.47	-4.7	-6.7	2.1	4.1
	CD MW/ SE/ WE SPECIAL CLIENTS	-	0.0	0.0	-	-	0.0	0.0
	WM AFFLUENT CLIENTS AMERICAS	1'182	53.0	1.68	-0.1	3.1	1.7	3.3
	WM AFFLUENT CLIENTS AME LG	55	59.4	1.84	-0.1	-0.1	0.1	0.2
	WM AFFLUENT CLIENTS AME GE	286	51.9	1.95	-1.0	-2.1	0.5	0.9
	WM AFFLUENT CLIENTS AME ZH	840	53.0	1.58	0.9	5.3	1.1	2.2
LONDON	NAM ADVISORS	1'205	23.1	0.5	-7.9	23.1	0.4	1.0

UBS

BS North America Report
Overview Figures NAM
March 2005
Contact: Jana Kurth Tel. 1923 - 74795

Overview Figures North America

		Assets (in CHFm)	AMS (in %)	ROA (in %)	Mar 05 NNM* (in CHFm)	YtD Mar 05 NNM* (in CHFm)	Mar 05 Revenue (in CHFm)	YtD Mar 05 Revenue (in CHFm)
North America		27'290	54.3	1.18	-135.8	-47.0	29.2	79.9
SFA	UBS SFA AG	1'055	38.5	0.49	-9.7	-7.6	0.5	0.8
W9	[redacted]							
CAN DOM	WM CANADA DOM	2'104	23.4	0.56	-31.9	21.4	1.0	2.9
CAN INTL	WM CANADA INTERNATIONAL	5'586	56.3	1.29	38.9	24.6	6.8	17.8
	CANADA INTL NASSAU	780	49.1	0.90	19.7	24.9	0.6	1.7
	CD CANADA INTERN. GENEVA	1'206	58.0	1.31	3.2	-3.9	1.6	4.0
	CD CANADA INTERN. ZURICH	3'600	57.4	1.36	16.0	5.6	4.6	12.1
	CD CANADA EAST ZH	1'695	62.3	1.42	-0.0	3.8	2.3	6.6
	CD CANADA WEST/ONTARIO ZH	1'904	53.0	1.31	16.0	1.4	2.3	6.2
NON W9		15'614	62.7	1.31	-94.0	-157.2	18.7	50.9
	WBA ACQUISITION NAM GE	322	[illegible]	1.02	7.2	7.5	[illegible]	2.5
	[redacted]							
	WM US NORTH EAST	5'198	60.4	1.27	-99.4	-143.4	6.1	16.5
	CD US NE ZH HNWI	2'368	54.0	1.23	-111.0	-118.2	2.5	7.3
	CD MILLIONAIRES US NE ZH	1'391	73.3	1.50	-6.9	-0.4	2.1	5.2
	CD US NE LG	802	58.1	1.19	5.0	1.4	0.9	2.4
	MGT CT US NE	635	59.1	1.04	14.8	-23.2	0.6	1.7
	RETENTION CD US NE	2	74.3	2.53	-1.2	-3.0	0.0	0.0
	WM US MIDWEST/ SE/ WESTERN	4'254	67.6	1.32	-0.0	-17.6	5.2	13.9
	CD US MW ZH	1'110	71.8	1.23	1.7	4.3	1.2	3.4
	CD US SE ZH	1'457	46.1	1.04	-0.5	-14.0	1.4	3.8
	CD WESTERN ZH	1'686	83.4	1.61	-1.2	-7.9	2.6	6.7
	CD MW/ SE/ WE SPECIAL CLIENTS	1	0.0	5.43	-0.0	-0.0	0.0	0.0
	WM AFFLUENT CLIENTS AMERICAS	1'239	53.1	1.70	0.9	4.0	1.8	5.1
	WM AFFLUENT CLIENTS AME LG	57	58.5	1.82	0.3	0.2	0.1	0.3
	WM AFFLUENT CLIENTS AME GE	316	52.4	1.95	-0.0	-2.1	0.5	1.5
	WM AFFLUENT CLIENTS AME ZH	867	53.1	1.60	0.7	5.5	1.2	3.4
LONDON	NAM ADVISORS	1'253	22.4	0.5	-2.4	20.7	0.5	1.4

CONFIDENTIAL TREATMENT REQUESTED UPSI 00060254

UBS

BS North America Report
Overview Figures NAM
August 2005
Contact: Jana Kurth-Spiegl
Tel. 1923 - 74795

Overview Figures North America

	YTD 2005		YTD 2005		MtD 2005	YTD 2005	MtD 2005	YTD 2005
	Assets in bn	AMS %	ROA %	Discreationary Share %	Revenues in mio CHF	Revenues in mio CHF	NNM in mio CHF	NNM in mio CHF
North America	41.2	51.2	0.98	31.7	28.9	242.4	1799.2	3253.0
[redacted]	[redacted]	[redacted]	[redacted]	[redacted]	[redacted]	[redacted]	[redacted]	[redacted]
MILLIONAIRES ZH	[redacted]	[redacted]	[redacted]	[redacted]	[redacted]	[redacted]	[redacted]	[redacted]
MILLIONAIRES GE	[redacted]	[redacted]	[redacted]	[redacted]	[redacted]	[redacted]	[redacted]	[redacted]
AFFLUENT AME	[redacted]	[redacted]	[redacted]	[redacted]	[redacted]	[redacted]	[redacted]	[redacted]
W9 BUSINESS ROW	[redacted]	[redacted]	[redacted]	[redacted]	[redacted]	[redacted]	[redacted]	[redacted]
TOTAL US INTL MILLIONAIRES	5.7	67.9	1.56	40.2	7.6	55.7	33.0	343.0
HNWI GE 1	[redacted]	[redacted]	[redacted]	[redacted]	[redacted]	[redacted]	[redacted]	[redacted]
HNWI GE 2	[redacted]	[redacted]	[redacted]	[redacted]	[redacted]	[redacted]	[redacted]	[redacted]
HNWI NE ZH	[redacted]	[redacted]	[redacted]	[redacted]	[redacted]	[redacted]	[redacted]	[redacted]
HNWI MW/SE/WE ZH	[redacted]	[redacted]	[redacted]	[redacted]	[redacted]	[redacted]	[redacted]	[redacted]
ADVISORS LONDON	[redacted]	[redacted]	[redacted]	[redacted]	[redacted]	[redacted]	[redacted]	[redacted]
TOTAL US INTL HNWI	12.6	55.2	1.00	37.6	11.2	87.7	13.9	192.9
> SFA	2.1	37.6	0.66	37.0	1.3	6.1	-3.0	-12.5
[redacted]	[redacted]	[redacted]	[redacted]	[redacted]	[redacted]	[redacted]	[redacted]	[redacted]
EUROPE DESKS AMERICA NY	[redacted]	[redacted]	[redacted]	[redacted]	[redacted]	[redacted]	[redacted]	[redacted]
EUROPE DESKS BAHAMAS	[redacted]	[redacted]	[redacted]	[redacted]	[redacted]	[redacted]	[redacted]	[redacted]
JULIUS BAER NAM L.A.	[redacted]	[redacted]	[redacted]	[redacted]	[redacted]	[redacted]	[redacted]	[redacted]
> Can International	6.0	55.9	1.26	33.1	6.1	48.4	21.5	40.2
CD CANADA EAST ZH	1.8	62.6	1.36	44.7	1.9	15.9	-0.5	-15.8
CD CANADA WEST/ONTARIO ZH	2.0	52.9	1.28	25.5	2.1	16.6	5.2	19.1
CD CANADA INTERN. GENEVA	1.3	57.7	1.32	30.9	1.4	10.9	24.6	20.4
CANADA INTL NASSAU	0.8	45.9	0.94	29.7	0.7	5.0	-7.8	16.5
> Can Dom	2.6	21.1	0.58	16.5	1.4	9.2	0.6	281.7
CD CAN TORONTO	0.6	66.9	0.50	61.9	0.4	3.0	5.2	12.3
CD CAN MONTREAL	0.4	33.3	0.91	31.3	0.3	2.0	2.6	31.9
CD CAN VANCOUVER	0.6	12.7	0.61	9.0	0.7	2.2	8.1	36.8
CD CAN CALGARY	0.0	0.0	0.00	0.0	0.0	0.0	0.0	0.0
CD LATIN AMERICA TORONTO	1.1	2.6	0.82	1.6	0.3	2.0	11.4	246.5
> KeyClient Development NAM	2.9	0.8	0.07	0.1	0.1	0.3	1708.9	1726.3

Source: Figures based on GMIS/Domino (Facts&Figures Report on GCRS)

* US Dom. Figures MtD Aug with deficiencies, esp. Revenues (will be corrected in Sep 2005)

CONFIDENTIAL TREATMENT REQUESTED UPSI 00060255

UBS

B5 North America Report
Overview Figures NAM
September 2005
Contact: Jana Kurth-Spiegl
Tel 1923 - 74795

Overview Figures North America

	YTD 2005		YTD 2005		MtD 2005	YTD 2005	MtD 2005	YTD 2005
	Assets in bn	AMS %	ROA %	Discretionary Share %	Revenues in mio CHF	Revenues in mio CHF	NNM in mio CHF	NNM in mio CHF
North America	41.3	50.9	0.99	33.0	36.3	278.7	106.4	3359.4
[redacted]	[redacted]	[redacted]	[redacted]	[redacted]	[redacted]	[redacted]	[redacted]	[redacted]
MILLIONAIRES ZH	[redacted]	[redacted]	[redacted]	[redacted]	[redacted]	[redacted]	[redacted]	[redacted]
MILLIONAIRES GE	[redacted]	[redacted]	[redacted]	[redacted]	[redacted]	[redacted]	[redacted]	[redacted]
AFFLUENT AME	[redacted]	[redacted]	[redacted]	[redacted]	[redacted]	[redacted]	[redacted]	[redacted]
W9 BUSINESS ROW	[redacted]	[redacted]	[redacted]	[redacted]	[redacted]	[redacted]	[redacted]	[redacted]
TOTAL US INTL MILLIONAIRES	5.9	68.0	1.61	40.5	9.4	78.1	-13.1	356.1
HNWI GE 1	[redacted]	[redacted]	[redacted]	[redacted]	[redacted]	[redacted]	[redacted]	[redacted]
HNWI GE 2	[redacted]	[redacted]	[redacted]	[redacted]	[redacted]	[redacted]	[redacted]	[redacted]
HNWI NE ZH	[redacted]	[redacted]	[redacted]	[redacted]	[redacted]	[redacted]	[redacted]	[redacted]
HNWI MW/SE/WE ZH	[redacted]	[redacted]	[redacted]	[redacted]	[redacted]	[redacted]	[redacted]	[redacted]
ADVISORS LONDON	[redacted]	[redacted]	[redacted]	[redacted]	[redacted]	[redacted]	[redacted]	[redacted]
TOTAL US INTL HNWI	12.3	56.1	1.03	38.7	13.2	101.0	73.2	1265.7
> SFA	2.1	37.7	0.67	37.2	1.3	7.4	-2.4	-14.9
[redacted]	[redacted]	[redacted]	[redacted]	[redacted]	[redacted]	[redacted]	[redacted]	[redacted]
EUROPE DESKS AMERICA NY	[redacted]	[redacted]	[redacted]	[redacted]	[redacted]	[redacted]	[redacted]	[redacted]
EUROPE DESKS BAHAMAS	[redacted]	[redacted]	[redacted]	[redacted]	[redacted]	[redacted]	[redacted]	[redacted]
JULIUS BAER NAM L.A.	[redacted]	[redacted]	[redacted]	[redacted]	[redacted]	[redacted]	[redacted]	[redacted]
> Can International	6.2	56.2	1.29	33.1	7.6	56.0	-29.8	10.3
CD CANADA EAST ZH	1.9	62.5	1.40	44.6	2.7	16.6	-1.2	-17.0
CD CANADA WEST/ONTARIO ZH	2.1	52.5	1.29	25.2	2.5	19.1	-16.2	2.8
CD CANADA INTERN. GENEVA	1.4	59.5	1.34	31.6	1.7	12.6	4.0	24.4
CANADA INTL NASSAU	0.8	46.3	0.95	29.1	0.7	5.7	-16.4	0.1
> Can Dom	3.0	20.6	0.58	17.4	1.4	10.6	204.4	468.1
CD CAN TORONTO	0.6	66.6	0.80	60.0	0.4	3.4	11.5	24.6
CD CAN MONTREAL	0.4	34.2	0.91	31.8	0.3	2.9	10.0	11.9
CD CAN VANCOUVER	0.8	12.2	0.61	7.3	0.4	2.6	177.7	214.5
CD CAN CALGARY	0.0	0.0	0.00	0.0	0.0	0.0	0.0	0.0
CD LATIN AMERICA TORONTO	1.1	2.3	0.32	1.5	0.3	2.3	25.2	271.7
> KeyClient Development NAM	3.1	0.8	0.07	0.1	0.2	0.4	18.0	1744.3

Source. Figures based on GMIS/Domino (Facts&Figures Report on GCRS)
US Dom. Figures with deficiencies.

CONFIDENTIAL TREATMENT REQUESTED UPSI 00060256

UBS

BS North America Report
Overview Figures NAM
October 2005
Contact Jana Kurth-Spiegl
Tel 1923 74795

Overview Figures North America

	YTD 2005		YTD 2005		MtD 2005	YTD 2005	MtD 2005	YTD 2005
	Assets in bn	AMS %	ROA %	Discretionary Share %	Revenues in mio CHF	Revenues in mio CHF	NNM in mio CHF	NNM in mio CHF
North America	42.1	49.8	0.88	32.3	32.5	311.2	259.0	3628.4
[redacted]								
MILLIONAIRES ZH	[redacted]							
MILLIONAIRES GE	[redacted]							
AFFLUENT AME	[redacted]							
W9 BUSINESS ROW	[redacted]							
TOTAL US INTL MILLIONAIRES	[illegible]	[illegible]	[illegible]	[illegible]	[illegible]	[illegible]	[illegible]	[illegible]
HNWI GE 1	[redacted]							
HNWI GE 2	[redacted]							
HNWI NE ZH	[redacted]							
HNWI MW/SE/WE ZH	[redacted]							
ADVISORS LONDON	[redacted]							
TOTAL US INTL HNWI	[illegible]	[illegible]	[illegible]	[illegible]	[illegible]	[illegible]	[illegible]	[illegible]
> SFA	2.1	38.3	0.68	37.8	1.3	8.7	-8.9	-23.8
[redacted]								
EUROPE DESKS AMERICA NY	[redacted]							
EUROPE DESKS BAHAMAS	[redacted]							
DESK IB NAM LOS ANGELES	[redacted]							
> Can International	6.2	56.0	1.30	32.6	7.4	63.4	62.4	72.7
CD CANADA EAST ZH	1.9	62.1	1.39	44.3	2.1	20.7	12.3	-4.7
CD CANADA WEST/ONTARIO ZH	2.1	52.7	1.29	24.7	2.3	21.4	19.2	22.0
CD CANADA INTERN GENEVA	1.4	58.7	1.32	30.8	1.3	14.0	32.0	56.4
CANADA INTL NASSAU	0.8	46.4	1.10	29.2	1.7	7.4	-1.0	-0.9
> Can Dom	2.9	27.2	0.58	17.5	1.3	11.9	26.5	441.6
CD CAN TORONTO	0.6	67.2	[illegible]	59.8	[illegible]	3.7	[illegible]	21.1
CD CAN MONTREAL	0.4	[illegible]	0.90	37.5	1.3	2.6	[illegible]	[illegible]
CD CAN VANCOUVER	0.8	13.8	0.61	8.5	0.4	3.0	28.4	186.2
CD CAN CALGARY	0.0	0.0	0.00	0.0	0.0	0.0	0.0	0.0
CD LATIN AMERICA TORONTO	[illegible]	[illegible]	0.31	[illegible]	0.3	2.5	3.0	274.7
> KeyClient Development NAM	3.6	6.7	0.10	5.9	0.5	0.9	7.3	1751.5

Source: Figures based on GMIS/Domino (Facts&Figures Report on GCRS)

Case Studies Cross-Border Workshop NAM

- **Please go through each case. Put yourself into the concrete situation as it occurs in real life.**
- **Do not tackle the case with the perspective of what you think that Legal, Compliance, IT or Security Risk wants to hear.**
- **Compare your behaviours with the ones of your colleagues in the group.**
- **Identify and note questions you want to raise in the plenary session.**

Case 1

During your trip to the USA/Canada, where you wish to visit various clients, you are stopped at the border by the customs authority or during your stay by the police and confronted with the following questions:

- purpose of your visit
- your profession
- people you are going to visit
- content of your baggage incl. notebook, cell phone, PDA (SMS, MMS, digital photographing) or Blackberry

Question 1: How do you react? How do you prepare for such a potential confrontation? How did you fill out your immigration form?

You get a strange feeling about the way the way the questions are asked. You remember that, with the intention to avoid having to carry those documents with you, you had sent an envelope with some of the sensitive account related data to your hotel (alternatively: a friend in the respective country whom you know very well; a family member; a local business contact).

Question 2: How do you handle sensitive documents you want to use during your visit (such as account statements and similar documents) when planning a trip to the USA/Canada?

Case 2

During the discussion with a very interesting prospect in the USA/Canada he/she indicates that he/she has a substantial amount of money to transfer from his/her home country to your bank. The prospect queries whether the bank can assist him/her in this respect. He/She mentions in the same token that Bank XYZ had offered him/her very concrete services for his/her assistance.

Question: How do you react? Would it make a difference if the person was a long standing client of the bank?

Case 3

During a trip to the USA/Canada you intend to meet client X. He recently gave you a telephone call and asked you to bring his latest account statements with you at your next visit. He also mentioned that he would like to hand over to you a number of written trading orders and to discuss them at the proposed meeting. Finally, he refers to the telephone conversation you had with him some weeks ago regarding the advantages of a PM mandate and he asked you to also bring along the necessary documents for the conclusion of a PM contract.

Permanent Subcommittee on Investigations

EXHIBIT #92

Due to a conflict of dates you are not able to travel. As you do not want to disappoint your client, you consider making a call to the local UBS branch/subsidiary (where you know one of the officers very well) and ask an officer to meet your client and to satisfy his requests on your behalf.

Question 1: What do you think of this idea?

Question 2: Generally speaking, to what extent and in which activities can your colleague of the local branch/subsidiary be of assistance? Please go through concrete situations as they occur in your daily work.

Case 4

After passing the immigration desk during your trip to the USA/Canada, you are intercepted by the authorities. By checking your Palm, they find all your client meetings. Fortunately you stored only very short remarks of the different meetings and no names.

As you spend around one week in the same hotel, the longer you stay there, the more you get the feeling of being observed. Sometimes you even doubt if all of the hotel employees are working for the hotel. A lot of client meetings are held in your suite of the hotel.

One morning your are intercepted by an FBI-agent. He looks for some information about one of your clients and explains to you, that your client is involved in illegal activities.

Question 1: What would you do in such a situation?

Question 2: What are the signs indicating that something is going on?

Case 5

As you had a lot of documents to take with you to your trip to the USA/Canada, the carry on luggage was very heavy and you decided to put your notebook in the checked luggage. When arriving at your destination, you realise that your notebook is missing. You are not sure, whether you had a separate excel-file with a client summary still on your notebook.

Question 1: What would you do in such a situation?

Later on, when arriving at the hotel, you are contacted by an anonymous caller. He pretends having found your notebook at the airport and offers you a deal: He sends you the notebook if you pay him an amount of USD 100'000. Your notebook is equipped with the latest security features (encryption, token based authentication).

Question 2: Your reaction

Strictly Confidential

αβ

UBS AG
Postfach
8098 Zürich
Tel.+41-44-234 11 11

Memorandum

15 November 2007

to

cc

from

subject Internal Memo

Changes in business model for U.S. private clients

Dear Colleagues

As part of our ongoing efforts to better serve our clients and to streamline and simplify our business in compliance with applicable laws and regulations, we have decided to realign the business model for U.S. clients by focusing our resources on our wealth management operations based in the United States ("U.S. units") and UBS Swiss Financial Advisers in Zurich ("UBS SFA"). Our U.S. units provide a complete set of sophisticated wealth management services to private clients. UBS SFA is an SEC-registered investment advisor and Swiss-regulated entity that offers investment programs in the Swiss tradition, trained private bankers and expertise in global investment diversification.

After the acquisition of PaineWebber in 2000, UBS has worked to better accommodate the global needs of U.S. clients. The establishment of UBS SFA in 2005 was a further important step in that process. UBS SFA has proved to be very successful and clients have responded very positively. UBS also has provided limited services to U.S. private clients who chose to maintain assets with UBS AG, governed by our established policies and procedures.

Over the years we have periodically reviewed these offerings in order to provide the best level of service to our clients in compliance with applicable laws and regulations. As part of these periodic reviews, we have recognized for some time that the current business structure is complex and could benefit from being simplified and streamlined. UBS has decided to accelerate the consolidation of our offerings to U.S. clients on these two platforms, U.S. units and UBS SFA.

We decided to further realign the overall structure and service model for U.S. clients by:

- Increasing our focus on the U.S. units and UBS SFA by permitting new account opening for securities related services only within those units;
- Discontinuing client relationships with assets below CHF 50.000;
- Permitting new account openings for banking services only with a minimum asset size of CHF 250,000; and
- Servicing clients only in their respective booking center.

The changes are effective immediately.

469: (Colleagues)

Permanent Subcommittee on Investigations
EXHIBIT #93

FEB-08-2008 11:51 IRS P.08

TOTAL P.09

αβ

Internal Memo
15 November 2007
Page 2 of 2

Further Information and instructions will follow in the course of the ongoing implementation of the new business model.

If you have questions please contact our US competence center. (Thomas Christen 1923-44753 / Thomas.christen@ubs.com). In case of questions from clients please contact U.S. competence center prior to answering their questions.

Best regards
Raoul Weil, Chairman and CEO Global Wealth Management & Business Banking

UBS AG

Internal use only

αβ

TALKING POINTS FOR INFORMING U.S. PRIVATE CLIENTS WITH SECURITIES HOLDINGS ABOUT THE REALIGNMENT OF OUR BUSINESS MODEL PLUS Q&A

A. Information that must be relayed on the call:

CA: Please permit me to explain the important changes that UBS has decided to make to the private banking relationships with our U.S. clients.

- As part of our ongoing efforts to better serve our clients and to streamline and simplify our business, we have decided to realign the services we offer to U.S. clients by focusing our resources on our wealth management operations based in the United States ("U.S. units") and UBS Swiss Financial Advisers ("SFA") in Zurich. Our U.S. units provide a complete set of sophisticated wealth management services to private clients. SFA is an SEC-registered investment adviser and Swiss regulated entity that offers investment programs in the Swiss tradition, trained private bankers and expertise in global investment diversification. If you would like to explore the services available through the U.S. units or SFA, please let me know and I will have a representative of those businesses contact you.

- Because of our increased focus on servicing our U.S. clients through the mentioned units, we are making some modifications to our existing service model. Specifically, if you would like to remain with UBS and do not choose to transfer your relationship to our U.S. units or SFA, we will not be able to open new securities accounts for you or any other U.S. client. Client advisors, including myself, will no longer be traveling outside of Switzerland to meet you, and you will only be serviced in your booking center location here in Switzerland. Moreover, in accordance with established policies, we will not be able to communicate with you about your securities account when you are in the United States. In other words, if you choose to maintain your account at UBS, any communication between us, including telephone, e-mail, fax, and written correspondence that involves your securities account must occur when you are outside the United States (which is subject to verification).[NOTE TO CLIENT ADVISERS: THIS STATEMENT IS SUBJECT TO THE ONE-TIME EXCEPTION AS PER ANSWER 5 HEREAFTER]

We should emphasize that we will not be able to execute your securities instructions if we are not satisfied that you are outside the U.S. when giving such orders.

****

B. Questions and Answers

Q1. What do I need to do to transfer my assets to the U.S. units or SFA?

A. I will have a representative of U.S. units/SFA contact you to explain the services they offer and the account opening process. Please note that the U.S. units and SFA provide Form 1099 tax reporting services and will require that you supply a W-9 form.

Q2. What if I do not want U.S. tax reporting services or to supply a W-9?

A. Then you may retain your current account subject to the modifications I just described.

1

Permanent Subcommittee on Investigations
EXHIBIT #94

FEB-05-2008 11:50 IRS P.02

Internal use only

αβ

Q3. Is there any other option for me at UBS?

A. I am afraid not. Although we very much would like to retain your business, if none of these choices is satisfactory to you, we will follow your instruction to transfer your assets to another institution if that is what you decide to do. Although we may accept simple instructions from the United States to transfer custody of your securities, i.e. you do not instruct us to sell your securities holdings or part of it but to transfer it in its entirety to another institution, please note that, in accordance with established policies, any instructions to sell your securities holdings (even as part of a transfer) must be given when you are outside of the United States and are subject to verification.

More generally, as I have mentioned, all instructions about selling, buying, redeeming, exchanging or otherwise engaging in securities transactions must be given when you are outside the United States, which is, of course, subject to verification

Q4. If I decide to keep my existing account, how will I communicate with you?

A. You may visit us in Switzerland. Otherwise you can only communicate with us when you are outside the United States. These requirements apply to phone, e-mail, fax, and correspondence. For example:

If you contact us by telephone, we will need to be able to verify that your call originated from outside the United States or request that you provide a non-U.S. phone number and return your call. In either case, we will ask you to tell us from where you are calling.

If you contact us by written correspondence, we will need clear evidence (such as a postmarks indicating that the point of mailing occurred outside the U.S.), and we will continue to retain your mail or send any outbound correspondence only to a non-U.S. mailing address.

If you contact us by facsimile, we will need to be able to verify that your fax transmission originated from outside the United States or request that you provide a non-U.S. phone number through which fax communications may be made.

If you contact us by e-mail, we will request that you provide a non-U.S. phone number and respond via a telephone conversation.

We may, of course, implement additional measures to verify that any such contact we have with you occurs only when you are outside the United States.

Q5a. If I keep my existing account, may you provide me with information about my securities holdings when I am in the United States?

A. With one limited exception, the answer is "no". During this conversation, I may tell you the aggregate valuation of your securities portfolio and describe the overall performance of your entire portfolio in the aggregate compared to a past time period. I will not, however, after this conversation be able to have any further conversations about these subjects nor may I discuss the performance of particular securities products and/or the allocations of securities products in your portfolio (neither currently nor historically) while you are in the United States. So this is a one-time exception.

Q5b. If I keep my existing securities account with UBS, may I contact you from the United States to change my investment profile?

A. No. Unfortunately, this type of communication may only be made when you are outside the United States. Again, we will have to verify that you are outside the United States.

Q6. May I communicate with you from the United States about banking products?

A. We may discuss banking products and services, including cash deposits, precious metals, credit and debit cards, loans, and safe deposits.

Internal use only

αβ

Q7. May I sell my securities and place the proceeds with you in a cash account? If not, why not?

A. As I mentioned before, for reasons of client service and business considerations, UBS is looking to promote its U.S. units and SFA and not to transfer existing securities accounts at UBS AG into cash accounts. However, if you determine it to be an option for you to be invested in cash only, you may instruct us to sell your securities holdings as long as such instruction is given when you are outside the United States (again, subject to verification). I should underscore that, even if you only have a cash account with us, we will only be able to meet with you at the booking location of the funds.

Q8. You mentioned "business considerations" and "streamlining and simplifying." What on earth are you talking about?

A. By concentrating the U.S. private client business in our U.S. units and SFA, we are able to increase operational and management efficiency, and focus on the services and product delivery models that we believe should hold the most long-term promise for our private client segments.

Q9. Why did you decide to make this change now?

A. This is a continuation of the evolution of our offerings to US private clients. Since UBS acquired PaineWebber in the United States and formed SFA in Switzerland, U.S. clients have responded very positively to the investment opportunities and service models they offer. We believe now is the right point in time to accelerate the consolidation of our offerings to US clients on these platforms.

Q10. Are you doing this in response to pressure, especially from U.S. authorities?

A. These changes are the result of the periodic review of our business and our continuing efforts to offer excellent service in compliance with applicable legal and regulatory requirements.

Q 10a. Are you respectively UBS subject of an investigation of US regulators?

UBS has to keep specifics about its regulatory interactions confidential. We are therefore not in a position to answer your question.

Q 10b. Am I exposed because of the most recent events?

As you will appreciate, UBS is bound by strict client confidentiality provisions the bank will, of course, abide by. They can only be lifted under strict conditions as per applicable law.

Q11. If I decide to transfer my assets to SFA, will Swiss client confidentiality still apply?

A. An SFA representative would be the best person to answer that question, but my understanding is that, although your information would be reported to the IRS and potentially available to the SEC, it otherwise generally would be covered by Swiss financial privacy protections.

Q12. If I decide to keep my existing account, will you as my client adviser continue to service it?

A. I will remain in my current position for at least the near term. After that point, I might consider other opportunities within the bank, including working for SFA, where I could continue to manage your assets.

Q13. What are you going to do? Are you going to leave UBS?

A. I will remain in my current position for at least the near term. After that point, I might consider other opportunities within the bank, including working for SFA, where I could continue to manage your assets.

UNITED STATES DISTRICT COURT
SOUTHERN DISTRICT OF FLORIDA
Case No. 08-CR-60099-ZLOCH

UNITED STATES OF AMERICA

vs.

BRADLEY BIRKENFELD,

Defendant.

______________________/

STATEMENT OF FACTS

The United States Attorneys Office for the Southern District of Florida, the United States Department of Justice, Tax Division, and the defendant, Bradley Birkenfeld (hereinafter referred to as the "defendant Birkenfeld") and his counsel agree that, had this case proceeded to trial, the United States would have proven the following facts beyond a reasonable doubt, and that the following facts are true and correct and are sufficient to support a plea of guilty:

The Qualified Intermediary Program

Beginning in 2000, the Internal Revenue Services ("IRS") sought to increase the collection of tax revenues without raising tax rates. In furtherance of this mission, the IRS established the Qualified Intermediary ("Q.I.") Program. Pursuant to the Q.I. Program, foreign banks voluntarily entered into Qualified Intermediary agreements with the IRS pursuant to which these foreign banks agreed to identify and document any customers who held U.S. investments, which were generally marketable securities and bonds, or received United States source income into their off-shore accounts. In accordance with IRS requirements, foreign banks agreed to have their customers fill out IRS Forms W-8BEN, which required the beneficial owner of a bank account to be identified on the form, or IRS Forms W-9, which required United States beneficial owners of bank accounts to be identified.

Foreign banks further agreed to issue IRS Forms 1099 to United States customers for United States source payments of dividends, interest, rents, royalties and other fixed or determinable income paid into the United States customers' off-shore bank accounts. Alternatively, if a client refused to be identified under the Q.I. Agreement, foreign banks agreed to withhold and pay over a twenty-eight percent withholding tax on U.S. source payments and then bar the client from holding U.S. investments. In addition, the sales proceeds, interest and

Permanent Subcommittee on Investigations
EXHIBIT #95

dividends earned on non-United States investments, if the purchase or sale of the investment was made as a result of contact (in person, via email, telephone or fax) with the U.S. client in the United States, were subject to the Form 1099 reporting requirements or twenty-eight percent withholding. These transactions are referred to under the Q.I. Program as "deemed sales."

In January 2001, a large Swiss bank ("Swiss Bank"), entered into a Q.I. agreement with the IRS. Swiss Bank owns and operates banks, investment banks and stock brokerage businesses throughout the world, and has locations in the United States, with branch locations in the Southern District of Florida. This agreement was a major departure from historical Swiss bank secrecy laws under which Swiss banks concealed bank information for United States clients from the IRS. At all relevant times to this indictment, the Swiss bank represented to the IRS that it had continued to honor this Qualified Intermediary agreement.

Defendant Birkenfeld's Employment

During the entire period from 1998 through 2006, defendant Birkenfeld was employed by various banks in Switzerland as a private banker primarily servicing United States clients. From 1998 through July 2001, defendant Birkenfeld was employed by Barclays Bank in Geneva, Switzerland. In 2001, Barclays Bank entered into a Q.I. agreement with the IRS. In order to comply with the terms of the Q.I. agreement, Barclays Bank decided to terminate its off-shore private banking business for United States clients that refused to complete an IRS Form W-9. Accounts owned by United States clients that refused to fill out IRS Forms W-9 were known in the off-shore banking business as "undeclared" accounts.

From 2001 through 2006, defendant Birkenfeld was employed as a director in the private banking division of a large Swiss bank ("Swiss Bank"), which owns and operates banks, investments banks, and stock brokerage businesses throughout the world, including the United States, with offices in the Southern District of Florida. A manager at the Swiss Bank assured defendant Birkenfeld that even though the Swiss Bank signed a Q.I. Agreement, the Swiss Bank was committed to continue to provide private banking services to United States clients who wished for their accounts to remain undeclared. Swiss Bank managers authorized and encouraged defendant Birkenfeld and other private bankers to travel to the United States to solicit new clients and conduct banking for existing United States clients. The Swiss Bank sponsored events in the United States where Swiss bankers met with U.S. clients, including Art Basel in Miami and the NASDAQ 100 tennis tournament in Miami. The Swiss Bank trained bankers traveling to the United States in techniques to avoid detection by United States law enforcement authorities, including training bankers to falsely state on customs forms that they were traveling into the United States for pleasure and not business. Defendant Birkenfeld, Swiss Bank managers and bankers knew that they were not licensed to provide banking services, offer investment advice or solicit the purchase or sale of securities through contact with clients in the United States.

The Tax Fraud Scheme

When the Swiss Bank notified its U.S. clients of the requirements of the Q.I. agreement, many of the Swiss Bank's wealthy U.S. clients refused to be identified, to have taxes withheld from the income earned on their offshore assets, or to sell their U.S. investments. To these clients, the Q.I. reporting requirements defeated the purpose of opening a Swiss bank account; to conceal their accounts from the IRS and to evade U.S. income taxes. These accounts were known at the Swiss Bank as the United States undeclared business. Rather than risk losing the approximately $20 billion of assets under management in the United States undeclared business, which earned the bank approximately $200 million per year in revenues, managers and bankers at the Swiss Bank, including defendant Birkenfeld, assisted these wealthy U.S. clients in concealing their ownership of the assets held offshore by assisting these clients in creating nominee and sham entities. These entities were usually set up in tax haven jurisdictions, including Switzerland, Panama, British Virgin Islands, Hong Kong and Liechtenstein. Defendant Birkenfeld, Swiss Bank managers and bankers and U.S. clients prepared false and misleading IRS Forms W-8BEN that claimed that the owners of the accounts were sham off-shore entities and failed to prepare and file IRS Forms W-9 that should have identified the owner of the account, the U.S. client.

Managers and bankers at the Swiss Bank, including defendant Birkenfeld, maintained relationships with Swiss and Liechtenstein businessmen, such as Mario Staggl, who would set up these nominee and sham entities for the Swiss Bank's U.S. clients and pose as owners or directors of these entities. By concealing the U.S. clients' ownership and control in the assets held offshore, defendant Birkenfeld, the Swiss Bank, its managers and bankers evaded the requirements of the Q.I. program, defrauded the IRS and evaded United States income taxes.

In order to further assist U.S. clients in concealing their Swiss bank accounts, defendant Birkenfeld, Mario Staggl, other private bankers and managers at the Swiss Bank and others advised U.S. clients to:

place cash and valuables in Swiss safety deposit boxes;

purchase jewels, artwork and luxury items using the funds in their Swiss bank account while overseas;

misrepresent the receipt of funds from the Swiss bank account in the United States as loans from the Swiss Bank;

destroy all off-shore banking records existing in the United States, and;

utilize Swiss bank credit cards that they claimed could not be discovered by United States authorities.

On one occasion, at the request of a U.S. client, defendant Birkenfeld purchased diamonds using that U.S. client's Swiss bank account funds and smuggled the diamonds into the United States in a toothpaste tube. Defendant Birkenfeld and Mario Staggl accepted bundles of checks from U.S. clients and facilitated the deposit of those checks into accounts at the Swiss Bank, Liechtenstein and Danish banks.

The Billionaire U.S. Real Estate Developer

Defendant Birkenfeld's largest client was a billionaire real estate developer whose initials are I.O. (hereinafter identified as "I.O."). I.O. had residences in Southern California and in Broward County, within the Southern District of Florida. On several occasions, defendant Birkenfeld, Mario Staggl and Swiss Bank managers met with I.O. in Switzerland and in the United States. It was well-known at the Swiss Bank that I.O. was a U.S. citizen, that the income earned on his accounts was subject to Q.I. withholding and reporting requirements, however, during the period from 2001 through 2005, the Swiss Bank issued no Forms 1099 to I.O., nor did the Swiss Bank report any Form 1099 information to the IRS or withhold or pay over any taxes to the IRS.

From at least 2001 through the date of the Indictment, defendant Birkenfeld conspired with Mario Staggl, an owner and operator of a Liechtenstein trust company, I.O., additional private bankers and mangers employed by the Swiss Bank, and others to defraud the United States by assisting I.O. in evading income tax on the income earned on $200 million of assets hidden offshore in Switzerland and Liechtenstein. In order to circumvent the requirements of the Q. I. Agreement, the defendant and others conspired to conceal I.O.'s ownership and control of the $200 million of assets hidden offshore by creating and utilizing nominee and sham entities.

Defendant Birkenfeld, Mario Staggl, I.O, additional private bankers and managers employed by the Swiss Bank, and others committed numerous overt acts in Broward County in the Southern District of Florida, Central District of California, Switzerland, Liechtenstein, and elsewhere in furtherance of the conspiracy, including the following:

On or about June 21, 2001, I.O. caused to be sent completed bank account opening documents for an account at the Swiss branch of a large bank based in London to defendant Birkenfeld, including a Form W-8BEN, Certificate of Foreign Status of Beneficial Owner for United States Tax Withholding that falsely and fraudulently claimed that the beneficial owner of the newly opened account was a shell corporation located in the Bahamas.

On or about July 26, 2001, defendant Birkenfeld caused to be sent an email to I.O. and others that the large bank based in London was terminating North American clients, travel and resources, and that his new employer, the Swiss Bank, had a superior network, product range and management, and had recently acquired a large United States securities brokerage house in order to enhance United States investment expertise.

On or about October 19, 2001, defendant Birkenfeld caused to be sent via facsimile to I.O. at a United States facsimile number Swiss bank account opening documents from the Swiss Bank, including a form entitled "Verification of the beneficial owner's identity." This form, executed by I.O., falsely and fraudulently stated that I.O. was not the beneficial owner, and that a nominee Bahamian corporation was beneficial owner of the account. The application further listed I.O. as a signatory to the account.

On or about December 4, 2001, Mario Staggle recommended to I.O. that in order to further conceal I.O.'s ownership of off-shore assets, in addition to setting up Liechtenstein trusts and Dutch holding companies, I.O. should set up an entity in the British Virgin Islands, Panama or Gibraltar that "would lead to another 'safety break' in a tax and anonymity aspect."

On or about December 19, 2001, Mario Staggl caused to be executed a "Letter of Intent," which stated that New Haven Trust Company Limited, trustee of The Landmark Settlement, intended to hold the trust property for the benefit of I.O., and, after his demise, for his children.

On or about March 13, 2002, defendant Birkenfeld caused to be sent a facsimile to I.O. at a United States facsimile number listing $15 million of bonds that an investment manager at the Swiss Bank had purchased for I.O.

On or about March 25, 2002, I.O. caused to be sent a facsimile to defendant Birkenfeld authorizing defendant Birkenfeld to issue five credit cards from the Swiss Bank to I.O. and others.

On or about April 16, 2002, I.O. caused to be sent a letter to defendant Birkenfeld authorizing the wire transfer of $80 million from one account at the Swiss Bank to another account at the Swiss Bank.

On or about April 23, 2002, Mario Staggl caused to be sent an email to I.O. in the United States with instructions for I.O. to transfer a portfolio, worth approximately $60 million, containing United States securities from a brokerage house in London to an account in the name of a Danish shell corporation at a Liechtenstein bank.

On or about April 25, 2002, an unindicted co-conspirator caused to be sent an email to I.O., with a copy to Mario Staggl, that recommended that in addition to the Liechtenstein trusts and Danish holding companies, I.O. should set up United Kingdom companies to act as nominee shareholders. As stated in the email, "... the partners appear to be U.K. companies and Liechtenstein does not appear to be connected.... The role of the U.K. companies is simply to act as nominee shareholders."

On March 25, 2002, I.O. caused to be sent a fax authorizing defendant Birkenfeld to wire transfer $39 million from one account at the Swiss Bank to another account at the Swiss Bank.

On or about May 7, 2002, Mario Staggl caused to be sent a reply email advising I.O. not to put his name on any Liechtenstein accounts because doing so could "jeopardize the structure," and reminded I.O. that he had executed blank account signature cards that Mario Staggl could use.

On or about April 15, 2003, I.O. filed his United States Individual Income Tax Return, Form 1040, for the 2002 tax year, listing his address as Sanctuary Cove, Florida that fraudulently omitted income earned on off-shore assets.

On or about May 19, 2003, Mario Staggl caused to be sent an email to I.O., with a copy to defendant Birkenfeld, that stated that Mario Staggl's lawyers in Gibraltar told him "that everything is now in order to proceed with the application to transfer ownership to Gibraltar" of I.O.'s 147 foot yacht.

On or about March 24 and March 25, 2004, defendant Birkenfeld traveled to the Southern District of Florida to meet with I.O. and a banker from the Swiss Bank's New York branch in order to solicit I.O. to take out real estate loans with the Swiss Bank using his undeclared off-shore assets as collateral.

On or about April 15, 2004, I.O. filed his United States Individual Income Tax Return, Form 1040, for the 2003 tax year, listing his address as Lighthouse Point, Florida that fraudulently omitted income earned on off-shore assets.

On or about April 15, 2004, I.O. filed his United States individual income tax return, Form 1040, for the 2003 tax year, listing his address as Lighthouse Point, Florida that fraudulently omitted income earned on off-shore assets.

On or about April 15, 2005, I.O. filed his United States Individual Income Tax Return, Form 1040, for the 2004 tax year, listing an address in Lighthouse Point, Florida that failed to report the income earned on off-shore assets.

On or about June 12, 2005, defendant Birkenfeld and Mario Staggl met with I.O. at a Liechtenstein bank and advised him to transfer all of his assets held by the Swiss Bank to a Liechtenstein bank because Liechtenstein had better bank secrecy laws than Switzerland.

The tax loss associated with the conspiracy involving the evasion of income taxes of the approximate $200 million I.O. concealed offshore is $7,261,387 million, exclusive of penalties and interest.

Respectfully submitted,

R. ALEXANDER ACOSTA
UNITED STATES ATTORNEY

Date: 6/10/08 By: ______________________
KEVIN DOWNING
SENIOR TRIAL ATTORNEY
MICHAEL P. BEN'ARY
TRIAL ATTORNEY
UNITED STATES DEPARTMENT OF JUSTICE
TAX DIVISION

Date: 6/13/08 By: ______________________
JEFFREY A. NEIMAN
ASSISTANT UNITED STATES ATTORNEY

Date: 6/10/08 By: ______________________
DANNY ONORATO
PETER RABEN
ATTORNEYS FOR DEFENDANT

Date: 10/06/08 By: ______________________
BRADLEY BIRKENFELD
DEFENDANT

THOMAS P. O'BRIEN
United States Attorney
WAYNE R. GROSS
Assistant United States Attorney
Chief, Santa Ana Branch Office
BRETT A. SAGEL (CBN: 243918)
Assistant United States Attorney
Ronald Reagan Federal Building
411 West Fourth Street, Suite 8000
Santa Ana, California 92701
Telephone: (714) 338-3598
Facsimile: (714) 338-3708
Email: Brett.Sagel@usdoj.gov

Attorney for Plaintiff
United States of America

UNITED STATES DISTRICT COURT

FOR THE CENTRAL DISTRICT OF CALIFORNIA

SOUTHERN DIVISION

UNITED STATES OF AMERICA, Plaintiff, v. IGOR M. OLENICOFF, Defendant.	SA CR No. 07-227-CJC PLEA AGREEMENT FOR DEFENDANT IGOR M. OLENICOFF

1. This constitutes the plea agreement between IGOR M. OLENICOFF ("defendant") and the United States Attorney's Office for the Central District of California ("the USAO") in the investigation of into tax violations regarding defendant and numerous entities related to defendant. This agreement is limited to the USAO and cannot bind any other federal, state or local prosecuting, administrative or regulatory authorities.

PLEA

2. Defendant gives up the right to indictment by a grand jury, waives venue, and agrees to plead guilty to the one-count

information in the form attached to this agreement or a substantially similar form.

NATURE OF THE OFFENSE

3. In order for defendant to be guilty of count one, which charges a violation of Title 26, United States Code, Section 7206(1), the following must be true: (1) The defendant made and subscribed a return, statement, or other document which was false as to a material matter; (2) The return, statement, or other document contained a written declaration that it was made under the penalties of perjury; (3) The defendant did not believe the return, statement, or other document to be true and correct as to every material matter; and (4) The defendant falsely subscribed to the return, statement, or other document willfully, with the specific intent to violate the law. Defendant admits that defendant is, in fact, guilty of this offense as described in count one of the information.

PENALTIES

4. The statutory maximum sentence that the Court can impose for a violation of Title 26, United States Code, Section 7206(1) is: 3 years imprisonment; a 3-year period of supervised release; a fine of $100,000 or twice the gross gain or gross loss resulting from the offense, whichever is greatest; and a mandatory special assessment of $100. The Court may order defendant to pay any additional taxes, interest and penalties that defendant owes to the United States. Also, the Court must order defendant to pay the costs of prosecution, which may be in

addition to the statutory maximum fine stated above.

5. Supervised release is a period of time following imprisonment during which defendant will be subject to various restrictions and requirements. Defendant understands that if defendant violates one or more of the conditions of any supervised release imposed, defendant may be returned to prison for all or part of the term of supervised release, which could result in defendant serving a total term of imprisonment greater than the statutory maximum stated above.

6. Defendant also understands that, by pleading guilty, defendant may be giving up valuable government benefits and valuable civic rights, such as the right to vote, the right to possess a firearm, the right to hold office, and the right to serve on a jury.

7. Defendant further understands that the conviction in this case may subject defendant to various collateral consequences, including but not limited to, deportation, revocation of probation, parole, or supervised release in another case, and suspension or revocation of a professional license. Defendant understands that unanticipated collateral consequences will not serve as grounds to withdraw defendant's guilty plea.

FACTUAL BASIS

8. Defendant and the USAO agree and stipulate to the statement of facts provided below. This statement of facts includes facts sufficient to support a plea of guilty to the charge described in this agreement and to establish the

sentencing guideline factors set forth in paragraph 12 below. It is not meant to be a complete recitation of all facts relevant to the underlying criminal conduct or all facts known to defendant that relate to that conduct.

Defendant is the President and Owner of Olen Properties Corporation (hereinafter "OPC"). During the years 1992 through 2004, defendant owned, controlled, and had signatory authority over financial accounts outside of the United States. At least as early as August 1997, defendant listed himself as chairman of Sovereign Bancorp Ltd. (hereinafter "SBL") and President and Director of National Depository Corporation, Ltd. (hereinafter "NDC") on signature cards for Barclays Bank in the Bahamas, which also listed defendant as an authorized signatory on these accounts. Defendant also had signatory authority and controlled several financial accounts with Solomon Smith Barney, which were held in Solomon Smith Barney's office in London, England. Defendant's accounts in Solomon Smith Barney's England offices included accounts in the names of SBL, NDC, Guardian Guarantee Company, Ltd. (hereinafter "GGCL"), Continental Realty Funding Corporation (hereinafter "CRFC"), and Swiss Finance Corporation. Defendant opened several accounts at UBS, formerly known as Union Bank of Switzerland (hereinafter "UBS") in Switzerland, in which defendant had signatory authority and listed himself as Vice President and Director of accounts under the name of GGCL and New Guardian Bancorp APS (hereinafter "NGB"). In addition, defendant also had signatory authority and control over several financial accounts at Neue Bank in Liechtenstein, including an account in the name of NGB.

Defendant directed and authorized transactions from his off-shore financial accounts, including, but not limited to the following transactions. On or about March 9, 1992, defendant transferred approximately $61,000,000 from an OPC account at First Interstate Bank in Newport Beach, California, to a Bank of Montreal account in Canada under the name of NDC. On or about October 5, 1998, defendant directed Solomon Smith Barney to transfer approximately $40,000,000 from an SBL account at Solomon Smith Barney (England) to an SBL account at Barclay's Bank (Bahamas). On or about June 4, 2001, defendant directed Solomon Smith Barney to transfer approximately $17,000,000, $43,000,000, and $58,000,000 from CRFC, NDC, and SBL accounts, respectively, at Solomon Smith Barney (England) to NDC and SBL accounts at Barclay's Bank (Bahamas). On or about December 10, 2001, defendant directed Barclay's Bank to transfer approximately $89,000,000 from a GGCL account at Barclay's Bank (Bahamas) to open the GGCL account at UBS (Switzerland). On or about February 27, 2002, defendant directed Solomon Smith Barney to transfer approximately $38,000,000 from CRFC, NDC, and CRFC accounts at

Solomon Smith Barney (England) to an GGCL account at Barclay's Bank (Bahamas).

For the calendar years 1998 through 2004, defendant filed his United States Individual Income Tax Returns (hereinafter "Form 1040") with the Internal Revenue Service for the respective tax years. Defendant signed his 1998, 1999, 2000, 2001, 2002, 2003, and 2004 Form 1040s under penalties of perjury. Defendant attached a Schedule B, Interest and Ordinary Dividends, to each of his Form 1040s for tax years 1998 through 2004. Each of the Form 1040s that defendant filed included Part III of Schedule B, Foreign Accounts and Trusts, whereby the Internal Revenue Service asked on Line 7a, "At any time during [calendar year], did you have an interest in or a signature or other authority over a financial account in a foreign country, such as a bank account, securities account, or other financial account?" Line 7b stated, "If 'yes,' enter the name of the foreign country." Lines 7a and 7b of Part III of Schedule B attached to the Form 1040s called for material information in that the requested information is necessary for a correct computation of the tax due and owing and has a natural tendency to influence or impede the Internal Revenue Service in ascertaining the correctness of the tax due and owing of the taxpayer. On each of the 1998 through 2004 Form 1040s, defendant falsely answered "No" to line 7a and left the space blank next to line 7b, even though, as he then well knew and understood, he had an interest in, signatory authority, and other authority over financial accounts in foreign countries during these years.

On or about April 15, 2003, in the Central District of California and elsewhere, defendant, a resident of Laguna Beach, California, did willfully make and subscribe a 2002 U.S. Individual Income Tax Return, Form 1040, which was verified by a written declaration that it was made under the penalties of perjury and was filed with the Internal Revenue Service, which defendant did not believe this 2002 U.S. Individual Income Tax Return to be true and correct as to every material matter in that Schedule B Part III, Foreign Accounts and Trusts, Line 7a asked "At any time during 2002, did you have an interest in or a signature or other authority over a financial account in a foreign country, such as a bank account, securities account, or other financial account?" to which said return falsely stated "NO," whereas, as defendant then and there well knew and believed, was a false statement, as defendant had ownership, control, and signatory authority over financial accounts in England, Switzerland, the Bahamas, and Liechtenstein. When defendant signed his 2002 Form 1040, defendant knew that it contained false information as to a material matter, and in filing the false 2002 Form 1040, defendant acted willfully.

WAIVER OF CONSTITUTIONAL RIGHTS

9. By pleading guilty, defendant gives up the following rights:

a) The right to persist in a plea of not guilty.

b) The right to a speedy and public trial by jury.

c) The right to the assistance of legal counsel at trial, including the right to have the Court appoint counsel for defendant for the purpose of representation at trial. (In this regard, defendant understands that, despite his plea of guilty, he retains the right to be represented by counsel - and, if necessary, to have the court appoint counsel if defendant cannot afford counsel - at every other stage of the proceedings.)

d) The right to be presumed innocent and to have the burden of proof placed on the government to prove defendant guilty beyond a reasonable doubt.

e) The right to confront and cross-examine witnesses against defendant.

f) The right, if defendant wished, to testify on defendant's own behalf and present evidence in opposition to the charges, including the right to call witnesses and to subpoena those witnesses to testify.

g) The right not to be compelled to testify, and, if defendant chose not to testify or present evidence, to have that choice not be used against defendant.

By pleading guilty, defendant also gives up any and all rights to pursue any affirmative defenses, Fourth Amendment or

Fifth Amendment claims, and other pretrial motions that have been filed or could be filed.

WAIVER OF DNA TESTING

10. Defendant has been advised that the government has in its possession the following items of physical evidence that could be subjected to DNA testing:

Documents obtained via search warrants

Defendant understands that the government does not intend to conduct DNA testing of any of these items. Defendant understands that, before entering a guilty plea pursuant to this agreement, defendant could request DNA testing of evidence in this case. Defendant further understands that, with respect to the offense to which defendant is pleading guilty pursuant to this agreement, defendant would have the right to request DNA testing of evidence after conviction under the conditions specified in 18 U.S.C. § 3600. Knowing and understanding defendant's right to request DNA testing, defendant knowingly and voluntarily gives up that right with respect to both the specific items listed above and any other items of evidence there may be in this case that might be amenable to DNA testing. Defendant understands and acknowledges that by giving up this right, defendant is giving up any ability to request DNA testing of evidence in this case in the current proceeding, in any proceeding after conviction under 18 U.S.C. § 3600, and in any other proceeding of any type. Defendant further understands and acknowledges that by giving up this right, defendant will never have another opportunity to have the evidence in this case, whether or not listed above, submitted for DNA testing, or to employ the results of DNA testing to support a claim that defendant is innocent of the offense to which defendant is pleading guilty.

SENTENCING FACTORS

11. Defendant understands that the Court is required to consider the United States Sentencing Guidelines ("U.S.S.G." or "Sentencing Guidelines") among other factors in determining defendant's sentence. Defendant understands, however, that the Sentencing Guidelines are only advisory, and that after considering the Sentencing Guidelines, the Court may be free to exercise its discretion to impose any reasonable sentence up to the maximum set by statute for the crimes of conviction.

12. Defendant and the USAO agree and stipulate to the following applicable sentencing guideline factors:

Base Offense Level :	6	[U.S.S.G. § 2T1.1(a)(2)]
Acceptance of Responsibility:	-2	[U.S.S.G. § 3E1.1(a)]

Defendant and the USAO agree not to seek, argue, or suggest in any way, either orally or in writing, that any other specific offense characteristics, adjustments or departures, from either the applicable Offense Level or Criminal History Category, be imposed. If, however, after signing this agreement but prior to sentencing, defendant were to commit an act, or the USAO were to discover a previously undiscovered act committed by defendant prior to signing this agreement, which act, in the judgment of the USAO, constituted obstruction of justice within the meaning of U.S.S.G. § 3C1.1, the USAO would be free to seek the enhancement set forth in that section.

13. There is no agreement as to defendant's criminal history or criminal history category.

14. The stipulations in this agreement do not bind either the United States Probation Office or the Court. Both defendant and the USAO are free to: (a) supplement the facts by supplying relevant information to the United States Probation Office and the Court; (b) correct any and all factual misstatements relating to the calculation of the sentence; and (c) argue on appeal and collateral review that the Court's sentencing guidelines calculations are not error, although each party agrees to maintain its view that the calculations in paragraph 12 are consistent with the facts of this case.

<u>DEFENDANT'S OBLIGATIONS</u>

15. Defendant agrees that he will:

a) Waive Indictment by Grand Jury, waive venue, and Plead guilty as set forth in this agreement.

b) Not knowingly and willfully fail to abide by all sentencing stipulations contained in this agreement.

c) Not knowingly and willfully fail to: (i) appear as ordered for all court appearances; (ii) surrender as ordered for service of sentence; (iii) obey all conditions of any bond; and (iv) obey any other ongoing court order in this matter.

d) Not commit any crime; however, offenses which would be excluded for sentencing purposes under U.S.S.G. § 4A1.2(c) are not within the scope of this agreement.

e) Not knowingly and willfully fail to be truthful at all times with Pretrial Services, the U.S. Probation Office, and the Court.

f) To fill out and deliver to the USAO, prior to sentencing, a completed financial statement listing defendant's assets on a form provided by the United States Attorney's Office.

g) Prior to sentencing, abandon his claim for a refund on the 1999 Corporate Return for Olen Properties Corporation ("OPC") seeking a refund based on interest income "paid" from OPC to Sovereign Bancorp Ltd. ("SBL"), another corporation controlled by defendant.

h) Prior to sentencing, defendant will move all money held in foreign financial accounts, including bank and securities accounts, which defendant has an interest in, signature authority, or any other authority, to financial accounts within the United States. Defendant further agrees that during the period of supervised release or probation, that defendant will not have any interest in, signature authority, or any other authority over a financial account in a foreign country, such as a bank account, securities account, or other financial account.

i) Cooperate with the Internal Revenue Service in the determination of defendant's civil tax liability and the tax liability of corporations owned and/or controlled by defendant for the Tax Years 1998-2004. Defendant agrees:

1) That defendant will, prior to the time of sentencing, enter into closing agreements for the years 1998 through 2004 for his Individual Income Tax Returns, correctly reporting unreported income and/or correcting improper deductions and credits, and will, if requested to do so by the Internal Revenue Service, provide the Internal Revenue Service with information regarding the years covered by the returns, and will pay at sentencing all additional taxes, and will pay promptly all penalties and interest assessed by the Internal Revenue Service to be owing as a result of any computational errors.

2) That nothing in this agreement forecloses or limits the ability of the Internal Revenue Service to examine and make adjustments to defendant's closing agreements.

3) That defendant will not, after entering into the closing agreements, file any claim for refund of taxes, penalties, or interest for amounts attributable to the closing agreements filed in connection with this plea agreement.

4) That defendant is liable for the fraud penalty imposed by the Internal Revenue Code, 26 U.S.C. § 6663, on the understatement of civil tax liability for Tax Years 1998-2004.

5) To give up any and all objections that could be asserted to the Examination Division of the Internal Revenue Service receiving materials or information obtained during the criminal investigation of this matter, including materials and information obtained through the execution of search warrants or

through grand jury subpoenas.

THE USAO'S OBLIGATIONS

16. If defendant complies fully with all defendant's obligations under this agreement, the USAO agrees:

a) To abide by all sentencing stipulations contained in this agreement.

b) At the time of sentencing, provided that defendant demonstrates an acceptance of responsibility for the offense up to and including the time of sentencing, to recommend a two-level reduction in the applicable sentencing guideline offense level, pursuant to U.S.S.G. § 3E1.1, and to recommend and, if necessary, move for an additional one-level reduction if available under that section.

c) Not to further prosecute defendant for violations arising out of defendant's conduct described in the stipulated factual basis set forth in paragraph 8 above or tax violations associated with moneys transferred to and held in foreign bank accounts from 1998 through 2004, or any other conduct known to the Government at the time this agreement is signed by defendant. Defendant understands that the USAO is free to prosecute defendant for any other unlawful past conduct or any unlawful conduct that occurs after the date of this agreement. Defendant agrees that at the time of sentencing the Court may consider the uncharged conduct in determining the applicable Sentencing Guidelines range, where the sentence should fall within that range, the propriety and extent of any departure from that range, and the determination of the sentence to be imposed after consideration of the sentencing guidelines and all other relevant factors.

BREACH OF AGREEMENT

17. If defendant, at any time between the execution of this agreement and defendant's sentencing on a non-custodial sentence or surrender for service on a custodial sentence, knowingly violates or fails to perform any of defendant's obligations under this agreement ("a breach"), the USAO may declare this agreement breached. If the USAO declares this agreement breached, and the Court finds such a breach to have occurred, defendant will not be able to withdraw defendant's guilty plea, and the USAO will be relieved of all of its obligations under this agreement.

18. Following a knowing and willful breach of this agreement by defendant, should the USAO elect to pursue any charge or any civil or administrative action that was either dismissed or not filed as a result of this agreement, then:

a) Defendant agrees that any applicable statute of limitations is tolled between the date of defendant's signing of this agreement and the commencement of any such prosecution or action.

b) Defendant gives up all defenses based on the statute of limitations, any claim of preindictment delay, or any speedy trial claim with respect to any such prosecution or action, except to the extent that such defenses existed as of the date of defendant's signing of this agreement.

c) Defendant agrees that: i) any statements made by defendant, under oath, at the guilty plea hearing; ii) the stipulated factual basis statement in this agreement; and iii) any evidence derived from such statements, are admissible against defendant in any future prosecution of defendant, and defendant shall assert no claim under the United States Constitution, any statute, Rule 410 of the Federal Rules of Evidence, Rule 11(f) of the Federal Rules of Criminal Procedure, or any other federal rule, that the statements or any evidence derived from any statements should be suppressed or are inadmissible.

LIMITED MUTUAL WAIVER OF APPEAL AND COLLATERAL ATTACK

19. Defendant gives up the right to appeal any sentence imposed by the Court, and the manner in which the sentence is determined, provided that (a) the sentence is within the statutory maximum specified above and is constitutional, (b) the Court in determining the applicable guideline range does not depart upward in offense level or criminal history category and determines that the total offense level is 4 or below, and (c) the Court imposes a sentence within or below the range corresponding to the determined total offense level and criminal history category. Defendant also gives up any right to bring a post-conviction collateral attack on the conviction or sentence, except a post-conviction collateral attack based on a claim of ineffective assistance of counsel, a claim of newly discovered evidence, or an explicitly retroactive change in the applicable Sentencing Guidelines, sentencing statutes, or statutes of

conviction. Notwithstanding the foregoing, defendant retains the ability to appeal the conditions of probation or supervised release imposed by the court, with the exception of the following: standard conditions set forth in district court General Orders 318 and 01-05; the drug testing conditions mandated by 18 U.S.C. §§ 3563(a)(5) and 3583(d); and the alcohol and drug use conditions authorized by 18 U.S.C. § 3563(b)(7).

20. The USAO gives up its right to appeal the sentence, provided that (a) the Court in determining the applicable guideline range does not depart downward in offense level or criminal history category, (b) the Court determines that the total offense level is 4 or above, and (c) the Court imposes a sentence within or above the range corresponding to the determined total offense level and criminal history category.

COURT NOT A PARTY

21. The Court is not a party to this agreement and need not accept any of the USAO's sentencing recommendations or the parties' stipulations. Even if the Court ignores any sentencing recommendation, finds facts or reaches conclusions different from any stipulation, and/or imposes any sentence up to the maximum established by statute, defendant cannot, for that reason, withdraw defendant's guilty plea, and defendant will remain bound to fulfill all defendant's obligations under this agreement. No one - not the prosecutor, defendant's attorney, or the Court - can make a binding prediction or promise regarding the sentence defendant will receive, except that it will be within the

statutory maximum.

NO ADDITIONAL AGREEMENTS

22. Except as set forth herein, there are no promises, understandings or agreements between the USAO and defendant or defendant's counsel. Nor may any additional agreement, understanding or condition be entered into unless in a writing signed by all parties or on the record in court.

PLEA AGREEMENT PART OF THE GUILTY PLEA HEARING

23. The parties agree and stipulate that this Agreement will be considered part of the record of defendant's guilty plea hearing as if the entire Agreement had been read into the record of the proceeding.

This agreement is effective upon signature by defendant and an Assistant United States Attorney.

AGREED AND ACCEPTED

UNITED STATES ATTORNEY'S OFFICE
FOR THE CENTRAL DISTRICT OF CALIFORNIA

THOMAS P. O'BRIEN
United States Attorney

[signature] 10/29/07

BRETT A. SAGEL
Assistant United States Attorney

Date

I have read this agreement and carefully discussed every part of it with my attorney. I understand the terms of this agreement, and I voluntarily agree to those terms. My attorney has advised me of my rights, of possible defenses, of the

Sentencing Guideline provisions, and of the consequences of entering into this agreement. No promises or inducements have been made to me other than those contained in this agreement. No one has threatened or forced me in any way to enter into this agreement. Finally, I am satisfied with the representation of my attorney in this matter.

10/17/07

IGOR M. OLENICOFF
Defendant

Date

I am IGOR M. OLENICOFF's attorney. I have carefully discussed every part of this agreement with my client. Further, I have fully advised my client of his/her rights, of possible defenses, of the Sentencing Guidelines' provisions, and of the consequences of entering into this agreement. To my knowledge, my client's decision to enter into this agreement is an informed and voluntary one.

10/17/07

EDWARD M. ROBBINS, JR.
Counsel for Defendant
IGOR M. OLENICOFF

Date

Subject: Meeting in California
Date: Thu, 26 Jul 2001 15:23:07 +0100
From: "Bradley Birkenfeld" <birkenfeld@attglobal.net>
To: "OLENICOFF, Andrei" <aolenicoff@olenproperties.com>
CC: "OLENICOFF, Igor" <iolenicoff@olenproperties.net>

Dear Andrei,

It was nice to speak to you the other day after some time. As we discussed, I needed to pursue a more advantageous firm to do my business, since Barclays was terminating North American clients, travel and resources. This was not suitable for me, so I have signed a contract as a Director with UBS to commence on October 2 (my assistant will be joining me as well). UBS has a superior network, product range, credit rating, senior management etc. Additionally, they just acquired Paine Webber to enhance their investment expertise.

I will call you next week when I return to Geneva and we can review some dates in August that would be mutually convenient to set up a meeting in your neighborhood. I hope all is well and I look forward to seeing you. Take care.

Regards,

Brad

Set up Hen. Conesp file for Mario? New Haven

Permanent Subcommittee on Investigations
EXHIBIT #97

SW 067087

OLEN

October 11, 2001 Via Fax: VFP
bcc BRAD BIRKENFELD

Hartis Pinder
McKinney, Bancroft & Hughes
Mareva House
4 George Street
Nassau, Bahamas

Dear Hartis:

I hope this letter finds you well, in all respects.

We are in the process, on behalf of Guardian Guarantee Co. Ltd., of establishing an account with UBS Bank, in Geneva. The representative for the bank is Mr. Bradley Birkenfeld. Mr. Birkenfeld felt that it would be best handled if he forwarded his requests for information to your office, as the corporate office for Guardian. He indicated that he may also call you, should there be any questions, relative to the opening of the account with UBS.

The signatories on this Guardian account will be Andrei Olenicoff, Natalia Olenicoff, Jeanette Bullington and myself. The purpose of the account is to be a clearing account for the investments Guardian Guarantee Co. Ltd. will be making through the UBS network of financial managers.

Should you need additional information, please reach me by phone, E-mail or fax.

Best regards,

Igor M. Olenicoff

7 Corporate Plaza • Newport Beach, CA 92660
(949) 644-OLEN • Fax (949) 719-7200
www.olenproperties.com

Permanent Subcommittee on Investigations
EXHIBIT #98

SW 066661

OLEN

October 23, 2001

Bradley C. Birkenfeld
UBS AG
Rue de la Corraterie 16
P.O. Box 2600, CH-1211
Geneva 2, Switzerland

Re: Guardian Guarantee Co. Ltd.

Dear Brad:

Pursuant to our discussions, enclosed please find the completed forms for the opening of the above referenced account. Also enclosed are copies of the signatories passports and the corporate documents requested.

I look forward to getting the account opened at your earliest convenience. Once the account is opened, please give me a call so that we can make further arrangements.

Best regards,

Igor M. Olenicoff
President

IMO:cs
Enclosures

7 Corporate Plaza • Newport Beach, CA 92660
(949) 644-OLEN • Fax (949) 719-7200
www.olenproperties.com

SW 066645

ructure ,

Subject: Structure
Date: Sat, 02 Jan 1904 06:43:10 +0200
From: Mario Staggl <mstaggl@newhaven.li>
To: Igor Olenicoff <iolenicoff@olenproperties.com>
CC: <aolenicoff@olenproperties.com>

Jan
Bole @ him

Dear Igor

Subsequent to our telephone discussion of last week your most recent e-mail made it very clear to me - you want to become on-shore - but still maintain an off-shore status in tax and protection point of view.

I have had a chance to review the structure based on the latest findings and should like to summarize as follows:

Danemark definitely provides for an on-shore status in an appearance point of view as well as for a "tax exemption" status in a tax point of view. With regard to the banks, both UBS and Neue Bank would not have to charge VAT on their managment fee since the Danish Holding Co. is not liable for VAT. Moreover, a Danish Holding Co. Is not even allowed by law to apply for a VAT number if it in itself does not have a turnover/activity in Danemark. Our Danish Co will without any doubt not perform any turnover in Danemark and the VAT problem would not exist. There is no need to escape to Gibraltar, latter being a traditional tax-haven jurisdiction and not necessarely advantageous to the appearance aspect. The banking / VAT aspect Sitzerland, UK and Liechtestein is covered if Danemark or Gibraltar is used but Danemark got a much better reputation. ? secrecy "yes"

The proposed company name "New Guardian Bancorp" is available and could be used.

It is further anticipated that the Danish Holding Co. will absorb/acquire the Olen US bearer shares presently allocated to the Bahamian Company. This is basically possible without any foreseeable problems but I should recommend to you to seek advice from a local US Tax Adviser because we will have to take the FIRPTA rule into account. Would you please check this with your domestic Tax Adviser and let me have his thoughts. Stock for stock exchange

Again, I strongly recommend not to use a Swiss Company since Swiss Holding Companies in conjunction with the US is the worst you can have (at least in this structure). The VAT is also an issue. I am sure your local Tax Adviser will share my opinion. ✓

Looking forward to hearing from you, I remain,

Personal regards,

Mario

12/10/01 10:27 AM

of 1

Permanent Subcommittee on Investigations
EXHIBIT #99

SW 067200

UBS **A** Master no.

Verification of the beneficial owner's identity

(Form A as per Art. 3 and 4 CDB)

Account/Custody Account No.:

Contracting partner:
IGOR OLENICOFF
ANDREI OLENICOFF

Category:
Company

The undersigned hereby declares:

(mark with a cross where appropriate)

☐ that the contracting partner is the beneficial owner of the assets concerned.

☒ that the beneficial owner of the assets concerned is:

Last name/First name (or firm)	Address/Domicile, Country
Guardian Guarantee Company Limited	4 George Street Mareva House Nassau, Bahamas

The contracting partner undertakes to inform the bank immediately of any changes.

Nassau, Bahamas 23/10/01

Place/Date

Signature(s)

For internal bank use only

Signature(s) verified
OU-Ref.:
OU-Ref.:
(as per Directives PF/1/005)

Customer Advisor's signature:
Supervisor's signature: 19.10.2001

63050 E V0 03.2000 J2

Permanent Subcommittee on Investigations
EXHIBIT #100

SW 066648

UBS

Master no. ....

▬▬▬	= Redacted by the Permanent Subcommittee on Investigations

Authorized signatories

Tel. No.: 242-322-4195

Company: ~~Guardian Guarantee Company Limited~~

Exact address of domicile: 4 George Street - Mareva House - Nassau, Bahamas

We hereby advise you of the following persons with unlimited authority to sign (without right of substitution) and who are authorized to carry out any legal acts and to enter into other obligations vis-à-vis UBS AG (hereinafter UBS) in connection with claims or assets deposited under the above master number and enter into other obligations vis-à-vis UBS:

Authority to sign:

Authorized signatory 1
Last name/First name: Olenicoff, Igor
Nationality/Date of birth: USA/ [redacted]
Signature:
☐ by sole signature
☒ by joint signature of 1

Authorized signatory 2
Last name/First name: Olenicoff, Andrei
Nationality/Date of birth: USA/ [redacted]
Signature:
☐ by sole signature
☒ by joint signature of 1

Authorized signatory 3
Last name/First name: Olenicoff, [redacted]
Nationality/Date of birth: USA/ [redacted]
Signatu[redacted]
☐ by sole signature
☒ by joint signature of 1

Authorized signatory 4
Last name/First name: [redacted]
Nationality/Date of birth: USA/ [redacted]
Signature: [redacted]
☐ by sole signature
☒ by joint signature of 1

(Please cross out unused fields.)

In particular, said authorized signatories are authorized to deposit, buy and sell, pledge, loan, convert and withdraw securities/book entry securities with binding effect in our name, to make deposits or withdraw funds in any manner whatsoever, be it by cheque or otherwise, to sign all settlements of account, receipts, discharges, verifications, transfers and assignments, to issue, accept, endorse or give discharges on bills of exchange, cheques, orders or similar instruments of every kind, to receive communications, statements of account/custody account and all other statements, to conclude agreements with UBS on the use of electronic services and to use same, to elect a jurisdiction and generally to do everything he/she/they may deem expedient or necessary. The authorized signatories are also authorized to take out any type of credits/loans in our name with binding effect and to give UBS legally binding instructions for the management of assets or to place an investment order. Furthermore, he/she/they are authorized to open and close accounts/custody accounts. It is his/her/their responsibility, and not the responsibility of UBS, to inform me/us at once of his/her/their actions.

Several authorized signatories
Without explicit restriction to joint signature the authorized signatories are authorized to act severally (sole signature). Provided that there is no other provision in writing the authority to sign by joint signature means joint signature of two.

The power of attorney of the authorized signatories shall be applicable without restriction until UBS receives an explicit revocation in writing. The power of attorney, therefore, shall remain in effect irrespective of any other or missing entries in a public register (e.g. the commercial register).

The present power of attorney shall be exclusively governed by and construed in accordance with Swiss law. The place of performance of all obligations of both parties, the place of debt collection, the latter only for Customers domiciled outside Switzerland, as well as the exclusive place of jurisdiction for any disputes arising out of and in connection with this power of attorney shall be Geneva, Switzerland.

UBS reserves the right, however, to take legal action against the grantor of the power of attorney before the authority of his/her/its domicile or before any other competent authority, in which event exclusively Swiss law shall remain applicable.

Company Name* Guardian Guarantee Company Limited
Last name/First name: Olenicoff, Igor
Function: President
Signature
Last name/First name: Olenicoff, Andrei
Function: Secretary
Signature

Place/Date: NASSUA, BAHAMAS 23/10/01

* The word «company» also stands for legal entities such as foundations, public entities, associations, etc.

For internal bank use only
Signature(s) verified
OU-Ref.:
OU-Ref.:
(as per Directives PF/1/005)
Customer Adviser's signature:
Supervisor's signature:
19.10.2001

63054 E V3 02.2001 JS

UBS

Master no.

Account no.

Waiver of right to invest in US securities

The undersigned instruct(s) UBS AG with respect to the above mentioned account not to invest in or hold US securities within the meaning of the relevant Qualified Intermediary Agreements (IRS Rev. Proc. 2000-12).

Name of Account Holder: Guardian Guarantee Company Limited

Street: 4 George St. Mareva House

Postal Code/Place: Nassau

Country of domicile: Bahamas

Nassau Bahama 23/10/01

Place/Date

Signature

For internal bank use only

Signature(s) verified/Signed in my presence

DU-Ref.

Signature

61526 E VO 10.2001 J3 · This Form will be kept in the records of UBS AG

SW 066652

THANK YOU !

Subject: THANK YOU !
Date: Sat, 01 Dec 2001 16:16:34 -0800
From: Igor Olenicoff <iolenicoff@olenproperties.com>
To: MARIO STAGGL <newhaven@newhaven.lol.li>
BCC: Bradley Birkenfeld <birkenfeld@attglobal.net>

THANK YOU AND KLAUS FOR MEETING WITH US LAST WEEK. WE FELT IT WAS A PRODUCTIVE MEETING FOR US AND ONE WHICH WILL LEAD TO PRODUCTIVE BUSINESS FOR BOTH OF OUR FIRMS .

AFTER RETURNING TO GENEVE , IT BECAME CLEAR THAT WE NEED TO RECONSIDER CERTAIN ASPECTS OF WHAT WE TALKED ABOUT AND MAYBE REDUCE THE NUMBER FROM THREE TO TWO TRUSTS . THE PRIMARY REASON FOR THIS IS THAT WE WERE INFORMED BY BRAD THAT THEY WOULD HAVE TO CHARGE THE VAT. CHARGE IS WE WERE TO DO BUSINESS THROUGH THE TRUST YOU FORM AND THAT WE NEED A FIRM IN A NON -SWISS ENTITY TO AVOID THIS TAX AND AS SUCH MAYBE WE ARE BETTER OFF SIMPLY RENAMING THE EXISTING ENTITY WE HAVE TO MATCH THE ENTITY NAME WE WERE GOING TO FORM WITH YOU AND ONLY HAVE THE STOCK OF THAT ENTITY ISSUED TO ONE OF THE OTHER TRUSTS , NAMELY LANDMARK. THIS WAY LANDMARK WOULD OWN THE MISC., ASSETS AND THE INVESTMENT COMPANIES STOCK WHICH WOULD BE IN THE EXISTING JURISDICTION . PLEASE GIVE ME YOUR ADVISE ON THIS ISSUE SO WE CAN DECIDE HOW MANY TRUSTS YOU NEED TO FORM. IT MAY EVEN BE ONLY ONE IF THE STOCK OF THE REAL ESTATE ENTITIES CAN BE OWNED BY A SWISS ENTITY AND THE STOCK OF THAT ENTITY WOULD BE OWNED BY THE TRUST YOU FORM .

PLEASE GIVE THIS SOME THOUGHT AND LET ME KNOW. WE ARE PREPARED TO GO FORWARD WITH ARNOLD AND PAUL , BUT NEED TO KNOW WITH WHICH ENTITY TO ESTABLISH THE RELATIONSHIP WITH THEM WITH . IT APPEARS THAT IT SHOULD BE THE SAME ENTITY THAT CURRENTLY HAS THE ACCOUNTS AT THE CURRENT INSTITUTION , WITH A NON-SWISS JURISDICTION TO AVOID THE VAT. ASSESSMENT ? PLEASE ADVISE YOUR THOUGHTS ON THIS BEFORE WE LAUNCH OFF TO A START THAT MAY NOT BE IN THE PROPER FORMAT.

THANK CLAUS AGAIN FOR THE TIME AND ADVISE AND WE LOOK FORWARD TO SEEING YOU AGAIN SOON AS WE ALL ENJOYED OUR STAY IN YOUR BEAUTIFUL COUNTRY AND THE WONDERFUL FOOD WE WERE ABLE TO SAMPLE.

10/31/2003 7:53 AM

of 1

Permanent Subcommittee on Investigations

EXHIBIT #101

SW 065109

arious

Subject: Various
Date: Tue, 04 Dec 2001 18:24:50 +0200
From: Mario Staggi <mstaggi@newhaven.li>
To: <oleinicoff@olenproperties.com>

Dear Igor

Thank you for your message of December 2. It was a pleasure to meet with you, Andrej and Jeanette and I am sure that this was the beginning of an excellent relationship.

I have read your aforementioned e-mail and should like to comment as follows:

The strucutre could basically be cut down to two trusts but I would still not recommend to do so. We were talking about three different components which would become part of the structure and in our opinion these should be kept and treated separate for reasons discussed.

The shares in OLEN US are "owned" by the Bahamian Company. In order to avoid any potential exposure in a tax point of view we would recommend to transfer the Bahamian company shares into a Danish Holding Company. The Danish Holding Company would be owned by the first of the Liechtenstein Trusts. Advantage is that Denemark is not a "off-shore" jurisdiction. Any dividends wich might be paid from Olen to the Cayman Company could be disposed by way of dividend to the Danish Holding Company without being liable to Danish Taxation and would become "offshore" assets.

The cash available for UBS and Neue Bank can basically be held by the second Liechtenstein Trust. If this is the case 7,6% VAT would become due on the bank's management charge as well as on the trustee fees. There is an easy way to get around this VAT by interposing an "off-shore" jurisdiction since services rendered and charged to non Swiss or non Liechtenstein entities are not liable to VAT. We would recommend the second Liechtenstein Trust being the sharholder of the investment "off-shore" vehicle. The jurisdiction could be the British Virging Islands (BVI), Panama, Gibraltar. The investment "off-shore" vehicle would be the contracting partner to the banks. The administration would be looked after by New Haven in Liechteinstein. The second advantage of interposing the "off-shore" vehicle would lead to another "safdty-break" in a tax and anonymity aspect.

There is basically no objection to have Landmark, provided it is an off-shore company, becoming the "Cash Box" (account holder) with both banks either in its existing name or re-named. The share in either Landmark or Landmark in its renamed form could be transferred to the third Liechtenstein Trust. Either a new "offshore-entity" or the existing Landmark could become the account holder/contracting partner to UBS and Neue Bank.

Finally, I should stress that a Swiss Holding Company would not be the appropriate jurisdiction is particular keeping in mind the 35% Withholding Tax Switzerland applies.

Please let me have your thoughts.

Kind regards

Mario

10/31/2003 7:54 AM

of 1

SW 065110

Subject: STRUCTURE DISCUSSION
Date: Sat, 08 Dec 2001 15:55:22 -0800
From: Igor Olenicoff <iolenicoff@olenproperties.com>
To: MARIO STAGGL <newhaven@newhaven.iol.li>
CC: Bradley Birkenfeld <birkenfeld@attglobal.net>, Andrei Olenicoff <aolenicoff@olenproperties.com>

MARIO , BASED ON OUR LAST CONVERSATION , YOU WERE GOING TO LOOK INTO A STRUCTURE WHICH MAY AVOID THE VAT TAX , BUT STILL HAVE AN ON-SHORE PRESENCE , SUCH AS IN DENMARK OR ____?

BARRING THE ABILITY TO DO IT ON SHORE , WHICH IS OUR PREFERENCE SIMPLY FROM AND APPEARANCE STANDPOINT , WE ARE RESOLVED TO DOING OFFSHORE THROUGH A JURISDICTION OF YOUR RECOMMENDATION . I BELIEVE THE MOST PREFERRED OF THE ONES WE DISCUSSED IS GIBRALTAR .

THE STRUCTURE WOULD BE TO HAVE YOU FORM LANDMARK SETTLEMENT , WHICH WOULD THEN FORM THE DANISH OR GIBRALTAR ENTITY AND OUR PREFERENCE OF A NAME AT THIS TIME , ASSUMING IT IS AVAILABLE WOULD BE NEW GUARDIAN BANCORP, LTD. . THIS NEW ENTITY WOULD THEN OPEN THE INVESTMENT MANAGEMENT ACCOUNTS AT UBS , WITH BRAD AND WE WILL PUT YOU IN TOUCH WITH THE LONDON INVESTMENT BANK WHERE ANOTHER ACCOUNT WOULD BE OPENED.

LANDMARK SETTLEMENT WOULD REMAIN THE HOLDING TRUST COMPANY FOR THESE INVESTMENTS AND THE ACCOUNTS AT THE INVESTMENT BANKS WOULD BE OPENED REQUIRING TWO SIGNATURES TO MAKE ANY WITHDRAWALS FROM THE ACCOUNTS , YOURS AS TRUSTEE AND ONE OF US AS THE MANAGERS OF THE ACCOUNTS . YOU WOULD ISSUE AUTHORIZATION FROM THE TRUST TO THE INVESTMENT BANKS TO TAKE MANAGEMENT DIRECTION FROM ANDREI, JEANNETE OR MYSELF RELATIVE TO THE INVESTMENTS.

IF THE VAT TAX CAN NOT BE AVOIDED FOR THE INVESTMENT ACCOUNT MANAGEMENT FEE THROUGH A DANISH CORPORATION , THEN PERHAPS WE CAN NEXT FORM A DANISH OR SWISS ENTITY TO BE THE PARENT COMPANY AND HOLDER OF THE REAL ESTATE COMPANY STOCK. IN SHORT , IT IS THE PREFERENCE OF THE CURRENT HOLDER OF THE STOCK , A BAHAMIAN CORPORATION TO MOVE THE OWNERSHIP TO AN ONSHORE ENTITY , BUT ONE WHICH PROVIDED COMPLETE ANONIMITY AS TO THE BENEFICIAL OWNERS. I AM THINKING THAT A SWISS ENTITY MAY BE THE BEST VEHICLE TO DP THIS WITH , AND IF YOU AGREE THEN WE WOULD NEED TO ESTABLISH A SWISS ATTORNEY CONTACT WHO WOULD AGREE TO SERVE AS THE DIRECTORS AND OFFICERS OF THE SWISS ENTITY WITH THE STOCK BEING ISSUED TO LANDMARK SETTLEMENT.

I WILL BE IN FLORIDA NEXT WEEK , HOWEVER ANDREI WILL BE AT OUR OFFICES IN CALIFORNIA AND YOU CAN CALL HIM OR SIMPLY EMAIL BOTH OF US --WHICH EVER IS EASIER FOR YOU .

THANK YOU FOR YOUR ASSISTANCE

SW 065111

Subject: Structure
Date: Fri, 08 Jan 1904 20:52:22 +0200
From: Mario Staggi <mstaggi@newhaven.li>
To: <iolenicoff@olenproperties.com>, Igor Olenicoff <iolenicoff@olenproperties.com>

Dear Igor

Thank you for your email of December 13 which is indeed very clear. We agree to proceed accordingly.

First, we will establish the Liechtenstein Trust to be known as "The Landmark Settlement". All the information we need in order to proceed are available at our offices. New Haven will be the trustee.

Sheltons, our correspondent in Danemark, agreed to incorporate "New Guardian Bancorp" wholly owned tby the Liechtenstein "The Landmark Settlement" and in order for them to proceed they require to have the share capital (Danish Krona 125'000) approx USD 20'000 in their client accounts. I will provide you with the account details tomorrow. Once the New Guardian is incorporated this money will be for free disposal of the company. With regard to Sheltons I should mention that this firm is rated within the top 3 leading tax firmsin Danemark. For your information their web-site is: www.sheltons-tax.com. The managing director Mr. Ned Shelton who is personally known to New Haven and its directors for many years is considered to be "The Leading Tax Advisor" in Danemark. There is no need to mention that I will negotiate a discounted fee.

I do not see any problem for New Guardian to enter into a Management Agreement with Andrej and yourself and suggest that such an agreement will be drafted by Sheltons once the company is duly incorporated.

With regard to the second Danish company I will ask Sheltons to clear the proposed name "Landmark Realty Holding Co. and if this name is available I am sure it can be translated into Danish and incorporated in its Danish translation. If the name should not be available we use a name which includes "Real Estate Investment" or "Real Estate Holding" not making refernce to any of the entity names in the structure. Again, in order for Sheltons to proceed they will need a further $ 20'000 being the share capital for the second Danish company.

I basically agree for the second Danish company to be owned by the Landmark Settlement (latter also owning the first Danish company New Guardian Bancorp, but should stress, in order to have "things" separated (we are also using a name for the second Danish company which will not lead to the others) to establish a second Liechtenstein Trust. Please let me have your thoughts.

I will be in touch with you on Monday December 17.

Kind regards,

Mario

10/31/2003 7:51 AM

copy done to s.a. acct.

[Click here and type return address and phone and fax numbers]

THE OLEN COMPANIES

Fax

FAX

To: Bradley Birkenfeld		**From:** Igor M. Olenicoff	
Fax: 41-22-375-69-49		**Pages:** 6	
Phone:		**Date:** 12/27/01	
Re: Structure		**CC:**	

☐ **Urgent** ☐ **For Review** ☐ **Please Comment** ☐ **Please Reply** ☐ **Please Recycle**

Pursuant to our discussion, enclosed is a signed copy of an e-mail from myself to Mario wherein he requests the transfer of $40,000 (Forty Thousand Dollars), as initial capital, for the formation of the two entities referenced. Please accept this letter as our authorization for you to make such a transfer.

Igor M. Olenicoff

Andrei Olenicoff

lst. a elran ?
UBS

[redacted]

Permanent Subcommittee on Investigations
EXHIBIT #102

SW 067081

■ = Redacted by the Permanent Subcommittee on Investigations

Subject: Smith Barney Transfer
Date: Tue, 23 Apr 2002 11:35:37 +0200
From: Mario Staggl <mstaggl@sewhaven.li>
To: Igor Olenicoff <iolenicoff@olenproperties.com>

Dear Igor,

We are looking forward to seeing you and Andrej in the near future. The account is kept in the name of New Guardian Bancorp Aps and you may remember that you and Andrej have signed the signature cards at the occasion of our firts visit at Neue Bank.

Smith Barney can now be instructed to wire the securities according to the co-ordinates set out below:

Neue Bank's correspondant:	Brown Brothers Harriman & Co. New York, DTC 010
For further Credit to:	Intersettle Zurich acc.-no: [redacted]
In favour of:	Neue Bank AG LI-9490 Vaduz acc.-no: [redacted]

For secrecy purpose, there is no need to mention "New Guardian Bancorp. Aps", but, if you prefer to do so the name of the beneficiary can be mentioned.

Please do not hesitate to contact me if anything needs to be discussed.

Regards,
Mario

Permanent Subcommittee on Investigations
EXHIBIT #103

Re: Smith Barney Transfer

▬▬ = Redacted by the Permanent Subcommittee on Investigations

Subject: Re: Smith Barney Transfer
Date: Thu, 25 Apr 2002 16:13:34 -0700
From: Igor Olenicoff <iolenicoff@olenproperties.com>
Organization: Olen Properties
To: Mario Staggl <mstaggl@newhaven.li>

MARIO , WE GAVE THEM INSTRUCTIONS TODAY TO SHIP THE SECURITIES AS NOTED BELOW SO NEUE SHOULD BE RECEIVING IT IN A MATTER OF A FEW DAYS . WHEN THEY DO , PLEASE SO ADVISE.

AFTER THEY HAVE REVIEWED THE PORTFOLIO RECEIVED , AND HAVE ANY SUGGESTIONS FOR IMPROVING THE PERFORMANCE OF THE PORTFOLIO , WE WOULD WELCOME THEIR INPUT .

PLEASE THANK THEM AND WE LOOK FORWARD TO MEETING WITH THEM AGAIN.

BEST PERSONAL REGARDS ,

IGOR

Mario Staggl wrote:

> *Dear Igor,*
>
> *We are looking forward to seeing you and Andrej in the near future. The*
> *account is kept in the name of New Guardian Bancorp Aps and you may remember*
> *that you and Andrej have signed the signature cards at the occasion of our*
> *firts visit at Neue Bank.*
>
> *Smith Barney can now be instructed to wire the securities according to the*
> *co-ordinates set out below:*
>
> *Neue Bank's correspondant:* *Brown Brothers Harriman & Co.*
> *New York, DTC 010*
>
> *For further Credit to:* *Intersettle Zurich*
> *acc.-no:* [redacted]
>
> *In favour of:* *Neue Bank AG*
> *LI-9490 Vaduz*
> *acc.-no:* [redacted]
>
> *For secrecy purpose, there is no need to mention "New Guardian Bancorp.*
> *Aps", but, if you prefer to do so the name of the beneficiary can be*
> *mentioned.*
>
> *Please do not hesitate to contact me if anything needs to be discussed.*
>
> *Regards,*
> *Mario*

IGOR OLENICOFF <iolenicoff@olenproperties.com>
PRESIDENT
OLEN PROPERTIES

1 of 2

Tax Haven Bank Secrecy Tricks

- Code Names for Clients
- Pay Phones, not Business Phones
- Foreign Area Codes
- Undeclared Accounts
- Encrypted Computers
- Transfer Companies to Cover Tracks
- Foreign Shell Companies
- Fake Charitable Trusts
- Straw Man Settlors
- Captive Trustees
- Anonymous Wire Transfers
- Disguised Business Trips
- Counter-Surveillance Training
- Foreign Credit Cards
- Hold Mail
- Shred Files

Prepared by the U.S. Senate Permanent Subcommittee on Investigations, July 2008.

Permanent Subcommittee on Investigations
EXHIBIT #104

Liechtenstein Secrecy Laws

Article 14 of the Banking Act: "The members of the organs of banks and their employees as well as other persons acting on behalf of such banks shall be obliged to maintain the secrecy of facts that they have been entrusted to or have been made available to them pursuant to their business relationships with clients. The obligation to maintain secrecy shall not be limited in time."

Article 11 of the Trustee Act: "Trustees are obliged to secrecy on the matters entrusted to them and on the facts which they have learned in the course of their professional capacity and whose confidentiality is in the best interest of their client. They shall have the right to such secrecy subject to the applicable rules of procedure in court proceedings and other proceedings before Government authorities."

Article 10 – Data Confidentiality: "Whoever processes data or has data processed must keep data from applications entrusted to him or made accessible to him based on his professional activities secret, notwithstanding other legal confidentiality obligations, unless lawful grounds exist for the transmission of the data entrusted or made accessible to him."

Processing of Personal Data - § 1173a, Art. 28a ABGB (General Civil Code): "The employer may not process data relating to the employee unless such data concern his or her qualification for the employment or are indispensable for the performance of the employment contract. In addition, the provisions of the Data Protection Act shall apply."

Article 8 – Transborder Data Flows : "No personal data may be transferred abroad if the personal privacy of the persons affected could be seriously endangered, in particular where there is a failure to provide protection equivalent to that provided under Liechtenstein law. This shall not apply to states which are party to the EEA Agreement.; whoever wishes to transmit data abroad must notify the Data Protection Commissioner beforehand in cases where: a) there is no legal obligation to disclose the data and b) the persons affected have no knowledge of the transmission."

Prohibited Acts of a Foreign State - Art. 2 of the Liechtenstein State Security Law: "Prohibited Acts for a Foreign State: Whoever, without being authorized, performs acts for a foreign state on Liechtenstein territory that are reserved to an authority or an official, whoever aids and abets such acts, shall be punished by the Liechtenstein court (Landgericht) with imprisonment up to three years. "

Prohibited Acts for a Foreign State – Art. 271 of the Swiss Penal Code: "Whoever, without being authorized, performs acts for a foreign state on Swiss territory that are reserved to an authority or an official, whoever performs such acts for a foreign party or another foreign organization, whoever aids and abets such acts, shall be punished with imprisonment up to three years or a fine, in serious cases with imprisonment of no less than one year."

Economic Intelligence Service (Art. 273 SPC): "Whoever seeks out a manufacturing or business secret in order to make it accessible to a foreign official agency, a foreign organization, a private enterprise, or their agents, whoever makes a manufacturing or business secret accessible to a foreign official agency, a foreign organization, a private enterprise, or their agents, shall be punished with imprisonment up to three years or a fine, in serious cases with imprisonment of no less than one year. Imprisonment and fine can be combined."

Prepared by the U.S. Senate Permanent Subcommittee on Investigations, July 2008.

Permanent Subcommittee on Investigations

EXHIBIT #105

CHAPTER SOURCES

The following chapters have been previously published:

Chapter 1 – This is an edited, excerpted and augmented edition of an United States Senate Permanent Subcommittee on Investigations, Committee on Homeland Security and Governmental affairs publication, of a dated July 17, 2008 hearing.

Chapter 2 - These remarks were delivered as testimony by U.S. Senator Carl Levin, before the Permanent Subcommittee on Investigations on Tax Haven Banks hiding Billions from the IRS dated July 17, 2008.

Chapter 3 - These remarks were delivered as testimony by Douglas Shulman, Commissioner of Internal Revenue Service, before the Senate Committee on Homeland Security and Governmental Affairs' Permanent Subcommittee on Investigations Hearing on Tax Haven Financial Institutions dated July 17, 2008.

Chapter 4 – This is an edited, excerpted and augmented edition of a Department of Justice statement of Kevin J. O'Connor, Associate Attorney General, hearing entitled "Tax Haven Banks and U.S. Tax Compliance" presented July 17, 2008 before the United States Senate Committee on Homeland Security and Governmental Affairs, Permanent Subcommittee on Investigations.

Chapter 5 – These remarks were delivered as testimony by U.S. Senator Carl Levin before U.S. Senate Permanent Subcommittee on Investigations on Tax Haven Banks and U.S. tax compliance dated July 17, 2008.

Chapter 6 - These remarks were delivered as testimony by U.S. Senator Norm Coleman Ranking Minority Member, Permanent Subcommittee on Investigations, on Tax Haven Banks and U.S. Tax Compliance dated July 17, 2008.

Chapter 7 – This is an edited, excerpted and augmented edition of a United States Senate Permanent Subcommittee on Investigations committee on Homeland Security and Governmental Affairs, Exhibit List hearing on Tax Haven Banks and U.S. tax compliance dated July 17, 2008.

INDEX

9

A

B

C

D

E

F

S

T

U

V

W